ANNALS and FAMILY RECORDS

of

Winchester
Connecticut

with Exercises of the Centennial Celebration, on the 16th and 17th Days of August 1871

John Boyd

HERITAGE BOOKS
2010

HERITAGE BOOKS
AN IMPRINT OF HERITAGE BOOKS, INC.

Books, CDs, and more—Worldwide

For our listing of thousands of titles see our website
at
www.HeritageBooks.com

A Facsimile Reprint
Published 2010 by
HERITAGE BOOKS, INC.
Publishing Division
100 Railroad Ave. #104
Westminster, Maryland 21157

Index Copyright © 2002 Heritage Books, Inc.

Originally published
Hartford
Press of Case, Lockwood & Brainard
1873

— Publisher's Notice —
In reprints such as this, it is often not possible to remove blemishes from the original. We feel the contents of this book warrant its reissue despite these blemishes and hope you will agree and read it with pleasure.

International Standard Book Numbers
Paperbound: 978-0-7884-2167-9
Clothbound: 978-0-7884-8346-2

PREFACE.

As early as 1856, the compiler of these Annals conceived the plan of collecting materials for a history of his native town, and its early settlers. His life-long residence, reaching back to 1799, and the custody of its records during no inconsiderable portion of the last fifty years, made him more familiar than most living men, with its documentary history and its traditions. Frequent calls by descendants of Old Winchester families, and by genealogists, for information derivable from the town records, impressed him with the belief that a compilation of historical events and family records, however imperfect, would be received with favor alike by citizens of the town and descendants of emigrating families.

It soon became apparent that the settlement and growth of one of the most recent of the original towns of the State, was attended with no thrilling incidents or romantic tales, with which to embellish its transition from barbarism to civilization. If its territory had ever been possessed by an aboriginal race, that race had long ago disappeared, leaving no trace behind. The dispirited remnants of the once warlike tribes of the Narraganset region, had only roamed through its tangled forests, and made temporary halts along the shores of its lakes and the banks of its streams. They claimed no right of domain, and contested no settler's possession of its soil. No fort nor block-house was ever needed for protection or defence of its pioneer settlers; and no hostile armament ever approached its borders.

Lacking historical material of this nature, in its origin, and destitute of sensational events in its slow and prosaic growth, the idea of a readable town history seemed preposterous. And yet there are unrecorded incidents and traditions in the growth of every community, which, however uninteresting to the outside world, may deeply interest residents and the descendants of residents, of that community. There are traits of character, and memories of worth or unworthiness, customs, and habits of thought and action, that should not be lost to posterity by want of brief record. There is also a growing desire among the descendants of New England families, to trace their ancestry and family connections; not so much in search of an illustrious origin, as with the desire to establish a connection with progenitors and kindred of solid worth.

ANNALS OF WINCHESTER.

With the purpose of aiding in these researches, the following circular letter was printed, and largely distributed among the descendants of early settlers and residents of the town:

CIRCULAR.

DEAR SIR:—

I am making a compilation from the Winchester Records, of all the facts ascertainable in reference to the settlers and inhabitants of the town prior to 1800;— and am desirous of incorporating therein such other facts as may be furnished by the descendants of old Winchester families, in reference to their origin and expansion. Such a compilation will have a value proportioned to the accuracy and extent of the information it will afford to future inquirers in reference to their family history;—and this must mainly depend on the prompt and liberal aid of those taking an interest in the perpetuation of family history.

The items desired are, the births, marriages, and deaths, of all members of inhabitant families—the dates of their settlement in, and their departure from the town—their prior and subsequent residence—the names, residences, and other particulars before enumerated, of their ancestors as far back as can be ascertained—and the names of all descendants;—also the offices and appointments in church and state, and the professions or occupations which any of them held or followed, together with peculiarities of character or history.

Family Bibles should be made the basis of reports, and such other facts added thereto, as are attainable. Communications, while they are comprehensive, should be brief and well digested—and must be promptly furnished to be available.

As the labors of the compiler will be arduous, and without remuneration, he feels assured that no son or grandson of old Winchester will withhold the aid he can furnish towards perfecting the work proposed.

Yours truly,
JOHN BOYD.

WEST WINSTED, CT., June 12, 1857.

The responses to this call were so few, and the materials furnished so scant, as to discourage any attempt in the way of perfected genealogies. Nevertheless, a systematic digest of the materials of family history furnished by the public records, supplemented by reliable additions from other sources, seemed to promise essential aid to genealogists, and to the widely scattered descendants of Winchester families. By adding personal notices of every known early settler and resident of the town, and incidents of town history, in the form of Annals, it was hoped that a readable book could be compiled, which would prove interesting and instructive to citizens of the town and their widely scattered descendants.

The plan adopted was, to trace out the land title of the township, to note the action of the proprietary body, the subdivision of the lands into divisions, tiers, and lots, and the assignment of these lots to individual proprietors or purchasers. The carrying out of this plan required a diligent search of the land records and assessment lists, to ascertain the order and dates of immigration, the location of immigrants, by means of descriptions and references in recorded deeds, and by personal inquiries of cotemporaries and descendants, for such items of family history as the records do not furnish.

PREFACE.

With these data obtained, and with the aid of town, society, and church records, the compiler entered on his task. How successfully he has accomplished it, amid the constant interruption of official duties, it is the province of others to judge; while it is his right to assume that few critics will discover more of its demerits than he is painfully conscious of.

In his treatment of the work his endeavor has been to make it readable and instructive to residents and the descendants of residents of the town, by embodying with statistical and historic facts, incidents and illustrations unappreciable by the outside world. If in this he has assimilated to the illustrious Boswell, the work will probably be not the less acceptable to the readers for whom it is specially designed. The home reader will hardly object to being conducted slowly along the path of the first settlers, as one of their number, learning about the divisions of the township domain into tiers and lots and their landmarks; sitting at the primitive fireside of Caleb Beach; partaking of Joel's collation of bear's meat or venison, supplemented by a wooden bowl of toast and cider; calling of an evening at landlord Mott's hostelry and hearing the news of the outer world, and perchance witnessing the descent down the chimney of his stalwart boys; going to meeting at the old Sab-a-day house, or, later, at the new meeting-house, and joining in the prayers and praises of the assembled worshipers; discussing at the store or tavern the merits or demerits of the half-way covenant and the impending Revolutionary crisis; attending the trainings, school exhibitions, and public whippings at the post; watching the growth of the settlement, and becoming acquainted with each new settler.

The experiences of a town in small things as well as in large, make up its history. Its legendary anecdotes, apocryphal though they may be, relieve the dullness of description or narrative, and illustrate manners and customs. Their absolute truth or falsity should not trouble the conscience of the sober-sided, unimaginative reader, who eschews all levity and humor as of the evil one. All that is demanded of such an one is, to receive them as traditions which, in the nature of things, cannot be authenticated or belied.

For assistance and encouragement in prosecuting this work, a grateful acknowledgment is due to D. Williams Patterson, Esq., late of Winsted and now of Newark Valley, N. Y., for essential aid in collecting and arranging the family records, for persistent urgency in stimulating the jaded, not to say indolent compiler, to perseverance in prosecuting his task.

To Deacon Ira Hills, of Vernon, N. Y., the oldest living native of the town, and the most filial of her sons, and to Mrs. Nellie M. Swift, of Colchester, Conn., both descendants of the early settlers of the town, and both residents elsewhere during most of their lives, we are indebted for many interesting reminiscences of men and customs of the past. We have copied liberally from the sprightly sketches of the latter, and from the former have obtained valuable material. We are also indebted to the venerable Father Marsh for extracts from his manuscript historical sermon, deposited in the archives of the Connecticut Historical Society. With these aged worthies it is fitting to associate Deacon Abel S. Wetmore, of the active generation now on the stage, as versed with traditional lore beyond any other living native of the town.

Credit is also due to Dr. Henry H. Drake, Recording Secretary of the Centennial Association, for securing and arranging accurate reports of the centennial exercises herein published, and for his efficient services in obtaining a list of subscribers exceeding in number the most sanguine anticipations of the compiler; also to C. A. Alvord, a native, and S. A. Hubbard, a former resident of the town, both now of Hartford, and to George M. Carrington, of Winsted, for the kind interest they have taken in the work, and the assistance they have rendered in its preparation for the press.

Before this work was projected, most of the generation connecting the present with the primitive stock had passed away. Among those then living and now departed, a tribute of grateful remembrance is due to Rev· Abel McEwen, D. D., of New London, whose analysis of character and fund of anecdote were unrivaled. A series of sketches of early Winchester men was commenced by him, but soon discontinued by reason of infirmities of age, of which we have availed ourselves. To the late Dr. Truman S. Wetmore, the compiler is also specially obliged for valuable information obtainable from no other living source. Also to the family of the late Deacon Lewis M. Norton, for free access to his manuscript volumes of Goshen genealogies, — a work of great interest and value, which should be made available to the public, in printed form.

The compiler originally contemplated publishing these Annals as early as 1862, but on ascertaining the expenses of publication and the probable patronage the work would receive, it appeared very doubtful whether the actual pecuniary outlay would be refunded, and therefore the project was abandoned.

The occurrence of the town centennial in July, 1871, created a new interest in the history of the town. A publication of the centennial exercises was demanded, of which the Historical Address formed a part. This was an epitome of this work; too long to be fully read to a public audience, and yet too brief to prove a satisfactory exposition of the town history. Under these circumstances the compiler decided to bring his whole work before the public, and by an arrangement with the town, engaged to publish in connection with it the other centennial exercises.

PREFACE.

The engraved portraits embellishing this volume are, with two exceptions, of deceased natives or citizens of the town; and all of them were provided at the expense of friends of the parties. Others would have been in like manner provided, had there existed satisfactory portraits from which to engrave them.

It is hardly an excusable weakness in a writer to deprecate criticism of a production which he has deliberately brought before the public, but it is hoped that the limited public for whose perusal the work was designed, and to whom it is dedicated, will consider that it was compiled in snatches of time amid other occupations, then laid aside for several years, and on finally taking it up for immediate publication, finding much to add, more to suppress, and the whole to correct and condense, and at an age when mental and bodily vigor is essentially impaired, will excuse its defects and the seeming unreasonable delay in carrying it through the press; and will find in its pages items of town and family history, and of tradition, which would have been lost had they waited for a more able chronicler to embody them.

CHAPTER I.

PRELIMINARY HISTORY—LAND TITLE.

The oldest conveyance of land recorded in Winchester bears date November 28, 1729, by which John Kilbourn, of Hartford, conveys to Jonathan and David Hills, of Hartford, "all (his) right, title, share, and interest in and to a large Tract of Land, commonly known as the Western Lands, belonging to the Towns of Hartford and Windsor, as it abuts on the Towns of Woodbury and Litchfield, west on the Colony Land, north on the Colony line, and east on Farmington and Simsbury, or however butted and bounded."

This title was derived from a hasty and ill-advised grant of the General Court, made in January, 1686, to the towns of Hartford and Windsor, in anticipation of the annulling of the colonial charter, and the sequestration by Sir Edmund Andross of the unoccupied lands of the colony. Besides several minor tracts undisposed of in Hartford and New Haven counties, the colony owned the whole territory of Litchfield county lying north of New Milford and Woodbury.

On notice of the arrival of Andross at Boston, with authority from the crown to revoke the colonial charter, and to assume the government of the colony, the grant referred to was made by the panic-stricken General Court. The series of votes, of which this grant was one, bore a resemblance to an assignment in bankruptcy, and had some badges which, in strict legal construction, might have been esteemed fraudulent had the usurpation of Andross been sustained.

The first vote constituted Major John Talcott and Ensign Nath. Standley trustees of all the bills secured to, and all claims due the colony, to be improved by them for paying the colonial debts, and to pay over the surplus, if any, to the several counties, for the encouragement of Grammar Schools. Another vote granted to Wethersfield, Middletown, and Farmington, all the vacant lands between Wallingford bounds and the bounds of those towns; another vote granted to the Town of Kenilworth, "all those lands north of their bounds and Guilford, and west of Haddam"; and by another vote, granted to Hartford and Windsor, "those lands on the north of Woodbury and Matatock, and on the west of Farmington and Simsbury, to the Massachusetts line north, and to run west to Housatunnuck River (provided it be not, or part of it, formerly granted to any particular persons) to make a plantation or villages thereon."

Andross, after repeated but fruitless efforts to induce the General Court to make a voluntary surrender of the charter, came to Hartford in October, 1687, dissolved the charter government, and assumed supreme control. The charter, however, was never surrendered to him, nor was it ever set aside by the English Courts, on the writ of *quo warranto* then pending. His usurped government, after a period of about sixteen months, came to an end on news of the deposition of James II., and the accession of William and Mary to the British throne.

On the flight of Andross early in 1689, the charter government was resumed, and the old magistrates, and civil and military officers, were reinstated, until a new election under the charter could be held. The land grants referred to had not been perfected by the issue of charters, which by law were indispensable to their validity, nor was any action taken in reference to them for nearly twenty years. It is probable that the General Court, while composed mainly of those who voted the grant, were unwilling, by a revocation, to incur the imputation of having made a fictitious disposal of the lands, and that the grantees, while the well-known intent of the grants was fresh in their remembrance, were slow to repudiate the implied trust by any overt acts of ownership.

By the town records of Hartford it appears that nearly twenty-two years after the grant, and after most of those then on the stage had passed away, it was voted in town meeting, "that whereas, a grant was made to the plantations of Hartford and Windsor, on the 26th of January, 1686, of those lands on the north of Woodbury and Matatuck, west of Symsbury and Farmington, to the Massachussetts Line North, and to run west to Housatonuck or Stratford River; that two or three persons be appointed to join with two or more from Windsor, to survey, or view, the said tract of land, and make return of the quantity and quality thereof, and to bring in a map of the same." In January, 1708, another committee was appointed by Hartford to compound with claimants of any part of the lands, to settle the boundaries, and, if need be, to sue, defend, eject, and recover, in course of law, all disputants of their title or trespassers on their lands. In 1710, a committee was raised to devise measures to secure the propriety of the lands, and to move the assembly "to grant them such deed in writing, or other thing" as might be deemed necessary.

Other votes, of a similar nature, were passed from time to time, with a view to establish a possessory right, and in 1715 it was decided to lay out one or two townships, probably with a view to fortify their right of ownership by compliance with the only expressed condition of the original grant. Pursuant to this policy, the township of Litchfield — originally named New Bantam — was surveyed and] laid out about 1717; and it being found that parties in Farmington had secured Indian titles to portions of this territory, they were compromised with, by allotting to them one-sixth part of the township, in consideration of their release of all claim to any other portion of the granted territory, and of procuring a confirmation to Hartford and Windsor of all the lands in the township claimed by Farmington Indians.

Litchfield having been surveyed and its lands disposed of to settlers who had entered on the same, the location and survey of a new township, north of Litchfield, was resolved on, and a committee appointed for that purpose. This committee reported their laying out of a township of about the dimensions of Litchfield, embracing a gore from the east side of Cornwall, the whole of Goshen, the west half of Torrington, and the southwest corner of Winchester. The report was accepted in 1723, and a committee was appointed to dispose of the lands, admit settlers, and convey the lands to purchasers.

At this stage of the proceedings, the General Assembly seems for the first time to have interposed to check the fillibustering operations of these powerful and arrogant towns; and the state of things imperiously demanded prompt and energetic action. Not Hartford and Windsor alone were interested in establishing the defective grant of 1686, but also the towns of Wethersfield, Middletown, and Killingworth — the grantees of smaller tracts. Farmington had become specially interested by its compact securing to it a sixth part of the township of Litchfield. Prominent men in other towns had purchased fractional shares of the territory from Hartford and Windsor proprietors, and were thereby brought into the combination, which became so strong that civil process against the trespassers could not be executed in Hartford county, which then comprehended the disputed territory. In this emergency, the Assembly, at the Spring session of 1723, directed the King's Attorney for New Haven county to prosecute the trespassers in the name of the Governor and Company. John Seymour, Samuel Catlin, William Baker, Thomas Moore, and Job Ellsworth, of the committee appointed by Hartford and Windsor to dispose of the allotments in the Goshen township, appear to have been the first parties prosecuted and arrested.*

---

* Doctor Trumbull, in his *History of Connecticut*, assigns an earlier period for the arrest and imprisonment of trespassers on the western lands, and ascribes to the men of Hartford and Windsor the famous uprising and jail-delivery in 1722, with the purpose of rescuing those trespassers. Recent investigations of the Colonial and Court Records of that period, by Hon. J. Hammond Trumbull, go to show that this high-handed outrage was perpetrated by men of Windham and Tolland counties, in no way concerned in the Hartford and Windsor controversy, but neighbors and friends of Captain Jeremiah Fitch, a popular and influential man in eastern Connecticut, who, after a protracted suit at law in defence of a land title, and, as he and his neighbors

The apprehension of a vigorous prosecution of these and other offenders, may have induced the following whimpering vote, passed in Hartford town meeting, in April, 1773:

"*Voted*, That Joseph Talcott, Esq., Lieut. Thomas Seymour, and James Ensign be a committee, in conjunction with a committee of Windsor, to represent to the General Assembly, in May next, the true state of our western lands by grant and purchase, and pray their favorable construction of our right thereto, and pray them for a further confirmation thereof by patent, or otherwise enquire of them their further intentions with us, as their children, who freely pay all obedience to them as our father." This language indicates a change of tone and policy. The asking of a confirmation of title shows a growing doubt of the validity of their action in appropriating Litchfield and attempting further appropriations of territory. Another vote of Hartford, October 7th, 1723, reciting the original grant, and the great expenses and charges of the towns in buying out the native claimants, and assigning as the reason why the Assembly refused their grant, that many members of the Assembly apprehended the quantity of land embraced in their grant of 1686 was far greater than was understood or intended at the time; therefore they appointed a committee to act with a Windsor committee in applying to the coming October session of Assembly "for a confirmation of said lands; or, if the General Assembly shall remain unwilling, for the reasons aforesaid, to grant a patent of the whole of said lands, the said agents are empowered to concert with the Assembly for obtaining a patent for a part of said lands, releasing the rest as said agents shall judge most conducive to the benefit of said towns and the quiet settlement of said lands." The vote then goes on to limit the agents to a proposed division, by a compromise line from the northwest corner of Litchfield, north, to the Massachusetts line, the eastern division to be confirmed to Hartford and Windsor, and the western to be relinquished to the colony. This division would have

---

conceived, a wrongful judgment rendered against him, was committed to Hartford jail, on an execution for costs. His neighbors, against some of whom similar actions were pending or threatened, — there being scarcely a farm in that region over which there were not two or three conflicting titles, — were indignant at his committal, and determined to liberate him. On the 22d of October, 1722, these neighbors and some East Windsor men — about fifty in all — in open day crossed the Hartford ferry, marched up to the jail, and demanded the release of Captain Fitch. The jailor refusing, a battering-ram was improvised out of a timber near at hand, the door was broken in, and Cap*. Fitch and the other prisoners were set free. The party then retreated to the ferry, which they seized, in spite of the sheriff's posse hastily assembled, and made good their retreat without further interruption. Capt. Fitch was afterwards tried as a participator in the riot, and acquitted of any knowledge, act, or part in the matter. He subsequently obtained a reversal of the judgment against him, the costs of which were the basis of his arrest and imprisonment.

LAND TITLE.

given to the towns more than three-fourths of the territory, and to the colony less than one-fourth.

Though not acceeded to, and probably not expected to be, the proposition became a basis of negotiation.

At the October Session, in 1724, the Assembly appointed a committee to examine the claims of the towns, to receive propositions, and to report. "The Committee," in the words of Dr. Trumbull, "found it an affair of great labor and difficulty to examine the claims, and obtain such concessions and propositions as they judged reasonable, or as the Assembly would accept. After laboring in the business nearly two years they made their report. The Legislature, wishing to preserve the peace of the colony, and to settle the lands as expeditiously as might be, on the report of their committee resolved, (May Session, 1726), " that the lands in controversy should be divided between the colony and the towns — that the colony should have the western, and Hartford and Windsor the eastern division."

The line of division coincided with the dividing line between Colebrook, Winchester, and Torrington, on the east, and Goshen and Norfolk on the west.

The township of Litchfield was conceded to the two towns, and their grants to New Milford and to Benjamin Fairweather were confirmed. The survey of the new township north of Litchfield was abandoned, and the area absorbed in other townships afterward laid out.

The territory conceded to Hartford and Windsor embraces the towns of Colebrook, Hartland, Winchester, Barkhamsted, Torrington, New Hartford, and Harwinton, making an area of 291,806 acres, to which is to be added the township of Litchfield, with an area of not less than 35,000 acres.

The territory reserved to the colony embraced the towns of Canaan, Norfolk, Cornwall, Goshen, Warren, and about two-thirds of Kent, making not far from 120,000 acres.

To the excess of area conceded to the two towns is to be added the advantage of location in considering the concession made to them by the Assembly, in order to quiet their tumultuous spirit, and secure a speedy settlement of the only remaining unoccupied territory of the Colony. Yet, the concession of this splendid domain was so unsatisfactory to the two towns that the ratification of the compact was not perfected until August 30, 1729, when a patent of one moiety of the 145,303 acres was duly issued to Hartford, and of the other moiety to Windsor.

The lands being surveyed and divided into townships, Hartford and Windsor proceeded to a dissolution of partnership by deeds of partition dated February 11, 1732, by which the inhabitants of Hartford became the sole owners of Hartland, Winchester, New Hartford, and the eastern half of Harwinton, and the inhabitants of Windsor of Colebrook, Barkhamsted, Torrington, and the western half of Harwinton. A law of the Assembly was enacted, providing for a subdivision by each of the towns among its taxable inhabitants, of their individual rights, by assigning to each his whole interest in one or other of the townships. The law also provided that the land-owners of each township should have a corporate existence as "proprietors" of the respective towns, with powers to survey and allot to each individual his *pro rata* share, according to the lists of 1720, of the land in the township to which he was assigned.

Under this enactment the seven proprietary townships were so organized as to constitute each tax-payer of Hartford and Windsor on their lists of 1720, or their heirs or assigns, a proprietor of an undivided share, in proportion to his list in some one of the townships; and the quantity of land to which each was entitled on subdivision was at the rate of more than three acres to the pound of his list.

CHAPTER II.

"PROPRIETORS OF WINCHESTER."

In the preceding chapter we have briefly detailed the events which resulted in settling the title of the western lands and vesting the township of Winchester in a proprietary body. It would seem as if, on this consummation, after a controversy of more than forty years, our proprietors would at once have organized and opened their lands for sale or settlement; but it appears they were in no haste to do so. In 1744, May 14, eight years after Hartford and Windsor had made a division of their illgotten territory, the proprietors of Winchester were called together, and were organized by choosing William Pitkin as moderator, and Thomas Seymour as clerk and register of deeds.

The names of individual proprietors, and the amounts set to them, was made out in these words:

Here follows a list of the names of the original proprietors of the township of Winchester, in the county of Hartford, with the severall sums annexed to their names by which the respective rights and shares of sd. proprietors of the township of Winchester afores'd are to be apportioned and holden or divided to and amongst them, their heirs and assigns, according as the same is sett and apportioned in the deed of partition made of that part of those lands called the Western Lands, which was sett out to and among the inhabitants of Hartford, viz.:

	£ : s : d		£ : s : d
Wm. Pitkin, Esq., Heirs,	251 : 0 : 0	Joseph Keeney,	44 : 0 : 0
Mr. Richard Lord's Heirs,	161 : 0 : 0	John Porter,	33 : 0 : 0
Rev. Mr. Thos. Buckingham,	100 : 0 : 0	William Cole,	52 : 0 : 0
Wm. Whiting, Jun.,	21 : 0 : 0	Capt. Thos. Seymour,	206 : 0 : 0
Peter Pratt,	41 : 0 : 0	Joseph Wells' Heirs,	20 : 10 : 0
Nath'l Jones,	39 : 10 : 0	Sam'l Church's Heirs,	31 : 0 : 0
Dan'l Smith,	23 : 0 : 0	Stephen Andruss,	35 : 0 : 0
Sam'l Burnham,	24 : 0 : 0	Henry & John Arnold,	93 : 0 : 0
Thos. Hopkins,	97 : 0 : 0	Wilterton Merrill,	134 : 0 : 0
Jacob Merrill's Heirs,	64 : 0 : 0	Thos. Burr,	91 : 0 : 0
Aaron Cook's Heirs,	171 : 0 : 0	Col. Wm. Whiting,	35 : 0 : 0
John Pratt, Jun.,	55 : 10 : 0	Capt. Jos. Wadsworth,	44 : 10 : 0
John Ensign,	38 : 10 : 0	Mr. John Whiting,	125 : 0 : 0
Wm. Roberts, Jun., Heirs,	29 : 0 : 0	John Pellett,	21 : 0 : 0
Joseph Easton,	40 : 10 : 0	Wm. Williams,	105 : 10 : 0
Tim. Phelps' Heirs,	71 : 0 : 0	John Cole,	40 : 0 : 0

	£. s. d.		£. s. d.
Thos. Wells,	79 : 10 : 0	Thos. Whaples,	26 : 10 : 0
Jona. Barrett,	49 : 0 : 0	Ephraim Tucker,	32 : 0 : 0
Thos. Pellett,	46 : 0 : 0	John Hazletine,	21 : 0 : 0
Jos. Keeney, Jun.,	49 : 0 : 0	Richard Seymour,	61 : 10 : 0
Isaac Kellogg,	48 : 0 : 0	William Day,	23 : 0 : 0
Richard Olmsted,	73 : 0 : 0	John Goodwin,	52 : 10 : 0
John Shepard,	64 : 10 : 0	John Williams' Heirs,	46 : 0 : 0
Jona. Olcott,	41 : 0 : 0	William Pratt,	31 : 0 : 0
Ensign Nath'l Goodwin,	124 : 10 : 0	Jacob Webster's Heirs,	38 : 0 : 0
James Ensign,	121 : 10 : 0	Mr. John Haynes' Heirs,	121 : 0 : 0
Edw'd Dodd's Heirs,	22 : 0 : 0	John Benjamin, Jun.,	18 : 0 : 0
Thos. Judd's Heirs,	61 : 10 : 0	Thos. Burnham's Heirs,	51 : 0 : 0
Eben'r Webster,	38 : 10 : 0	Jona. Bull,	44 : 10 : 0
Thos. Day's Heirs,	38 : 0 : 0	Jona. Ashley,	52 : 0 : 0
Jas. Bidwell's Heirs,	18 : 0 : 0	John Pantry,	109 : 0 : 0
John Skinner,	138 : 0 : 0	Caleb B. & Thos. Bunce's H'rs,	115 : 0 : 0
Josep Root,	1 : 0 : 0	Joseph Cook,	77 : 0 : 0
Thos. Meekin's Heirs,	24 : 0 : 0	David Forbes,	75 : 0 : 0
Jos. Sedgwick,	28 : 0 : 0	James Williams, Jun.,	43 : 0 : 0
Jona. Burnham,	21 : 0 : 0	John Burnham, Jr.,	30 : 0 : 0
Richard Goodman,	77 : 0 : 0	Sam'l Burr,	45 : 10 : 0
Caleb Watson,	21 : 0 : 0	Jos. Farnsworth,	25 : 0 : 0
Lem'l Deming's Heirs,	15 : 0 : 0	John Butler,	29 : 0 : 0
Obadiah Spencer,	161 : 0 : 0	John Easton's Heirs,	90 : 0 : 0
Thos. Dickinson's Heirs,	51 : 0 : 0	Charles Kelsey,	38 : 0 : 0
Aaron Cook's Heirs,	51 : 10 : 0	Samuel Spencer,	60 : 10 : 0
John Kellogg's Heirs,	54 : 0 : 0	Joseph Butler,	66 : 10 : 0
Thos. Burnham, Jr., Heirs,	29 : 0 : 0	John Abby,	27 : 0 : 0
James Porter,	27 : 0 : 0	Phebee Russell,	8 : 0 : 0
Richard Gilman,	58 : 0 : 0	Ozias Goodwin,	78 : 0 : 0
Caleb Benton,	41 : 10 : 0	Ichabod Wadsworth,	62 : 10 : 0
John Camp's Heirs,	2 : 0 : 0	Tim. Porter,	52 : 0 : 0
Rev. Mr. Benj. Colton,	100 : 0 : 0	John Kilborn,	51 : 0 : 0
Thos. Burr, Jun.,	51 : 10 : 0	James Poisson,	18 : 0 : 0
Joseph Gilbert,	53 : 0 : 0	Jonathan Tayler,	27 : 10 : 0
Sam'l Hubbard,	25 : 0 : 0	Thos. Day, Jr., Heirs,	18 : 0 : 0
Thos. Hosmer,	193 : 0 : 0		
Richard Burnham, Jr.,	56 : 0 : 0		

After an interval of more than six years, another meeting was called and held at Hartford, October 8, 1750, which appointed a committee "to proceed to and view the lands, and make report to the next meeting; and to warn the Indians not to set fire on any of the lands, upon peril of suffering the penalties of the law in case they so do."

The next meeting, held in January, 1751, voted, "That whenever twenty proprietors should signify their wish to proceed to the settlement of the township, the clerk should call another meeting." The next meeting, held in October, 1753, appointed a committee to form a plan for dividing and settling the township, but without result. More than two years later, January 22, 1756, another committee was raised, to view the lands, survey and renew the bounds and corners thereof, and to report to the next meeting a plan of laying out and settling the same. The plan reported and adopted at the next meeting, November, 1757, was to lay out two acres on the pound to each of the proprietors, in two divisions; and that Col. Samuel Talcott, Capt. Thomas Seymour, William Pitkin, Jr., and Mr. John Robins, Jr., be a committee, before the next meeting, to adjust and make up the interests of each of the proprietors, for the more speedy settling and laying out of said two divisions; and in January, 1758, a committee was appointed " to make and draw a lott for the proprietors, for their precedence and succession in laying out the two divisions in manner and form following, viz.: By making so many uniform papers as there are to be allotments, and on each of said papers write the name of the proprietor to have his share or allotment governed or laid out by said draft, and in a just and proper manner cause said papers to be drafted out of some covered instrument, as Providence shall direct the lotts, No. one, two, three, &c., in order as they come out, and make a return thereof to the proprietors under their hands;" and any proprietor owning by purchase or otherwise, to have all his rights added together in one allotment.

The committee was instructed to divide the township into six tiers, running northerly and southerly, parallel with the eastern line of the township: the first five to be one mile and six rods wide (including a reservation for a six-rod highway, northerly and southerly, where it will best accommodate), and the sixth, or westernmost tier, so broad as to take up the rest of the land. They were then to begin at the southwest corner of the township, and lay out the lot first drawn by lines at right angles to the tier lines, and so proceed northward, in course, as the lots were drawn (each lot containing one acre to the pound of the proprietor's interest) not less than three and a-half miles, unless the next lot will extend more than three and three-quarters miles northward; and then begin at the south end of the next tier east, and then to proceed northward, as in the first tier; and then to proceed with the third tier east in the same manner.

In laying out the second division, the committee were to begin at the northeast corner of the township, and lay out the first lot to the same proprietor who had the first allotment in the first division; and then to proceed southerly, laying out lots to the proprietors of the corresponding lots in the first division, in successive tiers, of the same extent southward as those in the first division were to extend northward.

In the first division the committee were instructed to locate the rights of Caleb Beach, Landlord Mott and his son Mott, and of Ebenezer and Joseph Preston, so as to take into their allotments the lands and buildings then occupied and improved by them. They were also to reserve, in the second division, two mill lots of six acres each — one on the Still river, embracing the Gilbert Clock Company's works, and the other " The Old Forge Privilege," on the lake outlet, now owned by the Winsted Manufacturing Company.

On the fourth Monday of May, 1758, the committee reported their action, and exhibited a plan of their survey and allotments of the two divisions to a meeting of the proprietors, which was accepted and ordered to be recorded.

The third and final division of lands in the township was ordered in November, 1763, and the committee reported their laying out of the same December 1st following; which report was accepted and ordered to be recorded. The undivided land in the northwest, or Danbury quarter, was laid out in three half-mile tiers, and one tier of one hundred rods, running northerly, from the first division lands to Colebrook line, parallel with the west line of the town and reaching easterly to the third or westernmost tier of the second division, and allotments of one acre to the pound were made on a new drawing of lots, beginning at the southerly end of the westernmost tier and proceeding northerly to Colebrook line; then beginning at the north end of the second tier and proceeding to the south end, then proceeding northerly on the third tier, and returning southerly on the one hundred-rod tier to its southerly end. The remaining allotments were made on the west, south, and east shores of Long Lake, so as to appropriate all the undivided lands of the township, except a section about a mile square at the southeast corner of the township, afterwards taken on execution by parties who had made the " Old North Road," by order of the General Assembly, — and known as the " Henshaw Tract."

Reservations of six-rod highways were made, running northerly and southerly, " where they would best accommodate," in all the tiers; and located reservations, four rods wide, were made easterly and westerly, at irregular intervals, across the tiers; but the reservations in the aggregate fell far short of the requirements of the town.

So far as the general plan and mechanical execution of this survey is concerned, it seems excellent. The tier lines — except a blunder in their bearings in the first division — were accurately laid out and well defined. The lines of marked trees between the lots and on the tier lines, are still readily found and traced, wherever the primitive forest remains. The center bounds, with stones containing the initials of the original owners, are generally still to be found in sections outside of the villages. But the system of triple division of owners' rights operated very unfairly on the small proprietors, and this injustice was aggravated by the width of the tiers on which the rights were laid. This operation may be illustrated by examples.

Joseph Root had a proprietary right of one pound on the list of 1720 It entitled him to three acres of land. One of these was set to him unless he had sold his right to some larger proprietor, in a strip of land in the first division, one mile long and half a rod wide; another acre in the second division, of the same dimensions, and the third acre in a strip half a mile long and one rod wide. John Camp's heirs had a two-pound interest, which in like manner was allotted to them in two detached strips of one rod wide and a mile long, and a third of two rods wide and half a mile long. In this way all the small proprietors found their allotments made in three detached driblets, instead of in one saleable plot; and only eighteen out of one hundred and six proprietors had allotments in parcels of one hundred acres or more.

The reservations for northerly and southerly highways could be located within each tier, where the road would best accommodate, but the located reservations for easterly and westerly highways could not be used unless the nature of the ground was adapted to a traveled road. As a consequence of this, so hilly and precipitous is the territory of the town that scarcely one of these reservations has been opened for public travel, and not one in its whole extent. The result is that probably no town in the State has afforded as little encouragement to its settlers in the matter of highways.

In another respect there was a meanness in the allotment of the land which it is to be hoped is unparalleled. It had been the uniform custom of township proprietors to make a liberal reservation of lands to aid the settlers in the support of the gospel and of common schools. Our stepfathers gave not a rood of land for support of schools, at home or abroad, and as to religious endowments, they allotted three hundred acres each to two of their own resident clergymen, who, not being subject to taxation could not regularly come in for their shares of the ill-gotten spoil.

CHAPTER III.

PHYSICAL CONFORMATION.

The physical conformation of the township was so forbidding as to offer few inducements to settlers, especially to the dwellers on the rich meadows and uplands of the Connecticut Valley. At all events, not one of the original proprietors ever came to occupy his new domain. The intervale lands of the township along the streams were narrow and lean, hemmed in by abrupt hills, mainly abounding with rocks of all sizes, projecting above the soil. Mountain ridges, with precipitous cliffs, ran through the town in northerly and southerly directions. The forests made up the deficient size of their trees by their number and variety. The lordly pine was rare. The hemlock predominated in the eastern section, and the sugar-maple and beech in the western. The chestnut, though in few parts of the town so frequent as others, was the patriarchial tree. majestic in size, and venerable in age. Many of them are still to be found from four to five feet in diameter at the butt, while the stumps of others show a still larger size. The birch, ash, bass, white wood and black oak everywhere abounded. The hickory and white oak were rare. The elm grew to some extent on the intervale lands. Beneath the hemlock forests, thick and almost impenetrable growths of laurel, or calmia, were often found covering many acres. The shores of ponds and marshes were lined with thorny vines, as impenetrable as the chaparral of more southern latitudes.

The mountain ridges are low continuations of the Green Mountain ranges, generally precipitous on the eastern side, and sloping westward. The first of these forms nearly a continuous range through the town, parallel with its eastern boundary, and a mile distant therefrom, with only one opening of less than a half mile, where east and west roads are practicable. A second range, more irregular in its direction and less continuous, borders the west side of the two lakes, and extends northward to Colebrook. Spurs of this range occupy a considerable portion of the northwest or "Danbury Quarter" of the town. Picturesque views, some of them of great beauty, are obtained from every mountain summit. The highest elevation in the town, west of Long Lake, in the old Winchester parish, commands a view of the Talcott and Bolton

Mountains in the east, and the mountains of Berkshire in Massachusetts, and the Taconic range in New York.

The geological formation is wholly primitive, and mainly of Gneiss rock in contorted strata, generally dipping westward, at a considerable angle. Pure granite occurs in veins and boulders in the western portion of the town. Veins and boulders of fine-grained gneiss, colored by an intermixture of epidote, and well adapted to building purposes, are found in the eastern section. Ill-defined veins of limestone are found on the extreme eastern border, but not in quantity or quality to make them available. Metallic veins are unfrequent.

A vein of specular magnetic oxide of iron, near the top of Street Hill in the northeast part of the town, was partially worked late in the last century, and abandoned.

The ore was bloomed at a forge in Colebrook, and found to produce a good quantity of bar iron. Other veins, or beds, of larger size, in the same vicinity, are so impregnated with sulphur as to be worthless. These veins were traced by Doctor Percival, in a southwestern direction, to the highlands in Putnam County, N. Y., where they have been extensively worked for smelting in the blast furnaces at Cold Spring on the Hudson.

Recently a very rich specular ore has been found in the Danbury section of the town, bordering on the Connecticut Western Railroad. The location has been explored by Professor Hall, of Albany, who describes it as an imperfect vein or bed in the contorted Gneiss Rock, which promises to grow wider as the shaft is carried downward. It is between three and four feet thick at the surface, descending into the hill nearly perpendicularly, and trending easterly and westerly. The ore is free from admixture of sulphur or other deleterious substances, and a large portion of it will yield from eighty to ninety per cent. of metal. It is held by joint-stock owners, whose explorations have, as yet, been very imperfect. Its location at a high point of hill, sloping rapidly down to Mad River and the Connecticut Western Railroad, gives it a high prospective value. Indications of this, or other veins of similar quality of ore, are frequent in the adjacent region.

Minerals are rare in this formation. Garnets and schorl are occasionally found. Quartz crystals, of considerable size, but imperfect formation, are found in a decomposed vein, near the Dugway School House and elsewhere. Rose quartz, in beautiful specimens, but not in situ, have been found in the borough of Winsted. Large and beautiful specimens of flesh-colored feldspar, with crystalline faces well defined, have been thrown out from the rock cuttings of the Connecticut Western Railroad.*

---

* For description of the geology of this region, see "Percival's Survey," page 119, and onward.

The soil of the township is mainly a reddish, gravelly loam, adapted to grasses, corn, oats, and potatoes, but not to other cereals. Clay lands are found occasionally on the higher ridges. The alluvial along the water courses is generally sandy loam of little fertility. Nearly all of the lands are devoted to dairy and stock-raising purposes. The smoother dry lands, where not choked with stones, are occasionally broken up and subjected to a rotation of potato, corn, and oat crops, perhaps more to improve their grass-growing capacity than for direct profit. Milk for the New York market is the staple product, save in the vicinity of the villages, where market products are in demand.

Springs of the purest water everywhere abound, and rarely is a dwelling to be found, out of the borough limits, which has not its aqueduct.

Long Lake extends from near the Torrington line northerly, a distance of three and a half miles, and forms the dividing line of the two parishes for that distance. It is surrounded by mountainous ridges on the eastern and western shores, and at the northeasterly end pours its waters over eleven factory wheels, down a ravine, into Mad River, distant half a mile from its outlet, and one hundred and fifty feet below its surface, in the center of West Winsted village. It is alike the pride and the source of the prosperity of the town.

In June, 1771, the proprietors of Winchester granted to Richard Smith, the proprietor of the "Old Forge," at Robertsville, a right "to draw off or lower the Long Pond in Winchester one and a half feet, for the benefit of his iron works, during the pleasure of proprietors." During the same year, David Austin became the owner of the land at the outlet of the lake, and soon after built a grist-mill and saw-mill on the premises now owned by the Henry Spring Company, and with the concurrence of Mr. Smith lowered the channel of the outlet, and erected a dam and bulkhead, so as to raise the surface of the lake some four feet, and to draw the water through a gate at the bottom of the channel, thus securing a reservoir six feet in depth over the whole lake surface, and controlling the drawing and closing of the bulkhead gate at his own pleasure. The uncontested exercise of this right for a long series of years secured to him a good title to control the water of the lake. This individual control, and a prudent drawing of the water during working days, and working hours only, almost threefolds the working power of the stream running night and day through the week. The seasons when a regular supply of water, during the whole year, has failed, have been very rare indeed. It is this certainty of a regular supply, alike in flood time and drought, which has attracted manufacturing enterprises, and sustained them in successful operation.

In 1806, or 1807, the frail wooden dam which raised the water above its original level, gave way on the east side of the bulkhead, during a

PHYSICAL CONFORMATION.

spring freshet. The danger of an outflow, most disastrous to the works on the stream, and the village at the foot of the hill, was imminent, but the disaster had been apprehended, and a good working force of men and teams was on the ground when the break occurred. Hardly had the rush of water through the breach begun, when a tree trunk was floated to the breach, and securely fastened at each end. Spars and plank from the neighboring mill were at hand, and a temporary dam was forthwith improvised by the use of swingling tow, straw, and gravel. During the following summer and fall, a solid causeway, between two substantial stone walls, and wide enough for a roadway, was laid down and raised to a safe height, some three rods outside of the original dam, and a new bulkhead of a permanent character was erected on the line of the causeway. This raised the high-water line about one foot higher than before.

In 1860, the borough of Winsted was authorized by the Legislature to raise the high-water level of the lake four feet above the previous high-water mark, and to take water therefrom by aqueduct, and convey and distribute the same into and through the borough, in such quantities as the conveniences of the borough should require. The same season, an imperfect embankment was raised to the required height, which during the following year was perfected by raising the former causeway to the same elevation, and protecting it by a thoroughly-built outer wall and two wide waste-weirs. This raises the surface, and expands the shores of the lake, so as to make a reservoir of about twelve feet in depth from high-water mark to the bottom of the bulkhead gates.

The Little Pond is a smaller body of pure and limpid water, covering a surface of about fifty acres, lying about a third of a mile northwesterly of Long Lake, at an elevation of ninety feet above, and discharging its waters into it by "Sucker Brook," running southerly between the two bodies of water, a distance of one mile. Neither of these lakes are fed by large streams of water, but both are mainly supplied by springs. Both of them, in early times, abounded with trout of large size, some of them reaching a weight of six to seven pounds. Perch, roach, bull-heads, and eels were abundant. About 1815, pickerel were introduced from the Southwick Ponds, by Colonel Samuel Hoadley. The Farmington river "Dace," as they are called, were introduced several years since as live bait, by pickerel fishermen, and escaping from their hooks, grew and multiplied, reaching the size and shape of a shad. Like the pickerel, it is a gamy fish, and these two intruders had exterminated the trout, and largely thinned out the smaller fish, when, about 1860, the black bass was transferred by E. S. Woodford, Esq., and has become the gamiest champion of our lakes.

Mad River, which rises in Norfolk, runs its rapid course southeasterly, receiving the lake stream, and emptying into Still River, in the borough of Winsted, has until recent years been little used above the junction of the lake stream, except for saw mills. It now furnishes water for a cutlery establishment, and for two of the largest tanneries in the state, and will, when proper reservoirs are built near its sources, furnish an important addition to our water power. The Connecticut Western Railroad, by an average grade of about eighty feet ascent to the mile, finds its way through the town, along the banks of this stream, to its summit level in Norfolk.

Still River, rising in Torringford, runs with little fall along the border of the Naugatuck Railroad to its junction with Mad River, and thence still northerly through the borough, furnishing near the borough line the power of two of the best water privileges of the town. The fall of water from the lake surface to the northern limit of the borough, exceeds 225 feet, all of which is profitably employed for manufacturing purposes.

The other streams in the Winsted section of the town are small, and unfitted for manufacturing purposes. In the west section, the two head branches of the Naugatuck River have their source. The eastern branch proceeds from a small pond near Norfolk line, and runs southerly to Wolcottville, and affords good water power as it approaches Torrington line. The other runs along Hall Meadow, and passes through the southeast corner of the town to its junction with the east branch at Wolcottville, where the united streams take the name of Naugatuck River.

CHAPTER IV.

INDIANS—GAME—THOROUGHFARES.

The Green Woods section of Litchfield County, though abounding with game, seems not to have been a permanent abiding place of the Indian, save along the Tunxis or Farmington River on the east, and the Housatonic on the western border. The Scaticoke Indians dwelt along the Housatonic, their chief residence in Kent. The Weatogues, of Simsbury, crowded out from the Tunxis valley by the white settlers, took refuge on the meadows of the Housatonic in Canaan.

On the east, a small tribe, or fragment of a tribe, probably crowded out of Farmington, took up their abode in New Hartford, near the gorge where the Farmington River breaks through a mountain ridge, which spot was designated by the early settlers as "the Kingdom," and eventually by the specific name of "Satan's Kingdom."

A portion of this tribe moved up the Farmington, to the foot of Ragged Mountain in Barkhamsted. Modern wiseacres assert that their council fire was the mythical "Barkhamsted Light House," of which so much has been said and so little known. The head man, or the last man of this tribe, named Chaugum, lived and reigned to near the close of the last century. His descendants in the female line, a race of bleached-out, basket-making, root-gathering vagabonds, with high cheek bones and bow-and-arrow eyes, have continued to dwell on the Ragged Mountain domain, and kept up the council fires until a very recent period. A daughter of Chaugum married a runaway servant of Secretary Wyllys of Hartford. They settled in the Danbury quarter of Winchester, and their descendants are the only known representatives of the aboriginal race in this town.

Not a single mountain, lake, or river, bears an Indian name. The flint arrow-head is occasionally found on the intervale lands, and in considerable numbers along the south shores of Long Lake, together with some other stone implements, indicating a resort there for fishing and hunting. There was also a cleared spot around a copious spring of water on the east shore of the lake, on land of Deacon Joseph W. Hurlbut, where numerous arrow-heads have been found.

Game was abundant at the early settlement of the town. A hunting lodge was erected on the bridle-path from New Hartford to Norfolk, near the south line of the town, before any settlement was made, and a deer park was enclosed near the reservoir pond, on the west branch of the Naugatuck, at a very early period.

Bear's meat was by no means a rare dish among our early settlers. It was in some families almost their ordinary fare. The records of Justice Alvord show frequent prosecutions for killing deer, out of season, up to 1790. Wolves abounded as late, or later, than the Revolutionary War. Mr. Levi Norton, while living in the red house between the two ponds, after 1783, returning from a neighbor's after nightfall, encountered a drove of these border ruffians on his own clearing, and was saved from an attack by the timely help of his powerful mastiff, which, on hearing his cry of alarm, rushed from his house and put them to flight.

Panthers, or "painters" as they were called in olden times, were not unfrequently shot by early settlers. Wild cats are still indigenous to the mountain range east of the lake, and running southerly into Torrington, as well as the Danbury quarter, where one was killed in November, 1871. Foxes and raccoons are still sufficiently numerous to afford good sport to huntsmen. Wild turkeys were brought in by our hunters as late as 1810, and probably later. A full-grown female hedgehog, or porcupine, the nursing mother of a living brood, was killed as late as 1860, on the Colebrook border.

Speckled trout, of large size and rare beauty, abounded in all our lakes and streams. In the boyhood of the writer, almost every ripple of Mad River, within the borough limits, had its trout ready to seize the bait or fly of the fisherman. In the lake some of them have been taken weighing five to six pounds. Perch, roach, and bull-heads of large size, and in great numbers, formerly occupied our lakes, but since the introduction of pickerel they have essentially fallen off in size and numbers. Fresh water eels may be caught in large numbers, in weirs along the lake stream, when descending at the fall equinox to deposit their spawn in some lower region, and in the following August their offspring, from three to six inches long, return in immense numbers. The basin of the Still River Falls, near Colebrook line, is for several days alive with them. They may be seen laboriously crawling up every rock which is moistened by the spray of the fall, and endeavoring to reach their ancestral lake or dam. At the foot of the Niagara Falls this phenomenon may be witnessed on a large scale at the same season of the year, or later, and probably in other places where the fall is too high and the current too swift for the young eels to stem it without contact with the rocks.

From these slippery reptiles the transition is natural to their finless congeners. Of these the rattle snake is the only one of a venomous

GAME—THOROUGHFARES. 27

character. They were numerous when the country was new, and are not yet extinct. One or more of them has, within twenty-five years, been killed in the wood-house of a residence on Main Street, in the borough of Winsted, and others in the contiguous region. The milk snake still, on occasions, robs the birds' nests in the shrubbery around our houses, and is sometimes suspected of milking our cows in the fields. The peaceful striped snake is not unfrequently caught in a disabled state for running away by reason of his gormandizing propensity for swallowing toads and frogs, and, when caught in the act, incurs the penalty of a bruised head, though in other circumstances he may, in these lax times, be carefully let alone, notwithstanding the scriptural malediction.

Before the survey and allotment of the Winchester lands, settlements in Goshen, Norfolk, and Canaan had begun, rendering it necessary for settlers from the eastern towns to pass through our township to their new homes. The Lawrences, and other settlers of Canaan, about 1738 to 1740, came from Windsor and Simsbury, first entered the wilderness by way of New Hartford, the northeast part of Winchester and southwest part of Colebrook, to the center of Norfolk. They left their families and stock at points along the way, where openings in the forests could be found for grazing, and went forward with their axes and cut down the trees and cleared a trail from one such opening to another, and then moved their caravan. Tradition says they made one of their halts on the Hoyt Farm in Colebrook, and went forward with their trail to a natural meadow at the northerly border of the small pond, a mile east of Norfolk Center, where they found a dead loon, and hence the name by which the location is still known. They returned, and brought forward their families and flocks to this oasis. From Loon Meadow they cleared their way to the foot of Hay Stack Mountain, and thence along the Blackberry River, to the land of Canaan, which to them must have been a happy land indeed after the toils and privations of their journey.

Where this trail passed through Winchester is not definitely known. It was, doubtless, the first that penetrated the town, and continued to be the traveled path in the direction of Albany for more than twenty years.

The General Assembly, at its May Session in 1758, "being advised that the road or way now often traveled through the towns of Simsbury, New Hartford, and Norfolk, to and through the northwestern parts of Canaan, towards Albany, is in many respects ill-chosen and unfit for use, and that some new and better road through said towns, or some of them, or the towns adjacent, may probably be discovered more direct and convenient, as well for carriages as traveling, to the great accommodation and benefit of his Majesty's subjects, and especially in time of war, occasionally traveling or marching, either from the eastern or central parts of the colony," therefore — " *Resolved*, that Colonel John Pitkin of Hartford, Seth Wetmore of Middletown, Mr. Wells of Glassenbury, and Colonel David Whitney of Canaan, be appointed a committee, as soon as conveniently may be, to repair to and through said towns (and towns adjacent if need be), and with all care and diligence to view and observe said roads now used; and also, with the utmost care to explore and find out how and where any other shorter and better way, in whole or in part, may be practicable, and their full description thereof, with their opinion thereon, to make report to the Assembly at their session in October (then) next."*

This committee, at the May Session in 1759, reported a new line of road, not departing in any instance more than two miles from a straight line, extending from the Court House in Hartford, to Colonel Whitney's in Canaan, and a plan of the intervening towns, with the line pricked thereon.

The Assembly accepted this report, and directed the committee " to lay out and make plain and certain, the said new country road from the mansion house of Samuel Humphrey in Simsbury, to Colonel David Whitney's in Canaan." In May, 1760, the committee having discharged their duty, the Assembly ordered the way to be cleared and made passable for traveling before November 20, 1761, by the towns and proprietors of townships through which it ran, and in case of non-compliance by any such towns and proprietors, the committee was to take such other measures to that end, at the expense of the delinquents, as would without fail accomplish the service, before May 1, 1762.

This thoroughfare, known to a former generation as " The North Road," and now almost a myth, had in its day an importance and renown which justifies our detailed history of its origin and progress. According to tradition, it was a wonder of the age that a direct and practicable route could be found and opened through the jungles and over the succession of steep rocky hills and mountains of the Green Woods for travel, and the movement of troops and munitions between Hartford and Albany. It soon became, and continued until 1800, the great and almost the sole thoroughfare of the colony in the direction of Albany. Continental troops passed over it for frontier service. Detachments of Burgoyne's army, as prisoners of war, marched over it to the quarters assigned them.

---

* Colonial Records, vol. 9, pp. 94–5.

There is a tradition that Col. Ethan Allen, while on military service in the Revolutionary War, presumed to desecrate the Sabbath by traveling over this road, instead of spending the day in sacred meditations at the hostelry of Landlord Phelps, or Roberts, on Wallen's hill, or of Landlord Freedom Wright, further westward, when a little bushy-headed Grand Juror, of our town, emerged from his log cabin on the road-side, siezed the bridle-rein of the Colonel's charger and attempted to arrest him as a Sabbath-breaker. The Colonel, sternly eying the legal dignitary, drew his sword, and flourishing it aloft, irreverently exclaimed, "You d—d woodchuck! get back into your burrow, or I'll cut your head off!" Grand Juror Balcomb, finding what a Tartar he had caught, prudently abandoned his captive and retired to his cabin.

It should not be inferred from the amount of travel that this road was an Appian Way. On the contrary. direct as it was, it went up and down the highest hills, on uneven beds of rocks and stones, and passed marshy valleys on corduroy of the coarsest hemlock log texture, commencing at the Northend village in New Hartford, it ran westerly up a steep hill, then turned northwesterly through the Bourbon region, crossing the Green Woods turnpike, a little west of the toll-gate, then northerly by zigzags to the top of a lofty hill, then over Wallen's Hill by the northeast school house, down to Still River near Daniel Wilson's, then up Dishmill Hill and onward by the Rowley Pond, to Colebrook, and onward through Colebrook center to Pond Hill, in Norfolk, and thence by Norfolk center and Canaan toward Albany.

Another bridle-path entered the township from the vicinity of Burrville and passed northwesterly by Landlord Mott's Tavern to the south part of Norfolk before any settlement was made. In 1762, a committee of the Assembly, previously appointed, reported a highway along this route, "beginning at a rock about three rods west of the fore door of the house belonging to Rev. Mr. Gold in Torringford, and running in a northwesterly direction a little more than a mile to Still River, about a hundred rods south of Yale's Mill, (at Burrville,) thence in a northwesterly direction by Spectacle Pond and Mott's house, to a stake and stones in Norfolk line."

This was the South Road, by which emigrants from the southeastern towns wended their toilsome way to the western townships, in process of settlement. It was so "hard a road to travel" that good Landlord Burr, living near the Hayden brick yard, used. as it was said, to detain his traveling guests until after morning worship that they might have the benefit of his prayers in aid of their arduous efforts to get up the old dug-way road, west of Burrville, an aid greatly needed.

The first of these roads was for many years the only way of access from the east to the Winsted section of the town. By the second, many, but not all of the immigrants, came into the "Old Society." Several of the earliest pioneers came in from Torrington and Goshen, at the extreme southwest corner of the township, and located in Hall Meadow and the Blue Street region. The later roads will be adverted to as the settlement of the town progresses.

CHAPTER V.

RESUMÉ—PIONEER SETTLERS.

WE have, in the preceding chapters, opened the way for the long-delayed settlement of our town. It seemed necessary to show, first, why the large domain of our western lands — the only unoccupied territory of the colony, Litchfield excepted — remained unsurveyed and unavailable for settlement from 1686 to 1729, a period of forty-three years. Second, if possible to learn why, after the two giant towns had secured and divided between them what may be aptly called their conquered territory, our Hartford step-fathers should still have held their assigned portion of the spoil from sub-division and settlement, twenty-nine years longer ; and third, to solve, if possible, the wisdom of the sub-divisions finally made. If the wisdom consisted in working out the problem — given, the settlement of a new town ; required, how not to do it ? — we have nearly reached a solution.

The triple division gave to each rich proprietor, at the rate of one acre to the pound, three detached farms of large size and compact forms ; to each forehanded owner, three small farms, two of them with average length and width as one to six, and one of half the same length and twice the width ; to the poorest men, two driblets a mile long, and from half a rod to five or ten rods wide, and one of half the length and twice the width.

There was not sufficient variation in the quality of lands to render the triple division expedient, for the whole area of the township was hilly and mountainous, except narrow intervales of gravelly or marshy lands along the streams.

The rich owners, with hardly an exception, held their lands, awaiting a rise in their value, to grow out of the life-and-death struggle of poor settlers on adjoining lands. None of the forehanded or rich owners ever personally occupied their land, and the poor owners could not if they would ; they could only sell out for mere songs their driblets to owners of larger tracts of adjacent lands. Not one of the one hundred and six original proprietors to whom allotments were made, ever occupied his lands or dwelt in the town, and only one son* of a proprietor ever had

---

* Thomas Hosmer, Jr., was an early settler on a portion of his father's land. He removed to Canaan after about ten years, and left no descendant behind him.

a permanent residence among us; and only three known descendants* of a proprietor now reside in the town.

We have already adverted to the scant and, to a great extent, unavailable reservations of land for highways, and to the endowment of two Hartford ministers by grants of three hundred acres of land to each; and the want of any endowment to aid the poor and almost starving settlers in supporting the gospel and common schools among themselves. A show of liberality, on a small scale, is made in the reservation of two mill lots, apparently designed to encourage the erection of mills to grind the corn and rye of the early settlers. If they were reserved for this purpose, they were not so appropriated. Both of them were disposed of by leases of nine hundred and ninety-nine years, without conditions, for the benefit of the proprietary body.

During the twenty-nine years that the Hartford proprietors were maturing a plan of division of their joint lands, many individual owners sold and conveyed away their undivided rights, by deeds, which were recorded in the proprietors' records. *Caleb Beach*, named of Goshen, became the owner of one of these undivided rights, by a deed dated May 21, 1750. Either despairing of a division ever being made, or hoping against hope for such consummation in the future, he at once, or in a very short time after his purchase, appropriated a small tract of land and erected thereon the first dwelling house in the township. It stood on the east side of the Hall Meadow road, about half a mile north of Torrington line, and about forty rods east of the line of Goshen, and some thirty rods south of the new house of Rufus Drake. This house or shanty disappeared more than a hundred years ago, and was replaced by a one-story frame house with stone chimney, erected on the same site, which is still standing — venerable in its marks of age, and still more venerable from its associations with the first human habitation in the town.

In the proprietors' vote of January, 1758, ordering the survey and allotment of the first and second divisions of land, the committee were instructed "to lay out to Mr. Caleb Beach or his assignees, his share or allotment in the Division where his house now is, so as to take in his house, barn, and orchard, if his allotment shall be wide enough to take [them] in." The lot set out to him or his assignees under these instructions, is a lot of sixteen and two-thirds acres, within lot No. 6, in the first division. He conveyed away his right to this allotment, March 18, 1756, and probably soon after moved back to Goshen, where he died January 13, 1760, aged sixty-one years. His will was probated and recorded in the Litchfield Probate Court, and contained the following bequests of his earthly possessions:

---

* Solomon R. Hinsdale and his child, and Mary P. Hinsdale, descended from William Pitkin.

"Imprimis, to my present beloved wife, Hannah, I give and bequeath one chest and one bed, and one great spinning-wheel, and one double spinning-wheel, to be her own and at her dispose.

Item, To my eldest daughter, Sarah Andros, the wife of Elon Andros, of Wallingford, I give and bequeath to her, out of my estate, but five shillings; she having received her portion of my estate before.

Item, To my sons Caleb and Hezekiah Beach, of Goshen, I give and bequeath my plough irons, and drag teeth, and plow chains, viz: to my eldest son, Caleb, two third parts; and to Hezekiah, one third part, to be their own and at their dispose.

Item, To my son, Joel Beach, of Torrington, I give and bequeath three steel traps, with the chains belonging to them, and my shaving knife, to be his own and at his dispose.

Item, To my daughter, Margit Beach, I give and bequeath three chests, one table, six puter platters and plates, three puter basins, four puter porringers, one pair of tongs, one fire shovel, and one tramel, one pair of andirons, one brass warming pan, one brass skillet, a brass kettle, one iron kettle and three iron pots, to be her own and at her dispose."

Mr. Beach was grandson of Thomas Beach, an early planter of Milford, son and youngest child of Deacon John, of Wallingford, and brother of Deacon John, of Goshen, from whom Beach street took its name. He was born at Wallingford, in 1699, where he married the first of his three wives. Thence he first removed to Goshen, and afterward to Winchester.

CALEB BEACH, born at Wallingford, in 1699; died January 13, 1761. He married first, May 26, 1726, Eunice Tyler. She died January 10, 1733. He married, second, October 4, 1733, Margaret Thompson. He had a third wife, named Hannah.

CHILDREN BY THE FIRST WIFE.

I. SARAH, b. at Wallingford, Oct. 26, 1728; m. Elon Andrews, of Wallingford.
II. CALEB, b. " May 10, 1732; m. Lois Preston.

CHILDREN BY THE SECOND WIFE.

III. HEZEKIAH, was in Goshen in 1760, and moved to New Ashford, Mass.
IV. JOEL.
V. MARGARET.

JOEL BEACH, third son of Caleb, and inheritor of his traps and shaving knife, came into the town with his father, at about fifteen years old, and is named as of Winchester in the record of his first marriage, in 1757. He afterwards lived in Torrington until 1761, when he purchased his life-long residence on Blue street, a little south of the stone school-house.

He is described by a cotemporary* as "a conservative of the first water,—conservative in his dress, in his food, and in all his habits—six

---

* Rev. Abel McEwen, D. D., of New London.

feet four or five inches high, gaunt and erect, with a pock-marked, weather-beaten face, large hands and feet, clothed in butternut colored coat, vest, and small clothes, garnished with long pewter buttons, stockings of black and white sheep's wool, cow-hide shoes of enormous size; crowned with a broad-brimmed, round-topped hat of dubious color; his costume on week days, Sundays, and training days, always the same, from early manhood to extreme old age. His fare was simple, consisting of bears' meat, venison, and wild turkey, when game abounded, and beef, pork, and mutton in after years, with toast and cider, mush and milk, and bean porridge, as his only luxuries."

He was, withal, a mighty hunter, never failing to bring down the deer, fox, or wild turkey with his six foot shooting-iron.

He was also a fish-fancier, and had stoned up a tank around a copious spring on the side of the road in front of his house, in which he kept a speckled trout of great size. There is another legend that a neighbor, with a long hooked nose, tinged at the end with deep red, coming along the road one day, stooped down to drink from the tank. The trout seeing the red protuberance, as it touched the water, and fancying it a gaudy insect, sprang upward and seized it. The nose recoiled, but too late. The fish was drawn out of the water, and dropped on dry land. Great was the rage of the man of the nose for a few moments, but as he surveyed the poor floundering fish, and reflected that he had got the worst of it, pity superseded wrath. Looking around and seeing no witness of his successful angling, he kindly restored the fish to the water and went on his way a happier man for his magnanimous act.

Mr. Beach's wife was also a dead shot. One day, near sunset, she discovered a panther* in a tree near the house. Her husband was away but his loaded gun was at hand. She seized and primed it, took deliberate aim, and lodged a bullet in its brain.

Mr. Beach was always a hard-working, temperate, and inoffensive man, who, in the words of the cotemporary before referred to, "had but little of religious theory, but in old age he became pious; and thence, down to the grave, his zeal for duty and worship glowed noiselessly but unquestioned. He died November 28, 1820, aged eighty-four; leaving his original farm, neither increased nor diminished by a single acre."

He married, at Torrington, October 18, 1757, widow Abiah Filley, of Torrington. He married, second, October 15, 1767, Amy Johnson, of Torrington.

---

* The *Felis Concator*, vernacularly named the "painter," was indigenous to this region, and is said to have been killed in Guilford or its vicinity, within the past fifteen years.

CHILDREN BY SECOND WIFE.

I. HEZEKIAH, b. July 19, 1768; bap. at Tor., Oct. 16, 1768.
II. JOEL, b. Oct. 3, 1769; bap. at Norfolk, Nov. 26, 1769. Killed by discharge of a gun, Oct. 19, 1771.
III. BENJAMIN, b. Dec. 7, 1770.
IV. JEREMIAH, b. April 19, 1772; d. Sept. 25, 1776.
V. JOSHUA, b. March 23, 1774.
VI. SEBA, b. Sept. 24, 1776.
VII. CALEB, b. Nov. 27, 1777.
VIII. PHEBE, b. May 15, 1779; d. June 2, 1780.
IX. SUSANNA, b. Jan. 18, 1783.

CALEB BEACH, seventh son of Joel, lived in the town landless, until his death, March 10, 1851. He married, June 25, 1797, Sarah Blakeslee.

CHILDREN.

I. ELIZABETH, b. July 3, 1798; d. December 2, 1804.
II. JONATHAN, b. November 19, 1799.
III. WILLIAM, b. January 25, 1802.
IV. SEBA, b. January 8, 1804.
V. CALEB, b. January 6, 1806.
VI. SUSAN SEREPTA, b. December 10, 1807; m. July 18, 1837, Friend Holcomb.
VII. HEZEKIAH, b. July 13, 1810.
VIII. SARAH, b. July 31, 1812.
IX. JULIA, b. April 25, 1815.
X. PHEBE, b. May 26, 1817.
XI. CLARISSA, b. June 2, 1819; m. December 31, 1837, Major Thorp, of Barkhamsted.

SAMUEL GILBERT, from Coventry, became a landowner and resident of the town in 1752, and is named of Winchester, in a deed of 1754, when he probably moved into Torrington, where his son, Samuel, was baptized August 25, 1754.

EBENEZER PRESTON, from Wallingford, and JOSEPH PRESTON, from Farmington, became owners of an undivided right of land in 1754, under which they entered upon, and improved, a small tract of land adjoining Torrington line, extending from Blue Street Road eastward to the north, and South Road in the second tier, which, under a vote of the proprietors, was allotted to them in the division of 1758. Here was their first dwelling place. They afterward lived, in various parts of the town, to a good old age, leaving sons and daughters, none of whom — nor any of their descendants bearing the name — now reside among us. The race was not a thrifty or vigorous one, physically or intellectually.

From the scant records of the family it is not possible to determine the relationships to each other of those of the name who were early residents.

MARTHA, wife of EBENEZER PRESTON, d. May 16, 1770, and he m. February 20, 1771, Martha Catling and had

CHILDREN.

I. PHEBE, b. July 20, 1773.
II. REBECCA, b. August 27, 1774; bap. Tor., Sept. 18, 1774.

JOSEPH PRESTON (senior), died in 1774.

JOSEPH PRESTON d. in Winsted in 1824, aged 85. He is believed to have been son to Joseph, the pioneer. He and his wife, known as "Uncle Joe and Aunt Keziah," lived early in this century, in a log shanty on Sucker Brook. They were a simple-minded couple, who lived by basket-making and renovating splint-bottomed chairs. They once lost the day of the week, and made Sunday a day of labor. They started for meeting on their old pillioned horse on Monday, and learning on the way their unintended desecration of the Sabbath, returned home and spent the rest of the day in penitential and devotional exercises.

JONATHAN and JOHN PRESTON, father and son, from Waterbury, named of Winchester in 1767, lived on a lot 41 first division, until 1769, after which their names disappear.

SAMUEL PRESTON, son of Ebenezer, owned and occupied a part of his father's land in 1768, and afterwards, until 1790, lived in the extreme south-west corner of the town. He was bap. Tor., Sept. 17, 1769; m. Jan. 4, 1770, Elizabeth Gleason.

CHILDREN.

I. MARTHA, b. Oct. 7, 1770.
II. SALMAN, b. Oct. 25, 1772.
III. SAMUEL, b. Dec. 20, 1776.
IV. MILLA, b. Aug. 22, 1779.
V. ELIZABETH, b. Feb. 16, 1785.

LANDLORD ADAM MOTT, originally from Windsor, erected his hostelry on the bridle-path that preceded the Old South Road, as early as 1754. It stood opposite the Hurlbut Cemetery, and on or near the site of the house of John Neth. The building was neither imposing nor spacious. Its walls were of unhewn logs, its roof of hemlock bark, with an opening in the ridge for the escape of smoke from the capacious stone chimney which ascended to the level of the garret floor. The landlord had two strapping boys, who slept under the roof, and occasionally worked off their superfluous animal force by a wrestling match before getting into bed. One cold winter night, when the hearth was all aglow with coals and embers of the consumed firewood, the boys, in their shirt tails, grappled for a trial of strength. They struggled long and vigorously. At length one of them got the dead lock of the other, at the edge of the yawning chimney. Both of them went headlong down the crater, into the coals and embers in the fireplace. Whether the tavern fare of the next day was called pork or bear's meat tradition does not say. It is presumable, however, if it was of the last night's roast, that it *was done brown*.

How a tavern could be sustained in this uninhabited region is hard to conceive. Landlord Mott, however, took courage and made the best of his business. To an inquiry as to how he succeeded in retailing his first keg of rum, he replied that he was doing remarkably well: that hunters, when they came along would fill their bottles, and that nearly every day he bought a glass of tanzy bitters of his wife, and that she would then buy one of him, with the same fourpence-halfpenny.

The bark-roofed tavern, in the course of years, gave way to a red lean-to mansion of the old Windsor order of architecture, and this in its turn to a pleasant modern cottage, drawing its water from the original well.

Landlord Mott became poor, and died in his native Windsor. He had children (as appears by deeds on record), Jonathan, Adam, junior, Lent, and Eunice, wife of Aaron Neal of Farmington, and may have had others.

JONATHAN MOTT, son of Adam, senior, came into the town with his father, and lived in a house on the slope of the hill, southeast of the tavern, which has long since disappeared. He died in 1818, aged 103, and was buried at the town's charge. His wife died in 1820.*

They had a son, SIMEON, baptized at Torrington, Dec. 23, 1653.

---

* On the anniversary of his 100th birthday the old man proposed to have some kind of a celebration, and requested that Uncle Reuben, Aunt Eunice, and Br. Daniel iCoe be invited to come around, which was done. Having been a "Singing Master" n his young manhood he thought nothing could be more appropriate to the occasion than the singing of "Old Hundred," during the performance of which he wielded the wand, which was his witch-hazel staff. He got through with that part of the programme quite satisfactorily, Br. Coe joining most vehemently, but when he came to try the *minuet* (and try it he would) he thought he could have gone through it much better if he had not been so long out of practice.

ADAM MOTT, Jr., succeeded his father in the homestead until 1767, and afterward lived west of the old Everitt Tavern. He went to Ticonderoga in 1775, in Captain Sedgwick's Company; served in Captain Beebe's Company in 1776, at Long Island, and was in other service during the Revolution. He removed to Vernon, N. Y., in his old age, where he was frozen to death at the age of about one hundred years.

He married Jan. 3, 1760, Abiah Filley. She died Oct. 19, 1784, and he married (second), February 14, 1786, Anna Cyrena Filley. She died June 5, 1806.

CHILDREN BY FIRST WIFE.

I. ELIZABETH, b. Nov. 12, 1760; bap. in Tor., March 30, 1761.
II. IRA, b. Feb. 13, 1764; bap. Tor., March 20, 1764.
III. DIANTHA, b. June 12, 1766.
IV. LODEMA, b. Sept. 9, 1768; bap. Tor., June 18, 1769.
V. SABRA, b. Nov. 1, 1770.
VI. ORANGE, b. Oct. 17, 1772.
VII. LOAMMI, b. May 5, 1775; m. Ap. 18, 1795, Polly Clark.
VIII. ABIAH, b. July 18, 1780.

CHILDREN BY SECOND WIFE.

IX. ANNA, b. Sept. 14, 1786.
X. ELIHU, b. Ap. 13, 1789.
XI. WAKEMAN IRA, b. Dec. 1, 1791.
XII. SOPHIA, b. June 15, 1794; d. Jan. 6, 1808.
XIII. ALVA GLEASON, b. Ap. 18, 1798.

LENT MOTT, son of Adam, senior, had land from his father near the old Everitt Tavern, on which he early resided. He served in the Northern Campaign, in 1775, and probably did other service. The name of his first wife, the mother of two of his children, does not appear. He married (second), January 1, 1766, Mary Filley.

CHILDREN.

I. SAMUEL, b. Goshen, Feb. 21, 1762; bap. Tor., Dec. 31, 1769.
II. MARY, bap. Tor., Dec. 31, 1769; d. W., July 15, 1783.
III. JOSIAH, b. Dec. 11, 1767; bap. Tor., Dec. 31, 1769.
IV. JERUSHA, bap. Norfolk, June 2, 1770.
V. JEMIMA, b. Ap. 19, 1771.
VI. LENT, b. May 12, 1773; m. Nov. 16, 1798, Lucy Ives.
VII. JERUSHA, b. Feb. 7, 1776.
VIII. SYLVANUS, b. July 3, 1778; removed to Vernon, N. Y.
IX. ITHAMAR, b. Feb. 26, 1781.

PIONEER SETTLERS. 39

LOAMMI MOTT, son of Adam, junior, married, April 18, 1795, Polly, daughter of Samuel Clark, of Winchester, and moved with his father-in-law, about 1800, to Stockbridge, Mass.

CHILDREN.

I. MERRITT, b. Jan. 3, 1796.
II. WILLARD, b. June 28, 1800.
III. LODEMA, b. Feb. 3, 1803, at Stockbridge, Mass.

IRA MOTT, son of Adam, junior, owned land on the Brooks Street Road in 1784, and on Blue Street in 1788.

The foregoing list comprises all the pioneers and their families who settled in the township before the survey and allotment in 1758, of whom we have any record or tradition, except Moses Miller and Joshua Merrills, who for a short period owned land on Hall Meadow, and in their deed conveying away the same, are named of Winchester.

CHAPTER VI.

PIONEER SETTLERS.

The Motts and Prestons seem to have been the only continuous residents of the town up to the division of lands in 1758, and for nearly three years afterwards.

WILLIAM FILLEY, the next settler, called in the deed "late of Torrington, now of Winchester," bought in 1761, seventy acres of land on Hall Meadow, south of Rufus Drake's, which included the land and house previously occupied by Caleb Beach, the first settler. He married in Torrington, June 11, or 13, 1759, Dinah Preston, of Winchester. He was drowned in a deep pool, called the tub, in the west branch, August 3, 1774, aged 39.

He was son of William Filley, of Torrington, whose widow, Abia, married Joel Beach. His brothers and sisters, who inherited his estate, were Abraham, Remembrance, Abia, wife of Adam Mott, Jr., Mary, wife of John Curtis, of Torrington and Marcy.

DEACON ABRAHAM FILLEY, inherited a portion of his brother William's estate and resided in the town most of his life. In 1772 his homestead was a part of the Col. Ozias Bronson farm. In 1774 he was of New Hartford, whence he removed to Winsted and had charge of Doolittle's mill; and afterwards lived and died in Old Winchester. He is said to have made a wooden clock with a pen-knife. In his later years he became a maniac, and was confined in a detached building. He and his wife Mary owned the convenant in Torrington church, June 6, 1762, and were admitted to full communion November 27, 1768. His children were:

    I. ISAAC, baptized in Torrington June 6, 1762.
    II. JESSE,   "   "   Sept. 9, 1764.
    III. LEVI,   "   "   May 31, 1767; was taxed from 1789 to 1802; residence not known.
    IV. RHODA, baptized in Torrington, April 9, 1769.
    V. ROGER,   "   in Winchester, May 25, 1771.

REMEMBRANCE FILLEY, baptized, Torrington, August 11, 1754;* inherited in 1774 a portion of his brother William's estate, which he exchanged for other lands. Before 1787 he lived on Blue Street, nearly one and a half miles north of Torrington line; and afterwards in Hall Meadow, near Rufus Drake's. He served in the revolutionary war, and in his old age became a pauper.

He married, August 20, 1774, Anna Cyrena Gleason, who was probably divorced from him, and afterward became second wife of Adam Mott, Jr. He married (2d), December 28, 1783, Hannah Hubbard.

CHILDREN BY FIRST WIFE:

I. WILLIAM, b. May 2, 1775.
II. ARUNAH, b. February 23, 1777.

CHILDREN BY SECOND WIFE:

III. CHARLOTTE, b. February 28, 1786.
IV. ABIGAIL, b. April 24, 1788,
V. HANNAH, b. June 25, 1790.

THOMAS HOSMER, Jr., son of Thomas Hosmer, Esq., of Hartford, one of the original proprietors, came into the town soon after 1761, and settled on the farm now owned by Abel S. Wetmore, which, after improving until 1771, he sold to Samuel Wetmore, Jr., of Middletown. His dwelling is supposed to have been on the Old South Coventry road, near the house named to widow Blake on the engraved map of the town. He was a leading man in the township and identified with all measures for its improvement during his residence. He sold out and removed to Canaan, in 1771, the year of the incorporation of the town.

It is noteworthy that he was the only known descendant of an original proprietor who ever settled on an ancestral lot; and that not one of the original proprietors ever occupied his land.

No record of Mr. Hosmer's family is found, except his (probable) second marriage (March 2, 1774) to Hannah Averet.

CORNELIUS MERRY, of Hartford, is grantee in a deed of January 14, 1762, conveying to him the John Pantry lot, first division, the western half of which became the Robert McEwen farm, now owned by Marcus Munsill; and the eastern half, on which his dwelling stood, on the Old South Coventry road, near Hurlbut Cemetery, became the property of John Hills. In a deed of 1770 he is named of Hartland.

JOHN SMITH, Jr., of Derby, is grantee in a deed of 1763, and John Smith, of Winchester, in another of 1754. He lived adjoining the Ebe-

---

* Son of William Filley, who, with his wife Abiah, joined the church in Torrington, July 17, 1754.

nezer and Joseph Preston lot, near the Torrington line, until 1771, when his name disappears.

DAVID AUSTIN'S name first appears as grantee in a deed from Cornelius Merry, of 1764, in which he is described as of Winchester. He probably came from Suffield. For thirty years or more he was perhaps the most prominent and enterprising citizen of the town. His first residence was on the Pantry lot above mentioned. In 1769 he purchased the Ensign lot, extending east and south from the outlet of the Long Pond so far as to embrace the pond stream and all the village of Winsted between Lake Street Bridge and Clifton Mill, a region then literally a howling wilderness, unapproached by roads and nearly unapproachable by reason of its jagged mountain ridges and heavy growth of timber, shrubs, and brambles. In 1771, he opened a cart-path through the forest, down to Sucker brook, and thence over the hills west of the Pond to its outlet, by which he conveyed the materials for the first grist mill in the town. This mill, and a saw-mill contiguous, were erected at the turn of Lake Street near the summit of the hill. The mill stood where the road now runs, a little northeastward of the Henry Spring Company's shop; the road as first opened running down the hill close to the old white dwelling now known as the Factory House. The water of the lake was raised some three feet above its natural level, by a frail dam of hemlock logs and plank, about three rods south of the present causeway, and let out by a new channel through a bulk head — the decayed parts of which are still to be seen in their place — and conveyed across the road nearly opposite the old stone-chimney mill-house and thence on the east side to the junction of Rockwell and Lake streets, and then again turned across Lake street and poured on the wheel of the mill.

This mill was, for about twenty years, the eastern terminus of civilized habitation towards Mad River valley. Mr. Austin's first residence in Winsted was in a log house nearest to the pond outlet. He subsequently built the stone-chimneyed lean-to house now known as the mill-house already mentioned. In one of the rooms he kept a small store of goods, at the same time personally attending his mill and saw-mill and his other concerns. A contemporary says of him: "The Deacon* commonly tended his own mill. In times of drought, when other mills failed, he ran his day and night, and had so disciplined himself that he would turn a grist into the hopper, lie down to sleep on a bench, with his old turnip watch ticking at his head and wake at the precise moment when the last kernel was running out."

---

*He was chosen first deacon of the Congregational Church, on Wallen's Hill (Ancient Winsted) in 1785.

It seems passing strange that with such results attained and with a sure prospect of increasing wealth and ease, a man of his advanced age should desire to renew his pioneer life on another field. He was induced by crafty misrepresentations to exchange his Winsted property, now worth hundreds of thousands, for wild lands in the State of Vermont which he had never seen, and which proved to be nearly worthless. He closed the bargain in 1796 and removed with all his family to Watertown, Vermont, where he spent his remaining days in straightened circumstances. His name appears in the records of the town as one of its prominent officers and efficient agents during the revolutionary period and his subsequent residence. His wife was a help-meet for such a man — industrious, thrifty, and prudent. Their hospitality was characteristic of the hard times in which they lived. The apples handed round to visitors were divided into halves or quarters, according to their size. A venerable citizen who, were he living, would be a hundred years old, once told me of his working the Deacon's saw-mill and living in his family when a young man and about to be married. On leaving, Madam Austin presented him with a complete assortment of garden seeds of her own raising, with the injunction thereafter to save his own seeds, and never to come to her for more, as she never gave to any person a second time.

CHILDREN OF DAVID AND MARY AUSTIN.

I. DAVID,   b. Aug. 5, 1761.
II. DANIEL,   b. Mch. 25, 1764 ; d. Oct. 13, 1775.
III. MARY,   b. July 8, 1766.
IV. RUTH,   b. Mch. 16, 1769.
V. ASA,   b. May 24, 1772 ; d. Feb. 12, 1776.
VI. DANIEL HARMON, b. Feb. 2, 1778.
VII. ASA,   b. May 7, 1781 ; d. Jan. 23, 1785.
VIII. PHEBE,   b. Oct. 4, 1783.

DAVID AUSTIN, junior, built and resided in the house adjoining the pond outlet. He married, September 30, 1782, Sarah Adkins. He moved to Vermont with his father.

CHILDREN.

I. SARAH,   b. Feb. 22, 1785.
II. BETSEY, b. Dec. 7, 1786.
III. ASA,   b. Aug. 12, 1788.
IV. DAVID,   b. July 16, 1791.
V. ORIN,   b. May 1, 1793.
VI. PATTY,   b. May 13, 1795.

BENONI HILLS,[1] born in Suffield in 1701 ; removed to Durham in

1724–5; to Goshen about 1740; afterwards to Torrington, and finally to Winchester, where he died, "ripe for heaven," June 24, 1793, in his ninety-second year. Several years before his death he selected two rough stones of Mica Slate, and shaping them to his liking, engraved in rude letters on one of them "Benoni Hills, this is my house," and on the other, "O eternity, death is come," to which is added, "June 24, 1793, B.H. act. 93." Working at these stones was the special enjoyment of his leisure hours. He brought them with him from Torrington, and gave special directions to have them placed over his grave, where they now stand, in the old Winchester burying ground. He married, December 19, 1723. His wife, b. June 3, 1700; died October 21, 1776.

CHILDREN.

I. HANNAH, b. Suffield, Oct. 5, 1724; m. — Wilson; died Tor., March 29, 1812.
II. ZIMRI, b. Durham, Dec. 16, 1725; d. Goshen, June 4, 1760.
III. BERIAH, b. D., Aug. 31, 1727.
IV. MEDAD, b. D., Ap. 27, 1729; d. Ap. 9, 1808.
V. MARY, b. D., Jan. 1, 1731; d. Jan. 28, 1732.
VI. JOHN, b. D., Dec. 13, 1732; d. Charlotte, Vt., March 15, 1808.
VII. MARY, b. D., Sept. 25, 1734; m. Epaphras Loomis.
VIII. SETH, b. D., Sept. 13, 1736.
IX. RACHEL, b. D., July 8, 1739; m. Dr. Joel Soper; d. Augusta, N. Y., Jan. 7, 1832.
X. BELA, b. Goshen, Aug. 24, 1741; d. May 29, 1756.
XI. ANN, b. G., June 11, 1743; m. Luman Beach; d. Norfolk, Jan. 22 1777.

SETH HILLS "of Winchester," is grantee in a deed of October 9, 1765, conveying to him fifty acres bordering on Torrington, in the third tier, first division, which he had probably occupied earlier.

Mr. Hills was first deacon of the church, and first representative of the town; a man of hardy constitution, indomitable energy, sound, good sense, and sincere piety; his integrity without a stain. He served as Wagon Master in the Saratoga campaign; was present at Burgoyne's surrender, and assisted in clearing the field of the dead and wounded when the battle was ended.

He sold out his homestead in 1798, and in the winter of 1798 went to Vernon, Oneida Co., N. Y., then without a white inhabitant, save two or three who went with him, where he cut down four acres of the heavy forest, on which to build his future home, and in the following autumn, with the assistance of his son Ira, then a lad of sixteen, burned, cleared, and fitted it for seed. He removed his family in the winter of 1799, and with the beginning of a new century, at the age of sixty-four, began the settlement of a new puritan town. His former neighbors, to the number

AND FAMILY RECORDS. 45

of nearly forty families, rallied around him, and laid the foundation deep and strong. A church was soon organized, made up mainly of Winchester members, of which Mr. Hills, Levi Bronson, and Samuel McEwen, all Winchester men, were the first deacons.

He married, November —, 1760, Abigail Soper. He died, Vernon, N. Y., June 3, 1826, aged nearly ninety years.

CHILDREN.

I. STATIRA,[3] b. July 6, 1762; m. Mch. 30, 1780—first, John Marshall of Torrington; second, Andrew Everitt, 1799.
II. JESSE,[3] b. May 17, 1764; m. Jan. 9, 1790, Mary Wheeler.
III. ELISHA,[3] b. May 8, 1766; d. June 11, 1766.
IV. ELISHA,[3] b. Dec. 9, 1769.
V. CANDACE,[3] b. June 1, 1772.
VI. HANNAH,[3] b. May 19, 1776.
VII. SETH,[3] b. Ap. 20, 1779.
VIII. IRA,[3] b. June 22, 1788.

CAPTAIN JOHN HILLS is named of Winchester, December 6, 1776, and doubtless came in earlier. He lived in a house that stood in or adjoining the Hurlbut Cemetery. He was a gunsmith by trade, and his shop stood near his house. He sold his homestead to James Atkins in 1781, and afterwards removed to Charlotte, Vt., where he died March 15, 1808, aged seventy-six. He was great grandfather of Deacon Abel S. Wetmore, now a resident of this town. He and his wife Jerusha, had

CHILDREN.

I. JERUSHA,[3] b. Nov. 26, 1755; m. May 12, 1774, Abel Wetmore; d. May 1, 1780.
II. LORRAIN LEWIS,[3] b. Feb. 6, 1758; d. Oct. 14, 1763.
III. ZIMRI,[3] b. Oct. 2, 1762; m. Mille Catlin, Jan. 17, 1782.
IV. ESTHER[3] (twin), b. June 1, 1766.
V. JOHN[3] (twin), b. June 1, 1766; d. July 21, 1766.
VI. LORRAIN,[3] b. May 30, 1768; d. Mch. 7, 1772.
VII. CLARAMAN (dau.), b. Oct. 5, 1770.
VIII. OLIVE,[3] b. July 23, 1773.
IX. LEWIS,[3] b. Sept. 8, 1775.
X. ROGER,[3] b. Jan. 9, 1779; d. Oct. 1, 1780.

BERIAH HILLS came into the town after 1769, and lived on Torrington line on the east side of the road, in the third tier, second division, running north from Fyler's. He was for several years appointed "to read the psalm" in the old meeting house, and died March 25, 1778, in his fifty-second year. His wife Mary survived him. Their

CHILDREN WERE:

I. MARY,³ bap. in Torrington, Mch. 20, 1748.
II. BENONI,³ " " Dec. 24, 1749.
III. LOIS,³ " " Feb. 2, 1751-2.
IV. CHAMERY,³ " " Feb. 17, 1754 ; m. Lois Grant.
V. BELA,³ " " Aug. 22, 1756.
VI. ROGER ENO,³ " " Mch. 4, 1759.
VII. ZIMRI,³ " " Ap. 23, 1763.
VIII. HULDAH,³ " " Aug., 1767.

MEDAD HILLS of Goshen, third son of Benoni, a gunsmith, who made muskets for the state during the Revolution, was a large landowner in Winchester, and resided at one period in the Norris Coe house. He had a son, Hewitt, who came into the town in 1788, and became one of its most prominent citizens. He will be spoken of hereafter.

JESSE HILLS, son of Deacon Seth, lived on the farm recently occupied by Samuel Hurlbut second, which he sold to Elijah Blake in 1798, and removed to Windham, Green Co., N. Y., and afterwards to Vernon, N. Y., and a few years later to Kirtland, Lake Co., O., where he died April, 1841, aged 81. He had a second wife.

CHILDREN BY FIRST WIFE.

I. LAURA, b. Oct. 14, 1790; m. Benj. D. Allen.
II. HULDAH, b. Jan. 19, 1793; m. Augustus Allen.
III. LUCY, b. Sept. 11, 1795; m. Ira Brown.

CHAUNCEY HILLS, second son of Beriah, "a noted stammerer," lived in his father's homestead bordering on Torrington line, until about 1802, when he sold out to Luke Case and William Bunnell, and removed to Litchfield, Herkimer Co., N. Y.

BENONI HILLS, oldest son of Beriah, had no real estate during the life of his father. One of his daughters married Chauncey Humphrey. He married, October 28, 1773, Elizabeth Agard, and had

CHILDREN.

I. THEODOSIA, b. Feb. 1, 1775.
II. ELIZABETH, b. Oct. 20, 1776.
III. AMANDA, b. Tor., June 18, 1780 ; bap. Aug. 27, 1780.

SETH HILLS and IRA HILLS, third and fourth sons of Deacon Seth, moved with their father to Vernon, N. Y. To the latter, the compiler is indebted for much valuable information respecting the family, and respecting Vernon families generally which originated in Winchester.

The Hills' in a body seem to have pulled up stakes and abandoned the town at the great exodus about 1800. Not a single descendant of Benoni Hills[1] bearing the name has lived in the town for several years. Descendants in the female line are not unfrequent.

Deacon Abel S. Wetmore is descended from Benoni[1] in the fifth generation.

In 1751 Captain Josiah Avered, of Woodbury, (Bethlem Society) became the owner of undivided lands in Winchester, and was soon after disabled by the kick of a horse, and confined to his bed until his death in 1765. His property being almost exhausted during his protracted confinement, his widow, Mrs. Hannah (Hinman) Avered, or Everett, as now spelled, soon after his death removed with her aged mother and seven children to the wilds of Winchester, while there were as yet but three families in the central part of the old society. They stayed in a house on the farm now owned by Deacon Abel S. Wetmore, until a clearing had been made and a house erected on their land about two miles north of the center, on the old South Country road, as it then ran toward Norfolk. This house is the oldest now standing in the town.* It has never been painted, and had not, when built, an iron hinge or latch on any of its doors.

Here this energetic and godly woman reared her young family, and so discharged the duties of a mother and revolutionary matron, that her children and fellow-townsmen might well rise up and call her blessed. Her aged grand-daughter, Mrs. Swift, now of New York, has permitted the copying from her reminiscences the following account of the experiences of the pioneer family:

"It is evident that my grand-mother removed from Bethlem in 1765; and with her children, came also her mother, Mrs. Mary Noble Hinman, who died in Winchester, at 92 years of age. The date of her death is not known. Her grave is on the left hand of her daughter's, as you face the head-stone of the latter. She is said to have been born in Northampton, and to have removed to old Milford at the age of 16, and that soon afterward, on a Sabbath morning, she and her sister went into the forest to collect thorns with which to dress themselves in order to attend church at New Haven. This sister was ancestress of President Day.

"During the severe winters of that period, the hungry wolves howled in the little enclosure of my grand-mother's cottage during the nights, and

---

* It was crushed to the ground by the weight of snow in the winter of 1870–71.

were seen to jump over the fence when any one opened the door. Many are the incidents related in my childish ears, of the sufferings of the family during the revolutionary war, particularly in the 'hard winter' of '83.

"No grinding could be done at the mill — snow fell every other day for six weeks — and the wind and drifting seemed only a continuation of the storm! Grain and corn were *boiled* for family use. Wood was drawn on the tops of the drifts, on a hand-sled by my Uncle Andrew (the youngest son) on snow shoes, and received by his sisters through a window at the back of the house. My Uncle Noble at this period was a chaplain in the army, and my father (Josiah), also away getting his profession, and afterwards in command of a company on the Canada frontier.

"During the hard winter a piece of check-woolen for soldiers' shirts was put into the loom, but it was impossible to weave it on account of the cold; so it was all wound out in balls, then doubled (one thread white and the other blue) and twisted on the 'great wheel'; and thus prepared, my grand-mother and her four daughters sat in a circle, — enclosed by blankets suspended from the joists over head around the high fire-place — and knitted the yarn into stockings for the army. One night during these times, my grand-mother and her children sat up amid the howlings of the winter blasts, in consultation whether they should break up housekeeping and each take care of themselves. After retiring and passing the remaining night sleepless, grand-mother arose in the morning, and told her family that 'by the help of God they would keep together.'

"When she was 84 years old, she often rode on horseback from her home two miles to the village, went to the store, then stopped at my father's to rest, and then rode home alone. She was 89 at her death.

"During the war my Aunt Diana, one Monday morning, received an invitation to a wedding just one week from that evening; she must, therefore, have a 'new gown.' The only store in the town was south of the burying-ground, near Torrington line, nearly four miles distant. My grand-mother rode over the hills to the store, where she found a pattern of chintz, which she could have for eleven and a half yards of checked woollen shirting for soldier's wear; but could not buy it with 'continental bills.' The old lady returned about one hour before 'sundown,' and told her story. 'We had,' says my aunt, 'wool, cards, wheel, net, loom, and blue dye all in the house, but not a thread of yarn. That night, before I went to bed, I carded, spun, washed, and put into the dye-tub, one run of yarn, and so the work went on; the cloth was wove, the 'gown' pattern purchased, made up, and worn to the wedding at the week's end. I have often seen this gown; and in 1843 I slept under a bed-quilt, made principally from its remains, in a good state of preservation.

"On another occassion, years afterwards, (within my own memory) this Aunt Diana, being engaged at her cheese-tub, heard the cry of a chicken at the open door; looking out, she perceived a large hen-hawk pounced on a poor fowl, her back towards her. With a long cheese knife in her hand she sprang lightly forward and sat down over the hawk, took him by the head and, with her knife, cut it off. 'He acted as if he felt ashamed when I was doing it,' she said, when she told me the story. Often have I played with its great talons.

"Aunt Diana, — afterwards wife of Deacon Theophilus Humphrey, of Canton — was almost 91 years old at her death, December 11, 1843. She was remarkable for her piety and talents — was educated beyond what was common at that early period — had spent three years at school in New London."

Richard Everitt, one of the founders of Dedham, Massachusetts, had a son, Israel,[2] born July 14, 1657; who had a son, Josiah,[3] born August 3, 1768; who had a son, Josiah,[4] born August 5, 1710, at Guilford, Connecticut; who married Hannah Noble Hinman. He died in Bethlem; will proved March 19, 1765. She died in Winchester, May 19, 1803, aged 88.

CHILDREN:

I. ELIHU,[5]   b. March, 5, 1741, d. October 25, 1759.
II. MARY,[5]   b. February 13, 1743; d. March 9, 1760.
III. AARON,[5]   b. April 3, 1745; d. December 4, 1761.
IV. REV. NOBLE,[5] b. March 3, 1747.
V. DOCT. JOSIAH,[5] b. February 27, 1749.
VI. HANNAH,[5]   b. January 1, 1751; m. March 2, 1774, Thomas Hosmer.
VII. DIANA,[5]   b. February 14, 1753; d. December 11, 1843; m. Dea. Theophilus Humphrey.
VIII. ANDREW,[5] b. July 30, 1755; } Twins. d. Jan. 31, 1835.
IX. MABEL,[5]   b. "   "   "   }   d. February 24, 1804; m. May 30, 1776, Daniel Corbin.
X. AMELIA,[6]   b. May 14, 1757; d. October 22, 1843; m. May 15, 1782, Doct. Sol. Everitt.

REV. NOBLE EVERITT, graduated at Yale, in 1775, served as a chaplain in the revolutionary army, afterwards settled in the ministry at Wareham, Massachusetts, and died in the discharge of his pastoral duties December 30, 1819.

DOCTOR JOSIAH EVERITT,[5] married December 5, 1776, Esther Hinman. She died September 30, 1783, in her 30th year. He married (2d) February 23, 1785, Nelly, daughter of Captain Samuel Pease, of Enfield, Connecticut; born December 23, 1762; she died, November 2, 1791;

and he married, (3d) September 26, 1794, Hannah Stanley, who died, June 27, 1826. He died, February 5, 1829, aged 80. He studied medicine with Doctors Bird, of Bethlem, and Hall, of Woodbury, and settled in Winchester as a physician, living first in the store building, recently torn down, that stood in front of Mr. Theron Bronson's new store at Winchester centre, and afterwards, through his remaining life, in the house now occupied by his son, Noble J. Everitt, a quarter of a mile south of the centre.

He served as captain of a company of Connecticut troops in the Northern army in the first year of the revolutionary war.

CHILDREN OF DOCTOR JOSIAH[5] AND NELLY (PEASE) EVERITT.

I. NELLY MINERVA,[6] b. July 30, 1786; m. Doct. Zepheniah Swift.
II. JOSIAH NOBLE,[6] b. December 10, 1788; m. Roxy L. Cook, daughter of Elisha Cook, Esq.
III. CHESTER P.,[6] b. November 12, 1790; d. April 24, 1807.

CHIDREN OF DOCTOR JOSIAH[4] AND HANNAH (STANLEY) EVERITT.

IV. HANNAH B.,[6] b. June 7, 1798; m. March 8, 1825, Rev. Henry Bushnell.
V. MARY,[6] b. December 29, 1799; d. May 29, 1807.

ANDREW EVERITT,[5] married, May 18, 1780, Abigail North. She died, June 2, 1795, aged 31; and he married (2d), December 26, 1799, Statira, daughter of Deacon Seth Hills, and widow of John Marshall. He resided with his mother in the old homestead until her decease, and continued to own and occupy it until 1809, when he sold it, and removed to Vernon, New York, where he died.

CHILDREN OF ANDREW[5] AND ABIGAIL (NORTH) EVERITT.

I. ELIHU,[6] b. December 16, 1780; d. September 11, 1781.
II. ELIHU,[6] b. January 21, 1783; m. Roxy, daughter of John Marshall.
III. ANDREW HINMAN,[6] b. October 27, 1788; d. March 9, 1791.

CHILDREN OF ANDREW[5] AND STATIRA (HILLS) EVERITT.

IV. ANDREW HINMAN,[6] b. November 26, 1800.
V. TRUMAN,[6] b. December 26, 1801; d. October 9, 1804.
VI. ELISHA,[6] b. February 15, 1805.

JONATHAN COE,[5] of Torrington, purchased 100 acres of land at the south end of the third tier, first division, lying immediately north of the farm of Deacon Seth Hills, in 1764, which remained in his family ninety-nine years. In 1765 he conveyed one half of this lot to his son Oliver, and the other half to his son Robert. He was born in Durham, Connecticut, about 1710; son of Robert⁴ and Barbara (Parmele) Coe; grand-son of John³ and Mary (Hawley) Coe; great-grand-son of Robert² and   Coe; and great-great-grand-son of Robert¹ Coe, who was born in Suffolkshire, England, in 1596, and came to New England with his wife Anna, in 1634; settling successively in Watertown, Massachusetts; Wethersfield and Stamford, Connecticut; and in Hempstead, Newtown, and Jamaica, Long Island. He married in Durham, September 23, 1737, Elizabeth Elmer, and was one of the first settlers of Torrington. They came to Winchester when old. She died June 28, 1794, aged 84; he died April 23, 1795, aged 84.

CHILDREN.

I. OLIVER,⁶ b. in Torrington, September 3, 1738.
II. ROBERT,⁶ b. in " March 28, 1740.
III. JONATHAN,⁶ b. in " August 20, 1742; m. April 15, 1767, Eunice Cook; she d. April 12, 1818; he d. August 21, 1824.
IV. ELIZABETH,⁶ b. in Torrington, September 5, 1743.
V. JERUSHA,⁶ b. in " March 27, 1746.
VI. MARTHA,⁶ b. in " January 5, 1748–9.
VII. EBENEZER,⁶ b. in " December, 2, 1750; d. in Torrington, October 18, 1784.
VIII. LUCRETIA,⁶ b. in " June 9, 1755; m. March 18, 1776, Daniel Murray, she d. June 1792.

OLIVER COE,⁶ moved on to the south half of the above lot at or soon after the date of his deed and occupied the same until his death, December 31, 1775, at the age of 37. He served in the continental army under Captain Sedgwick, and Colonel Hinman, at Ticonderoga, in 1775; was discharged November 20th; was taken sick on his way home near Lake George; procured a horse on which he reached home November 28th; and was confined to his bed with the camp or typhoid fever, until his death, five weeks afterward. He left a widow and six children, from three to thirteen years old, all of whom were sick with the same disease. These facts are gathered from a memorial to the assembly by his administrator, asking a reimbursement of the expenses of his sickness and death on which a grant was allowed of £14 6s. He married, October 7, 1762, Mary Agard, of Torrington.

CHILDREN.

I. ABNER,⁷ b. in Torrington, April 12, 1763; m. May 20, 1784, and had Wealthy, b. Oct. 16, 1785; moved to Burk, Vt., had five more children; and d. Aug. 15, 1846.
II. OLIVER,⁷ b. November 7, 1764.

III. MARY,⁷ b. September 2, 1766; d. September 13, 1766.
IV. JUSTUS,⁷ b. September 1, 1767; m. 1789, Ruth Bailey; they moved to Jewett, N. Y., where she d. March 4, 1838; and he in June 1850.
V. MARY,⁷ b. December 6, 1769; m. Doctor Abraham Camp, of Mt. Morris, N. Y.; she d. 1846.
VI. JOB,⁷ b. April 22, 1772.
VII. JAMES,⁷ b. May 31, 1774.

ROBERT COE,⁶ settled on the north half of the hundred acre lot aforesaid, and remained until 1768, when he sold out to his brother, Jonathan Coe, Jr. He afterwards owned and lived on the Levi Bronson farm near the southeast corner of Norfolk, until 1788, when he removed to Cooperstown, New York. He married, December 26, 1764, Chloe Thrall.

CHILDREN.

I. JOEL,⁷ b. May 4, 1765.
II. ARMANDA,⁷ (son), b. July 3, 1767.
III. ABIJAH,⁷ b. October 23, 1769.
IV. ARIEL,⁷ b. October 31, 1772.
V. ROSWELL,⁷ b. February 5, 1780.

JONATHAN COE, Jr.,⁶ known as Ensign Jonathan Coe, moved with his father and mother in 1768 on the farm until then occupied by Robert Coe, where Jonathan Coe, senior, died. He removed to Winsted in 1796 and resided until near his death in the house afterward occupied by Col. N. D. Coe. He married, April 15, 1767, Eunice Cook. She died April 12, 1818; he died August 1, 1824.

Ensign Coe may be considered the father of the Methodist denomination in the town; having been perhaps the earliest convert and a consistent and earnest supporter of the order through his life.

CHILDREN.

I. LOVINA,⁷ b. February 11, 1768; m. October 26, 1788, Asahel Miller.
II. JONATHAN,⁷ b. March 23, 1770.
III. EUNICE,⁷ b. March 27, 1772; m. January 20, 1793, Abiel Loomis.
IV. ROGER,⁷ b. July 27, 1774, (see 1795).
V. RHODA,⁷ b. March 27, 1777; m. Eben Woodruff, of Barkhamsted.
VI. HULDAH,⁷ b. January 3, 1779; m. May 16, 1796, Major Lloyd Andrews.
VII. DAVID,⁷ b. February 11, 1781.
VIII. DANIEL,⁷ b. February 2, 1783.
IX. EBEN,⁷ b. July 9, 1785.

OLIVER COE, Jr.,⁷ owned and lived on the Henry Drake farm, near Torrington line, in the second tier, first division, from 1805 to 1814, when he moved to Hudson, Ohio, and died there August 14, 1825, aged 61.

He served on several tours of duty in the revolutionary war, and on the breaking out of the Indian war again enlisted for three years, and served in General Harmer's campaign down the Ohio, and was one of seven survivors of Col. Harden's detachment which was cut off by the Indians on the headwaters of the Scioto in the fall of 1791. He also served as military guard of the surveying party that surveyed the Ohio Company's purchase; after which he returned to the place of his nativity and became a thrifty and wealthy farmer, enjoying in a high degree the respect and confidence of the communities in which he lived. He married, December 1, 1791, Sarah Marshall, daughter of Thomas. He married (2d), Chloe Spencer, daughter of Thomas. He died in Hudson, Ohio, August 14, 1825.

CHILDREN BY FIRST WIFE.

I. NORRIS,[8] b. May 1, 1792; m. March 10, 1814, Chloe Hubbell, b. January 25, 1788, daughter of Silliman Hubbell.
II. DEMAS,[8] b. January 11, 1794; m. April 15, 1819, Eliza Ward. He d. December 1, 1853.
III. ARTEMISIA,[8] b. December 5, 1799; m. 1815, George Chase.

JONATHAN COE, Jr.,[7] married, October 3, 1792, Charlotte Spencer, daughter of Thomas. She died July 15, 1842, aged 70. He married (2d), Huldah (Spencer) Wetmore, widow of John Wetmore, 2d, and sister of his first wife. She died July 10, 1845; and he married (3d), November 30, 1848, Mrs. Betsey (Miller) Wetmore, of Wolcottville. He died May 31, 1849; she died September 18, 1850, aged 80.

CHILDREN.

I. JEHIAL,[8] b. October 5, 1794.
II. CHLOE,[8] b. February 24, 1797; m. Chauncy Eggleston.
III. WEALTHY,[8] b. March 1, 1799; m. May 10, 1820, Nelson Wilson; she d. February 2, 1845.
IV. CHARLOTTE,[8] b. August 24, 1801; d. February 15, 1814.
V. ASAHEL,[8] b. April 4, 1804.
VI. SYLVIA,[8] b. August 12, 1806; m. September 20, 1825, Samuel Boyd.
VII. HULDAH,[8] b. April 6, 1809; m. October 13, 1834, Erastus Sterling Woodford; she d. April 18, 1859.
VIII. JANE,[8] b. August 14, 1812; m. October 13, 1834, Henry Hinsdale; she d. October 5, 1839; he d. October 14, 1846.
IX. RUTH,[8] b. April 5, 1814; m. November 30, 1837, Abel A. Smith; he d. May 11, 1841; she d. April 18, 1847, childless.

DAVID COE,[7] married, March 15, 1804, Prudence Ward. She died February 23, 1823, aged 42; he married (2d), Esther Wright. He died June 12, 1834.

CHILDREN.

I. SAMUEL WARD,[8] b. June 10, 1805; m. August 16, 1831, Abigail B. Sanford; she died December 23, 1838; he married (2d), May 10, 1841, Julia M. Starks. In company with Luman Hubbell and E. S. Woodford, he engaged in trade at Winsted about 1830, and continued the business until his death, September 20, 1868, and was largely identified with the public interests of the town, filling with ability many offices of trust and honor. He was Justice of the Peace from about 1830 to the time of his death; Town Clerk from 1833 to 1837, and from 1841 to 1851; Judge of Probate from 1843 to 1850; State Senator in 1850. He was also a faithful member and office-bearer of the Methodist Episcopal Church from early manhood. As a citizen, public spirited and a faithful worker in the Temperance and Anti-Slavery causes; as a neighbor, kind and obliging — especially to the sick and dying. Social in disposition, respected and beloved in life, and lamented in death. Children by first wife; 1. Charles Betts,[9] b. January 15, 1838; 2. David Ward,[9] b. May 11, 1836. By second wife: 3. Francis Abby,[9] b. June 26, 1842; 4. Wilbur Fisk,[9] b. November 23, 1844.

II. EMERY,[8] b. March 17, 1809; m. May 7, 1837, Almira Griswold; he d. August 27, 1861; she m. (2d) March 22, 1866, Milo Burr, of Torrington. Children: 1. Sarah Jane,[9] b. March 29, 1840; 2. Edward Griswold, b. April 3, 1847.

III. SALLY,[8] b. June 24, 1811, m. November 17, 1834, Alvin Gilbert.

IV. DAVID FLETCHER,[8] b. June 30, 1819; d. September 7, 1823.

V. PRUDENCE,[8] daughter of David[7] and Esther W. Coe, b. July 1, 1828; d. September 11, 1829.

REV. DANIEL COE,[7] married, October 17, 1803, Mrs. Anna (Sweet) Keyes, daughter of Rev. John Sweet; she died November 29, 1818. He married (2d), January 20, 1820, Lucy Hall; he died January 12, 1847.

CHILDREN.

I. CAROLINE,[8] b. September 20, 1804; m. April 15, 1833, Wm. Currie.

II. CLARISSA ANNA,[8] b. April 16, 1807; m. December 30, 1829; Shadrack Manchester.

III. LOUISA,[8] b. April 11, 1809; m. March 14, 1836, Oliver H. Loomis; he d. December 25, 1838; she m. (2d), September 9, 1845, Chas. Hall.

IV. COL. NELSON DANIEL,[8] b. November 8, 1811.

V. REV. JONATHAN,[8] b. June 1, 1815.

VI. REV. JAMES ROGER,[8] b. March 30, 1818.

EBEN COE,[7] married, December 1, 1806, Eliza Kirkham; he died September 10, 1818.

CHILDREN.

I. JULIA,[8] b. August 26, 1807; m. Voorhies.

II. SAMUEL MILLS,[8] b. February 21, 1809; d. December 26, 1809.

III. ELIZA,[8] b. December 23, 1811; m. Porter, of Cleveland, Ohio.

IV. CHARLES,[8] b. October 25, 1816.

AND FAMILY RECORDS. 55

JEHIAL COE,[3] married, September 4, 1816, Amanda Betsey Case, born in Simsbury, April 28, 1797, daughter of Luke and Betsey (Adams) Case. She died February 18, 1855; and he married (2d), September 25, 1856, Mrs. Harriet E. Sage.

CHILDREN.

I. CHARLOTTE,[9] b. December 21, 1817; m. September 14, 1841, Lemphier B. Tuttle.
II. LUKE CASE,[9] b. June 13, 1821; m. July 18, 1844, Sarah Jane Andrews, and has Lillie, adopted April 7, 1855, b. August 17, 1847; and Florence Amanda,[10] b. July 11, 1857.
III. SPENCER WALLACE,[9] b. October 15, 1827; m. June 3, 1856, Carrie Capron, of New York; and has 1. Spencer Capron,[10] b. April 4, 1858.
IV. WILLIAM GILMORE,[9] b. September 10, 1829; m. September 15, 1852, Martha A. Williams; she d. October 6, 1854, leaving a daughter, Martha Jane,[10] b. in Jonesville, New York, February 17, 1854; and he m. (2d) May 27, 1856, Jeannette T. Lee; and has Minnie Agnes,[10] b. October 31, 1857; and Alice Lee,[10] b. August 12, 1859.*
V. MARY JANE,[9] b. June 20, 1831.

ASAHEL COE,[3] married, April 26, 1826, Louisa Hale, born in Glastonbury, July 31, 1803, daughter of Ebenezer and Sarah (Cornwall) Hale; they removed to Pennsylvania, settling finally at Lock Haven.

CHILDREN.

I. ANNA,[9] b. in W., October 2, 1827; m. E. S. Woodford.
II. JONATHN HALE, b. in Honesdale, Pennsylvania, March 6, 1831; d. May, 1832.
III. WILLIAM HALE,[9] b. in Rome, Pennsylvania, January 23, 1843.

COL. NELSON D. COE,[3] married, February 5, 1834, Maria H. Seymour; he died November 1, 1856.

---

* He died of a disease of the brain, after a long and distressing illness, May 31, 1872. He studied law with Hon. O. S. Seymour; was admitted to the Litchfield bar in 1851; entered into successful practice at New Britain, Connecticut; whence he returned to Winsted in 1856, where he engaged in manufacturing business as Agent of the Clifton Mill Company, and soon became prominently identified with the public interests of the community — originating our Borough Corporation and Water-works, and efficiently aiding all other measures of public improvement. Though not the originator, he was the leading organizer of the Connecticut Western Railroad Company, and acted as its Secretary from its organization to the time of his prostration by the disease that caused his death. He served in two sessions of the General Assembly, acquitting himself with decided ability, and wielding a large influence. He was gifted with a magnetism that made him a natural leader of others, and secured to him the warm attachment of many friends and admirers. At the centennial of the town in August, 1871, he presided with a dignity and ability creditable alike to himself and to the community he represented.

CHILDREN.

I. LUCY ANN,[9] b. November 18, 1834; m. December 24, 1857, Rufus E. Holmes; has children: 1. Anna Louisa, b. September 17, 1860; 2. Susan Beecher, b October 27, 1862; 3. Rufus, b. April 4, 1865, d. March 16, 1866; 4. Edward Rufus, b. March 7, 1867; 5. Ralph Winthrop, b. October 6, 1869.
II. JAMES NELSON,[9] b. October 20, 1836; m. July 19, 1857, Kate R. Goddard. He was Lieut. in 2d Connecticut Heavy Artillery. Children: 1. Nelson Daniel,[10] b. October 17, 1858; 2. Kate Goddard,[10] b. July 6, 1865; 3. Harriett Maria,[10] b. September 20, 1869.
III. A SON,[9] b. 1838; d. same day.
IV. DANIEL SIDNEY,[9] b. August, 1840.
V. ELLEN MARIA,[9] b. March 31, 1845.

REV. JONATHAN COE,[8] married, in Bridgewater, Massachusetts, October 15, 1844, Sarah Wales Whitman; born March 30, 1815; she died September 5, 1848; and he married (2d), January 1, 1850, Susan L. Whitman, sister of his first wife. He was a graduate of Trinity College, Hartford, a minister of the Protestant Episcopal Church, and first Rector of St. James' Church, Winsted. He died of a railroad accident at Athens, New York, about 1867.

CHILDREN.

I. JAMES HERBERT,[9]   b. July 22, 1845.
II. WILLIAM WATSON,[9]   b. November, 1846.
III. HARRIET WHITMAN,[9]   b. September 2, 1848; d. September 4, 1848.
IV. ALLEN WHITMAN,[9]   b. August 27, 1851; d. April, 1852.
V. ROBERT HENNING,[9]   b. October   1852; d.
VI. REGINALD,[9]   b. July 22, 1854.
VII. MARY CLEVELAND,[9]   b. July 22, 1856; d.   1857.
VIII. ANNA CAROLINE,[9]   b. October, 1858.

REV. JAMES R. COE,[8] a clergyman of the Protestant Episcopal Church; married, October 4, 1848, Mary Cleveland; born December 23, 1830, daughter of Charles C. and Rachel (Talcott) Cleveland.

CHILDREN.

I. ANNA HIGLEY,[9]   b. August 10, 1849.
II. SARAH WHITMAN,[9]   b. January 13, 1851.
III. GEORGE JARVIS,[9]   b. May 7, 1853.
IV. CHARLES CLEVELAND,[9]   b. June 13, 1855.
V. MARY CLEVELAND,[9]   b. December 17, 1857.

ROBERT MCEWEN, a native of Dumfries, Scotland, a covenanter, who fought at Bothwell Brig, was apprehended by the English government, and with others, was allowed to come to America, in the Henry and Francis; he landed at Perth Amboy, New Jersey, December 18, 1685, and the next summer walked to Stratford, Connecticut, arriving there July 18, 1686, where he married, June 20, 1695, Sarah, daughter of Timothy Wilcoxson. He died in Stratford, February, 1740.

CHILDREN.

I. JOHN,[2] b. in Stratford, September 20, or 23, 1697.
II. ELIZABETH,[2] b. " " November 7, 1699.
III. ROBERT,[2] b. " " March 7, 1702.
IV. SARAH,[2] b. " " November 5, 1704.
V. TIMOTHY,[2] b. " " April 11, 1707.
VI. GERSHOM,[2] b. " " April 7, 1711; m. January , 1737, Martha, daughter of Samuel Pickett. He bought in 1766, of David Austin, the farm now owned by Marcus Munsill, about a quarter of a mile south of Winchester center. He was called of "Winchester," in 1773. He owned and occupied land next south of Sylvester Platt's farm, until his death, August 31, 1794. She d. in Sangersfield, New York, in 1798, aged 86.

CHILDREN OF GERSHOM[2] AND MARTHA (PICKETT) M°EWEN.

I. MARY,[3] b. S., Apr. 1, 1738; m. Apr. 17, 1760, Peter Blackman.
II. ROBERT,[3] b. S., June —, 1743; came to Winchester soon after his father made the first purchase in 1766, and began to clear and improve the land. He married October 10, 1770, Jerusha Doolittle. She died December 10, 1815, aged sixty-three. In 1769 his father conveyed the lot to him, and he continued to own and occupy it until his death, Nov. 17, 1816, at the age of seventy-three. He was a member, and was constituted moderator of the Church at its organization in 1770, and became one of its deacons in 1799; was a representative in nine sessions of the assembly from 1781 to 1797; filled nearly every office of trust in the town, and performed several terms of military duty in the Revolutionary War. This record indicates the estimation in which he was held. He inherited from his covenanting ancestors rectitude, shrewdness, and thrift, which, when combined with earnest piety, made him a strong pillar of the infant Church and town. He was father of Rev. Abel McEwen, D.D., late of New London, deceased.
III. SARAH,[3] b. S., Apr. —, 1747.
IV. SAMUEL,[3] b. S., December, 1749; came with his father to Winchester; married October 7, 1773, Lois Sherman. He owned and occupied the Deacon Platt farm until 1798, when he removed to Vernon, N. Y., and became a pioneer of that town, and one of the deacons of the Church at its organization.
V. GERSHOM,[3] b. S., ——; married April 24, 1777, Thankful Andrews. He came into the town with his father, and owned and occupied a house and land north of and adjoining the homestead of Deacon Abel S. Wetmore, until 1796, when he removed, as is believed, to Sangersfield, N. Y.

CHILDREN OF ROBERT³ AND JERUSHA (DOOLITTLE) M°EWEN.

I. SARAH,⁴ b. February 6, 1772; died March 23, 1772.
II. SARAH,⁴ b. March 2, 1775; m. Solomon Rockwell, Esq.
III. ABI,⁴ b. April 8, 1777; m. May 29, 1800, James Beebe, Esq.
IV. ABEL,⁴ b. February 13, 1780; graduate Yale College 1804; m. January 21, 1807, Sarah Battell, b. May 29, 1781, daughter of William Battell, Esq., of Tor. He died at New London, September 7, 1860. She died March 9, 1859. He was pastor of Cong. Ch. in New London, nearly fifty years.

CHILDREN OF SAMUEL³ AND LOIS (SHERMAN) M°EWEN.

I. CLARK,⁴ b. October 26, 1774.
II. EZRA,⁴ b. January 10, 1776.
III. HANNAH,⁴ b. November 13, 1777.
IV. PHEBE,⁴ b. April 4, 1779.
V. LOIS,⁴ b. January 28, 1781.
VI. ZENAS,⁴ b. March 23, 1784. Living in Lisbon, Kendall Co., Illinois, in 1863.

CHILDREN OF GERSHOM³ AND THANKFUL (ANDREWS) M°EWEN.

I. MARY,⁴ b. August 18, 1777.
II. ELI,⁴ b. November 30, 1778.

CHILDREN OF REV. ABEL⁴ AND SARAH (BATTELL) M°EWEN.

I. ROBERT,⁵ b. June 22, 1808; m. Betsy, daughter of Ebenz. Larned, b. May 30, 1803; grad. Yale, 1827; clergyman.
II. CHARLOTTE,⁵ b. February 9, 1810; m. July 7, 1834, Cortland L. Latimer, of Norwalk, O., b. February 8, 1810.

CHILDREN.

1. Lucius,⁶ b. Feb. 11, 1835; d. same day.
2. Cortland,⁶ b. February 20, 1836; d. September 26, 1836.
3. Cortland,⁶ b. March 19, 1838; d. May 14, 1840.
4. Charlotte McEwen,⁶ b. December 13, 1841; d. August 7, 1847.
5. Abel McEwen,⁶ b. July 18, 1843; d. January 15, 1853.
6. Everton Judson,⁶ b. October 14, 1848.

III. SARAH,⁵ b. May 25, 1812; m. January 5, 1838; Henry Garrett, of Buffalo, N.Y.; b. August 8, 1812. He d. Feb. 9, 1849.

CHILDREN.

1. Sarah Battell,⁶ b. December 24, 1839.
2. Charlotte McEwen,⁶ b. January 26, 1842.
3. Anna,⁶ b. February 14, 1844.
4. Henry,⁶ b. November 26, 1845; d. March 1, 1863.

IV. WILLIAM,⁵ b. May 29, 1814.
V. ANN BUCKINGHAM,⁵ b. January 15, 1817; d. November 18, 1832.
VI. HARRIET,⁵ b. September 15, 1819; d. July 18, 1832.
VII. JOHN BATTELL,⁵ b. April 19, 1821; d. October 1, 1861, unmarried.

ENOCH PALMER from Farmington came to Winchester in 1767, and lived in the late homestead of Adam Mott, junior, which stood on the site of Noble J. Everitt's house, next north of the Robert McEwen house, now owned by Marcus Munsill, until 1773, when he removed to a farm on the old north country road, near the Wallen's Hill School-house, where he died in 1795. His sons Lazarus, Solomon, and Reuben, who resided near him in Winsted, will be hereafter adverted to. His daughter Mary was wife of Reuben Sweet. His wife, Jemima, died May 28, 1790; he married (second) November 23, 1790, Elizabeth Soper. He died 1795, in Winsted.

SIMEON LOOMIS, supposed from Torrington, is named of Winchester, in a deed of June 29, 1767, conveying to him a part of the Salmon Bronson Farm, lying south of the road running west from the Wade Tannery, which he occupied until his death after 1790, and which was afterwards owned and occupied until 1801 by Seth Griswold, who married Loomis's widow. He married, November 29, 1770, Huldah Priest. Administration granted on his Estate in Simsbury, Probate Court, January 9, 1777. His widow, Huldah, married December 31, 1778, Seth Griswold of New Hartford.

CHILDREN OF SIMEON AND HULDAH (PRIEST) LOOMIS.

I. ELISHA, b. August 14, 1771; had wife Mary, and a daughter Sabra Maria, b. November 14, 1804.
II. LOIS, b. August 12, 1773.
III. JOAB, b. June 2, 1775.

AARON COOK from Torrington purchased in 1767, and occupied during his life, the lot at the southeast corner of the second tier, first division, immediately north of the Preston reservation, and lived on south part of Blue Street. He died May 19, 1804, aged fifty-nine.

CHILDREN OF AARON AND LYDIA COOK.

I. ABIGAIL, b. November 19, 1768.
II. ASENATH, b. April 22, 1771; m. May 10, 1792, Jonathan Hall.
III. RUTH, b. March 12, 1773.
IV. HANNAH, b. January 20, 1775; m. November 26, 1801, Merritt Bull.
V. JOSEPH, b. December 1, 1776.
VI. ROGER, b. December 20, 1781.
VII. REUBEN, b. October 31, 1784.
VIII. LENA ALSON, b. March 25, 1796.

ELEAZER SMITH had a child born in Winchester in 1768, but is named of Barkhamsted in a deed of June 22, 1770, conveying to him land at the angle of the old road to Winchester Center, north of Sylvester Platt's. He built and occupied the old house recently torn down that stood east of the north and south road opposite the turn westward of the road to the center. In 1791 he sold to Thomas Spencer, junior, after which his name disappears. He had ten children born in the town, but it is not known that any of his descendants remain among us.

CHILDREN OF ELEAZER AND MARY SMITH.

I. MARY, b. October 2, 1768.
II. ROXY, b. June 21, 1770.
III. NOADIAH, b. July 5, 1772.
IV. SARAH, b. December 13, 1774.
V. LUCINA, b. August 6, 1777.
VI. MERCY, b. June 6, 1779; d. July 1, 1779.
VII. DOROTHY, b. July 4, 1780.
VIII. ZADOC, b. February 15, 1783.
IX. ELEAZER, b. September 10, 1785.
X. DAVID WILLIAMS, b. August 3, 1787.

NOAH GLEASON from Torringford bought a house and lot of John Smith in 1769, on the east side of Blue Street, near Torrington line, which he occupied until about 1776. In 1783 he bought and lived on the west side of Blue Street, now a part of the farm of Henry Drake. He afterwards lived until 1793 on Brooks Road, a little above N. T. Loomis.

NOAH GLEASON, junior, owned and occupied land adjoining his father, on the west side of Blue Street, from 1783 to 1787, and afterwards on the Brooks Road. Both father and son occasionally shifted their residence from Winchester to Torrington, and back again.

DANIEL GROVER of Stratford, a shoemaker, bought in 1769 a lot of land at the parting of the Norfolk and Brooks Street roads, in first tier, first division, which he occupied, living in a house near N. T. Loomis, until 1785. He had six fingers on each hand, and six toes on each foot. He moved to Unadilla, N.Y. Daniel Grover and Mercy Stannard married April 11, 1773. She died June 5, 1776.

CHILDREN.

I. MERCY, b. May 26, 1776.

AND FAMILY RECORDS.

Daniel Grover and Betsy Stanclift married October 13, 1778, and had

CHILDREN.

II. Mary,   b. July 28, 1783; d. July 30, 1783.
III. Daniel,   b. January 18, 1787.
IV. Timothy,   b. March 4, 1792; d. March 6, 1792.
V. Betsy,   b. May 3, 1796.

Joseph Hoskin from Torrington came to Winchester probably in 1769, and lived on a road bordering on Torrington line, at the south end of the third tier, first division. He served as trumpeter in the cavalry detachment that went down from Litchfield County to Long Island, whose gaunt appearance, rusty equipments, and pacing horses excited the ridicule of Washington's army, until their good service in the battle and retreat from Brooklyn Heights made them better appreciated. He was a kind-hearted jovial man, as was indicated by his life-long sobriquet of " Uncle Joe." He died in Winsted, December, 1818, aged eighty-two.

Joseph Hoskin, junior, married August 20, 1761, Eunice Coe, eldest daughter of Ebenezer Coe,[5] b. September 22, 1742.

CHILDREN.

I. Rachel,[2]   bap. April 12, 1762; m. December 27, 1783, Lazarus Palmer.
II. Theodore,[2]   bap. in Tor. May 20, 1764; died young.
III. Theodore,[2] b. April 1766; bap. Tor., June 29, 1766; m. Eunice, daughter of Thomas and Mary Coe, b. July 24, 1766.
IV. Roswell,[2]   b. in W., August 30, 1769.
V. Alexander,[2] b.   "   August 31, 1773; lived in Winsted a short time, and went to Vernon, N. Y.
VI. Loranda,   b.   "   December 19, 1778; m. November 22, 1803, Ichabod Loomis.
VII Gustavus,   b.   "   March 4, 1784.

CHILDREN OF THEODORE[2] AND EUNICE (COE) HOSKIN.

I. Clarissa,[3]   b.   ; m. December 12, 1808, Christopher Lyon.
II. Mariah,[3]   b.   ; m. Luther Phelps.
III. Erastus,[3]   b.   ; removed to Ohio. } twins
IV. Augustus,[3]   b.   ;   "   "
V. Silas,[3]   b. January 20, 1798; m. October 13, 1823, Priscilla Bailey, b. Groton, October 26, 1799, daughter of Ransford and Priscilla Bailey. He d. September 9, 1870.
VI. Roxana,[3]   m. May 25, 1826, m. Alva Oakley.

CHILDREN OF SILAS AND PRISCILLA (BAILEY) HOSKIN.

I. RANSFORD BAILEY,⁴ b. June 24, 1825; d. October 17, 1828.
II. TRUMAN SILAS,⁴ b. March 23, 1827.
III. THEODORE BAILEY,⁴ b. April 26, 1829.
VI. THOMAS COE,⁴ b. March 15, 1831.
V. ERASTUS,⁴ b. April 9, 1833.
VI. CHARLES SHERMAN,⁴ b. February 4, 1835.
VII. GEORGE,⁴ b.   "   5, 1837.

REUBEN TUCKER, from Bolton, bought lands adjoining Norfolk line on both sides of Mad River in 1769, on which he resided after 1770, until his death in 1811, at the age of 64. He left a large family of children, most of whom removed from the town early. His son, Isaac Tucker, lived in the town as late as 1830. Mr. Tucker built the first saw-mill on the site near the Norfolk line, now owned by the Brooks's. He married December 17, 1772, Martha Carrier. He died July 24, 1811, aged 64; she died March 27, 1814, aged 64.

CHILDREN.

I. REUBEN, b. February 15, 1774;   of Elmore, Vermont, in 1814.
II. MARTHA, b. October 13, 1775; m. Thayer.
III. CHLOE, b. February 25, 1778; d. October 6, 1783.
IV. IRA, b. March 19, 1780; d. June 6, 1801.
V. MOSES, b. June 25, 1782; d. July 5, 1782.
VI. ISAAC, b. January 11, 1784; m. Nov. 5, 1805, Pamelia Benedict.
VII. HIRAM, b. February 13, 1786; d. April 14, 1794.
VIII. ZEBINA, b. January 19, 1788; of Elmore, Vermont, in 1813; of Sodsbury, Erie County, Pennsylvania, in 1817.
IX. PHEBE, b. February 9, 1790.
X. CHARITY, b. May 7, 1792; wife of Stephen Ackley, 3d, of Chatham, in 1817.

TIMOTHY GROVER, brother of Daniel, owned land south of and adjoining Daniel's, which he occupied until his death in 1780. He left no family.

CAPTAIN JONATHAN ALVORD, of Chatham, came into the town in 1770 and lived in a house, long since taken down, near the northwest corner made by the Dugway road where it turns west to Winchester center, until he sold out to Rev. Joshua Knapp, in 1773. He married, October 16, 1739, Elizabeth Sanford, of Milford. She died at East Hampton, Connecticut, April 7, 1764; he married (2d) East Haddam, November 21, 1765, widow Mary Brainard. He died June 28, 1784, in his seventy-third year.

ELIPHAZ ALVORD, ESQ., son of Jonathan above named, born at East Hampton, town of Chatham, January 13, 1742; married, November 29, 1764, Esther Hart, of New Britain, born April 1764. In 1770 he came to Winchester, and following the marked trees to the land he had purchased, cleared and planted a garden and built a log house, in three weeks, and then returned and moved his family and effects to his new home, carrying one child in his arms, and another behind him on one horse, and his wife riding another horse with an infant in her arms, while their effects were drawn on an ox-cart. He afterwards built, opposite his first log house, on west side of the Dugway road a red lean-to house, a little north of the line of the road westerly to the center, in which he resided during his remaining life. Both houses have long since disappeared, and no new structures mark their sites.

He was chosen Town Clerk at the organization of the town in 1771, and continued to hold the office, with the exception of two years, until his voluntary resignation in 1819. His records are a model of accuracy and penmanship; and the vote of thanks for his faithful services was well merited. In 1779 he was appointed the first Justice of the Peace in the town, and held the office until disqualified by age, discharging the duties with equal ability and rectitude. If in doubt as to the law of any case before him on trial, he almost invariably went to Litchfield and consulted Judge Reeve, or some other able counsel before deciding the points. His cases were invariably recorded at large, with great precision, and in perfect legal form,—even to the taking of recognizances and administering of oaths. His records give a better insight to the prevailing habits, customs, and vices of his day than can be obtained from any other source.

Rev. Frederick Marsh, in his commemorative sermon, deposited with the Connecticut Historical Society, says of Mr. Alvord:—

"He had a better education than most men of that day in the ordinary walks of life. He possessed a strong mind, mature judgment, and decided piety. His punctuality, accuracy, and weight of character, and talent for business, with his remarkably fair and legible hand-writing, were well appreciated by his fellow-townsmen. He held, and admirably executed the office of Town Clerk about forty-six years, and it is said, as an illustration of his fidelity, that of one hundred and seventeen Town Meetings holden during his life, he was present at all but one of them. When not detained by special cause, he was almost never absent from public worship on the Sabbath, or from stated and occasional meetings of the Church. He held and performed the duties of Justice of the Peace for many years, and represented the town in the Legislature more frequently than perhaps any other man. Having been chosen a Representative when past seventy — in a very handsome and appropriate address to the people, he acknowledged their former respect and confidence toward him, and declined the appointment, desiring that he might never again be considered a candidate for any office.

His influence in the school-room, in the Church, in the society and town, and wherever he was known, was great and eminently salutary."

His wife died November 18, 1818, aged 76. He died April 15, 1825, aged 83 years. No descendants bearing his name remain in the town.

CHILDREN OF ELIPHAZ[2] AND ESTHER (HART) ALVORD.

I. ELIZABETH,[3] b. November 22, 1765; d. June 26, 1818, unmarried.
II. ESTHER,[3] b. January 18, 1768; m. February 5, 1792, Dea. Levi Platt.
III. SYLVESTER,[3] b. February 21, 1770; d. March 13, 1770.
IV. LOIS,[3] b. March 4, 1771; m. Levi Ackley, January 6, 1795.
V. JOHN,[3] b. May 27, 1773; m. Winchester, January 16, 1800, Experience Webb, b. Hillsdale, Mass., Jan. 13, 1778; he d. October 20, 1841.
VI. ANNA,[3] b. November 11, 1774; m. Abel Tibballs.
VII. ACHSAH,[3] b. August 14, 1778; d. July 2, 1779.
VIII. ELIPHAZ,[3] b. September 29, 1780; d. October 27, 1780.
IX. ACHSAH,[3] b. May 21, 1782; d. same day.
X. ELIAS,[3] b. March 4, 1784; d. April 23, 1784.

CHILDREN OF JOHN[3] AND EXPERIENCE (WEBB) ALVORD.

I. ACHSAH,[4] b. November 11, 1800; m. February 22, 1829, James Lewis, of Wethersfield; settled in Berlin, Connecticut; he d. in 1860; had children, Celestia Chappel, b. January 20, 1830; Edward James, b. December 3, 1836.
II. ISAAC HYLAS,[4] b. July 15, 1802; m. at Evansburg, Pennsylvania, February, 1836; d. February 1, 1847; had children, Esther, b. February, 1837, d. February, 1842; Mary, b. November, 1839, d. November, 1843.
III. HULDAH ELTHY,[4] b. November 4, 1803; m. October 3, 1827, Elijah M. Gaylord, of Gainesville, New York; she d. July 6, 1855; had children, Silas M., b. June 9, 1830; Margarette Experience, b. April, 1834; Mary Elizabeth, b. April, 1838; all of whom married and settled in Plainview, Minnesota.
IV. ELIPHAZ,[4] b. March 13, 1807: m. October 14, 1832, Mary Cravath; she d. May 4, 1861; he m. (2d) November 23, 1861, Ruby Bissell; he had children, Eugene Stow, b. April 9, 1835, d. June 29, 1841; Coridon Alexis, b. March 18, 1839, d. May 8, 1840; Mary Brainerd, b. March 17, 1844; m. October 29, 1863, Capt. Sterling Manchester; Sarah Cravath, b. September 27, 1846; Emma Salome, b. May 5, 1851. He d. Nov. 9, 1871.
V. DAVID SANFORD,[4] b. October 18, 1809; m. October 5, 1835, Sarah Andrus; settled in Austinburg, Ohio; had children, Ellen Maria, b. August 26, 1836; Elizabeth Louisa, b. December 20, 1837; Sarah Jennet, b. January 15, 1840; Mary Loretta, b. April 19, 1841; Eugene David, b. April 30, 1843; d. ; George Nelson, b. July 14, 1848; Coridon Alexis, b. December 2, 1849.
VI. CORIDON ALEXIS,[4] b. May 12, 1813; m. September 6, 1836, Mary Ann Buckland; for many years engaged in the printing business in New York city; retired in 1871, and now resides near Hartford, Conn.; had children: Coridon Alexis, b. in Hartford, May 30, 1827; Mary Elizabeth, b. in Hartford, March 20, 1839, d. October 8, 1843; Huldah Amelia, b. in Hartford, May 31, 1841, m. December 5, 1860, Henry Howard, and had a

child, Adeline H., b. November 1, 1861, and her husband d. December 16, 1861; Mary Elizabeth, b. in Hartford, March 26, 1843; m. May 31st, 1866, Charles Perret. Children: Frank Alvord, b. August 2, 1867; Léon Louis, b. April 22d, 1872; Eliphaz Eugene, b. in Brooklyn, New York, May 5, 1845, d. January 25, 1846; Caroline Experience, b. in New York, September 18, 1847; m. February 6, 1867, Charles B. Coe. Children: Coridon Ward, b. December 5, 1868; Charles Frederick, b. in New York, August 31, 1851, d. April 3, 1852; Florence Nightingale, b. in New York, June 7, 1857; George Mather, b. in New York, October 25, 1860.

VII. JOHN CALVIN,[4] b. November 26, 1818; d. June 6, 1857; unmarried.
VIII. LOIS ELIZABETH,[4] b. May 5, 1820; m. April, 1841, Cornelius Vrooman; he d. October 20, 1848; she d. July 9, 1850; had children, Coridon Alexis, b. February 6, 1844; d. November 1, 1850; Daniel McKinney, b. January 31, 1847.

WARHAM GIBBS, from Litchfield, came into the town in 1770, and lived on the east side of a road now discontinued, running southerly from Winchester center, by the first meeting-house to the Luther Bronson place. The road, the house of Mr. Gibbs, and the old meeting-house, and all other traces of civilization in that vicinity, except a few ancient apple trees, have disappeared for near half a century.

Mr. Gibbs was Moderator of the first Town Meeting, and the first Constable of the town — also frequently appointed " to assist in reading the psalm" on Sundays, and to discharge other public trusts and duties. He went to Ticonderoga and Canada in 1775 and 1776 as lieutenant and captain, and did other service in the revolutionary war. He removed from the town in 1780. He married in Suffield, March 3, 1756, Eunice Spencer.

CHILDREN.

I. DARIUS,   b. in Litchfield, February 9, 1759.
II. DORCAS,   b. "   "   July 15, 1763.
III. MIRIAM, b. "   "   January 19,   ; d. September 3, 1774.
IV. EUNICE,   b. "   "   June 11, 1772.
V. ZEBULON,   b. "   "   June 2, 1774.
VI. WOODRUFF, b. "   "   October 15, 1776.
VII. AZUBAH, b. "   "   November 1, 1778.

LEWIS WILKINSON, from New Milford, with his sons, Jesse and Levi, came to Winchester in 1770, and lived until 1773 on the farm on the Brooks road, — afterwards owned by Abram Andrews, — and afterwards until 1784 on the farm on the west side of the Brooks road, recently owned by Nathan Tibballs. He died August 31, 1785.

JESSE WILKINSON, son of the above, lived on lands adjoining his father's in a red lean-to house. He married, May 16, 1772, Eunice Roberts.

CHILDREN.

I. EUNICE, b. December 17, 1772.
II. MILES, b. June 6, 1773.
III. LOIS, b. April 16, 1774; d. December 26, 1774.
IV. LOIS, b. May 6, 1777.
V. LUCINA, b. June 18, 1781.

LEVI WILKINSON, son of Lewis, lived between his father and his brother Jesse, on the west side of Brooks road until 1789. He married, April 23, 1776, Bathsheba Tucker.

CHILDREN.

I. LEVI CLARK, b. January 23, 1778.
II. ELIZABETH, b. September 19, 1782.
III. IRA, b. April 18, 1785.
IV. ASAHEL, b. November 10, 1788.

SAMUEL WETMORE,[1] born in Middletown, Middlefield Society, March 13, 1692; married, June 21, 1722, Hannah Hubbard, born July 21, 1700. He came to Winchester at the age of 79 years in 1771, and settled with his son, Samuel Wetmore, Jr., on the farm now owned and occupied by his great great-grand-son, Deacon Abel Samuel Wetmore. He died December 30, 1773, aged 81, — and is said to have been the first person whose remains were deposited in the Winchester burying-ground.* She died June 4, 1797.

CHILDREN.

I. SAMUEL,[2] b. December 24, 1723.
II. HANNAH,[2] b. " 18, 1725.
III. JOHN,[2] b. October 27, 1727.
IV. NOAH,[2] b. April 16, 1730; graduated at Yale 1757; ordained in November 1760; settled as pastor at Bethel, Connecticut, November 25, 1770; had two children bap. in Torrington, Irenia, March 30, 1761, and Ann, February 12, 1768.
V. MEHITABEL,[2] b. August 5, 1732.
VI. SARAH,[2] b. March 31, 1734.
VII. LOIS,[2] b. " 6, 1736.
VIII. JOEL,[2] b. " 9, 1738; m. November 23, 1763, Sarah Lyman; had three children bap. in Torrington, Olive, March 10, 1765; Ebenezer Lyman, December 28, 1776; and Millicent, January 19, 1772.
IX. MILLICENT,[2] b. September 15, 1739.
X. MARY,[2] b. July 23, 1741.

---

* This burying-ground is held by a lease for the term of 999 years, from Samuel Wetmore, Jr., to Seth Hills, Warham Gibbs, Committee in behalf of the Society, — the lessor reserving the use and improvement of the same as to the herbage.—See Winchester Land Records, Book 2, page 563.

SAMUEL WETMORE, Jr.,[2] better known as Deacon Samuel, came to the town with his father in 1771, and became a prominent and eminently useful member of the infant community. He was chosen one of the selectmen of the town at its first annual meeting, and one of the deacons of the church after its institution. He married Anna Roberts, born March 16, 1723; she died September 22, 1804; he died March 2, 1809, aged 86.

CHILD.

I. ABEL,[3]　b. in Middletown, April 6, 1753.

JOHN WETMORE,[2] married Elizabeth Leaming; they settled in Torrington, where he died August 27, 1795.

CHILDREN.

I. ELIZABETH,[3]　bap. in Torrington, October 15, 1758; m. David Alvord.
II. SETH,[3]　b. " " March 20, 1761.
III. SAMUEL,[3]　b. " " December 31, 1763.

ABEL WETMORE,[3] an only child, came to Winchester with his father on the first Wednesday in May, 1771; married, May 12, 1774, Jerusha Hills, daughter of John. She died April 30, 1780; and he married (2d), April 17, 1783, Mrs. Mary (Smith) Allen. He died May 20, 1796, and his widow married　　　Loveland.

CHILDREN.

I. TRUMAN,[4]　b. August 12, 1774.
II. ANNA JERUSHA,[4]　b. March 6, 1776; m. January 21, 1801, to Elijah Starks or Starkweather.
III. JOHN,[4]　b. February 6, 1778.
IV. SAMUEL,[4] (known as Samuel H.) b. March 24, 1780.
V. ABEL,[4]　b. September 23, 1783.
VI. ELISHA,[4]　b. April 11, 1785.

MAJOR SETH WETMORE,[3] born in Torrington, March 20, 1761; lived in Winchester; married December 9, 1779, Lois, daughter of Colonel Ozias Bronson of Winchester. He died in Canajoharie, N. Y., April 16, 1836.

CHILDREN.

I. JOHN, 2d,[4]　b. in W., October 7, 1780.
II. SETH,[4]　b. " October, 1784; d. at Lake Pleasant, N. Y., November, 1831.
III. ABIGAIL BEACH,[4]　b. " January, 1787; d. at Eagle Village, N. Y., October 1858.
IV. ARTEMISIA,[4]　b. " November, 1789; d. at Canajoharie, N. Y., July, 1813.

V. ALPHONSO,[4] June, 1849. b. in W., February 5, 1793; d. at St. Louis, Mo.,
VI. SALMON B.,[4] b. " September 5, 1795.
VII. PYTHAGORAS,[4] b. " April 2, 1798, a lawyer at Canajoharie, N. Y.
VIII. LOIS MELINDA,[4] 1841. b. " June 15, 1800; d. in Kentucky, July,

MAJOR SETH WETMORE,[3] had by a second wife two children, born in Canajoharie, N. Y.

IX. LUCY ELIZABETH,[4] b. May 9, 1802.
X. GEORGE CLINTON,[4] b. June, 1809.

SAMUEL WETMORE,[3] born in Torrington, December 31, 1763; married May 15, 1788, Hannah Griswold; he was known as Samuel Wetmore 2d; he lived in W.

CHILDREN.

I. SELINA,[4] b. in W., March 13, 1789.
II. LEAMING,[4] (son) b. " February 13, 1791.
III. RUBY[4], b. " June 27, 1793.
IV. ALMEDA,[4] b. 1795.
V. CANDACE,[4] b. 1797.
VI. CALVARY,[4] b. 1799. { m. Jan. 10, 1827, Athea Skinner, m. 2d Jan. 14, 1834, Elizabeth, daughter of Isaac Bronson.
VII. SAMUEL,[4] b. 1801.
VIII. HANNAH,[4] b. 1804.
IX. HARRIET T.,[4] b. 1806.
X. HURLBUT G.,[4] b. 1808.
XI. CLARISSA,[4] b. 1811.

DR. TRUMAN WETMORE,[4] married October 18, 1799, Sylvia Spencer, daughter of Thomas; she died March 27, 1800, and in her memory he added the name "Spencer" to his Christian name, December 27, 1800; he married (second) Elizabeth Jarvis; she died May 7, 1844, aged 58; he died July 21, 1861, aged 87. Soon after the death of his first wife he began the study of medicine, under Drs. Woodward of Torrington, Moore of Winsted, and McEwen of Albany, N. Y. Receiving his diploma in 1802 he commenced practice in Vermont, but in 1806 returned to Winchester, and in the following year, on the breaking out of the spotted fever in this county, he was the first who treated it successfully. He was a well-read and successful physician of the old school, a poet of local celebrity, a musical composer (some of his tunes being still retained in the worship of the churches), a man of genial humor and tender feelings, and a chronicler of olden times to whom the compiler is largely indebted. He continued in practice until the age of 75. His residence until about 1828 was on the south side of Cooper Lane, about half a mile west of the center, and during his remaining life in the old Parsonage house, now owned by his son-in-law, Leonard B. Hurlbut.

CHILDREN.

I. SYLVIA ELIZA,[5]   b. October 20, 1805 ; m. Leonard B. Hurlbut.
II. DARWIN WOODWARD, b. September 2, 1807 ; d. August 20, 1853.
III. WILLIAM JARVIS,[5]   b. June 30, 1809 ; resides in the city of New York ; a physician, poet, and popular musical composer. He delivered the poem at the Centennial of the Winchester Church, August 16, 1871.
IV. GEORGE WHITEFIELD,[5] b. October 11, 1812 ; graduated M.D., at Pittsfield, 1838 ; m. November 29, 1843, Sarah Ann Thompson, b. April 28, 1819, daughter of Deacon Seth and Anne (Burton) Thompson ; has children. George Thompson, b. Amenia, N. Y., February 9, 1845 ; Elizabeth Jarvis, b. A., April 6, 1846 ; Mary Fitch, b. W., April 16, 1855.
V. CHARLES FITCH,   b. August 21, 1815 ; grad. Washington College in 1841.

JOHN WETMORE,[4] born February 6, 1778 ; married November 19, 1801, Lucy Nash, daughter of John. He settled on the homestead of his ancestors, where he died May 24, 1832 ; she died August, 1869, aged 85.

CHILDREN.

I. ABEL SAMUEL,[5]   b. November 16, 1802.
II. LUCY ESTHER,[5]   b. December 12, 1806 ; m. September 11, 1833, Fred. P., son of Miles Hill.
III. HANNAH JERUSHA,[5] b. June 11, 1809 ; m. October 13, 1840, Lewis Whiting.
IV. CLARISSA WHITING,[5] b. May 14, 1816 ; m. March 30, 1836, George L. Whiting.
V. REBECCA NASH,[5]   b. December 8, 1812 ; m. November 11, 1846, Alonso Whiting.

JOHN WETMORE,[4] 2d, born October 7, 1780 ; married December 30, 1802, Huldah Spencer, daughter of Thomas. He first lived in the house next north of A. S. Wetmore, then about 1817 to 1820, in the red house at the crossing of the roads between the two lakes, and finally in the house at the center now owned by Washington Hatch, where he died November 12, 1823, aged 43. She married (second) Jonathan Coe.

CHILDREN.

I. HORATIO LUCIUS,[5]   b. September 24, 1803 ; m. May 20, 1829, Hannah, Catlin, daughter of Horace; she d. September 20, 1856, leaving a daughter Sarah Louisa, b. April 12, 1833 ; he m. (second) ? 1862, Abigail Kilburn, daughter of Elisha.
II. CELESTIA,[5]   b. in W., May 30, 1805 ; m. January 20, 1831, Luman Catlin.

III. SAREPTA,[5]   b. in W., August 2, 1807; d. unmarried January 4, 1862.
IV. LOUISA MATILDA,[5] b. " May 25, 1810; m. October 19, 1830, Jabez Gillett Curtis.
V. WILLARD SPENCER,[5] b. " May 8, 1813; m. October 24, 1839, Julia Ann Woodford, daughter of Erastus. Children: Willie, b. Nov. 2, 1841; d. same day; Julia, b. May, 1849; d. same day
VI. JOHN GRINNELL,[5]   b. in W., April 27, 1817; m. October 3, 1841, Eliza F. Rossiter. She d. March 9, 1847, leaving a daughter, Eliza Rossiter, b February 20, 1847. He m. (second) November 1, 1848, Eliza P. Lee.
VII. HULDAH ANN,[5]   b. July 1, 1821; m. April 17, 1844, Jonathan A. Rossiter.

SAMUEL WETMORE,[4] known as Samuel H., married December 2, 1802, Sally Beach, daughter of Adna. They removed to Vernon, N. Y., where he died March 23, 1813.

CHILDREN.

I. MARY SOPHRONIA,[5]   b. May 10, 1803; m. (first) Silas H., and (second) Samuel A. McAlpine.
II. HARRIET ELIZA,[5]   b. November 8, 1806; m. John McAlpine, Jr.

DEACON ABEL SAMUEL WETMORE,[5] married November 24, 1829, Lucy Almira Hills, born March 18, 1810, daughter of Miles. He owns and occupies by regular descent the farm of his ancestor Deacon Samuel Wetmore. Possessing a retentive memory, and a large fund of traditional lore, his aid in the compilation of these annals has been highly prized.

CHILDREN.

I. JULIA ANN,[6]   b. August 18, 1830; d. June 5, 1831.
II. JOHN NASH,[6]   b. in W., March 8, 1833.
III. ELLEN ELIZA,[6]   b. " October 29, 1834; m. August 14, 1856, Stephen G. Beecher, New Milford.
IV. LE ROY WHITING,[6] b. " September 28, 1836.
V. MILES HILLS,[6]   b. " September 6, 1840.
VI. SAMUEL ABEL,[6]   b. " September 25, 1842.
VII. HUBERT PORTER,[6] b. " February 21, 1847.

DAVID GOFF's name is on the petition for incorporation of the town dated August 4, 1767, but it does not appear that he was ever a landowner, nor is his residence ascertainable. He was an early member of the Church, and is occasionally named on the records as holding subordinate town offices. From an affidavit of Colonel Aaron Austin accompanying a petition of Goff for compensation for military service, it appears that he served as sergeant in Captain Griswold's Company, in an expedition to Canada in 1775, and that in 1776 he and his son enlisted in the company of which Austin was captain, and that in the retreat from Canada in that year, he was the means of saving the army from destruction by devising and carrying out a plan of getting the boats up the Chamblee Rapids by means of drag-ropes, with men on the shores to tow them, instead of carrying them and their freight a circuit of some miles by land, as had been the custom, which it was impossible to do without teams, of which the army was destitute. It appears by the same document that he was afterwards a lieutenant in the Continental Army. It also appears by Sedgwick's "History of Sharon" that he resided in that town during a part of the revolutionary period.

CHILDREN OF DAVID AND MARY GOFF.

I. IRENA, b. January 9, 1770.
II. SARAH, bap. February 10, 1771.
III. ESTHER, b. November 10, 1772.

CAPTAIN BENJAMIN BENEDICT, from Danbury, was chosen a Surveyor of Highways at the first annual town meeting. His first deed dated April 4, 1771, in which he is named Benjamin Benedict, junior, conveys to him the Colonel Whiting Lot on both sides of Mad River where the Danbury School-house stands. His homestead stood on a discontinued road east of the present road, running east of the school-house, on the hill south of Mad River. He built a saw mill on the south side of Mad River, above the bridge, nearly all traces of which have now disappeared. He removed to Coventry, Chenango Co., N. Y., in 1807. He married, May 27, 1762, Mary Bouton.

CHILDREN.

I. NOAH,[2] b. May 28, 1763; m. May 22, 1788, Chloe Andrews; lived on part of his father's homestead; his last deed on record is dated 1805; had son Noah, b. March 18, 1789.
II. ABIJAH,[2] b. April 30, 1765; m. June 11, 1789, Abigail Corbin; lived south of Noah, on part of his father's original homestead; he probably left town before 1800; had Daniel, b. February 26, 1790; Sylvester, b. December 4, 1794.
III. BENJAMIN,[2] b. July 18, 1767; m. July 3, 1788, Sibyl Loomis. He was a deacon; had Wealthy, b. March 9, 1793; Sylvia Melissa, b. May 15, 1811. He lived on the east side of the old country road, south of the Corbins.
IV. EDEN,[2] b. May 6, 1770; m. May 24, 1792, Miranda Culver; had son Ira, b. May 16, 1794.
V. MARY,[2] b. November 10, 1772; m. October 25, 1792, Levi Bronson, second.

VI. PHEBE,² b. May 30, 1775 ; m. August 1, 1796, Levi Daw.
VII. ELIAKIM,² b. March 9, 1778.
VIII. HULDAH,² b. April 6, 1782; m. November 1, 1799, Lorrain Sweet.

CAPTAIN TIMOTHY BENEDICT, from Danbury, named in his first deed, Timothy Benedict, Jr., bought in 1771 the eastern half of the lot originally purchased by Captain Benjamin Benedict, lying on both sides of Mad River, and enclosing the Danbury school-house, on which he resided until his death. His wife, Mrs. Lydia Benedict, died in this town February 21, 1824, aged 95.

The land records show that he had three sons, Timothy, Jr., William, and Joshua, who came with him to Winchester and to whom he conveyed portions of his land. There was an Elizabeth Benedict, married to Hezekiah Elmer, September 7, 1774, who may have been his daughter.

TIMOTHY BENEDICT, Jr.,² owned land on both sides of Mad River east of the highway and running south from the Danbury school-house, and lived on the east side of the road nearly opposite the Danbury burying-ground until his decease. He married, October 5, 1773, Mary Judd. She died September 8, 1822, aged 75 ; and he died November 27, 1836, aged 89.

CHILDREN.

I. DEBORAH,³ b. August 29, 1774 ; m. William Crocker.
II. TIMOTHY,³ b. March 8, 1777.
III. SARAH,³ b. August 17, 1781.
IV. MELA,³ b. October 23, 1784.

WILLIAM BENEDICT,² son of Timothy, is named of New Marlboro, Massachusetts, in a deed of 1786, July 5. No record of his family is found.

JOSHUA BENEDICT,² son of Timothy, is not found on the records after 1786. He married, November 15, 1784, Mary Wilcox, and had a child, Anna, born March 13. 1786. He removed to Montreal, L. C., and is supposed to have died there.

TIMOTHY BENEDICT,³ son of Timothy,² lived and died (Mch. 29, 1820) in the house now owned by Joel Tuttle, on the easterly side of the turnpike above the toll-gate. He married Lydia, daughter of John Crocker, and had by her

CHILDREN.

I. RHODA,⁵ b. September 1, 1800 ; m. Willard Hart; d. in 1824.
II. HANNAH,⁵ b. November 2, 1802 ; m. Eleazer Andrews.
III. LYDIA,⁵ b. December 8, 1809 ; m. Charles Selden ; d., 1834.

DEACON NATHANIEL DUTTON, from Woodbury, purchased in 1771, Lot 33, first tier, first division, and built a house thereon. He sold a part of the lot to John Bradley the same year, and sold the remainder to Ichabod Loomis in 1773, and returned to Woodbury. He afterwards came and finished the second meeting-house in 1785. He afterwards had his permanent residence in Litchfield (Northfield parish). He was father to the late Professor Mathew Rice Dutton, of Yale College, and of ex-Governor Henry Dutton, of New Haven.

JOHN BRADLEY is described as of Winchester in Nathaniel Dutton's deed of December 19, 1771, conveying to him seventy acres from the north side of Lot 33, first division, lying on the west side of the road a little south of the Widow Everitt house, which he conveyed to Daniel Loomis in 1778, and probably then left the town.

DANIEL PLATT, from Danbury, bought of Benjamin Benedict a lot of land on Waterbury River turnpike, a little south of the Potter place, in 1771, which he conveyed to Phillip Priest in 1776. He and his wife, Thankful, had a son, Stephen, baptized March 13, 1774.

LEMUEL STANNARD, Jr., from Saybrook, is a signer of the petition for incorporation of the town in 1771, and is a grantee of land in 1772. He first owned land on Blue street, and afterwards a little west of the center. His name disappears from the records about 1780. He was born April 13, 1750; married, April 14, 1774, Christian Spencer.

CHILDREN.

I. CHAUNCEY, b. December 23, 1774.
II. MARGARET, b. August 29, 1776.

ABEL STANNARD, supposed to be son of Lemuel, Senior, bought in 1779 a lot, lying immediately north of the Little Pond, and built and lived in a square-roofed house on the road running along the east side of the pond — nearly opposite the Dan. Beckley lane — and sold out to Amasa Wade in 1803. He married, June 23, 1774, Phebe Stevens.

CHILDREN.

I. PHEBE, b. September 4, 1776.
II. TOMESIN, b. April 10, 1781.
III. ABEL, b. " 20, 1784.
IV. SARAH, b. March 28, 1786.
V. HERVEY, b. February 18, 1788.
VI. RUTH (twin), b. March 27, 1790.
VII. LYDIA (twin), b. " " "
VIII. ZENAS, b. July 23, 1793.
IX. GILES, b. September 14, 1795.

LEMUEL STANNARD, Senior, from Saybrook, is grantee, in 1778, of a lot in second tier, first division, near Reuben Chase's, which he conveyed to his son, William, in 1789, describing it as his homestead. In 1796, he is alluded to in a deed as "Lemuel Stannard, late of Winchester, deceased."

WILLIAM STANNARD occupied his father's homestead until 1790, when he sold out to Col. Ozias Bronson; and afterwards owned land in Danbury quarter, which he conveyed to his father-in-law, Peleg Sweet, in 1800. He married, September 15, 1779, Hannah Sweet.

CHILDREN.

I. WILLIAM, b. December 2, 1780.
II. MERCY, b. October 15, 1782.

SETH STANNARD, married, November 13, 1785, Martha Preston. He owned no land in town.

CHILD.

1. SETH, b. February 15, 1786.

EZRA STANNARD, son to Lemuel Stannard and Ruth, his wife, born "at Saybrook, March 13, A. D. 1766," married, January 19, 1786, Margaret Norton. He owned in 1793 and 1794, the Humphrey farm, on the east side of Long Pond, south of the Pratt farm, which he sold to Levi Ackley and Ozias Spencer. In 1795, he is named of Torrington.

CHILDREN.

I. CHARLES, b. October 16, 1786.
II. LORRAIN, b. May 9, 1788.
III. ORLOW, b. April 13, 1790.
IV. GRINNELL, b. January 30, 1792.

CHAPTER VII.

SOCIETY OF WINCHESTER ORGANIZED—FIRST HOUSE OF WORSHIP.

We have followed out the slow settlement of the town, from the first entry of Caleb Beach in 1750, to the year 1768, and endeavored to locate and commemorate its pioneers. We find them as yet confined to the corner of the township bordered on the northeast by the Old South Country road, comprising little more than one-eighth of the territory. Of the families whose prior residence is ascertained, six were from Torrington, two each from Goshen and Hartford, and one each from Woodbury, Wallingford, Derby, Suffield, Stratford, and Farmington.

Their first utterance as a social community seems to have been a petition to the Colonial Assembly, dated August 4, 1767. It so graphically sets forth their condition and needs as to render it worthy of transcribing:

"To the Honorable the General Assembly of the Colony of Connecticut, to be convened at New Haven on the 2d Tuesday of October, 1757.

"The memorial of us the subscribers, Inhabitants of the Township of Winchester, in the County of Litchfield, humbly sheweth,

"That whereas there is about 18 families, containing 82 souls, have begun a settlement in said Township, and by reason of our distance from any place of Public Worship, it being near or quite seven miles to the nearest, makes it extremely difficult for any of us to attend public worship at any of said places, and utterly impossible for us to convey our families, so that we are laid under a necessity of bringing up our families in Ignorance, and Strangers to publick Gospel Preaching. not being able to hire preaching ourselves by reason of our infant state of settlement, and the greatest part of the land in said Township belongs to men of Wealth, who are under no necessity either to sell or to settle their land, which makes our case peculiarly difficult, and as the welfare of the soul is of vastly more importance than that of the body, your memorialists humbly pray that your honours will take the state of our Case into serious consideration and comiterate our miserable Circumstances, and that you would incorporate and form us into a Town with Town privileges, and lay a small tax on all the divided lands in said Township, in the first and third Divisions lying south and west of the Long Pond, such as may enable us to support the Gospel among us, or otherwise provide for our relief as you in your wisdom shall think best and most for the honour of God and interest of said religion amongst us, and your memorialists as in duty bound shall ever pray, &c. Dated at Winchester the 4th day of August, 1767.

SETH HILLS,	LENT MOTT,
AARON COOK,	ABEL BEACH, Proprietor,
ROBERT COE,	JOHN SMITH,
ROBERT MACUNE,	DAVID AUSTIN,
DAVID GOFF,	BERIAH HILLS, Proprietor,
WILLIAM FILLEY,	JOEL BEACH,
ENOCH PALMER,	NOBLE AVRED,
THOMAS HOSMER,	SIMEON LOOMIS,
ADAM MOTT,	OLIVER COE,
JOHN HILLS,	SAMUEL PRESTON."

Of these petitioners eighteen were residents of the town, and ten of them became members of the church at, or immediately after, its organization.

It does not appear that any action was had by the Assembly on this petition. Another petition was brought to the May Session in 1768, similar in substance to the former, and signed by fifteen of the former memorialists, and also by John Preston, Jonathan Preston, John Wetmore, and Ebenezer Preston; in which the population is stated to be about twenty-one families and 110 souls. Upon this memorial, the General Assembly resolved "that the inhabitants living on the west side and south end of the Long Pond, and the lands south of the same, as far as Torrington line, and all those west of said Pond to Norfolk line, and north upon said line until it comes to Colebrook line, and east upon Colebrook line, so far as to include the westernmost tier of lots on the second or northeast division of lots in said township of Winchester, be and remain for the future, one entire and distinct Ecclesiastical Society, * * * * * * and that a tax of one penny half-penny per acre per annum be laid upon all the lands lying within the lines and limits aforesaid, as well those belonging to non-resident proprietors as others, for the term of three years now next ensuing, and that David Austin be a collector with full power to collect and pay said rate or tax toward the support of the ministry in said Society," &c.

Under this act of incorporation, a Society meeting was held, June 29, 1768, and the following votes passed:

" Voated, that John Smith should be Moderator for sd. Meeting.
" that Seth Hills should be Clark for sd. Sosiety.
" that all free agents be lawful voaters.
" that Thomas Hosmer should be fust Commety man for sd. Sosiety.

ORGANIZATION OF WINCHESTER. 77

"Voated, William Filey secnd Commety man for said Sosiety.
" Seth Hills be third Commety man for sd. Sosietay.
" that the Sosiety will except 74 pounds of the tax yearly."

September 20, 1768, at an adjourned meeting, it was "voated, that the meeting on the Saboth should be continued att John Hills til December next."

"That the Sisiety will aply to the Association for advice." October 13, 1768, "Voated that ye Society wil wait til week after next for Mr. Mills."*

"Voated, that the Comity shall try for Mr. Pitkin proid Mr. Mills don't com."

At the Annual Meeting, first Tuesday of December, 1768, Thomas Hosmer, Seth Hills, and John Hills, were chosen Society Committee: Seth Hills, Clerk, and Thomas Hosmer, Treasurer; and the Committee were instructed to apply to Samuel John Mills to supply them.

At the Annual Meeting, December 28, 1769, the privilege of voting extended to "all free agents by vote of a former meeting, was confined to all the inhabitants that are of age"; — and after choice of Committee, Clerk, and Treasurer, the following additional appointments were made: "John Hills, Corester; Abram Filley, Corester; David Austin, to read the Psalm; Beriah Hills, to assist to read the Psalm."

And was voted "that our anuel meeting shall be warnid by the Comity by setting up a paper on a post by the *Meeting House* at least eight days before ye meeting, telling the place and time of day."

At the Annual Meeting, December 11, 1770, after appointment of officers, the sweeping of the meeting house was set up to the lowest bidder, and bid off by Jesse Wilkinson, at 5s. 6d. for the year. The expenses of the year were reported to be £60 4s. 3d., and of the years 1768 and 1769, £69 8s. 9d. — and the meeting adjourned to the first Monday of March, 1771, at which adjourned meeting it was "voted, that we will send a petition to the Assembly next May for tound privileges."

"Voted, that we will send a Petition to the assembly next May for a Tax for the Settlement of a Minister and building a Meeting House."

"Voted, that Beriah Hills and Warham Gibbs shall assist in reading the Psalm."

"Voted, that John Hills and Abram Filley shall sett the Psalm."

The first mention of a meeting house in the infant society is made in a vote in 1769 already quoted. No record is found referring in any way to the building of this sanctuary; nor is any traditionary account of its erection, or by whom it was erected, discoverable. No tax was laid to pay for it, and no building committee was appointed to superintend it.

---

* Rev. Samuel J. Mills, afterwards the venerable and eccentric pastor of Torringford.

On the 20th September, 1768, it was voted that the Sabbath meeting should be held, until the next December, at John Hills' house, which stood near the Hurlbut Cemetery; — then follows, in December, 1769, the vote requiring notices of society meetings to be placed on a post by the meeting house. These votes would indicate 1768 as the year of its erection. It stood on the slope of a hill, on the west side of a road long since discontinued, coming up from the Luther Bronson house, and passing immediately in front of the houses of Marcus Munsill and Noble J. Everitt, to Winchester center. The traces of the old road are indistinctly visible, but no indication of a church having once stood on the sloping ground on its borders are visible. The place has no feature of convenience or beauty to recommend it. Its uneven and rocky surface would utterly preclude all attempts at improvement, while no village could have grown up around it. In the absence of facts as to its origin, it might be theorized that it was originally a barn, and was extemporized into a meeting house, — were it not that the height of the building fell short of the

FIRST MEETING-HOUSE.

requisite of a barn, and that no farmer would ever have put a barn in such an inaccessible position. A dwelling it could not have been intended for, as there was no cellar, and the rocky formation would have precluded excavating one.

It was a low, steep-roofed building, thirty feet long and twenty-four feet wide, with nine-feet posts, covered with wide rabbeted boards one

ORGANIZATION OF THE CHURCH.

inch thick. It stood on a side hill above the road, the rear resting on the ground, and the front supported by sections of Chestnut logs, three to four feet in diameter, lying diagonally under the corners. A huge chestnut butt, set up perpendicularly at the front door, with a series of steps cut crosswise of the timber, gave access to the ground floor. Opposite the door was the pulpit or rostrum, three to four feet high. The seats were rough planks or slabs with legs at the ends inserted in augur holes. Originally there was no floor overhead; but as more room was required to accommodate the worshippers, joists were inserted in the cross beams, and boards laid down loosely for a floor, except on a space of nine feet square, over the rostrum. This was the gallery. Access was gained to it by a plank ladder outside, at one of the ends of the building ascending to a door in the gable. The interior was neither ceiled nor plastered. The space beneath the building was open on three sides, affording a shade and shelter for vagrant sheep, pigs, and calves.

In this primitive edifice our fathers worshipped summer and winter for seventeen years, with no warming apparatus but the foot stoves of the women, and the sound doctrine of the minister. Two choristers to lead the singing, and two readers to line the psalms were regularly appointed at each annual meeting.

Near this church edifice there appears to have been another religious building peculiar to New England in the last and early in the present century, called a Sabbath-day House, or, as spelled in the one of the two instances in which it occurs in our records, a "Saba-day House." It is first mentioned in a vote of temporary adjournment of a Society meeting in December, 1761, probably by reason of the extreme cold in the meeting house. The second mention of it is in the survey of the road formally laid out and established in 1772, along the line of the bridle path which had previously been the only means of access to the meeting house, in which two prominent land marks are "a birch tree near a saw-mill, then N. 13 E. to a Sabbath-day house." Such buildings were erected by individuals living distant from places of worship for the accommodation of their families before and during the intervals of worship in the inclement weather of winter. They were generally long, low buildings of two apartments, with a fire place in each attached to one chimney. A supply of fuel was provided in the fall. Some member of the family or families owning those apartments went forward early on the Sunday morning and made up the fires, and the rest of the parties followed in such season as to thoroughly warm themselves before going into meeting. At the noon intermission, they returned to their rooms, warmed themselves, and such homely fare as they had brought with them, ate their dinners, discussed the morning sermon, and returned to the afterooon exercise; at the close of which they again warmed themselves at the fires, and returned to their distant homes with a far better appreciation of their Sabbath worship than could otherwise have been enjoyed.*

Such buildings, nearly unknown to the present generation, are well remembered by the aged people of New England. Probably some of them still exist in retired parishes. There were two or more of them in a dilapidated state near the Carmel Meeting House, eight miles north of New Haven, as late as 1820. There were one or more of them attached to the old Town Hill Meeting House in New Hartford until after the secession of the Northenders not far from 1830, in which the compiler was hospitably entertained in 1822, during the interval of worship on one of the coldest winter days of that year. The pleasant memory of the refreshing warmth of that snug little room, contrasted with the shivering exercise of the unwarmed old barn-like house of worship and the freezing solemnities at the grave of a deceased classmate, on a still higher elevation, renders the old Sabaday House worthy of special notice as one of the by-gone institutions of New England.

In the early part of this century, the Old Meeting House was removed by the owners of the land on which it stood, to the rear of the new store of Theron Bronson, Esq., at Winchester Center, where it stood in the last stage of dilapidation, having served for some fifty years as a barn, until Sunday, June 9th, 1867, when it was blown down in a violent thunder storm.

---

* Prior to the late centennial, a diversity of opinion was found to exist among the residents of "Old Winchester," in respect to the precise location of this meeting house. There was no one of them who had seen it before its removal to another location, and apparently not understanding of the requirements of the ancient records in reference to its location above quoted, and other records of a dwelling house once owned by Reuben Miner, and located on the east side of the road, "near the meeting house." This was the only dwelling ever erected in that vicinity. The location of the ancient saw-mill is ascertainable, and not many rods west of it, is the trace of an ancient sunken northerly and southerly road, along the center of which is a modern stone wall. On the east side of this road track, and in a northwesterly direction from the saw-mill site, are the undoubted traces of the site of a dwelling house and garden, such as a continued growth of "live-for-ever," and traces of cellar walls, with fragments of ancient bricks, such as might have been used in constructing the oven. The stones in the wall immediately west of this location are more angular and square than in other places, and were probably taken from the old chimney stack and foundations of the house. The land on the west side of this old road, near this chimney place, slopes down from the west in the manner required by the traditions of a meeting house resting its rear sills on the ground, and raised to a level in front by the large logs under the corners, and the steps cut into a stump under the front door.

The location adopted by the centennial committee, and on which they placed a stone monument and flagstaff, is on the top of an eminence several rods west of where the road must have run, and some forty rods northerly or northwesterly from the spot indicated by the record land marks. As a fancy location, it would be preferable to what is here claimed to be the true one: but authenticated facts do not warrant its selection.

CHAPTER VIII.

INCORPORATION AND ORGANIZATION OF THE TOWN.

At the Society meeting on the first Monday of March, 1771, it was voted to petition the Assembly for a town corporation. The Petition prepared and sent in to the May session of that year is as follows:

To the Honorable General Assembly to be holden at Hartford on the second Tuesday of May next,

The memorial of Seth Hills and John Hills, inhabitants of the Ecclesiastical Society lately established in the Township of Winchester, and the rest of the inhabitants of said society humbly showeth;

That your Honors, at your session at Hartford, in May, 1768, did make and establish a distinct Ecclesiastical Society in said Winchester, and were also graciously pleased to grant a tax of one penny half-penny upon the acre of all the lands within the limits of said society; as well to those of non-resident proprietors as others for the term of three years, toward the support of the Gospel ministry in said society (which term is now expired), and the moneys arisen by virtue of said tax have been duly expended for the purpose for which they were granted; by means whereof the lands lying within the limits of said society, and especially those near the center thereof, are much increased in price, and some almost or quite, doubled, which lands near the center chiefly belong to non-resident proprietors, who have received by far the greatest benefit in the rise of lands by means of said premises: yet so it is that all of the lands in said Township have been laid out for the sole use and benefit of the Proprietors, without appropriating any part thereof for the support of the Gospel, or schools, or any other pious or public uses whatever; as has been usual and customary in many towns lying in the northwesterly part of this colony, which were formerly granted to the Proprietors of the towns of Hartford and Windsor, excepting only some little part reserved for highways, which is by no means sufficient to answer the purpose, even for necessary highways at present, but many more must in a short time be purchased at the expense of the inhabitants.

Your Memorialists would further beg leave to observe to your Honors, that the number of families at present in the limits of said society amount to twenty-eight, and the number of souls to 179, and that there are but four at present who live within the limits of said Township, but which also live without the limits of said society; and that the greatest part of your Memorialists are under very low circumstances; as they laid out a chief part of what they had towards purchasing their lands of the Proprietors at a much greater price than they otherwise would have given, upon a full expectation that they should be assisted by the non-resident Proprietors by way of general tax upon all the lands for the purpose of building a Meeting House, settling a minister, &c., as has been heretofore done in some of the new townships; and that your Memorialists have been at very great expense since their settlement in said township in the supporting of schools, building of mills and bridges, and in purchasing and making of highways, as well as in clearing and cultivating their lands, a very considerable part of which is rough, and the residue very heavy timbered: By means whereof, they are not able at present, (without some assistance) to build a Meeting House, settle a minister, support proper schools, &c., which they are very desirous of doing, that they might be enabled to attend upon institutions and ordinances of the Gospel themselves, but also to bring up their children in the nurture and admonition of the Lord, which cannot be otherwise obtained by reason of their distance from any other place of public worship.

Your Memorialists would further beg leave to inform your Honors that they are under many similar inconveniences and difficulties, by reason of not having town privileges among themselves.

Thereupon your Memorialists humbly pray your Honors to take their unhappy circumstances into your wise consideration, and to grant a tax (for such time and sum as to your Honors wisdom shall seem meet) upon all the lands lying within the limits of said Society, as well those belonging to the resident population as others, for the purpose, and to be improved in building a Meeting House, and settling a minister in said Society, or to be collected and laid out and improved according to the direction of your Honors; and that your Honors would also make, incorporate and establish the inhabitants living within the limits of said Township of Winchester into one distinct and entire town, with all the powers and privileges that other towns by law have, and do enjoy, or under such particular limitations and restrictions as to your Honors may seem just and reasonable. And your Memorialists as in duty bound shall ever pray, &c.

Dated at Winchester, this 4th day of April, 1771.

ADAM MOTT,
JOSEPH HOSKIN,
LEMUEL STANNARD, JR.,
DAVID GOFF,
REUBEN TUCKER,
OLIVER COE,

INCORPORATION AND ORGANIZATION.

ABRAM FILLEY,
ROBERT MACUNE,
JONATHAN ALVORD,
JOSIAH AVERIT,
WARHAM GIBBS,
ELIPHAZ ALVORD,

BERIAH HILLS,
BENONI HILLS,
AARON COOK,
BENJAMIN PALMER,
JESSE WILKINSON,
JOEL BEACH.

In compliance with the prayer of this Memorial, the Assembly at the May Session, 1771, Resolved as follows:

"That a tax of two pence on the acre annually, for two years from the last day of May, 1771, be granted on all the lands in said Society;— and that said Township of Winchester, with all the inhabitants thereof be, and they are hereby declared to be one distinct and entire town; with all the rights, powers and privileges, and subject to the same rules and orders, and to be under the same regulations as other towns in this colony have, enjoy, and are subject to."

Under this corporate act, the first Town Meeting was held, the Record of which is as follows:

At a Town Meeting of the Inhabitants of Winchester, lawfully assembled on Monday the 22d day of July, 1771.

Warham Gibbs chosen Moderator of sd. meeting.

Eliphaz Alvord chosen Town Clerk, and sworn.

Jonathan Alvord and Seth Hills, and Samuel Wetmore, Jr., chosen Townsmen.

Robert Mackune chosen Treasurer.

Warham Gibbs chosen Constable.

Abram Filley chosen Grand Jury Man.

Oliver Coe and Noah Gleason and David Goff chosen Surveyors of Highways.

Josiah Averit and Joseph Hoskin chosen Fence Viewers.

Beriah Hills and David Austin and Jonathan Coe chosen Listers.

Robert Mackune chosen Leather Sealer.

Adam Mott and Benoni Hills chosen Tything Men.

Voted, that David Austin's cow yard be a pound for the present.

Voted, that a Maple tree near the Meeting House shall be a sign-post.

David Austin chosen Key-keeper.

Voted, that the Annual Town Meeting in this Town shall be on the first Monday of December at nine of the clock in the morning, at the Meeting House of said Town, and that the Selectmen shall set up a notification on the Sign-post twelve days before the said first Monday for sd. meeting.

Test, ELIPHAZ ALVORD, *Town Clerk.*

The settlements of the town thus organized were all embraced within the limits of the first, or "Old Society" of Winchester, with the exception of four families along the old north road, running across the extreme northeast corner of the town, a section which had little, if any community of interest with the original settlements. As set forth in the memorials of 1768 and 1771, the physical conformation of the township was such as to preclude free mutual intercourse between the two sections. South of the long lake, mountainous ridges extend to the borders of Torrington, the old south road entering the town from the southeast at a point westward of these ridges. The long lake thence extends northerly to a point near the center of the town, where it approaches within a quarter of a mile of the Little Pond which extends half a mile further north, at which point the mountain range on the west side of Mad River commences, and extends northerly to Colebrook. Prior to 1780 it is believed there was no road across this barrier. The communication through the town between the old north and old south roads was by a crooked and difficult bridle path across the Still River and Mad River valleys, thence winding around between the two ponds and up the dugway to the highest elevation of the town above the Deacon Alvord place, and thence to the center of Old Winchester.

The most feasible lands in the town were west of this barrier. The first settlers came largely from Torrington and Goshen, and settled along the borders of those towns, or along the old south road already described. None of them were rich, and most of them had scant means to purchase the small tracts of uncleared, heavy timbered lands they occupied.

In a former chapter we have alluded to the unshapely and inconvenient lots set out to the smaller proprietors, the scant reservations of land for highways, and their unavailability to a great extent by reason of improper location, the want of reservations for the endowment of schools, and the reservations to their own resident clergymen instead of grants for the support of religious institutions of the impoverished and benighted settlers. Add to these drawbacks the withholding of their lands from sale by the larger proprietors, that their value might be enhanced by the improvement of lands of adjoining resident proprietors, and the exemption of their lands from taxation in aid of the outlays for roads, bridges, ministers, churches, and schools. Considering all these hindrances, and adding to them the hardships and privations of pioneer life, it is not surprising that at the twentieth anniversary of Caleb and Joel Beach's advent the number of resident families in the town were less than 180.

It is rather a wonder that any but outlaws should have resorted to a region so forlorn alike in its physical characteristics and proprietary management. None but the toughest of the puritan Anglo-Saxon race could have made headway against such impediments.

INCORPORATION AND ORGANIZATION.

Names of settlers not a few appear on the land records, who, after a short buffeting with hardships and discouragements retired from the forbidding field, and large numbers of others fled to the rich lands of Western New York as soon as they became accessible.

The names of those who participated in the organization of the town, as far as it is possible to ascertain them, and their prior residence, are as follows :—

JONATHAN ALVORD,	from Chatham.
ELIPHAZ ALVORD,	" do.
DAVID AUSTIN,	" Suffield.
JOSIAH AVERED,	" Woodbury (Bethlem).
BENJAMIN BENEDICT,	" Danbury.
JOHN BRADLEY,	" Unknown.
OLIVER COE,	" Torrington.
JONATHAN COE,	" do.
AARON COOK,	" do.
NATHANIEL DUTTON,	" Woodbury.
ABRAM FILLEY,	" Torrington.
NOAH GLEASON,	" Unknown.
WARHAM GIBBS,	" Litchfield.
DAVID GOFF,	" Unknown.
THOMAS HOSMER, Junior,	" Hartford.
SETH HILLS,	" Torrington.
BERIAH HILLS,	" do.
BENONI HILLS,	" do.
JOSEPH HOSKIN,	" do.
JOHN HILLS, (?)	" do.
SIMEON LOOMIS,	" do.
ROBERT McEWEN,	" Stratford.
ADAM MOTT,	" Windsor.
ADAM MOTT, Junior,	" do.
EBENEZER PRESTON,	" Wallingford.
ENOCH PALMER,	" Farmington.
DANIEL PLATT, (?)	" Danbury.
LEMUEL STANNARD,	" Unknown.
REUBEN TUCKER,	" Bolton.
SAMUEL WETMORE, Junior,	" Middletown (Middlefield).
JOHN WRIGHT, Junior,	" Wethersfield.
JESSE WILKINSON,	" New Milford.
LEWIS WILKINSON,	" do.

This list comprises five more names than the number of families stated to be residents of the Society in the petition dated April 4, 1771, but it can hardly be doubted that all these, if not some four or five others, were inhabitants and voters on the 22d of July following. Some of them may have come in during the intervening time, or may not yet have become heads of families.

CHAPTER IX.

ORGANIZATION OF CHURCH AND SETTLEMENT OF FIRST PASTOR.

Immediately after the organization of the town, during the same year, the Congregational Church of Winchester was gathered. We copy the original minutes as follows:

"The Church of Christ in Winchester was gathered by the Rev. Messrs. Roberts of Torrington, and Robbins of Norfolk, October 30, A. D. 1771."

The Confession of Faith, which they assented to and adopted as their rule for admission of members, &c., is as follows, viz:

"You, and each of you do believe the articles of ye Christian faith as contained in ye Scriptures of ye old and new Testament, particularly.

"1. You believe that there is one only living and true God in three persons, Father, Son and Holy Ghost, ye great Creator, Preserver, and Governor of ye world.

"2. You believe that God did make man in His own image, consisting in knowledge, righteousness and holiness, but man, by his disobedience, has fallen from that holy and happy state, and plunged himself into a State of Sin and misery, and of which he is unable to recover himself, and in wh. he might have been justly left of God, to perish forever.

"3. You believe that God, out of his mere goodness, has opened a new way of life to a fallen, guilty, sinful world, by wh. the mediation of [his] own Son, Jesus Christ, who has offered up himself a sacrifice of atonement to God for ye sins of ye world, and that all are invited to put their trust in him and return to God through him, and that there is no salvation in any other way.

"4. You believe that mankind, in their present fallen State, are dead in Sins, and so contrary to God and averse to a reconciliation, that without the special influence of divine grace, they will never savingly hearken to and comply with ye gospel call; so that ye Conversion and Salvation of Sinners is only owing to ye distinguishing sovereignty of God.

"5. You believe that altho. we are justified by faith, and saved by grace, yet the law, as a rule of life, remains in full force to believers; so that perfect holiness of heart and life is their duty; nor does the gospel of free grace in any sort Countenance or incourage them to live in ye least Sin.

ORGANIZATION OF CHURCH.

" 6. You believe that all true saints shall persevere and finally be recovered by ye grace of God, to perfect holiness and happiness — and be perfectly happy in ye enjoyment of the blessed God to all eternity, while the wicked and impenitent shall go away into everlasting punishment."

The above being publicly and unanimously owned and assented to by all those hereafter named, — they then, after solemn prayer, entered into a Covenant with God, and with one another, to walk in Christian fellowship and all the ordinances of the Gospel.

The form of the Covenant here follows:

"A COVENANT.

" You, and each of you, do now, in the presence of God, Angels and men, solemnly chuse and avouch the LORD JEHOVAH to be your God, taking JESUS CHRIST to be your only redeemer, and the HOLY SPIRIT to be your sanctifyer, — and do give up yourselves, souls and bodies, to be the Lords, with yours, — and you do Covenant & ingage faithfully to serve him in all the ways of his appointment, — seeking his glory as your last * * * * You sincerely promise, by assistance of divine grace, that you will deny all ungodliness and every worldly lust, and live soberly in ye world, — and renouncing Sin, Satan and world, do bind yourselves to walk together in christian fellowship and Communion, in all the Ordinances of the Gospel, — and that you will watch over one another and your fellow-members in meekness and in love, — and submit yourselves to the discipline and government of Christ in this Church, in the administration and services of it, — so far as you are therein directed by ye unerring word of God."

The Covenant being exhibited, the following persons publicly owned and assented to it, and were thereupon declared to be a visable church of Jesus Christ, viz:

WIDOW MARY LOOMIS,	LENT MOTT,
WIDOW HANNAH AVERIT,	ABRAHAM FILLEY,
DINAH, WIFE OF WM. FILLY,	ROBERT MACUNE,
JOHN HILLS,	JOSEPH PRESTON,
SETH HILLS,	MARY PRESTON,
ADAM MOTT,	AMY,. wife of JOEL BEACH,
ABIAH MOTT,	ELIZABETH AGARD.

" After ye Church was gathered, ye following persons were admitted members in full Com^n. with the Church, viz:

DAVID AUSTIN,
MARY AUSTIN,
MARY WILKINSON,
MARY GOFFE,
MERCY FILLEY.

"The Church then proceeded to, and made choice of Robert Macune to be the Moderator or Clerk of this church,

"Attest,

"NATH¹. ROBERTS, Pastor of y⁰ Ch., Torrington,
"A. R. ROBBINS, Pastor of Ch., Norfolk."

The cursory reader of these annals will be very likely to pass over this record as a mere form, without significance in its bearing on the destinies of the newly organized community. While he recognizes the importance of a social compact, such as the heterogeneous gathering of settlers had just adopted for their civil guidance, he little realizes the vitalizing principle imparted by a humble band of believers walking in Christian fellowship, and in the ordinances of the gospel. It is this inner life of a town or state that determines its character and destinies. If strong and vigorous, healthful morals prevail; if feeble, vices are tolerated; if dead, anarchy succeeds to order, and licentiousness becomes rampant.

The following members were added to the church prior to the ordination of its first pastor in 1772.

Nov. 3, 1771, Warham Gibbs and Eunice his wife, by profession.

Jan. 19, 1772, Ebenezer Preston, by letter from ch. at Torrington.

"   "   "   Martha Preston (his wife) "   "   Harwinton.
"   "   "   Eliphaz Alvord   "   "   Chatham.
"   "   "   Esther Alvord (his wife) "   "   "
Feb. 10, "   Capt. Jon. Alvord   "   "   "
"   "   "   David Goff, by profession.

July 26, "   Samuel Wetmore and Anna his wife, by letter from Middlefield.

July 26, 1772, Simeon Loomis, by profession.

The records of the society show that endeavors were made, both before and after the gathering of the church, to secure a permanent minister. Mr. Peter Starr, afterwards the life-long minister of Warren, was invited to preach, on probation, in July, 1771. A Mr. Hale was employed four "Saboths"; a Mr. Potter was invited, on probation, in Sept. 1771, and in case he could not come, a call, on probation, was voted to Mr. Judson; and it was also voted to have Doctor Bellamy of Bethlem, and Rev. Mr. Robbins of Norfolk, act for them in hiring a candidate "that they think will sute the society." Sept. 30, 1771, it was left "with the comity to hire a candidate as they shall think best, but not to hire one that is Determined not to settle." Oct. 31, 1771, the committee was directed to "apply to Mr. Jonson to supply us six Saboths." Feb. 13, 1772, it was voted "that the society will give Mr. Samˡˡ Jonson amedeat call for a settlement. Feb. 17th following, the committee were directed to apply

SETTLEMENT OF PASTOR.

to Mr. Brooks to supply for three Sabbaths; and on the 31st March following, an application was voted to Mr. Napp to supply for six Sabbaths, and the committee was directed to go or send after him. July 10th, following, "Mr. Napp" was applied to to preach twelve Sabbaths on probation.

Sept. 23, 1772, it was voted "that the Society will give Mr. Joshua Napp a call for a settlement in the ministry amongst us"—and a settlement was proposed of £200, payable in instalments, and a salary beginning at £35, and increasing £5 annually, until it should reach £65, which was modified so that it should increase in proportion to the increase of the grand levy, until it should reach £65. The first Thursday in November was fixed on for the ordination, and it was voted that the Council should meet at Robert Macune's, and that he should provide for them, and that John Hills, Samuel Wetmore, Jr., Enoch Palmer, Ebenezer Preston, Oliver Coe and John Bradley should keep houses of Entertainment for Ordination. By a subsequent vote, Mr. Knapp was allowed to invite his friends to Robert Macune's, upon the society's cost.

No record appears of the action of the church in calling Mr. Knapp. The entry of his Ordination in the church records in his own hand is as follows:

NOVEMBER 11, A. D. 1772.

This day I was ordained to ye pastoral charge of ye Church of Christ in Winchester. The whole Association were sent to by letters missive. Present the Rev'd Messrs.

DR..BELLAMY,	[of Bethlem.]
MR. ROBBERTS,	[" Torrington.]
MR. LEE,	[" Salisbury.]
MR. BRINSMAID,	[" Washington.]
MR. FARRAND,	[" Canaan.]
MR. CANFIELD,	[" New Milford.]
MR. NEWEL,	[" Goshen.]
MR. BENEDICT,	[" Woodbury.]
MR. DAY,	[" New Preston.]
MR. ROBBINS,	[" Norfolk.]
MR. HART,	[" North Canaan.]
MR. STAR,	[" Warren.]

with these delegates, also a delegate from Torringford.

Mr. Benedict made ye first prayer, Mr. Robbins preached ye sermon,— Mr. Farrand made ye ordaining prayer,— Dr. Bellamy gave ye charge,— Mr. Hart ye right hand of fellowship,— Mr. Day made ye concluding prayer, ... the whole was performed with ye greatest Decency and Solemnity.

Test,

JOSHUA KNAPP, *Pastor.*

We copy from Rev. Mr. Marsh's Commemorative Sermon, the following notice of Mr. Knapp:

"Rev. Joshua Knapp, — a native of Danbury, graduated at Yale College in 1770, — was ordained Nov. 11, 1772, — and dismissed Oct 13, 1789. He was a ready and easy speaker. Few ministers possessed a happier talent at extemporaneous speaking. This operated somewhat unhappily in his case, as it has in others, by becoming a temptation to neglect that application to study and mental discipline which is essential to a minister's bringing forth out of his treasures things new and old.

Subsequent to his dismission, Mr. Knapp preached at North Canaan, New Hartford and Milton, in this county. From Milton he removed to Hamilton, Madison Co., N. Y., where he preached a considerable time, and from thence removed to Torrington, where he spent his old age in the family of his son-in-law, Deacon Abel Hinsdale. Occasionally he visited the people of his former charge, and as health permitted, preached to them. He departed this life March 23, 1816, in the 72d year of his age, and the 44th of his ministry. His grave is in this parish, among those of his early charge, who have finished their earthly course. A marble slab, erected by his friends in this place, marks the spot where his remains await the summons of the Archangel's trump. Previous to his settlement in Winchester, Mr. Knapp married Mary Keyes, a worthy and excellent lady, from the eastern part of Massachusetts. They had two sons and three daughters, most of whom are deceased. Mrs. K. survived her husband a few years, and while visiting friends in New Marlboro', Mass., became sick, and died at that place at the age of about 72."

The besetting sin of our first minister, as hinted by his worthy successor, was constitutional weariness. He is said to have tripped and fallen, while leisurely walking across his floor, with no impediment in his way, and thereby *broken his leg.* Want of thrift was an element of his character incident to his torpidity. He could not eke out his support from the scanty salary of ministers of that day. On one occasion he called together the society's Committee and Deacons, and set forth to them his privations, and his need of a more adequate support, closing with the remark that they ought to so provide for him that he could live as comfortably as Parson Robbins, who was a model of economy and good living. Good Deacon Hills replied to this remark, — "Mr. Knapp, if we should put a barrel, full of dollars, behind your buttery door, you couldn't live as Mr. Robbins does, *for it ain't in you.*"

This trait of his character, however, did not impair his firm adherence to principle in his pastoral duties. The churches in that day abounded with half-way covenant members, an anomalous class of professors, who had found their way into the Christian folds in the lax state of religion prevailing at the middle of the last century. Mr. Knapp seems to have

SETTLEMENT OF PASTOR. 91

set his face against these interlopers, and to have barred their entrance so the new church under his charge. Heart-burnings grew out of his somewhat arbitrary exercise of pastoral prerogative; an opposition grew up, not only to him, but to the church; which opened a way for Methodism, then in its infancy, to obtain a footing in the parish. As a consequence the growth of the church, though perhaps more pure and healthy, was slow, and the influence of the pastor was undermined.

CHAPTER X.

1771 to 1775. RESUMÉ AND NEW SETTLERS.

BEGINNING our annals with the hasty vote of the Colonial Assembly granting to Hartford and Windsor nearly all the unoccupied territory of the Colony, ostensibly for a single plantation, but really to place it beyond the grasp of the usurping Governor Andros, we have traced step by step the long controversy growing out of this ill-advised and unperfected* grant. We have seen these powerful towns assuming a vested ownership, first of the large township of Litchfield, and then of the whole territorial grant, thereby repudiating the implied, but doubtless understood, trust incident to the grant when made. We have viewed, with a modified sympathy, the awkward predicament of the Assembly when attempting to resume its control of the lands in the face of its semi-fraudulent grant; and with no sympathy at all, the persistent efforts of those pampered towns to hold their ill-gotten domain; especially the portion of it remaining after their appropriation of the large township of Litchfield by metes and bounds, thereby determining the extent of the "Plantation," provided for in the grant. We have followed the windings and turnings of sharp practice, by which the Assembly was finally badgered into a division of the remaining territory between the rightful owners and the unscrupulous claimants; a division securing to the latter 139,778 acres of land, which of right belonged as a common property to all the inhabitants of the colony.

We have detailed the sub-divisions of these lands until our own township fell into the hands of the niggardly "Proprietors of Winchester," and have seen how the long-delayed sub-division to individual proprietors was so made as to preclude any concerted measures for its settlement, and to withhold all inducement to that end, which the customary reservation of lands for religious and educational purposes would have held out to settlers. We have searched out the squatters who, after waiting in vain for an allotment of their individual rights, had selected their own locations; and have made ourselves acquainted, as far as possible, with the succeed-

---

* No patent of this territory was ever issued by the Assembly to these towns.

NEW SETTLERS.

ing pioneers — have ascertained whence they came, where they lived, and how they fared. We have seen the distinctive elements aggregate and crystallize into a religious society and a civil commonwealth.

But as yet the settlement of the town has only begun. All the inhabitants, with the exception of some half dozen families, are located on and west of the old South Country Road, a section not exceeding one-sixth part of the township. The whole population, as stated in the petition of April 4th, 1771, is twenty-eight families and 179 souls within the society of Winchester, and only four families without the society and within the town. The "Danbury Quarter," embracing the four half-mile tiers in the northwest corner of the town, is, as yet, nearly unoccupied. The four families located without the society are on the North Country Road, at the northeast corner of the town, and will be again referred to.

The slow growth of a remote country town affords few events that can interest others than those connected with it by personal or parental residence. To each and all of these, it is hoped that the minute details embodied in these annals will furnish some matters of interest and instruction, and that their affectionate regard for their fatherland or residence will lead them to appreciate our labors.

We propose to continue our History, if it can be so dignified, mainly in the form of annals, embracing in each year its public events, and accessions of inhabitants, with such biographical and genealogical notices as our scanty materials will afford, leaving the settlement of Winsted to be separately treated.

1772.

We find in the records of town meetings during this year, no votes or proceedings of special interest. The customary town officers were chosen, and a tax of "one penny half-penny on the pound" was laid.

The following new inhabitants are found on the records of this year, in Old Winchester Society: Thomas Spencer, Alexander Leach, John Corey, Levi Bronson, Roswell Coe, Elisha Smith, Samuel Hurlbut, and Reuben Thrall.

THOMAS SPENCER, from Saybrook, this year moved on to the farm recently purchased of Bronson and Munsill by Rufus Eglestone, lying north of his homestead, and bordering on the west side of the Long Pond south of Sucker Brook. The house which he built and occupied during his remaining life, remained standing until the winter of 1862-3, and then yielded to the wintry blasts. He was a prominent man of the town, and nine of his children became heads of large and influential families; but, of more than twenty of his descendants now residing in this town, not one bears the name of Spencer. He was born January 16th, 1736, O. S.;[*] married April 10th, 1760, Phebe Grenell, born July 20th, 1736, O. S.; he died May 1st, 1807, aged 71; she died October 2d, 1812.

CHILDREN.

I.	PHEBE,	b. April 20, 1761; m. Rev. John Sweet.
II.	JOHN,	b. October 18, 1762.
III.	CHLOE,	b. December 15, 1764; d. May 16, 1767.
IV.	THOMAS,	b. November 19, 1766.
V.	GRENELL,	b. September 9, 1768.
VI.	CHLOE,	b. December 4, 1770; m. Oliver Coe.
VII.	CHARLOTTE,	b. April 4th, 1773; m. Jonathan Coe, Jr.
VIII.	CANDACE,	b. June 14, 1775; m. January 17, 1798, Ashbel Munson, of Waterbury.
IX.	SYLVIA,	b. April 12th, 1778; m. Dr. T. S. Wetmore.
X.	HULDAH,	b. October 1, 1780; m. John Wetmore, 2d.

JOHN SPENCER,[2] oldest son of Thomas,[1] in 1784 bought of David Austin 39 acres of land in the heart of the West Village of Winsted, embracing all of Main street from Camp's Block southerly and easterly to Clifton Mill Bridge, and the whole of High street, Elm street, the Green Woods Park and adjacent streets. He entered on this purchase, cleared a few acres, and built a loghouse, on the flat near the corner of Elm and Main streets, before any bridge had been erected across Mad river at Lake street, or any road opened south of the bridle path now known as Hinsdale street. Despairing of ever having access by a road and bridge to the civilized part of the town, and unwilling to rear a family in this savage region, he sold his purchase for three dollars an acre, and bought a two hundred acre farm in Danbury Quarter, lately owned by Edward Rugg, then a well-populated section of the town, on which he lived until 1799. In 1800 he removed to Peacham, Caledonia county, Vermont, where he accumulated a fortune of $15,000, and lost it by becoming surety for the sheriff of the county. He then removed to Westmoreland, Oneida county, and after two years, again lost his all by the burning of his house. In 1816 he purchased a farm in the adjoining town of Vernon, on which he resided until his death, February 14th, 1826, aged 63. He married February 14th, 1793, Abigail, daughter of Abner Marshall, of Torrington, who died in 1849.

CHILDREN.

I.	JULIUS,	b. Winchester, January 31, 1794; living in 1857 at Lisbon, Ill.

---

[*] Probably descended from Sergt. Jared Spencer, who died in Haddam in 1685, through Thomas, who d. in Saybrook before 1703. See Godwin's Genealogical Notes, pp. 200 and 201.

II. ALMEDA,	b. Winchester, April 19, 1795; m. —— Carter, of Worthington, O.
III. GEO. GRINNELL,	b. Winchester, November 17, 1796; living in 1857 at Lexington, Va.
IV. HARLOW,	b. in Vermont; d. at 23 years of age.
V. SYLVIA,	b. " m. Marshall of Westmoreland, N. Y.
VI. WM. SCOTT,	b. " of Warsaw, Ill., in 1857.
VII. LAURA,	b. in Vermont; m. — Green, of Westmoreland, N. Y.
VIII. ORPHA,	b. " m. — Hiscock of Rochester, N. Y.
IX. JOHN,	b. " d. at the age of 8 years.
X. FRANKLIN AUGUSTUS, recently Congregational Minister of New Hartford, Conn., now living in Clinton, N. Y.
XI. RILEY, of Lexington, Ky., in 1857.

THOMAS SPENCER,[2] a millwright by trade, lived until about 1795, in a house that stood on the east side of the Dug-way road, nearly opposite a road that turns west to Winchester Centre Village. In 1795, in company with Benjamin Jenkins and James Boyd, he built the first forge in the town, on the "Old Forge Site," on which the grinding works of the Winsted Manufacturing Company now stand. He also built a store in which he traded in company with Hewett Hills, on the depot grounds of the Connecticut Western Railroad Company, on the north side of Lake street; and also the rear part of the tenant house on south side of Lake street, directly opposite the store building, in which he lived until his removal to Vernon, Oneida county, N. Y., about 1801 or '2. He died at Vernon, N. Y., about 1828. He married May 28th, 1795, Lucy, daughter of Hewitt Hills. Their children were three sons, Hilamon,[3] Thomas,[3] and Alpha,[3] and six daughters, Clarissa,[3] Lucy,[3] Sylvia,[3] Huldah,[3] Elizabeth,[3] and Sabrina.[3] The two sons, Hilamon and Alpha, died between the ages of fifteen and twenty. All the daughters, except Clarissa, were married. The particulars of this and the preceding household were furnished by Rev. F. A. Spencer, of Clinton, N. Y.

CAPTAIN GRINNELL SPENCER settled in Winsted, and first lived on a high hill about 100 rods west of the Spencer Street road, adjoining his original orchard, which can be seen from the west village of Winsted. About 1808 he built and occupied until his death the house on Spencer Street road now owned and occupied by his son-in-law, Amos Pierce. He improved more than 200 acres of land as a dairy farm, and for many years spent his winters in Charleston, S. C., as a dealer in cheese. He was an energetic, public-spirited, warm-hearted man, always the foremost to turn out and break the winter roads, to attend upon the sick, or to relieve the misfortunes of his neighbors. He died of a cancer March 5, 1843, aged 74. He married first Abigail ——, who died August 29, 1811, and second Mrs. —— Case of Farmington, who survived him but a few years, and died of the same disease.

CHILDREN OF GRINNELL[2] AND ABIGAIL (   ) SPENCER.

I. MATILDA,   b.   ; m. Elisha Kilbourn.
II. HARRIET,   b.   ; m. first, Sheldon Norton of Bethany, Wayne Co., Pa., and second, Rufus Grinnell.
III. ABIGAIL,   b.   1801; m. September 26, 1826, George Goodrich, d. September 13, 1828.
IV. PHEBE,   b.   ; m. Grinnell.
V. HELEN,   b.   ; m. Amos Pierce.

ALEXANDER LEACH, a Scotchman, came from New Haven to Winchester, and owned a farm in the Danbury Quarter, immediately north of the Edward Rugg farm. By his will, proved in Simsbury Probate Court, it would appear that he died in 1777, leaving Catharine, his wife (executrix), and Alexander, William, Catharine, and Elizabeth, their children. His wife is said to have been kidnapped from Holland when a child, and brought to this country. She died March 19, 1815, aged 80. Their daughter, Elizabeth, born January 18, 1774; married November 16, 1786, Nathan Brown.

ALEXANDER LEACH, Junior, lived on the homestead as late as 1791.

WILLIAM LEACH also lived on the homestead for many years, and afterwards in other parts of the town. He served in the continental army, and drew a pension. He died, probably, after 1830, leaving a son, Alva, and perhaps other children. He married March 24, 1783, Sarah Thompson.

JOHN COREY, from Goshen, owned and occupied in 1772–3, a part of the W. F. Hatch farm on the Little Pond, and probably soon after left the town.

LIEUTENANT THOMAS HURLBUT, immigrant, ancestor of Captain Samuel Hurlbut of Winchester, belonged to the first company that garrisoned the Fort at Saybrook in 1636. He served and was wounded in the Pequot War in 1637; settled in Wethersfield, and is supposed to have died soon after 1671. His wife was Sarah

STEPHEN,[2] fifth son of Lieutenant Thomas,[1] and Sarah Hurlbut, was born in Wethersfield about 1649, and there resided until 1690, after which no further record is found of him. He married, first, Dorothy   , December 12, 1678; second, Phebe

THOMAS,[3] son of Stephen,[2] and Dorothy Hurlbut, born in Wethersfield January 28, 1680, became a farmer and settled there. He married, January 11, 1705, Rebecca   He died April 10, 1761; she died March 22, 1760.

AMOS,⁴ son of Thomas³ and Rebecca, born in Wethersfield, April 14, 1717, settled there, and married June 10, 1742, Hannah Wright of Wethersfield, who died July 25, 1756; he married, second, March 3, 1757, Sarah Hill, who died in 1764; he married, third, March 10, 1766, Sarah Lattimer. He died in 1777 or earlier, administration having been granted on his estate February 22 of that year. He had by his first wife Hannah, Samuel,⁵ born about 1746; married at Torrington, December 1, 1768, Rebecca Beach; by his second wife, Sarah Stephen,⁵ born in Wethersfield, December 12, 1760, and Martin,⁵ baptized in Wethersfield, June 12, 1763.

CAPTAIN SAMUEL HURLBUT,⁵ from Newington Society (Wethersfield), came from Torrington to Winchester, and first purchased, with his brother in-law, Levi Bronson, the Artemus Rowley farm, near Torrington line, in the third tier, from whence he removed in 1774 to the center, and built the red lean-to house which stood on the site of his grandson, Samuel Hurlbut's present dwelling, where he lived until his death, March 23, 1831, at the age of 83. He began the world as a carpenter and joiner, afterwards became a tavern-keeper, at a period when "The Land Lord" stood next in rank after the minister and merchant, at the same time managing a large farm and a saw mill; and in later years engaged with his sons, Samuel and Lemuel, in country trade.

He was a sedate, thinking, methodical man of great energy and thrift, the second magistrate of the town, and a representative in seventeen sessions of the General Assembly.

In the words of Rev. Mr. Marsh, "he closed a useful life, after having lived in the parish fifty-nine years, and enjoyed a good share of respect and confidence as a magistrate, and in other departments of public business. Having been one of the earliest inhabitants, and having purchased a large quantity of land in the center of the parish, he did much to promote the settlement of the place, by disposing of his lands on so easy terms as to induce others to settle here. The public green and ground, on which the meeting house stood until recently, were given to the Society by him. He manifested great respect for the institutions of the Gospel, and gave some evidence of piety, though not a professor."

From the town records and a memorandum in his handwriting, we compile the following account of his family:—

Samuel Hurlbut,⁵ married in Torrington, December 1, 1768, Rebecca, daughter of Abel Beach. He died March 23, 1831, aged 83. Rebecca (his widow) died October 27, 1829, aged 84.

CHILDREN.

I. SILAS,⁶   b. July 6, 1769; died unmarried December 24, 1793.
II. LEONARD,⁶ b. May 18, 1771.

III. MARGARET,⁶ b. March 2, 1773; m. John McAlpine.
IV. SAMUEL,⁶ b. March 13, 1775; d. October 4, 1776.
V. LUCY,⁶ b. October 6, 1777; m. May 12, 1797, Sylvester Hall of Burke, Vermont.
VI. REBECCA,⁶ b. November 30, 1779; m. Church of Vernon, N. Y.
VII. SAMUEL,⁶ b. October 2, 1783.
VIII. LEMUEL,⁶ b. September 20, 1785.

GENERAL LEONARD HURLBUT,⁶ oldest son of Captain Samuel, lived and died in the house recently occupied by his son in-law, William H. Rood, about a mile northeasterly from Winchester Center. He was a large dairy farmer, and an unassuming, exemplary man. He married, October 17, 1798, Huldah Case. She died August 16, 1800, aged 23. He married, second, February 14, 1805, Elizabeth, daughter of Daniel Hurlbut Cone, born January 29, 1784; died June 16, 1839. He died December 21, 1851, aged 81.

CHILDREN BY FIRST WIFE.

I. HILAMON,⁷ b. October 14, 1799; d. about 1861, in Platte Co., Missouri.

CHILDREN BY SECOND WIFE.

II. SILAS,⁷ b. May 16, 1806.
III. HULDAH,⁷ b. February 7, 1808; d. January 25, 1818.
IV. LEONARD BEACH,⁷ b. July 23, 1811; m. October 21, 1835, Sylvia, daughter of Dr. Truman S. Wetmore.

CHILDREN.

1. Sylvia Elizabeth,⁸ b. September 29, 1840.
2. Charlotte Jarvis,⁸ b. September 13, 1845.

V. ELIZABETH HULDAH,⁷ b. November 19, 1818; m. November 5, 1845, Wm. H. Rood.

SAMUEL HURLBUT, Junior,⁶ second son of Captain Samuel, went into trade at Winchester Center in early life, with Chauncey Humphrey, and afterwards, in company with his brother Lemuel, continued the business, until his death, at the age of 74. He was a man of good education and studious habits, a close applicant to his business, and a careful manager, rarely leaving home except to make his semi-annual purchases of goods, and never indulging in any useless expense or hazardous speculations. With these characteristics, and with the co-operation of his more energetic brother, an estate of more than $200,000 was accumulated and transmitted to their heirs.

Mr. Hurlbut was a man religiously educated and inclined, but not a professor; a supporter of good order and religious institutions; charitable to the poor, and occasionally liberal to public benefactions. The death of his younger brother, who had for so many years pushed forward the business which he had regulated, came upon him with stunning force.

His mind lost its balance. He attempted to make a will, and after bequeathing legacies of five thousand dollars each to the American Bible, Home Missionary. and Tract Societies, and appointing executors, he executed the instrument, leaving the bulk of his estate to be legally divided to his heirs. He lived a consistent bachelor, and died at the age of 74, on the 22d day of October, 1857.

LEMUEL HURLBUT,[6] youngest child of Captain Samuel,[5] was endowed with a hardy constitution, a manly person, pleasing address, and a sanguine temperament. His perceptive faculties predominated over his intellectual, and his tastes ran to fine animals and highly cultivated lands. Though a large trader, he was rarely seen at the desk or behind the counter. His department of the business of the brothers, S. & L. Hurlbut, was to receive and market the cheese, of which they were extensive purchasers, and to cultivate and improve their lands. For more than thirty years he spent his winters at Baltimore in the sale of cheese which had during the fall been purchased from the dairy farmers of this region. His summers were occupied in superintending his farming operations. and in raising and improving domestic animals. for which he had a passionate fondness. His horses, sheep, and oxen were unsurpassed in excellence and beauty. About 1820, he introduced upon his farm the pure Devon breed of cattle, the first of this beautiful and serviceable stock brought into the State. From his herd the breed has been largely diffused through the Northern and Western States. The unrivaled strings of pure red working oxen that grace the agricultural fairs of this county, attest the valuable service he performed for the agricultural interest of this region; while the ample profits realized attest his sagacity and thrift.

During a period of seventy years from his birth, Mr. Hurlbut had never been visited with sickness requiring the attendance of a doctor. In the fall of 1855, he came home from the Massachusetts State Fair. suffering from a severe cold contracted during his absence, and aggravated by imprudent exposure. After confinement to his bed for one hundred days, his strong frame yielded to decay, and he expired February 19. 1856, at the age of seventy and a half years. He made a profession of religion, and united with the Congregational Church May 1, 1853. He married Ann H. Phelps, of Norfolk; she died July 18, 1867, aged 76.

CHILDREN.

I. CAROLINE,[7] b. May 20, 1811; m. October 24, 1832, John Rutherford, of Macon, Ga.
II. ELIZABETH ANN,[7] b. December 13, 1813; m. June 23, 1838, Dr. John H. T. Cockey, of Frederick Co., Md.
III. LEMUEL,[7] b March 8, 1816; m. Florania, daughter of John Westlake.

IV. SAMUEL,⁷   b. January 12, 1818.
V. JEREMIAH PHELPS,⁷ b. January 16, 1821 ; d. January 27, 1821.
VI. REBECCA,⁷   b. March 9, 1826 ; m. June 7, 1848, Henry P. Chapman of Brooklyn, N. Y.

STEPHEN HURLBUT,⁵ born December 12, 1760; half brother of Samuel,⁵ from Wethersfield, Newington Society, came into the town about 1782; he bought and settled on a lot of land south of, and near, Rufus M. Eggleton's. At the time of his death, April 14, 1807, aged 46, he resided in the farm house of Mrs. Boyd, on East Lake Street. He married Abigail Meeker; she was born August 14, 1768, and died in 1856.

CHILDREN.

I. SARAH,⁶   b. July 11, 178⁻; m. Walter Dickinson; d. 1855.
II. EUNICE,⁶   b. "   29, 1789; m. David Hubbard, of W. Hartford.
III. AMOS,⁶   b. February 13, 1792; m. Eleanor Elmore.
IV. LUCY,⁶   b. April 21, 1794 ; m. Daniel Phelps, Jr.
V. MARY,⁶   b. August 27, 1796 ; m. Charles Clark.
VI. SAMUEL,⁶   b. October 31, 1798; is known as Samuel Hurlbut, 2d; m. March 19, 1822, Lavinia Blake; she d. May 26, 1864, aged 63; he d. in the spring of 1872.
VII. HULDAH,⁶ b. February 15, 1801 ; d. unm. October 31, 1830.
VIII. SILAS,⁶ b. March 27, 1803 ; m. Ruth Goodwin.
IX. CLARISSA,⁶ b. August 18, 1806; m. Sherman Goodwin.

MARTIN HURLBUT,⁵ from Wethersfield, came, when a boy, to live with his half-brother, Captain Samuel,⁵ and continued to reside in the town until his death, April 5, 1810, at the age of 47. He built and lived in the old part of the house, on the height of land a mile south of the Winsted depot, known as the Pratt House, and now owned by James W. Ward, which he sold to Andrew Pratt in 1801 : after which he lived on South Street, in Winsted, until 1808, when he bought and occupied the farm on the easterly shore of Long Lake, now owned by his son and only child, Deacon Joseph W. Hurlbut. He married, September 10 1787, Elizabeth Wheeler; she died May 27, 1849, aged 85. They had one child,

JOSEPH WHEELER HURLBUT,⁶ born July 20, 1793 ; m. April 25, 1817, Sarah Merrill, born June 18, 1794 ; daughter of Stephen. She died October 29, 1864, aged 70 years.

CHILDREN.

I. JAMES MARTIN,⁷   b. January 5, 1818 ; d. August 14, 1847, unmarried.
II. JOSEPH MERRILL,⁷ b. September 28, 1824 ; m. June 2, 1869, Anne Augusta Field.
III. WARREN PHINEAS,⁷ b. January 4, 1827.
VI. WM. FLOWERS,⁷   b.   "   27, 1835.

DEACON LEVI BRONSON, from Berlin, married, October 25, 1769, Hannah Hurlbut, sister of Samuel, and came with him to Winchester. He built the Artemas Rowley house, in which he lived until about 1795, when he moved to Cattskill, New York. A cotemporary says of him: "Mr. Bronson was a large and prosperous farmer, and withal a merchant. His goods for trade he mainly bought of Sheldon Leavitt, of Bethlem. He made a large amount of potash. He was a prudent, straight-forward man in all his business. His store was in his dwelling-house, — the first, and for many years, the only store in the town. Upright, kind, generous, and exemplary, he made his life adorn his religious profession. After he settled in Cattskill he engaged somewhat in navigation; — and by it, lost money; and afterwards, with property diminished, he removed to Vernon, Oneida County, New York, where he spent his remaining days." He married, October 25, 1769, Hannah Hurlbut.

CHILDREN.

I. LEVI, b. July 30, 1770; d. April 18, 1775.
II. LEMUEL, b. Oct. 23, 1772; d. March 6, 1775.
III. DAVID, b. Dec. 23, 1774.
IV. LEVI, b. May 15, 1777.
V. HANNAH, b. July 21, 1784.
VI. LUCY, b. Dec. 9, 1786.
VII. SARAH, b. Nov. 28, 1789.

CAPTAIN ROSWELL COE came from Torrington and bought a farm in the southwest part of the town, which he occupied until his sale of the same to John Lucas in 1789, when he returned to Torrington.

ELISHA SMITH, ESQ., from Torrington, bought of Enoch Palmer, the Noble J. Everitt place, about a hundred rods south of Winchester center, which he occupied until 1776, when he sold to Martin North and returned to Torrington, where he spent his remaining life as a farmer and trader, occupying a high position as a magistrate and representative of the town. He was born in the ancient town of Farmington, August 14, 1751; married in Torrington, November 25, 1773, Lucy Loomis. He died January 9, 1813.

CHILDREN.

I. ELISHA, b. July 19, 1775; d. in Tor., August 9, 1776.
II. ORREL, b. in Tor., Jan. 30, 1778; m. Russell C. Abernethy.
III. ALMIRA, b. " " 12, 1780; d. April 20, 1780.

REUBEN THRALL, from Torrington, bought and occupied until his death, May 23, 1777, a farm immediately north of Roswell Coe's, in the southwest part of the town, afterward a part of the Wade farm ; he died May 20, 1777, and his widow married William Barbour, September 26, 1778; and about 1798, removed with him to Burke, Caledonia County, Vermont.

CHILDREN OF REUBEN AND RUTH THRALL.

I. ALEXANDER, d. Oct. 27, 1786.
II. ERASTUS, b. Feb. 14, 1773.

1773.

The town records of 1773 show that the customary town officers were chosen, and a committee appointed to straighten the line between Winchester and Torrington ; a vote was passed to restrain swine from running at large, and another directing the Proprietor's committee to lay out the road from the Dugway, to Colebrook, already mentioned.

The Society records show that the usual officers were chosen, including three choristers and two readers of the psalms. It was provided that the psalms should be read before singing for four months, and that thereafter they should be sung without reading. It was also voted to raise two pence on the pound of the rateable estate for the support of schools; and the society was divided into three School Districts, which were to receive their rateable portions of the money raised; but an adjourned meeting in January of the following year reconsidered all the votes concerning schools.

The last vote of the year was, " that we desire Mr. Farrand and Mr. Newell and Marsh, shall come out and give their advise concerning some difficulty in this place." The difficulty referred to grew out of a disagreement of the church and society, in respect to the privileges of halfway covenant members of the church. Prior to the ordination of Mr. Knapp, the church had voted, " That upon persons owning the covenant, they may have their children baptized, while they cannot see yr. way clear to come to ye Lord's table."

About a month after Mr. Knapp's ordination (Dec. 16) a series of standing rules were adopted by the church ;—the seventh of which was, " that all persons who in other places have owned what is called the halfway covenant, in order to be admitted to special privileges in this church, shall renewedly and explicitly own ye Gospel Covenant." After the adoption of this rule, Joseph Hoskin and Jonathan Coe applied for admission to membership on letters from Mr. Robert's church in Torrington. This application brought the disputed question to a practical issue. The church passed an explanatory vote " that the vote of the church which allowed baptism to ye children of persons owning the covenant, was in our view, and as we account, to be understood a whole covenant, without any clause left out ;" and thereupon refused to receive the applicants.

Upon this state of the question, the counsel of Messrs. Farrand, Newell, and Marsh was asked by the concurrent vote of the church and society. The council met, on the 25th day of January, 1774, and came to a divided result. Messrs. Marsh and Newell were of opinion that the church rules above quoted were not consistent. They further say "that certain persons also applying to us, and complaining of injury done them by ye church in not accepting of ye letters of recommendation from ye Rev. Mr. Roberts, and claiming privileges by virtue of their recommendation. It is our opinion, y^r letters ought to be read to this chh. and ye persons recommended be admitted to ye privileges of baptism for yr. children, agreeable to y^s vote of sd. ch. before ordination of Mr Knapp."

Mr. Farrand dissented from the opinion of his colleagues, for the following reasons:

"1. As the church declares they never meant to have any other but a gospel covenant, and 'twould be strange if a chh. of Jesus Christ, covenanting to walk together in his holy ordinances, should have only a political covenant, or a mere legal covenant, which they must have, if not a gospel one, or no covenant at all.

"2d. The Chh. had a covenant written and assented to at their incorporation by ye members of y^r Chh., which they say they agreed that all future members should own; and ye same covenant is what they now call a Gospel Covenant.

"3d. They say that they never meant to divide ye covenant but only to indulge tender consciences 'til they could receive further light, wh. they are willing to do now; but ye judgment (of the majority) was that ye covenant must be divided, and this clause left out, that obliged them to walk in all ye ordinances of ye Lord, so that such may come into covenant, who will not promise to walk in all ye ordinances of ye Lord, but only such as they pick out and chuse.

"4th. The first vote says that all that have their children baptized shall own their covenant, wh. must mean either a Gospel covenant or ye covenant y^t ye Chh. of Winchester had adopted; but if their vote meant a Gospel covenant, they require no more of 'em now, but if they meant to distinguish ye covenant which ye Chh. had then, from a Gospel covenant, they require no more of them but to adopt the same covenant they then had, and are ready to indulge tender consciences; whereupon I conclude they have not broken covenant, nor gone off from their first plan in their 2d vote."

This divided counsel, of course, satisfied neither party, and in no way tended to heal the dissention. At a subsequent meeting, May 3, the society voted "to choose four men to treat with Mr. Knap concerning the difficulty among us, and to see if he will join with the society in chusing a mutual council." The church on May 9, unanimously voted "that it is our opinion that y⁰ association to which we belong is y⁰ proper board for us to be tried by, and by them we are ready to be tried at any suitable time."

Whether the matter was carried before the Association (or Consociation?) does not appear, but it may be inferred that under some new advice or counsel, a new gloss was added to the church covenant, at a meeting Dec. 14, by inserting the clause "only, in case you may labor under any scruples of conscience with respect to immediate attendance upon y⁰ Lord's supper, you may be indulged in your absenting until you have had proper light for conviction." It was also voted "that we understand y⁰ import of y⁰ covenant entered into by this Chh. to be consistent with indulging persons that have any scruples of conscience about coming immediately to y⁰ Lord's Supper, in absenting themselves from that ordinance until they have had sufficient light to convince them that it is their indispensable duty to attend upon it agreeable to the vote of y⁰ Chh. relating to persons owning yr. covenant being allowed to have y⁰ children baptized, tho. they cannot see their way clear to come to y⁰ Lord's table." It was also voted 'that persons bringing letters from other churches, previous to their being admitted into this Chh. shall explicitly renew y⁰ covenant with us."

This controversy in our infant church might well remain in the obscurity of our imperfect and scattered records, and consigned to oblivion, were it not for the results of good and evil that flowed from it in all the subsequent history of the parish and town. Good men became disaffected towards the standing order, and arrayed themselves in hostility to the pastor, who set his face determinedly against the compromise of principle involved in a half-way consecration to the Lord, and may have displayed more of arbitrary zeal than of wise consideration in his efforts to annul the unholy compact.

Luther Lee,* or some other early apostle of Methodism, came into this region about that period ; and the new evangel was welcomed by the opponents of the standing order. A number of the patriarchs of this town received it gladly, and left it as a legacy to their children. A church was organized at "Noppit" in Torrington, near the border of this town, where the opponents of Mr. Knapp found refuge. Another was organized at an early day in Winsted, which has grown into a large and influential body. The asperities of early years have died away. Sectarianism has yielded to Christian love, and the members of the two communions differ little but in name from each other. Their combined influence in advancing and extending the cause of religion is far greater than could be effected by one united body.

---

* The compiler has recently learned that the two earliest Methodist ministers preaching in the town were named Covill and Stoneman.

1773.

The new comers of the year 1773, were Abram Andrews and his sons, Theophilus, Abram, Jr., Daniel and Eli, John Austin, Rev. Joshua Knapp, Hawkins Woodruff, Reuben Miner, and Gideon Wilcoxson.

CAPT. ABRAM ANDREWS, SENIOR, from Danbury, bought a farm of eighty acres, lying north of the old Everitt house, in the Danbury Quarter, now in part belonging to Mr. Tibball's farm, a part of which he occupied until his death. Out of his eighty-acre lot he successively apportioned as advancements to his four sons, ten acres each, and to two of his daughters five acres each, in parallel strips running north and south through the farm, and eventually sold out the remainder in driblets, and died landless October 29, 1805, aged 84. Over his grave in the Danbury Quarter is a marble slab "erected by his daughter Laurana." He was born about 1721, at Grassy Plain, in Danbury, son of Robert and Anna (Olmsted) Andrews, grandson of Abraham and Sarah (Porter) Andrews, and great-grandson of John and Mary Andrews, who were among the first settlers of Farmington. He married Sarah Taylor, of Bethel; from whence she brought a letter of dismission to the church in W., November , 1774.

CHILDREN.

I. THEOPHILUS,[2] m. October 4, 1764, Phebe Benedict.
II. ABRAM,[2] m. April 24, 1773, Sarah Young.
III. ENSIGN DANIEL,[2] b. 1749, m. Sarah Hall; she d. October 3d, 1822.
IV. ELI,[2] m. August 29, 1787, Ruth Rockwell.
V. CHLOE,[2] m. May 22, 1768, Noah Benedict.
VI. LAURANA,[2] m. September, 1804, Israel White, of Sharon.

THEOPHILUS ANDREWS, son of the foregoing, is described by a cotemporary as "a Yankee, dyed in the wool; by profession a tinker, he traversed the northern part of the county, with his kit of tools in a pair of leather saddle-bags swung over his shoulders, mending brass kettles and molding pewter spoons and buttons." He continued his peregrinations as late as 1810, and afterwards went to live with a son in central New York. None of his descendants remain in the town. He married October 4th, 1764, Phebe Benedict.

CHILDREN.

I. ELIAKIM, b. April 17, 1765.
II. JAMES, b. January 17, 1767.
III. THEOPHILUS, b March 18, 1768; d. March 19, 1768.
IV. NAOMI, b. April 30, 1769.
V. PHEBE, b. February 20, 1772; d. May 29, 1775.
VI. BETSEY, b. April 28, 1774.
VII. PHEBE, b May 9, 1776; d. February 14, 1777
VIII. LUCY, b January 1, 1778.
IX. ROSWELL, b. October 8, 1779.

ABRAM ANDREWS, JR., is described by the same cotemporary as "a Yankee diverse from 'Theof.,' but of equal doodle. Both were wise-acres, but neither of them added more than a cubit to his ten acre patrimony." He removed to central New York after 1805. He married April 24, 1773, Sarah Young.

CHILDREN.

I. LEVI, b. January 21, 1777.
II. ABRAHAM, b. August 15, 1779.
III. SARAH, b. April 4, 1782.
IV. JOHN SPRAGUE, b. May 22, 1784.
V. CHLOE, b. January 10, 1788.
VI. SYLVESTER, b. November 26, 1795.

ENSIGN DANIEL ANDREWS, third son of Abram, Senior, "was a man of sense, energy, industry and uprightness." He built, and occupied until his death, July 20th, 1828, aged 79, the lean-to house a little east of the Danbury school house, now owned by Lyman H. Gilbert. He married April 2d, 1771, Sarah Hall; she died October 3d, 1822, aged 69.

CHILDREN.

I. RHODA, b. June 24, 1771; m. Levi Grant, of Norfolk.
II. DANIEL, b. October 25, 1772.
III. ANNA, b. April 3, 1774.
IV. HULDAH, b. October 14, 1775.
V. SARAH, b. February 16, 1777.
VI. EZRA, b. September 13, 1778; had wife, Paulina. Children: Paulina Louisa, b. June 22, 1804; Huldah Emeline, b. May 17, 1806; and Jerusha Fidelia, b. October 15, 1807.

ELI ANDREWS, fourth son of Abram, Senior, lived on a part of his father's original farm until his removal to central New York, after 1801. He married August 29, 1787, Ruth Rockwell.

CHILDREN.

I. JOEL, b. December 29, 1787.
II. CLARA, b. June 4, 1789.
III. ABIGAIL, b. March 27, 1792.
IV. POLLY, b. August 15, 1793.

DANIEL ANDREWS, son of Ensign Daniel, married Sarah Platt; she died December 16, 1848, aged 72; he died October 4, 1854, aged 82.

CHILDREN.

I. PLATT, b. March 6, 1799; m. March 6, 1828, Nancy Gilbert; she d. June 25, 1850; he m. (2d) the widow of Ira Hull. He d. June 16, 1860, s. p.
II. AMOS, b. July 15, 1801; d. September 20, 1845.

III. Augustus,   b. January 23, 1806; d. August 2, 1853, at Council Bluff, Iowa.
IV. Maria,   b. November 15, 1808; m. Willard Hart.
V. Hiram,   b. May 12, 1813.
VI. Lewis,   b. December 10, 1814; m. October 5, 1840, Caroline P. Culver.
VII. Huldah,   b. September 1, 1817; m. Milo M. Wadsworth.
VIII. Harriet,   b. November 4, 1819; m. (1st) Albert Jaqua; (2d) Correl, Manchester.

John Austin bought this year of David Austin, thirty-five acres of land within the present village of Winsted, and sold the same to John Walter in 1779, and is described in the deeds as of Winchester. Whence he came and where he went is not ascertained.

Rev. Joshua Knapp, from Danbury, the recently ordained Pastor, purchased and lived on a lot next South of the homestead of Eliphaz Alvord, Esq., at the north-west corner made by the parting of the east and west road to Winchester Centre, from the north and south Dug-way road. His dwelling-house was demolished early in this century.

CHILDREN OF THE REV. JOSHUA AND MRS. MARY KNAPP.

I. Mary,   b. December 8, 1772.
II. Abigail Bracy,   b. August 16, 1774.
III. Elizabeth,   b. October 11, 1776; d. June 29, 1777.
IV. Joshua,   b. July 2, 1778.
V. Elizabeth,   b. January 28, 1781.
VI. Caleb Bushnell,   b. June 16, 1783.
VII. Martha,   b. October 21, 1785.
VIII. Florilla,   b. May 12, 1787; d. June 1, 1787.
IX. Florilla,   b. July 23, 1788.

Hawkins Woodruff bought, and lived a few years on the farm now owned by Frederick Murray, on the old road from Winsted to Winchester Centre. He sold out to Samuel Clark in 1777. Whence he came and where he went is not ascertained. He married June 4, 1773, Lois Hills.

CHILD.
Clara, b. March 24, 1774.

Reuben Miner came from New London, was a blacksmith by trade, and first built a house and shop near the original meeting house, from whence he removed in 1775 to the centre of the township, and built and occupied until his death the old house now owned and occupied by Joel G. Griswold, on the old road from Winsted to Winchester. He was a man of earnest piety and zeal and an estimable citizen. He married Mrs. Sanderforth.* He died February 15, 1826, aged 85, leaving no record of

---

* The marriage of this worthy couple was said to be of the Enoch Arden order. They were both residents of New London. Mrs. Sanderforth's first husband was a sea captain, who was shipwrecked on a distant voyage, and not being heard from for

his family. He had two daughters, Esther and Lucy. Lucy lived and died single. Esther married David Strong.

JONATHAN SWEET is described on the land records of this year as of Winchester, and subsequently as of Goshen, and then again as of Winchester. He first owned the B. B. Rockwell farm, between the two ponds, and afterwards a tract of land on Blue street, adjoining Goshen line. He may have temporarily resided on both places. He sold out his land in 1781, and probably then left the town. He married August 29, 1773, Esther Lewis.

CHILDREN.

I. SARAH, b. May 16, 1774.
II. LORRAIN, b. February 16, 1776; d. March 24, 1778.
III. JONATHAN LEWIS, b. June 26, 1778.
IV. LUCY, b. June 30, 1780.

GIDEON WILCOXSON, from Stratford, owned and is supposed to have lived on land lying north and northeast of the Little Pond, probably the Daniel Beckley place. He served in the Revolutionary War, and died, while a prisoner, in the Sugar House in New York. His estate was administered in the Simsbury Probate Court, and distribution made to his brothers Elisha, David, and John, and his sisters Elizabeth Lake, Ruth Hubbell, Martha Beach, Huldah Coe, and Abia McCune.

1774.

We find the following votes of 1774, which reflect no credit on the infant town:—

"It was put to vote whether Lent Mott should be an inhabitant of this town, and it was voted in the negative."

"It was put to vote whether Widow Sarah Preston should be an inhabitant of this town, and it was voted in the negative."

"It was put to vote whether Benjamin Preston should be an inhabitant of this town, and it was voted in the negative."

When it is considered that each of these parties was a pioneer settler, that the first was one of the original members of the Church, still in good

---

several years, was believed to be lost. Mrs. Sanderforth, after some years of supposed widowhood, married Mr. Minor; and soon afterwards, Capt. Sanderforth re appeared and claimed his wife. The two husbands finally agreed that the wife should decide to which of them she would adhere; and that she and her selected husband should move out of New London county. She adhered to Mr. Minor, and they forthwith moved to Winchester. Their marriage was in some way legalized, and their lives were exemplary, affectionate, and pious. She was a refined woman, and highly esteemed. Some of her Sanderforth children followed her to this town, one of whom, a daughter, married William, son of John Miner.

standing, and that the other two were admitted to membership in 1775, it is hard to assign any other cause than poverty for these disfranchising votes.

The new comers of this year were Ozias Brownson and his sons, Ozias, Junior, Levi (second), Salmon, Asahel, Abijah P., and Isaac; Joseph Frisbee, Phineas Griswold, Ambrose Palmer, Joel Roberts, Peter Corbin, and his sons, Peter, Junior, and Daniel; John Videto and his son, John, Junior; Stephen Wade and his son, Amasa; Ichabod Loomis, William Castel, Benjamin Preston, and Gideon Smith.

COL. OZIAS BROWNSON lived on the farm now owned by Reuben Chase, about a mile and a half southerly from the center. He was a blacksmith and farmer, and is described by a cotemporary as a "professor of religion, somewhat fierce and overbearing, industrious and thrifty, abounding in horses. He had children, one daughter and six sons. These sons were of gigantic strength, and the Colonel worked the five oldest to a great profit." He served as a Lieutenant and Captain of Militia in several tours of duty during the Revolution. He died March 12, 1810, aged 68. His wife, Abigail (Peck), died August 21, 1831, aged 78. His youngest son, Isaac, Esq., was born in Winchester, January 22, 1776.

OZIAS BROWNSON, Junior, built the house at Winchester Center now owned by Rev. Frederick Marsh, in which he lived until 1802, when he sold out to Rev. Archibald Bassett, and soon after removed to Amsterdam, N. Y. He married, January 12, 1792, a daughter (Grace) of Daniel Coe Hudson of Torrington,* and called his eldest son George Washington Jefferson, a name which somewhat dumb-founded Parson Robbins at the

---

* The compiler heard Mr. B. relate an incident of his marriage, illustrating the customs of that day. On the morning after the wedding he started from Torringford to Winchester in a sleigh, with his bride and a two-gallon bottle of rum, and on his way home found the road fenced up in three successive places, with gatherings of neighbors at each fence, prepared to salute his wife, or bottle, before allowing him a passage homeward.

* * * * Another Winchester man, about this time married a wife in North Goshen, and was rather select in his invitations to the wedding. The roystering boys of Goshen Center were "left out in the cold." The marriage ceremony having been performed, and the "cushion dance" or some other kissing game commenced, a gang of the uninvited "he ones," who had secreted themselves around the open outside door, suddenly sprung upon the bride as she was passing, and rushed her into their sleigh. The horses were put to their full speed, the bride was taken to a tavern in the south part of Norfolk, and treated to flip, music, and dancing until the early hours of the morning, before the frantic husband could rescue her. He resorted to law instead of pistols for redress, but settled the suit before trial, so that it was never ascertained what a Litchfield county jury would award in dollars and cents for "stealing a bride."

baptism. "He could build a house, a cart, or a plough, or any other article of wood and iron. He worked all day at the anvil, or on his land, and journeyed two-thirds of the nights. At length he pulled up stakes and moved to the German Flats to grow hemp."

LEVI BROWNSON, second son of Ozias, Senior (known as Levi Bronson, second), owned, and occupied until his death, an extensive farm near the southeast corner of Norfolk, living in the red house near the Norfolk line. He was a hard-working, wealthy farmer. He married, October 25, 1792, Mary Benedict, daughter of Benjamin Benedict, Sen. She died March 9, 1824, aged 51. He married (second), November 14, 1824, Widow Clarissa L. (Higley) Morgan, who died September 14, 1827, aged 50. He died October 16, 1846, aged 81.

CHILDREN.

I. URIEL B., b. May 6, 1796; m. May 13, 1823, Clarissa Lawrence.
II. ALMA, b. July 4, 1798; m. March 14, 1825, Russell Cowdry.
III. HULDAH, b. June 4, 1800; m. May 2, 1826, Chester Humphrey.
IV. SALIMA, b. March 31, 1802; m. — Stevens of Coventry, N. Y.
V. MARY, b. April 8, 1804; m. October 20, 1827, Seth Benedict of Coventry, N. Y.
VI. LEVI, b. February 4, 1806; m. May 2, 1826, Susan Morgan.
VII. LYMAN, b. December 23, 1808; m. May 3, 1836, Jerusha Wright.
VIII. LUCY, b. August 29, 1811; m. April 11, 1833, David R. Barnes.
IX. FREDERICK, b. July 2, 1815.
X. ASAHEL HERVEY, b. June 16, 1817.

SALMON BROWNSON, third son of Colonel Ozias, lived and died on the farm now or lately owned by his son, Luther Bronson. "He was industrious, frugal, honest, moral and steadfast. His religion was something more than profession." He married, November 3, 1800, Mercy Wheadon. He died February 18, 1832, aged 64.

CHILDREN.

I. GALPIN PECK, b. May 13, 1802; had wife, Freelove L., and a daughter, Lucretia Wheadon, b. June 22, 1830.
II. SALOME WHEADON, b. Jan. 17, 1804.
III. PAMELIA R., b. Feb. 28, 1807; d. unmarried, 1871.
IV. CHARITY, b. Oct. 28, 1809; m. March 6, 1827, Samuel C. Ford, Waterbury.
V. CLARINA, b. April 19, 1812; m. September 9, 1833, Chas. Bently, N. Stonington.
VI. ELECTA, b. Jan. 28, 1816.
VII. LUTHER, b. Feb. 6, 1821.

ASAHEL BROWNSON, fourth son of Colonel Ozias, lived and died in the house on Blue Street, lately occupied by Archibald Dayton, now deceased, who married his widow. He was a retiring, laborious and successful farmer. He married, July 26, 1824, Lophelia Richardson, and died childless, October 13, of the same year, aged 54.

ABIJAH PECK BROWNSON, fifth son of Colonel Ozias, lived on Brooks Street, north of Nelson T. Loomis, until his removal to Vernon, New York, about 1800. "He was the Anak of the family: — a man of pleasant temperament, and brim-full of courage and fortitude." Many a strong wild colt did he shoe; many a wild steer did he yoke, — and many a time did he bind his neighbor, John Lucas, a respectable man, but strong and occasionally crazy. Soon after his marriage (November 16, 1797, to Mary, daughter of Hewitt Hills), he removed to Oneida County, New York, where. at middle age, he died, less successful than his brothers in the acquisition of property.

ISAAC BRONSON,* youngest son of Colonel Ozias, and the only one born in the town, built and resided until his death, in the house at the center now owned by his son, Theron. He was the largest land owner in the town. He was also a trader for many years, and a large dealer in dairy products from his own farms and purchased from others. He was a prominent and influential man in the town, — a Justice of the Peace, and three times a Representative to the General Assembly. Having divided up his large estate among his children, he died January 13, 1849, aged 74. He married, September 18, 1800, Eliza, daughter of Hewitt Hills.

CHILDREN.

    I. BIRDSEY,   b. June 16, 1801; m. Nov. 7, 1826, Elizabeth Garret Beebe, daughter of Hon. James Beebe. He owned and occupied the house at the corner of the Norfolk road and Waterbury turnpike, until his removal to New London, where both he and his wife died not far from 1840. Children:
        1. William B., b. May 10, 1829; m. Sept. 23, 1858, Katie McAlpine.
        2. Ellen Elizabeth, b. May 16, 1833; m. Jan. 29, 1855, Dr. L. P. Woods. She m. (2d), March 7, 1867, Oscar F. Potter, of Desmoines, Iowa.
  II. ELIZA,   b. Dec. 19, 1802; m. Jan. 14, 1834, Calvary Wetmore.
 III. NEWBURY,   b. April 13, 1804.
 IV. EMELINE,   b. Feb. 19, 1806; d. July 27, 1806.
  V. ORPHA,   b. June 30, 1807; m. June 10, 1851, Jas. Reynolds, Esq., of Orange, Ct.
 VI. THERON,   b. March 20, 1809; m. — Maria Munsill.
VII. LOUISA,   b. Nov. 28, 1810.

---

* The "w" was retained in the name of the Winchester Brownsons, until after 1810; by some of them, as appears by their recorded deeds, as late as 1825.

VIII. DELIA,	b. Dec. 25, 1812; d. Dec. 26, 1816.	
IX. EDWIN,	b. Feb. 2, 1815; d. Jan. 8, 1817.	
X. ABIGAIL,	b. Dec. 13, 1817.	
XI. ISAAC A.,	b. June 16, 1820; m. Nov. 4, 1845, Susan R. Nash.	

LOIS, daughter of Colonel Ozias Brownson, married, December, 9, 1779, Seth Wetmore, and in advanced life, Major Benoni Bronson.

The family of Bronson, once the most numerous, with one exception, in the town, has but few representatives remaining. But two of the third generation (Theron and Isaac A.) bearing the name are now residents.

ENSIGN JOSEPH FRISBIE, from Torrington, first lived on Lot 6, in the southwest corner of the town, and afterwards, in 1782, removed to a lot opposite the original meeting house, with a saw-mill thereon, probably erected by him. He removed to Vernon, New York, about 1800. He married, October 7, 1767, Sarah Kelsey; she died May 25, 1783, and he married (2d), February 21, 1785, Diantha, daughter of Adam Mott.

CHILDREN BY FIRST WIFE.

I. ELIJAH, b. July 12, 1768; m. Jan. 10, 1792, Lodemia, daughter of Adam Mott; she d. March 27, 1801.—Child, Marcus, b. May 7, 1792. He went to Vernon, N. Y., about 1801.
II. ELI, b. June 8, 1772.
III. PARDA, b. May 19, 1775.

CHILDREN BY SECOND WIFE.

IV. JOSEPH, b. Feb 4, 1786.
V. SALLY, b. March 22, 1789.

ELIJAH FRISBIE, son of Joseph, in 1791, owned the Silas Hoskin place in Winsted, which he sold to Benjamin Whiting in 1793, and afterward owned and occupied the Samuel A. McAlpin place, about a mile south of Winchester center, until his removal to Vernon, New York, about 1800.

PHINEAS GRISWOLD, from Wethersfield, lived, until 1784, near Torrington line, on the old South Country Road, — when he bought and occupied until his death (March 11, 1815, aged 74), the Newman B. Gilbert farm, in the Danbury quarter. His wife, Lois, was sister of the oldest Samuel Hurlbut. She died December 5, 1808, aged 64.

CHILDREN.

PHINEAS, MATTHEW, BENJAMIN, and AMOS, born in Wethersfield.
PATTY, b. in Winchester, Feb. 1, 1778.
BENA, b. "   "   Dec. 26, 1779.
SABRA, b. "   "   Aug. 26, 1781.

AMBROSE PALMER, son of Job, of Litchfield, lived on a part of the John J. Fanning farm, in the Danbury quarter, until 1791, when he returned to Litchfield. Had wife, Susanna.

CHILDREN.

I. MINERVA, b. July 24, 1778.
II. SUSANNA, b. Oct. 24, 1781.
III. AMBROSE, b. Sept. 15, 1784.
IV. CALVIN, b. March 30, 1786.

BENJAMIN PRESTON, from Goshen, lived near the Widow Everitt place on Brooks Street, in Danbury quarter. He was a cripple from his birth, and lived by making baskets, birch brooms, and splint chair bottoms. He married, May 3, 1775, Sarah Videto. She died October 23, 1780, and he married (2d), August 20, 1782, Mary Curtis.

CHILDREN BY FIRST WIFE.

I. THANKFUL, b. Dec. 31, 1775.
II. "LYSUF" [Eliasaph], b. Aug. 17, 1777; d. Aug. 17, 1777.

CHILDREN BY SECOND WIFE.

III. PATIENCE, b. March 16, 1779; d. March 16, 1779.
IV. BENJAMIN, b. Dec. 29, 1783.
V. EPHRAIM, b. Feb. 22, 1787; d. March 12, 1794.
VI. SETH, b. April 25, 1789.

JOEL ROBERTS owned and lived on a farm now absorbed in the B. B. Rockwell, J. G. Griswold, and Emory Coe farms, until his death in 1780. The probate records of Norfolk District show that he had sons, Judah, (baptized in Torrington, September 28, 1783), Joel and Loomis, and daughters, Mary, Naomi (she died unmarried October 1, 1782), Chloe and Esther; and left Esther, his widow. His son, Judah, lived on the Kelsey farm, near the small pond in the northeast part of the town, from 1802 to 1810, and died in Hitchcocksville at an advanced age.

His grand-son, Judah, son of the above, owned and occupied the B. B. Rockwell farm, from 1848 to 1857, and thence migrated to Kankekee, Illinois, where he died about 1861.

CAPT. PETER CORBIN, with his sons, Daniel and Peter, Jr., came from Danbury and lived on the Asaph Brooks farm in the Danbury quarter. His house stood on the east side of the way, opposite Mr. Brooks. He removed to Colebrook in 1805, and spent his remaining life with his son Peter, Jr. He was captain of the first company of the

Alarm Regiment of Conn., in 1780. He was b. in 1733, and m. Nov. 18, 1756, Abigail Benedict, at Danbury.

CHILDREN.

I. DANIEL, b. in Danbury, Oct. 1, 1757; m. May 30, 1776, Mabel Everitt; he died in Colebrook, 1809.
II. PETER, JR, b. in Danbury, Aug. 6, 1762.
III. ABIGAIL, b. " Feb. 26, 1766; m. in 1788, Abijah Benedict.
IV. LUCY, b. " Jan. 20, 1770; m. in 1806, —— Jennings, of Coventry, N. Y.
V. ANNA, b. " Feb. 6, 1772; m. 1795, Ashbel Humphrey, of Goshen.
VI. ESTHER, b. in Winchester, Jan. 3, 1776; m. 1797, Zeri Hoyt.

PETER CORBIN, JR., lived in the old part of the house of Asaph Brooks, above mentioned, until his removal to Colebrook, about 1805. He m. in 1790, Villette Nearing, of Simsbury, N. J.

CHILDREN.

I. JOSEPH, b. March 31, 1791; m. in 1815, Lois Cady.
II. URIEL, b. " 1793; died in Colebrook, 1842.
III. JOHN S., b. Feb. 25, 1797; m. Maria, dau. of Asa Nearing of B'oomfield.
IV. AMOS, b. Dec. 25, 1800; m. Jan. 1822, Louisa, dau. of Samuel Cowles, of Colebrook.
V. PETER, b. Jan. 27, 1808; m. May 11, 1835, Caroline, dau. of Seth Whiting, of Colebrook.

DANIEL CORBIN lived on a hill, west of Asaph Brooks, about half way to the house of Lloyd Humphrey, in Norfolk. He died in Colebrook in 1809, aged 52.

JOHN VIDETO, a foreigner, came from Danbury, and lived on the old South Country Road, next south of the Widow Everitt farm, until his death Nov. 29, 1799, at the age of 85 years, 18 days.

JOHN VIDETO, JR. came with, and lived in the same house with his father, until his removal to Austinburg, O., in 1807, with his son Jasper. He m. Aug. 13, 1776, Mary Grover. She d. Sept. 8, 1779; and he m. (2d) Dec. 12, 1780, Achsah North.

CHILDREN BY FIRST WIFE.

I. HANNAH, b. May 26, 1777; m. —— Cowles, of Austinburg, O.
II. MARY, b. July 2, 1779; d. Nov. 21, 1779.

AND FAMILY RECORDS.   115

CHILDREN BY SECOND WIFE.

III. JASPER, b. Sept. 12, 1783; m. Jan. 1, 1806, Rebecca Williams, dau. of Obed W., of Colebrook. Child, Sally, b. Nov. 7, 1806.
IV. LORA,   b. June 13, 1785.

JACOB WADE,[1] came from England to Lyme, Conn., where he died aged 99 years. His children were:

I. JACOB.[2]
II. LUCY.[2]
III. STEPHEN,[2] moved to Branford, where he m. Maria Abigail Hoadley. He came with his son Amasa,[3] to Winchester, in 1774, where they settled on the farm recently occupied by Isaac Wade,[4] in the southeast part of the town. He d. Feb. 8, 1817, aged 93.

CHILDREN.

I. SOLOMON,[3] b. Nov. 23, 1748; d in Rupert, Vt., aged 92 yrs. 5 mos. 3 d. He had children, Abigail, Matilda, Amasa, Stephen, and Lucy.
II. AMASA,[3] b. March 16, 1751.
III. EDWARD[3], b. May 25, 1754.
IV. ABIGAIL,[3] b. Aug. 18, 1759; m. Nov. 22, 1780, Benj. Baker, of Litchfield, - and had children: Edward, John, Stephen, David, Lucy, Sally, and Anna.

AMASA WADE,[3] resided on the same farm until his death, Aug 30, 1838, aged 87 yrs. 5 mos. 3 d. He was. by trade, a Tanner and Shoemaker; and by frugal industry acquired a large estate. He is described by Rev. Mr. Marsh as a useful and worthy ci izen, respected and honored for his love of order, his puritanic habits, his steady attention to business, and firm regard to the interests of religion and the welfare of the church and society. He m. Jan. 22, 1777, Anna Hale; she d. Ap. 27, 1837, aged 85 years.

CHILDREN.

I. ISAAC,[4]   b. Dec. 9, 1777.
II. STEPHEN,[4] b. May 9, 1779.
III. ANNA,[4]   b. Oct. 2, 1781; m. Allen Burr; 2d, Lyman Barber.
IV. AMASA,[4]   b. Dec. 5, 1785.
V. WEALTHY,[4] b. Oct. 30, 1788; m. Stephen Baker, son of Benjamin, and had children:— 1, Amasa Hale, b. May 16, 1815; 2, Clarissa, b. Jan. 20, 1818; 3, David G., b. Jan. 11, 1824, d. Jan. 14, 1843.

EDWARD WADE,[3] third son of Stephen,[2] lived in Vermont, and died at the age of 96 yrs. 5 mos. His children were Edward,[4] Hannah,[4] Abigail,[4] Alenam,[4] (?) Isaac,[4] Phebe,[4] Anna,[4] Jacob,[4] and Stephen.[4]

ISAAC WADE,[4] in his earlier years, lived in the house late owned by Sage W. Grant, half a mile west of the centre, next near the Elmore Tannery, and after the death of his father, in the paternal homestead. He died Aug. 28, 1862, aged 85. He m. Sally Anderson.

CHILDREN.

I. LUCIA,[5] b. May —, 1809; m. Dec. 25, 1839, James L. Williams, of Brooklyn, N. Y.
II. SIDNEY,[5] b. Nov. 6, 1810; m. June 15, 1840, Louisa Bronson. He m. (2d) July 1, 1857, Mary E. Huntting.
III. HARRIETT,[5] b. Ap. —, 1814; m. William Sanford.
IV. ANDERSON,[5] b. Nov. 19, 1816; m. Dec. —, 1847, Clara G. Bartlett.
V. SARAH ANN,[5] b. Ap. —, 1819; m. June 19, 1845, Ruel O. White.

STEPHEN WADE[4] lived on Brooks Street, Danbury Quarter, until his removal to Vernon, N. Y., about 1825. He m. March 25, 1802, Lovisa, dau. of Hewitt Hills.

CHILDREN.

I. TRACY,[5] b. July 7, 1802; d. Jan. 14, 1811.
II. ELIZA,[5] b. Aug. 14, 1803.
III. SCHUYLER,[5] b. June 9, 1806.
IV. AMASA HALE,[5] b. June 8, 1808; d. Jan. 21, 1809.
V. ABERNETHY,[5] b. Jan. 9, 1810.
VI. TRACY HALE,[5] b. Ap. 12, 1814.
VII. STEPHEN FRANKLIN, b. Oct. 28, 1818.
VIII. VIRGIL BOOTH, b. March 15, 1823.

AMASA WADE[4] lived on a farm adjoining his father's, and, in partnership with his brother Isaac, owned and carried on the tannery afterwards owned by the Elmores. He removed, about 1835, to Harmony, Chautauqua County, N. Y., and afterwards to Union Mills, Erie Co., Penn. He m. July 15, 1811, Abigail, dau. of Abner Coe.

CHILDREN.

I. HOMER HALE,[5] b. July 15, 1811.
II. HARMON COE,[5] b. Feb. 19, 1813.
III. HIRAM WHITE,[5] b. Aug. 12, 1815.
IV. MARY LEDYARD,[5] b. July 18, 1817.
V. HIEL DWIGHT,[5] b. Sept. 18, 1820.
VI. HARRIS EATON.[5]

EDWARD WADE,[4] son of Edward,[3] b. Nov. 7, 1778, lives in State of New York, has 17 children, as follows, all by one wife.

I. Sally,	b. Ap. 21, 1804.	X. Melissa,	b. Feb. 28, 1820.
II. Loring,	b. Feb. 21, 1806.	XI. Samantha,	b. Dec. 4, 1821.
III. Temperance,	b. June 4, 1807.	XII. Alex'nd. McD.,	b. Ap. 5, 1823.
IV. Florain,	b. Ap. 8, 1809.	XIII. Hannah V.,	b. Jan. 10, 1825.
V. Peter S.,	b. Nov. 5, 1810.	XIV. Lewis S.,	b. Sept. 6, 1826.
VI. Grant E.,	b. Mch. 26, 1812.	XV. Harrison,	b. Oct. 10, 1829.
VII. Marcia G.,	b. Jan. 17, 1814.	XVI. Eleanor,	b. July 4, 1831.
VIII. Patty M.,	b. March 2, 1816.	XVII. Helen M.,	b. Mch. 22, 1833.
IX. Loly Jennett,	b. Dec. 14, 1817.		

Joseph Loomis,[1] Senior, came from Bristol, England, to Windsor, about 1639.

Deacon John Loomis,[2] son of Joseph, Senior, married Elizabeth, daughter of Thomas Scott, of Hartford, February 6, 1648.

Timothy Loomis,[3] son of Deacon John, born at Windsor, July 27, 1661, married Rebecca Porter, March 20, 1689.

Ichabod Loomis,[4] son of Timothy, born at Windsor, July 25, 1692, married Dorothy Loomis, January 25, 1738, and died February 25, 1796, aged 84.

Ichabod Loomis,[5] son of Ichabod,[4] born ; married January 29, 1766, Mindwell Lewis. He migrated to this town from Torrington, in 1774, and died July 31, 1785. She died August 6, 1807, in her 66th year. He lived on a farm in the Danbury Quarter, lying on a road parting northeasterly from the South Country Road, a little south of the Widow Everitt house.

CHILDREN.

I. Thaddeus,[6]	b. November 27, 1766.	
II. Sibyl,[6]	b. June 25, 1770; m. Dea. Benjamin Benedict.	
III. Abiel,[6]	b. August 8, 1773.	
IV. Ichabod,[6]	b. June 14, 1775.	
V. Minie,[6]	b. February 15, 1779; m. Asahel Wells.	

Thaddeus Loomis,[6] lived near Goshen line, north of the Norfolk road, on land that was afterward a part of the farm of Levi Bronson, second. He removed in 1802 to Salisbury, Herkimer Co., N. Y., where he was for many years a Justice of the Peace, and for four years an Assistant-Justice of the County Court. He married May 26, 1789, Lois Griswold, daughter of Phineas. She died in 1827; he died in Holley, N. Y., June 14, 1832.

CHILDREN.

I. HULDAH,[7]   b. September 12, 1789.
II. LUCY,[7]   b. November 2, 1790.
III. MATILDA,[7]   b. October 20, 1793; m. Loring S. Williams.
IV. ARSENOE,[7]   b. June 28, 1796.
V. ARPHAXAD,[7]   b. April 9, 1798.
VI. HORACE,[7]   b. March 4, 1800.
VII. LEWIS,[7]   b. Salisbury, N. Y.
VIII. MALINA,[7]   b. S.; m. Alden S. Gage.
IX. ALGERNON,[7]   b. Salisbury, N. Y.

HON. ARPHAXAD LOOMIS,[7] son of Thaddeus, settled in Little Falls, N. Y., in the practice of law in 1825, and continued to reside there during his life. He held the office of county surrogate eight years, was first Judge of the County Court five years, member of Congress two years, member of the State Legislature three years, and member of the Constitutional Convention in 1846. His defective hearing prevented his appointment to high judicial stations for which his integrity of character and legal acquirements eminently fitted him. He married in 1832, Ann, daughter of Doctor Stephen Todd of Salisbury, N. Y., and has had eight children, five of whom were living in 1857. (See Kilbourne's "Biographical History of Litchfield Co.," p. 315.)

CAPTAIN ABIEL LOOMIS[6] lived in Winsted, on Spencer Street, in a house that stood on the site of Widow Lucy Coe's residence, until about 1809, when he removed to the farm now owned by William Johnson, on the dugway road in Old Winchester. About 1815, he purchased the Dudley Tannery in Winsted, and removed to the house on Main Street next west of the Tannery, where he died October 16, 1818, aged 45. He was a man of ardent temperament, highly respected and influential. He married June 20, 1793, Eunice Coe, daughter of Ens. Jonathan. She died May 15, 1841.

CHILDREN.

I. ALVAH,[7]   b. October 25, 1793; d. September 4, 1794.
II. ALMIRA,[7]   b. April 19, 1795; m. November 17, 1844, Thomas Williams of Winsted; he died May 10, 1870, aged 63, s. p.
III. EUNICE,[7]   b. February 16, 1797; died March 3, 1797.
IV. CALISTA,[7]   b. July 16, 1798; d. October 13, 1818.
V. ABIEL,[7]   b. August 19, 1800; was prepared to enter College, when the death of his father, in 1818, threw on him the care of the family. He manifested great energy and skill in extricating the embarrassed affairs of his father's estate, and subsequently in his own business transactions. After carrying on the tannery business and a country store for several years, he removed to New York in 1826, where he died November 25

1830, leaving a widow and son. He was a model son and brother, generous and noble in his nature.

 VI. NORMAN,[7]   b. November 27, 1802 ; d. January 14, 1819.
 VII. ALANSON,[7]   b. January 21, 1806 ; m. Sarah Richards. He succeeded his older brother in the tannery business in Winsted, where he resided, with the exception of three years, until 1848, when he removed to Fulton, N. Y., where he now lives, and has a family of children. His wife died in 1863.
 VIII. ELIHU LEWIS,[7]   b. March 19, 1808, known as Lewis E. ; lived in New York from 1826 to 1840, and in Winsted from 1840 to 1845, when he removed to Fulton, N. Y., where he now resides. He m.   Camp, daughter of Moses Camp, and has a family of children.
 IX. HARRIET,[7]   b. January 27, 1811 ; wife of Joshua K. Richards, removed with her husband from Winsted to Salmon River, N. Y., in 1850, where he died. She now resides in Winsted.
 X. MARY,[7]   b. July 10, 1815 ; d. November 24, 1834.

ICHABOD LOOMIS[6] lived until about 1824 in Old Winchester, and afterward until his death, April 23, 1833, in the house now owned by his daughter Sally on Spencer Street, in Winsted. He was by trade a butcher ; a kind-hearted man, without an enemy. He married November 22, 1803, Loranda Hoskin, daughter of Joseph. She died Winsted, March 16, 1855, aged 76 years.

CHILDREN.

 I. LUCY,[7]   b. December 14, 1804 ; m. Hiram Root, September 1, 1828.
 II. FANNY LORANDA,[7]   b. August 6, 1806 ; m. Noah Hall, N. Marlboro.'
 III. EUNICE MATILDA,[7]   b. June 28, 1808 ; m. August 10, 1831, Sidney Eggleston ; lives in Guilford, N. Y.
 IV. SALLY AMANDA,[7]   b. May 26, 1813 ; lives in Winsted unmarried.
 V. JOSEPH ICHABOD,[7]   b. August 13, 1816 ; twice married ; he left Winsted about 1855 for the city of New York, where he now lives.

DAVID ALVORD (brother of Eliphaz), from Chatham, came from Torrington as early as this year, as appears by the records of births. In 1776, he bought the lot on which the parsonage house of Rev. Mr. Booge (lately owned by Dr. T. S. Wetmore), was afterwards erected, on which lot he lived until 1785. He afterwards lived near the Leonard Hurlbut place, and finally removed to Neversink, Sullivan county, and thence to Vernon, N. Y. He married September 8, 1774, Elizabeth, daughter of John Wetmore, of Torrington.

CHILDREN.

 I. PERSIS,   b. December 18, 1774.
 II. URSULA,   b. February 13, 1778.

WILLIAM CASTEL, from Ridgefield, owned land between the Alva Nash and Leonard Hurlbut places, and near the Edward Rugg farm, in the old

Society, and resided, as is supposed, on the former tract. The land records show that he had two sons, Elijah and Samuel, to whom he conveyed lands in 1784, and who must have been born before he came here. Whether he died in the town is not ascertained. His last conveyance of land was in 1786, and his name is not on the tax list of 1790.

CHILDREN OF WM. AND KATHERINE CASTEL, RECORDED IN WINCHESTER.

I. MIRIAM, b. July 28, 1771.
II. WILLIAM, b. July 10, 1773.
III. ELIZABETH, b. September 27, 1775; d. June 23, 1778.
IV. MARY, b.—date not given; d. April 25, 1778.
V. AARON, b.—date not given; d. March 15, 1783.

ELIJAH CASTEL, son of William, owned and lived on land south of the Edward Rugg farm in Danbury Quarter. He is described in a deed of April 12, 1787, as of the Manor of Livingston, Columbia county, N. Y., and in 1789 of Winchester. He probably left the town soon after the latter period.

SAMUEL CASTEL, son of William, disappears from the record in 1789. It does not appear where he lived in the town nor where he went to.

JOHN BEACH came into town this year from Torrington, and lived on the farm recently owned by Artemas Rowley, near the south end of third tier, first division, until 1781, when he returned to Torrington. He was born in Torrington May 2d, 1750, fifth child of Abel Beach of Torrington, who was born in Durham, February 9, 1712; g. son of Benjamin (born in Stratford, October 1, 1683) and Martha (Curtis) Beach; g. g. son of Benjamin (born in Stratford, October 28, 1642) and Sarah (Wells) Beach; and g. g. g. son of Benjamin Beach, the immigrant to Stratford from England [MS. Records of Deacon Lewis M. Norton, of Goshen.] He died at Torrington April 1, 1824, aged 76. He married June 9, 1774, Mercy Bassett. She died at Torrington, May 22, 1832, aged 76.

CHILDREN.

I. ABEL, b. January 3, 1775.
II. MARY, b. August 19, 1778.
III. REV. JAMES, b. in Winchester, June 10, 1780. Graduated at Williams College. Studied theology under Rev. Asahel P. Hooker, of Goshen, 1804-5. Ordained Pastor of Winsted Church. Dismissed. He married October 28, 1806, Hannah Clarissa Baldwin, born Goshen, March 10, 1784, only child of Isaac and Lucy (Lewis) Baldwin. He died at Winsted June 11, 1850, of apoplexy. She died May 7, 1852. His friend, Deacon L. M. Norton, of Goshen, writes of him, "It will be for those of a

coming generation to speak or write of the ability, the fidelity, the affectionate labors and the success of this servant of Jesus Christ."

Children : 1. Lucy Baldwin, b. August 20, 1807 ; m. Henry Hyde; 2. Hannah Clarissa, b. March 20, 1809, d. October 26th, 1815 ; 3. Mary, b. December 16, 1814, m. Caleb J. Camp.

CHILDREN OF HENRY AND LUCY B. (BEACH) HYDE.

1. James Beach, b. November 14, 1831, d. a member of Yale College at New Haven, January 8, 1850 ; 2. Henry Baldwin, b. February 15, 1834 ; 3. Lucy B., b. August 20, 1841 ; 4. Mary, b.

IV. JOHN,   b. February 26th, 1783 ; d. May 7, 1817.
V. ADAH,   b. March 12, 1787.

CHAPTER XI.

POPULATION—TOWN VOTES—NEW SETTLERS.

1774.

The first census of the Colony, on record,* taken in 1756, gives twenty-four as the population of Winchester.

The next census, taken in 1774, shows a population of 327 white, and twelve blacks.

We copy the figures of these two enumerations of Litchfield County, to show the relative population and growth of the towns at these periods:

1756.	1756.	1774. White.	1774. Black.	Total.	
Barkhamsted,	18	250	0	250	
Col. brook,	0	150	0	150	
Canaan,	1100	1573	62	1635	
Cornwall,	500	957	17	974	
Goshen,	610	1098	13	1111	
Hartland,	12	500	0	500	
Harwinton,	250	1015	3	1018	
Kent,	1000	1922	74	1996	
Litchfield,	1366	1509	45	1554	
New Hartford,	260	985	16	1001	
New Milford,	1127	2742	34	2776	Blacks in 1756, 16.
Norfolk,	84	966	3	969	
Salisbury,	1100	1936	44	1980	
Sharon,	1205	1986	26	2012	7 Blacks in 1756.
Torrington,	250	843	02	845	
Winchester,	24	327	12	339	
Woodbury,	2911	5224	89	5313	31 Blacks in 1756.
Westmoreland,†		1922			

1775.

In annual town meeting for 1775, the approaching revolutionary struggle was foreshadowed by the following votes:

"That the troopers be freed from paying any thing for their colors."

"To raise two-pence half-penny on the List of 1775, to purchase a town Stock of powder and lead, and also to pay other necessary charges arising in the town."

---

* To be found in the Comptroller's office.

† Westmoreland, then one of the towns of Litchfield County, comprised the whole of the beautiful valley of Wyoming, Pennsylvania.

In Society Meeting, besides the routine business, it was "Voted, to come into Mr. Bron-on's mode of singing." Levi and Ozias Bronson were chosen choristers; — Beriah Hills to read the Psalms, and Jesse Wilkinson to sweep the meeting house for 5s. 6d. per year.

The new comers of this year in Winchester Society, were Lemuel Bassett, Daniel Loomis, James Sweet, Jonathan Sweet, Reuben Sweet, Hezekiah Elmer, John Miner, and Elisha Wilcoxson.

LEMUEL BASSETT, a crippled tailor, from New Haven, first owned seventy-three acres of land, embracing a considerable portion of Winchester center village, which he sold in 1777, and afterwards bought and lived on a small lot near Colonel Ozias Bronson's. He had wife, Patience, and

CHILDREN.

I. EZRA,   b. in Goshen, March 23, 1774.
II. MIRAM,   b. May 12, 1776.
III. LYDIA, b. April 7, 1778.
IV. ERASTUS, b. July 5, 1780.
V. HARVEY,   b. Feb. 20, 1783.
VI. BEDE,   b. Jan. 20, 1786.

DANIEL LOOMIS, son of Ichabod,[4] of Torrington, lived on the old Country Road, immediately north of his brother, Ichabod,[5] and south of Widow Everitt's. He removed to Delhi, New York. He married, April 30, 1783, Anna Phelps.

CHILDREN.

I. MILO,   b. Sept. 26, 1783.
II. ELIZABETH, b. Nov. 30, 1786.
III. TRYPHENA, b. Oct. 23, 1788.

JAMES SWEET, supposed from Goshen, owned a lot on Blue Street, north of the Stone School House. In 1780, he conveyed away this lot by a deed, in which he is named of Norfolk.

REUBEN SWEET owned the lot next south of James Sweet's, which he conveyed to Jonathan Sweet, in 1777, and moved to Wallen's Hill in Barkhamsted, near the first Winsted meeting house.

JONATHAN SWEET is named of Goshen in a deed of 1774, and of Winchester in 1775. He owned lands adjoining those of James and Reuben, and also a part of the B. B. Rockwell farm, between the two Lakes, all of which he disposed of in 1771, or earlier. He probably lived on the Blue Street land. He married, August 29, 1773, Esther Lewis.

CHILDREN.

I. SARAH, b. May 16, 1774.
II. LORRIN, b. Feb. 16, 1776; d. March 24, 1778.
III. JONATHAN LEWIS, b. June 26, 1778.
IV. LUCY, b. June 30, 1780.

HEZEKIAH ELMER married, August 11, 1775, Elizabeth Benedict.

CHILDREN.

I. ELIZABETH, b. Sept. 7, 1776.
II. DANIEL, b. Oct. 14, 1778.

Nothing is to be learned from the records of the place of Mr. Elmer's residence, or the time of his removal from the town.

JOHN MINER, from New London, brother of Reuben of Winchester, came from Torrington, and settled and died on the farm lately owned by Emory Coe, now deceased, and now owned by George Cramer and wife. He was a man of pleasing address, and social in his habits. He married, in Torrington, April 9, 1775, Hannah Strong, born in Torrington, November 30, 1753, daughter of Asahel. He died March 23, 1813, aged 61; she died November 23, 1835, aged 80.

CHILDREN.

I. JOHN STRONG, b. in Tor. Aug. 15, 1775; tradition says he never lived in this town.
II. PHINEAS, b. Nov. 27, 1777.
III. FLORINDA, b. " 9, 1780; m. March 26, 1807, Roger Root.
IV. WILLIAM, b. March 17, 1783.
V. SARAH, b. Jan. 16, 1786; d. unmarried.
VI. PAMELIA, b. June 3, 1791; d. unmarried.

HON. PHINEAS MINER,[2] second son of John,[1] lived in the old parsonage of Mr. Booge, (lately owned by Dr. T. S. Wetmore) until his removal to Litchfield, in 1816. He died in Litchfield in 1839.

Mr. Miner, with only a common school education, studied law under Judge Reeve, of Litchfield, and entered on the practice in Winchester, in 1798. By close study and faithful preparation of his cases, — as well as by his ardor in trying them, he early attained a good standing at the bar; and eventually ranked among the ablest advocates in the County. He was by nature unfitted for legal trickery, or for any dishonorable act. He repeatedly represented Winchester, and afterward Litchfield, in the Legislature, having served in this capacity during eleven sessions. He was chosen to the State Senate in 1830 and 1831; was elected a Representative in Congress during the sessions of 1832 and 1833, and was Judge of Probate for Litchfield District at the time of his death. He m. May —, 1801, Zerviah W. Butler; she died April 24, 1811, aged 32. He m. (2d) —— Parsons, of Granville, late the wife of Tertius Wadsworth.

CHILDREN.

I. HENRY BUTLER, b. June 1, 1803; he m. and died childless.
II. ZERVIAH RUTH, b. March 18, 1811; died unmarried.

WILLIAM MINER,[2] third son of John,[1] owned and lived in the Daniel Murray house, on the Dugway road, until his removal to Ohio, in 1816. He m. Feb. 23, 1809, Lucy Denison Sandiforth.

CHILDREN.

I. EMELINE ADELIA, b. Feb. 23, 1811.
II. WILLIAM SANDIFORTH, b. Sept. 22, 1812.
III. DANIEL, b. Nov. 22, 1815.
IV. LUCY,

CAPTAIN ELISHA WILCOXSON, from Stratford, owned the farm and built the house on the Dugway road, now owned and occupied by William Johnson, which he sold to Augustus Humphrey in 1800, and removed to Vernon, New York. He was a surveyor, — an extensive dealer in lands, and largely employed in the business of the town. He married in Stratford, May 1, 1771, Mary Clark.

CHILDREN.

I. SARAH ANNA, b. in Stratford, Nov. 2, 1772.
II. CHARITY, b. June 17, 1775.
III. MARTHA, b. May 4, 1777.
IV. MARY, b. Feb. 25, 1779.
V. GIDEON, b. April 25, 1781.
VI. RUTH, b. Aug. 8, 1783.

1776.

At the annual town meeting, 1776, in addition to the routine business, the Selectmen were instructed to provide the camp equipage ordered by the Assembly, viz: Three tents, six pots, and nine bottles, or canteens for the town.

It was also voted, "that Swine be free commoners this year."

In Society meeting, as a result of the half-way covenant troubles, before referred to, Lemuel Stannard, Jonathan Coe, John Bradley, and Samuel Hurlbut, were excused from paying taxes this year, for Mr.

Knapps' salary. If this was done with a view of quieting the disaffection toward the minister, it appears from subsequent action of the Society to have failed to effect the object.

The new comers of the year were Philip Priest, Daniel Forbes, Martin North and his sons, Martin, Jr., and Rufus, Truman Gibbs, Joseph Agard, and Gershom Fay.

PHILIP PRIEST, from Barkhamsted, purchased of Daniel Platt, his lot near the Danbury school-house, and sold the same in 1779. He probably then left the town. He had wife, Trube, and

CHILDREN.

I. TRUBE,	b. Feb. 4, 1764.
II. NOAH,	b April 1, 1766.
III. ABI,	b. " 15, 1768.
IV. ZADOC,	b. " 19, 1770.
V. CHARITY,	b. July 18, 1772.
VI. DINAH,	b. Jan. 3, 1775.
VII. ELIZABETH,	b. March 25, 1777.
VIII. MERRIT,	b. June 11, 1779.

DANIEL FORBES, from Wethersfield, bought of Noah Gleason his homestead, bordering southerly on Torrington line and the Ebenezer and Joe Preston lot, and northerly on Amasa Wade. He died, as appears by the Norfolk Probate Records, in 1779, leaving a wife, Lydia, who, with Ozias Hurlbut, of Wethersfield, administered his estate.

MARTIN NORTH, with his sons, Martin, Jr., and Rufus, came from Danbury, and bought of Elisha Smith the Noble J. Everitt place, immediately south of Winchester center village. He built the lean-to house standing thereon, and occupied it until 1791. He afterwards lived with his son, Martin, Jr., in the house next west of the Doctor Wetmore house, on the north side of the Norfolk road, until he removed to Colebrook, in 1797. He married in Torrington, April 2, 1760, Abigail Eno; she died, January 5, 1782; and he married (2d), June 27, 1782, Mary Coe; he died in 1806.

CHILDREN BY FIRST WIFE.

I. MARTIN,	bap. in Tor., Sep. 13, 1761; named in his father's will.
II. ABIGAIL,	bap. " June 17, 1764.
III. LUCINA,	bap. " Aug. 2, 1767; named in her father's will.
IV. RUFUS,	birth record not found; named in his father's will.

CHILDREN BY SECOND WIFE.

V. NOAH,	b. May 25, 1783; d. June 13, 1783.
VI. NOAH,	b. July 22, 1785; named in his father's will.

MARTIN NORTH, Jr., built, and lived in, the house next west of the Doctor Wetmore house, on the north side of the Norfolk road, until 1802, and afterwards owned and lived in a house, lately torn down, on the west side of the Dugway road a little north of Joel G. Griswold's, until about 1805, when he removed to Colebrook. He was Town Clerk during the year 1802. He married, September 24, 1781, Mary Fay.

CHILDREN.

I. ABIGAIL, b. Jan. 13, 1783; d. Oct. 5, 1783.
II. MARY, b. Aug. 16, 1785.
III. SYLVESTER ENO, b. Dec. 6, 1792.

RUFUS NORTH, son of Martin, Senior, owned a twelve acre lot, — probably the one on which Luman Munsill now resides, — immediately north of his father's first homestead, which he sold in 1791, soon after which he removed to Colebrook. He married, August 27, 1789, Esther Roberts, and had by her a son, Ebenezer, born March 2, 1790.

TRUMAN GIBBS, "of Litchfield," bought of Hannah Everett, and probably lived until 1778, on the lot now owned and occupied by Asaph Brooks, on the old Country Road.

1777.

In town meeting, April 10th, of this year, it was voted, "that we adopt the late acts passed by the General Assembly, holden at Midd'etown on the 18th day of April, 1777; and that we will firmly abide thereby." This vote probably refers to the "Abstract and Declaration of the Rights and Privileges of the people of the State," adopted by the General Assembly, after the adoption of the Declaration of Independence by the Continental Congress, in these words:

"The People of this state being by the Providence of God free and independent, have the sole and exclusive Right of governing themselves as a free. sovereign, and independent sta'e; and having from their ancestors derived a free and excellent Constitution [Charter] of Government, whereby the Legislature depends on the free annual election of the People, they have the best security for the Preservation of their civil and religious Rights and Liberties. And forasmuch as the free fruition of such Liberties and Privileges as Humanity, Civility and Christianity call for, as is due to every Man in his Place and Proportion without Impeachment and Infringement, hath ever been, and will be the Tranquility and Stability of Churches and Commonwealths; and the denial thereof, the Disturbance. if not the Ruin, of both.

"Be it enacted and declared by the Governor, Council and Representatives in General Court assembled, and by the authority of the same, that the ancient Form of Civil Government, contained in the charter from Charles the Second, King of England, and adopted by the People of this state, shall be and remain the Civil Constitution of this state, under the Sole authority of the People thereof, independent of any King or Prince, whatever. And that this Republic is, and shall forever remain, a free, Sovereign and independent State, by the name of the state of Connecticut."

" And be it further enacted and declared by the Authority aforesaid, That no man's Life shall be taken away; No Man's Honor or good Name shall be stained; No Man's Person shall be arrested, restrained, banished, dismembered, nor any ways punished: No Man shall be deprived of his Wife or Children; No man's Goods or Estate shall be taken away from him, nor in any ways indamaged under the Color of Law, or Countenance of Authority; unless Clearly warranted by the Laws of this State."

" That all the free Inhabitants of this or any other of the United States of America, and Foreigners in Amity with this state, shall enjoy the same Justice and Law within this State, which is general for the State, in all Cases proper for the cognizance of the civil Authority and Courts of Judicature within the same, and that without Partiality or Delay.

" And that no Man's Person shall be restrained, or imprisoned, by any Authority whatsoever, before the Law hath sentenced him thereto, if he can and will give sufficient Security, Bail or Mainprize for Appearance and good behavior in the mean Time, unless it be for capital Crimes, contempt in open Court, or in such Cases wherein some express Law doth allow or order the same."

By this act the Governor and company formally severed their connection with the Crown of Great Britain; and retained the Charter of Charles the Second, so strenuously and successfully defended and preserved amid repeated attempts of the Crown to wrest it from them,— as the fundamental law or constitution of an independent State.

Those who have but casually examined this charter are little aware of its thoroughly republican features and its delegation of powers which made the Colony, save in name, a free and independent Commonwealth. The " declaration of Rights and Privileges " above quoted, which is the introductory statute in the revised code of 1784, was all that was needed to put the charter in perfect working order as a republican form of government.

It was claimed by the advocates of the new Constitution adopted in 1818, that the State was and had been without a constitutional form of government; and that the retention of the charter as a basis of law, was a remnant of kingly rule unworthy of freemen, and dishonorable to the State. If, as is probable, the other towns of the State formally recognized the Declaration of the Legislature, in manner similar to the action of this town, it had all the sanction of other written constitutions since adopted by other States of the Union. It had moreover a ring of pure democracy, more clear and distinct than was probably ever found elsewhere in a modern republic. It restored the whole Legislative and Judicial power to the people twice in each year. The lower house of the General Assembly came, by election, fresh from the people to the May and October Sessions, and elected the Judges annually. The "Steady habits" of the people prevented an abuse of this power by arbitrary changes of the incumbents. The same men were re-elected from year to year, until incompetent through age. The Constitution of 1818 provided only for an annual election of Representatives, one regular session a year, and a choice of Judges to hold their office until seventy years old, unless removed for incapacity or crime. The working of this provision has led to a recent amendment of the Constitution limiting the term of a Judge to eight years.

Before returning from this digression to the distinctive annals of our town, we would urge upon every lover of his Connecticut forefathers, to study carefully the early history of our State, and find therein a record of prudent and wise legislation, — of firm and undeviating patriotism, and of devoted service in establishing and defending our republican institutions, of which the most imperial State in the Union might well be proud.

Sept. 25th, 1777. — "Voted to provide the articles mentioned in the Governor's Proclamation, for the Soldiers, at the town's cost, and to give them to them, viz: to the Soldiers," and "that Deacon Samuel Wetmore and Sergt. David Austin be a committee to procure the above mentioned articles, and to take care of them."

It was also voted that Gershom McCune, Jonathan Alvord, and Martin North, be a committee to provide for the families of those men that are enlisted into the Continental Army, according to the Act of Assembly.

December 1st, of the same year, Samuel Wetmore, Gershom Fay, Capt. John Hills, David Austin, and Jonathan Coe, were appointed a committee for supplying the families of such soldiers belonging to this town, now in the Continental army, with such clothing and provisions as may be necessary for their support.

It was also voted, "that those men that went volunteers to the Northward, and Southward, shall receive Five Pounds each out of the treasury;" and "that those men who went with Ensn. Brownson last April, and with Sergt. Timothy Benedict, in August, and with Lieut. Benedict, shall receive five pounds for going volunteers."

It was further "voted that Deacon Samuel Wetmore, and the owners of the Saw Mill, by the Meeting House, shall have the privilege of the dam by Capt. Hill's, as agreed."

This Saw Mill was the first erected in the town. It originally stood near the country road, at the foot of the hill, north of the burying ground, and was carried by means of a dam on the east side of the road, which flooded the meadows, east and northeast of the road. It was probably at this time moved down the stream to the vicinity of the old meeting house, in order to get a better head of water. It was eventually removed down to the site of the mill and cheese box factory, recently owned by the McAlpines.

An incident connected with this Mill has been handed down, which pleasingly illustrates the characters of the first two Deacons of the Winchester church. Deacon Wetmore sawed the logs of his neighbors in regular order, according to their priority of claim. A certain day was fixed for sawing the logs of his bosom friend and colleague, Deacon Seth Hills; but in the morning, before Deacon Hills had come to draw his logs on to the logway, another neighbor came, who was in pressing and immediate need of some lumber, and prevailed on Deacon W. to let him draw in the logs he required to be sawed. Some of the logs were drawn in when Deacon Hills arrived. Irritated at finding himself superseded, he made some sharp remark, which was sharply replied to by his colleague. Both of them fell from grace to wrath. "I'll never draw another log to your mill," says Deacon Hills. "And if you do, I'll never saw it for you," says Deacon Wetmore. Other defiant words were bandied back and forth, until their wrath, by repeated blowing off, came down from high to low pressure. Several world's people were listening to their unedifying abjurgations. A pause ensued. One of the Deacons beckoned the other to follow him. They retired to a neighboring clump of bushes, whence the voice of penitent prayer arose. Grace prevailed over passion, and on returning to the Mill, Deacon Hills assisted in drawing in his neighbor's logs, cheerfully postponing his own turn until his neighbor could be accommodated.

In Society Meeting this year, in addition to society committee, clerk, and collector, three choristers and three readers of the psalms were appointed, and directions were given for repairing and enlarging the Meeting House, a measure obviously needed, to enable those officials to effectively discharge their duties.

The new comers of the year were Nathan Blackman, Peter Blackman, Samuel Clark, Joseph Dodge, Timothy Fay, William Fay, James Stevenson, Joseph Sweet, and Jonah Woodruff.

NATHAN BLACKMAN, from Stratford, a remarkably tall, athletic man, lived in a house that stood on the cross road, leading from the Dugway road, in rear of the house of Mrs. Sophronia Leonard. He m. April 24, 1783, Phebe Orvis of Norfolk. He d. Dec. 18, 1786.

CHILDREN.

I. ABIGAIL, b. Jan. 17, 1784.
II. ELIZABETH, b. Sept. 1, 1785.

PETER BLACKMAN came from Stratford, and lived on the easterly side of the Dugway Road, nearly opposite Mrs. Sophronia Leonards, on land recently purchased by John T. Rockwell. He is believed to have removed to Sangersfield, N. Y., about 1794. He was b. June 23, 1735 (old style); m. April 17, 1760, Mary McEwen, b. April 1, 1738, dau. of Gershom.

CHILDREN.

I. ABIGAIL, b. Sept. 28, 1761.
II. TRUMAN, b. July 12, 1763.
III. MARTHA, b. March 27, 1765.
IV. SARAH, b. May 1, 1767.
V. JOSEPH PICKET, b. June 24, 1769.
VI. SALMON, b. June 18, 1771.
VII. GERSHOM, b. Feb. 2, 1774.
VIII. MARY, b. April 28, 1776.
IX. WILLIAM ADAMS, b. Dec. 11, 1778.
X. PETER, b. March 6, 1781; d. Aug. 16, 1783.

TRUMAN BLACKMAN, oldest son of Peter, lived until 1793 in the house, a mile east of Winchester center, at the turn of the road towards the Dugway, which he sold to Theodore & Russell Goodwin, and afterwards lived on the Asher Case farm until 1794, when he removed to central New York. He married, January 8, 1789, Hannah Sherman. They had one son, Adin, born October 23, 1791.

JOSEPH PICKETT BLACKMAN, second son of Peter, had an interest in land on the east side of the Long Pond, but probably never resided there.

None of the Blackman family remained in this town. They are reported to hold a highly respectable standing in central New York.

SAMUEL CLARK built and lived in the house recently occupied by Daniel Murray on the Dugway road. He built, in company with Reuben Miner and Christopher Whiting, a saw-mill on Sucker Brook, near the site of the mill recently built by McPherson Hubbell. He also built in the same vicinity a trip-hammer shop for welding gun-barrels;—and lost his thumb in attempting to hold the bed-piece under the hammer, in his haste to see the working of the hammer before the bed-piece had been secured. He built a wind-mill near his house for the purpose of sawing fire wood. His dam flooded the meadows above so as to cause a law-suit between him and his neighbor, Miner. He seems to have been an active, stirring body,—somewhat restive as a neighbor and Church member,—traded largely in lands; and about 1800, removed to Stockbridge, Massachusetts. He married, November 7, 1770, Mary Cooper.

CHILDREN.

I. MARY, b. June 20, 1778; m. April 18, 1795, Loammi Mott.
II. SAMUEL, b. March 17, 1783.

JOSEPH DODGE, from Wethersfield, lived, until 1782, near the old meeting house, and afterward in the previous homestead of Aaron Cook, near the south line of the town, on Blue Street. His name disappears from the records after 1783. He had wife, Elizabeth, and

CHILDREN.

I. JOSEPH, b. June 22, 1777.
II. CLARA, b. July 28, 1779.

TIMOTHY AND WILLIAM FAY, brothers, owned and lived on a part of the B. B. Rockwell farm, between the two lakes. One, or both of them lived in a log cabin adjoining an old orchard, south of the present road passing Mr. Rockwell's. It is believed that one of them died there. They disappear from the records about 1788. A Tyringham Shaker of that name told the compiler, several years ago, that he was born there.

TIMOTHY FAY had wife, Sarah, and a son, Timothy, born November 16, 1781.

WILLIAM FAY married, October 22, 1778, Bethia Bassett, and had

CHILDREN.

I. WILLIAM, b. Dec. 21, 1778.
II. AARON, b. Nov. 9, 1781; d. Nov. 19, 1782.
III. AARON, b. Sept. 11, 1783.
IV. JONATHAN, b. June 4, 1785.

GERSHOM FAY had a daughter, Dinah, baptized June 30, 1776; he took the oath of fidelity in the town January 13, 1778; was not a land holder, and no further note of him appears.

JAMES STEVENSON is named of Winchester, in a deed of 1777, conveying to him a lot of land near the original meeting house. He conveyed away the same land in 1784, by a deed, in which he is named of Goshen.

JOSEPH SWEET, named of Voluntown, bought of Adam Mott, a lot of land with a dwelling thereon, not far north of the stone school-house, on Blue Street. He is also named of Winchester in 1779, and in 1780 is named of Goshen.

JONAH WOODRUFF, from Litchfield, bought and sold several tracts of land in the 1st division, among which was a lot on the east side of the old discontinued road near the first meeting house, where he is supposed to have resided until 1784, when his name disappears from the records. He and his wife, Mary, had a son, Benjamin, born May 12, 1778.

CHAPTER XII.

WAR RECORDS—HALF-WAY COVENANT TROUBLES—NEW SETTLERS.

1778 TO 1783.

At a Town Meeting, January 13, 1778, the articles of Confederation of the thirteen United States were presented for approval, and by vote on each successive article, were accepted;—and thereupon the oath of Fidelity to the State of Connecticut was administered to those present and certified in the records. The names of others who took the oath afterwards were also recorded. We subjoin the names in alphabetical order, giving the dates of administration only of those taking the oath subsequent to January 13, 1778.

DAVID ALVORD,
ELIPHAZ ALVORD,
JONATHAN ALVORD,
ABRAHAM ANDREWS,
DANIEL ANDREWS,
DAVID AUSTIN,
JOHN AUSTIN,
LEMUEL BASSETT,
JOEL BEACH,
JOHN BEACH, Feb. 12, 1779.
BENJAMIN BENEDICT,
TIMOTHY BENEDICT,
LEVI BROWNSON,
OZIAS BROWNSON,
WILLIAM CASTEL,
JOHN CHURCH, July 18, 1782.
SAMUEL CLARK,
JONATHAN COE,
ROBERT COE,
ROSWELL COE,
DAN¹ HURLBUT CONE, Dec. 2, 1782.
RICHARD COIT,
PETER CORBIN,
DANIEL CORBIN,
JOSEPH DODGE,
HEZEKIAH ELMER,

NOBLE EVERITT,
ANDREW EVERITT,
Mrs. H. EVERITT, Jan. 18, 1782.
GERSHOM FAY,
REMEMBRANCE FILLEY,
JOSEPH FRISBEE,
WARHAM GIBBS,
PHINEHAS GRISWOLD,
BELA HILLS, Dec. 2, 1782.
SETH HILLS,
JOHN HILLS,
BENONI HILLS,
JOSEPH HOSKIN,
SAMUEL HURLBUT,
REV. MR. KNAPP,
WM. KEYES, Feb. 12, 1779.
DAVID LOOMIS, Dec. 2, 1782.
ICHABOD LOOMIS,
ROBERT McCUNE,
SAMUEL McCUNE,
GERSHOM McCUNE, Dec. 4, 1778.
REUBEN MINER,
JOHN MINER,
ADAM MOTT,
LENT MOTT,
MARTIN NORTH,

AMBROSE PALMER,
JOSEPH PLATT, Feb. 5, 1778.
EBENEZER PRESTON,
SAMUEL PRESTON,
BENJAMIN PRESTON,
PHILIP PRIEST,
CHAUNCY SMITH, Dec. 2, 1782.
ELEAZER SMITH,
THOMAS SPENCER,
WM. STANNARD, Dec. 2, 1782.
LEMUEL STANNARD, Jr.,
ABEL STANNARD, July 25, 1782.
LEM'L STANNARD, Mch. 10, 1782.
JAMES SWEET,
JOHN SWEET,
JONATHAN SWEET,
PELEG SWEET,
REUBEN TUCKER,
JOHN VIDETO, Jr.,
AMASA WADE,
SAMUEL WETMORE,
ABEL WETMORE,
ELISHA WILCOXSON,
JESSE WILKINSON,
REUBEN WILKINSON,
JONAH WOODRUFF.

An examination of the list shows that of the seventy-eight inhabitants therein named, but fifteen are now represented in the town by descendants bearing their family names.

In Town Meetings this year, taxes were laid, in all amounting to four shillings and three pence on the pound, for meeting the expenses of the town.

Sergt. Freedom Wright and John Balcom, Jr., were allowed five pounds each for doing a tour of duty, the previous year, in the Northern army.

It was voted, that if the committee on trial cannot procure a sufficiency of provisions for the families of those men who are gone into the Continental army, the Selectmen shall be empowered to lay the matter before the Governor and Council or Assembly, and pray them to point out some way for our relief; and also to pray for a tax on non-resident proprietors to support the country roads.

Ensign Ozias Bronson, Joseph Hoskin, Samuel Hurlbut, Roswell Coe, Ambrose Palmer, Samuel Preston, and Phineas Griswold, were appointed a Committee to provide for the families of the soldiers.

From the records of the Society meetings of this year, it appears that owing to disaffection of many members, it was decided, after consultation with Mr. Knapp, "to throw by the civil law in collecting Mr. Knapp's rate, and [to] support him some other way."

The new comers of this year were, Lemuel Stannard, Senior, Seth Griswold, James Hale, and William Barbour.

LEMUEL STANNARD, SENIOR, has been noticed under the year 1771.

SETH GRISWOLD, of New Hartford, married, December 31, 1778, Huldah, widow of Simeon Loomis, and settled on the Loomis homestead, now composing a part of Luther Bronson's farm, in the southwest part of the town, and there resided until 1801, when he removed to the southwest corner of Colebrook, and there resided in the house now occupied by Isaac Jacklyn, until his death, about 1810.

CHILDREN.

I. ROSWELL, b. Feb. 8, 1780; m. Nov. 3, 1802, Lucretia Wheadon, daughter of Solomon. She d. and he m. (2d), Nov. 1808, Mrs. Jerusha (Grant) Walter, daughter of Joel Grant and widow of Cyrus Walter. She d. in Colebrook, March 3, 1828; he m. (3d) Anna (Hall) Preston, who was a widow Clark before she m. Preston. Children by first wife: 1. Wyllys, lives in Auburn, Iowa; 2. Lucretia, m. Asahel Northway; 3 Hiram, grad. Western Reserve College, lived at Canton and Cleveland, Ohio, a lawyer senator of Ohio, lives at Leavenworth, Kansas. Children by second wife: 4. Lucius, b. July 12, 1810; 5. Almira, b. July 23, 1811; 6. Joel Grant, b. March 15, 1813; 7. Lavinia, b. Feb. 25, 1817; 8. James, b. Jan. 20, 1819; 9 Nelson, b. Aug. 20, 1820; 10. Edward, b. April 13, 1824; 11. Ellen Amanda, b. April 6, 1825, m. March 18, 1850, William S. Phillips, a trader, of Winsted, who d. Aug. 19, 1860—she lives in Winsted; 12. Mary Ann, d. unmarried. These children were all born in Colebrook.

II. ASA, b. May 26, 1781.

JAMES HALE, from Wethersfield, bought the Ensign lot at the southwest shore of Long Lake, west of the mouth of Taylor's Brook, where he lived until 1784, when he left the town. By his wife, Sarah, he had three

CHILDREN.

I. ABIGAIL, b. May 12, 1778.
II. SARAH, b. Aug. 8, 1780.
III. WILLIAM, b. March 16, 1784; is said to have become a sailor, was pressed into the British navy, and obtained his discharge by procuring a certificate of the record of his birth in Winchester.

WILLIAM BARBOUR, from Paisley, Scotland, deserted the British army brought to this country at the beginning of the revolution, and became a resident of this town as early as 1778. He married, September 26, 1778, Ruth Thrall, widow of Reuben Thrall, who died in the town the previous year. He resided in the Thrall homestead, near Reuben Chase's present residence, until 1798; soon after which he removed to Burke, Caledonia County, Vermont. He was by trade a tailor,—a pious and highly estimable man.

CHILDREN.

I. CLARA, b. July 19, 1781.
II. ESTHER, b. Nov. 19, 1784.

1779.

The town records of this year are mainly confined to routine business.

Martin North and Joseph Hoskin were appointed "to provide for the families of Continental soldiers"; and Dr. Josiah .Everitt, Samuel McCune, and Phineas Griswold, to provide clothing for the soldiers.

The Society records are also barren of interest. The "civil law" having been "thrown by in collecting the minister's rate," no Society tax was laid.

The new comers were Elijah Hubbard, Daniel Clark, and Christopher Whiting.

ELIJAH HUBBARD, from Middletown, bought and occupied Lot 8, first Tier, first Division, on Blue Street, near the southwest corner of the town. In 1805 he sold what remained to him of this tract to Jared Curtis. His wife, Ursula, died May 3, 1786. Anna, their daughter, was born April 16, 1783. Tradition says he was an eminently pious man, and that he died alone in a house on the hill, east of the original meeting house.

DANIEL CLARK's name appears only in the record of births. He had, by wife Eunice,

CHILDREN.

I. BELA (son), b. Feb. 25, 1779.   II. PATTY, b. June 28, 1781.

BENJAMIN WHITING,* married in Torrington, October 17, 1755, Esther Marcum.

CHILDREN.

I. CHRISTOPHER,[2] b. in Tor., Aug. 3, 1757.
II. WILLIAM,[2]   b. "   Sept. 4, 1759.
III. ESTHER,[2]   b. "   " 13, 1763.
IV. BENJAMIN,[2] b. "   Dec. 11, 1765; see 1793.

CHRISTOPHER WHITING,[2] settled on the old road from Winsted to Winchester, north of Sucker Brook bridge, and built and occupied, during his life, the house now owned by Frederick Murray. He died July 6, 1812, aged 54; — an industrious, unassuming, and worthy man. He married, January 9, 1782, Mary Wilcox.

---

* Not a resident of Winchester.

CHILDREN.

I. LORRAIN,[3]	b. Dec. 19, 1782.
II. RILEY,[3]	b. Jan. 16, 1785.
III. CLARA,[3]	b. March 11, 1785; m. Samuel Westlake; she d. Jan. 27, 1815.
IV. LUMAN,[3]	b. May 5, 1792; m. Anna Hayden.
V. ESTHER MIRIAM,[3]	b. Sept. 13, 1796.
VI. NORMAN,[3]	b. Aug. 5, 1796; d. Aug. 5, 1815, by kick of a horse.

LORRAIN WHITING[3] built the brick house on Wallen's Hill, in Winsted, near Barkhamsted line, recently owned and occupied by his son, Hiram C. Whiting, in which he resided until his death September 6, 1833, aged 51. He married, May 1, 1806, Polly Mallory, born in Winchester, May 24, 1784, daughter of Elisha. She died January 10, 1851, aged 66.

CHILDREN.

I. ALGERNON SIDNEY,[4]	b. March 7, 1807; m. June 20, 1832, Loritta M. Sage.
II. LAURA,[4]	b. Jan. 22, 1809; m. Feb. 7, 1828, Martin Johnson.
III. CHLOE AMELIA,[4]	b. Oct. 17, 1810.
IV. URSULA JENET,[4]	b. April 20, 1812; m. Oct. 8, 1833, John Camp; d. June 3, 1839.
V. ORSON,[4]	b. July 5, 1813.
VI. LUCIEN,[4]	b. April 12, 1816.
VII. LORRAIN CHRISTOPHER,[4]	b. Feb. 22, 1819.
VIII. HIRAM CHATTERTON[4] (twin),	b. March 29, 1821.
IX. HOMER WILCOX[4] (twin),	b. March 29, 1821; m. July 30, 1850, Sophronia C. Wheelock.
X. NELSON,[4]	b. Feb. 25, 1823.
XI. DEWITT CLINTON,[4]	b. Aug. 29, 1824; d. Nov. 27, 1846.
XII. POLLY MALLORY,[4]	b. Feb. 19, 1826.
XIII. SARAH JANE,[4]	b. April 29, 1827.
XIV. SYLVIA ANN,[4]	b. Dec. 4, 1828.
XV. EDWARD GAYLORD,[4]	b. Feb. 27, 1832.

RILEY WHITING came to Winsted about 1810, and soon after built and occupied until his death, the house on the east side of Still River, near the clock factory recently owned and occupied by R. L. Beecher. He went into the clock making business as partner with Samuel and Luther Hoadley, and about 1815 became sole owner of the concern;— and carried on the business until his death, with great energy and perseverance. He was a man of quiet, unassuming manners and feeble constitution, who, more than most men, minded his own business and prosecuted it with the same perseverance in adverse, as in prosperous circumstances; and, though twice compelled to assign his property, yet in both instances succeeded in paying off his debts, and left a handsome estate at his death, which took place at Jacksonville, Illinois, August 5, 1835, at the age of fifty-one, while on a business journey. He was a man highly esteemed. He represented the town in the Legislature in the years 1818 and 1832. He married, February 9, 1806, Urania Hoadley. She married (2d), Erasmus D. Calloway; she died December 8, 1855.

CHILDREN.

I. EMILY,[3] b. May 23, 1807; m. August 17, 1826, Dr. Lyman Case.
II. MARY,[3] b. June 11, 1810; m. Feb. 3, 1835, James Litchfield; she d. at Lima, Michigan, Oct. 7, 1837.
III. URANIA,[3] b. Sept. 9, 1812; m. May 26, 1840, Thomas Wilder.
IV. LEMUEL HOADLEY,[3] b. Dec. 11, 1815; d. Dec. 25, 1815.
V. RILEY,[3] b. Sept. 25, 1820; m. August 28, 1843, Clarissa Jane Webster.

1780.

At a Town Meeting, March 13, 1780, Robert McCune was appointed "an Agent to represent the circumstances of the town to the General Assembly and pray that a State Tax be not imposed on this town under our present circumstances; — and that he be empowered to imploy an Attorney to speak in behalf of the town at the General Assembly, viz, Col. Adams, if he may be had, — and if he cannot be obtained, then sd. Agent to employ some other Attorney."

It was also voted, " to give John Videto, Jr., and those in partnership with him their fine for killing one Deer after the law forbid."

July 17, it was voted to grant some relief for those men who are, or may be detailed to serve in the army between the first day of June last, and the first day of January next.

Whereupon Lieutenant John Wright and Enoch Palmer entered their protest against anything being recovered on the foregoing vote, for that it was (as they say) obtained by illegal voters.

At the Society meeting, February 3, 1780:—

Voted, to give Mr. Knapp sixty-five pounds for his last year's service, to be paid in specie as it went in 1774, or an equivalent in cash, to be adjusted by a committee to be chosen for that purpose, which committee are to adjust the price of all kinds of specie as well as cash, which adjustment shall be made once in three months.

Voted, Ichabod Loomis, Samuel McCune and Reuben Miner, a committee to adjust the price of all kinds of specie collected for Mr. Knapp, and also, to estimate money once in three months.

Voted, Levi Brownson, Andrew Everitt, Bela Hills and Abel Wetmore, choristers to tune the Psalm on the Sabbath the year ensuing.

Voted, Deacon Joseph Mills (of Norfolk), Mr. Noah North, and Lieut. Asahel Case, be a committee to hear the complaints of any agrieved members of this Society, respecting paying to Mr. Knapp for his support, and if the said committee judge the complaints or objections of said agrieved members against paying to Mr. Knapp sufficient, then said agrieved members to be exempt from paying to Mr. Knapp.

Voted, Capt. Jonathan Alvord to sweep the meeting house at forty dollars the year ensuing.

At a meeting, March 7, 1780, the doings of the meeting February 3d, were reconsidered ; — and it was then

Voted, to give Mr. Knapp 65 pounds for his last year's service, to be paid in specie — wheat to be valued at six shillings the bushel, and the price of all other kinds of specie to be regulated by wheat at 6s. the bushel in proportion as they were valued in the year 1774, or cash equivalent to specie at the rate above prescribed.

It was further voted, that the Society mean to have Mr. Knapp join with the Church and Society in accommodation of matters of difficulty now subsisting in this Society previous to voting another salary.

December 5th of the same year, another year's salary was voted to Mr. Knapp, " to be paid in Specie as it was valued in 1774, or in Cash equivalent, to be adjusted by a Committee," — and that "if any Persons in the Society shall, within one Month from this, appear before the Society Committee and say that they cannot in their conscience support Mr. Knapp, they shall be exempt from supporting him, and the Rate be made on the remainder of the Society."

It would seem from the foregoing votes, and from the action of the church, this year, that the exclusion from the church of Half-way-covenanters was still working dissension in the Society and occasioning irreconcilable hostility to Mr. Knapp, who strenuously persisted in the exclusion.

The church voted, December 29, 1779, "That it is our opinion y^t a visible appearance of Holiness is necessary for ye Church to admit members into their communion."

What was the occasion of this vote does not appear, but it probably had reference to applications made for half-covenant membership.

A meeting was held March 7th following, " by ye desire of a number of members of ye Society that call themselves greived, in order to see if ye chh. and they could not come understandingly to agree " — the meeting was adjourned to the next Friday — " the agreived members agreeing to bring their greivences in writing at or before the next meeting ; " — another adjournment was had to the next Thursday ; no greivences being brought in — " after considerable of discourse, 3 of ye members of yᵉ society were willing yᵗ yᵉ chh. should have their greivances in writing wh. [are] here recorded."

The first was Abel Wetmore's, as follows:

"Mr. Knapp told me, He will have nothing to do with any man whatever of a spiritual nature, that refuses to give me an account of his spiritual estate previous to reading his letter, nor read his letter."

The second matter of grievance was exhibited by Ensign Wilcoxson, as follows:

"1. I exhibited to Mr. Knapp a letter of recommendation from yᵉ chh. of New Hartford to yᵉ chh. of Winchester, wh. Mr. Knapp never communicated to yʳ chh.

"2. Mr. Knapp told me he did not desire yᵉ use of Civil law to support yᵉ gospel — and now he insists c ᴑ yᵉ use of Civil law."

"3. Mr. Knapp hath neglected to visit and converse with me so much as I have thought was his duty."

Third matter of grievance was exhibited by Eliezer Smith:

"1. Respecting Baptized persons — Mr. Knapp said to me that there was no more connexion between yᵉ chh. and yᵉ rest of yᵉ world, any more than between heaven and Hell.

"2. Mr. Knapp signified he did not desire yʳ use of yᵉ Civil law to support yᵉ Gospel, but now he desires yᵉ Civil law to take place to make men Honest."

The record proceeds to say:

"These following things are what yᵉ chh. attended to and voted;

"1. of a chh. — A chh. is a number of persons mutually covenanting together to walk in gospel fellowship and communion in all yᵉ ordinances of yᵉ gospel.

"2. of a covenant — The covenant of grace is yᵗ covenant wh. in reality subsists only between God and true believers. The covenant implies on our part, repentance toward God and faith towards our Lord Jesus X. * * * * love as yᵉ spring of all our obedience, * * * God's part, spiritual blessings & privileges are promised, together with yᵉ everlasting enjoyment of God in heaven, the covenant subsisting between God and his visible chh. is yᵉ visible exhibition of this covenant.

"3. Baptism and yᵉ Lord's Supper are Seals of this covenant. By baptism yᵉ parent in behalf of yᵉ child gives it up to God yᵉ Father, Son and Holy Ghost, to God as his God and portion and Chief good; to God yᵉ Son as yᵉ only Redeemer, and by yᵉ Holy Ghost as its Sanctification — By baptism yᵉ parent not only gives it up to God yᵉ Father, Son & Holy Ghost, but he puts it under yᵉ watch & Care of yᵉ chh. — the import of it to yᵉ chh. is, pray watch over me and my child, and admonish us when we go astray; — it is yᵉ duty of yᵉ chh. to watch over them, —

to reprove, rebuke and admonish them, — they are to be called upon when come to adult years to take upon themselves ye vows of ye covenant and cordially, understandingly and heartily come up to its terms. — If, after forbearance towards them, they refuse to comply with ye terms of ye covenant, yy. are to be cut off, and the chh. to withdraw their watch and Care from them."

" 2. Voted, that upon any persons bringing a letter of recommendation from any other chh. to be communicated to this, that Mr. Knapp stay ye church by themselves, and exhibit ye letter to ye chh., and if Mr. Knapp have any objection against ye person bringing such, then to communicate his objections to ye chh., and also any person having been propounded for admittance into ye chh., on ye day he is to be admitted Mr. Knapp stay the chh. at noon y^t if there be any objections yy. may then be made manifest.

" 3. Voted, that no person can be indulged in absenting himself from ye Sacrament of ye Lord's Supper only upon point of tender conscience.

" 4. Voted, that persons who shall desire to be propounded for communion in this chh., ye chh. be stayed, and if Mr. Knapp have objections, y^t he then inform ye chh. of them."

These votes indicate that the church, while agreeing with Mr. Knapp in respect to qualifications for membership, was not disposed to yield to him the prerogative of receiving or excluding members; — and the whole record quoted leads to the conclusion that a less arbitray, though equally firm adherence to sound principles of church order, would have resulted in greater peace and unity.

The vote in 1778 "to throw by the Civil Law" in collecting the ministerial rates, and the adoption of the voluntary system of support, proved a failure; — and the return to taxation seems to have been attended with great difficulties, which were but partially obviated, by allowing the malcontent members to relieve themselves from taxation by avowing conscientious scruples in respect to the support of Mr. Knapp. This plan of relieving the malcontents, after three years' trial, was abandoned, and the tax was thereafter levied on all the inhabitants of the Society. It is stated on good traditional authority that the taxes were rigorously collected by attachment of the property or persons of those who refused to pay; — that Ensign Jonathan Coe (grand-father of Jehial and Samuel W. Coe), had his cow attached and sold for a minister's rate; — that there was a surplus of money left of the sale, beyond the tax and costs, which the constable, Deacon Platt, offered to pay him back, but which he indignantly refused to receive; — telling the constable to "put it under Mr. Knapp's pillow and let him sleep on it if he could." The same tradition tells of the attachment of Joseph Hoskin's great coat in the fall and its retention until spring; — and also of the carrying of the late venerable Jonathan Coe to Litchfield Jail, — and how he finally paid the tax under protest.

These occurrences, and others of a similar nature, prepared the way for the introduction and growth of Methodism; and in connection with a subsequent division in the Winsted Society, hereafter detailed, led to the establishment and growth of the large and stable Methodist Church in Winsted; — of which the Coe family have ever been among the most useful and valued members.

The financiers of the present day would be troubled to comprehend the "Specie" currency referred to in the tax votes of this and subsequent years. Hard money was literally too hard in those days, as well as these, to be obtainable as a circulating medium. Continental Bills had so depreciated that it took forty dollars to pay a year's sweeping of the meeting house, which had been done six years before for five shillings and sixpence. The term specie then had a well received meaning not given in Webster's Unabridged Dictionary. It comprehended in its meaning, wheat, rye, corn, meslin, beans, beef, pork, mutton, tallow, suet, lard, and all other farm products; — and these were the tithes for the most part brought into the minister's storehouse in payment of his salary. They were also the kind of specie largely gathered by Washington's "Brother Jonathan,"* from all parts of the State in aid of the revolutionary war. They were received and appraised by committees appointed for that purpose, and forwarded to general depots, in lieu of money taxes.

The standard of specie value adopted in the vote of this year was a wise and equitable one. By taking wheat at the price ruling in 1774, and regulating other articles at proportionate values, the difficulty of determining what amount of a depreciated and fluctuating currency would be equal to the salary originally voted Mr. Knapp, was obviated in an equitable manner.

On the 19th of September of this year, for the first time, freemen were admitted, preparatory to an election of the first Representative sent by the town to the General Assembly, as appears by the following record:

"This certifies that Eliphaz Alvord, Adam Mott, Capt. John Hills, Lt. Ozias Brownson, Samuel McCune, Seth Griswold, Lent Mott, David Austin, Ens^n. Josiah Everitt, David Crissey, Phinehas Potter, John Miner, Ebenezer Preston, Robert Coe, Roswell Coe, Samuel Preston, Reuben Tucker, Dea. Seth Hills, Ens^n. Elisha Wilcoxson, Robert McCune, Andrew Everitt, Martin North, Dea. Samuel Wetmore, David Alvord, Thomas Spencer and Abel Wetmore, are persons of quiet and

---

* Gov. Jonathan Trumbull — Washington's sheet-anchor.

peaceable behaviour and civil Conversation, and qualified to take the Freeman's oath, and had said oath administered to them September 19th, A. D. 1780.

> SETH HILLS,
> ROBERT MCCUNE, } Select Men."
> ELISHA WILCOXSON,

The new comers of the year were Stephen Spencer, Simeon Hurlbut, John Church, Thomas Cannon, Stephen Schovil, Benjamin Woodruff, William Barnstable, and Prince Negro.

STEPHEN SPENCER, — a relative, probably a cousin of Thomas, — is supposed to have come from Saybrook. He owned and lived on the farm recently owned by William F. Hatch, on the east side of the Little Pond, in a house on a road now discontinued, which turned out of the Winchester road, nearly opposite the Stabell House, and extended northwesterly to the Little Pond road. This house, the two barns and cider mill around it, have now disappeared, together with all the cherry, damson and peach trees which once profusely abounded. A few antiquated apple trees alone indicate the location.

Mr. Spencer also owned lands extending down to Mad River, along the north side of the pond stream, and built a saw-mill on the site of Lathrop and Barton's Cutlery Works. In 1800 he sold his farm to Jenkins and Boyd, and removed to Westmoreland, Oneida County, New York. He married, January 18, 1776, Elizabeth Turner.

CHILDREN.

I. ELIZABETH, b. Nov. 30, 1777.
II. LOVISA, b. Dec. 29, 1779; m. Nov. 28, 1795, Zacheus Munsill.
III. SUBMIT, b. Nov. 15, 1781.
IV. SARAH, b. Sept. 1, 1783.
V. AI (son), b. April 25, 1786.
VI. TEMPERANCE, b. " 20, 1789.
VII. HANNAH, b. Oct. 10, 1795.

SIMEON HURLBUT, "of Wethersfield," was owner of lands in Winchester as early as 1776, and is named of Winchester in 1780, when he sold his home lot on which he then lived, lying south of the south end of Long Lake, and bordering on Torrington line. He probably then removed to Torrington. His wife's name was Mary, by whom he had a daughter, Olle, born in Winchester, August 4, 1780.

JOHN CHURCH, from Chatham, was a raw-boned, grim-visaged man, who served under Arnold at Quebec and Saratoga. The precise time of his coming to Winchester is not ascertainable. His first deed is dated

July 7, 1780. He built and lived and died in the ancient red lean-to house on the Little Pond road, recently occupied by Sylvester Hurlbut. He was, during his early residence, a zealous religionist of some hardshell order, and preached on his own hook, from house to house. He married, March 29, 1780, Deborah Spencer. He died December 6, 1834, aged 79. She died December 5, 1834, aged 75.

CHILDREN.

I. HANNAH,[2] b. July 25, 1781; m. Ansel Shattuck; she d. April 10, 1847.
II. EUNICE,[2] b. July 18, 1783; m. Jan. 7, 1808, John Storer.
III. JONATHAN,[2] b. Sept. 17, 1785.
IV. DAVID,[2] b. June 1, 1788; moved to Beaver Dam, Erie Co., Penn.
V. ISAAC,[2] b. Sept. 11, 1790; " " " " " " "
VI. URI,[2] b. Aug. 4, 1792.
VII. LUCY,[2] b. Sept. 5, 1794.
VIII. WEALTHY,[2] b. Jan. 20, 1796.
IX. WEALTHY,[2] b. Jan. 14, 1799; m. Dec. 1, 1834, Rensellaer Sheldon.
X. SIMEON,[2] b. March 5, 1801.

JONATHAN CHURCH[2] was a blacksmith, and lived in a house now torn down on the east side of Green Woods turnpike, nearly opposite the Mad River bridge leading to the Little Pond road. He died in this town. He married Lucy   , and had

CHILDREN.

I. TIMOTHY CHARLES,[3] b. Oct. 25, 1809.
II. AMOS CHARLES,[3] b. July 3, 1812.
III. MARY,[3] b. " 2, 1814.
IV. WEALTHY,[3] b. Oct. 25, 1816.
V. SARAH,[3] b. July 7, 1818.
VI. LUCY,[3] b. Nov. 15, 1820; d. Aug. 30, 1831.
VII. JONATHAN SETH,[3] b. Oct. 12, 1822; was graduated at the Wesleyan University in Middletown, Conn., and died while engaged in teaching in one of the Western States.

URI CHURCH[2] lived in the red house next north of his father's, on the Little Pond road, where he died August 12, 1856, aged 64, leaving a wife, who died in 1861; and a daughter, Amanda, their only child, who still lives on her father's homestead. He was a well educated, industrious and worthy man.

THOMAS CANNON, and Mary, his wife, are named on the records of this year as residents of the town, and addicted to hard swearing, breaking the peace and other explosions. They seem to have lived not far from the old society burying-ground. No trace of them is found after 1781.

OF STEPHEN SCHOVIL, nothing is ascertained, save that he was this year appointed " Key-keeper " of the Pound, and had been a soldier in the Continental service, hired by the town as one of its quota ; — as appears by a certificate of the Select Men on file in the Comptroller's office. In 1784 he is named of Torrington, as defendant in a suit before Justice Alvord. He married Elizabeth   , and had a daughter, Lucy, born August 19, 1781.

There was also a STEPHEN SCHOFIELD, Jr., of Winchester, in 1781, as appears by Justice Alvord's records, who " personally appeared and confessed himself guilty of a breach of the Sabbath, by striking Martin Hurlbut on the ham, and laughing and playing in an undecent and unlawful manner, on ye Sabbath, or Lord's Day, being ye 25th day of March, 1781, in ye Meeting House, in sd. Winchester, in ye time of publick worship," whereupon he was fined 3 shillings and cost four shillings, State money.

BENJAMIN WOODRUFF was colleague " Key-keeper " of the Pound with Mr. Schovil, and lived near the first meeting house.

WILLIAM BARNSTABLE leaves no record except the birth of Pede his daughter, by his wife Hannah, March 4, 1780.

PRINCE, a negro, who seems to have had no surname, died in the town this year, leaving several State Notes received for military service in the Continental army, on which administration was granted to Robert McEwen by the Norfolk Probate Court.

1781.

The records of the town in these years afford many striking analogies to the war of 1861. The patriotic ardor of the earlier years of the revolution had become chilled by the protracted struggle and sad reverses of the war. The continually succeeding drafts of militia-men for short terms of service, rendered it nearly impossible for the towns to raise their allotted quotas of men for the Continental army. Substitute brokerage was a refinement of baseness then unsystematized. The people were too poor to furnish means for hiring middle-men, to buy up on speculation New York roughs and Canadian Frenchmen, to do the fighting for able-bodied, well-dressed, stay-at-home patriots.

The following votes of town meetings in 1781, would not seem strange if found in the records of the third year of the slave-owners' rebellion:

Voted, to appoint Capt. Benj. Benedict and Dea. Seth Hills, to hire the two men now required.

Voted, to give forty shillings State money to Aaron and Joseph Agard for securing Joseph Preston for the town.

Voted, Dea. Seth Hills, Eliphaz Alvord and Lt. Josiah Smith, a Committee to procure clothing for the Soldiers, according to act of Assembly.

Voted, to make out our quota of Continental Soldiers as soon as the number we are deficient can be known.

Voted, Capt. Benedict, Capt. Corbin and Capt. Wright be a Committee to procure Soldiers to fill our deficiency in the Continental army.

Voted, Lieut. Brownson to represent the town before the Committee appointed by the Assembly to adjust matters respecting Soldiers.

Voted, Lt. Brownson go to Hartford to get Dolphin's son* to count for Winchester.

Voted, Capt. Corbin to make application to Gen'l Parsons, or some other General Officer, to procure a pardon for Jonathan Preston on account of his deserting the army.

Voted, to raise a man to supply the place of George Hudson in the Continental Army.

Voted, Lt. Josiah Smith and Ens^n. Jesse Doolittle be a Committee to hire a man for the State Guard.

Voted, to raise Sixpence, hard money, on the Pound to hire the soldiers now called for, and to pay the Soldiers already procured.

Voted, that Neat Cattle, or Sheep, or Pork or English Grain, or Indian Corn, shall be accepted in lieu of hard money granted in the last vote, — said articles to be delivered in Winchester, at the house of Eliphaz Alvord at the appraisement of a committee to be appointed for that purpose.

Voted, to raise fourpence on the Pound, to purchase Beef for the use of the Army, agreeable to the act of Assembly in May last, with an abatement of said rate according to the bill of form by which Winchester is taxed.

Voted, Robert McCune, Sam'l Hurlbut and Jesse Doolittle a Committee to procure Barrels, receive and salt, pack and secure the Beef and Pork that shall be brought in and necessary to be salted, and to store other articles delivered in payment of State Taxes.

Voted, Dea. Wetmore to receive the Cattle and Sheep into his pasture, that may be delivered in payment of aforesaid Taxes.

The following freemen were admitted and sworn, April 9th of this year: Rev. Mr. Knapp, Capt. Benj. Benedict, Capt. Abraham Andrews,

---

* This "Dolphin's son" was one of the small number of colored men, then resident in the town. Two of his grand-sons recently went from here to Rhode Island, and enlisted into one of the colored regiments there; — there being at the time no organization for colored volunteers in this State. One of them, James Dolphin, died in the service at Plaquemine, La., August 5, 1864; the other, Edward H. Dolphin, returned.

John Beach, Jonathan Coe, Eleazer Smith, Gershom McCune, Jr., Phineas Griswold, Aaron Cook, Timothy Benedict, Jr., Abram Filley, Nathan Blackman, John Walter, Joel Beach and Samuel Hurlbut.

The town was for the first time represented this year in the General Assembly, by Deacon Seth Hills and Robert McEwen.

In Society meeting December 4, 1781, Mr. Knapp's salary was voted "to be paid in Specie as things went in 1774, or Cash equivalent," and exempting such persons from payment thereof as could not in conscience support Mr. Knapp.

It was also voted, that the women singers sit in the cross fore-seats, and the men singers as usual.

The new comers of this year were Elijah Andrews, and his son, Elijah, Jr., James Adkins, Isaac Adkins, Richard Coit, Aaron and Joseph Agard.

ELIJAH ANDREWS, with his son Elijah, Jr., came from Windsor, and lived on the east side of the Colebrook road, on land now a part of the farm of William E. Cowles. He was fined by Esq. Alvord, in 1784, twenty shillings for traveling on the Sabbath — and not long afterward removed to Colebrook. Had wife Mary.

ELIJAH ANDREWS, JR., lived from 1810 to about 1815, in the late homestead of James Crocker, on the Green Woods turnpike.

JAMES ADKINS came from Middletown, and bought the homestead of Capt. John Hills, on the Old Country road, near the Hurlbut Cemetery. He is described by a contemporary as "an old man with broad coat skirts, and beaver, old and smooth." — "He brought with him a famous calico Narraganset pacing mare, which he said he once rode on a single day, between sun-rising and sun-setting, one hundred miles from Middletown up the Connecticut River valley." Being asked if he stopped to bait his horse, — "No," said he, "I had my coat pockets full of ears of corn, — and going up hills, I now and then reached round and gave her a nubbin."

One of his daughters married David Austin, Jr., and another Daniel Hurlbut Cone.

ISAAC ADKINS, probably a son of James, owned lands, and lived in a house on the east side of Blue Street, until 1788, when he sold out to Hewitt Hills, — after which his name disappears from the records:

RICHARD COIT, a shoemaker, came from New London, and lived two-thirds of a mile northwest of the center, on the Old Country road, in the house recently owned by Nelson T. Loomis. He served in the unsuccessful siege of Quebec, and subsequently on the quota of this town in the Continental army. In the words of a contemporary, — "he was impulsive and fractious, — talked a volume every day, — disciplined his children and hogs severely, was not dainty about his words, — was poor, until in old age, his brother bequeathed him forty thousand dollars, which was nearly squandered before his death." He was born in New London, December 25, 1752; married, August 27, 1778, Hepzibah Smith, born in Middletown, August 9, 1750; she died March 15, 1828, aged 77; he died March 25, 1834, aged 81.

CHILDREN.

I. JOSEPH, b. Aug. 29, 1780; m. Nov. 13, 1807, Francis Ursula Adams, and had children: 1. Lucy, b. Jan. 5, 1809; 2. Joseph Richard, b. March 28, 1811. In 1807 he was "of Trumbull Co., Ohio." In 1809 and 10, he owned and occupied the Luman Munsill house, a little south of the center; and soon after removed to Monticello, N. Y., where he died.
II. SARAH, b. May 16, 1785; m. Feb. 13, 1815, William S. Marsh; d. s. p. March 10, 1833.
III. LUCY, b. Dec. 2, 1790; d. June 7, 1794.

AARON AND JOSEPH AGARD are named in the record of a town meeting this year. They, or one of them, lived in the Noble J. Everitt house, half a mile south of the center. They came into the town probably earlier than 1776, but were not land owners. Elizabeth, probably wife of Aaron, was one of the original members of the Church.

Joseph and Tabitha Agard, his wife, had

CHILDREN.

I. JOSEPH, b. May 11, 1776. II. TABITHA, b. May 17, 1779.

BENAJAH ABREW, or ABRO, is mentioned in a vote of this year as a Continental soldier, claimed as serving on the quota of Winchester. His name is on the list of 1785 as a resident tax-payer. By another vote in 1788 the tax was given up as uncollectable.

1782.

In Town Meeting February 26, 1782, it was voted "to hire the men now called for, for the Guard at Horse Neck, and to fill the deficiencies in the Continental Army 'til December next." Also "to raise fourpence on the pound in money or specie at money prices, in the specific articles of neat cattle, sheep, wool, flax, wheat, rie, and indian Corn, at the price the said articles were valued at in 1774; and that the above rate be appropriated to the sole purpose of procuring the soldiers, if needed, that are or may be called for by the Assembly."

November 7, 1782, voted to build a bridge over Mad River in the most convenient place in, or near, the road now leading to the Society of Winsted, ... and Lt. Uriah Seymour, Col. Seth Smith and Samuel Mills were appointed as an indifferent committee from other towns, to view and report which place is the best on the whole, for the public and private interest, for a road to, and a bridge over, Mad River ; —whether the road now established and traveled to and over said river, or a new proposed place east of Mr. Austin's mill.

The traveled road here referred to probably crossed the river, either near Rockwell's tannery or on the site of Dudley's Block; — and the proposed route was Lake street as it now runs.

The freemen admitted this year were Reuben Miner, William Barbour, Jonah Woodruff, and Jonathan Alvord.

The new comers were Daniel H. Cone, John Deer, Jonathan Deer, John Marshall, Levi Norton, Samuel Roberts, Chauncy Smith, Elijah Thompson, and David Ward.

DANIEL HURLBUT CONE, from Middletown, first lived on a part of the John Hills farm, near the burying-ground, and afterward on a new farm near the Leonard Hurlbut place, where he died May 17, 1842, aged 88. His wife, Elizabeth, died February 27, 1829, aged 74. He was by trade a shoemaker ; — had served nearly the whole war, as an artilleriest in the Continental army ; — was a good man in every sense of the word.

CHILDREN.

I.	SUSANNA,[2]	b. June 22, 1781.
II.	DANIEL,[2]	b. Oct. 14, 1782.
III.	ELIZABETH,[2]	b. Jan. 29, 1784.
IV.	SAMUEL,[2]	b. Oct. 18, 1785; lived and died in Norfolk.
V.	HURLBUT,[2]	b. Jan. 5, 1788.
VI.	WARREN,[2]	b. Aug. 19, 1789; lived and died in Norfolk.
VII.	SULLIVAN,[2]	b. Jan. 14, 1793.
VIII.	SILAS,[2]	b. " 27, 1795; lived and died in Granby.

Two twin sons of Samuel,[2] James and John, and a daughter of Silas, are now residents of Winsted.

JOHN DEER, from Goshen, this year bought a tract of land, now composing mainly the farms of Orren Tuller and Dudley Chase. He lived on the discontinued part of the Blue Street road which extended north of the road passing the houses of Tuller and Chase, until his death. He married, November 22, 1780, Hannah Stow; she died February 28, 1786; he married (2d), May 6, 1787, Rhoda Filley; she died April 8,

1793; and he married (3d), Lucy Foresbey, or Frisbey. He was a soldier of the revolution. He died August 30, 1828, aged 73 years. His father, John or George Deer, was also a soldier in the revolution, and was killed by a cannon shot, while on a boat on Lake Champlain. His mother, Abigail Deer, died October 5, 1792.

CHILDREN OF JOHN AND HANNAH (STOW) DEER.

I. RUTH, b. Jan. 28, 1781.
II. HANNAH, b. Aug. 30, 1782; d. same day.
III. LAURANNA, b. July 19, 1784.
IV. ABIGAIL, b. Feb. 5, 1786; d. same day.

CHILDREN OF JOHN AND RHODA (FILLEY) DEER.

V. HANNAH, b. April 15, 1788.
VI. ABIGAIL, b. Aug. 11, 1789.
VII. ROGER, b. Oct. 3, 1791.
VIII. AMAN, b. Feb. 3, 1793.

JONATHAN DEER, supposed to be brother to John, bought of him the south part of his lot, and first lived in a log house on Hall Meadow Road, near its junction with the Tuller and Chase road; and in 1796, lived a little west of the center on the Old Country road, near the school house. In 1797 he is described as "absconded to parts unknown," in Esq. Alvord's Justice Records. He married, January 26, 1785, Mary Reed; they had one

CHILD.

I. JONATHAN WHEELER, b. Aug. 14, 1786.

JOHN MARSHALL, from Torrington, owned lands between the Norfolk and Brooks roads, and is supposed to have lived on or near the latter road, above Nelson T. Loomis. He probably died in the town before 1800;—as his widow married Andrew Everitt in December of that year. He married, March 31, 1780, Statira Hills, daughter of Deacon Seth.

CHILD.

I. OLIVER, b. Aug. 3, 1780. (Removed to Vernon, N. Y.)

LEVI NORTON, youngest child of Samuel and Mabel Norton, of Goshen, Connecticut, was born May 13, 1759. At sixteen he entered the Continental army under Putnam, and served until late in the fall of 1779, a period of nearly five years. In 1780 he made a rude cabin under a chestnut tree between the two lakes, and began clearing the land of his future farm, and studying Dilworth's arithmetic by the blaze of his cabin fire. In 1782 he built his first dwelling, a few feet north of the red one and a half story house, which he erected in 1795, and thence occupied until 1812. In this first dwelling, he introduced his newly married wife on the 23d of January, 1783; — and here labored day and night in clearing and cultivating one of the largest and best farms of the town.

In May 1812 he removed to the wilderness of Wayne County, Pennsylvania, where he foreclosed 5,000 acres of land and gathered an unmixed Yankee settlement around him. He died January 21, 1823, aged 64 years.

He was a prominent, intelligent, and influential man of the town, and a zealous Jeffersonian.

He married, January 21, 1783, Olive Wheeler, born in Bethlem, Connecticut, September 19, 1759; she died May 25, 1838.

CHILDREN.

I. WARREN WHEELER, b. Nov. 12, 1783; m. Oct. 26, 1800, Polly, daughter of Martin and Mary North, of Winchester. Children: Hiram, Sidney M.

II. ALVA W., b. Aug. 10, 1791; [living in 1872], m. Nov. 21, 1816, Sallie Freeman, of Chester, Mass. Children: Emily A., Olive A., Maria S., Harriet C., and Lucius F.

III. SHELDON, b. Nov. 26, 1793; m. Sept. 14, 1818, Harriet, daughter of Grinnell Spencer, of Winchester, Ct.; he d. Sept. 15, 1838. Children: 1. Edmund Kirby; 2. Oscar Montgomery; 3. Abigail Catlin; 4. Mary Elizabeth; of whom Edmund K. and Abigail C. were living in Wayne Co., Pa., in 1872. He was an early clerk of Wayne Co., and afterwards during his life an Agent of the American Sunday-School Union in Missouri, Iowa, and Wisconsin.

IV. CLARISSA, b. March 28, 1796; m. in 1821, Hon. Isaac Dimick, of Ottawa, Ill., in 1872. Children: 1. Levi Norton; 2. Philo J.; 3. Ann; 4. Olive.

V. SAMUEL, b. June 11, 1799; m. in 1822, Jerusha Tracy. Children: 1. Levi; 2. Philander; 3. Phebe; 4. Luther; 5. Tracy; 6. Washington.

SAMUEL ROBERTS, probably from Torrington, bought of the executor of Joel Roberts, deceased, the farm of said Joel, and lived in the house above mentioned as the subsequent residence of Warren W. Norton, until 1802. His name appears as plaintiff or defendant in Justice Alvord's Records more than fifty times during the years 1796 and 1797, from which it is inferred that he was not of the most amiable disposition. We extract a single record in 1799 as a sample of many others.

Stephen Carter, one of the grand jurors of Winchester, complained "that Samuel Roberts, of said town, did, at Winchester aforesaid, on the 17th day of September last past, in an angry manner, sinfully and wickedly curse or damn the person of Preserved Crissy of said Winchester," whereupon he was found guilty and fined one dollar with costs, amounting to two dollars and fifty-nine cents. He married, December 11th, 1783, Mary Brooks. He sold out to Martin North in 1802, and thereafter disappears from the records.

CHILDREN.
I. NAOMI, b. May 20, 1785.
II. SYLVESTER, b. March 30, 1787; d. May 20, 1787.
III. WARREN, b. June 27, 1788.
IV. MINERVA, b. October 14, 1790.

CHAUNCEY SMITH owned and lived on lot 36, 3d division, on the Brooks road, in a house on the west side, about 100 rods north of the Everitt House. The inventory of his estate was returned to the Norfolk Probate Court November 18, 1794. He married, April 9th, 1783, Sarah Page.

CHILDREN.
I. LUCINDA, b. October 23, 1784.
II. ABEL, b. December 19, 1785.
III. ORILLA, b. October 3d, 1786.
IV. SARAH, b. January 21, 1790.

ELIJAH THOMPSON owned and lived on lot 19, 3d division, in the neighborhood of Newman B. Gilbert, Danbury Quarter. He conveyed to his sons Daniel and Elijah two portions of the same lot, on which they are supposed to have lived.

DANIEL THOMPSON married, November 2, 1788, Roxy Smith.

CHILDREN.
I. HULDAH, b. November 15, 1790.
II. ROXALANA, b. September 20, 1791.

SAMUEL THOMPSON married, March 3, 1788, Hannah Wolcott.

CHILDREN.
I. SAMUEL, b. May 17, 1790.
II. HANNAH, b. February 5, 1792.
III. DAVID WOLCOTT, b. February 13, 1794.

DAVID WARD came to this town as a schoolmaster, and this year bought lands on Blue street; and the next year bought a part of the John Hills farm, near the burying ground. He married, January 1, 1784, Mary, daughter of David Austin, senior, and soon after became the owner of the farm in Winsted, lately owned by Colonel Hosea Hinsdale, which he sold in 1796, and probably removed with his father-in-law to Vermont.

CHILDREN.
I. MARY, b. Friday, January 28, 1785.
II. LUCY, b. November 14, 1786.
III. SAMUEL, b. March 27, 1790.
IV. DANIEL, b. May 8, 1792.
V. LAURA, b. May 7, 1794.
VI. AUSTIN, b. March 27, 1796.

20

1783.

In the record of a town meeting, September 26, 1783, we are reminded of modern war times by a vote condemning the "commutation" adopted by the convention at Middletown, as "unconstitutional, and altogether unjust and unreasonable."

In society meeting, the project of a new meeting-house was ventilated, and an application to the county court for a committee, to set a stake therefor, was voted. The committee having been appointed, and having set a stake, another meeting was held, which rejected the site selected, and set another stake, in Sam'l Hurlbut's lot, north of Dr. Everitt's, and about eight rods west of the allowance, and near the middle of said lot north and south, and appointed Captain Brownson to go to the county court, to get the doings of the society established. These doings were upset by the vote of a subsequent meeting, reconsidering the aforesaid doings.

The freemen admitted this year were Captain Peter Corbin, Levi Brownson, David Ward. Ichabod Loomis, Stephen Spencer, Samuel Smith, William Fay, David Austin, Jr., John Church, Benoni Brownson, and Levi Norton.

The new comers of the year were Benoni Brownson, William Chamberlin and William Chamberlin, Jr., Jedediah Coe, Timothy Cook, Joseph Elmore and Joseph B. Elmore, his son, Isaac Filley, Benjamin Judd, Joseph Platt, Samuel Smith and Benajah Smith, his son, Ephraim Smith, Samuel Stancliff, Josiah Wade, Daniel Ward, Hopkins West, Nathaniel White.

MAJOR BENONI BROWNSON, from Berlin, distantly related to the other Brownsons in the town, lived in a house, now torn down, immediately north of John J. McAlpine's late residence, until a few years before his death, when he removed to the Major Seth Wetmore house, then standing immediately south of the Hurlbut store, where he died December 15th, 1833, aged 76. He is described as "a man of pleasant temperament, tolerably industrious, and a great talker." He married Mary Percival, of Berlin, and after her death he married (2d) Mrs. Lois Wetmore, daughter of Colonel Ozias Brownson, and the divorced wife of Major Seth Wetmore.

CHILDREN BY FIRST WIFE.

I. CHAUNCEY,   b. February 26, 1778.
II. ORENTUS,   b. December 3, 1779.
III. AMELIA,   m. Elijah Blake, Jr.
IV. POLLY,   m. Herman Munson.
V. PARLIAMENT,
VI. GEORGE, went South, d. unmarried.

CHAUNCEY BROWNSON lived for some years in the original homestead of his father; and after the breaking up of his family, in consequence of his partial derangement, he lived mainly in Winsted, until his death in 1853. He married May 1, 1806, Fanny Thrall, born August 9, 1783.

CHILDREN.

I. EDWIN WORTHY, b. October 24, 1807; d. of yellow fever at New Orleans, October, 1841, unmarried.
II. SAMUEL JOHN, b. April 17, 1809; d. at the South, unmarried.
III. HIRAM CHARLES, b. February 1, 1811; d. at Columbia, S. C., May, 1863.
IV. PARLIAMENT HART, b. July 15, 1816; d. at New Orleans, of yellow fever, October, 1841, unmarried.
V. GEORGE WASHINGTON, b. May 10, 1820; d. aged 7 years.
VI. MARY JANE, b. April 2, 1826; m. lives in Missouri.

ORENTUS BROWNSON migrated about 1800 to Burke, Vermont, whence he returned to Winchester, and at one time kept a tavern in the house of Washington Hatch, at the Centre. About 1835, he built and moved into the house now owned by Samuel Smith, in Winsted, and followed the business of building through his remaining active life, during which he built, mainly by unassisted labor, nearly twenty dwellings. Though never educated as a mechanic, he did all the carpenter and joiner work, and not unfrequently, the masonry and brick and stone laying; selling the house, when finished, to buy the lot and materials for building another; changing his own residence from time to time, and closing his laborious and inoffensive life in the house now owned by Samuel A. McAlpine, August 19, 1859, aged 80. He married, October , 1804, Abiah, daughter of Wm. R. Case. She died June 20, 1836, aged 56. He married, May 15, 1848, widow Huldah Munson. He had one child, Huldah L., born January 29, 1818; died March 18, 1838.

HON. PARLIAMENT BROWNSON removed in early life to Auburn, N. Y., where he became a lawyer of some eminence, and a man of great uprightness and independence of character. He married, about 1847, a Miss Wood, and died childless some years afterwards.

WILLIAM CHAMBERLIN, from Colchester, settled on the farm late owned by James L. Bragg, and occupied it until his death, January 6, 1821, at the age of 86. His wife Mary died December 26, 1820, aged 87.

WILLIAM CHAMBERLIN, Jr., owned and occupied a farm immediately north of his father's, now owned by Harlow Fyler, until 1809, when he migrated to Hudson, Ohio, where his descendants now reside. He married May 4, 1780, Joanna Skinner.

CHILDREN.

I. ANNA, b. June 13, 1782.
II. JOSEPH, b. November 12, 1784.
III. WILLIAM, b. December 9th, 1786.
IV. MARY, b. December 15, 1788.
V. LYDIA, b. January 11, 1791.
VI. AMOS, b. July 24, 1793; d. at Hudson, Ohio, April 14, 1861. An obituary notice says, "He has contributed a large share towards the improvement of this township for the last fifty-two years. He was a man of the strictest honesty, and of unswerving integrity. He leaves a wife and eight children, besides a large circle of relatives and friends, to mourn his loss."
VII. ASAHEL, b. August 13, 1795.
VIII. REUBEN, b. December 23, 1797.
IX. SAMUEL, b. April 9, 1800.
X. LUCY, b. March 17, 1802.
XI. PHILEMON, b. January 31, 1804.
XII. HIRAM, b. December 27, 1807.

JEDEDIAH COE is on the assessment list of this year. He owned land adjoining, or a part of, the Bragg farm, which he sold to John Nash in 1809, and then migrated to Burke, Caledonia county, Vermont, where some of his descendants now reside.

TIMOTHY COOK, from Windsor, owned a lot and built a house on Wallen's hill, where he resided some years, after which it became the property of his father-in-law, Simeon Moore, of Windsor. In 1792, he bought a sixty-acre lot on Colebrook line, west of Green Woods turnpike, on which he afterwards resided. His wife's name was Hannah.

CAPT. JOSEPH ELMORE, a blacksmith from Danbury, owned and occupied the place afterwards owned by Silliman Hubbell, and now by Norris Coe's widow, on the Norfolk road, a third of a mile west of Winchester Centre. His will was proved in Norfolk Probate District, December 26, 1801. He had, by wife Lucy, a son, Joseph Benedict, born in Danbury, November 16, 1769.

DOCTOR JOSEPH B. ELMORE, son of the foregoing, owned a house and lot previously owned by Dan'l Grover, on the discontinued north and south road, west of Orrin Tuller's, which he sold in 1799 to John Beecher, soon after which he removed to Granville, Massachusetts.

ISAAC FILLEY, son of Abram and cousin of Remembrance, is on the list as a resident tax payer. Nothing further is known of him except the following town legislation, recorded on January 7, 1787:

"*Voted*, that Isaac Filley shall mend and make good the gun he broke, belonging to James Hale, as good as when he received the gun."

He married, December 9, 1782, Elizabeth Curtis, of Winchester.

BENJAMIN JUDD'S name is on the list of this year, but his residence and history are unknown. His marriage to Dinah Filley, April 24, 1783, is recorded in the Church Records, and he is there described as of Danbury.

JOSEPH PLATT, from Danbury, uncle to Deacon Levi Platt, lived on a lot north of the Edward Rugg Farm. He was a clothier, and had a fulling mill on the brook, a little south of the Potter negro house. He sold out in 1787, and afterwards moved to Ohio.

SAMUEL SMITH owned and resided on land near Winchester Centre, and was assessed as a tavern keeper this year. It is not easy to locate his residence, or to ascertain how long he dwelt in the town. In 1795, he is described in a deed of land as of Litchfield.

BENAJAH SMITH, son of Samuel, is grantee in 1784, of the above-mentioned land of his father, which he conveyed in 1787, to Roswell Coe.

EPHRAIM SMITH, known as "Deaf Smith," is on the list of this year. In 1794, Chauncey Smith conveyed to him his homestead above the Everitt house, which he sold to Levi Brownson in 1796. He is described as of Kent in a Recognizance dated June 27, 1797.

JOSIAH WADE, of Litchfield, bought, November 11, 1783, a wedge lot in the second tier, first division, bordering on Torrington line, on which he afterward resided, and which he sold to Amasa Wade, April 23, 1786, when he probably left the town.

DANIEL WARD, from Middletown, owned a lot on Blue Street, on which he probably lived until 1789, when he bought and lived on land near the parting of the Norfolk road and the Brooks road. He had a rough tongue, which he kept in vigorous exercise, in wordy contests with his neighbor-in-law, Richard Coit, who was an able combatant in this species of warfare. Squire Alvord's records show that he was somewhat addicted to profanity and breaches of the peace.

HOPKINS WEST, from Chatham, owned land near the Leonard Hurlbut place, and probably resided there until about 1785, when he is described, in his conveyance of the same land, as of New Cambridge district, Albany county, New York.

NATHANIEL WHITE, from Chatham, owned land east of the little pond, now a part of the farm, late of Wm. F. Hatch. Where he lived, or when he left the town, is not ascertained.

CHAPTER XIII.

CLOSE OF THE REVOLUTIONARY WAR—RESUMÉ.

The close of the revolutionary war is a fitting period for summing up the growth of our infant settlement since its incorporation as a town in 1771.

The population at that period, as given in the petition of April 4, 1771, was,

In the Society of Winchester, 28 families, embracing - - 179 souls.
In the township and out of the Society, 4 " estimated at - - 26 "

Total, 32 " 205 "

The census of 1782, in the Comptroller's office, gives the population at that period as 683 whites and 5 blacks; Total, 688.

The oldest complete Assessment List of the town now to be found, is that of 1783, which has the names of 109 resident male tax-payers in Winchester Society, and thirty-nine in Winsted; making the total of the town 148.

We copy this assessment, as showing who were then the inhabitants of the town, — their relative condition as property owners, — the amount of improvements and accumulation of property.

WINCHESTER SOCIETY.

NAMES.	Amount of Taxable Property. £. s. d.	NAMES.	Amount of Taxable Property. £. s. d.
Daniel Andrus,	50: 5: 0	Wm. Benedict,	26: 5: 6
Abram Andrus,	31: 8: 6	Benoni Brownson,	39: 2: 6
David Alvord,	33:11: 6	Peter Blackman,	40: 3: 0
Theophilus Andrus,	15: 0: 0	Joseph Bown,	21: 0: 0
Abram Andrus, Jr.,	26: 5: 6	Lemuel Basset,	6: 2: 6
Eliphaz Alvord,	68: 0: 0	Capt. Benedict,	81: 8: 6
Isaac Adkins,	49:11: 0	Timothy Benedict, Jr.,	48: 1: 6
Jonathan Blackman,	38:13: 9	Joel Beach,	44: 0: 0
Levi Brownson,	59:15: 9	Elijah Castle,	22: 8: 0
Timothy Benedict,	49: 7: 6	Aaron Cook,	51: 7: 6
Capt. (Ozias) Brownson,	98: 4: 0	Richard Coit,	3: 8: 3

FAMILY RECORDS. 159

NAMES.	Amount of Taxable Property. £. s. d.	NAMES.	Amount of Taxable Property. £. s. d.
Abner Coe,	30 : 3 : 0	Lent Mott,	32 : 2 : 6
Capt. (Peter) Corbin,	56 : 16 : 0	Gershom McCune, Jr.,	56 : 1 : 0
John Church,	35 : 1 : 6	Adam Mott,	22 : 6 : 6
Peter Corbin, Jr.,	21 : 0 : 0	John Minor,	43 : 18 : 3
Jedediah Coe,	21 : 0 : 0	Samuel McCune,	62 : 2 : 6
Jonathan Coe,	70 : 15 : 0	Gershom McCune,	49 : 13 : 6
Sam'l Clark,	30 : 14 : 0	Robert McCune,	94 : 19 : 6
Robert Coe,	52 : 9 : 9	Reuben Minor,	34 : 0 : 6
Sam'l Castle,	21 : 0 : 0	Martin North, Jr.,	23 : 17 : 6
Daniel Cone & David Ward,	78 : 7 : 3	Martin North,	49 : 13 : 6
Wm. Chamberlin,	25 : 15 : 6	Levi Norton,	40 : 8 : 6
Rozel Coe,	91 : 17 : 6	Joseph Platt,	37 : 6 : 6
Wm. Castle,	32 : 2 : 0	Benjamin Preston,	4 : 16 : 0
Timothy Cook,	22 : 16 : 6	Ambrose Palmer,	51 : 0 : 0
Daniel Clark,	29 : 1 : 1	Samuel Preston,	59 : 1 : 0
Joseph Dodge,	33 : 4 : 6	Ebenzer Preston,	34 : 2 : 0
John Dear & Salmon Hoskin,	50 : 5 : 0	Moses Roberts,	21 : 0 : 0
Eli Dolphin,	37 : 14 : 0	Samuel Roberts,	33 : 2 : 0
Andrew Everit,	36 : 19 : 0	Ephraim Smith,	22 : 0 : 0
Hannah Everit,	14 : 1 : 6	Ephraim Smith (deaf),	19 : 13 : 0
Joseph Elmer,	42 : 0 : 0	Samuel Stanclift,	0 : 12 : 0
Josiah Everit,	30 : 10 : 0	Eleazer Smith,	32 : 19 : 6
Wm. Fay,	24 : 10 : 6	Lemuel Stannard,	27 : 3 : 6
Rem'b. Filley,	1 : 18 : 6	Abel Stannard,	28 : 2 : 0
Isaac Filley,	27 : 0 : 0	Chauncey Smith,	25 : 13 : 6
Abm. Filley,	79 : 1 : 6	Samuel Smith,	14 : 15 : 3
Joseph Frisbie,	51 : 2 : 0	Stephen Spencer,	37 : 8 : 3
Daniel Grover,	23 : 19 : 6	Thomas Spencer,	69 : 13 : 0
Phineas Griswold,	47 : 2 : 0	William Stannard,	20 : 10 : 6
Seth Griswold,	51 : 0 : 0	Reuben Tucker,	45 : 18 : 0
Joseph Hoskins,	39 : 7 : 6	Elijah Thomson,	42 : 4 : 6
Stephen Hurlbut,	20 : 15 : 0	John Videto,	28 : 16 : 6
Elijah Hubard,	23 : 15 : 6	Jonah Woodruff,	36 : 17 : 6
Samuel Hurlbut,	93 : 17 : 6	Nathan White,	38 : : 6
Seth Hills,	83 : 6 : 0	Daniel Walter,	23 : 0 : 0
Widow Mary Hills,	5 : 7 : 3	Christopher Whiting,	48 : : 9
James Hale,	29 : 11 : 6	Samuel Wetmore,	61 : 0 : 9
Benjamin Judd,	17 : 2 : 0	Elisha Wilcoxson,	74 : 7 : 9
Seth Kellogg,	38 : 2 : 0	Abel Wetmore,	47 : 0 : 0
Ichabod Loomis,	66 : 13 : 6	Amacy Wade,	60 : 17 : 9
Daniel Loomis,	34 : 0 : 6	Lewis Wilkinson,	23 : 7 : 3
Widow Leach,	2 : 9 : 6	Jesse Wilkinson,	27 : 18 : 3
William Leach,	12 : 15 : 0	Levi Wilkinson,	24 : 12 : 0
John Marshall,	26 : 8 : 9	Hopkins West,	46 : 0 : 0

Total Winchester Society, £4242 14s. 10d.

WINSTED SOCIETY.

NAMES.	Amount of Taxable Property. £. s. d.	NAMES.	Amount of Taxable Property. £. s. d.
David Austin, Jr.,	35 : 18 : 6	Eleazer Porter,	36 : 15 : 3
David Austin,	45 : 13 : 3	Enoch Palmer,	59 : 5 : 0
Elijah Andrews,	55 : 5 : 6	Benjamin Palmer,	23 : 14 : 0
Nathan Balcam,	27 : 0 : 0	Samuel Stanclift,	18 : 0 : 0
Jonathan Balcam,	28 : 0 : 0	Elisha Spencer,	23 : 10 : 0
John Balcam,	43 : 4 : 9	John Sweet,	23 : 18 : 0
Samuel Clark 2d,	21 : 13 : 0	Josiah Smith,	84 : 14 : 6
Uzal Clark,	28 : 16 : 0	Comfort Stanclif,	24 : 0 : 0
David Crisse,	73 : 18 : 0	Simeon Rogers,	32 : 4 : 9
Silas Dunham,	25 : 0 : 0	Ebenezer Rowlee,	46 : 10 : 0
Jesse Doolittle,	54 : 14 : 0	Zebulon Thomson,	4 : 2 : 0
Abijah Fuller,	21 : 19 : 9	Henry Walter,	37 : 17 : 0
Comfort Goff,	19 : 8 : 0	Freedom Wright,	42 : 13 : 3
Samuel Hayden,	46 : 4 : 3	John Wright,	21 : 6 : 0
Abel Hoskin,	55 : 16 : 0	Charles Wright,	34 : 13 : 3
Stephen Knowlton,	28 : 19 : 9	John Wright, Jr.,	45 : 9 : 6
David Mills,	76 : 6 : 0	John Walter,	31 : 1 : 0
Phinehas Potter,	30 : 14 : 0	Lemuel Walter,	28 : 6 : 6
Lazarus Palmer,	21 : 0 : 0	David West,	47 : 2 : 0
Reuben Palmer,	21 : 0 : 0		

Total, Winsted Society, ... £1425 12s. 9d.

This list was made up of the following items:

- 134 Polls from 21 to 70 years, at £18 : 0 : 0.
- 40 do. " 16 to 21 " at £9 : 0 : 0.
- 122 Oxen, 4 years old or upwards, at £4 : 0 : 0.
- 271 Cows and Steers, 3 years old or upwards, at £3 : 0 : 0.
- 100 Steers and Heifers, 2 years old or upwards, at £2 : 0 : 0.
- 77 " " " 1 " " " at £1 : 0 : 0.
- 120 Horses, 3 years old and upwards, at £3 : 0 : 0.
- 9 " 2 " " " at £2 : 0 : 0.
- 7 " 1 " " " at £1 : 0 : 0.
- 154 Swine, at £1 : 0 : 0.
- 28 Smokes or fire place, at £0 : 7 : 6.
- 92 do. " do. at £0 : 3 : 9.
- 586 Acres of Plow Lands, at £0 : 10 : 0.
- 1027 " " Meadow Lands, at £0 : 8 : 0.
- 51 " " Bog Meadow Lands, at £0 : 5 : 0.
- 409 " " Bush Pasture Lands, at £0 : 2 : 0.
- 12219 " " Timber Land, at £0 : 0 : 6.
- 3 Silver Watches, at £3 : 0 : 0.
- 5 Taverners assessed at £15 : 0 : 0.
- 1 Store, at £25 : 0 : 0.
- 1 Grist-Mill and Saw-Mill, at £24 : 5 : 0.
- 1 Saw-Mill, at £8 : 15 : 0.

2   do.   at £4 : 0 : 0.
1 Physician, at £10 : 0 : 0.
2 Shoemakers, at £5 : 0 : 0.

The number of dwellings is not specified on the list; the tax being levied on the "smokes" or fire-places. From an examination of the list, the number of dwellings may be estimated at from seventy to seventy-five; and their quality is indicated by the low assessment of the smokes, which are rated at 7s. 6d., or 3s. 9d. each, while the rate for smokes in houses in good repair is 15s. each.

The cleared lands of all kinds, — bush pasture included, — amounted to 1015 acres; being about one-twentieth of the territory, and less than eight and a half acres to each resident land-owner.

The quantity of land put in the list falls short of the whole territory of the town by more than six thousand acres. It is difficult to account for so large an omission, except on the ground that lands "on mountains, inaccessible to teams," were not considered as taxable, even at the rate of sixpence per acre.

We have quoted largely from year to year, the votes passed and the measures adopted to recruit the army, and aid the government with supplies for carrying on the war, as showing how much the success of that struggle depended on the legislation of the New England towns, and how zealously it was sustained by the efforts of our infant settlement.

It is often said that the settlement of this and other neighboring towns was greatly accelerated by immigration of men of more prudence than courage or patriotism, who hoped in this remote region to escape from compulsory military service. If this is true, they found it a poor refuge for non-combatants, for it would be difficult to find an able-bodied man of that period who had not seen hard service, either as a volunteer or detached militiaman. Our infant town had her representatives at Ticonderoga, Bunker Hill, Quebec, Long Island, Saratoga, and many other battle fields.

The following soldiers from this town went to Ticonderoga in 1775, in Captain Sedgwick's Company, Colonel Hinman's Regiment:—

Warham Gibbs, Lieut.,	Nathan Balcom,	William Stannard,
Charles Wright, Jr.,	Hawkins Woodruff,	Lemuel Walter,
Adam Mott,	John Derby,	Noah Gleason, Jr.,
Ebenezer Shepard,	David Goff,	Abraham Wilkinson,
Stephen Arnold,	Peleg Sweet,	Elisha Smith,
Freedom Wright,	Oliver Coe, Sen.	

Charles Wright and Ebenezer Shepard marched to the relief of Boston on the Lexington alarm.

Samuel Hurlbut, John Sweet, and Lemuel Stannard served in the 7th Regiment in 1775.

Daniel Hurlbut Cone and William Lucas served in Colonel Meigs' Regiment in 1775.

Benoni Brownson served in Captain Hooker's Company in 1775.

Stephen Knowlton served 5th company, 3d Regiment.

Judah West, " 8th " 2d "
Gideon Wilcoxson,* " 10th " 7th "
Shubael Cook, " 4th " 8th "
Ebenezer Rowley, " 9th " 8th "
Nathan Blackman, Capt. Smith's " 8th "
David Beebe, " " 8th "

Truman Gibbs, Major Weld's Company.

Benjamin Palmer, " "

Josiah Adkins, Captain Arnold's Company, Wooster's Regiment.

John Arnold, Captain Denny's Company, Hosford's Regiment, in 1776.

William Leach, Colonel Ducher's (4th) Regiment, in 1779.

Do. Captain Converse's Company, 7th Regiment, in 1780.

Lemuel Walter, Captain Alden's Company, Colonel Butler's Regiment, in 1780.

Samuel Roberts, Captain Alden's Company, Colonel Butler's Regt., in 1780.

John Balcom, Captain Alden's Company, Colonel Butler's Regiment, in 1780.

Daniel Walter, Colonel Swift's Regiment, in 1780.

Oliver Coe, Jr., Captain Porson's Company, Col. Butler's Regt., 1780.
Samuel Mott, " " "
Peter Corbin, Sherman's Company, 8th Regiment, "
Daniel Wright, " " "
Ebenezer Coe, " " "

The following other men served in the continental army prior to 1780, as appears by a certificate of the selectmen:—

George Hudson,	Stephen Hurlbut,	Gershom Fay,
Peabody Stannard,	Levi Wilkinson,	William Fay,
Jonathan Preston,	Stephen Schovil,	Timothy Fay,
Prince Negro,	Adam Mott,	Seth Stannard,
John Fay,	Remembrance Filley,	Jesse Wilkinson.

---

* He served in Captain Beebe's Company in 1776, and died while a prisoner of war in the Sugar House, New York.

Of these, Remembrance Filley, Gershom Fay, and William Fay, belonged to Captain Beebe's Litchfield Company.

Oliver Coe, Jr., and Wait Loomis, also served under General Harmer, in the Indian War in Ohio.

David Austin, Daniel Corbin, and William Leach belonged to Captain Medad Hills' Company, enlisted in 1776.

William Stannard served in Captain Morris's Company, Bradley's Regiment, in 1781.

Richard Coit served in the 6th Troop in 1781, and in various regiments during the war.

David Goff and his son, served in the Northern Army in 1776.

The names here given are found on such of the muster and pay-rolls and other documents as are preserved in the state archives, the series of which is very imperfect, and embraces only a limited portion of the military service performed. Scarcely a vestige is found of the service of drafted militia, repeatedly called out from Litchfield County to Danbury. Horse Neck, Long Island, Peekskill, and other points on the North River, during the long, protracted struggle for the possession of the Highlands. Probably not an able-bodied man of the town failed of being called out more than once on this harrassing service.

The town records refer, in 1777, to "those who went out with Ensign Ozias Brownson last April, with Sergeant Timothy Benedict in August, and with Lieutenant Benedict;" in 1778, "to Sergeant Freedom Wright, and John Balcom, Jr., for doing a tour of duty last year in the Northern Army;" in 1780, "to those men who are or may be detailed with the army between the 1st day of June last and the 1st of January next." In 1781 it was voted to try to get Dolphin's son (a negro) " to count for Winchester," and " to make application to General Parsons, or some other general officer, to try to procure a pardon for Jonathan Preston, on account of his deserting the army," and " to raise a man to supply the place of George Hudson in the Continental Army." In 1782 it was voted " to hire the men now called for, for the guard at Horse Neck, and to fill the deficiencies in the Continental Army 'till December next."

Many other inhabitants, not named in any of the pay rolls or votes of the town referred to, are known to have been in the service.

John Church served in the Canada invasion under Arnold, and was in the battle at Saratoga.

Deacon Seth Hills served at Saratoga, and was present at Burgoyne's surrender.

Joseph Hoskin served as a trooper on Long Island, and was in the rear guard at the retreat from Brooklyn Heights.

Captain Moses Hatch enlisted at sixteen, and served through the war.*

A company of which John Hills was Captain, and Ozias Brownson Lieutenant, served at New York while General Putnam commanded in that department.

We have before us a "Muster Roll" of Captain John Hills' Company, for the year 1778, from which we copy the names, embracing all the subjects of military duty in the town at that period, though it is not supposed that all, or a major part of them, were on the special service at New York.

   Captain John Hills,
   Lieutenant Benjamin Benedict,
   Ensign Ozias Brownson,
   Sergeant Elisha Wilcoxson,
    " Jonathan Coe,
    " Eliphaz Alvord,
    " Joseph Frisbee,
   Corporal Samuel Hurlbut,
    " Abel Wetmore,
    " Josiah Smith,
    " John Wright,
   Fifer Belah Hills,
    " Levi Brownson,
   Drummer Joseph Dodge,
    " Andrew Avret,
    " John Austin.

---

* The late Dr. T. S. Wetmore informed the compiler that on the passage of the Revolutionary Pension Law, Captain Hatch made application for a pension, which was rejected for want of documentary proofs of his service. He was then advised by the Doctor to make another application, and to detail the events connected with his service, which might lead to his identification. It was drawn up by the Doctor, and among other incidents he related the occurrence of his capturing a Tory spy while on picket guard, and bringing him before his colonel, who instantly recognized the spy, and ordered him to be taken out and shot, remarking that the fellow had once betrayed him into the hands of the enemy, and tried his best to get him executed as a spy.

This application, with many others, remained undecided on the files of the War Department, until the Secretaryship of John C. Spencer, during President Tyler's administration, who determined to bring them to a final adjudication. While examining Captain Hatch's application, the identical colonel called on him on business. Mr. Spencer read him the statement, and enquired whether he remembered the circumstance. He replied, "Yes, I remember it well, and the name of the captor of the scoundrel was Moses Hatch, as good a soldier as ever shouldered a musket." The pension was at once awarded.

PRIVATES:

Daniel Andrus,
Eli Andrus,
Steven Arnold,
Joel Beach,
Nathan Balcom,
Jonathan Balcom,
John Balcom, Jr.,
John Beach,
Timothy Benedick,
Azariah Bradley,
Aaron Cook,
Hezekiah Elmer,
Remembrance Filley,
Daniel Grover,
Zimri Hills,
Chauncey Hills,
Seth Kellogg,
William Kies,
Ichabod Loomis,
Samuel McCune,
Gershom McCune, Jr.,
Reuben Miner,
Samuel Preston,
Joseph Plat,
Philip Priest,
William Fay,
Phineas Griswold,
Ambrose Palmer,
Reuben Sweet,
Peleg Sweet,
William Stannard,
Reuben Palmer,
Lazarus Palmer,
Lemuel Stannard, Jr.,
Jesse Wilkinson,
Reuben Wilkinson,

Reuben Tucker,
David Alvord,
Lemuel Walter,
John Walter,
James Stevenson,
Richard Coit,
Thomas Spencer,
Amasa Wade,
Joel Roberts,
Timothy Fay,
Steven Hurlbut,
Phineas Potter,
Preserved Crissee.
Abraham Andrews, Jr.,
John Austin, Jr.,
Samuel Mott,
Phineas Smith,
David Mills,
Daniel Corbin,
Simeon Hurlbut,
Samuel Roberts,
Elijah Castel,
Benjamin Palmer,
Silas Filer,
Peter Corbin, Jr.,
Samuel Castel,
Moses Derbye,
William Leach,
Isaac Filley,
John Spencer,
Moses Roberts,
Jacob Palmer,
Daniel Loomis,
Abner Coe,
John Church,
—— Palmer.

This list embraces but few of the names of those who served in the early part of the war, — while many of the names copied have either been canceled or encircled with lines, to indicate that by active service or for some other cause they had become exempt.

It is proper to say that some of the persons whose names have been extracted from the pay rolls, performed the services referred to before becoming inhabitants of the town.

On a general survey of the town at this period, it appears that the first or old Society was mainly settled; and had nearly as large a population as it has at the present time. Then, as now, the southern portion had a denser population than the northern, or Danbury quarter.

The portion of Winsted on or near the old North Road, was in a good measure settled, and inhabitants were thinly scattered along the Spencer Street Road, from Colebrook line down to the northern outskirt of the Borough of Winsted, and along the Still River valley from the crossing of the North road to Still River Bridge;—and a few families had located on the South Street road.

Deacon Austin had located himself and built his mill at the outlet of Long Lake, and a few other families had settled around him, but no settler had yet ventured down the hill into the savage and almost impenetrable valley now populated with more than three thousand inhabitants and active with a business exceeding that of any other village in the County.

CHAPTER XIV.

WINCHESTER SOCIETY CONTINUED.

1784 TO 1791.

In annual town meeting of this year, in addition to routine business, it was voted "That swine be free commoners, with a good and suitable yoke."

The society records show the doings of thirteen meetings during the year, none of which were of special interest. Efforts were made to collect arrearages on old rate bills, and a large number of them were wiped out by excusing the delinquents from payment. Six choristers were appointed, the difficulties between Mr. Knapp and disaffected parishioners were ventilated, and Rev. Messrs. Sherman of Goshen, Mills of Torringford, and Robbins of Norfolk were named as an advisory council "in matters between Mr. Knapp and y° Society;" Mr. Knapp's accounts were settled, and a three and three-quarter-penny tax was laid to pay up the arrearages found due him. A place for building a new meeting house had been established by the county court, which, not proving acceptable, a new location was agreed on (by a vote of 33 to 16), near the burying ground, and then a new locating committee was appointed, whose doings were accepted, but it does not appear what place was designated.

The new comers of the year 1784 were as follows:—

DAVID GAYLORD from Cambridge, Hartford County, had an interest in the two wedge lots adjoining Colebrook line, at the northwest corner of the town. In 1792, in his deed conveying away these lots, he is named of Bristol. There was said to have been a man of this name who kept a tavern in that region in early times.

SAMUEL HAWLEY from Salisbury, owned the farm in Danbury Quarter a little north of the burying ground, afterwards occupied by his son-in-law, John Benedict, and recently owned by William Price. He died on this farm, February 10, 1820, aged 74. He married July 30, 1782, Rebecca Taylor, who died March 9, 1820, aged 69.

DIDYMUS SHEPARD, named of Winchester, was tried before Justice Alvord, February 5, 1784, for "prophane swearing," and on his plea of guilty was fined 6s., and costs 2s. On April 26 following, he was again brought before Esquire Alvord, and tried for a like offence, on his plea of not guilty, whereupon he was acquitted, and ordered to be dismissed *on paying the cost of prosecution,* taxed at £1 0s. 6d., and to stand committed until the costs were paid. As his name no where else appears, it is probable that he fled the town through fear of another acquittal!

PELEG SWEET, named of Torrington, July 10, 1784, and of Winchester, August 24, 1785, owned and lived on the Harry Brooks Farm, Danbury Quarter, until 1807, when he moved to Ashtabula, Ohio. The house he occupied is believed to be the wing of the present residence of Mr. Brooks. He married November 20, 1777, Mary Wilkinson.

CHILDREN.

I. LORRAIN, b. September 17, 1778; m. October 6, 1799, Huldah Benedict, and had one child, Candace, b. April 22, 1800.
II. SUSANNA, b. December 6, 1780.
III. ISAAC, b. March 13, 1783.
IV. MARY, b. March 11, 1785.
V. CLARISSA, b. March 13, 1787; d. August 19, 1797.
VI. ARA (twin), b. February 13, 1789.
VII. IRA (twin), b. February 13, 1789.
VIII. LEWIS, b. April 7, 1791.
IX. FREDERICK ALDRIDGE, b. June 10, 1793.
X. PELEG, b. August 10, 1795.
XI. CLARISSA, b. August 19, 1797.
XII. WILLARD, . b. March 13, 1800.

1785.

No business of special interest was transacted in the town meetings of this year.

The Society held eleven meetings during the year, with a view to locating and building a new meeting-house. A location would be fixed at one meeting, and reconsidered, and a new one established at another, and then the doings of the second meeting reconsidered, and the first location re-established. The size of the house to be erected was first fixed at 46 by 56 feet, then it was changed to 50 by 40, and then four feet was added to the length, and then a tax of one shilling on the pound was voted, and a committee appointed to apply to the Assembly for power to tax non-resident landowners eightpence on the acre. A building committee was appointed, who were instructed "to carry on the building forthwith." At this stage of the business, a new meeting was held, which reconsidered the previous doings, and petitioned the Assembly to free the Society from public taxes, until it can build a meeting-house.

A subsequent meeting instructed Mr. Hurlbut " to repair the old meeting house, viz. : lay down boards on the joists, that people may sit above; also, make a ladder or stairs to go up into the upper part of the meeting-house, and make seats to sit on above, and that he do the same at the cost of the Society." The old meeting-house, of unknown origin, and located nearly a mile south of the present center, has been already described.* It would be incredible that such a place "for men to sit above," as was constructed pursuant to the foregoing vote, could have been resorted to, were not the frame of the structure still† a standing witness to the fact that the attic gallery existed, with the rafters coming down to the floor, the floor having an opening of not more than nine feet square over the pulpit, through which the good Parson Knapp was required to throw up his preaching to the hungry sinners who had made their venturous way up the outside ladder, through a gable door, into this cock-loft. It is equally hard to conceive that three readers and four or five choristers should be needed to conduct the psalm-singing in a building of such modest dimensions.

The conflicting votes above referred to were all adopted between the first of January and last of May. In September it was voted "to build a meeting house near the crotch of the roads by Mr. Hurlbut's, at a stake and stones within Doctor Everitt's home lot, about twelve or fifteen rods from his dwelling house, if on application made to the county court said place shall be established," and " if the court do not establish the above-mentioned place, to apply for a new committee."

October 6, five choristers were appointed, and the vote to build the meeting house on the spot designated was reiterated.

December 12 it was voted to build, cover, and close it in, and lay the lower floor by the first of the following October; also, "to raise one shilling on the pound of the list of August, 1785, to be paid in good pine boards, or whitewood clapboards, or neat cattle, or labor, or good pine shingles, the boards and shingles to be delivered by ye 10th day of June next, and what is not paid by said 10th of June, to be paid in beef cattle by y^r 10th day of October next, and ye above articles to be delivered at ye meeting house spot."

The building spot selected, and on which the new house was erected, and in process of time completed, was on the green nearly in front of the dwelling of Theron Bronson, Esq. The ground was then covered with a heavy growth of chestnut trees.

1785.

The new comers of this year were as follows :—

SALMON HAWLEY from Stratford, who built and lived in the first

---

* Page 78.

† This paragraph was written before the building fell, in 1867.

house above the Dugway, on the old Winchester road, lately owned by Sophronia Leonard, and now torn down. He sold out in 1795, and his name is not found on the tax list afterwards. He married Jane ———.

CHILDREN.

I. Jerusha,	b. in Stratford,	January 28, 1778.	
II Wm. Salmon,	b.	"	December 25, 1779.
III. Eunice,	b.	"	April 20, 1782.
IV. Susanna,	b.	"	March 9, 1784.
V. James,	b. in Winchester,	April 27, 1786.	
VI. Daniel,	b.	"	February 16, 1789.
VII. Avis,	b.	"	May 17, 1793.

Charles Kent, who lived in Hall Meadow, near Rufus Drake's, until 1787, was fined for profane swearing in 1787, and is described as an absconding debtor in 1788.

Zeba Meacham is on the tax list of this year, and onward to 1789. He owned land on the old south road, north of the Everitt place.

Simeon Moore, Jr., son of Simeon of Windsor, this year received by conveyance from his father the James Crocker farm, and other adjacent lands. He lived in the Crocker house (now torn down), at the parting of the old Waterbury Turnpike from the Green Woods Turnpike, until about 1808, when he removed to Ohio. His wife, Hannah, died October 22, 1794.

CHILDREN.

I. Lovina,	b. April 16, 1786 ; m. Elijah Benedict.
II. Wealthy,	b. March 24, 1789.
III. Simeon,	b. June 8, 1791.
IV. Hannah,	b. January 15, 1794.

Captain John Nash[6] came from Torrington to Winchester in early life, and for many years followed the joiner's trade, after which he became a highly respected and wealthy farmer. He first owned and occupied a house at the center, afterward burned down, which stood on the site of Rev. Frederick Marsh's residence. He afterward built and occupied during his remaining life the house now owned by his son, Alva Nash, Esq., half a mile north of the center. He was a man of pure life and kind heart, universally respected, and often employed in the affairs of the town.

He was born in West Hartford, July 18, 1758, son of John[5] (born December 1, 1728), and Mary (Graves) Nash ; g. son of Moses[4] (born Hadley, July 2, 1696), and Rebecca (Kellogg) Nash; g.g. son of Lieutenant John[3] and Elizabeth (Kellogg) Nash ; g.g.g. son of Timothy[2] (born 1626) and Rebecca (Stone) Nash, and g.g.g.g. son of Thomas[1] and Margery Nash, who were among the first settlers of New Haven. He married Esther Whiting, born Torrington, September 13, 1763, daughter of Benjamin and Esther Whiting. She died March 4, 1835, aged 71 years; he died October 21, 1835, aged 77 years.

CHILDREN.

I, Lucy,[7]   b. May 8, 1783; m. December, 1801, John Wetmore.
II. Hannah,[7]   b. December 23, 1787; m. October 22, 1811; Wm. Crum.
III. Alvah,[7]   b. September 26, 1793.
IV. Mary Graves,[7]   b. January 21, 1797; m. 1819, October 27, Calvin Sage of Colebrook.
V. Nancy,[7]   b. June 2, 1801; m. May 30, 1827, Stephen Monson.
VI. Samuel John,[7]   b. September 25, 1806; d. September 8, 1808.

Alva Nash,[7] Esq., a clothier and farmer, resides in the paternal homestead, half a mile north of the center. He has twice represented the town in the General Assembly, and has held the office of justice of the peace. He married March 16, 1819, Rebecca Sage.

CHILDREN.

I Susan Rebecca,   b. October 12, 1820; m. November 4, 1845, Isaac A. Bronson. She d. April 7, 1857.
II. Lorenzo Samuel,   b. December 30, 1823; m. January, 1852, Caroline E. Tuller.

Daniel Sandiforth's name is on the tax list of this year. He was son of the wife of Reuben Miner by her first husband, and is believed to have removed to New Hartford.

Nathan L. Wade's name is also on the tax list of this year.

Justus Wright, a carpenter, who was of Torrington, December 29, 1783, was named in the tax list of 1785. He owned and occupied the former homestead of Aaron Cook in Blue Street, which he sold in 1795; he married December 2, 1784, Abigail Blackman; had son, Calvin, born October 5, 1785.

The freemen admitted this year were William Castel and Bela Hills.

1786.

The following vote in town meeting this year, indicates a prudent care of the people to prevent improper allowances, by the Selectmen, of claims against the town.

Voted, that not any person whatever, who shall do any service for the town the present year, shall be allowed to receive any reward therefor, until he shall exhibit his account before the next annual town meeting, and have his account allowed by said meeting.

Another, appointing a committee "to examine into the debts due to and from the town, and make out an exact statement of accounts respecting the town's debts and credits and lay the same before the next town meeting," seems to show that the chronic tendency of the town's affairs to get into a snarl, had an early beginning.

The Society, this year, voted a tax of 3 pence on the Pound, to enable the meeting house committee to procure glass and nails; — to be paid in beef, cattle or pork, or flax seed, or one-quarter of it in butter or cheese, at the current market price, or in cash at a deduction of 10 per cent.

The electors admitted this year were John Wright, Martin North, Jr., and Richard Coit.

The new comers of the year were:

WILLIAM KEYES, whose name is on the tax list of 1786, resided in the town until near the close of the last century. He is named of Torrington in 1797. He owned in 1786, for about a year, nineteen acres of land in the vicinity of Alva Nash; and afterward had an interest in land on the Green Woods turnpike, near the Green Woods Hotel. He married, January 2, 1777, Seba Smith.

CHILDREN.

I. WILLIAM,[2]   b. Jan. 12, 1778.
II. PRUDENCE,[2] b. Dec. 7, 1779.
III. SALLY,[2]   b. " 24, 1783.
IV. TRUMBULL,[2] b. Oct. 3, 1787.

WILLIAM KEYES,[2] married, November 23, 1797, Anna, daughter of John Sweet; lived in the house at the east corner of Lake and Rockwell streets, and died about 1800, leaving a son, William. She married (2d), Rev. Daniel Coe.

LONDON, OR LUNNON, a negro, a resident of the town, was, this year, brought before Justice Alvord on a complaint for breach of the peace. The complaint was quashed. He had wife Phillis.

1787.

A petition was brought to the October session of the General Assembly of 1786, for incorporating the east part of Winchester and the part of Barkhamsted west of Farmington River as a town, which was continued through the years 1787 and 1788, and finally rejected. In the annual town meeting of this year the town voted its assent to the prayer of the petition, provided the new town should not extend westerly beyond the Long Pond and the west boundary of the second tier; which would have excluded all the inhabitants on Coe Street, north of the Indian Meadow bridge.

The following document was entered on the Society records of this year.

Winchester, October 9th, 1786. This may certify that I have received from the Society's Committee in full all that was due me from the Society, from the beginning of the world to the year 1782.

Witness my hand,   JOSHUA KNAPP.

The following freemen were admitted this year: John Marshall, Abraham Andrews, Jr., John Nash, William Chamberlin, Ozias Brownson, Jr., Lemuel Bassett, and Martin Hurlbut.

Only one new resident of Winchester Society is found this year, while the new comers into Winsted were more numerous than in any previous year.

DAVID HUNGERFORD, of that part of Farmington which is now Bristol, was a soldier in the French war, and died near Saratoga, New York, of camp fever, aged 45 years. He had five children, of whom David died about the same time as his father, of the same disease, aged 18. Joel and Jonah settled in Watertown, Connecticut, and had families. Ann married Rev. Mr. Tiler, and was the youngest.

REUBEN HUNGERFORD, born in Bristol September 9, 1748; married, April —, 1776, Olive Gaylord, born June 24, 1760. He bought land in Winchester, February 4, 1780, when he was named of Farmington; again June 14, 1783, when he was of Norfolk; and September 6, 1787 he was of Winchester, and so appears by frequent deeds thereafter. He first lived near the Norfolk line, until April 6, 1795, he bought of Moses Wright, of Colebrook, the place directly opposite the Green Woods Hotel, where he spent the rest of his life.* He served three months in the war

---

* He was a man of great energy and marked peculiarities. The story is told of an assessment in old Winchester for building the second meeting house, in which he was assessed beyond all reason by the committee appointed for that purpose. At the meeting to which the committee reported their assessments, Mr. Hungerford protested in his nervous Saxon that he wouldn't pay such an extortionate assessment, — that they might build their own meeting house; — and he would go down to Noppit to meeting. The meeting was adjourned without action on the subject matter for a week. At the adjourned meeting Mr. Hungerford entered another appearance with a changed mind. "Mr. Moderator," said he, "I told you t'other day I'd go to Noppit to meeting before I'd pay my tax. I've been thinkin' it over since, — and I now think, for a man who haint got no religion to go deviling off down to Noppit to get it, is a mean business. I won't do it, but I'll pay my tax like a man."

of the revolution. He died November 10, 1828. His wife was the professional mid-wife of the region, attending all calls, and often riding six or eight miles on horse back, with one of her own nursing babes in her arms, until incapacitated by age. Her last professional service being at the birth of George E. Woodford, March 27, 1836, when she had to be carried in a rocking-chair. She is entitled to this notice for assisting the compiler of these annals into the world in 1799. She died in Winchester July 6, 1839, aged 79.

CHILDREN.

I. LOIS, b. in Winchester, Jan. 29, 1777; m. Nov. 20, 1794, Joseph Cowles; they were among the first settlers of Austinburgh, Ohio in 1801. She d. March 9, 1841.
II. POLLY, m. Shubael Coy, settled in Oxford, N. Y., where she d. in 1832.
III. AMOS, b. Dec. 17, 1781; m. 1814, Betsey Latourette; settled at Mt. Morris, N. Y. He d. May 6, 1861.
IV. CHAUNCEY, b. ; d. aged 7 years.
V. REUBEN, b. June 3, 1786; d. Jan. 27, 1809.
VI. OLIVE, b. April 19, 1788; m. Noah North; settled in Alexander, N. Y., where he d. Sept. 28, 1824, and she March 11, 1849.
VII. SALLY, b. Feb. 12, 1790; m. Jan. 23, 1813, Halsey Phillips; settled in Colebrook, Ohio; she d. Feb. 2, 1867.
VIII. ANN, b. April 5, 1793; m. Salmon Drake; she d. Aug. 26, 1866, leaving a son Henry Hungerford, b. Feb. 21, 1833, who m. May 18, 1862, Mariam Roberts, b. in Colebrook, Sept. 7, 1840.

CHILDREN.

1. George F., b. May 12, 1864.
2. Anna, b. Sept. 8, 1866.

IX. LUCINDA (twin), b. Dec. 30, 1794; m. April, 1825, Ethan Pendleton; she d. in Norfolk, June 29, 1829.
X. DELINDA (twin), b. Dec. 30, 1794; d. Jan. 10, 1809, of hydrocephalus.
XI. CANDACE, b. Sept. 5, 1798; m. May 19, 1819, Samuel D. Gilbert; she d. June 17, 1840.
XII. AMANDA, b. Sept. 16, 1801; d. unmarried, Feb. 26, 1847.
XIII. CHAUNCEY, b. March 11, 1803; m. April 20, 1825, Cynthia Allen, b. Oct. 22, 1804; settled in Mt. Morris, N. Y.

1788.

The town manifested its appreciation of the services of its officers and agents, by the following vote in annual meeting this year:

Voted, that none that shall do business for the town, in the town, the year ensuing, shall have any wages therefor, except one meal of victuals a day.

In Society meeting, a tax of 1½ pence on the pound was laid, "to enable the Meeting House Committee to pay the debts they have contracted

for building the meeting house, and also to procure glass for the glazing of the meeting house, to be paid by the 15th day of December next."
This is the only record indicating the progress thus far made in the work, which by a former vote was directed to be finished by 1st October, 1786.

The freemen admitted this year were, Justus Wright, Samuel Roberts, Peter Blackman, John Videto, Christopher Whiting, Levi Wilkinson, Joel Coe, Zalmon Benedict, and Jesse Hills.

The new comers were as follows:

ZALMON BENEDICT, son of Silas Benedict, from Danbury, who was killed in the Wyoming massacre. He returned with his mother to Danbury, and thence removed to Winchester this year as is supposed. He first lived in a log house in Danbury quarter, some thirty rods south of the iron mine; afterward on Taylor's Brook near Torrington line,—and after 1805, in Danbury quarter, not far from the burying ground. He m. Chloe Perry, of Danbury.

CHILDREN.

 I. JOHN,[2]   b. Oct. 22, 1789.
 II. LOVISA,[2]   b. Nov. 12, 1791; m. Feb. 2, 1820, Norman Baldwin.
 III. RUAMA,[2]   b. June 1, 1794; m. — Pratt.

JOHN BENEDICT,[2] resided on the Samuel Hawley place, 100 rods north of the Danbury Burying Ground, till about 1869, and now lives in Norfolk. He m. Jan. 30, 1811, Rebecca, dau. of Samuel Hawley; she d. May 10, 1857.

CHILDREN.

 I. SAMUEL HAWLEY,   b. Jan. 25, 1814; m. Lavina Canfield.
 II. LAURA,   b.   1816; m. Samuel Hart.
 III. LYMAN,   b.   1818; m. Polly Simons.
 IV. CAROLINE,   b.   1820; m. William Price.
 V. WILLIAM,   b.   1822.
 VI. HELEN.   b. Aug. 13, 1838; m. Newman B. Gilbert.

NATHAN BROUGHTON lived until 1792 in a log house on Sucker Brook road, near the house built by James B. White, now owned by Fittus Stack. He probably left the town before 1800. He had wife, Elizabeth.

CHILDREN.

 I. CHARLES,   b. Jan. 23, 1782.
 II. MARY,   b. Sept. 17, 1784.
 III. DARIUS CLARK,   b. Aug. 31, 1786; d. Sept. 5, 1788.
 IV. NATHAN,   b. July 31, 1788.

V. Darius Clark, b. Nov. 14, 1790.
VI. Uriel, b. Oct. 12, 1792.
VII. Esther, b. Aug. 13, 1794.

Ephraim Foot, from Colchester, owned and lived on the Edward Rugg Farm, in Danbury Quarter, from 1788 to 1795, after which he removed to Hamilton, Herkimer Co., N. Y.

Roswell Grant, son of Elijah Grant of Norfolk, resided until 1804 in the northwest corner of the town, on part of the Richard Beckley farm, and afterward lived for many years on the same farm in Norfolk. He was a large farmer and laborious man, honest and conscientious in a way of his own. Having carelessly left his barn doors open through a mid winter night, he punished himself the night following by again opening them and sitting in the draft of a bitter northwest wind until morning. In his declining years he became poor, and worked in Winsted as a hired man. Such was his love for work, that he would steal off on Sundays and hoe his pious employer's potatoes, without his knowledge, and without compensation.

He joined the Continental Army when seventeen years old, and endured hard service with characteristic fortitude. When Baron Steuben was selecting his corps for special discipline, he passed in front of Grant's company while on parade. Grant was surprised to find himself the only man taken from the company, being, as he said, "such a little nubbin' of a fellow, I had no idea he would take me." While in the Highlands, he was posted as guard on one of the bleakest points, in extremely cold weather; the army moved, without recalling him, but he stuck to his post till relieved, two days after.

Going to Litchfield in his advanced life, on foot, a neighbor entrusted him with a letter to be delivered there. He had reached within a mile of his home, after dark, on his return, when he discovered that he had brought the letter back. He immediately turned and walked fourteen miles to Litchfield, delivered the letter, and came home before daylight the next morning.

He m. Anna Coy, who d. March —, 1810, aged 50 years; and he m. (2d) May 16, 1811, Mrs. Elizabeth Lawrence. She d. Oct. 6, 1815, aged 45. He d. July 7, 1837, aged nearly 75 years.

CHILDREN.

I. Mahala, b. Norfolk, July 31, 1785; m. Elijah Pinney.
II. Amarilla Minerva, b. N., March —, 1789; d. W., Ap. 23, 1852, unm.
III. Deidamia A., b. N., May —, 1794; m. Edwin M. Strong.
IV. Sage Washington, b. N., Aug. 13, 1800; m. Lucy Spaulding of New Marlborough, Mass. He d. W., Nov. 4, 1866. She m. (2d) Roswell Smith. They had a son, Ward Grant, now living.

CHILDREN BY SECOND WIFE.

V. A Daughter (twin), b. N., Feb. 11, 1812.
VI. Anna Elizabeth (twin), b. N., Feb. 11, 1812.

Hewitt Hills, son of Medad, of Goshen, a large farmer, and prominent business man of the town, this year settled on the farm, and built the house thereon, now owned by Henry Drake on Blue Street, near Torrington line. He was a representative to the General Assembly between 1790 and 1800, and filled at various times most of the town offices.

In company with Thomas Spencer, Jr., about 1796, he built and traded in the building on Lake Street, where the depot of the Conn. Western R. R. now stands. He was a man of good person and address, shrewd in his business, and influential in the community. He removed to Vernon, Oneida Co., N. Y., about 1805. No record of his family is found, except the following marriages of his daughters.

I. Lucy Hills, m. May 28, 1795, Thomas Spencer, Jr.
II. Mary Hills, m. Nov. 16, 1797, Abijah Brownson.
III. Eliza Hills, m. ——— Isaac Brownson.
IV. Louisa Hills, m. March, 1802, Stephen Wade.

Jacob Kimberly is named of Goshen, in a deed of January 23, 1788, conveying to him a half acre lot, with a house thereon, on the west side of the Hall Meadow stream near Torrington line, which he thereafter occupied until 1791 or later. He was of Goshen in 1794, of Winchester in 1801, of Torrington in 1802, when he bought the farm now owned by Amanda Church, on the Little Pond road, near Green Woods Turnpike, and resided there until 1804, and then bought and occupied the George Raymond farm on Wallen's Hill, which he sold to Jesse Clarke in 1805. He was living in Otis, Mass., in 1815. He was a convivial man, of great humor. His witty sayings are still quoted by the old people in this community.

Jacob Kimberly, Jr., in 1800, became the owner of the old Caleb Beach place, in Hall Meadow, and resided there until his death, December 24, 1813. He married June 11, 1797, Nancy Pond.

CHILDREN.

I. Laura, b. April 15, 1798.
II. Freelove, b. November 2, 1799; d. September 17, 1801.
III. Olive, b. April 14, 1801; d. November 3, 1808.
IV. Freelove, b. January 21, 1804.
V. Horace Sidney, b. July 26, 1805.
VI. Esther Emily, b. June 22, 1807.

VII. MARY MEHITABEL, b. March 17, 1810.
VIII. SILAS, b. April 29, 1812 ; d. December 6, 1812.
IX. JACOB HARVEY, b. November 8, 1813.

JOEL AND ELISHA KIMBERLY, sons of Jacob, Senr., received from him a deed of land in 1802, east of Green Woods Turnpike, opposite the Little Pond Road Bridge over Mad River, which they parted with in 1804, and are no more found on the records.

DAVID MURRAY, a Scotch-Irishman, was assessed on the list of this year. In 1789, his wife, Sarah, became the owner of a lot, with a log shanty thereon, on the easterly side of the Dugway road, nearly opposite Mrs. Sopronia Leonard's, in which they lived until 1793, or later. It is believed that they removed to Vernon, N. Y.

Their son, William, had a family, and lived in various parts of Winsted, until he removed to Colebrook about 1840. He married, not far from 1806, Ann Hewitt.

HEMAN SMITH, from Goshen, this year bought and moved on to the farm of Noah Gleason, on the south part of Blue Street, which he occupied until 1801, when he sold out to Isaac Brownson, and removed to Vernon, N. Y. He was a man highly esteemed, prominent in town affairs, and three times a representative of the town between 1795 and 1800. He was a son of Stephen Smith from Farmington, was born in Goshen, and married Hannah Dunning. He left no record of his family in Winchester.

1789.

The records of town meetings this year embrace routine business only. No freemen were admitted.

Eleven society meetings were held. Much action was had on the matter of arrearages in the collection of society rates. Numbers who were too poor to pay were excused, and those delinquents not excused were allowed to pay in good merchantable sheep at a penny a pound, in lambs at a penny and a farthing, in good well-washed wool at sixteen pence, to be delivered to the Society's Committee at the parsonage by the 29th of June.

A bad habit of unpunctual attendance at society meetings was attempted to be corrected by a vote "that all society meetings to be hereafter held, either by warning or adjournment, shall be opened within one hour after the time appointed," and "that no vote passed in such meetings after sun setting shall be deemed a legal vote."

The absence of any allusion to discontent with Mr. Knapp for a few years past seemed to indicate a wearing away of old grudges. We are therefore surprised to find the following vote of July 17 :—

Voted—That Lieutenant Samuel Hurlbut, John Minor, Levi Norton, Thomas Spencer, and Huitt Hills, be a committee to attend with the Church Committee in stating the matters of grievance with Rev. Mr. Knapp's past conduct. July 24 it was voted, to lay our matters of difficulty between Mr. Knapp and the Church and Society before the Association, and to invite the Association to meet at the house of Levi Brownson, on Tuesday, three weeks from next Tuesday, at 11 A.M. August 19 it was voted "that it shall be lawful to transact business in this meeting until midnight," and before midnight it was voted to accept the advice of the Association.

What causes of grievance were presented, and what advice was given, does not appear, either on the society or church records, but probably a dismission was recommended, as it was voted, September 8, to join with the church in calling the Consociation to dismiss Rev. Mr. Knapp from his pastoral charge on the day appointed by the church, the second Tuesday of October next. On the church records is entered a request of Mr. Knapp, and a vote of concurrence by the church, passed on the day assigned for meeting of Consociation, that the pastoral relation of Mr. Knapp to the church should be dissolved.

"Mr. Knapp was a talented preacher, and a good man. He retained the affection of a large portion of his people as long as he lived ; preached to them whenever he visited the town during his labors in other fields ; came back among them to spend the last years of his life, and had a handsome stone erected over his grave by his life-long friends."

The new comers of this year were as follows :—

FRANCIS BACON, named " of Farmington," bought, August 21, 1789, a forty-one-acre lot between Harvey L. Andrews' and the Bragg house, on which he probably lived until 1794, when his name last appears on the tax list. He is named of Barkhamsted in 1798.

JOHN BACON'S name appears on the tax list of this year. He lived on a lot immediately south of the one owned by Francis Bacon, which came by inheritance to his wife, Sarah, from her father, Joseph Foot of Simsbury. They sold out in 1798, and left the town. He married, January 4, 1782, Sarah Foot.

CHILDREN.

I. SARAH, b. July 31, 1785.
II. ABIAH, (dau.) b. April 10, 1788.
III. LAURA, b. August 18, 1790.

IV. John,   b. November 7, 1792.
V. Seth,   b. December 8, 1794.
VI. George, b. March 23, 1797.

Levi Brownson 2d, son of Ozias, before referred to, this year purchased the first portion of his large farm, on which he afterwards lived until his death, October 16, 1846, in the red house on the Norfolk road, near the extreme northeast corner of Goshen. He was connected with his brothers Asahel and Isaac in trade, at the center, for several years early in this century.

David Deer's name is on the tax list of this year, and is not found elsewhere.

John Lucas, son of Thomas Lucas of Goshen, came from Norfolk to this town this year, and bought and occupied the Roswell Coe farm, subsequently owned by Amasa Wade, Jr., being lot 42, second division. He sold out and moved to Blanford, Mass., about 1808, where he died three or four years later. For more than half of the last twenty years of his life he was so deranged as to need confinement. According to record of Deacon L. M. Norton he married Jerusha Coe of Torrington, and had

CHILDREN.

I. Roxana, b. September 12, 1765; m. N. Stanley Parmelee.
II. Esther, b. July —, 1768; m. Thadeus Fay, and Ira Gleason.
III. Jerusha, b.   , 1770; m. Thomas Porter; d. 1837.
IV. Thomas, b. April —, 1784; m. Hannah Turner.

Deacon Levi Platt came from Danbury to this town when a boy, with Joseph Elmer, of whom he learned the blacksmith's trade. He was a schoolmaster in his early manhood. In 1790 he bought of Martin Hurlbut, land now composing, it is believed, part of the farm of Harvey Andrews, — on which he lived until about 1794, when he bought, and occupied during his remaining life, the farm recently owned by his son, Sylvester Platt, Esq., now deceased. He died August 14, 1856, aged 91.

Deacon Platt was a Puritan of the Puritans; firm as the everlasting hills in his political and religious principles; and withal, a man of humble, sincere piety, faithful to every duty as a father, a church member, and citizen of the town. He succeeded his father-in-law, Eliphaz Alvord, as Town Clerk and Register, and as Deacon of the Congregational Church, and was a member of the Convention of 1818, which formed our State Constitution.

His Pastor, Rev. Frederick Marsh, thus speaks of him in 1852: "This truly venerable and patriarchal man still lives among us. At the age of

86 he enjoys good health, retains in an unusual degree his mental powers, reads much, and converses sensibly and interestingly. It is now 68 years since he joined the church by profession. In the education of his family, in his observance of the Sabbath, attendance on public worship, regard for the institutions and duties of religion, and general course of life, Deacon Platt has been a striking representative of the Puritan character. He and his wife both united with the church before they were 19 years old, and six or seven of his children became hopefully pious before they were twenty-three years old." He m. Feb. 5, 1792, Esther Alvord, dau. Eliphaz, Esq. She d. March 28, 1840. He d. Aug. 14, 1856, aged 91.

CHILDREN.

I. ABI, b. July 25, 1793; m. Jan. 7, 1850, Hiram Royce of Norfolk.
II. ELIPHAZ ALVORD, b. May 3, 1796; d. May 7, 1807.
III. EZRA HART, b. Sept. 18, 1798.
IV. SYLVESTER, b. May 17, 1800.
V. LEVI, b. April 11, 1802; m. Parmela R. Munger; went to Collinsville, Conn., and thence to Hartford, where he now resides.
VI. LUCY, b. Oct. 31, 1804; m. March 10, 1847, Hiram Royce of Norfolk.
VII. ELIZABETH, b. Sept. 19, 1806.
VIII. ELIPHAZ ALVORD, b. Feb. 6, 1809.
IX. WILLIAM, b. Dec. 16, 1816; d. Feb. 28, 1840.

SYLVESTER PLATT resided on the farm owned by his father, until some three years before his death; he filled the office of Justice of the Peace and Town Representative, besides other minor stations, and died at Winsted, Sept. 18, 1870. He m., Norfolk, Sept. 4, 1833, Mary, dau. of Wilcox Phelps.

CHILDREN.

I. LEVI WILCOX, b. Aug. 27, 1834; d. Dec. 9, 1844.
II. HELEN REBECCA, b. Sept. 6, 1837; d. Jan. 19, 1840.
III. EDWIN SYLVESTER, b. Sept. 30, 1839; m. Feb. 12, 1863, Elizabeth Brooks.

LEVI PLATT, Jr., m. Pamelia R. Munger.

CHILDREN.

I. HELEN ESTHER, b. Dec. 27, 1824.
II. RUTHY SMITH, b. Oct. 10, 1826.
III. ELIZABETH, b. Sept. 5, 1828.
IV. MARY JANE, b. Aug. 22, 1831.

DANIEL THOMPSON, named of Wethersfield, in a deed of land to his wife, Hannah, lived on the Brooks street road, above the old Everitt house, until 1793. He m. Nov. 2, 1788, Roxy Smith.

CHILDREN.

I. HULDAH, b. Nov. 15, 1790.
II. ROXALANA, b. Sept. 20, 1791.

1790.

The matter of incorporating the Society of Winsted, as a Town, was again ventilated in Town Meeting this year; and a vote of acquiescence was passed, in case the dividing line should run northerly along the reservation in the second tier, to Mad River, and thence, along the east line of the tier, to Colebrook. This line would cross the Pond Stream, near Hurlbut's Forge, thence diagonally, through Meadow Street, to Mad River, a little east of Dudley's Tannery, and thence along the Street Hill range, a division "not fit to be made." The General Assembly failed to pass the act of incorporation; and it is believed that no petition has since been carried to the Legislature for a division of the town. No freemen were admitted this year.

The Society of Winchester, being without a Pastor, devoted itself assiduously to finding and settling a successor to Mr. Knapp. Fortunately they were spared the calamity of a succession of candidates, and the consequent dissensions growing out of divided preferences. Parish hunters were rare in those days; for the supply of ministers was hardly equal to the demand; and the salaries given, or promised, in the new towns, offered small inducements to the class of men caring more for the fleece than for the flock.

It was the custom of those days for a vacant parish to apply to neighboring ministers for advice in the selection of a candidate for settlement, and to employ only such as were thus accredited.

Fathers Mills of Torringford, and Robbins of Norfolk were repeatedly called in during the year, to help on and guide the church and society in wooing their new spouse. Early in January, Rev. Publius V. Booge (pronounced Bogue), a graduate of Yale, in the class of 1787, was applied to, "to preach with us on probation." This application was repeated in April, and Messrs. Robbins and Mills were invited to come and counsel with them on the 26th. On that day the society voted "to continue Mr. Publius Virgilius Booge to preach with us longer with a view for a settlement, if hereafter he and we should agree." Another very provident vote was passed at the same meeting in these words: " that the Committee be directed not to contract with Mr. Booge, unless he will agree to receive for his pay not more than one quarter part thereof in cash, and less, if the committee can agree with him to take less, — and the remainder in the produce of our farms."

June 21 and 25, it was voted, " to invite Mr. Booge, to preach with us four Sabbaths, after the time expires for which he is now engaged at New Cambridge," and " that the committee invite the inhabitants of the north part of Torrington" (the " Noppit," or " Newfield " people) " to apply, if they see cause, to the General Assembly to annex them to this society.

September 1st, it was voted to give Mr. Booge a call, with a " settlement" of one hundred and fifty pounds, and a salary of seventy-five pounds a year. This vote was modified September 6th, so as to make the Settlement payable in three successive annual installments of fifty pounds each, — and to be payable in neat cattle, good merchantable shipping horses, and sheep, at current market prices ; — the settlement to be absolute in case he continued in the pastorate fifteen years ; — if not, then he was to refund ten pounds a year for such time as falls short of fifteen years ; — and that the salary should be paid, four-fifths of seventy pounds in farm produce, and one-fifth thereof in cash, — the remaining five pounds to be paid in wood at four shillings (67 cents) a cord, in eight feet lengths, delivered at the parsonage.

October 8th, Messrs. Robbins and Mills were again called in to the meeting, and the proceedings of the two previous meetings were laid before them for their advice thereon ; — after which a formal vote was taken to settle Mr. Booge according to the modified terms above. The result was, twenty-eight affirmative, five negative, and four " neuter " votes. It was then voted to send to the Association for advice and to desire Messrs. Robbins and Mills to write to Mr. Booge to meet a Committee of the Society, and wait on the Association for their advice.

It was voted, October 21st, to accept the advice of the Association and that the Committee wait on Mr. Booge as quick as may be, and see if he is suited with the proposals, and ascertain what alteration, if any, he would choose.

November 15, the terms of the settlement were so altered as to exclude horses, and stand for cattle and sheep only, — and that the time and mode of delivery should be made more specific. The farm products were specified to be Wheat, Rye, Indian Corn, Oats, Flax, Beef, Pork, Tallow, Butter, and Cheese. The refunding of a portion of his settlement was to be contingent on his failing to serve in this ministry fifteen years, by reason of death or otherwise, if he be the blamable cause of separation ; — this question to be determined by a mutual council.

November 30th, the several votes respecting settlement and salary, as amended and modified, were consolidated into one clear, formal vote, which was duly passed, and all former votes in reference thereto were reconsidered, annulled and made void, — and the Committee were directed to lay before Mr. Booge the doings of the meeting. They were also directed to furnish Rev. Mr. Robbins with copies of the votes of the Church and Society, to be laid before the Examining Committee of the Association.

December 27th, the provisions of the amended vote were so altered as to change the time of delivery of the farm products, — and so to change the wood contract as to make the supply twenty-five cords per year without reference to price; — and the Committee were directed to lay the newly amended vote before Mr. Booge, — and in case of his approval thereof, to invite him into the meeting to agree with them on a time for ordination. The result of these votes, and the conference with Mr. Booge were, that the 12th of January, 1791, was fixed on for the ordination, and that the Consociation meet at the house of Major Brownson, and that he make provision for their entertainment.

The ordination did not come off on the 12th of January, as voted; probably by reason of Mr. Booge's hesitation to accede to the terms of settlement, so painfully and carefully elaborated. On that day it was voted "that the Committee wait on Mr. Booge and request his answer whether he will settle with us in the work of the ministry," — an adjournment of half an hour, — and then another of eight minutes, — was had; — after which the 26th of January was fixed for the ordination — a day of fasting and prayer was appointed for the 18th, and Rev. Messrs. Robbins and Mills were invited to attend; — Capt. Elmer was directed to make provision for the ordaining council, and Robert McCune. Major Ozias Brownson, Levi Brownson, Esq. Alvord, Dr. Everitt, Richard Coit, Huitt Hills, John Nash, Jesse Hills, Capt. Wilcox and Andrew Everitt were appointed to be tavern-keepers on the day of ordination.

The Church records make up in brevity for the prolixity of the Society records of this event. They simply contain a vote passed November 30, 1790, "to give Rev. Mr. Publius V. Booge a call to take the pastoral charge of this Church."

No record of the ordination council, or of the exercises, is to be found; — and it is impossible to ascertain whether the new meeting house was so far completed as to be used for the occasion, or whether the exercises were in the old house.

The conclusion naturally arrived at by inspecting the interminable proceedings of seventeen Society meetings from which we have quoted, is that the Society and its minister were keen at a bargain, and were determined to understand each other fully. The nature of the arrangements also shows the extreme scarcity of money, and the rigid economy necessarily practiced in those days. Long as the quotations are we trust they will interest the reader of the history of our little commonwealth, as an illustration of the customs of the times in regard to the hearing, calling, and settling of a life-long minister.*

The only new comer of this year in Winchester seems to have been ISAAC SKINNER, named of Colchester in his deed of land from Martin Hurlbut. This land, on which he probably lived, is supposed to be now a part of the farm of Harvey Andrews; but no conveyance of it by Mr. Skinner can be found. He is assessed on the list of 1795, and not afterward. He married, November 11, 1790, Mary Saxton.

CHILDREN.

I. MARY, b. Oct. 20, 1791.
II. ISAAC, b. April 4, 1793.
III. ALVA, b. July 10, 1795.

---

* We find among our papers, a memorandum of the names and length of the pastorates of the ministers composing the council which ordained the Rev. Mr. Knapp, which was omitted in connection with that event. As showing the permanency of pastoral settlements in the last century we here transcribe it.

DR. JOSEPH BELLAMY,	Bethlem,	1738 to 1789,	51 years.
REV. NATHANIEL ROBERTS,	Torrington,	1741 " 1776,	35 "
" JONATHAN LEE,	Salisbury,	1743 " 1788,	45 "
" DANIEL BRINSMADE,	Washington,	1749 " 1793,	44 "
" DANIEL FARRAND,	Canaan,	1752 " 1803,	51 "
" THOMAS CANFIELD,	Roxbury,	1744 " 1795,	51 "
" ABEL NEWELL,	Goshen,	1755 " 1781,	26 "
" NOAH BENEDICT,	Woodbury,	1760 " 1813,	53 "
" JEREMIAH DAY,	New Preston,	1770 " 1806,	36 "
" AMMI R. ROBBINS,	Norfolk,	1761 " 1813,	52 "
" ASAHEL HART,	North Canaan,	1770 " 1775,	5 "
" PETER STARR,	Warren,	1772 " 1829,	57 "
	Total years,		506 "
	Average length of pastorate,		$42\frac{1}{6}$ "

CHAPTER XV.

ANNALS AND RECORDS.

1791 TO 1801.

THE town records of this year are devoid of interest otherwise than as showing that the revolting system of bringing town paupers to the auction block was initiated by the following vote :—

"Voted, that the selectmen be directed to take charge of Remembrance Filley, and conduct with him as they shall think most for his comfort, and will be least expensive to the town, whilst he remains in his present state of delirium, either to set him up at vendue to the person who will keep him the cheapest, or dispose of him in any other way which may appear to the selectmen more convenient, and for such time as they may think reasonable, and on the cost of the town."

The record then states that "Ensign Bronson bid off Remembrance Filley at eight shillings per week, for two weeks, and at ten shillings for two weeks after," and "Samuel Wetmore second bid him off to keep him two weeks at ten shillings per week." In this case the step may have been necessary and justifiable, by reason of the want of lunatic asylums at that early day. Another vote of the same meeting shows that the auctioning of paupers had not yet been fully adopted. It was voted "that Daniel Loomis take the oversight of building the house of Benjamin Preston, and inspect the labor done, and the stuff provided for said house, and make return to the selectmen."

As a specimen of the economical spirit of the town we extract the following :—

"Voted, to sell the two Congress Laws and Kirby's Reports. Ensign Coe bid off one Congress Law, at ten shillings. Samuel Wetmore second bid off second Congress Law, at six and ninepence. Hewitt Hills bid off Kirby's Reports, at thirteen shillings."

ADNA BEACH from Goshen, this year bought a farm on Blue Street, recently owned by Archibald Dayton, on which he lived until 1811, when he sold to Asahel Bronson, and removed to the farm on the old

Waterbury turnpike, Danbury Quarter, lately owned by John A. Bidwell, where he died April 20, 1820, aged 63. He was a man of standing in the town, and executed many public trusts. His father, Adna, was son of Deacon John Beach, one of the thirteen members of the Goshen Church, at its formation in 1740. His grandmother was Hannah Miles from Wallingford. He was born at Goshen, November 10, 1757; married October 11, 1781, Mary, daughter of Captain Timothy Stanley of Goshen. She died September, 1837.

CHILDREN.

I. SALLY, b. June 4, 1783; m. Samuel H. Wetmore.
II. HORACE V., b. September 10, 1784; studied medicine, and practised at Lexington, N. Y.; afterward at North Goshen, Conn., and in 1847 removed to Memphis, Michigan. He m. Harriet A. Camp, and after her death he m. (2d) Huldah H. Bailey. He d. in Flint, Michigan. Children by first wife: 1. Horace A. Children by second wife: 2. Cicero B., b. 1815; m. Semantha Bailey; she d. and he m. (2d) Zelia Chamberlain; 3 Albert Nelson, b. January 19, 1818; m. April 24, 1844, Sarah Ann Trafford, b. Cornwall, September 25, 1825; lives in Winsted, and has children, Elizabeth Lucell, b. Canaan, October 19, 1846; Delia Lucelia, b. C., August 18, 1848; d. October 11, 1850; 4. Adna S., b. 1820; 5. Joseph M., b. 1822; 6. Harriet U., b. 1824; m. Royal Lewis; 7. Sophronia, b. 1826; d. unmarried; 8. Sarah, b. 1828; m. and d.; 9. Mary, b. 1830, m. — Wedge.
III. POLLY, b. July 7, 1786; resided, unmarried, in Liberty, N. Y., in 1860.
IV. FISKE, b. March 26, 1788; owned and occupied the Edward Rugg farm, in Danbury Quarter, from 1814 to 1827, when he moved to Hunter N. Y. He m. February 24, 1814, Roxa, daughter of Captain Stephen Fyler of Torrington; she d. and he m. (2d) Mrs. Pryor. He had children: 1. Frederick; 2. George; 3. Mark; 4. Charles; 5. James; 6. Roxa.
V. HANNAH L., b. November 15, 1789; m. October 28, 1812, Harry Blake.
VI. ADNA, b. December 8, 1791; m. at Hunter, N.Y., Widow Abigail (Bailey) Showers. He moved in 1826 to Hunter, N.Y., and afterward to Liberty, N.Y.
VII. SIBYL, b. January, 1794; m. September 16, 1814, John Lockwood of Hunter, N.Y., and had children: 1. Harriet, m. Charles Beach; 2. Mary, m. Dr. Robinson; 3. Elizabeth, m. Alfred Green; 4. Horatio, and 5. John.
VIII. MABEL, b. November 3, 1795; m. October 28, 1812, Deacon Allen Blake of Winchester.
IX. SILAS, b. November 11, 1797; m. Lovina Ford. He moved to Hunter, N. Y., in 1826, and afterward to Liberty, N. Y.

REV. PUBLIUS V. BOOGE, the second pastor of the Winchester Church, bought in 1791 the lot on which he built the lean-to house, west of the center, on the Norfolk Road, now owned by Leonard Hurlbut. He sold to Hon. Phineas Miner, in 1799, and followed a large number of his parishioners to Vernon, N. Y. He married Catharine, daughter of Colonel Timothy Robinson of Middle Granville, Mass.

CHILDREN.

I. DECIUS ROBINSON, b. January 29, 1792.
II. HULDAH MAY, b. August 31, 1793.
III. TIMOTHY LESTER, b. December 7, 1794.
IV. HORACE P., b. December 22, 1796.
V. SOPHIA, bapt. June 12, 1799.

NATHAN BROWN, named " of Winchester," this year bought a thirty-acre lot south of the Edward Rugg place, in Danbury Quarter, which he conveyed to Ambrose Palmer in 1792.

LEVI COY married Anna, daughter of Ensign Daniel Andrews. He lived on the north side of Mad River, near the Danbury School-house, and sold out to Phineas Griswold in 1802.

SILAS FYLER bought land in Torrington, came to make a clearing preparatory to moving his family, and while so engaged he lived with Chauncey Hills, where he was taken sick, and died April 12, 1779, aged 69 years. He was born about 1710; son of Zerubabel and Rachel (Gillett) Fyler; g. son of Zerubabel and Experience (Strong) Fyler, and g.g. son of Lieutenant Walter Fyler, one of the early settlers of Windsor, and Jane, his wife. He married about 1747, Catharine Drake, who was born about 1730. She settled, with her family, on the farm he was preparing in Torrington.

CHILDREN.

I. ABI, b. 1748; m. 1782, Josiah Everitt.
II. CATHARINE, b. 1750; married 1770, Samuel Rowley.
III. SILAS, b. 1752; m. Lucy Drake.
IV. JANE, b. 1754; m. Ephraim Loomis [mother of Oliver].
V. STEPHEN, b. May 27, 1755; m. 1779, Polly Collier. He d. Tor., July 15, 1836.
VI. JOHN (twin), b. May 27, 1760; m. December 27, 1787, Esther Bacon.
VII. BETHURSDA (twin), b. May 27, 1760; m. Asahel Bronson.
VIII. SABRA, b. April 24, 1764; m. May 18, 1804, Juna North.
IX. ROMAN, b. August 12, 1769.

ROMAN FYLER from Torrington, bought from Martin North, Jr., the Noble J. Everitt place, a third of a mile south of the Winchester Meeting-house. In 1794, in company with Reuben Marshall, he built the Washington Hatch house at the center, in the north wing of which they kept a country store, while Mr. Fyler kept a tavern in the body of the house. About 1800 he removed to Burke, Caledonia Co., Vt., where he resided during his remaining life. He was a prominent and influential man of the town, and was a pioneer settler of Burke, to which a large number of families from this and the neighboring towns migrated with him. During his residence there he laid down the first aqueduct in Troy, N. Y., and opened the first road through the White Mountains of New Hampshire, which became the thoroughfare of travel from Vermont to Boston. He married February 8, 1793, Hannah Barton, born April, 1770; she died November 15, 1795, and he married (2d) 1797, Mrs. Sally (Bray) Lyman of Goshen.

CHILDREN.

I. ORSEMUS ROMAN, b. Nov. 4, 1793; d. unm. at Harlow Fyler's.
II. BARTON NICHOLS, b. Oct. 19, 1795; had a twin sister d. at birth.

CHILDREN BY SECOND WIFE.

III. ALFRED BRAY, b. Jan. 17, 1799.
IV. HORACE R., b. 1801.
V. MARCUS W., b. 1805.
VI. CALVIN, b. 1808.
VII. MINERVA, b. 1810; d. 1811.
VIII. CARLTON C., b. 1812.

THEODORE and RUSSELL GOODWIN, hatters, from Hartford, this year bought the homestead of Rev. Joshua Knapp, a mile east of the center near the intersection of the Easterly and Dugway roads.

THEODORE GOODWIN sold his interest in this property to his brother Russell in 1795, and bought the Noble J. Everitt place, which he exchanged in 1798 with Dr. Josiah Everitt for the old yellow store building and lot, until recently occupied successively by Isaac Bronson, and Theron Bronson, as a country store, and which has recently given place to the new store building of the latter. This one story building Mr. Goodwin occupied as a tavern and hatter's shop until 1809, when he removed to Granville, Mass., where he died at a good old age. He was a man of keen intellect and humor, whose sayings are often quoted by the old people of the town. He was Town Clerk and Register in 1798. He m. Nov. 11, 1792, Lucy Adams. She d. March 6, 1804, aged 31; and he m. (2d) June 24, 1805, Harriet Prior.

CHILDREN BY FIRST WIFE.

I. LAURA, b. Nov. 23, 1793.
II. ABIGAIL, b. Sept. 11, 1796; d. June 26, 1810.
III. LUCY, b. Apr. 11, 1800.

BY SECOND WIFE.

IV. HARRIET PRIOR, b. Aug. 17, 1806.
V. SIDNEY WADSWORTH, b. April 13, 1809.
VI. THEODORE.

RUSSELL GOODWIN removed in 1795 to a house on the east side of the Dugway road, now torn down, nearly opposite the junction of the East and West roads; and thence in 1808, to the old Thomas Spencer farm on the Sucker Brook road, next north of the Rufus M. Eggleston place, and resided in the old house, the chimney of which now remains standing, until about 1825, when he removed to Litchfield, Conn., where his son Leonard (now deceased) then resided. He too, was a humorist, enlivening every social circle which he entered, by his genial wit and hearty laughter.

It is a singular coincidence, that both of these brothers, and their brother George, the venerable printer of Hartford, should have lived to the ordinary age allotted to man in religious indifference, and should at their extreme age have become humble and trusting followers of their Saviour, and exhibited undoubted evidence of their acceptance as his disciples. He m. Ruth Church; she d. in 1831.

CHILDREN.

I. CLARISSA, m. Erastus Hurlbut; d. in Ohio, 1864.
II. LEONARD, m. Mary A. Galpin; he d. Sept., 183–.
III. DAVID ELMORE, d. when less than ten years old.
IV. HEPZIBAH, d. under ten years of age.
V. MARANA, m. Austin Fuller; d. Trenton, N. Y., 1828.
VI. PHILENA, m. Philo Whitmore.
VII. HIRAM, m. Nancy Jones; he d. Aurora, Ill., Aug. —, 1864.
VIII. HARRIET, m. Jesse Schovill.
IX. EMILY, m. Frederick McNeil.
X. HEPZIBAH, m. Parker Sedgwick, living in Ill., 1867.
XI. DAVID ELMORE.
XII. JEREMIAH, b. Feb. 21, 1815; m. Mary D. Sedgwick.

ZEPHENIAH HATCH,[1] father of Capt. Moses, came from England, and settled in Wethersfield. He had

CHILDREN.

I. LUCY[2], b. May 6, 1752.
II. JERUSHA,[2] b. June 11, 1755.
III. JAMES,[2] b. Oct. 26, 1757.
IV. MOSES,[2] b. March 15, 1760.
V. MARY,[2] b. April 13, 1762.
VI. JOHN,[2] b. Aug. 22, 1764.

VII. SIMEON,[2]	b. Nov. 26, 1766.
VIII. SAMUEL,[2]	b. Feb. 19, 1768.
IX. LEVI,[2]	b. Oct. 13, 1770.
X. ESTHER,[2]	b. Sept. 10, 1772.
XI. ELIAS,[2]	b. March 19, 1775.
XII. DANIEL,[2]	b. Aug. 26, 1778.

CAPT. MOSES HATCH,[2] from Wethersfield, was for many years a sea captain, in the employ of Justus Riley, the Wethersfield merchant. Prior to this, at the age of sixteen, he enlisted into the Revolutionary Army, and served in various capacities during the war. In 1791, he removed to this town and took charge of a large tract of wild land, belonging to Mr. Riley, at the south end of the Long Lake. He built the house which he occupied during his remaining life, some fifty rods south of the house of his son, Elias T. Hatch, on a road now discontinued, leading from the center down to the Still River valley. He d. Dec. 21, 1837, aged 77, a kind-hearted whole-souled man. He m., Wethersfield, Abigail Loveland, b. March 16, 1763. She d. Winchester, Nov. 3, 1850.

CHILDREN.

I. LEVI L.,[3]	b. Dec. 13, 1785.
II. ABIGAIL,[3]	b. Oct. 21, 1787.
III. POLLY,[3]	b. April 5, 1790; d. Feb. 10, 1791.
IV. POLLY,[3]	b. Nov. 4, 1792.
V. ESTHER,[3]	b. Feb. 7, 1795; m. May 8, 1829, Silas Crocker, Jr., of Vernon, N. Y.
VI. WASHINGTON,[3]	b. March 14, 1797; d. March, 1872.
VII. WM. FRANKLIN,[3]	b. March 4, 1801; m. Sept. 28, 1832, Emeline Baldwin; she d. Sept. 22; 1870, aged 62 years and 2 days. He m. (2d) Sept. 20, 1871, Lizzie M. Eells; lives in Winsted.
VIII. TRUMBULL,[3]	b. May 11, 1803; d. June 1, 1807.
IX. ELIAS T.,[3]	b. Oct. 6, 1805; m. Cornelia M. Foote, and lives at the south end of Long Lake.
X. LUCY,[3]	b. June 3, 1807.

SIMEON HATCH.[2] came to Winchester, with his brother Moses, and probably lived with him until about 1800, when he removed to Vernon, N. Y.

JOSIAH HULL, from Hartford, a shingle splitter, owned land on both sides of the Little Pond, from 1791 to 1794, and his name is found on the tax lists until 1804.

The freemen admitted and sworn this year were John Spencer, Elijah Frisbee, Levi Brownson, Salmon Brownson, Silas Hurlbut, Roman Fyler, Jonathan Deer, Ezra Stannard, Elisha Hills, Peter Corbin, Jr., Noah Benedict, Zebina Smith, Chauncey Mills, Nathan Wheeler and Benjamin Wheeler.

1792.

In Town Meeting this year, the town tax was made payable in wheat, Indian corn, beef, pork, oats or flax, if delivered at the house of Captain Samuel Hurlbut, or the mill of Deacon Austin, by the first of May following at prices to be set by the Selectmen.

In Society Meeting, a tax of one penny on the pound was laid "to hire a Singing Master four months, to instruct in singing psalm tunes and anthems."

JOHN B. HALL, of New Fairfield, became joint owner with Eliud Taylor, of the farm on Mad River adjoining Norfolk line in Danbury quarter, and half of the saw-mill afterwards owned by Micajah Hoyt, and now by Nelson Brooks. They sold out in 1796 to Deacon Hoyt, and Mr. Hall afterward left the town. In 1810 the Church voted him a letter of dismission to the Church in Durham, New York. He was grandfather to Hon. Highland Hall, late M. C. from Vermont.

ELIUD TAYLOR, from Danbury, continued to reside in Danbury quarter until 1799, when he sold his dwelling-house and adjoining land to Luther Holcomb, being the premises recently owned by John J. Fanning. He afterwards lived from 1803 to 1806 in the Widow Leach house in the same vicinity. In 1807 the Winchester Church voted him a letter of dismission to the Union Society Church in New Haven. By wife Mary, he had Polly, born January 25, 1794.

WAIT HILL, a blacksmith, was admitted a voter this year. In 1795 he built the house on the Waterbury turnpike a little south of the center, now owned and occupied by Luman Munsill. In 1797 he bought and lived in Winsted, on the Spencer street road, a house that stood near Widow Lucy Coe's dwelling, and worked in a shop long since burned down, which stood on Main street near the dwelling of Samuel W. Coe. He removed to Vernon, New York, in 1798, or 1799. He married, June 26, 1794, Hannah Hills, of Winchester.

The freemen admitted and sworn this year were Rev. Publius V. Booge, Jonathan Coe, 3d, Thomas Spencer, Jr., Harvey Marshall, Theodore Hoskin, Daniel Russell, Elisha Spencer, John Church, Samuel Clark, Truman Blackman, Wait Hill, and Joseph Elmore, Jr.

1793.

The records of Town and Society meetings this year are of little interest. It appears by the Society records that the interior of the new meeting house was not yet finished.

DANIEL ANDREWS, JR., a native of the town, whose record has been given already, came of age this year; built and occupied through life the red house, at the parting of the Danbury school-house road from the Green Woods turnpike.

WILLIAM R. CASE, from the Society of Wintonbury, now the town of Bloomfield, this year, bought and thereafter occupied until 1799, a lot of land now composing a part of the Harvey Andrews farm; he returned to Wintonbury after 1810. He was born February 20, 1751; married Huldah Loomis, born December 12, 1756. He died November 29, 1828. She died January 1, 1835.

CHILDREN.

I. WILLIAM, b. Aug. 20, 1775; d. April 9, 1793.
II. HULDAH, b. Nov. 17, 1777; d. Aug. 16, 1800.
III. ABIAH, b. Sept. 1, 1779; m. Orentus Bronson; d. June 20, 1836.
IV. RUTH, b. April 4, 1782; d. Sept. 27, 1853.
V. HORACE, b. July 5, 1784; d. Oct. 29, 1823.
VI. ASHER, b. Dec. 12, 1786; m. Nov. 13, 1826, Charlotte Pettibone; he d. Sept. 7, 1858; had children George and Edward.
VII. WILLIAM, b. April 25, 1794; grad. Yale College 1821; Cong. minister at Chester, Ct.; d. April 28, 1858.
VIII. CHESTER, b. Sept. 20, 1796; d. in Penn., Oct. 2, 1857, a bachelor.

REUBEN MARSHALL, son of Thomas and Desire Marshall, born at Torrington, May 19, 1765; came to Winchester this or the preceding year, and became a trader in company with Roman Fyler. In 1810 he bought the farm near the center of the town, lately owned by Daniel Murray, now deceased, which he occupied until his removal to Granville, Mass., about 1811. During the last ten years of his residence here he was largely engaged in purchasing cheese for the Southern market. He married Widow   Hills, of Torrington, who had a son Reuben, by her first husband, — and two or more daughters by Mr. Marshall, — one of whom, Orpha, married Patrick Boice, Esq., of Westfield, Massachusetts.

JOHN MCALPINE, JR., son of a Scotchman, is named "of Hartford" in his first deed of land in Winchester. He was a joiner by trade, and a man of great industry and energy, — was a Selectman for many years, — and highly esteemed as a neighbor and citizen. He built, and occupied during his remaining life, the house about sixty rods east of the center, now owned and occupied by his son, John McAlpine; he married, May 16, 1794, Margaret, daughter of Samuel Hurlbut, Esq. He died August 30, 1850, aged 81. She died February 28, 1845, aged 72.

CHILDREN.

I. SILAS HURLBUT, b. Sept. 2, 1794.
II. ELIZABETH ANN, b. Feb. 18, 1798; m. March 11, 1819, Horace Jay Humphrey.
III. SAMUEL AVERY, b. Nov. 15, 1802; m.   ; d.
he lived for many years in Penn., and after the death of his wife returned to Winchester; m. (2d), May 15, 1845, Mary S. McAlpine, widow of his brother, Silas H.; now lives in Winsted.
IV. JOHN, b. Nov. 1, 1805; m. Aug. 6, 1845, Harriet E. Wetmore, and has since resided on his father's homestead at the center; she d. Dec. —, 1869, childless.
V. LEMUEL, b. Oct 21, 1808; a physician, lives in Illinois.

SILAS H. MCALPINE, oldest son of John and Margaret, married, Jan. 11, 1842, Mary S. Wetmore, and lived on the Waterbury turnpike, half a mile south of the center. He was a man of literary and scientific tastes, — a poet, and a warm philanthropist. Standing as he did in the front rank of the despised little band of early Abolitionists, it is fitting that his name should be identified with the once feeble, but now triumphant, cause which he advocated. He died childless, August 12, 1842.

SOLOMON WHEADON, from Branford, owned and occupied until his death, the farm of Harvey Ford in Hall Meadow, adjoining Goshen line. He died December 12, 1814, aged 65. His wife Sarah died January 10, 1821, aged 73.

No record is found of the births of Mr. Wheadon's children. The death of Lomisa, daughter of Solomon and Sarah Wheadon, Jan. 8, 1799, and the marriage of Benjamin Wheadon, their son, to Deborah Merriman, April 21, 1803, are recorded. This Benjamin Wheadon is named "of Hudson, Portage County, Ohio," in a deed of January 28, 1826, conveying his interest in land of Stephen Wheadon, deceased, by which it would appear that Stephen died childless, leaving a widow, not named, and sisters, Sally Wells, Mercy Bronson (wife of Salmon), Esther Pond, and heirs of Lucretia Griswold.

Lucretia Griswold was the first wife of Roswell Griswold of Colebrook, and the mother of Wyllys, Lucretia, and Hon. Hiram Griswold, formerly of Canton, Ohio.

DEACON STEPHEN WHEADON, son of Solomon, owned and occupied the paternal homestead until his death, December 2, 1824, aged 40. He was chosen Deacon of the Winchester Church in 1823. The family of Wheadons was held in high esteem in the community. His wife, Polly, was sister of Moses Drake, Jr., and afterwards married successively Deacon Humphrey of Goshen, and Deacon Rogers of Cornwall; died in 1867, a widow.

RUFUS CRANE, from Killingworth, this year bought of David and Sarah Murray, a house and lot on the Dugway road, nearly opposite the Sophronia Leonard house, which he occupied until after 1796.

JOHN JOES is on the Winchester tax lists of 1793 and 1794.

The freemen admitted this year were Daniel Marshall, Laurence Barber, and Levi Platt.

1794.

The prices of labor in payment of highway taxes were this year established as follows:—

For a man's work in May or June, three shillings and sixpence per day.
" a man and team, " seven shillings "
" a man in October or November, three shillings "
" a man and team, " six shillings "

The new comers of the year were as follows:—

MAJOR LLOYD ANDREWS, a joiner, from Meriden, purchased land in the town, November 20, 1794. He first lived, after his marriage, in the old homestead of his father-in-law, Ensign Jonathan Coe, in the south part of the society, since owned by Samuel Mills Munsill. About 1799 he bought the farm now owned by his son, Harvey Andrews, and there resided until his death, October 23, 1833, aged 60, an unassuming, industrious, and worthy man. He was born in Meriden, February 10, 1773; married May 16, 1796, Huldah Coe. She died December 27, 1866.

CHILDREN.

I. ORSON, b. February 16, 1798; d. November 29, 1836, unmarried.
II. HIRAM, b. December 22, 1799; d. March 15, 1808.
III. HULDAH, b. January 8, 1802; d. September 8, 1808.
IV. GEORGE, b. March 19, 1805; m. in New York.
V. SAMUEL LLOYD, b. October 22, 1811; m. May 23, 1839, Sophia Case of Canton; has a son Geo. L., who served as 1st Sergt., Co. F., 28th Regt. Conn. Volunteers.
VI. HARVEY, b. July 13, 1814; m. Susan (Merwin) Sage.
VII. HELEN, b. May 1, 1821; d. September 13, 1823.

FRANCIS BACON owned from 1794 to 1798 a part of the farm now owned by Harvey Andrews. In his deed of sale of this land in 1795, he is named "of Barkhamsted." In 1795 he is named in a record of judgment as of Simsbury.

DAVID BEEBE, "of Winchester," a blacksmith, this year bought a lot of land in the Jacklin neighborhood. In 1795 he bought a house and lot on Danbury Hill, northwest of William Price's, and there resided while he remained in town. In 1808 the Church in Winchester voted him and his wife a letter of dismission to the Church in Coventry, N. Y.

DOCTOR NATHANIEL ELMORE is on the tax list of this year. He was a native of Sharon, a schoolmaster and physician. He lived in the town a few years, and then removed to Granville, Mass. He was father of Harvey B. Elmore, now of Winsted.

GILLETT HINKLEY this year bought 38 acres of land, which now forms a part of the Harvey Andrews or Wm. H. Rood farm, which he sold in 1801, and then moved to the West.

EPAPHRAS LOOMIS, married, Torrington, September 9, 1755, Mary Hills. They came to Winchester to live with their son Lorrain, about 1809. He died September 10, 1812, aged 80; she died February 12, 1813, aged 78.

CHILDREN.

I. EPAPHRAS, b. March 31, 1756; m. December 1, 1777, Phebe Bacon. He d. in Hannibal, N. Y., in 1850.
II. REMEMBRANCE, b. February 27, 1759; was taken prisoner by the British at Fort Washington in the Revolution; was poisoned by the water, and d. January —, 1777.
III. JERUSHA, b. February 6, 1761; m. Noadiah Bancroft; d. October, 1827.
IV. LORRAIN, b. June 9, 1764.
V. WAIT, b. November 23, 1765.
VI. ARAH, b. July 7, 1767.
VII. IRA, b. September 14, 1770.

DEACON LORRAIN LOOMIS from Torrington, became a resident of Winchester this year. He bought the Truman Blackman farm and other lands, now composing the farm owned by the children of Asher Case, and built and lived in the house now occupied by them. About 1818 he removed to Cornwall, and acted as steward of the Foreign Mission School during its continuance there, after which he returned to his old homestead in Winchester. Pecuniary losses came upon him in later life. He gave up all his property to his creditors, and worked as a farm laborer for several years, paying his earnings to his creditors, until the larger part of their claims were satisfied. Age and infirmities compelled him to relinquish his cherished design of paying in full, out of his hard earnings, the balance of his indebtedness.

In his later years, until his death, he lived with his son, Nelson T. Loomis, on the Richard Coit place, near the south end of the Brooks road. He died July 7, 1857, at the age of ninety-three years and six months. Winchester has had hundreds of men richer in worldly goods and popular talents, but probably not one combining in so high a degree all the qualities of a good man and humble Christian. He was the loved schoolmaster of a large portion of the youth of the town from 1788 to 1810. The writer of these annals remembers him as his first male teacher, with an affection accorded to no other. With the sick he was ever the welcome visitor and kind watcher; with the afflicted, the sympathizer and consoler; in the Church an example of faith and good works; in the world, a humble follower of Him who went about doing good. He married Abigail Rainsford of New Marlboro,' Mass.; she died August 26, 1832, aged 65.

CHILDREN.

I. LOPHELIA, b. July, 1790; d. January, 1791.
II. DORRANCE, b. September, 1792; d. March, 1793.
III. NELSON T., b. March, 1799; m. November, 1827, Abigail Hills of Goshen. He lived near the parting of Brooks str et and the Norfolk road.

CHILDREN.

1. Sarah L., b. January, 1829.
2. Frederick L., b. August, 1834.

IV. EDWARD R., b. August, 1806; lives in Napiersville, Illinois.

ORANGE MOTT, son of Adam, is on the tax list of this and the following year. In 1798 he is described in a deed as of Bridgewater, Herkimer Co., N. Y.

DANIEL WELLS, probably from West Hartford, a tanner, bought a quarter acre lot west of the Booge Parsonage, on the Norfolk road, on which he built a tannery, and two years after built, on the opposite side of the road, the dwelling house since owned by Sage W. Grant. In 1798, he sold out to Asahel Wells, and removed to Augusta, Oneida Co., N. Y.

ERASTUS THRALL, son of Reuben, was admitted a voter this year, and soon after went into trade at the center, buying dairies and other farm products, and exchanging them for goods in the New York market and elsewhere. He is said to have gone with his products to the West Indies, and brought home his sugar, molasses, etc., for home trade. He was a young man of fine person and address, active and *fast*. He ran through his business in 1798,—left the town,—and died soon after in prison, before his trial, on a charge of forgery, of which he was believed to be innocent. He died unmarried.

The freemen admitted and sworn this year were Erastus Thrall, Theophilus Andrews, Benjamin Benedict, Jr., Jedediah Coe, Caleb Munson, Abijah Benedict, and Abiel Loomis.

1795.

In special Town Meeting, April 27 of this year, the following vote was passed: "That this meeting disapprove of the appropriation of the avails of the Western Lands, belonging to this state, as passed in the Honorable Upper House of Assembly, in October last."

This vote probably refers to the project, well nigh carried out, to appropriate the proceeds of the lands in Ohio, reserved by Connecticut in her cession to the general government, to the support of the churches of the standing order. The measure, after passing the Upper House, sitting with closed doors, was resisted in the Lower House, and after a severe struggle of the friends of common schools with the adherents of the clergy, was defeated; and the lands were subsequently appropriated to the endowment of our School Fund. They were eventually sold to the Connecticut Land Company for one million two hundred thousand dollars, and constituted the basis of the splendid endowment from which our common schools have ever since been mainly supported.

It is doubted by many, whether our common schools have been really benefited by this gratuitous aid, which, while it relieves the people in a great measure of the burden of educating the children, at the same time makes them careless as to the management of the schools, sustained without their immediate contributions. The fact is unquestionable, that our common schools have fallen far behind those of some of the neighboring states with smaller endowments, in the efficiency of their management, and the results of good education. But whatever may have been the effect on our common schools, no one can doubt that a diversion of this fund to the support of our churches, would have deadened whatever of vital piety then existed; and it is creditable to the fathers of our town that they set their faces against the measure.

A vote of the society this year, giving permission to other denominations of Christians to use the new meeting house, now completed, on any days when not wanted by the church or society, indicates a catholic spirit.

ROGER COE (see 1765) son of Ensign Jonathan, this year became the owner of his father's homestead in the south part of the society,—

his father removing to Winsted. He lived here from his birth to the year 1857 or 1858, when he came to Winsted with his adopted son, Rev. James R. Coe, third son of his brother Daniel. He was for many years a prominent citizen of the town, which he represented in the Legislatures of 1814 and 1815, and was much employed in town affairs. He m. March 5, 1797, Anna Higley; she d. June 26, 1857. He d. Winsted, Jan. 14, 1859, aged 84 years; *s. p.*

JOSHUA BEACH, son of Joel, came of age this year, and is entered on the Tax List as a resident of the society.

WILLIAM CROCKER's name is on the Tax List of this year. He came from New London County; and in 1799 bought the farm in Danbury Quarter now partly owned by John J. Fanning, on which he lived until about 1825, and then removed to Vernon, N. Y. He m. Dec. 20, 1796, Deborah, daughter of Timothy Benedict, b. Aug. 29, 1774; she d. Sept. 18, 1823; they had a son, *Silas*, and perhaps other children. Silas removed, at or about the same time, with his father, to Vernon, N. Y. His wife's name was Mary Breen. They had a son, Lemuel, born in Winchester, June 27, 1825. The father (Joseph) and two brothers (Joseph and James) of William Crocker, became inhabitants of the town after 1800, and all of them died here.

PHINEAS, JR., and MATTHEW GRISWOLD, sons of Phineas of Winchester, are on the Tax List of this year. Matthew removed to Vernon, N. Y., before 1800. Phineas was of Beaver Dam, Erie Co., Penn., in 1822.

LUTHER HOLCOMB, from Danbury, came into the town this year, and in 1797, bought the farm in Danbury Quarter, on the east side of Brooks street, not far south of Mad River, which he owned and occupied until 1803. His name disappears from the Records after 1804. He was said to be the same Luther Holcomb mentioned in Barber's Historical Collections, who brought the British Army of 3,000 men to a dead halt on its march through Bethel to Danbury in 1777. By wife Joanna, he had

CHILDREN.

I. FRIEND RANSLEY, b. Oct. 1, 1795.
II. LLOYD HOLMES, b. July 27, 1797.

LEVI MARSHALL owned land on the North and West side of Little Pond, and lived in the Daniel Beckley house until his removal to Vernon, N. Y., in 1799.

LOAMI MOTT, son of Adam, Jr., of Winchester, is on the tax list of this and the following years to 1801. In 1797 he bought and lived in a house on Sucker Brook, below the Dugway road, near the Hubbell Saw Mill. In 1803 he is named of Stockbridge, Mass.; and at a later day he removed to Vernon, N. Y. He married April 18, 1795, Polly, daughter of Samuel Clark, of W.

CHILDREN.

I. MERRITT, b. at Winchester, Jan. 3, 1796.
II. WILLARD, b. " June 28, 1800.
III. LODEMA, b. at Stockbridge, Mass., Feb. 3, 1803.

DANIEL PHELPS, from East Windsor, purchased, with Horace Higley, the Artemas Rowley farm in the southeast part of the Society, on which he lived until 1809. He afterwards lived in the house on the west side of Brooks Street next south of the old Everitt place. He was a sedate man, — highly esteemed, and often employed in town affairs. He represented the town in the Assembly in 1818 and 1828. He died March 19, 1850, aged 83. His wife, Huldah, died March 4, 1839, aged 70 years.

CHILDREN.

I. DANIEL, bap. in E. Windsor, Nov. 3, 1793.
II. HULDAH, bap. " " " " "
III. BENJAMIN, bap. " " Aug. 2, 1795; he lived in Danbury quarter near the Everitt place until his death, July 12, 1849, aged 54; he m. Feb. 16, 1826, Abigail Brooks, of W.
IV. FREDERICK, b. Winchester, June 30, 1795; m. May 22, 1826, Lucy W. Hurlbut, and moved to Valatie, N. Y.
V. A SON (not named), b. July 14, 1803; d. Sept. 7, 1803.
VI. JONATHAN, b. March 17, 1805; d. July 1, 1822.

DANIEL PHELPS, JR., married, April 18, 1816, Lucy Hurlbut, daughter of Stephen, and lived in Winchester until after 1826, when he removed to Norfolk, and after 1840 to Wellington, Ohio, where he died not far from 1860. His first wife died in Ohio, and he there married a second wife. He seems to have owned no real estate in Winchester.

CHILDREN BY FIRST WIFE.

I. LOUISA ABIGAIL, b. March 13, 1817.
II. JAMES WHITING, b. April 4, 1819.
III. JOSEPH, b. March 26, 1821.

JOHN CHESTER RILEY, from Goshen, came to Winchester this year and, in company with Seth Holmes, commenced trade as a country merchant in a house south of Jonathan Blake's, near the center. In 1800 he bought of Fyler and Marshall the Washington Hatch place at the center, where he traded and kept a tavern. In 1807 he built a store at the parting of the Old Country road and the Waterbury turnpike, in which he did an extensive business until his failure in 1816. Being a Jeffersonian in politics, while most of the traders of his day and vicinity were of the Federal School, he drew in to a large extent the trade of those of his own faith in this and the neighboring towns. After his failure, he was confined on the jail limits at Litchfield for a considerable time, and continued to reside there during his remaining life. He lived a bachelor until past middle age, and married at Litchfield.

SETH HOLMES, from Torrington, came to Winchester with John C. Riley this year, and for one or two years they were partners, under the firm name of Holmes & Riley. He lived while in town on the discontinued road west of Waterbury turnpike, near the site of the first meeting house. He removed to Vernon, New York, prior to 1802. His wife's name was Phebe.

EZRA HOLMES was "of Winchester" in 1801, and probably became a resident earlier. In 1802 Seth and Phebe Holmes conveyed to him their late homestead above described. Three years after he bought the Luman Munsill place, a little south of the center, which he sold in 1807, and thereafter owned and lived on a farm two miles north of the center on the Danbury burying-ground road, which he sold in 1809 to Birdsey Norton, of Goshen. He is last on the tax list in 1810, and probably that year removed to Ohio. By wife, Grace, he had

CHILDREN.

I. POLLY, b. Oct. 21, 1801.　　II. DANIEL, b. Aug. 27, 1804.

SILAS TAYLOR, from Danbury, owned and lived in the shingled house that stood until about 1860 on Taylor's Brook, at the junction of the old highway south from R. M. Eggleston's, with the new road from the center by Elias T. Hatch's. He died April 24, 1819, aged 67. He had sons, Clark, who died January 22, 1826, leaving a widow. and Ira, who lived on his lands until 1827. He had also a daughter, Clarissa, married, November 28, 1816, Alva Hyde, of Oxford, or Guilford, Chenango County, New York.

DOCTOR TRUMAN S. WETMORE,[4] whose record has been given, appears on the tax list of this year.

REUBEN TUCKER, JR., a native of this town, is on the tax lists of this and the two succeeding years. He is named of Elmore, Vermont, in a deed dated in 1814.

MILES WILKINSON, son of Jesse, born in this town, is on the tax lists of this and the following years. He married, December 2, 1796, Lydia Ives.

The tax list shows that there were four licensed taverns in the town this year, to wit: Samuel Hurlbut, in the house that stood at the center on the site now occupied by the house of Samuel Hurlbut; John Miner, in the house between Winsted and Winchester, lately owned by Mrs. Almira Coe; Zerah Doolittle, in the old Pease House that stood where North Main street now runs, nearly in front of the house of Isaac B. Woodruff, in Winsted, and Freedom Wright, in the Kelsey house, lately burned down, near the small pond on the Old North Country road.

The freemen admitted and sworn were Abijah Bronson, Leonard Hurlbut, Nathan Elmore, and Zaccheus Munsill.

1796.

The town records of this year refer only to routine business; no freemen were admitted.

In Society meeting, a "Pall or Funeral Cloth" was ordered to be purchased and to be kept at the house of Doctor Everitt, when not in use.

A committee was appointed with instructions to contract for the finishing off of the interior of the new meeting house, and, if no offer could be obtained more favorable than that of Deacon Dutton, of Watertown, then to contract with him.

By the records of the following year it appears that the work was done, so as to require the appointment of "seaters" to assign to the parishioners their respective pews and seats.

This edifice stood near the center of the triangular green nearly south of the dwelling of Theron Bronson. It was nearly square, with a steep roof, — the gables, with a round window in each, facing east and west, and without a tower or steeple, and in all respects conforming to the principles of country church architecture of that period. The pulpit stood in the north, with an alley extending to the south door; another alley from the east to the west doors, gave access to the gallery stairs and wall pews. The pews were square with paneled sides, surmounted with low banisters. The galleries occupied the three sides of the interior in front and at the right and left of the pulpit. The altar had a folding leaf which was dropped down when not in use; — an unfortunate arrangement, as it proved, when, some forty years ago, a self-opinionated and partially deranged parishioner conceived himself divinely commissioned to testify against the corruptions of the Church, and took an opportunity to do so by presenting himself at the altar at the close of the communion service, and reading the history of the Saviour's overturning the tables of the money changers in the temple; — and suiting his action to the words, knocked away the support of the leaf, and scattered the sacred elements and contribution box on the floor. The culprit was tried for this outrage before two Justices of the Peace, who decided that he was crazy; but lest an acquittal on that ground should embolden him to commit other acts of the same nature, they found him guilty and imposed a fine.

The pulpit had the usual decorations of vines and clusters of grapes carved in wood, in humble imitation of the gorgeous adornments of the Jewish Sanctuary, and an imposing sounding-board set into the wall above.

Here worshipped the fathers and mothers of the town and their offspring, for about fifty years, a race of honest, hard-working, self-denying, pious, rigid Puritans. The like of Deacons Samuel Wetmore, Seth Hills, Robert McEwen, Eliphaz Alvord, Lorrain Loomis, and Levi Platt, to say nothing of other worthies, who here dispensed the symbolic bread of life, and digested the severe doctrines of the Calvinistic creed, is not to be found in these days of diluted orthodoxy.

ROGER BARBER, a blacksmith, plied his trade in the shop vacated by Wait Hills, until 1798, when he gave way to William Bunell, and went to Sandisfield, Mass.

EPHRAIM BOWERS is on the tax list of this and the following year.

LEVI DAW is on the tax list of this and the following years until 1804. He married August 1, 1796, Phebe, daughter of Benjamin Benedict of W.

WILLIAM GRAY, a Scotchman by birth, and a shoemaker by trade, owned and occupied a part of the Nathan Tibball's farm in Danbury Quarter, until 1799.

SYLVESTER HALL, a millwright, is on the tax list of this year. He married May 12, 1797, Lucy, daughter of Captain Samuel Hurlbut, and probably thereafter lived with his father-in-law, until his removal to Burke, Caledonia Co., Vermont, about 1803, where he resided until his death.

Their children, as appears by the Probate Records of Winchester, were :—

  I. A DAUGHTER, who married — Lawton.
  II. HULDAH,   " — Bemis.
  III. ELECTRA,   " — Trull.
  IV. DAVID, a resident of Virginia.
  V. ELIZA, who married — Bemis.

VI. SILAS, residing in Winchester.
VII. HARRIS B , died in Vermont.
VIII. A SON, who died leaving two sons, Elbridge and Sylvester.

NATHANIEL HOYT from Danbury, owned and lived on land in Danbury Quarter, between the farm late of John J. Fanning and Mad River. In 1811 the Church voted him and Lucretia his wife a letter of dismission to the Church in Locke, N. Y., where they then resided.

DEACON MICAJAH HOYT, son of Nathaniel, owned and lived on the farm in Danbury Quarter now owned by Harry Brooks, until 1844, when he removed, as is believed, to Locke, N. Y. He was chosen Deacon of the Winchester Church in 1825. He was born December 12, 1770; married November 1, 1792, Esther Trowbridge, born October 22, 1773.

CHILDREN.

I. ELIAKIM D., b. May 16, 1794.
II. DELIA, b. October 4, 1796; m. November 27, 1814, Robert Andrews of Danbury.
III. JAMES T., b. December 27, 1798.
IV. ORPHA, b. May 3, 1801; married — Curtice of Vernon, N. Y.
V. SIDNEY, b. April 2, 1804; m. October 9, 1828, Huldah A. Starkwether. They settled in Barton, Tioga Co., N. Y. Children: Harriet, Julia, Louisa, a son, name not known, and Delia.
VI. LORUHAMA (fem.), b. January 16, 1806; m. November 6, 1832, Charles Dunning of Whitehall, N. Y.
VII. ANSEL, b. October 31, 1809.
VIII. MARIA, b. October 31, 1812.

ZERI W. HOYT, son of Nathaniel, lived successively on the Jacklin farm in Danbury Quarter, next on the Norfolk Road, a little west of the Doctor Wetmore place, then on Lake Street, in Winsted, and last in a house near John W. Fanning. He left the town after 1803.

NATHANIEL HOYT, Jr., lived on a part of the John W. Fanning farm, in Danbury Quarter, from 1799 to 1802. He afterwards lived not far from the old Everitt house in the same quarter, until 1810. In 1816 the Church voted him a letter to the Church in Litchfield, Conn., where he then resided.

GEORGE KINGSBURY is assessed on the list of this year for his faculty as attorney-at-law, being the first legal luminary that shed its light on this benighted town. His stay seems to have been as brief as a comet's visit, there being no other note of him extant, save a record of trial before Justice Alvord, on a grand juror's complaint, setting forth that "Daniel Ward and George Kingsbury did, at Winchester, on the

27th day of July, 1796, in a tumultuous and offensive manner disturb and break the peace, by quarrelling, beating, and striking each other," &c. Kingsbury pleaded not guilty, but failed to sustain his plea, and was fined one dollar and costs. Ward had been before the Court so often, as Sabbath-breaker, hard swearer, &c., that he thought it wisest to admit his guilt, and was fined two dollars, he probably having fought hardest, or been most blamable. It is to be regretted that our new juris consult had not left this kind of pastime to Ward and his next door neighbor, Coit, who were well matched and thoroughly trained to wordy objurgations by years of practice.

DAVID STRONG, named of Charlotte, Vt., is on the tax list of this year. He was born in Torrington, May 31, 1768, son of Asahel; married August 28, 1794, Esther, daughter of Reuben Miner of Winchester, and lived in a house long since torn down, which adjoined the house of his father-in-law, now owned by Joel G. Griswold and wife, at the geographical center of the town. About 1808 he removed to New Pultz, Ulster Co., N. Y., where he died. He had a son, George D. Strong, who was for many years a liquor dealer, prominent politician, and alderman of the City of New York. Another son, Edwin M., was adopted by his grandfather Miner, who left him his homestead, on which he lived until about 1836, when he removed to East New York, on Long Island, where he died after 1850.

EDWIN M. STRONG, born July 25, 1795; married September 18, 1816, Deidamia Grant of Norfolk.

CHILD.

I. GEORGE WASHINGTON, b. February 7, 1818.

ELIJAH STARKWETHER, son of Thomas of East Windsor, born January 7, 1777; married January 21, 1802, Anna Jerusha, daughter of Deacon Samuel Wetmore of Winchester, and received a conveyance of his homestead, and lived in a house that stood between the houses of Abel S. Wetmore and Widow Allen Blake, until about 1816, when he built a house on the Waterbury River turnpike, about a mile north of the center, in which he died December 3, 1819. His children have abbreviated the family name to "Starks."

CHILDREN.

I. JERUSHA ANN, b. November 12, 1802; m. October 31, 1822, Sheldon Miller.
II. LAURA HILLS, b. October 26, 1804; d. October 26, 1805.
III. HULDAH ANDREWS, b. August 28, 1806; m. October 9, 1828, Sidney Hoyt of Winchester.

IV. JULIA MARIA,   b. January 6, 1809; m. May 10, 1841, Samuel W. Coe of Winsted.
V. SAMUEL WETMORE, b. August 31, 1812; m. May 8, 1839, Flora, daughter of Daniel Murray.

CHILDREN.
1. Jane Flora,   b. March 18, 1840.
2. Darwin Samuel,* b. August 24, 1843.
3. Huldah Annie,   b. December 11, 1846.
4. Hattie Murray,   b. March 30, 1856.

VI. SYBIL ANDERSON, b. May 14, 1815; m. May 14, 1845, Amos E. Hull of Tolland, Mass.
VII. FREDERICK ELIJAH, b. November 21, 1819.

1797.

The notable event of this year was the success of the Jeffersonian or Democratic party, in electing a majority of the Selectmen, and in displacing our excellent town clerk. The violent party feelings and dissentions of that day have long been forgotten; but the changed appearance of the records by the substitution of the scrawny hand writing of the new town clerk for the clear and precise hand of Squire Alvord, marks a period of change, but not of improvement.

It is easy to find causes for the growth of Democracy in the forced collections by the "Standing Order" of parish dues from disaffected and dissenting members; the frequent prosecutions for profane swearing, sabbath breaking, and especially for playing in meeting, not only against young men and boys, but frequently against young women of respectable families, — all go to show that the reins of civil power were held pretty taut by our worthy old Federal grandfathers, and warrant the conclusion that moral suasion was imperfectly applied for the correction of social evils. That the Democratic ascendency at this time lasted but one year, goes to show that the conservative element was yet too strong to be effectually put down.

The Society records show that by change of prices of provisions, and lax payment of dues, Mr. Booge's salary had become inadequate for his support; in consequence of which a vote was passed adding fifty dollars to his salary, and increasing his allowance of firewood to thirty cords a year. It was also provided that notes of the society, on interest, should be given him from year to year for such arrearage of salary as should be found due him. Another wise provision was adopted by which the wood

---

* The above-named Darwin S. Starks was a private in Company E, 2d Conn. Heavy Artillery, and died in the service, at Alexandria, August 16, 1863.

contract was taken by some responsible individual, at a fixed price. The contract was taken this year by Col. Brownson, at three shillings a cord. The sweeping of the meeting house for the year was also undertaken by Col. Brownson at three dollars.

ELI FRISBIE, son of Joseph, this year bought land near Torrington line on the third tier road, which he sold in 1799, and soon after removed to Vernon, N. Y. He m. April 17, 1794; Sarah Hills; had dau. Lucia, b. Sept. 1, 1794.

CLARK MCEWEN, son of Samuel, is on the tax list of this year. He removed with his father to Vernon, N. Y.

STEPHEN GAYLORD owned a house and land near where the two chimney school-house stood, at the parting of the third tier road from the old country road, which he sold in 1806. He m. May 12, 1797, Mary Rhodes.

CHILDREN.

I. SALLY, b. Nov. 11, 1797.
II. ANSON, b. July 30, 1799; d. May 18, 1803.

The assessment of Trades and Professions this year, were Josiah Everitt and Joseph B. Elmore, Physicians, in Old Society.
Fyler & Marshall and Holmes & Riley, Traders, "
Samuel Hurlbut, Tavern-keeper, "
Lloyd Andrews and John McAlpine, Joiners, "
Roger Barber, Blacksmith, "
Amasa Wade and Daniel Wells, Tanners and Shoemakers, "
Isaac Wheeler and Freedom Wright, Taverners, in Winsted.
Hine Clemmons and Wait Hills, Blacksmiths, "
Jenkins & Boyd, Scythe Makers, "
Asher Loomis, Tanner, "
John Sweet and Chauncey Mills, Millers, "

The freemen admitted and sworn, were Daniel Corbin, Thaddeus Loomis, Daniel Wells, Sylvester Hall, Asahel Bronson, Asher Loomis, Eli Frisbie, Israel Douglass, Roger Coe, Amos Tolles, Seth Lucas, and Daniel Eggleston, Jr.

1798.

Inoculation for small pox was regulated this year, by vote in town meeting, "that Doctors or other men may have liberty to carry on inoculation for the small pox in this town, from the 20th of February to April 10th, under such regulations as shall be agreed on by the Civil Authority and Select Men; provided they shall give a Bond of One thousand Pounds, with sufficient surety, to carry on the business in such a prudent manner as not to expose any inhabitant of the town to said disorder, and to be continued at the houses heretofore occupied, and within the same limits." The location of the "pest houses," as they were called in Winchester Society, is not known. In Winsted, a house was built for this purpose, near the large spring on the old Pratt Road, which was used for a time, and afterward the farm house of Mrs. J. R. Boyd on East Lake Street was appropriated to that purpose. The head and foot stones of the graves of several persons who died of the disease, at the latter place, are still standing in an adjoining field.

The Pest Houses, remote from other dwellings, were established by the civil authorities, who prescribed certain limits around them, within which the patients should confine themselves, and all other persons not authorized to enter, were excluded therefrom by fines and penalties.

JOHN BISSELL, supposed from Litchfield, succeeded Fyler & Marshall as a trader, and continued in town but one year. The last record found of him is a complaint of the Grand Jurors and Tithing Man against him, dated May 9, 1799, for unnecessarily and unlawfully traveling on the Sabbath, to which he pleaded guilty, and paid a fine of $2.50, and costs.

ELIJAH BLAKE, a native of Middletown, came to Torrington in early life, and removed thence to Winchester, in February of this year. He was by trade a tanner, and lived and died in the house afterwards occupied by his son-in-law, Samuel Hurlbut, 2d. He d. Oct. 2, 1833, aged 77. He m. Sept. 27, 1779, Sarah Hamlin, of Middletown, who d. Oct. 27, 1811, aged 53.

CHILDREN.

I. SALLY, b. Tor., Dec. 12, 1780; d. June 17, 1798.
II. POLLY, b. " Sept. 15, 1782; m. Feb. 2, 1803, Timothy Loomis, of Riga, N. Y.
III. ELIJAH, b. " June 26, 1784.
IV. JONATHAN, b. " Aug. 13, 1786.
V. HARRY, b. " June 29, 1788; m. Oct. 28, 1812, Hannah, dau. of Adna Beach.
VI. ITHUEL, b. " Aug. 1, 1790; m. March 17, 1812, Wealthy, dau. of Benj. Benedict.
VII. ALLEN, b. " May 19, 1792; m. July 9, 1817, Mabel, dau. of Adna Beach.
VIII. SALLY, b. " Dec. 16, 1794; unmarried.
IX. MARIA, b. " Oct. 18, 1797; d. Sept. 21, 1805.
X. LOVINA, b. Winchester, Oct. 16, 1799; m. Samuel Hurlbut, 2d, of W.

ELIJAH BLAKE, JR., m. Amelia Bronson, dau. of Benoni, and early removed to Springfield, Mass., where he still resides. He had four sons and two daughters. Both of the daughters are dead. The sons, William and Charles, are in trade in Boston, and Marshall and Hamlin, in New York.

JONATHAN BLAKE, ESQ., resided during his married life on the east side of the old Waterbury River turnpike, in the first house south of its parting from the Old Country road at the center. He was for some years a Justice of the Peace, and represented the town in the General Assembly in 1851. He married, May 12, 1808, Sabra Bronson. He died May 14, 1868, aged 81 years and 9 months. She died March 30, 1870, aged 86.

CHILDREN.

I. INFANT SON, d. Aug. 19, 1809.
II. INFANT DAUGHTER, d. Nov. 30, 1810.
III. MARCIA, b. Feb. 13, 1812; m. Jan. 24, 1845, Silas B. Crocker, of Vernon, N. Y.
IV. MARY ANN, b. Jan. 17, 1814; m. Sept. 8, 1835, Lorenzo Mitchell, of Collinsville; he d. Sept. 17, 1838, aged 26. Their son, Ward Blake, d. July 31, 1837, aged 1 year and 1 month.
V. CHARLES HAMLIN, b. Oct. 17, 1817; m. May 11, 1842, Jane, daughter of James C. Cleveland.

CHILDREN.
1. James Cleveland, b. Feb. 9, 1847; d. Jan. 24, 1848.
2. James Cleveland, b. July 12, 1849.
3. Lorenzo Mitchell, b. April 26, 1851.

VI. A SON, b.   ; d. Feb. 17, 1822.

HARRY BLAKE, lived for twenty years or more on the west side of the north and south road in the third tier, in the second house south of the Dugway. He moved to New Britain about 1867, where he soon died. He married Oct. 28, 1812, Hannah Beach, daughter of Adna.

CHILDREN.

I. SARAH HAMLIN (twin), b. July 21, 1813; m. Aug. 12, 1847, Giles L. Gaylord, of Tor.
II. MARY STANLEY (twin), b. July 21, 1813; m. Dec. 17, 1851, John Moore; d. Aug. 5, 1854.
III. REV. HENRY BEACH, b. May 20, 1817; graduate of Williams College and East Windsor Theological Institute. He settled in the ministry at South Coventry, 1845; afterwards in Belchertown, Mass., and now lives in Newbern, N. C. He m. Sept. 23, 1845, Mary R., daughter of Harvey Wolcott, of West Springfield. He delivered the historical sermon at the Centennial Celebration, in Winchester, Aug. 16, 1871.
IV. LUCIUS DODDRIDGE, b. Sept. 9, 1819; m. March 29, 1843, Susan Griswold, resides in W. Hartford.

V. HANNAH H. (twin), b. May 6, 1824.
VI. HARRIET H. (twin), b. May 6, 1824; d. April 4, 1825.
VII. GEORGE, b. April 16, 1826; m. July 8, 1856, Lucy Case; lives at Indiantown, Iowa.
VIII. DEA. ELIJAH F., b. May 22, 1830; m. May 1, 1856, Julia M., daughter of Jared Clark.
IX. HUBERT, b. Aug. 31, 1832; d. June 18, 1841.

ITHUEL BLAKE, removed in 1818 to Coventry, N. Y. He has for many years been deacon of a church in that place. He married, March 17, 1812, Wealthy, daughter of Benjamin Benedict, and had ten children.

DEACON ALLEN BLAKE lived at the parting of the road running north by Abel S. Wetmore's from the Old Country road, until his death, March 10, 1850, aged 58. He succeeded his father in the tanning business, which he carried on in the tannery on the stream southeast of his dwelling. He was Deacon of the first Congregational Church for several years before his death. He married, July 9, 1817, Mabel Beach, daughter of Adna.

CHILDREN.

I. HERVEY VINCENT, b. June 29, 1818; m. Nov. 20, 1844, Catherine E. Caul; she d. July 13, 1845, aged 24.
II. MARIA ELIZABETH, b. April 16, 1822; m. Hopkins Barber.
III. SAMUEL A., d. Dec. 6, 1847, aged 23.
IV. CELIA C., m. Denison Lambert; d. Sept. 7, 1849, aged 23.
V. LOUISA, d. Nov. 16, 1851, aged 18.

CAPT. WILLIAM BUNNELL, this year, succeeded Roger Barber as blacksmith at the center. He resided in the house at the parting of the Norfolk road and the old Waterbury turnpike, west of Theron Bronson's store, until his death, July 27, 1820, aged 46.

CHAUNCEY HUMPHREY, a native of Simsbury, came from Torrington this year, and first lived on the Deacon Seth Hills place near Torrington line. In 1802 he bought the Jonathan Blake place, and built a tinner's shop at the south parting of the Old Country and Waterbury River roads. In this shop he afterwards went into trade in partnership with the Samuel Hurlbuts, Senior and Junior. From 1810 to 1813 he kept tavern in the yellow store building recently torn down, that stood in front of the new store of Theron Bronson. During the war of 1812 he was connected with the introduction of British goods to the States from Canada, a quantity of which were seized at Hartford, as smuggled, thereby reducing him to poverty. He removed to Ohio in 1816. He was a man of great activity, — of fine personal appearance and address, — and filled a large space in the society where he lived.

ASAHEL WELLS, from Farmington (now Bloomfield), a tanner, this year bought from Daniel Wells, the house west of the center, recently owned by Sage W. Grant, and the tannery on the north side of the road, a little west of the old parsonage, now owned by Leonard B. Hurlbut, which he occupied until 1807, when he returned to Farmington. He afterward removed to Winsted and lived some three or four years on the hill road to Colebrook, near David N. Beardsley's, and again left the town. He married, January 27, 1799, Mine Loomis, daughter of Ichabod.

CHILDREN.

I. ALMIRA, b. Nov. 1, 1799.
II. SIBYL, b. Jan. 25, 1801 ; d. May 3, 1807.
III. ASAHEL HARLOW, b. Feb. 16, 1805.

The freemen admitted and sworn were Benjamin Whiting, Jr., Giles Russell, Asahel Wells, Vine Utley, Phineas Miner, Timothy Benedict, Jr., Benjamin Wheadon, Ichabod Loomis, Benjamin Carter, Chauncey Hills, William Crocker, John Miner, Jr., Miles Wilkinson, and John Alvord.

1799.

The Winsted settlement had this year assumed such proportions, as to induce a vote of the town " that the Select men be directed to appoint one third of the town meetings to be holden at the house of Horace Higley during the pleasure of the town."

The opening of the Green Woods turnpike, this year, from New Hartford to Sheffield, Massachusetts, by a new and more direct route, avoiding as far as practicable the high hills, and following the course of the streams diverted all the long travel from the old north road over Wallen's hill and the old south road through old Winchester.

The only new comer of the year was

JOHN BEECHER, " of Cheshire," who bought a house and lot on the Brooks street road next north of Nelson T. Loomis, which he owned until 1807, when the Church granted him a letter of dismission to the Church in Waterbury.

1800.

The town votes of 1800 present no matters of special interest. Joseph Preston, Jr., had died, leaving it to the towns of Torrington and Winchester to decide by litigation, which of the towns was liable for his support while living, — and a committee was appointed to compromise the litigation or bring it to a final issue. The two towns had also a boundary question which Major Wetmore was appointed to settle. Phineas Miner, Esq., was directed to oppose, or stave off, the appointment by the County Court of a committee to lay a road from Winsted to Colebrook;—and rams were prohibited running at large from August to November.

The Republican, or Jeffersonian party, was again in the ascendant this year in the election of Town Officers. The veteran 'Squire Alvord, however, breasted the storm and was re-elected Town Clerk. A three per cent. highway tax was laid. The tax for town expenses,—other than roads,—was five mills on the dollar, which, if fully collected, would have raised $171.94.

The Society records of the year mainly relate to the dismission of Rev. Mr. Booge from his pastoral charge, on his own application, concurred in by the Church and Society, which was ratified by Revs. Robbins of Norfolk, Gillett of Torrington, and Mills of Torringford.

The following notice of Mr. Booge we extract, by permission of its author, from the manuscript account of the Winchester Church, which Rev. Frederick Marsh furnished to the Connecticut Historical Society:

" Mr. Booge was born in the parish of Northington, now the town of Avon, March 30, 1764. His father was a clergyman, and died in Northington when his son was about two years and ten months old. He continued under the care of his mother until fourteen years old. Though a good reader, his education at this time was very limited. He then began to act for himself, and after laboring a short time on a farm, he entered the American Army, as substitute for an older brother. He served principally at West Point. When about 18, he became anxious to know what he should do to be saved. His convictions issued in hopeful conversion. . . . . His mind was thus turned to the Gospel Ministry, and after struggling with various difficulties, he entered Yale College at 19, and graduated in 1787. He became the pastor of this Church, January 26, 1791. His dismission took place March 20, 1800, much to the regret of his people. He was licensed to preach the Gospel by Springfield Association, at Feeding Hills, Mass. After preaching a while at East Granville, Mass., then at Cornwall, Ct., he came to this place. About the time of his settlement here, he was married to Catharine Robinson, daughter of Colonel Timothy Robinson, of Granville, Mass. The leading cause of Mr. B.'s dismission from here was the failure of his health, and a strong conviction on his own mind that it was necessary to remove to a new country. Soon after his dismission, Mr. B. removed to Vernon, Oneida Co., N. Y. After preaching in that county about two years, as his health would permit, he removed to Georgia, Vt. After having the charge of that people eleven years, enjoying the satisfaction of seeing his labors blessed to the hopeful conversion of many souls, he took the pastoral charge of a congregation in Paris, Oneida Co., N. Y., called Union Society. Here he labored twelve years, happily and successfully, enjoying several interesting revivals. While enjoying peace, and the prospect of spending the remnant of his ministerial life with that people, a young man of Hamilton College, professedly very good, was the means of such difficulties among his people as led to his dismission.

"Mr. B. was several times employed as a missionary by different societies, and aided in forming many churches. He was able in council, and often employed in aiding others with his advice, much respected and beloved. He died suddenly in Clinton, Oneida Co., N. Y., in his own dwelling, August 28, 1836, aged 73 years, and five months after the death of his wife. He exercised his ministry about forty-four years.

"Most of the above account of Mr. B. is taken from a letter of his son, Rev. Horace P. Booge of Vernon Village, N. Y.

"Mr. B. was in person above the middle stature of men, handsome, had a good countenance, pleasant voice, and an unusually prepossessing appearance. As a preacher he was very acceptable and edifying.

"The kindest feelings appear ever to have existed between him and his people. His repeated visits and preaching since my settlement here were apparently very acceptable and pleasant to the people, and gratifying to himself. His surviving parishioners still remember him with interest."

The Church applied to the dismissing council for advice in reference to a successor of Mr. Booge, and Rev. Archibald Bassett, a graduate of Yale College, in the class of 1796, was soon employed as a candidate, and continued his ministrations as such through the year.

The electors admitted this year were Selah Hart, Loammi Mott, James Boyd, Ezra Andrews, Daniel Andrews, Jr., Levi Andrews, Benjamin Jenkins, Merritt Bull, Ezra Doolittle, and Roswell Marshall.

BENJAMIN WHEADON, supposed to be son of Solomon, of Winchester, is this year certified as equipped for military duty, November 5, 1807; the Church voted him a letter to the Church in Hudson, O.

ELIAKIM BENEDICT, son of Benjamin, Senior, and a native of the town, came of age in 1799, and is this year certified as equipped for military duty. He married November 29, 1798, Anna Beebe.

LENT MOTT, Jr., son of Lent, of Winchester, and native of the town, was this year certified as equipped for military duty. He seems to have had no permanent residence, though he probably died in the town. He married November 16, 1798, Lucy Ives.

CHILDREN.

I.	LAURA,	b. November 17, 1799.
II.	ALMA,	b. April 28, 1800.
III.	JERUSHA,	b. October 28, 1801.
IV.	LUCY,	b. August 2, 1803.
V.	JOSIAH,	b. March 28, 1805.

SILLIMAN HUBBELL came from Danbury to Winchester in 1800, and bought the house and lot on the south side of Cooper-lane, or Norfolk Road, about one-third of a mile westerly of the center, now owned by his grandson, Andrew E. Hubbell, in which he resided until his death, July 27, 1847, aged 83. He was one of the last and best esteemed humorists who abounded in Old Winchester at the close of the last century. His descent from his immigrant ancestor was in the following line:—

Richard Hubbell,[1] Senr., from England in 1647, to Fairfield in 1664.

Samuel,[2] son of Richard.

Jeptha,[3] son of Samuel; married Sarah Brindle or Brintnell.

Silliman,[4] their son, who married 1st, April, 1787, Hannah Taylor, daughter of Timothy Taylor of Bethel, who died January 12, 1814; 2d, Nov., 1815, Polly, daughter of Wm. Chamberlin, who died s. p. May 6, 1864.

CHILDREN BY FIRST WIFE.

I. CHLOE,[5] b. January 25, 1788; m. 1814, Norris Coe. He died s. p., June 25, 1866.

II. AMMON,[5] b. April 15, 1790; m. ; died s. p., August 8, 1823.

III. POLLY,[5] b. January 17, 1792; m. April 18, 1819, Ira Dexter. She died March 25, 1856.

IV. IRA,[5] b. October 10, 1794; m. (1), Irene Strong; (2), — Hart; (3), Urania Patton. Children by first wife: 1. Henry[6]; 2. Mary[6]; 3, Laura.[6] By second wife: 1. Silliman J.[6]

V. LUMAN,[5] b. August 28, 1797.

VI. ANDREW,[5] b. January 17, 1800; m. November 16, 1826, Marian Rogers. He died s. p., Charleston, S. C., September 14, 1827.

VII. McPHERSON,[5] b. August 24, 1803; m. September 27, 1830, Minerva Seymour.

VIII. ANNA,[5] b. March 8, 1806; d. April 20, 1807.

IX. LYMAN,[5] b. February 18, 1808; d. unmarried April 19, 1833.

X. SILLIMAN,[5] b. February 7, 1810; d. September 30, 1826.

LUMAN HUBBELL,[5] son of Silliman,[4] married 1st, June 22, 1831, Jane Munro Boyd, daughter of James and Mary (Munro) Boyd. She died January 8, 1836, aged 22; 2d, Oct. 7, 1837, Henrietta, daughter of Benj. Jenkins.

AND FAMILY RECORDS. 215

CHILDREN BY FIRST WIFE.

I. ANDREW LYMAN,[6] b. March 5, 1834; m. September 10, 1857, Martha W. Woodworth of Great Barrington, Mass., b. April 15, 1836.
II. JAMES BOYD,[6] b. March 18, 1836; m. September 9, 1858, Katie Amelia Tew, b. December 17, 1836.

CHILDREN.

1. Louis Boyd,[7] b. Mankato, Minnesota, July 5, 1859.
2. Grace,[7] b. Mankato, July 11, 1860.
3. Henrietta May,[7] b. Winnebago Indian Agency, May 11, 1862.
4. James Boyd,[7] b. Mankato, December 22, 1866.*
5. Andrew Lyman,[7] b. Mankato, October 8, 1870.

CHILD BY SECOND WIFE.

III. LUMAN SILLIMAN,[6] b. May 24, 1844: residing in 1872 at Mankato. Min., unmarried.

JOSIAH COWLES lived near Colebrook line on the Jacklin road, from 1800 to about 1805.

AUGUSTUS HUMPHREY, last from Torringford, this year bought of Elisha Wilcoxson the William Johnson farm, above the Dugway, on the old Winsted and Winchester road, where he lived until 1810, when he sold to Abiel Loomis, and left the town.

1800.

CALEB BEACH, son of Joel, and grandson of Caleb, the first settler of the town, is on the tax list this year, and spent his life in the town; his residence not ascertained. He died March 10, 1851, aged 72. He married June 25, 1797, Sarah Blakesley.

CHILDREN.

I. ELIZABETH, b. July 3, 1798; d. December 2, 1804.
II. JONATHAN, b. November 19, 1799.
III. WILLIAM, b. January 5, 1802.
IV. SEBA, b. January 8, 1804.
V. CALEB, b. January 6, 1806.
VI. SUSANNA SEREPTA, b. December 10, 1807.
VII. HEZEKIAH, b. July 13, 1810.
VIII. SARAH, b. July 31, 1812.
IX. JULIA, b. April 25, 1815.
X. PHEBE, b. May 26, 1817.
XI. CLARISSA, b. June 2, 1819; m. December 31, 1837, Major Thorp of Barkhamsted.

ARAH LOOMIS, son of Epaphras, lived from 1800 until his death (September 10, 1844, aged 77), in the house now occupied by Samuel

W. Starks, on the road turning west above the Dugway, and leading to the center. He married May 15, 1799, Margaret Loomis. She died September 28, 1841, aged 69.

CHILDREN.

I.	HARRIET,	b. February 4, 1800; d. March 10, 1807.
II.	MARY,	b. January 27, 1802.
III.	HARRY,	b. March 14, 1803; d. March 26, 1803.
IV.	ABIGAIL,	b. May 9, 1804.
V.	RUBY,	b. April 27, 1806.
VI.	HARRIETT,	b. March 16, 1808.
VII.	LUCY (twin),	b. February 5, 1810.
VIII.	LURY (twin),	b. February 5, 1810.

ISAAC WILCOX, Jr., from Simsbury, in 1799 bought a house and land near Colebrook line, in third tier, third division, near Richard Slocum's, which he conveyed to Luther Phelps by a deed in which he is named "of Pompey, Onondaga Co., N. Y." He is assessed this year as a resident of the town.

CHAPTER XVI.

EARLY SCHOOLS.

WE have found scant materials for a history of the rise and progress of schools, and have made no mention of them hitherto in our Annals, preferring to bring together all that we have learned of their history and condition in a separate chapter. The first recorded action in reference to schools is found under date of December 17, 1773, the year of Rev. Mr. Knapp's settlement; it was voted "to raise two pence on the pound of the rateable estate for the support of schools in this [1st] Society." It was also voted that the north district begin at the house now owned by Medad Hills, and contain all the north part" (of the society), "that the west district contain all the inhabitants on the west road from the crotch of the paths and all west," and "the east district to contain all the rest of the Society;" "that the money raised by the tax be divided according to the list, and that Warham Gibbs, Reuben Thrall, Ebenezer Preston, Seth Hills, Oliver Coe, Samuel McCune, Benjamin Benedict, Abram Andrews, and Daniel Platt be school committee;" "that money [raised?] in each district be laid out in each district as shall best accommodate the same, if it shall be laid out in the year; if not laid out in the year, to be returned to the society treasury."

The foregoing votes promised an excellent provision for the educational interests of a community that as yet had only paths instead of roads by which to define the limits of its school districts. But unfortunately at an adjourned meeting, January 6, 1774, it was voted "to reconsider all the votes that have been passed in this meeting concerning schooling." Here the matter rested, so far as taxation and the organization of school districts was concerned, until December 2, 1777, when it was voted "to raise two pence on the pound on last August list, to support schools," and Deacon Seth Hills, Ensign Ozias Brownson, Philip Priest, Eliphaz Alvord, Captain Gibbs, Phineas Griswold, Lieutenant Benedict, and Eleazer Smith were appointed school committee.

Whatever may have been done pursuant to these votes, there is no record of their repeal, and at the annual meeting in 1778 similar votes were renewed, and a rate of sixpence on the pound was granted, and a collector in each district appointed to collect the same.

We have no means of ascertaining when or where the first school houses were erected, or what teachers were employed, or for what length of time; but we have reason to suppose that schools were first opened in private houses by voluntary associations, and that these were aided, but not wholly sustained, by taxation.

The next action appears on the society records in 1786, when a new school district was organized, "beginning at Torrington line, by a stream called the Branch, and to extend up said Branch so far as that an east line will include Captain Elmer [now Widow Norris Coe], from thence down ye country road, including Doctor Everitt [now Theron Bronson], John Nash, and all on the north side of said country road, and to include Phinehas Griswold's, from thence south to Torrington line," and Jonathan Coe and Levi Browrson were appointed district committee. This description is not very definite, but probably is intended to designate the district which built about this time the "Two-Chimney School House" that stood, until burned down, in a southeast direction from the burying-ground.

In 1788, on the petition of Eliphaz Alvord, and others, another district, to be called the Second District, was organized, beginning on Long Lake, at the mouth of Sucker Brook, and extending up said brook to the north end of the third tier, first division (near the Dugway school house), then to the northwest corner of the tier, then southerly along its west line to the southwest corner of Gershom McCune, Jr. (late Sylvester Platt's) lot, thence easterly along his south line, direct to Long Lake, and thence northerly along the shore thereof to the mouth of Sucker Brook.

In January, 1790, we find the following appointment of district school committees:—

Samuel Clark, who lived in the Daniel Murray house, for the northeast district, which embraced the east part of Danbury Quarter, and extended south to Mr. Clark's.

Andrew Everitt, who lived in the old Everitt house, for the northwest district, embracing the principal part of Danbury Quarter.

Amasa Wade, for the southwest district, embracing the territory west of Branch Brook, nearly as far north as the Norfolk road.

Captain Joseph Elmore, for the southeast district, embracing the center and the southern portion of the society, lying west of Branch Brook, and southwest of Sucker Brook.

Captain Elisha Wilcoxson, who lived in the William Johnson house, for the second or Sucker Brook District.

In 1798, by vote of the town, a new district was established, partly out of Winchester Society, and partly out of Winsted Society, the boundaries of which were directed to be placed on file in the Town

Clerk's Office, but as no such file is to be found, its limits cannot be ascertained. It probably embraced the northern half of the present Sucker Brook district, and extended easterly to the Austin Mill, or Mad River, in Winsted. The committee were—Deacon David Austin, Levi Norton, and John Miner.

In 1792 another district was formed, embracing essentially the territory of the present West Winsted district, there then being no village in existence, all the inhabitants living on the Coe and Spencer street roads to Colebrook, the two roads there diverging from the original school house, which stood on the site of the present West Winsted school house, and was burned down about 1808 or 1809.

In the records of Winsted Society, under date of December 27, 1784, we find a vote that the districts set off for schooling by a committee chosen for that purpose be established according to their doings, but no record of the districts so established is to be found. October 5, 1785, a tax of "one penny halfpenny" on the pound was laid for the "use of schooling," but was reconsidered and annulled at an adjourned meeting on the 26th of the same month. December 8, 1788, Ebenezer Rowley, and Ensign Eleazer Kellogg were appointed school committee. No further reference to school matters is found until December 8, 1794, when it was voted to divide the society into school districts, and a committee was appointed for that purpose, who reported January 12, 1795. The report was accepted and placed on file, but not recorded, and the file is not to be found.

In the foregoing minutes and extracts we have collated all of the essential doings of the town, and of the two societies prior to the act of General Assembly, May Session, 1795, which appropriated the interest of the proceeds of the western reserve lands to the support of schools in the several societies constituted, or which should thereafter be constituted by law, and requiring such societies to hold distinctive meetings, as school societies, separate from their meetings for ecclesiastical purposes. This act left the ecclesiastical societies as it found them in respect to their religious functions, but invested them with new and distinct powers as school societies, so that persons qualified to vote on school matters might be disqualified as voters in ecclesiastical matters. As a consequence, the meetings and officers of each had a distinctive character, and distinctive records were kept.

Little of detail is known in respect to the schools supported in the districts prior to the act of 1795. We know, however, that several schoolhouses were built in the old society, and that they swarmed with pupils. We know, too, that good teachers were employed, and that the mass of the people were well instructed in all the branches of common school education.

We have before us some of the early reminiscences of a lady,* born in 1786, which illustrate the school customs and mental culture at the period referred to, from which we extract her notice " of the great day of examinations and exhibitions, when eight district schools assembled in the large, unfinished meeting-house in the winter of 1793-4.

" The reading and spelling of the schools occupied the forenoon, and the afternoon was devoted to dramas, comedies, orations, etc. One corner of the church was enclosed in curtains, and each school took its turn behind the scenes to prepare for their special exhibitions on the stage.

" The late Deacon Levi Platt was the teacher of the school to which I belonged. Well do I remember the directions given by him to the little girls, as to dressing their hair for exhibition, viz: The night previous, our mothers were to wet our heads with home-brewed beer, and our hair was to be combed and braided very tightly before going to bed. In the morning, the last thing after we were dressed for the exhibition, the braids were taken out, and the hair lay in waving lines all over our shoulders.

" Among the variety of things he taught us, was the practice of spelling a whole sentence, all together, or more particularly the first class. The sentence to be publicly spelled, was: 'Abominable Bumble Bee, with his Tail cut off'; but Mr. Platt thought best to shorten it to 'Abominable tail cut off.'"

" Imagine, if you can, in soberness, a large, thoroughly trained school-class, spelling, or chanting, before the assembled families of the town, in this wise:

" ' A—   there's your A.
" ' B-O—   there's your Bo, and your A-bo.
" ' M-I—   there's your Mi, and your Bo-mi, and your A-bo-mi.
" ' N-A—   there's your Na, and your Mi-na, and your Bo-mi-na, and your A-bo-mi-na.
" ' B-L-E—   there's your Ble, and your Na-ble, and your Mi-na-ble, and your Bo-mi-na-ble, and your A-bo-mi-na-ble.
" ' T-A-I-L— there's your Tail, and your Ble-tail, and your Na-ble-tail, and your Mi-na-ble-tail, and your Bo-mi-na-ble-tail, and your A-bo-mi-nable-tail.
" ' C-U-T—   there's your Cut, and your Tail-cut, and your Ble-tail-cut, and your Na-ble-tail-cut, and your Bo-mi-na-ble-tail-cut, and your A-bo-mi-na-ble-tail-cut.

---

* Mrs. Nelly M. Swift, daughter of Dr. Josiah Everitt.

"'O-F-F— there's your Off, and your Cut-off, and your Tail-cut-off, and your Ble-tail-cut-off, and your Na-ble-tail-cut-off, and your Mi-na-ble-tail-cut-off, and your Bo-mi-na-ble-tail-cut-off, and your A-bo-mi-na-ble—tail—cut—off.'

"In the afternoon, each school had its oration, poem, dialogue, comedy or tragedy. One of our dialogues was called 'Old Gibber,' in which the late Abel McEwen, D.D., of New London, took the part of Old Gibber; his wife was Charity Bronson. Oliver Marshall, Seth Hills, Joseph Coit, and myself, had parts.

"FIRST SCENE.— Old Gibber and wife talking about the war — wife stirring the hasty pudding — daughter Betty (myself) setting the table — John, the son, just home from the war, etc.

"Another scene is a bar-room, with such talk as we may suppose would take place there during the war of the Revolution.

"The boys of this period were remarkable for their successful imitations of every kind of business.

"The late Samuel Hurlbut, Senior, was Justice of the Peace. Samuel Stanley (son of Dr. Everitt's third wife, who died young), was a lawyer, also Sylvester Griswold. Lemuel Hurlbut was constable, etc. Mock Courts were held in my father's long kitchen. Writs, attachments, and executions were all made out in due form. A statute book of laws was compiled, specifying a great variety of things contrary to law, for which culprits would be arrested, tried, and punished by imprisonment for so many hours, etc., etc. Witnesses were summoned, examined, cross-examined, and impeached, etc.

"A newspaper was edited and published weekly by Samuel Stanley, before mentioned. It was ruled in columns, had editorials, news, anecdotes, advertisements, etc. These boys, at that time, were none of them over twelve years old!"

These glimpses of the common schools of that early day, before any School Fund existed, and of their results in stimulating the mental activity of the youth, seem almost incredible.

In this connection, a sketch of the first "General Training" in Winchester, by the same lady, seems appropriate.

"Up to this time (about 1793) the 'Green,' in front of the Meeting House, was ornamented with quite a number of chestnut stumps, which were then split down and drawn out piecemeal, by teams and chains, the holes were filled up and levelled, all the fences in every direction were removed, and the tables for dinner were set in my father's orchard. Never shall I forget the array of ladies in silks, satins, damasks, and changeable lustrings, of all colors, as they stood in a regular mass, directly opposite our house, on the other side of the road, for it was a new thing, and all the towns near contributed largely to this display of female beauty and rich dresses. It should be recollected that these robes were not worn every day, or even once a week, as they are now, and were of a far richer material than those flaunted by modern butterfly-belles. Every officer, and every soldier brought his wife, his lady-love, or his sister; it was the grand holiday of the year.

"Col. Ozias Bronson commanded the regiment, and I remember his coming to my father's to ask for my black ostrich plumes to wear on his hat. I also recollect that when the regiment was formed in a hollow square, the colonel tried to find a clergyman to make a prayer, but found none. He then took off his plumed cocked hat, as he sat on his horse, and said: 'I will pray'; so he did, and with great propriety.

"It was customary for those who had been officers and soldiers in the then late war, to ride on horseback, single file, past the train band, take off their hats and bow to the company, who returned what was called the 'General Salute,' by fife and drum. Well do I recollect seeing my father at the head of such a procession, riding past Captain Hurlbut's company. To play Indian, dressed like savages, and sound the 'War-Whoop,' used to fill one with terror, for nothing was so dreadful in the minds of children as 'Indians' and 'British Regulars.'"

CHAPTER XVII.

EMIGRATION WESTWARD—FAMILY RECORDS.

FROM 1801 to 1811.

AT the opening of the nineteenth century the old society of Winchester had reached or passed its culminating point, as to population and wealth, as well as social institutions. As we have traced its slow growth, we have found it a hard struggle of energetic men encountering and subduing a most forbidding and inhospitable territory. Victory has crowned their efforts. A virtuous, law-abiding, God-fearing community has been organized out of the heterogeneous materials gathered from every part of the state. The roads have been made, the mills built, the church organized, the minister settled, the meeting house erected, the schools organized. Blacksmiths, tanners, shoemakers, hatters and tailors have begun to ply their trades, and even the dancing-master has found a lodgment, and held his assemblies once a fortnight, during the winter of 1793-4, at Captain Hurlbut's tavern.

It would seem as if the labor worn denizens should now in comparative ease enjoy the fruits of their hard toils and privations. Such had doubtless been the fond hopes that cheered their exhausting labors: for as yet they knew of no more fertile lands to be possessed and enjoyed. The Dutch settlements along the Hudson, from New York to Lake Champlain, then formed a barrier to the westward march of the Yankee nation, and they knew little of the wilderness beyond. As new and improved roads were projected from Schenectady westward along the Mohawk to Utica and onward, enterprising men from this and neighboring towns contracted to build them. They hired their laborers and teamsters mainly from the Greenwoods towns, especially from Winchester and Torrington. These laborers bore no resemblance to the railroad gangs of our day. They were the élite of our young and middle-aged farmers. They went on a service not unlike a military expedition, camping out and working their toilsome way through the German Flats to the virgin soil of Oneida county. They found it "a goodly land, a land of brooks of water, of fountains and depths that spring out of vallies and hills, a land of wheat and barley, a land wherein they should eat bread without scarceness, and should not lack anything in it."

It was a region of beauty and fertility, well calculated to excite the desires of the hard-working and ill-compensated farmers of Western Connecticut to better their lot, and to make them discontented with their own hard-featured, unproductive region. The spirit of emigration was again aroused. The men who had subdued the rugged hill sides of Northern Litchfield county had accomplished labors, compared with which the clearing and bringing into cultivation the rich rolling lands of "the Oneida Country" was a mere pastime. They began to sell their newly-cleared lands before the stumps had decayed from their meadows, and to move away to the banks of the Mohawk, and to the shores of Oneida, Cayuga, and Seneca lakes.

All the new towns of Litchfield county were seriously retarded in their growth by this first emigration westward, and not one of them so irretrievably as Old Winchester. The old inhabitants speak of it as "the Great Exodus." The Danbury Quarter, which, prior to this movement, was thickly settled, in a few years became almost deserted, and has not to this day recovered from the exhausting drain of its inhabitants. Numerous old chimney places line the lonely roads where, in 1800, large families were reared, and school houses crowded. The late Dr. T. S. Wetmore is said to have counted up the remains of more than sixty chimneys, within the society, where the houses had never been rebuilt.

While many valued inhabitants were thus abandoning the town, immigrants were, to some extent, filling their places, whose names, residences, &c., we propose to continue through another decade, connecting therewith, as heretofore, the doings of the town and society.

The year 1801 is made memorable by the election of Thomas Jefferson to the presidency, and also by the occurrence of the great flood, which took his name in commemoration of the coincident events. The flood was one of unprecedented magnitude, carrying away nearly all the bridges, and doing other heavy damages throughout this region. An extra tax of five mills on the dollar was laid for replacing and repairing the bridges of the town.

In society meeting a call was voted to Rev. Archibald Bassett, and a salary offered him of one hundred pounds ($333.33), one-half "in merchantable pork, or beef, or butter, or cheese, or English grain, or Indian corn, or Wool, or Flax, if delivered by the first of each year, at current market prices." This not being accepted, the society proposed ninety-five pounds and twenty-five cords of wood; and finally agreed to pay one hundred pounds, and to furnish wood as they had done to the former pastor. On these terms the call was accepted, and the union was consummated by an ordination, of which no minute is found, either in the Church or society records.

The Waterbury River Turnpike, running through Colebrook and Winchester, and then down the Naugatuck valley, was chartered this year, and soon after was opened. It crossed the Green Woods turnpike at the Crocker house, passed through Winchester Centre village, and thence southerly to and along the Naugatuck branch to Wolcottville. Much benefit to stockholders and travelers was anticipated, but was never realized. Its income in course of years ceased to pay expenses, and about 1850 the company threw open their gates and surrendered their charter.

RICHARD BECKLEY, from Berlin, is on the list of this year; he lived and died on the cross-road or lane north of the Little Pond, in the house now occupied by his son, Daniel Beckley. He was father of Richard Beckley of Norfolk, Daniel and Norris Beckley of this town, and a daughter, who went West about 1815. His wife Susanna (Wilcox), died March 31, 1828, aged 62; he died May 2, 1841, aged 82.

RICHARD BECKLEY, Jr., married October 16, 1825, Sabrina Spicer; she died and he married (2d) March 16, 1834, Mary Cook of Colebrook.

CHILDREN.

I. ELISHA MORGAN, b. April —, 1827 (son of Sabrina).
II. JANE, b. September 16, 1828 (dau. of Sabrina).
III. JULIA SABRINA, b. March 4, 1833 (dau. of Sabrina).
IV. WILLIAM EDMUND, b. July 2, 1837 (son of Mary).

ROGER COOK, son of Aaron, of Winchester, is on this year's list, though according to the record of his birth only twenty years old. He lived in town — the place of residence not ascertained — until about 1810.

ABEL TIBBALLS and Jane, his wife, this year, bought the farm in Danbury quarter now owned and occupied by their grand-son, George Tibballs. She died on this farm, October 5, 1809, aged 58, after which he married (2d) Anna, daughter of Eliphaz Alvord, and lived until his death (April 6, 1822, aged 71,) in the house that stood on the east side of the north and south Dugway road, opposite the parting of the road westerly to the center.

NATHAN TIBBALLS, son of Abel, occupied the original homestead until a few years before his death. He married Rebecca Green.

CHILDREN.

I. GEORGE.
II.
III. HULDAH REBECCA, b. Jan. 6, 1821; m. May 20, 1841, Riley A. Grant, of Norfolk.
IV. NATHAN, d. April 1, 1841, aged 18.
V. SARAH, d. April 1, 1842, aged 15.

NEHEMIAH BAILEY is on the tax list of this year, and owned and occupied from 1802 to 1803 a lot of land on the old South Country road, near Torrington line.

The severity of the contest between the Federal and Republican parties is indicated by the number of new electors admitted this year. They were Abijah Wilson, Jr., Wm. Filley, James Gilbert, Newell Haydon, Eli Andrews, Levi Daw, Levi Filley, Jonathan Douglass, Elijah Benedict, Lorrin Sweet, Cyrus Patrick, Anson Cook, Reuben Rowley, Joseph Ellsworth, Levi Fox, Joel Wright, Jesse Porter, John C. Riley, Obadiah Platt, Levi H st, Reuben Scovill, Joseph Mitchell, Luther Holcomb, Daniel Wilcox, David Holmes, Ebenezer Rowley, Stephen Knowlton, Samuel Wetmore, 3d, Orrin Bronson, Stephen Hart, John C. Barber, Moses Hatch, Nathaniel Hoyt, Micajah Hoyt, John Wetmore, Joseph Cook, Isaac Bronson, Chauncey Bronson, Eden Benedict, Joseph Preston, Amasa Wade, Andrew Pratt, Anson Allen, Lyman Doolittle, Ozias Spencer, Zenas Wilson, Stephen Hurlbut, Abel McEwen, Levi Coy, Lloyd Andrews, Asahel Morse, Isaac Wade, Eliphalet Mills, Nathaniel Smith, Wm. Westlake, and William Chickley. Total, 56.

1802.

The political feature of this year was the defeat of the Jefferson party and the restoration of the Federal party to the supremacy.

The town and society records embrace only routine business.

MATHEW ADAMS, from Simsbury, this year bought a farm on both sides of the Winchester and Torrington line, partly in the third tier, first division, on which he resided forty-seven years. In 1849 his house was burned down, and he soon after removed to Granville, Ohio, where he died September 24, 1863, aged 93.

He lived and died without an enemy; — yet he was a man with decided traits of character. Integrity and kindness marked all his dealings and intercourse. He was a prominent citizen, often employed in town affairs, and five times elected to the Assembly. He was born in Simsbury, October 8, 1770, son of Matthew and Keziah Adams. Married Betsey Coe, of Simsbury, by whom he had

CHILDREN.

I. MATHEW, who went while a young man to Gayamas, on the Gulf of California, and d. on the Pacific Coast within ten or fifteen years past.
II. SUSAN, ; m. Coleman, of Ohio.
III. ZELOTES, who lived and died in Georgia.
IV. GAYLORD, who lived and died in Granville, Ohio.

V. BETSEY, who m.   Atwood, and died in Ohio.
VI. NORMAND, residing in Winsted, who m. Betsey, daughter of Dr. Luman Wakefield.
VII. MARCIA ANN, who died in Winsted unmarried.
VIII. JOHN, who lived and died in Georgia.
IX. OSCAR, now residing in Portage, N. Y.

THEODORE BAILEY, probably from Goshen, this year bought the farm lately owned by John A. Bidwell, on the Waterbury River turnpike, in Danbury quarter, and lived on it a few years. He was "of Goshen" in 1807, and of Bath, Steuben County, New York, in 1817.

TIMOTHY BAILEY bought of Theodore above, part of the Bidwell farm and other adjoining lands, on which he lived until 1807, or later.

ITHAMAR BAILEY, described "of Winchester," this year bought thirty acres of land with a dwelling-house thereon, now a part of the Bidwell farm, and sold it in 1803.

JAMES BARTON, a hatter, resided in Winchester, and this year bought the house at the north angle of the road running east from the center and the north and south Dugway road, and sold it in 1804.

WILLIAM CHICKLEY, a blacksmith, this year bought a lot near Goshen line, in Danbury quarter, and sold it in 1805. He afterwards bought and lived on a place between N. T. Loomis and Asaph Brooks, on the east side of Brooks street, which he sold in 1813. He married, March 28, 1802, Hannah Moore.

CHILDREN.

I. HARRIET, b. March 16, 1803.   II. WILLIAM, b. Jan. 1, 1806.

JONAS ELLWELL, a blacksmith, is listed this year in the old Society. He afterwards lived in the "old mill house" on Lake street, in Winsted, until 1805 or 1806, working in a blacksmith shop then standing on the west side of Lake street, nearly opposite the mill house. He removed to Barkhamsted or New Hartford. One of his sons was drowned by falling from the Kingdom bridge into the Farmington River in New Hartford.

BENJAMIN PAYNE, named "of Bolton, Tolland County," this year bought the house and saw-mill property on Mad River, immediately south of the Danbury school-house, and sold the same in November, 1803, to Oliver Smith. He probably then left the town. The house and saw-mill have long since disappeared.

PHINEHAS WARREN, 2d, from Saybrook, this year bought of Samuel Clark, the farm on the old Winsted and Winchester road, late owned by Daniel Murray, and sold the same to Reuben Marshall, in November, 1806, — probably then leaving the town.

JESSE HORTON, "of Winchester," this year bought the Jonathan Blake house at the center, and sold it to Mr. Blake in 1812. He then bought and occupied, until 1823, the Samuel A. McAlpine place, half a mile south of the center, on the Waterbury River road. The Church voted him a letter to the Church in Trumansburg, New York, May 15, 1825. He had wife, Lydia, and

CHILDREN.

I. JULIA, b. July 10, 1804.
II. HARRIET REBECCA, b. Aug. 6, 1810.
III. WILLIS DORRANCE, b. Jan. 11, 1814.
IV. HENRY BISHOP, b. Sept. 1, 1819.

The freemen admitted and sworn this year were Deacon Josiah Smith, Nathaniel Balcom, Michael Grinnell, Silliman Hubbell, Abel Stannard, Levi Ackley, Gideon Hall, Asher Rowley, Levi Norton, Jr., John Wetmore, Jr., David Coe, Moses Camp, Samuel Camp, Salmon Treat, Horace Eggleston, Reynold Wilson, Josiah Apley, Arah Loomis, John Deer, Elijah Starks, Hawley Oakley, Fisher Case, Rufus Grinnell, James Henshaw, Ezra Rockwell, Truman Smith, Phinehas Warner, Rufus Holmes, and Roswell Grant.

1803.

The records of the town and society this year embrace only routine business.

ALLEN BURR, who lived in a hipped-roof house, now torn down, on the road east of the Little Pond, nearly opposite the lane to Daniel Beckley's, married, January 27, 1803, Anna Wade. He died June 22, 1806, aged 27.

CHILDREN.

I. ALMIRA, b. Dec. 24, 1803; m. Oct. 17, 1821, Marova Seymour.
II. AMASA, b. Oct. 24, 1805.

JOHN HAMILTON from Goshen, owned a hundred-acre lot on both sides of Waterbury River turnpike, immediately north of the J. A. Bidwell farm, from 1803 to 1806, and is not afterwards found on the records.

JUPITER MARS, a colored man from Norfolk, bought a small lot at the west end of the Amanda Church farm, on which he lived until 1805, and then bought thirty acres of land on the Waterbury turnpike, now owned by the heirs of Quashe Potter, on which he lived until his return to Norfolk in 1809.

Jupiter was originally a slave in Dutchess, or Ulster Co., N. Y., and was bought as such by a Reverend Mr. Thompson, a resident of Virginia, who brought him to Canaan, Conn., and there married him to a female slave, whom he brought from Virginia, and placed the married pair in charge of the farm on which his aged parents resided. They took good care of the old people, but did not make the farm pay. Their reverend master returning, and finding the state of things, took measures for carrying them back with him to Virginia. They found out his design, and fled with their children to the woods of Norfolk, where the few families around their place of refuge fed and concealed them. Mr. Thompson finding it impossible to get hold of them, or carry them out of the state, finally arranged that the two oldest boys should be sold within the county until twenty-five years old, when by law their slavery would end, and that Jupiter and his wife should at once go free.

Joseph, the oldest boy, died before he was twenty-five; James, the other boy, at twenty-one years of age told his master he would be a slave no longer, and finally arranged to pay him ninety pounds for his remaining five years of slavery, which he earned and fully paid.

The family thus freed from slavery proved worthy of the boon. Jupiter, the father, was a burly, jovial man, fond of good eating and drinking, and disposed to enjoy life as it moved on. Fanny, the mother, was the best cook in the region, and a most estimable woman. The children had a high degree of self-respect and refinement. James, the slave boy, became deacon, first of the Zion African Church, at Hartford, and afterwards of the African Church, at Pittsfield, Mass. John, a younger son, became a Methodist preacher in Worcester Co., Mass., and afterwards served in the late war, first as chaplain of a colored regiment, in North Carolina, and afterward as minister among the freed men. Elizabeth, one of the daughters, was educated at Philadelphia, and went out as a teacher to Liberia, where she married, and is still employed in teaching. A daughter of her brother James has since joined her in the same capacity. Sherman, another son, was a sailor out of Stonington for many years before his death. Three other daughters, two of them still living, have ever commanded the respect of all who knew them.

OLIVER SMITH from Southwick, Mass., this year bought and occupied a house and lot on the south side of Mad River, on the road running south from the Danbury school house. He afterward bought and occupied the red house next west of the Green Woods turnpike toll gate, until about 1816, when he removed to Tyringham. He became a Methodist exhorter, but had not attained to the priesthood when he left here.

In his zeal for purity and good morals, he was so exceedingly scandalized one day by the sight of Old Holcomb passing along the road with his beloved fiddle on his shoulder, that he incited a reckless neighbor to seize the profane instrument and dash it to pieces. Holcomb sued him as principal in the trespass, and made him pay heavily for his iconoclasm.

DANIEL RICE is assessed this year, but probably lived in the town earlier, as he had by wife Anna, a son, named Chester, born October 24, 1801.

The electors admitted and sworn were as follows:—Phinehas Reed, Amos Hungerford, Joel Kimberly, Elisha Kimberly, Samuel Hoadley, Ransley Bull, Ithamar Bailey, Jacob Seymour, Stephen Wade, Stephen Gaylord, James Barton, William Phillips, Nathan Potter, Timothy Bailey, and Eli Marshall.

1804.

The town and society meetings of this year were confined to routine business.

The electors admitted were:—Daniel Coe, Daniel Mills, and Elihu Everitt.

ELIHU EVERITT, son of Andrew of Winchester, came of age this year, and seems to have lived on the Norfolk road, near the west line of the town, from this year to 1809 or later, and is named of Vernon, N. Y., in a deed of 1812. He married Roxy, daughter of John Marshall of Winchester, as appears by the same deed.

ISAAC JACKLYN came into the town this year, and resided until his death (May 13, 1834, aged 90), on a farm in Danbury Quarter, still owned by his descendants, and now occupied in part by Noah Barber. He is said to have been a servant of Secretary Wyllys of Hartford, from whom he ran away before the Revolutionary War, and took refuge in the Ragged Mountain region of Barkhamsted. Here he won the heart of a daughter of Chaugum, the head or chief of the Narragansett Indians, who held their council fire at the "Light House," but could not get Chaugum to sanction their marriage; so they ran away, got married, settled down in Danbury Quarter, made baskets, and raised children, of whom John was the oldest, and lived and died (November 21, 1850, aged 58), on the paternal farm, leaving several children, among whom were Isaac of

Colebrook and Samuel of Pennsylvania, or elsewhere. A daughter of Mrs. (Chaugum) Jacklyn married into the family of Elwells, who, in conjunction with the Wilsons, still linger around the Light House, occasionally lighting up the old council fires.

SETH PORTER from Goshen, this year owned and lived in a house on the west side of Brooks Street, somewhere near the old Everitt place, and the next year removed to the Luman Munsill house, near the center, and soon after left the town.

ISAAC SWEET, son of Peleg, and a native of the town, came of age this year. He owned twenty-five acres of the southwest part of his father's farm, until 1807, and probably removed soon afterwards with his father to the Western Reserve, O.

1805.

In society meeting, December 30, 1805, "the question being put to said meeting by the moderator, on motion made and seconded, does this meeting feel satisfied with Mr. Bassett, as their minister?—and it was voted in the negative," whereupon a committee was directed to wait on Mr. B. and inform him of this vote, and to report the result of their conference to an adjourned meeting, on January 6, 1805.

The freemen admitted this year were:—Luther Hoadley, Oliver Smith, Timothy Porter, Jasper Videto, and Benjamin Johnson.

JAMES BEEBE, Esq., son of Colonel Bezaleel Beebe of Litchfield, is this year assessed as an inhabitant of the town. He lived on the McEwen homestead from this time until 1838, soon after which he removed to Hartford, Trumbull County, Ohio, where he died in 1865. He was a man of the old puritan stamp, prominent in town and church; was a justice of the peace for many years, a representative at three sessions of the assembly, and senator from the 15th district in 1836 and 1837. He married May 29, 1800, Abi, second daughter of Robert McEwen.

CHILDREN.

I. JULIA FRANCES, b. May 24, 1801; m. June 26, 1827, Darius Phelps of Norfolk.
II. ELIZABETH GARRETT, b. February 13, 1803; m. November 7, 1826, Birdsey Brownson of Winchester.
III. SARAH, b. July 3, 1805; m. May 12, 1829, Doctor Benj. Welch, Jr., of Norfolk.
IV. ROBERT MCEWEN, b. August 17, 1807; d. December 28, 1807.
V. MARY, b. April 8, 1809; d. June 23, 1838.
VI. ROBERT MCEWEN, b. April 28, 1811. Physician, Hartford, O.
VII. JAMES HERVEY, b. August 8, 1813.
VIII. EBENEZER, b. May 27, 1818.

JARED CURTIS, of Pompey, State of New York, m. Dec. 27, 1801, Submit Hubbard, daughter of Elijah Hubbard of W. He received a deed this year, from his father-in-law, of his homestead, in the vicinity of the Bronson & Rugg cheese box factory, and resided on the premises until 1816, when he bought the Rufus Drake farm, in Hall Meadow, which he occupied until 1823. He died in Norfolk, Jan. 1, 1861, aged 81.

CHILDREN.

I.	SYLVIA,	b. in Fabius, Onondaga Co., N. Y., Dec. 17, 1802.
II.	TRUE WORTHY (son),	b. Oct. 14, 1804.
III.	JANE WYLLYS,	b. Aug. 17, 1806.
IV.	CHESTER,	b. Aug. 25, 1808.
V.	HIRAM,	b. Aug. 19, 1810.
VI.	DANIEL,	b. Aug. 12, 1812.
VII.	EMILIA,	b. May 24, 1815.
VIII.	LORRAIN,	b. Oct. 23, 1817.
IX.	BERONA (dau.),	b. Feb. 16, 1819.
X.	LEDELIA,	b. April 4, 1822.

LEVI HOYT lived in a house on the north side of Mad River, and east side of the north and south highway, near the Danbury School-house, until 1807. In 1811 he lived in Litchfield.

ELIJAH PINNEY, this year lived in Winchester, and was "of Barkhamsted," in 1814, when he bought the Harry Blake farm, on the old road from Winsted to Winchester, on which he resided until 1835, when he removed to Erie, Penn., and died there. His widow, Mahala, died in Colebrook, in January, 1866, at the house of her son-in-law, Ralzemon Phelps.

ISAAC TUCKER, son of Reuben, of W., and a native of the town, came of age this year. He m. Nov. 5, 1805, Pamelia Benedict. In 1811, he became the owner of his father's homestead on Mad River, near Norfolk line, which he occupied until about 1827. He died some ten years later.

CHILDREN.

I.	PHINEHAS JUDD,	b. May 17, 1807.
II.	ANNA,	b. June 8, 1809.
III.	TIMOTHY BENEDICT,	b. Dec. 29, 1811.
IV.	WILLARD,	b. May 22, 1815.
V.	WYLLYS,	b. March 26, 1817.
VI.	SARAH PAMELA,	b. Oct. 16, 1820.
VII.	ISAAC,	b. Sept. 26, 1827.

CHAUNCEY WHITE, a tailor, lived until about 1810, on the Norfolk road, beyond L. B. Hurlbut's, and then built and occupied a small house that stood near the stone house of Isaac A. Bronson, until about 1813, when he removed from the town.

1806.

Either the "fathers of the town" had heretofore received the honor of their appointment as a sufficient compensation, or they had charged a higher price for services than their constituents approved, as would seem from a vote of this year, "to allow some compensation to select men for their services," and another vote fixing the compensation at fifty cents a day.

The geese of the town, perhaps by reason of affinity to the selectmen, seemed to have been deemed worthy of "some compensation," which was provided for by the following vote:

"*Voted*, that every goose found in the highway, if any person shall take up such goose, and drive the same to the owner, or to pound, shall be entitled to receive two cents for each goose or gander." *

Manifestations of discontent, on the part of the Church and Society, with the pastorate of Mr. Bassett, began to appear at the close of the year 1805. Early in 1806, Mr. B. was requested to join in the call of a council with reference to his dismission. Further steps were taken in April, which resulted in the call of a council, consisting of Rev. Messrs. Robbins of Norfolk, Hooker of Goshen, and Lee of Colebrook, and Deacons Norton and Frisbie, " to advise such measures as they in their wisdom should think proper." The advice given does not appear. In May, following, a vote of very questionable propriety was passed, appointing a committee " to enquire of any person they may think proper, whether any, and if any, what allegations can be brought and substantiated against Mr. Bassett's moral conduct as a gospel minister or a Christian." After the report of this committee, a series of allegations were embodied in a complaint, and submitted to the moderator of Consociation. The Consociation met in August. Neither the charges exhibited, nor the result of council thereon, are found on Record. Mr. Bassett was dismissed from

---

* That this was not a solitary instance of ambiguous legislation, is shown by the following extract from the records of Simsbury:

' At a Generall Town metting of the Inhabetanc of Simsbury, Regulerly convened fe'nery twenty-eight, 1718–19, these Sundery acts were past: Im:prs: Samuel barbor was chosen to take care to prowide a bull for hop meadow in the Room of Ephraim buell said buell being dead.''

his charge, but was not deposed from the ministry. In the following year he brought before the Association (or Consociation) a complaint against the Church, exhibiting eleven articles of charge for immoral conduct toward him. The church went into consideration of each of the articles of charge, and unanimously denied their being guilty of each and all of them. The church records do not show the nature of the charges, nor the result arrived at by Consociation; and the record of the trial, and result of that body, if in existence, has not been accessible to the compiler.

Rev. Mr. Marsh, in his account of the Winchester Church, before referred to, writes as follows:

" Mr. Bassett removed to Walton, Delaware Co., N. Y. How long he continued pastor of that church is not known to the writer. After his dismission from that people, he preached considerably in various places, but continued his residence at Walton.

" He was a man of talents, had a high standing in a good class — wrote able, sound and discriminating discourses, — and merely as a preacher, might have been acceptable to his people. But unhappily, in his dealings with men, and management of secular matters, he was so indiscreet as to create difficulties which led to his dismission. He married Kezia, dau. of Mr. Zebulun Curtis of Torringford, a worthy woman." Their daughter, Mary, was baptized June 23, 1805.

The electors admitted this year were Jared Curtis, Samuel Hurlbut, Jr., Warren W. Norton, Alexander Cleveland, Isaac Sweet, James Beach, Elizur Hinsdale, and Roger Root, Jr.

WAIT LOOMIS, from Torrington, brother of Lorrin and Arah of W., lived in the old house since torn down, at the parting of the roads above the Dugway, where he d. Feb. 25, 1849, aged 83. He m. in 1796, Sally Stone, who d. Sept. 25, 1845, aged 77 years, leaving one daughter, Sophronia, who has had two husbands, Swain and Leonard.

DANIEL MURRAY, b. Torrington, April 4, 1785, came to Winchester when a boy, and is on the assessment list of this year. In 1815, he bought of William Miner, the Samuel Clark farm, which continued to be his homestead until his death, Aug. 27, 1870. He m. March 25, 1810, Roxalany North, of Torrington; born Nov. 2, 1785.

CHILDREN.

I. PHILOMELA, b. July 7, 1811 ; m. Sept. 10, 1850, Wilkes, of Norfolk.
II. FREDERICK, b. " 28, 1813 ; m. June 2, 1847, Ann M. Caul.
III. FLORA, b. Sept. 4, 1815 ; m. Samuel W. Starks.
IV. JENNETT, b. April 2, 1818 ; m. George Phelps.
V. LUCRETIA, b. Dec. 15, 1820 ; m. Augustus Smith.

VI. SABRA, b. July 24, 1823.
VII. PRUDENCE, b. Sept. 1826; m. (1st), Lucius Curtis; (2d), Ralph I. Crissey.

ROGER ROOT, from New London county, a shoemaker, came to Winchester this or the preceding year. He owned no real estate in the town,—resided mainly in the Danbury Quarter,—and died Nov. 1, 1820, aged 84. His wife, *Temperance*, died July 2, 1833, aged 89.

ROGER ROOT, JR., lived in the house since torn down, some thirty rods north of Joel G. Griswold's, on the west side of the old Winsted and Winchester road, until he removed to Erie Co., Penn., about 1820. He m. March 26, 1807, Florinda, dau. of John Miner.

CHILDREN.

I. CAROLINE NANCY, b. Feb. 9, 1808.
II. HARRY OSCAR, b. Aug. 23, 1810.
III. LUCIUS MINER, b. Feb. 28, 1814.
IV. JULIETTE, b. June 26, 1816.

GURDON ROOT, son of Roger, and a bachelor, lived with his maiden sisters, Hannah and Nancy, in a house which was burned while occupied by them, on the old Waterbury turnpike, half a mile south of Mad River, and afterwards in the second house beyond the toll gate, on the north side of Green Woods turnpike, until his death, May 29, 1832, aged 50. Hannah resided with him and died in the same house, July 26, 1835, aged 58. Nancy, the other sister, in 1849, bought a house on north side of High street, Winsted, near Elm street, in which she came to her death by the accidental burning of her clothes, while alone in the house, Sept. 24, 1862.

ASAHEL SMITH, from Torrington, is on the tax list of this year. He m. Oct. 6, 1809, Elizabeth, widow of Luke Case, deceased, and lived on the east and west road, bordering the Torrington line, in a house now torn down, until 1828, when he removed to Winsted, and lived in the Russell house on the old Colebrook road until his death, May 29, 1832, aged 50. He represented the town in the General Assemblies of 1827 and 1831.

His first wife dying he m. (2d), Oct. 27, 1828, Widow Sophia (Munson) Rice, of Barkhamsted, who m. March 7, 1842, Reuben Brown of Norfolk.

CHILDREN BY FIRST WIFE.

I. ABEL ADAMS, b. March 10, 1811; m. Nov. 30, 1837, Ruth Coe; d. childless, May 11, 1841. She d. April 18, 1847.

II. MINERVA, b. Sept. 1, 1812; m. Nov. 7, 1825, Henry Stanton.
III. ELIZABETH, b. Aug. 14, 1814; m. March 16, 1836, Sheldon A. Wilcox.
IV. HARRIET, b. June 20, 1826.
V. EVELINE, b. Aug. 19, 1819.

CHILD BY SECOND WIFE.

VI. ANN, b.

1807.

REV. THOMAS ROBBINS, D. D., son of Rev. Ammi R. Robbins, of Norfolk, was employed to fill the pulpit made vacant by the dismission of Mr. Bassett;—and on the 20th of April of this year, a committee was appointed to ascertain his views of settling in the ministry; and to secure the continuance of his labors as a candidate. In May following it was voted, "that we do earnestly and sincerely wish that Mr. Robbins would agree to supply the pulpit personally, when he is able; but in case his health will not admit of it, that he should engage some one to preach in his absence,—and that he be indulged the liberty of taking all possible pains to gain his health."

At the annual meeting, November 2d, it was unanimously voted (53 members of the Society present and voting), to invite Mr. Robbins to a settlement, with a salary of $430. The Church, with equal unanimity, voted the call. Owing to his feeble health Mr. Robbins declined the call, and soon afterward withdrew from the Society.

The electors admitted this year were Jos. T. Cummings, Stephen Wheadon, Jos. Chamberlin, Chauncey White, Elisha Wetmore, and Jonathan Church.

SAMUEL W. BALDWIN, from Goshen, became the owner and occupant of the old Crocker house, at the parting of the Green Woods and Waterbury River turnpikes, half a mile above the toll-gate, and succeeded Simeon Moore as tavern-keeper, adding thereto the trade of blacksmith. In 1810 he sold out and left the town, but in 1818 resumed the ownership, and in 1819 conveyed the premises to his son, Norman Baldwin, who sold out to James Crocker in 1823 and removed to Vernon, New York. He had another son, George W., older than Norman, who was graduated at Yale College in 1811.

NORMAN BALDWIN, married, February 2, 1820, Lovisa Benedict.

CHILDREN.

I. MOSES LYMAN, b. Jan. 1, 1822.
II. ZALMON LUMAN, b. March 26, 1824.

His name is last on the assessment list in 1824.

LEVI L. HATCH, son of Moses, of W., is on the list of this and the following years, until 1811, after which he resided at Coxsackie, New York, until a short time before his death. He died in W., August 6, 1845, aged 59.

ZENAS NEAL, from Harwinton, owned and occupied a lot and house thereon, near Norfolk line, on the southern border of Danbury Quarter, until 1811, and thereafter disappears from the records.

LANCELOT PHELPS, SR., this year built the Green Woods Hotel building, at the parting of the Waterbury River and Green Woods turnpikes near Colebrook line, in which he resided about a year and then removed to Colebrook. He was father of Warren, and grand father of the late Wm. H. Phelps, of Winsted.

ROGER STARKWEATHER, from Windsor, bought and lived in the house at the parting of the north and south, and Old Country roads, below the burying-ground, now or lately owned by Nelson Hart. He died May 26, 1826, aged 44. Wife Martha.

CHILDREN.

I. EMILY, b. March 5, 1807; m. Jan. 17, 1827, Wm. Phippenny, of Tor.
II. HARRIET, b. Sept. 17, 1809; m. Oct. 6, 1829, John C. Barber, of Tor.
III. THOMAS, b. Jan. 1, 1815.
IV. CHARLES, b. March 26, 1817; d. Nov. 22, 1850.

1808.

In 1799, one-third of the town meetings had been carried to Winsted, and were held at the old Higley tavern, now standing in the West village; — all of the electors' meetings being still held in the old Society. This year Winsted had so increased in population as to claim that both the town and electors' meetings should be there holden each alternate year. The result was a vote to hold half the town meetings in the Winsted (east village) meeting house; — all the electors' meetings still to be held in the old Society.

In Society meeting, January 11, 1808, the committee were directed to employ Rev. Frederick Marsh to supply the pulpit for the future at their discretion.

February 12th, it was voted to paint the meeting house, — the body white, and the roof red.

At the annual meeting, November 7th, it was voted to unite with the Church in their call to Mr. Frederick Marsh, to settle in the work of the Gospel Ministry; — 33 in favor and 1 against the vote; — and to give him a salary of $430.

December 19th, Mr. Marsh declined the call, partly on account of lack of unanimity and partly on account of his inability to procure a residence without going into debt therefor; — whereupon the Society voted unanimously (42 present and voting) to continue their call, and to ascertain whether his first reason assigned would be insurmountable, provided the second were obviated. Mr. Marsh's answer to this overture was laid before a meeting on the 30th of December, and was as follows:

BRETHREN AND FRIENDS:

Your call to me to settle in the work of the Gospel Ministry has received from me a deliberate and solemn attention. After a mature and prayerful consideration of the call, and the several subjects connected with it; and after taking the advice of my particular friends, and others whose situation and experience enable them to assist me in making up my mind on so important a subject, I have thought it my duty to accept, and accordingly do accept your invitation to settle with you in the work of the ministry, provided at the time appointed for the ordination no difficulty should then exist in Church or Society, which would render it improper for me to receive ordination.

With sentiments of respect, and a desire for the peace and happiness of the people,   I am yours &c.,
Winchester, Dec. 30, 1808.   FREDERICK MARSH.

The 1st day of February, 1809, was appointed for the ordination, and the previous Friday assigned by the Church as a day of fasting and prayer, and one or more neighboring ministers were invited to attend the exercises.

Neither the records of the Society or Church, nor Mr. Marsh's historical notes give any particulars of the ordination.

It took place on the day appointed, and Mr. Marsh entered on his faithful and acceptable ministrations, and still lives, the venerable and beloved Patriarch of the ministers of Litchfield County.

He was son of Jonathan Marsh of New Hartford, where he was born September 18, 1780. He prepared for college with Rev. A. R. Robbins, of Norfolk, — graduated at Yale, September, 1805, — studied theology under Rev. Asahel Hooker, of Goshen, — was licensed as a preacher by the North Association of Litchfield County, — and was dismissed from his pastoral charge October 2, 1851, after a laborious ministry of more than forty-two years. He married, May 22, 1809, Parnal Merrill, of New Hartford, daughter of Joseph and Lydia (Flower) Merrill, born August 7, 1782; died March 11, 1860.

Frederick Marsh

CHILDREN.

I. LOUISA MERRILL, b. May 16, 1810; d. May 9, 1831.
II. CATHARINE, b. April 3, 1812; m. June 17, 1835, Rev. Geo. Carrington, of Hadlyme, who d. in Rushville, Ill., Oct. 31, 1843.
III. JONATHAN PITKIN (deaf and dumb), b. April 26, 1814; m. Jan. 24, 1840, Paulina Bowdish.
IV. FREDERICK EDWARD, b. Dec. 30, 1816; m. Jan. 2, 1844, Matilda Marsh; she d. Jan. 5, 1860, and he m. (2d), May 8, 1862, Mrs. Eliza A. Spencer.
V. SARAH ANN, b. Dec. 29, 1819; d. Sept. 15, 1823.
VI. JOSEPH MERRILL, b. Sept. 15, 1823; m. May 5, 1848, Candace G. Eggleston, of Winchester.
VII. HOWARD PITKIN (twin), b. April 12, 1826; m. June 10, 1856, Harriett E. Hotchkiss, of New Haven; d. New Hartford, Feb. 21, 1864.
VIII. HENRY FLOWER, (twin), b. April 12, 1826; m. June 11, 1855, Sarah E. Frissell, who d. Aug. 24, 1870.

ASAPH B. BROOKS, from Chatham, became a resident this year. In 1816, in connection with his brothers, Samuel and Chauncey, he bought the Peleg Sweet farm, in Danbury quarter, on Brooks street, on which he died November 27, 1866, aged 83.

ASHER CASE, son of William R., once of this town, this year became the owner of the Rufus Eggleston farm, on the West side of Long Pond, which he conveyed away in 1820, by a deed in which he is named "of Hartford." He returned to this town about 1825, and after 1845, lived on the farm now owned by his sons, Edward and George. He d. Sept. 7, 1858, aged 67.

SAMUEL CONE and WARREN CONE, sons of Daniel Hurlbut Cone, of W., and natives of the town, are on the list of this year. Samuel lived here until about 1810, and then went to Norfolk, and carried on the scythe making business until his death. He was a Deacon of the Norfolk Cong. Church, and a man of eminent piety. His twin sons, John and James, reside in Winsted. Warren Cone went to Norfolk with his brother Samuel, and was for some years partner with him in the scythe making business, and afterwards built and carried on a shop of his own. He was a prominent man of the town, which he represented in the Assemblies of 1834 and 1838.

ERASTUS G. HURLBUT, from Torrington, is on the list of this year. In 1816 he bought the Frederick Murray farm, adjoining Sucker Brook, on the old Winsted and Winchester road, on which he lived until his removal to Torrington, in 1825. He m. Dec. 16, 1812, *Clarissa*, dau. of Russell Goodwin of W.

AMMI MURRAY, brother of Daniel, of W., son of Daniel of Torrington, b. July 29, 1787, is on the list of this year as a resident. In 1822, he bought the old Roberts farm, and lived in the house thereon now torn down, on the old Winsted and Winchester road, some thirty rods north of Joel G. Griswold's, until his removal to North Bloomfield, Trumbull Co., Ohio, in 1831. He m. Feb. 23, 1814, Prudence, dau. of Remembrance North of Torrington.

CHILDREN.

I. EMELINE,   II. JULIETTE,   III. HELEN.

JOHN STORER, or STORY, is on the list this year as a resident. He was by trade a Joiner, owned no real estate in the town, and had no fixed residence. About 1825, he left his family and joined the Tyringham Shakers. He m. Jan. 7, 1808, Eunice, dau. of John Church.

CHILDREN.

I. SIMEON, b. Sept. 30, 1808.
II. DAVID, b. Dec. 3, 1810.
III. ELIZA, b. Nov. 4, 1812; m. July 3, 1834, Samuel D. Sheldon; both of them run-away Shakers.

GEORGE TUTTLE, a blacksmith, came to the town this year. In 1817, he bought the second house west of the toll gate, on the north side of the Green Woods turnpike, and had a shop on the opposite side of the road. He lived here until his removal to Colebrook, about 1825, where he died about 1850. He had several children, born in this town; among them, Joel, still a resident.

The electors admitted this year were Elijah Blake, Jr., Jonathan Blake, Joseph Coit, Jesse Clark, Elisha Rowley, Reuben Baldwin, Asa Mallory, Lemuel Hurlbut, Eben Coe, William Miner, Isaac Tucker, John Westlake, and Elisha Smith.

1809.

The records of these latter years indicate that our town enjoyed great quiet if not prosperity. All the doings of this year, election of town officers and laying of taxes included, are recorded on a single page.

The Society, too, under its new pastor, enjoyed great quiet; the only extra-routine business recorded being a vote " to pay a leader of Psalmody, to instruct the youth and others in the art of singing," or in other words to hire a singing master.

AND FAMILY RECORDS. 241

The only new names of residents appearing, are Fisk Beach, who has been noticed in connection with his father, and Noble J. Everitt, both natives of the town.

NOBLE J. EVERITT, son of Dr. Josiah, and grandson of Widow Hannah of W., lived with his father during his life, and still lives in the lean-to house on the West side of the Waterbury River road, between Luman Munsill on the North, and Marcus Munsill on the South. He m. Roxy E., dau. of Elisha Cook, Esq., of Torrington, and had one child, *Albert Chester*, b. Dec. 22, 1816, who died in childhood.

The electors admitted this year were William Chamberlin, 2d, Asher Case, Lyman Strong, Daniel Burnham, and Roger Starkweather.

1810.

The town and society records of this year are without interest.

The electors admitted this year were Ira Preston and Riley Whiting.

CAPT. ELI RICHARDS, from Torrington, this year bought the farm recently conveyed by the widow of Artemas Rowley to Alonzo C. Parcels, which he occupied until his death, Jan. 23, 1816, aged 66. By his wife, Lydia, who d. in W. Oct. 30, 1835, aged 74, he had an only child, Elizabeth, who m. Oct. 1, 1817, Joseph Miller, Esq., of Winsted, and d. in Michigan about 1855.

WILLIAM CRUM, a saddler and harness maker, is on this year's list as a resident. In 1813, he bought of Chauncey White the house which stood adjoining Isaac A. Bronson's new stone house, in which he resided until his death, Dec. 14, 1824, aged 49. He m. Oct. 22, 1811, Hannah, dau. of John Nash of W., who is still living in Winsted.

CHILDREN.

I. FREDERICK, b. March 21, 1813; resident of Unionville, Conn.
II. SOPHIA, b. Sept. 1, 1815; m. May 6, 1846, Abram G. Kellogg, of W.

CHAPTER XVIII.

STATE OF SOCIETY—CUSTOMS—FAMILY RECORDS.

1811 to 1831.

We find Old Winchester, at this period, in its full maturity and vigor —a staid agricultural community, with well-established institutions in good running order, with a homogeneous population, elastic in spirit, virtuous in morals, and orthodox in faith, with property as equally distributed as is consistent with the varied capacity of men to acquire and to hold it, with no overshadowing rich, and very few abjectly poor men.

The compiler's first personal knowledge of this section of the town was acquired by attending a Fourth of July celebration there solemnized in 1810 or 1811. To a boy of eleven or twelve years, whose experience of the world had been hitherto limited by the hills and mountains surrounding the Winsted valley, this outlook on the world was decidedly impressive. The elevated plateau of the centre village received the earliest rays of the rising sun, and the latest effulgence of the setting luminary. Around and near the village green were some half dozen most respectable lean-to houses, some of them in white paint and others in red, which were occupied by the clerical, legal, medical, and magisterial dignitaries. There were other houses indicating comfort and respectability: two gambrel-roofed stores, one Federal and the other Democratic, where they sold two and six-penny hum-hums for eighteen pence a yard, Barlow knives for nine-pence a piece, and New England rum for three shillings, and Jamaica for four and sixpence a gallon. The tavern was a one-story building of neutral tint, large on the ground, with a capacious garret. Two blacksmith shops and the pound were on the outskirts of the village.

The meeting-house stood near the centre of the triangular green, with its line of horse-sheds bordering the front line of Theron Bronson's premises. The whipping-post and stocks, those indispensable pillars of New England law and order, stood on the green near the meeting house. The post did extra duty as a sign post, on which public notices were fastened, and to which, when occasion required, the petty thief was tied, to receive from the constable his five or ten lashes " well laid on to his naked back."

The "stocks" were an upper and lower plank, say six feet long, eight inches wide, and two inches thick, the lower one lying edgewise near the ground, mortised at one end into the post and firmly fastened to the ground at the other. The upper plank was attached to the post at one end by a heavy hinge, so that its lower edge came in contact with the upper edge of the other, and they were held together by a hasp and padlock at their outer ends. At the line of junction of the two planks were four holes, half in the upper and half in the lower plank, about three inches in diameter, ranged at suitable distances for receiving the ankles of two culprits. How often our worthy forefathers and their young children were treated with the edifying spectacle of a public whipping at the post or of a culprit in the stocks, is not ascertainable.

A well authenticated tradition is handed down, of one Meacham, a hired laborer of old Squire Hurlbut, of very moderate intellect, who, after a faithful service and inoffensive life of several years, took it into his head to run away, and to carry with him a variety of articles of clothing, &c., purloined from his employer's premises. His theft being discovered, he was pursued, brought back, and tried on a grand juror's complaint, found guilty, and sentenced to be publicly whipped at the post. The sentence was duly executed on Saturday. On Sunday following, though not a church member, he attended public service, occupying a prominent seat. At the close of service, he arose, and the minister read to the audience his penitential confession, asking pardon of the church and the community, and that he might be restored to public confidence. The minister then exhorted the people to accept his confession, and to extend to him their sympathy and encouragement in aid of his reformation. He is said to have continued to live with his old employer for several years a blameless and exemplary life.

To return from this episode to the celebration:—the day was fine, the gathering large. The long booth of green boughs stood on the green in front of the tavern and shaded a table of equal length, loaded with baked beef and mutton, roasted pigs, baked Indian puddings, and pies of every variety the season afforded. The sayings and doings of the occasion were fully reported in the Connecticut Courant of the following week ; how the procession was escorted into the meeting-house by Captain Bunnell's full militia company, the singing led by Major Lloyd Andrews, the prayer offered by Rev. Ammi R. Robbins of Norfolk, the able and brilliant oration pronounced by Rev. Chauncey Lee of Colebrook, the table presided over by Captain Abial Loomis of Winchester ; then followed the toasts fragrant with sentimental patriotism and Malaga wine, each followed by a feu-de-joie of musketry and the asthmatic cough of a cast-iron four-pounder field piece, mounted on cart-wheels which had been brought from Litchfield for the occasion, no cannon having ever before been fired in the peaceful town.*

---

* The history of the old field-piece, prior to its advent in Winchester, whether it was a trophy of the Old French Wars or of the Revolutionary struggle, is lost in

Such was Old Winchester sixty years ago. Several of the old lean-to houses have passed away. The venerable mansion where Squire Alvord dispensed justice for nearly fifty years, is gone, leaving no trace behind. The dwelling place of Rev. Mr. Knapp is also gone, and its location undefined by any visible mark of a former habitation. Captain Hurlbut's tavern at the center has given place to the present residence of his grandson bearing his name. Four or five others, at and near the center, still remain decayed and venerable, but not dilapidated.

The old Meeting House, and the Tavern House of 1810, afterwards used as a store, are also gone, as well as the whipping post and stocks. The Green is no longer cumbered with church sheds, or other appendages. The more recent meeting house, a neat, well-repaired building, with its wooden Doric portico, tower, and bell, faces the Green at the east, end of the northern border, and the new and commodious store of Theron Bronson has superseded the former store building, while his dwelling occupies the intervening space in the rear of the old horse sheds. Several other large and commodious dwellings of modern date give to the village a cheerful and refined aspect.

The subsequent history of the Society is barren of notable incidents.

---

oblivion. Since it first gave voice to the patriotism of Old Winchester, its fate has been quite eventful. It never went back to Litchfield, having been bought of its former owners by old Uncle Richard Coit, who, some years after, parted with it to some unknown parties in Winsted. Here it was made to vomit small thunder from its rusty throat from Cobble Hill, Street Hill, and divers other places, on all festive occasions. It was brought into service to defend the liberty pole on the East Village Park against the assaults of the old Federalists during the War of 1812, and at a later period to break up meetings of the pestilent abolitionists. Some thirty years ago a couple of lusty old maids living at the East Village hotel, out of patience with the noisy thing, which had been fired off in front of the house half the night, and had been left on the ground, contrived to roll it into the garden, where they dug a grave and buried it. The gun was no more to be found for a dozen years, when the secret of its burial place leaked out. It was exhumed and again did service in celebrating the political victories of each party until the Buchanan campaign, during which the Republicans again secretly buried it, with the intention of resurrecting it for use in the event of Fremont's election. The Democrats discovered its grave in season to secure it for their use when the returns came in, showing the election of "the Old Public Functionary." They used it most savagely in front of the Herald office, breaking in the windows and doors and smashing things generally. Why it didn't burst with the enormous charges filling it to the muzzle, no one can tell. It was soon after taken by the Fremont men and thrown into the Clifton Mill pond, where it remained until mid-winter, when a West Village saloon-keeper and his patriotic customers turned out one cold night and made diligent search up and down the cold stream until they found and transferred it to a safe hiding place, where it was kept ready for renewed use in the Spring, to celebrate the election of General Pratt for Governor. His opponent was elected, and the gun wasn't wanted. It was liable to be discovered in its hiding place, so the party in possession again buried it in an unknown grave, where it is said to remain to this day.

With very limited accessions of population from abroad, and a continued though diminished drainage by emigration to the West; and with a soil growing less productive from generation to generation, it has made little, if any, gain in its aggregate wealth and productiveness, and has diminished in numbers. In its general tone of morals there has been little, if any, deterioration, though in Sabbath observances and attendance on public worship there has been a great falling off from the old puritan standard. Excitements and dissensions, some of them of a very serious nature, have arisen and died away. Religious institutions, sometimes greatly imperiled, now stand on a solid basis of unity and piety. No intoxicating liquors are openly sold, and few intemperate men are found. Education is in advance of the average of retired communities around it; property is more equally distributed now than it was twenty years ago, and the condition of the Society is prosperous and happy.

The new inhabitants appearing on the stage from year to year grow less frequent. We proceed to notice them in their order.

APOLLOS DEAN seems to have been a resident from 1810 for several years; whether married or single is not ascertained. He may have been a tanner or shoemaker in the employ of the Wades, from whom he received a conveyance of land in 1823, in which he is named of Boston, Portage Co., Ohio.

JOSEPH EGGLESTON, probably from Torrington, was a resident from 1810 to 1815, but not a land owner. His place of residence not ascertained.

JAMES BRAGG came into the town from Springfield, Vt., in 1812. In 1820 he became the owner of the William Chamberlin farm, one and a half miles northerly from the center, on which he lived till a short time before his death, January 30, 1871, aged 88. He married 1807, Susanna, daughter of Daniel H. Cone; she died February 11, 1816, in her 34th year, and he married (2d), 1821, Orpha, daughter of Wait Munson, of Barkhamsted; she died November 18, 1868, aged 76.

CHILDREN.

I. DANIEL HURLBUT, b. September 6, 1808; m. Lavinia Gould of East Granby. He m. (2d) Gracy N. Calvert of Lexington, Ky., where he d. in 1847.
II. WARREN, b. February 13, 1810; m. Julia, daughter of Deacon Warren Cone. He m. (2d) Almira Gray of Sauquoit, N. Y.
III. CLARISSA, b. December 22, 1811; m. Henry Griswold of Hartland
IV. MARY, b. April 19, 1813; d. December 28, 1813.
V. JAMES, b. September 27, 1814; d. October 5, 1819.

VI. JULIA LUCRETIA, b. November 10, 1823; m. Frank L. Whiting of Torrington.
VII. MARY ELIZABETH, b. December 5, 1824; m. Rufus T. Towne of New Hartford.
VIII. HULDAH, b. February 20, 1826; m. Deacon Samuel C. Newton of Hartland.
IX. SARAH, b. August 15, 1831; m. Henry M. Smith of Fairfield, a retired New York merchant.
X. JAMES LORENZO, b. February 24, 1833; m. Eliza, daughter of Hiram Sage of Colebrook. He m. (2d), Sarah Spaulding, daughter of A. A. Spaulding of Norfolk.

DOCTOR ZEPHANIA SWIFT married Nellie Minerva, daughter of Doctor Josiah Everitt of Winchester, and resided in the house recently owned by Samuel Hurlbut 2d, at the center, which he sold, and removed to Farmington before 1819, where he died.

CHILDREN.

I. HELEN ABIGAIL, born in Winchester July 10, 1814; other children were born to them after they left this town. Mrs. Swift still survives, living with a daughter, in New York or Brooklyn. To her the compiler of these annals is indebted largely for aid and encouragement in tracing out old families and delineating ancient customs.

LUMAN WHITING, third son of Christopher Whiting of Winchester, came of age May 5, 1813, and occupied his father's homestead until his removal to Ashtabula County, Ohio, about 1815. He married Anna, daughter of Samuel Hayden, Esq., of Barkhamsted.

MOSES DRAKE and MOSES DRAKE, Jr., of Torrington, in 1813 bought the farm of Oliver Coe, at the south end of Blue street, and occupied it during their remaining lives. Moses Drake, Sen., died July 3, 1831, aged 80, and Moses Drake, Jr., April 10, 1859, aged 71, leaving sons, Henry, who lives on the homestead, Martin V., who lives in Goshen, and several daughters.

EDWARD GRISWOLD and PHINEAS GRISWOLD, Jr., owned and occupied after the death of Phineas, senior, in 1815, the farm next west of the Danbury school house, on the Norfolk Road, until 1822. Phineas Griswold was named in their deed as of Beaver Dam, Erie Co., Penn.

LEWIS HART from Colebrook, purchased the above farm from the Griswolds in 1822, and occupied it until 1826, and then sold to Samuel D. Gilbert. He afterwards removed to Ohio, whence he returned to Colebrook about 1860, and died there in 1866.

CHILDREN.

I. ELMIRA,   b. October 23, 1816.
II. WILLIAM, b. September 12, 1819.
III. LUCY,   b. September 17, 1821.
IV. ERASTUS S.

SAMUEL D. GILBERT came to Winchester when a boy, and resided here during his after life. In 1826 he bought of Lewis Hart the above-mentioned farm, and occupied it until his death, August 24, 1844, aged 46. He married May 19, 1819, Candace, daughter of Reuben Hungerford of Winchester; she died June 17, 1840, aged 42.

They left three sons, Newman B., Lyman, and Charles, and two daughters, who are wives of Erastus S. Hart, late of Canton, and Riley Grant of Norfolk.

Charles Gilbert, son of Samuel D., was wounded and taken prisoner in the battle of Secessionville, S. C., and died of his wounds in prison at Charleston, aged 29, unmarried.

EBENEZER COWLES, from Norfolk, kept the Green Woods Turnpike Toll Gate, from 1816, for several years, and made coal baskets to eke out a living. He was a zealous religionist of the ultra Calvinistic school, — had a wife and two daughters.

JOEL CLARK is on the tax lists from 1816 to 1830. No real estate is found in his name, and his place of residence is not ascertained. No record of his family.

HENRY DAYTON, from Torrington, in 1816, owned and occupied a house and tannery in the south part of the Society, until 1824.

BENJAMIN PHELPS, son of Daniel of W., is on the tax lists from 1816. In 1823, he bought, and afterwards occupied a farm on Brooks street, near the old Everitt place, until his death, July 12, 1849, aged 54. He m. Feb. 6, 1826, Abigail Brooks.

FREDERICK PHELPS, son of Daniel, of W., came of age June 30, 1816, — owned and lived on land on Brooks street, near the old Everitt place, until his removal to Kinderhook, N. Y., not far from 1850, where he now resides. He m. May 22, 1826, Lucy W. Hurlbut, dau. of Stephen of W.

JONATHAN SAXTON first appears on the tax list of 1816, and continues until his death, April 19, 1843, aged 66. He owned no real estate in the town.

SALMON BAIL, son of a Hessian soldier, appears on the tax list of 1816. He lived in the society from that date to the time of his death, Sept. 30, 1853, aged 68. He was not a land owner, and his place of residence is not known. His wife Ursula is named on his gravestone, but no date of death given.

JONATHAN F. BALDWIN is on the tax lists of 1819, and onward to 1821. He owned a blacksmith shop at the centre, which he sold in 1821, and then left the town.

RANDALL COVEY is on the tax lists from 1817 to 1821; and owned a wagon maker's shop at the Center, which he sold the latter year.

GEORGE CHASE, son of Gedeliah of W., married Artemisia, dau. of Oliver Coe; owned and occupied from 1819 to 1823, the house on the north side of the Norfolk road, next west of the Center District school house.

DUDLEY CHASE, son of Gedeliah, of W., came of age Aug. 30, 1817; m. Simsbury, Sept. 27, 1826, Electa ———, b. Simsbury, Feb. 13, 1800. He settled first in Goshen, and since 1831, has lived on the farm where he now resides, on the road from the Center to Hall Meadow. He represented the town in the Legislature of 1858.

CHILDREN.

I. NATHAN, b. Goshen, Oct. 21, 1827; d. Feb. 3, 1856, unmarried.
II. HENRY E., b. G., June 3, 1829; drowned in N. J., March 19, 1852.
III. MARY A., b. G., Aug. 30, 1831; m. Rev. A. V. R. Abbott.
IV. ERWIN E. (twin), b. Nov. 8, 1834; m. Mary Commerford.
V. A SON " b. Nov. 8, 1834; d. Nov. 17, 1834.
VI. DUDLEY, b. Oct. 19, 1838; d. April 30, 1839.
VII. ELLEN E., b. Feb. 1, 1840.

REUBEN CHASE, son of Gedeliah, of W., in 1844 bought a house and land in the south part of the society, which he has since occupied to the present time. He was b. March 25, 1800; m. Oct. 17, 1823, Lucy, dau. of Asahel Curtis, b. Oct. 22, 1806.

CHILDREN.

I. ADELINE, b. June 8, 1825; m. Mathew Hart of Goshen.
II. LUCY E., b. Jan. 30, 1827.
III. HARRIET, b. Jan. 27, 1829; m. George H. Cook of Torrington; d. Nov. 3, 1858.
IV. DELIA, b. March 21, 1832; m. May, 1868, Henry C. Church, New Haven.
V. HARMON, b. Nov. 8, 1839; d. Nov. 21, 1839.
VI. LAURA, b. July 5, 1843; m. Lemuel Munger of Torrington.

SHELDON MILLER, son of George of Winchester, came of age Nov. 10, 1820; m. Oct. 30, 1822, Jerusha Ann Starkweather; lived in the Society until after 1825, and removed to Tyringham, Mass.

CHILDREN.

I. Lewis Allen, b. in W., Nov. 3, 1823.
II. George Hudson, b. in W., June 24, 1825.
III. Henry Elijah. b. in Tyringham, Mass., April 18, 1830.
IV. Laura Ann, b. in Lenox, Mass., Aug. 29, 1832.
V. Mary Maria, b. in Lenox, Mass., Dec. 6, 1841; d. March 23, 1842.
VI. Mary Jerusha, b. in Lee, Mass., Jan. 13, 1844.

HIRAM CHURCH, a native of Vernon, N. Y., and grandson of the first Samuel Hurlbut, — served his time as clerk to S. & L. Hurlbut, and continued in their employ several years; afterwards did business at St. Louis, and at Vernon, N. Y., and then returned to Winchester. He m. Nov. 7, 1838, Emily E. Eno, of Colebrook, who, after his death, m. Gail Borden, Esq., now of Texas.

SAMUEL BANDLE, a blacksmith, came from New Hartford; m. a dau. of Samuel Hart of W. Lived in the Society several years, and then moved to Ohio.

WILLARD HART, son of Samuel, of Winchester; m. Dec. 11, 1822, Rhoda Matilda, dau. of Timothy Benedict, deceased, of W., and (2d), Maria, dau. of Daniel Andrews, Jr., of W.; resided in Danbury Quarter; d. May 5, 1840, aged 45, leaving a dau. Rhoda, by his first wife, who m. in 1848, William Miner, and d. leaving one child. By his second wife he had

CHILDREN.

I. Sarah, b. Sept. —, 1829; m. Geo. G. Camp.
II. Henry, b. 1831; d. in 1846.
III. Elizabeth, b. in 1835; m. James G. Ferris.
IV. Lewis, b. in 1837.
V. Henrietta, b. 1839; m. Nelson Beers.
VI. Willard, b. in 1840; m. May 6, 1860, Marietta Hill; killed at Cold Harbor, Va., June 1, 1864, while in the Volunteer Service, as private in Company E., 2d Conn. Heavy Artillery.

RUFUS DRAKE. from Torrington, in 1823, bought the farm in Hall Meadow, on which he has since resided to the present time.

HARVEY FORD, m. June 26, 1825, Mary Ann, dau. of Noah Drake, of Torrington. About 1830, he bought the farm, on Hall Meadow, which he has occupied till recently.

John M. Galagher, an Englishman, not far from 1825, began manufacturing woollen cloths on the east branch of the Naugatuck River, in the south part of the Society, and removed from the town about 1830.

Archibald Dayton, from Torrington, m. Jan. 1, 1827, Lophelia, widow of Levi Bronson, and during his remaining life, lived on Blue Street, near the Stone School House. He d. Nov. 28, 1863. His son, Isaac Dayton, now occupies the same place.

William S. Marsh, from Hartford, m. for his second wife, Sally, dau. of Richard Coit, — and moved to Winchester in 1825, where he resided, on the homestead of his father-in-law, until about 1834, when he removed to Canaan, and died there in 1868.

Daniel Beckley, son of Richard, Sr., of W., has occupied the former residence of his father at the north end of Little Pond to the present time.

Norris Beckly, son of Richard, of W., has resided from his childhood, and still resides in the Society, mainly in Danbury Quarter.

Oliver Loomis, from Torrington, bought the farm between the two lakes in 1827, and lived thereon until 1844, when he bought, and occupied during his remaining life, the second house west of Dudley's Tannery, on the north side of Main street, in Winsted, and died, childless, Feb. 7, 1872, aged 84 years, 9 months, leaving the bulk of his estate to the Methodist Episcopal Church and Society of Winsted, and a legacy of $1,000 to the M. E. Church of Wolcottville. His wife, Mary (Barber) Loomis, d. March, 1870, aged 77 years. Mr. L. was a quiet, frugal citizen, of decided Methodistical and Anti-Slavery sentiments. He was elected a representative to General Assembly in 1834, by a nearly unanimous vote of both political parties.

CHAPTER XIX.

ROADS, PAUPERS, SELECTMEN, ECCLESIASTICAL AFFAIRS, MANUFACTORIES, SEMINARIES, &c.

FROM 1831 TO 1872.

AFTER reaching the matured growth of the Winchester Society, materials for continued annals have steadily diminished in variety and interest. A retired farming community, homogeneous in its composition, with its institutions in running order — so staid that deep ruts mark its pathway — furnishes few events worthy of record. Changes, imperceptible in their progress to a resident inhabitant, may become strikingly apparent to a former resident returning after long years of absence. He may find the possessions of the rich of one generation divided and diffused in another; the overshadowing influence of one class of men undermined, and another class or organization in the ascendant; the all-engrossing dissensions of one period quieted, and new subjects of heart-burning and strife grown up in another.

Such have been the course of events — of improvements and deteriorations — for the last forty years. We find no events of startling interest, no dissensions worthy of being resuscitated from the pall of oblivion, no special exhibitions of foul crime or eminent virtue.

In the way of public improvements, the laying out and opening of several new roads, and the alterations of old ones, are worthy of mention, and preliminary thereto it is fitting to advert to the conservative and narrow-sighted policy of the town in reference to roads and bridges. This pig-headedness may have had its origin in the heavy expense to which the early settlers were subjected in making their first roads by reason of the parsimonious allowances and reservations of lands for highways by the proprietary body, which has been referred to in our earlier annals. Sectional jealousies of the two societies may also have had an influence in fostering opposition to improvements tending to specially benefit one section more than the other. Whatever may have been the remote cause, the effect was a prevailing hostility to almost every proposed improvement. If a road was laid out by the selectmen and reported to the town, however important it might be for public convenience and necessity, if it promised a sectional benefit it was blindly voted down, regardless of the certainty of its being ultimately carried through and established by appeal to the county court.

Notable instances of this nature are found in the now traveled roads from Winsted to Wolcottville, and to Colebrook center, the first having been contested with blind obstinacy and reckless expense from 1822 to 1826, and the second from about 1830 to 1835. In both of these cases litigation was kept up, and long trials without number were had before the court and its delegated committees, at an expense in each instance exceeding the actual cost of the roads when finally constructed. Add to this the point blank, contradictory swearing by platoons and battalions of excited witnesses, the pettifogging tricks of counsel unlearned in the laws of fair dealing, and the vindictive hatreds engendered among neighbors, and the evils cannot be over-estimated.

The old roads from Winchester to Winsted were precipitous and circuitous beyond the average of original layings out of roads. A shorter and every way better route was apparent to every observer. A new road over this route was advocated from time to time early in this century, but was strenuously opposed by influential parties favoring entire non-intercourse rather than free access between the rival sections. In 1836 the selectmen were instructed to report this or some other better route for a road. Some sinister influence, or non-agreement of the board, prevented any lay-out being reported at that time, and the matter rested until after the opening of the Naugatuck Railroad to Winsted, when, in 1853, the selectmen laid out and reported a road along the south border of the Little Pond, and onward to near the General Hurlbut place, with alterations of the existing roads connecting at each end of the new lay-out. This report, according to ancient usage, was summarily rejected in town meeting. Application was soon after made to the court for a road along this line, which was referred to the county commissioners in 1855. The commissioners of that year proved to be men of more than ordinary judgment and independence. They laid out the new road and alterations of the connecting roads in a way that can hardly be in any way improved. The distance saved is nearly half a mile, while the grades are far better than on the old routes. The lay-out was accepted, and the work completed.

In 1871 a connecting link with these improvements was made by laying out a new road, known as Boyd street, from the Connecticut Western Railroad Station, northerly and westerly to the old road above the Stabell place, thereby avoiding the long and steep ascent of Lake street to the lake outlet. This road was accepted, and is now completed, opening an avenue of easy and pleasant communication between the two Societies heretofore greatly needed, and promising a freer communication and fellowship of the two sections.

About 1830, a new road was laid out and accepted, running westerly from the Norfolk or Cooper Lane road, by the residences of Orrin Tuller and Dudley Chase, to a new north and south road, along Hall Meadow in Goshen, which in 1831 was discontinued without being opened. It was soon afterward re-laid, either by the town or by order of Court, and opened to travel,—affording a long desired, and important avenue of intercourse with Goshen, Cornwall, and the Housatonic Valley.

In 1838, a new road was petitioned for, to run from the Center, southerly and easterly, by the house of Elias T. Hatch, near the south border of Long Lake, and thence in the direction of the Pine Knot, near the line of the Naugatuck Railroad,—to connect with a new proposed road through the south end of New Hartford to Canton. The town, according to usage, rejected the Winchester section, as did the town of Torrington the section within its borders;—whereupon the petitioners applied to the County Court, and got a committee, which made short work of laying out a line of roads, and improvements on the proposed route, which were confidently expected, by the projectors, to divert the Albany and Hartford travel from the old time route through Winsted, to this new thoroughfare. The road was petitioned for to the Court, laid and accepted, during the smoke of the great battle then raging over the Colebrook Road, without serious opposition from any quarter. The committee is reported to have carried with them a jug of rum, while examining the route and laying the road, which accounts for the profound wisdom of portions of their lay-out. The road has never fulfilled the sanguine expectations of its projectors, but has nevertheless vindicated its necessity and convenience.

Improvements and changes have been made in many other roads of the Society; but the greatest and most beneficial change has been wrought by the entire abandonment of the old system of repairing highways, by a wretched system of labor-taxation, inherited from "the fathers." Attempts were more than once made to get rid of it by allotment of sections of roads to individual contractors, and by money taxes; but this system failed to work satisfactorily, and others were tried until the annual town meeting in 1860, when it was voted, "that a thorough man be appointed in each district to repair the roads therein, and that the men so appointed bring in their bills for such repairs to the Selectmen for payment." This vote led to the most thorough repair and improvement of roads ever made in the town; yet the process did not prove so expensive as to prevent its being repeated with good results, until the annual meeting in 1865, when a commissioner was appointed in each society to supervise the repairs, under such a limitation of expense as not to exceed two thousand dollars for the whole town. The result was a partial repair of the Old Society roads, and an almost total neglect of those in Winsted. The same course was adopted in 1866, without a limitation of expenses, and repeated in 1867 and 1868, — when the appointment of district road masters was given to the select men, and so continued to 1870, when the entire supervision of the roads was restored to the selectmen, and it has continued in their hands to the present time.

Up to about 1850 the model selectman, — however fair, honorable, and humane he may have been in his private transactions, seemed to become penurious and heartless when invested with this dignity. A capacity to systematize the affairs of the town, and to manage them with a view to general and permanent advantage, was held in small estimation. It was not supposable that he could, at the end of the year, render an intelligent account of his doings or do-nothings. He entered on his duties with an abiding fear of indiscriminate censure of any liberal act or comprehensive policy. At the year's end his report was criticised, and his doings were scanned without reason or mercy. Lucky was he, if his report was so blind as to cover up his mismanagement, and conceal the true financial condition of the town. He thereby stood a chance of re-election, and ultimately of representing the incapacity of the town in the General Assembly.

On the other hand, instances have occurred of the election of independent, straight-forward men, who have blasted out obtruding rocks from the roads, or built permanent bridges, or kindly provided for the poor; or, worst of all, have investigated the financial affairs of the town, and produced a reliable balance sheet, showing a before unknown amount of indebtedness. Rarely, in former times, did such offences as these escape the penalty of deposition from office.

It has rarely been the wont of our town to avail itself of the experience of a competent selectman, by continuing him in office for a long course of years as in many other towns. The darling principles of rotation in office, and the maxim that to the party victors belong the spoils, alike forbade it.

These strictures, though applied specially to our own town, doubtless have a general application to many of the towns around us.

In many respects, improvement has become manifest in our affairs. The financial condition of the town is clearly made known in printed reports, from year to year. There is a readiness to vote the taxes that are clearly seen to be needful. The principle of cash payments of current expenses is established. About fifty-six thousand dollars of war loans have been paid off, and the financial condition of the town is prosperous.

But rare allusions have been made in our annals to the system, or rather want of system, of providing for the poor. We have quoted a few early instances of bringing these unfortunates to the auction block and of summarily attempting to vote them out of the town guardianship. Such cases are rarely found. As a rule the wants of the poor have been supplied at their own dwellings, or places have been provided for them in private families in the vicinity of their previous residences.

About 1845 the system of contracting with some responsible individual of approved character, to provide for all the poor of the town, either in his own family or at their dwellings, was initiated, and was continued until 1871. Few well founded complaints of unkind treatment by contractors have been made. The selectmen have been required to make monthly inspections and careful inquiries as to the treatment of the poor; and the ministers in charge of the different denominations have been invited by votes of the town to perform the same duties.

This course of management has not been pursued without a consciousness on the part of the community of its evils and abuses. The records of the last fifty years abound with votes instructing the Selectmen to take measures for selecting and purchasing a town farm, and other votes appointing special committees for the same purpose;—but no selection and recommendation was ever sanctioned by approval of the town until the month of June of the present year (1872), when the Whiting farm, on the east border of the town, was purchased, and is hereafter to be used, under the direction of the town as a home for the poor. The buildings are well adapted to the purpose; and it is devoutly to be hoped that a competent and humane manager will be selected and such preparations made, as will give a fair start and ensure a successful working of the institution. It is also to be hoped and devoutly prayed for, that whether or not, worthy or unworthy, members of any of our churches are consigned to this refuge, their associated followers of Him who went about doing good will imitate His example, by conscientiously and systematically visiting and ministering to the needs and comforts of the destitute and forsaken.*

---

* The following obituary notice of a worthy member of one of our churches who had for several years of poverty and disease, been an inmate of the poor-house, appeared in the Winsted Herald of December 9, 1864. It needs no comment. "Exchanged his poverty for eternal riches, and his rags for a crown which fadeth not away—at the Winchester poor-house, Nov. 5, 1864, James C. Smith, aged 67. The pall-bearers were few on this side—not so many perhaps as they that waited on the 'shining shore,' and went up with the old man to 'his Father's house.'"

Returning from this disquisition of town affairs, to the closing of our annals of the Old Society of Winchester, we find little more of history to be compiled; while the sources from which to compile family records are exhausted.

A noteworthy and creditable feature characterizing the Society, has been, and continues to be, the permanence, amid all divisions and excitements, of the Congregational Order, and the absence of all other organized denominations. At Noppit, beyond the Torrington border, — where Mr. Hungerford threatened going to get religion, — the fathers of the Drakes, Fylers, Norths, and others, were Baptists; and early erected a meeting house for their order. The Methodists, in process of time, became numerous, and the two orders united in enlarging, repairing, and adding a steeple to the Baptist house, under an arrangement that each order should use it on alternate Sabbaths. This plan worked well until the Methodist quarterly meeting occurred on the Baptists' Sabbath, and they of that persuasion refused to yield their right of worship for the exigency. At the fever heat of the resulting *odium theologicum*, — a new Methodist Church, with steeple and bell, was erected over the way. The process was the reverse of that of Peter Pinder's farmer, who burned his barn to kill the rats, but was equally unwise; — for there were now two barns to shelter the vermin of sectarianism; and the scant ability to sustain one house of worship became divided and utterly inadequate for the two. The Baptists have dwindled down to the shadow of a name, and the Methodists, overshadowed by the rising order of Adventists, yielded their house to the ownership and control of that persuasion about 1850. This new Evangel, for a few years, was gladly received by large numbers, and religious zeal pervaded the whole community. Both meeting houses became crowded with Sabbath worshipers, and continued so for a few years, when the flame of devotion and sectarianism died away leaving both houses permanently empty and dilapidated.

Only a few of these "sectarians" lived in Winchester, so that the Congregational order was slightly affected by their controversies. Rev. Father Marsh, amid many trials growing out of internal dissensions of his Church, pursued the even tenor of his way sole pastor until 1846, when Rev. James H. Dill, a graduate of Yale College and Theological Seminary, was ordained as his colleague pastor, and was so continued until October 2, 1851, when they were both dismissed at their own request. The pulpit was then supplied for a year or more by Rev. Alexander Cunningham, and afterwards by various ministers until October 1857, when Rev. Ira Pettibone, formerly pastor of the First Winsted Church, was installed its pastor, and officiated as such until his removal to Stafford, Connecticut, in 1866. He was succeeded by Rev. Wm. M. Gay, as a supply, for one year. On the 28th of December, 1870, Rev. Arthur Goodenough, the present worthy pastor, was installed, Rev. Mr. Pettibone having been on the same day formally dismissed.

The present state of the Church and Society appears more auspicious than for many past years.

In addition to the district schools in various parts of the Society, an academic school was for several years sustained at the center, under the successive charges of the late Silas H. McAlpine, Robert M. Beebee,

WINCHESTER INSTITUTE.

Henry Norton, James Coe, and others, in the lecture room of the Church. In 1858 Rev. Ira Pettibone, aided by other citizens of the Society, erected a commodious seminary building on an elevated site, immediately north of the village, which he opened as a boarding and day school, under the name of "The Winchester Institute," in conducting which he was assisted by his sons, Colonel Ira W. and Benjamin W. Pettibone, graduates of Yale and Amherst Colleges. The former entered the service in

1862, as Major of the 10th Regt. Conn. Volunteers, and served in the North Carolina campaign, was promoted to Colonel, — and on his resignation, caused by constant ill-health, he assumed the entire management of the school and successfully conducted it until his removal to Beloit College, Illinois, as principal of the preparatory department of that institution.

In 1869 the Seminary grounds and buildings were purchased by Mrs. Sabra Blake, and her daughter, Mrs. Mary Ann Mitchell, and were by them conveyed to seven trustees and their successors, "for the purpose of sustaining, carrying on, and maintaining a Seminary of learning similar to the Institute now and heretofore carried on in the conveyed premises and to possess all the powers necessary for that purpose." Since this purchase and dedication, the Seminary has been conducted by J. Walker McBeth, Esq., a graduate of Edinburgh University and an experienced educator, under whose auspices it is hoped that such a degree of success will be attained as will induce other wealthy citizens of the town to make similar endowments, and thereby raise the present standard of education among us.

The streams adapted to water power run through the northern and southwestern parts of the Society; and none of them are large and permanent enough for large manufacturing purposes. No grist-mill was ever erected in the Society. The early settlers had their grinding done at a mill in the northwestern corner of Torrington, until Austin's mill was erected in Winsted.

The first saw mill was built by Deacon Samuel Wetmore, near the burial ground, with a privilege of flowing the meadow and marsh land bordering the stream above. It was early moved down the stream to a point near the site of the first meeting-house; and, at a later period, was moved further down to the site of the McAlpine mill, below the junction of the east and west branches. A saw mill was early erected on Mad River, near Norfolk line, on the site of the Martin and Nelson Brooks mill; and another, long since abandoned, on the same stream, near the Danbury school-house. The Trumbull Brooks mill, still lower down the stream, was first built early in the present century. Another saw mill was built on Sucker Brook in the last century by Samuel Clark, Christopher Whiting, and others; and still another on the same site was erected by McPherson Hubbell, about 1848, which has now disappeared. Few branches of manufacturing have ever been undertaken in the Society, and none of them have been permanently successful. Dish and trencher mills were appendages of most of the early saw mills, for working up the slabs into primitive household utensils. The last one in the town, standing immediately west of Meadow street bridge, ceased operation as early as 1804.

A fulling mill is said to have been erected about 1776 by Daniel or Joseph Platt, on the small stream running north and emptying into Mad River, at the mill dam of Trumbull Brooks. Samuel Clark built a trip-hammer works for welding gun-barrels, late in the last century, on Sucker Brook, just below the Dugway bridge. A bark mill, connected with the Amasa Wade tannery, on the Naugatuck Branch, near Torrington line, was erected early in the present century. The tannery went into new hands about 1844, and was essentially enlarged and improved in capacity and business, but was abandoned as a tannery about 1850, and was afterwards used for a time in manufacturing cheese boxes. Another tannery and bark mill was erected early in this century by Elijah Blake, senior, and carried on after him by his son, Deacon Allen Blake, now deceased. It stood on Taylor's Brook, and is now abandoned. Early in this century, John McAlpine erected a shop on the east branch, near the burying ground, for cutting scale boards used in packing cheese in casks for marketing, which continued in operation until the packing of cheeses in separate boxes superseded the old method. In 1814 John Nash, James Beebe, and Dr. Zephenia Swift erected a clothiers' works, carding-machine, and fulling mill on the Naugatuck branch, between the McAlpine saw mill and the Wade tannery, which was operated a few years by Alva Nash, then sold to John Galagher, who introduced power looms, and went into the manufacture of broadcloths and satinets. David Bird succeeded Galagher in the business, and formed a joint stock company which operated the concern in a small way until the establishment was burned down about 1860.

Prior to 1825, all the usual handicraft trades, such as blacksmiths, tanners and shoemakers, joiners and carpenters, tailors, hatters, coopers, wheelwrights, &c., were carried on and sustained in the society; but since that period, in consequence of the growth of Winsted, most of them have been abandoned.

From almost the beginning of the century to the year 1857 a large portion of the mercantile and produce business of the Society was transacted by the brothers Samuel and Lemuel Hurlbut, who early placed their business on a solid basis, and enlarged it by transactions beyond the line of ordinary country traders, identifying their interests with those of the community around them, and sustaining its rights and privileges against all outside rivalries. For a long course of years, before Winsted had begun to abound in wealthy men, they were the bankers of this region, and especially so of the dairy farmers requiring loans for the purchase and stocking of their farms. We have already in another place analyzed their characters and capacities, and referred to their introduction of improved breeds of sheep and cattle. On their deaths, occurring within a year of each other, their large business was wound up, and their property distributed among numerous and widely-scattered heirs.

Compared with other farming communities around us, Old Winchester and the agricultural portions of Winsted are favored in a high degree with a distribution of wealth approaching equality, a freedom from embarrassing debt, good education largely diffused, temperate habits, refined morals, and intelligent patriotism.

WINSTED SOCIETY AND BOROUGH.

CHAPTER XX.

WINSTED SOCIETY—FIRST SETTLERS AND FAMILY RECORDS.

As already stated in our preliminary account of the township, the opening of the Old North Road was soon followed by a settlement in the northeast corner of the town, distinct and distant from the earlier settlement in the southwest section, to which our attention has thus far been directed. Long Lake, and the mountain ridges extending from its north end to Colebrook line effectually separated these communities from each other, until near the close of the last century; when the improvement of the splendid water power along the Lake Stream, and at the Still River falls, gradually drew settlers to the intermediate region. The Winsted settlement began some twenty years later than that of the old society. The records show but four resident land owners there in 1771, when the town was incorporated; and none of their names are found on the petition for the incorporation.

1770.

LIEUT. JOHN WRIGHT, from Wethersfield to Goshen in 1740, came thence to Winsted, it is believed in 1769 or 1770, and settled, with his large family, on the northeast side of the old North road, near Colebrook line, on the site of the homestead now occupied by Edward and Edwin Rowley. His title of Lieutenant is said to have been acquired during his service in the French War. His will was proved in the Norfolk Probate Court, Dec. 24, 1784, in which are named his wife Dorcas, and his children, John, Jr., Jabez, Charles, Freedom, Dorcas, Mary, and Lucia. L. M. Norton, in his Goshen Genealogies, names Samuel, David, and Moses, as sons of Lieut. John. The relative age of their children is not ascertainable. His wife was probably a dau. of Benjamin Deming, of Goshen.

SAMUEL WRIGHT, son of John, Sen., probably born at Wethersfield, lived and died at Goshen. L. M. Norton gives his children, born in Goshen, as follows:

CHILDREN.

I.	Josiah,	b. April 1, 1753.
II.	Ozias,	b. Sept. 1, 1755; d. young.
III.	Abigail,	b. Jan. 8, 1757.
IV.	Ozias,	b. Feb. 18, 1759.
V.	Andrew,	b. March 17, 1763.

Moses Wright, son of John, Sen., is probably the same Moses Wright who lived and died in Colebrook, and was father to Norton Wright, who formerly lived near the Old Hemlock Meeting-house, in Winsted, and Alvin Wright of Colebrook, who d. May, 1866.

David Wright, son of John, Sen., is not noted on the Winchester Records as an inhabitant, though he probably came to the town with his father. He enlisted into Capt. Sedgwick's company in 1775, and while on the march to the Northern frontier, died of the camp distemper, at Lanesborough, Mass., unmarried.

John Wright, Jr. probably came to Winsted with his father. He lived immediately east of his father, on the old North road, until his removal in 1801, to Morgan, Ohio. He m. Aug. 14, 1770, Lydia Mason, who d. Nov. 11, 1771. He m. (2d), March 24, 1774, Sarah, dau. of Lieut. Asahel Case, of Norfolk, by whom he had

CHILDREN.

I.	Lydia Mason,	b. Jan. 19, 1775.
II.	David,	b. Aug. 16, 1778; d. Sept. 1, 1784.
III.	John,	b. Jan. 11, 1780.
IV.	Amos Case,	b. Sept. 5, 1782; m. Lydia, dau. of Rev. Aaron Kinney.
V.	Sally,	b. April 16, 1785.
VI.	David,	b. July 27, 1787.
VII.	Alpha,	b. Dec. 26, 1789.
VIII.	An Infant,	b. April 25, 1791.

Charles Wright probably came from Goshen to Winsted about 1775, and lived near his father until his removal in 1801, to Jefferson Co., N. Y. He served as Sergeant in Capt. Sedgwick's company, on the northern frontier, in 1775. He m. Nov. 11, 1767, Ruth Smith.

CHILDREN.

I.	Tyrannus,	b. Goshen, March 20, 1768; probably died young.
II.	Sarah,	b. Jan. 29, 1770.
III.	Charles,	b. July 28, 1774.

AND FAMILY RECORDS.

IV. STEPHEN, b. Aug. 18, 1776; bap. July 30, 1797.
V. TYAGUSTUS, b. Feb. 6, 1779; bap. July 30, 1797.
VI. RUTH, b. April 30, 1781; bap. July 30, 1797.
VII. ERASTUS, b. ; d. Aug. 28, 1786.
VIII. ERASTUS, b. May 28, 1787; bap. July 30, 1797.
IX. CHESTER, b. Nov. 10, 1789; bap. July 30, 1797.
X. NATHAN, b. May 17, 1792; bap. July 30, 1797.
XI. MATTHEW MILES, bap. July 30, 1797.

CAPT. FREEDOM WRIGHT became a land holder in 1777, and lived and kept a tavern in the house now burned down, recently owned by Albert Kelsey and wife, in the same neighborhood with his father and brothers. He removed to Jefferson Co., N. Y., about 1801. He was a soldier in Capt. Sedgwick's company. He m. Sept. 1, 1777, Anna Horton. She d. Sept. 18, 1788, and he m. (2d), Aug. 10, 1789, Phebe Turner. She d. in 1793.

CHILDREN BY FIRST WIFE.

I. ASA DOUGLASS, b. Sept. 18, 1778.
II. JABEZ, b. Feb. 6, 1780.
III. LUCY, b. March 29, 1782; m. Abijah Wilson, Jr.
IV. ABIGAIL, b. July 6, 1784.
V. FREEDOM, b. Sept. 25, 1787; d. same day.
VI. FREEDOM, b. Sept. 13, 1788; d. same day.

CHILDREN BY SECOND WIFE.

VII. ANNA, b. March 16, 1790.
VIII. FREEDOM, b. Sept. 29, 1791; d. Oct. 20, 1791.
IX. FREEDOM, b. Oct. 6, 1792.

LUCIA or LUCY WRIGHT, a dau. of John Wright, Sen., named in his will, m. Elijah Rockwell, Esq., first Justice of the Peace and Town Clerk of Colebrook, and was the grandmother of John T. Rockwell, of Winsted. She was b. Oct. 7, 1756.

The Wrights were a highly intelligent, studious family; supporters of religion and good order, and earnest patriots in the revolutionary struggle.

1771.

EBENEZER SHEPARD, from Goshen, this year bought lands bordering on Colebrook line, on the road to Colebrook, by way of Nelson Beardsley's, on which he lived until 1775, when he sold out to David Crissey, and moved into Colebrook. He served in Capt. Sedgwick's company on the northern frontier, in 1775. Wife, Mercy.

CHILDREN.

I. PRUDENCE, b. June 8, 1771.
II. CAROLINE, b. July 26, 1773.

JOHN BALCOM, JR., from Mansfield, Windham Co., came into the town this year; he owned and lived on a lot of land east of Still River, nearly opposite the Horace Rowley place, and lived in a log house on the hill, adjoining Barkhamsted line. He lived in Winchester as late as 1808, and was of Sidney, Delaware Co., N. Y., in 1810, as appears by his conveyances on record. He m. Jan. 1, 1783, Lois Hudson.

CHILDREN.

I. ZILPHA, b. Oct. 18, 1783; bap. July 22, 1784.
II. LOIS, b. May 22, 1785; bap. June 18, 1786.
III. EBENEZER, b. June 15, 1786; bap. June 18, 1786.
IV. ELIZABETH, bap. Sept. 1, 1790.
V. UNA VILDA, bap. in Wd. Ch., Sept. 1, 1790.

1772.

JOHN BALCOM, Sen., is named of Winchester, in a deed of this year, conveying to him Lot 10, 2d Division, next south of the Daniel B. Wilson farm. He lived in a log house on the old North road, a little easterly of the Henry Dowd place. The Land Records show that he had sons: John, Jr., Jonathan, and Nathaniel. His wife's death in 1797, is noted in the Church Records. He renewed his church covenant in 1800, — and probably died in the town, though no record of his death is found.

JONATHAN BALCOM, son of John, Sr., lived on Wallen's hill, between Roswell Smith's and Joel Meade's. The inventory of his estate was returned to Norfolk Probate Court September 6, 1790. Administration to his widow, Molly; — distribution to his sons John, Jr., and Nathaniel, and to his daughters Keziah (who died unmarried), Mary, wife of Gates, Rhoda, Irena, wife of Seth Goodrich, and Esther (who died unmarried).

NATHANIEL BALCOM, son of John, Sr., lived on the homestead of his father until 1813 or 1814, when he removed to Wayne County, Pennsylvania. He married, September 2, 1782, Lois McEntire.

CHILDREN.

I. Francis, b.
II. Nathan, b. May 9, 1787.
III. Jonathan, b. Aug. 18, 1791; enlisted in the war of 1812.
IV. Silas, b.

Elias Balcom is named of Winchester in 1774. In 1776 he had some interest in the mill lot and the corn-mill, saw-mill, and dwelling-house thereon, which he quit-claimed to Stephen Chubb, of New Hartford. The nature of his ownership does not appear on the records. He then resided on the premises, and had probably erected the mills and dwelling on some arrangement with the proprietors of Winchester, who afterwards granted to Stephen Chubb, Jr., a lease of the lot for 900 years.

Jacob and Joseph, sons of Elias Balcom, were baptized in the Winchester Church in November, 1775. — The former is said to have carried on horseback the earliest mail between Hartford and Albany.

Elias Cabit Balcom (probably son of Elias above), married, December 30, 1782, Mary Dickinson.

CHILD.

I. Sarah, b. Feb. 6, 1786.

Nathan Balcom died August 7, 1808, aged 84.

1773.

John Austin, of Winchester, is this year grantor of thirty acres of land, extending from the east shore of Long Lake to first tier line, and embracing parts of Rockwell and Prospect streets, and the Naugatuck Railroad depot grounds, which he sold in 1779. There is an ancient cellar on the east side of East Lake street on this land, which may have been his residence.

Abel Hoskin, from Windsor, this year bought a lot, now a part of the farm of Anson Fosket, and lived thereon until after 1787. In 1790 he lived in Hartland.

Josiah Smith, from Wethersfield, owned, lived, and died on the farm, on the old Still River turnpike, now owned by Horace Rowley. He was a founder and one of the first Deacons of the Congregational

Church of Winsted, from which he withdrew during the dissensions in Rev. Mr. Woodworth's time, and became a member and Deacon of the Baptist Church then founded in the northeast corner of the town. He married, June 17, 1770, Elizabeth Merrill. She died November 26, 1829, aged 85; he died September 28, 1824, aged 81.

CHILDREN.

I. SALOME,	b. Oct. 12, 1770; m. Amasa Mallory.	
II. SARAH,	b. Jan. 5, 1772; m. Feb. 13, 1794, Elisha Mallory, Jr.	
III. JOSIAH,	b. Jan. 9, 1775; d. Oct. 3, 1777.	
IV. BENJAMIN,	b. Aug. 22, 1778.	
V. TRUMAN,	b. Nov. 22, 1780.	
VI. JOSIAH (twin),	b. Aug. 29, 1784.	
VII. ELIZABETH (twin),	b. Aug. 29, 1784; m. Grandison Newell.	

TRUMAN SMITH, son of Deacon Josiah, lived with his father and continued to occupy the homestead until after 1825, when he removed to Lenox, Ohio, where he died April 14, 1862, aged 81. He succeeded his father as Deacon of the Baptist Church.

His son, Luman Smith, now resides in Winsted.

JOSIAH SMITH, JR., lived in Winsted, and after 1810 was one of the Deacons of the Congregational Church till his removal to Windsor, after 1834, where he died, s. p., January 1, 1852, aged 67.

All of the members of this family were eminent for piety and good works.

1774.

STEPHEN ARNOLD'S prior residence does not appear. In 1774 he bought of John Darbe forty-one acres of land on Wallen's hill, adjoining Barkhamsted line, now composing part of the farms of Sylvester Treat and Homer W. Whiting, on which he then lived. He sold out and probably left the town in 1783. Wife, Lois.

CHILDREN.

I. MARY,	b. Aug. 29, 1778.
II. STEPHEN,	b. Jan. 29, 1781.
III. LOIS,	bapt. Nov. 9, 1782.

ZEBULON SHEPARD, of New Hartford in 1773, of Winchester, January 10, 1784, and of Barkhamsted, March 16, 1774, — was interested with Ebenezer Shepard in the Crissey farm on Colebrook line, and must have lived there, if he ever had a stated residence in the town.

PHINEAS POTTER, from Woodbury, owned land in the east village of Winsted, which embraced the Holabird place, and extended northward on North Main street to the late residence of John Camp, deceased. He first built a shanty against the large rock on Hinsdale street, near the Champion barn, and afterward built and lived in a house, now torn down, in rear of the ancient elm, where the Henry Champion house now stands. Tradition says that when Mr. Potter moved to Winsted there was no road from the Old South road in Torringford to Winsted, and that on reaching the tavern of Landlord Burr (father of Russell and Milo), near the top of Hayden hill, Mr. Burr assisted him in cutting out a path for his team; — that at the end of a hard day's labor, they accomplished a distance of five miles, — reaching the east bank of Still River, at or near the old Wheeler house, lately belonging to the Holabird estate, where they camped out for the night, — and on the following morning crossed to the west side of the river, and built the shanty before mentioned; and that his was the first family settled in the Still River valley, south of the Old North road. Wife, Dorcas.

CHILDREN.

I. SHELDON, came with his father.
II. DANIEL,   "   "   "   "
III. SALMON,   b. May 25, 1774.
IV. FREEDOM, b. Sept. 5, 1776.

SHELDON POTTER built and lived in the old Wheeler house, on the east side of Still River, nearly opposite the Holabird place, which he sold to Nathan Wheeler in 1786, and afterwards left the town. He married, November 2, 1786, Mary Knowlton, and had one

CHILD.

I. CYRUS,   b. Feb. 28, 1788.

DANIEL POTTER lived in a house which stood above the east bank of Still River, nearly due east of the east village hotel, on a road that then ran along the rear of the houses more recently built along the east side of the river. He sold out to Eleazer Porter in 1789. His name is on the tax list of 1796; he left town soon after 1798, and probably settled in Johnstown, Montgomery County, New York, as appears by a deed from him in 1801. He married, December 8, 1785, Naomi Crissey.

CHILDREN.

I. DANIEL,   b. Aug. 21, 1786.
II. ABIJAH,   b. April 19, 1788.
III. JOSEPH CRISSEY, b. March 24, 1790.

IV. ALVIN,   b. Nov. 4, 1791.
V. PHILO,   b. Dec. 6, 1793.
VI. CHESTER,   b. Feb. 13, 1796.
VII. HARVEY,   b. Nov. 10, 1798.

1775.

DAVID CRISSEY, from Waterbury, and originally from Woodbury, this year bought of Ebenezer Shepard, the farm adjoining Colebrook line, late owned by George Marvin. He died in 1803; his inventory was returned to the Norfolk Probate Court, March 14, 1804. He married at New Haven, Hannah Wilmot.

CHILDREN.

I. PRESERVED, b.   m., January 11, 1787, Rachel Kellogg.
II. MARY,   m. Joseph Loomis of New Hartford.
III. NAOMI,   m. Daniel Potter of Winchester.
IV. ISRAEL was 13 years old when his father came to Winchester.
V. JEMIMA,   m. ——— Fairchild.
VI. ASENATH,   m. Ira Mudge, of Pittsfield, Otsego Co., N.Y.
VII. LIBERTY,   m. ——— Brainard and moved to Chatham.
VIII. HANNAH,   m. Levi Dean of South Canaan.
IX. PHINEAS, b. in Winchester June 19, 1778.

PRESERVED CRISSEY,[2] a prominent citizen, first lived, until 1794, in a house then standing, where Mrs. Lucy Coe now lives, on Spencer Street, after which, until 1803, he lived in the house, now torn down, on West Lake street, nearly opposite the John Stabell house; soon after which he removed to Litchfield, Herkimer county, New York. He married, January 11, 1787, Rachel Kellogg.

CHILDREN.

I. ELECTA,[3]   b. March 14, 1788.
II. TRUMAN,[3]   b. February 22, 1790.
III. ALFRED,[3] b. March 19, 1792.
IV. PHILO,[3]   b. October 10, 1794.

ISRAEL CRISSEY lived on the eastern border of the Indian Meadow near Colebrook line. He removed in 1810 to Norfolk. He married February 7, 1788, Alice Woodruff.

CHILDREN.

I. MEHITABLE, b. July 21, 1789; m. Seth Barber, and removed to Western N. Y.
II. BENJAMIN WILMOT, b. May 19, 1791; m., 1828, in Norfolk, Eunice Burr, and had Warren, b. 1831; Ralph Israel, b. 1833; Olive Elizabeth, b. 1835; Theron Wilbert, b. 1837.
III. ALICE, b. June 15, 1793; d. unmarried in 1861.
IV. OLIVE, b. February 28, 1795; m. Seth Barber, Western N. Y.; living in 1859.

1776.

DAVID MILLS, from West Simsbury, now Canton, owned the lot which embraced the Winsted Manufacturing Company's and Cook Axle Company's premises, and extending easterly to Barkhamsted line. He lived on Wallen's Hill, where the clock-factory road joins the north and south roads, in the red house afterwards owned by Lemuel Clark and Daniel Burnham. He removed with his sons, Eliphalet and Daniel, to Colebrook, about 1804 or '5, where he died. He was son of John[1] (born 1690; died Canton, 1774) and Damaris (Phelps) Mills; grandson of John and Sarah (Pettibone) Mills; great grandson of Simon and Mary (Buell) Mills, and great-great-grandson of Simeon and Sarah (Bissell) Mills, who came from England. He married, about 1761, Huldah Edgecomb; she died February 7, 1787; and he married (2d) May 8, 1788, Jane Hungerford; he married (3d), December 26, 1789, Abigail Shortman.

CHILDREN.

I. DAVID, b. May, 1762; d. 3½ years old.
II. CHAUNCEY,
III. PHEBE, m. David Smith.
IV. ROSWELL, m. Ellis Apley.
V. ELIZABETH, m. February 4, 1795, Josiah Apley.
VI. HULDAH, b. in W. October 19, 1776; m., January 1, 1794, Thomas Boyd, of Amenia, N. Y.
VII. ELIPHALET, b. January 5, 1779.
VIII. DANIEL, b. February 6, 1782.
IX. SARAH, b. January 10, 1785; m. Wm. Shortman, of Kinderhook, N. Y.

CHAUNCEY MILLS lived in a house next north of his father's, which stood on the site of the house now owned by George Raymond. He sold out in 1803, and is named of Adams, Jefferson county, New York, in a deed of 1806. He married September 26, 1784, Ruth Doolittle.

CHILDREN.

I. SELOEN, b. September 27, 1788.
II. ANNA, b. February 14, 1790.
III. FYLER (twin), b. September 15, 1792.
IV. FANNY (twin), " " "

ELIPHALET MILLS learned the scythe makers' trade of Jenkins & Boyd, and resided in the town a few years after his majority; and then, with his brother Daniel, erected and carried on a scythe works at Colebrook River. He eventually migrated to Ohio, where he died. He married Eda Hurd.

DANIEL MILLS learned the hatters' trade and afterwards went into the scythe-making business at Colebrook River, where he died. He married Hannah Hurd.

His son, Daniel H. Mills, and his daughter, the wife of C. S. Norton, now reside in Winsted.

1777.

ENSIGN JESSE DOOLITTLE, from New Hartford, this year bought of Stephen Chubb, Jr., the mill lot reserved by the proprietors at the Still River Falls, where the clock factory is now located, and the land adjoining on the east side of the river. His house was burned, after which he built, on the same site, the Asaph Pease house, which has recently been taken down and removed, which stood where the road now runs, nearly opposite the house of Isaac B. Woodruff, and occupied it until his death, February 9, 1793, aged 55. The house previously occupied by Elias Balcom, and which Mr. Doolittle first occupied, stood on the site of the house next south of the Beecher store. His wife, Mary, died March 2, 1819, aged 82.

JESSE DOOLITTLE, Jr., oldest son of Ensign Jesse, lived about half way up Wallen's hill, on the south side of the road running east from the clock factory, in a house long since torn down. About 1812, he removed to Wolcott, Wayne county, New York, where he died about 1822. He married November 15, 1787, Hannah Jopp.

CHILDREN.

   I. MARION, b. July 6, 1788; m. Moses Hitchcock.
  II. LORRAIN, b. December 16, 1790.
 III. SILAS, b. September 17, 1794.
 IV. ZEBINA, b. July 20, 1796.
  V ERWIN, b. June 1, 1799; lived at Wolcott, N. Y., 1822.
 VI. ZERAH, b. October 1, 1802.
VII. HULDAH, b. August 26, 1804.
VIII. HANNAH HENSHAW, b. December 3, 1806.
 IX. EDWARD HOUGHTON, b. January 29, 1809.
  X. NELSON, b. November 4, 1810.

ZERAH DOOLITTLE, second son of Ensign Jesse, lived with his father, and continued to occupy the homestead until he removed to Vermont about 1800. He married Lucy Wheeler in 1793, who eloped with Major Seth Wetmore about eight years afterwards.

LYMAN DOOLITTLE, third son of Ensign Jesse, born June 5, 1779, lived in the old homestead until 1819, when he bought the Zenas Wilson place, now owned by William F. Roraback, on the old North Road, where he died March 14, 1851, aged 72. He married Achsah Davis. She died October 9, 1854. He had a son, Lyman Jr., who died a soldier in the U. S. army near the time of the Mexican War, leaving a widow. One of his daughters married Daniel B. Wilson, one married Julius Weaver, and another married Henry Dowd.

The name of this Doolittle family has become extinct in the town. The descendants in the female line are numerous.

SAMUEL HAYDEN, Esq., came from Goshen this year, and owned a farm on the old North Road; his dwelling stood on the north side of the road, nearly opposite the late Riley Smith's. Before 1790, he sold out and purchased a farm on Wallen's Hill, and built a house a little east of the town line, in Barkhamsted, which is still occupied by his daughter, Mrs. Laura Andrews. In his old age he removed with the family of his youngest daughter, to Ashtabula county, Ohio, where he died. He was a man of pure character, strong intellect, and quiet humor; a justice of the peace, and three times a representative of the town of Barkhamsted. In his advanced years, he united with the Winsted Congregational Church and honored his profession. He was born in Windsor, January 12, 1748, son of Samuel and Abigail (Hall) Hayden; grandson of Samuel and Anna (Holcomb) Hayden; great-grandson of Daniel and Hannah (Wilcoxson) Hayden; and great-great-grandson of William Hayden, one of the early settlers of Windsor, and afterward of Killingworth. He married Rebecca Smith; she died September 1, 1793; he married (2d) Sally Maybee.

CHILDREN BY FIRST WIFE.

I. SAMUEL, b. October 24, 1774; d. September, 1799.
II. MARY, b. December 4, 1776; m. 1797, Gideon Hall; d. March 16, 1830.
III. SETH, b. June 8, 1781; m. Huldah Soper; d. 1845.
IV. MOSES, b. October 30, 1783; m. May 8, 1806, Sally Jenkins.
V. ABIGAIL, b. March 27, 1788; d. 1805.
VI. LAURA, b. October 17, 1791; m. July 13, 1826, Charles Andrews.

CHILDREN BY SECOND WIFE.

VII. ANNE, b. November 2, 1795; m. Luman Whiting, Austinburg, O.
VIII. SALLY, b. June, 1803; m. Solomon Curtis Smith.

SETH HAYDEN, son of Samuel, Esq., lived on the southerly side of the Old North Road, adjoining Barkhamsted line, until 1827, when he migrated to Bethany, Wayne Co., Penn., where he died March 14, 1845, aged 64. He was a retiring man, of feeble constitution, and industrious habits, who reared and educated a large family of children, now occupying stations of usefulness and honor. The compiler affectionately remembers him, after a lapse of nearly sixty-five years, as a mild, kind-hearted, and faithful schoolmaster. He married Huldah Soper.

CHILDREN.

I. SAMUEL, b. May 4, 1805; m. ; d. New Harmony, Ia., March 7, 1842; had two children, Laura and Henry.
II. SETH, b. February 21, 1807; d. April 2, 1825; unmarried.
III. LUCIEN, b. October 31, 1808; graduated Hamilton College, 1836; ordained Pastor of Baptist Church, Dover, N. H., 1838; resettled Saxton's

River, Vt., 1843; received degree of A.M. at Madison University, 1854; resettled New London, N. H., 1857; m. (1st), Caroline C. Smith, Keene, N. H., by whom he had one child, Lucien Henry, b. May 21, 1839; he m. (2d), 1858, Mary J. Prescott of Concord, N. H.

  IV. COLIN MARCUS, b. January 15, 1811; farmer, J. P., and Deacon of Bapt. Church at Cornwall, Ill.; has two children, Samuel S. and Huldah Sophia.

  V. CORINTHIA, b. July 28, 1814; m. Benjamin Smith of Penn.

  VI. HULDAH REBECCA, b. February 28, 1817; m. Levi Bronson, E. Saginaw, Mich.

  VII. HENRY, b. February 28, 1817; m. Sophia Bowman, Town Hill, Penn.; lives in Muncy, Penn; has a son, William B., b. June, 1851.

  VIII. WILLIAM, b. September 9, 1821; graduated Castleton Medical College, Vt.; settled in Wyoming, Ill.; has children: 1. Isabella, b. 1848; 2. Frank, b. 1849.

  IX. LAURA ABIGAIL, b. May 30, 1826.

MOSES HAYDEN, Esq., second son of Samuel, resided, until his removal from the state, a little south of his father, in a house built for Rev. Mr. Woodworth, the first pastor of the Winsted Congregational Church. He, too, was a schoolmaster in his early years, less kind, but more efficient than his brother. He early succeeded his father as justice of the peace, was a member of the Assembly during seven sessions, and in the war of 1812 commanded a company of state troops called out for the defence of New London. In 1815 he migrated to Bethany, Penn., where he was a justice of the peace. He died suddenly in 1829, aged 46. He married May 8, 1806, Sally Jenkins.

CHILDREN.

  I. JAMES CARLETON, b. August 13, 1806; m. — Phillips; lives in Cornwall, Ill.; has two sons and one daughter.

  II. JULIA, b. October 25, 1807; m. Heman Arnold, Pa.; d. 1830.

  III. JOSEPH ADDISON, b. January 1, 1809; went to Michigan.

  IV. LUCIA, b. February 16, 1810; m. H. Ames.

  V. JANE, b. April 21, 1811; m. (1st), — King; (2d), M. Greiner.

  VI. HELEN, b. August 5, 1812; m. C. P. Sweet; d. October 10, 1842.

  VII. EDWIN, b. March 7, 1814.

  VIII. LAVINIA, b. July 15, 1815; m. — Miller.

  IX. SAMUEL SHERIDAN, b. November 9, 1822.

JAMES CARLETON HAYDEN, son of Moses, lived in Winsted for some fifteen years after coming of age; afterward at Wolcottville, whence he removed about 1855 to Cornwall, Illinois. His residence in Winsted was in the house on the south side of Main street, nearest to Still River Bridge. The family name has become extinct in the town, but several descendants in the female line still remain.

JOHN DARBE or DERBY, from Hebron, lived beyond the Barkhamsted line on Wallen's Hill, as early as 1773, and came into Winchester as early as 1778. He owned the land south of the road east from the clock shop up Wallen's Hill, afterward owned by Ensign Doolittle, and lived in the house near the top of the hill until 1782. He is named of Norfolk in 1787. He married September 22, 1773, Sarah Balcom; had one child, Phebe, b. July 8, 1774.

HENRY WALTER from Torrington, bought and occupied land on Spencer street, now a part of the Lockwood farm, and lived in a log house near the Lockwood dwelling. His land was taken on execution for debt in 1793.

JOHN WALTER, son of Henry, from Torrington, owned in 1779 a lot of land within the borough limits of Winsted, and in 1790 bought a part of the Lockwood farm, on which he lived until his removal to Burke, Vt., after 1798. He served in Captain Watson's Company, Colonel Burrall's Regiment, on the northern frontier. He married August 3, 1773, Sarah Gleason.

CHILDREN.

I. CYNTHIA, b. April 7, 1774.
II. NORRIS, b. October 25, 1775.
III. JERUSHA, b. January 18, 1777.
IV. ANDREW, b. December 5, 1779.
V. JOHN, b. February 25, 1782.
VI. EBER, a younger son, came back from Vermont, lived in Winsted several years, and removed to and died in Wayne Co., Pa. He married a daughter of Major Isaiah Tuttle of Torringford.

ANDREW WALTER returned from Vermont to Winsted not far from 1805; married Abby Westlake, and raised a family of children, one of whom married Silvester Hart. He lived several years on the William F. Hatch farm, and afterwards in various places. He died not far from 1840.

LEMUEL WALTER, probably brother of the foregoing, also lived on a part of the Lockwood farm in 1781, and afterward in a log house on Spencer street, between Hinsdale street and the district school house. He died in the town in 1792. He had wife Mehitabel, and

CHILDREN.

I. HANNAH, b. November 9, 1776.
II. ROXY, b. June 5, 1779.
III. LEMUEL, b. January 2, 1780; d. 1792.

DANIEL WALTER, in 1786, owned the western part of the Colonel Hinsdale farm, and sold the same in 1793. He married August 19, 1779, Mary Gleason.

CHILDREN.

    I. AUGUSTUS,   b. March 3, 1780.
   II. LEONARD,   b. April 19, 1782.
  III. POLLY,   b. September 29, 1784; d. July 17, 1785.
  IV. DANIEL,   b. November 13, 1787; d. June 17, 1792.

IRA WALTER, in 1793, bought land north of and adjoining John Walter's land, which he sold in 1797.

EBENEZER ROWLEY, JR.'s name first appears on the land records of 1781, but his name is on the Petition of 1777, for the incorporation of Winsted Society, as well as the recorded birth of his oldest child, indicates an earlier residence. He came from Chatham, and was probably the first settler on South street. He owned and occupied until his death, the dwelling and farm lately owned by Orson W. Jopp. He was a hard working, jovial, thrifty, and in earlier years, public-spirited man, who raised a large family, and by his practical jokes contributed largely to the cheerfulness of his associate pioneers.

His brother-in-law, Knowlton, occupied the adjoining farm. Their cleared lands extended down the hill westward to Still River at the base of the mountains. "Uncle Ebb." had been out cooning through the night on the mountains and was returning at early dawn, when he hears Knowlton calling to his cow which had strayed into the forest. To Knowlton's call Uncle Ebb. responded in cow language from the foot of the mountain. Knowlton wades the muddy stream to reach the spot from which he had heard the looing. Rowley, unseen, ascends the slope and gives another cow-like moo-o, and Knowlton follows; Rowley reaches the top of the ridge and gives another moo-o, — and while Knowlton climbs from crag to crag, wondering how the "tarnal critter" could get up there, Rowley slips down the mountain, crosses the stream to the cleared land and presents himself to the bewildered view of Knowlton from the mountain top, and explains the joke by another prolonged moo-o-o, and by throwing himself on all fours and kicking up his heels in the air, after the manner of sportive female oxen, and then sets off on the run for his chores and breakfast.

"Uncle Ebb." sometimes "found his match." It was in those days a stigma to a man's thriftiness to lay in a short stock of pork for the coming year, and our uncle was a self constituted inspector of his neighbors' pork barrels. Calling on the mild, sober-sided Squire Hayden, the squire lighted his candle to get a mug of cider from the cellar, when Uncle Ebb.

proposed to go with him and examine his pork. The squire assented, and showed him a barrel nearly full; the inspector examined and smelled. The squire then called his attention to another barrel in a dark corner which he thought might have a little pork at the bottom, — and so turning the light as to give an imperfect view, he raised the lid, — Uncle Ebb., in haste to complete the inspection, thrust his arm to the bottom of the barrel before discovering that it was filled to the brim with *soft soap*, which adhered to his arm from the hand to the shoulder.

A hardy race were these South street pioneers, from Still River bridge down to Major Isaiah Tuttle's, who sifted their corn-meal for hasty pudding "through a ladder." The Major remarked that by working barefooted in the stubble fields, their heels became so hard and flinty that if they happened to tread on the feet of their cattle it would make them bellow!

Apropos of the Major, — the horse-tamer, who could ride anything but chain-lightning. — With his boys he was felling timber on top of the same ridge of mountains. They felled a tall tree, so that one-third of its length extended over a precipice of some twenty or thirty feet. The Major ordered his oldest boy to go out on the trunk and cut away the top. Uriel went out and after striking a few blows came back with a swimming head. Daniel was sent out to finish the job, but soon came back equally dizzy. After blazing away in his characteristic manner at his boys for their want of pluck, the Major took up his axe and went out himself, and chopped away, until the top of the tree unexpectedly yielded. One of his feet was on each side of the chopping; and as the one on the top section yielded he lost his presence of mind, and instead of grasping the main body of the tree threw his arms round the falling section and went down with it. The boys, hastening round the precipice, came down to the landing place of the tree top, and found the Major bruised and wounded, but on his feet, wiping away with green leaves the blood that was flowing into his eyes and mouth from a wound in his forehead "Father," said one of the boys, "you've had a terrible fall." "Yes! yes!" said the Major, " a terrible fall! Adam's fall was nothing to it!"

Returning from this undignified digression, we remark that Mr. Rowley was a vivid type of the pioneers of this region; a hardy worker, turning his hand to any farming or mechanical labor, shaving his own shingles, splitting his own laths, hewing his own timber, and grafting his own trees. No man was more efficient and public spirited than he in getting up the East village Congregational meeting house and settling the pastor. A change in the mode of raising the salary of the minister by annual sale of pews instead of the old method of taxation, so disaffected him towards the society that he ceased to attend its worship and selected a spot on his farm for his own burial.* He died at the age of 79, Aug. 25, 1834. Wife, Abigail.

CHILDREN.

I. REUBEN,	b. Feb. 10, 1775.	
II. ABIGAIL,	b. Nov. 5, 1779; m.	Hazael Dunham.
III. ERASTUS,	b. April 17, 1782.	
IV. ANTHA,	b. July 10, 1784; m. April 3, 1806, Thos. R. Bull.	
V. ADA,	b. June 26, 1786.	
VI. FLORA,	b. April 15, 1789; m. June 1, 1809, John Westlake.	
VII. BETSEY,	b. June 10, 1791.	
VIII. ADNA,	b. about 1793.	
IX. ALPHA,	b. " 1795.	
X. MIRA,	b. " 1798; m.	Halsey Bailey.
XI. BEULAH,	b. " 1800; m. May 27, 1829, Benj. Fowler.	

ASHER ROWLEY, younger brother of Ebenezer, Jr., first appears on the list of 1789, though it is probable that he came to Winsted earlier. In 1794, his father conveyed to him the farm on South street, next north of his brother Ebenezer, which he occupied until his death. He was b. Jan. 18, 1765, at Chatham, Conn., and d. at Winsted, Sept. 7, 1844. He m. Mehetabel, dau. of Lieut. Jonathan Dunham, b. at Colchester in 1774. She d. June 21, 1839.

CHILDREN.

I. BETSEY, b. Jan. 10, 1794; m. Lewis McDonald, from Woodbury, Conn., and now (1872) living in Wisconsin.

II. ANSEL, b. Feb. 13, 1796; m. Lucy Clayborn, of Chesterfield, Va.; d. at Oakland, Missouri, Oct. 25, 1851.

III. ELIAS, b. March 22, 1798.

IV. WARREN DUNHAM, b. June 20, 1800; m. (1), Nancy Stanton; (2), Harriet Curry, both of South Trenton, N. Y., where he d. Sept. 25, 1854, highly respected, and entrusted with important offices.

V. SALLY M., b. June 28, 1802; m. Sept. 6, 1827, Chauncey Shattuck of W.; settled in Green Township, Pa., where he d. She now resides in Ackley, Iowa.

VI. HARRIET, b. July 20, 1804; d. Aug. 18, 1831, unmarried.

VII. GEORGE, b. July 16, 1806; supposed to be living in Wisconsin.

VIII. HARLOW, b. July 12, 1808; m. Sarah A. Haynes. Now living in Brighton, Canada West.

IX. HIRAM, b. April 7, 1811; drowned while fording a stream near Little Rock, Ark., Jan. 7, 1841.

X. CHARLES, b. May 3, 1813; d., unmarried, at Philadelphia, Dec. 21, 1833.

XI. CHARLOTTE, b. Dec. 6, 1815; d. Dec. 17, 1815.

---

* His remains, and those of his wife, were transferred to the Central burying-ground, after the farm went out of the hands of the family.

AND FAMILY RECORDS. 279

ELIAS ROWLEY, son of Asher, received a conveyance of his father's homestead and farm, in May, 1839. He sold the homestead on South street, and built his present residence on the Wolcottville road, about 1847. He m. Widow Laura Curtis, dau. of Lemuel Bushnell, of Hartland.

CHILDREN.

I. HIRAM D., b. Sept. 4, 1828; now of Delphi, N. Y.
II. GEORGE S., b. Oct. 20, 1830; m. Sophronia Buckman.
III. WARREN, b. Jan. 15, 1832. Supposed to be living in Idaho Ter.
IV. CHARLES L., b. Jan. 10, 1834; m. Martha J. Simonson, of Watkins, N. Y.; living at Willard, N. Y.
V. ANSEL, b. Dec. 28, 1836; m. Ruey Rogers, of Orwell, Vt., now of Hersey, Michigan.
VI. JOHN G., b. July 11, 1838; m. Anna C. Latham, of Granby, Conn.
VII. HENRY H., b. Aug. 26, 1839; m. C. Louise Grant, of Torrington; now (1872) of Burrville, Conn.
VIII. CATHARINE A., b. Dec. 11, 1841; m. Samuel H. Norton, of Otis, Mass.; d. May 18, 1861, leaving son Edward L.
IX. EDWARD, b. Feb. 28, 1844; d. Sept. 18, 1844.

CHAPTER XXI.

INCORPORATION OF WINSTED SOCIETY, AND CONTINUED IMMIGRATION.

1778.

THE families named in the preceding chapter, with those of the Austins on Lake street, composed nearly the whole population in 1778, while a settlement almost as large had been made in the west part of Barkhamsted.

The circumstances of the new settlement at this period are fully set forth in the following petition to the general assembly for the incorporation of the ecclesiastical society of Winsted.

"*To the Honorable General Assembly of the State of Connecticut, to be convened at New Haven on the second Tuesday of October next:*—

"The memorial of the subscribers hereunto humbly sheweth to your honors, that we are inhabitants of the east part of the town of Winchester, and west part of the township of Barkhamsted, to the number of about twenty-five families, and nearly 130 souls, being destitute of the privileges of a preached Gospel, and that there having formerly been a tax granted by your honors to promote the Gospel in that society, and no tax on the land east of the Long Pond, and that said pond so divides the town that the inhabitants on the east side of the pond cannot attend worship with those on the west side of the same; and that those inhabitants on the west side of Barkhamsted are so divided from those on the east side of said town by a rough and ragged chain of mountains and a rapid river, that it is impossible for them to have any communication as a society without the greatest inconvenience. We would further humbly shew to your honors that the greatest part of the lands are held by wealthy proprietors residing in other towns, who are not disposed to sell or settle, which is much to our detriment, in keeping out people that would otherwise come in, whereby the inhabitants are disabled from supporting the Gospel. We would not censure them too hard, but are humbly of the opinion that as we, by breaking the way and encountering the many difficulties and disadvantages that attend the first settlement of such a new, rough and heavy-timbered place have added to the value of their land, it is no more than equitable that they, with us, should contribute towards defraying the costs that will arise in having the Gospel set up among us.

"We, therefore, your honors' memorialists, would humbly pray that to so good an end your honors would form the part of Barkhamsted that is west of Farmington River, with the east part of Winchester, into one ecclesiastical society, with powers and privileges that other societies have, taking in all the land in said Winchester east of said pond, and to run by the end thereof with the line of the lots next to said pond, across the pond stream to the west end of said lots, and then running northward at the end of the lots to the river known by the name of Mad River, so as to take in all the land that has not been taxed before, and from thence up said river so far as to take in the third tier of lots, and from thence to Colebrook line, containing in the whole about 12,000 acres, and that your honors would grant a tax on all the above lands, sufficient for the purpose of hiring some suitable orthodox preacher, to preach the Gospel among us for the space of four years next coming, and that Mr. Charles Wright, whom we nominate for a collector, be empowered to gather said tax, and as in duty bound, your memorialists will ever pray.

"Dated at Winchester this 1st day of September, Anno Domini, 1777.

John Darbe,	Charles Wright,	Lemuel Walter,
Josiah Smith,	John Wright, Jr.,	Abraham Catling,
Enoch Palmer,	Freedom Wright,	Foster Whitford,
John Balcom,	Phinehas Potter,	Jonas Weed, Jr.,
David Mills,	John Walter,	Stephen Arnold,
Reuben Sweet,	Isaac Kellogg,	Nathaniel Crowe,
Ebenezer Rowley,	Eleazer Kellogg,	Robert Whitford."

1778.

This petition, after continuance to the February session in 1778, was granted, and the Society of Winsted, embracing the territory prayed for, was invested with all the powers and privileges by law belonging to other ecclesiastical societies in this state, with the power of taxing the lands of non-resident proprietors two pence on the acre of their lands not taxed by the Society of Winchester, for the term of four years, for supporting the gospel.

As we shall hereafter give in a connected form the history of the ecclesiastical society of Winsted, we proceed with our account of the settlers.

The inventory of JOHN STEEL, late of Winchester, deceased, was this year returned to the Simsbury Probate Court by Hannah Steel, his widow. He is not found on the records as a landholder, and his location is not known, but as the bondsman and appraisers lived near Barkhamsted line, his residence was probably in the same vicinity.

BARZILLAI HANDEE from Woodbury, this year bought a tract of land near Colebrook line, now composing a part of the Wm. E. Cowles farm, which he owned and occupied until 1781, when he probably returned to Woodbury, his name appearing in "Cothren's History" as one of a committee to provide for soldiers' families in 1783. Wife Mary.

CHILDREN.

I. CLEMONS, b. August 29, 1762.
II. CYRENUS, b. April 13, 1764.
III. ABEL, b. August 13, 1767; d. March 13, 1769.
IV. LUCY, b. May 13, 1769.
V. LYMAN, b. December 17, 1773.
VI. THANKFUL, b. November 13, 1776.
VII. LUCRETIA, b. August 4, 1779.

CLEMONS HANDEE is on the tax list of Winsted, from 1796 to 1799, when he lived in one of the houses attached to the Upper Forge. He is believed to have been an iron refiner or bloomer.

CYRENUS HANDEE lived as late as 1810 near the Old Forge in the southeast corner of Colebrook. He raised a family there, of whom three were Alpha, Hiram, and Leman, the latter of whom made extensive explorations in Africa and Central America, in pursuit of wild animals for the Westchester menageries.

During the years 1779 and 1780, we find the names of no new settlers of the Winsted section.

1781.

The following memorial shows more feelingly than any modern writing can do, the condition of this back-woods settlement, in this year.

To the Honorable General Assembly of the State of Connecticut convened at Hartford:

The Memorial of the subscribers hereunto humbly shows to your Honors, that we are inhabitants of the east part of Winchester, making part of the society called Winsted, and being the newest and youngest part of said Winchester, having just begun under low circumstances, on new and uncultivated and exceeding heavy timbered lands, the expenses of the town and this society being greater than in older places; having no meeting-house, nor minister settled in this society, most of us not having houses for ourselves scarcely to defend us from the inclemencies of the weather, and a number without barns; our families consisting chiefly of small children that cannot provide for themselves, having many of us a considerable part of our provision to buy at a distance in these difficult times: expenses arising almost on every hand, and but little profit arising from our labor or lands; our quota of men to find for the army, and to provide for, which comes very heavy on us; a considerable of a tax arising on these lands, which are wild and useless at present to us.

We therefore, your Honors' Memorialists, humbly pray that you would be pleased to compassionate us, in our infant and weak condition, and suffer us not to be crushed in the bud of our being by having more laid on us than we are able to bear; but that your honors would be pleased to exempt us from county taxes, until it shall appear your duty to lay them on us, and we have ability to pay them. As in duty bound your memorialists shall ever pray.

Dated at Winsted this 12th day of June 1781.

      Josiah Smith, } Committee for the
      Jesse Doolittle, } Memorialists.

Enoch Palmer,   Phinehas Potter,
Lazarus Palmer,   John Wright,
Joseph Bown,   Charles Wright,
David Crissey,   Freedom Wright,
John Walter,   David Mills,
Nathan Balcom,   Stephen Arnold,
Henry Walter,   Samuel Hayden,
Simeon Rogers,   John Balcom,
      Jonathan Balcom.

In Lower House.

On this memorial granted that the memorialists be abated of the 2 s. 6 d. tax payable December, 1781, and of the 9 d. tax payable March of '82.

          Test, Jedh. Strong, clerke.

Concurred in the Upper House.

        Test, George Wyllys, secretary.

(*Ecclesiastical Records*, vol. 15, p. 132.)

UZAL CLARK, from East Haddam, bought and occupied the lot next south of the Ebenezer Rowley farm, on South street, and sold the same to Stephen Knowlton in 1784. He afterward lived in Torrington and Barkhamsted. Wife Azubah.

CHILDREN.

I. FILENDA (dau.), b. October 29, 1780.
II. JOSEPH, b. January 1, 1783.

STEPHEN KNOWLTON, Jr., from Chatham, brother-in-law of Ebenezer Rowley, bought and lived on the farm on South street, next south of Mr. Rowley's farm, in a house now torn down, afterward bought and occupied by Samuel Camp. He migrated to Western New York in 1804. He married February 1, 1780, Deidamia Chubb.

CHILDREN.

I. RACHEL, b. March 31, 1781.
II. CALVIN, b. March 23, 1783.
III. DEADAMIA, b. October 5, 1785; m., 1804, Moses Camp.
IV. LAURA, b. September 21, 1788.
V. STEPHEN, b. August 25, 1790.
VI. SAMUEL, b. June 6, 1793.

SIMEON ROGERS owned a thirty-seven acre lot embracing the homestead lots of John Camp, Edward G. Whiting and others, on North Main street. He lived on the east side of Still river, a little north of the old Potter house, now standing, until 1789, when he removed to Barkhamsted. He was by trade a blacksmith. He married August 12, 1782, Hannah Potter.

CHILDREN.

I. JOSEPH, b. January 16, 1783. }
II. POLLY ESTHER, b. October 31, 1783. } So recorded.
III. CHARRY, b. May 16, 1785.

ABIJAH FULLER, from Chatham, owned and lived on 11 acres of land on Wallen's hill, adjoining Barkhamsted line, now a part of the farm of Homer W. Whiting. He is named of Barkhamsted in 1785.

ELISHA SPENCER, from Saybrook, bought and lived on land immediately west of the pond causeway, on West Lake street, in a log house that stood a little east of the new dwelling recently built by Sherman T. Cook. About 1793 he removed to a house, now torn down, on the original Spencer Street road, about sixty rods north of the Manchester place. In 1812 he removed with his son, Ozias, to Colebrook, where he died May 3, 1817. His wife Mary died July 23, 1828. He was born in Saybrook in 1744, and had a wife Rachel, who died before he came to W., by whom he had one

CHILD.

I. OZIAS, b. Saybrook, October 1, 1769.

AND FAMILY RECORDS.

CHILDREN BY SECOND WIFE.

II. RANNEY,   b. September 8, 1774; d. April 21, 1839.
III. ELISHA,   b. November 12, 1777.

OZIAS SPENCER resided with his father in both the houses above mentioned, and removed with him to Colebrook in 1812, where he died April 8, 1858. He married September 29, 1799, Hannah Shattuck; she died October 16, 1800; and he married (2d), October 5, 1801, Mary Shattuck.

CHILDREN.

I. HIRAM SHATTUCK, b. June 12, 1800, by 1st wife.
II. HANNAH,   b. March 21, 1804, by 2d wife.
III. ELVIRA,   b. October 8, 1805.   do.
IV. AMOS BARTLETT,   b. April 16, 1808; m. Susan H. Deland.
V. ROBERT SHATTUCK, b. September 7, 1810; married Charlotte Chapin.

RANNEY SPENCER married, 1796, Cynthia Walter; he moved to Vermont, and died March 21, 1839.

CHILDREN.

I. WILLARD,   b. August, 1798.
II. WILLIAM,   b. June, 1808.
III. LAURINDA,   b. 1821.

ELISHA SPENCER, Jr., left the town in early manhood, and probably settled in Vermont.

CHILDREN.

I. ERASMUS,   b. November 19, 1814.
II. CHESTER,   d. September 13, 1845.

HIRAM S. SPENCER, oldest son of Ozias, lived on his father's homestead, in Colebrook. He married, January 26, 1834, Mary Hill, and died Colebrook, 1869.

CHILDREN.

I. AMOS B., 2d, b. June 29, 1835.
II. HARRIET C., b. November 28, 1838.
III. MARY L.,   b April 25, 1841.

1782.

ELEAZER PORTER, from Hebron, this year bought the original lot which embraced all of the east village between the Episcopal church and the Green Woods turnpike. He lived on the original road from the Doolittle Mill to Torringford, in a house in the rear of the George Roberts and Jonas Le Roy houses. During his ownership of this lot, there was no road on the west side of Still river, south of Hinsdale street. He sold out the village lot in 1799, and his homestead in 1800, and soon after removed from the town. Wife Susanna.

CHILDREN.

I. ELIJAH, b. July 19, 1783.
II. ROSWELL, b. July 9, 1785.
III. ANNA, b. January 7, 1788.

SAMUEL CLARK, of Chatham, this year bought lands now composing part of the Lockwood farm. He is named as Samuel Clark, 2d, on the list of 1783, being then a resident proprietor. In 1788, he is named in his deed conveying away the same land, as Samuel Clark of Canajoharie, New York.

TIMOTHY COOK, from Windsor, this year became the owner of a lot on Still River and Wallen's Hill, embracing the Halsey Burr premises, on which he built a house and lived some years. In 1792 he owned and occupied a lot on Colebrook line, west of Green Woods turnpike. He was defendant in a suit in 1797, after which his name disappears. His wife, Hannah, was daughter of Simeon Moore, Sr., of Windsor.

1783.

SILAS DUNHAM, from Chatham, bought and occupied a lot afterwards a part of the Jonathan Coe farm in Winsted, and since owned in part by E. S. Woodford, about 100 rods east of the toll gate on Green Woods turnpike. In 1794, he is named of Chatham; and in 1787 of Nobletown, Columbia Co., N. Y.

COMFORT GOFF, owned and occupied a part of the Gillett farm, on Colebrook road, and conveyed the same to Nath. Russell, in 1784.

ELISHA MALLORY, from New Haven or Hamden, this year purchased the farm on Wallen's Hill, which he occupied during his remaining life. The house which he built and occupied, stands on the west side of the north and south road, nearly opposite the brick dwelling of his grandson, Homer W. Whiting. He was a man of great amiability and integrity of character; a founder of the Winsted Congregational Church, from which he withdrew during the troubles with the first minister, after which he united in organizing the Baptist Church at the north-east corner of the town. He was born in February, 1736; married, March 12, 1762, Esther Chatterton, born in June, 1742. He died March 23, 1812; she died August 27, 1828.

CHILDREN.

I. AMASA, b. February 20, 1763; m. Salome, daughter of Deacon Josiah Smith. He died November 9, 1855; she d. February 9, 1846, aged 75.

II. Samuel, b. May 1, 1765.
III. Lowly, b. November 9, 1769; m. Benjamin Wheeler, who went to Wayne Co., Pa.
IV. Lue, b. April 21, 1770, m. John Hawkins; d. August 20, 1835.
V. Elisha, b. July 7, 1772; m., February 13, 1794, Sarah, daughter of Deacon Josiah Smith. He d. November 6, 1853; she d. June 13, 1838, aged 36.
VI. Esther, b. November 10, 1794; m. Salmon Treat; she d. August 21, 1853; he d. March 30, 1858, aged 91.
VII. Lydia, b. July 19, 1777; m., November 26, 1801, Jesse Clarke, of Winchester.
VIII. Peter, b. September 19, 1779; d. May 10, 1780.
IX. Chloe, b. March 16, 1781, m. Reynold Wilson, son of Abija of W.
X. Mary, b. May 24, 1784; m., May 1, 1806, Lorrin Whiting of W. She d. January 10, 1851.
XI. Asa, b. December 7, 1786.

Amasa Mallory married Salome, oldest daughter of Deacon Josiah Smith, and lived on the farm now owned by his daughter, Salome Mallory, on the Green Woods turnpike, a mile easterly from the east village. He died November 9, 1855, aged 93. His wife died February 9, 1846, aged 75.

CHILDREN.

I. Sally, m. January, 1812, William Dexter; went to Illinois,
II. Amasa, settled in Illinois.
III. Nancy, m. Henry B. Crowe; lived and died in Winsted.
IV. Polly, m. Lorin Sexton of Hartford.
V. Betsey, m. Samuel S. Camp of Norfolk.
VI. Anne, m. Miles C. Burt of Hartford.
VII. Salome, unmarried.
VIII. Harriet, m. Dr. Myron H. Hubbard of New Hartford, and m. (2d) Harvey B. Elmore of Winsted.

Elisha Mallory, Jr., lived on the farm in Barkhamsted bordering on Winchester line, in the house now owned and occupied by his son Elisha 3d, and his daughter Sylvia. He married February 13, 1794, Sarah 2d, daughter of Deacon Josiah Smith. He died November 6, 1853, aged 81. She died January 13, 1838, aged 66.

Asa Mallory, son of Elisha, lived with his brother Elisha in Barkhamsted, until 1809, and afterwards in the old homestead with his father, until 1816, when he removed to Concord, near Painesville, Ohio He married December 8, 1807, Fanny Norton.

CHILDREN.

I. Riley, b. December 13, 1808.
II. Harmon, b. January 2, 1811.

Comfort Stanclift had a child born in the town this year. In

1786 he bought the Andrew Pratt farm, a mile south of the Naugatuck depot, on which he lived until 1792; wife Hannah.

CHILDREN.

I. MARGARET, b. July 26, 1783.
II. MARTIN, b. March 11, 1785.
III. HANNAH, b. January 30, 1787.

SAMUEL STANCLIFT from Torrington, first owned land in the old society, near Goshen line, and afterwards owned and lived on a farm adjoining that of Comfort Stanclift, in a log house, long since torn down, which stood on the north and south road, nearly east of the Pratt house. He sold to Aaron Marshall. In 1798 he is named of Norfolk. He married, November 12, 1783, Olive Balcom.

CHILD.

SAMUEL, b. August 10, 1784.

JOHN SWEET from Rhode Island, this year bought the Edward Manchester farm on Spencer street, and built the rear part of the dwelling thereon, in which he lived until he purchased the mill property and farm of David Austin, at the outlet of the lake, in 1796. He then lived in the house directly east of the bulkhead, at the pond outlet, a few years, and about 1800 sold out to the Rockwell Brothers, and bought the Erastus Woodford farm, on which he built the house at the parting of the turnpike and Colebrook roads. In 1806 he removed to Otis, Mass., whence he returned about 1812, and bought the farm between the lakes, and a few years later removed to Tyringham, Mass., thence to Staten Island, N. Y., and thence to East Hartland, where, at 90 years of age, he married his third wife, and died a few years later.

He was a shrewd, long-headed, restless man, who made sharp bargains, but attained to no more than ordinary wealth, owing to his frequent removals from place to place. He early became a local Methodist minister, and preached and traded to the close of his life. He married, December 7, 1780, Phebe, daughter of Thomas Spencer.

CHILDREN.

I. ANNA, b. August 16, 1781; m. November 23, 1797, William Keyes; she m. (2d) Rev. Daniel Coe.
II. PHEBE, b. January 20, 1783; m. October 18, 1798, Cyrus Bertrick.
III. RILEY, b. August 16, 1785; was a captain in war of 1812, and left the town soon after the close of the war.
IV. ADAH, b. September 29, 1787.
V. ORRA, b. January 20, 1790.
VI. JOHN WESLEY, b. February 18, 1792; m. Laura, daughter of Asahel Miller. He owned for a few years the farm between the lakes on the

	Winchester road.	He moved to Tyringham, Mass., in 1820, where he still lives.
VII. CHARLES WESLEY,	b. July 28, 1794; left the state about 1815.
VIII. BENEDICT,	b. October 15, 1796; m. Lois Lucena Grant.
IX. ADDISON,	b. September 5, 1800.
X. ALGERNON SIDNEY,	b. July 2, 1804.

The only descendants of John Sweet remaining in the town are the children of Colonel Nelson D. Coe, son of Anna, his oldest daughter.

ZEBULON THOMPSON'S name is on the tax list this year. In 1785 he lived in a log house then standing on the farm of Thomas Williams, on South street. In 1784 he and his son, Zebulon, Jr., were fined six shillings each for "prophane swearing" by 'Squire Alvord.

DAVID WEST, Jr., from Chatham, first lived in a log house at the base of Cobble Hill, on Spencer street, a little south of the Joshua Hewit dwelling. Prior to 1800 he built a small house on the site of George Dudley's residence, in which he lived until his death in 1822, at the age of 87. He was one of the early Methodists, a pious and worthy man. His wife, Judith, died February 24, 1816, aged 80.

JUDAH WEST, son of David, Jr., came to Winchester with his father, and first lived on the Halsey Burr place, on the old Still River turnpike, and afterward, until his death, April 9, 1825, aged 60, in a house on the east side of the same road where the toll gate was located. He married, December 26, 1785, Mary Todd.

CHILDREN.

I. MARY,	b. September 24, 1786; m. Erastus Burr.
II. DAVID,	b. February 20, 1789; d. February 22, 1790.
III. ALPHA,	b. September 4, 1790.
IV. NANCY,	b. September 6, 1792; m. Roswell Burr.

They had other children whose births are not recorded. Among them DAVID, probably born in 1794; a daughter, born about 1797, who married John P. Oviatt; EDGAR, about 1799, and FLORA, who married November 29, 1821, Hiram Wescott.

None of this family or their descendants now live in the town. Most or all of them removed to Western New York or Ohio.

CHAPTER XXII.

WINSTED IMMIGRANTS AND FAMILY RECORDS.

From 1783 to 1791.

NATHANIEL RUSSEL, from Wethersfield, Rocky Hill Society, came to Winsted this year and settled on the farm, on the old road to Colebrook, now owned by Junius Gillett, and there spent his remaining life. He represented the town in the General Assembly in 1801, held sundry town offices, and reared a large and influential family.

We are indebted to Hon. Edwin Stearns, late of Middletown, deceased, for the following extracts from his genealogy of the descendants of William Russell, who came from England in 1639.

MR. WILLIAM RUSSELL, born in England, October 11, 1612; came from England in 1639, and soon after came to New Haven and signed the covenant agreement of the first settlers and free planters of Quinnipiack; was a man of good standing and education, a member for several years of the General Court, assessor of taxes, &c. He died at New Haven, January 2, 1665. He married, 1649, Sarah, daughter of William and Martha Davis, of New Haven; she died December 3, 1664.

CHILDREN.

I. HANNAH,[2] b. July 29, 1650; m., November 21, 1670, Samuel Potter, of Wallingford, afterward of Newark, N. J.
II. JOHN,[2] b. November 12, 1653; died young.
III. WILLIAM, Jr.,[2] b. 1655; d. in infancy.
IV. JAMES,[2] b. 1657; d. in infancy.
V. NOADIAH,[2] b. July 22, 1659.

REV. NOADIAH RUSSELL,[2] graduated at Harvard in 1681; tutor in 1682 and 1683; studied for the ministry; settled over the first society of Middletown in 1688; was one of the founders of Yale College in 1700, and one of its trustees; one of the framers of the Saybrook Platform, and a distinguished divine, beloved of his flock. He died at Middletown, December 3, 1713, in his 55th year. He married, February 20, 1690, Mary, daughter of Captain Giles and Esther Hamlin. She died October 4th, 1743, in her 81st year.

CHILDREN.

I. Rev. William,[3] b. November 20, 1690; graduate and tutor of Yale, succeeded his father in the ministry at Middletown; m., August 19, 1719, Mary, daughter of Rev. James Pierpont; d. June 1, 1760.
II. Noadiah,[3] Jr., b. August 8, 1692; m. February 23, 1721; Desire Cooper, (daughter of ?) a farmer in East Middletown; he d. February 20, 1734.
III. Giles,[3] b. November 8, 1693; d. June 13, 1712.
IV. Mary,[3] b. December 30, 1695; d. unm. February 27, 1723.
V. John,[3] b. July 6, 1697; d. unm. October 17, 1780.
VI. Esther,[3] b. August 14, 1699; d. March 21, 1720.
VII. Rev. Daniel,[3] b. June 3, 1702.
VIII. Mehitabel,[3] b May 27, 1704; m. March 19, 1729, Daniel Deming, Jr., of Wethersfield.
IX. Hannah,[3] b. February 23, 1707; m. Joseph Pierpont, of North Haven.

Rev. Daniel Russell,[3] graduated at Yale in 1724; ordained first minister of S epney Society (now Rocky Hill) in 1724; died September 16, 1764. He married, November 13, 1728, Lydia, daughter of George and Rebecca Stillman. She died September 3, 1750, and he married (2d) July 29, 1752, Catharine, daughter of Rev. Nathaniel and Sarah Chauncey, of Durham, who died January 10, 1777, aged 71.

CHILDREN.

I. Giles,[4] b. November 8, 1729; graduated at Yale, 1751; lawyer at Stonington; Captain in Old French War; Colonel in Connecticut Line in the Revolution; mortally wounded at Danbury and d. October 28, 1779.
II. Lydia,[4] b. January 29, 1731; d. November 30, 1735.
III. Daniel,[4] b. June 21, 1732; m., October 16, 1755, Rachel, daughter of Joseph Stowe, of Middletown.
IV. John,[4] b. February 8, 1734; d. September 23, 1741.
V. Benjamin,[4] b. December 13, 1735; d. January 31, 1758.
VI. Mary,[4] b. August 18, 1737; m., November 25, 1784, John Robbins, of Stepney; she d. August 27, 1825, in 90th year.
VII. Lydia,[4] b. Nov. 26, 1739; d. September 24, 1741.
VIII. Nathaniel,[4] b. May 5, 1741.
IX. John,[4] b. December 26, 1742; d. in the army September 16, 1760.
X. Hannah,[4] b. May 31, 1746; d. August 23, 1753.

Nathaniel Russell,[4] of Winchester, married, December 25, 1766, Elizabeth Willard, born in Wethersfield, April 26, 1741, daughter of Stephen. He died December 10, 1810, in his 70th year, and she died February 26, 1819, in her 78th year.

CHILDREN.

I. Daniel,[5] b. in Rocky Hill, January 18, 1768.
II. John Willard,[5] b. in Rocky Hill, April 8, 1770.
III. Benjamin,[5] b. in Rocky Hill, November 26, 1772.
IV. Giles,[5] b. in Rocky Hill, July 27, 1775.

V. ELIZABETH,[5]   b. in Rocky Hill, November 23, 1778; unm.; removed to Mill Creek, Penn.
VI. HAMLIN,[5]   b. in Rocky Hill, March 5, 1781.
VII. GEORGE STILLMAN,[5] b. in Rocky Hill, October 21, 1783; d. unm. July 14, 1813, at Mill Creek, Penn.
VIII. MARY,[5]   b. in Winsted, July 28, 1787; unm.; removed to Mill Creek, Penn.

DANIEL RUSSEL,[5] came with his father to Winsted, whence he emigrated, about 1794, to the Genesee Valley, and settled in Williamson, Wayne Co., N. Y., as a farmer, and died in 1852. He married, 1792, Lucy Wright, of Colebrook. He married (2d) Lucy Aldridge.

CHILDREN BY FIRST WIFE.

I. EMMA,[6]   m. Stephen Sanford.
II. DANIEL W.,[6]
III. JOHN,[6] unm.
IV. JUDAH[6],
V. NATHANIEL,[6]   m., March 20, 1834, Rachel Prescott.
VI. MOSES,[6]
VII. GEORGE,[6]
VIII. LUCY,[6]

CHILDREN BY SECOND WIFE.

IX. MARY,[6]
X. ANN,[6]
XI. LOUISA,[6]
XII. CAROLINE,[6]
XIII. ALFRED,[6]
XIV. HAMLIN,[6]

JOHN WILLARD RUSSELL,[5] was a sea captain in the African trade, in the employ of the De Wolfs, of Bristol, R. I. He settled at Bristol, where he died August 20, 1814. He married, June 1, 1802, Nancy Smith; she died September 5, 1810, aged 35.

CHILDREN.

I. ELIZABETH B.,[6]   b. September 11, 1803; m. Rev. Royal Robbins.
II. PARNELL T.,[6]   b. October 18, 1805; unm.
III. NANCY SMITH,[6]   b. October 15, 1807; m. Henry Felix.
IV. JOHN,[6] Russell.   b. May 25, 1810; was adopted by his uncle Benjamin

BENJAMIN RUSSELL,[5] emigrated in 1796 from Winsted to Mill Creek, Erie Co., Penn., and married, September 29, 1807, Maria C. Buchler. He died June 10, 1829, and his wife died March 16, 1841, aged 67; *s. p.*

GILES RUSSELL[5] lived with his parents until their death, and removed, in 1825, to Erie Co., Penn., where he died March 16, 1842, aged 67 years. He was for many years a successful teacher; a man of literary taste and culture; a member of the General Assembly in 1810 and 1816; a selectman of the town, and sheriff's deputy for many years. Returning to Winsted on a visit, and finding the old cemetery in a neglected condition, he collected money enough to pay for clearing the ground, setting out the trees, and fencing the cemetery. He married, July 3, 1803, Lois, daughter of Urijah and Submit Cook. She died October 17, 1852.

CHILDREN.

I. LOUISA LAURETTA,[6] b. in Winsted, January 9, 1804; m. A. E. Austin, of Austinburg, Ohio; she d. April 5, 1855.
II. MARY ELIZABETH,[6] b. W., March 18, 1805; m. John Cook.
III. CAROLINE MATILDA,[6] b. W., February 27, 1807; m. 1835, Thos. G. Hurlbut.
IV. JULIA ANN RHODA,[6] b. W., July 24, 1809; m. May 7, 1831, David Smith.
V. GEORGE STILLMAN,[6] b. W., March 6, 1812; m. June 3, 1843, Jane Healey.
VI. SARAH SOPHIA,[6] b. W., October 23, 1814; m., January 15, 1844, Jason R. Orton, M. D.
VII. GILES WILLARD,[6] b. W., November 16, 1817; d. unm. August 4, 1836.
VIII. BENJAMIN COOK,[6] b. W., August 31, 1820; m., April 13, 1849, Sophia Parker.
IX. REV. EDWARD BRADFORD,[6] b. W., July 24, 1822; m. May 25, 1853, Mary Woods; she d. January 27, 1855; and he m. (2d) March 7, 1857, Mary E. Cable.

HAMLIN RUSSELL[5] removed from Winsted to Erie Co., Penn., in June, 1802, where he was a farmer. He married May 29, 1811, Sarah Norcross, born December 22, 1788, in New Jersey. She died February 11, 1831; he married (2d) November 4, 1834, Rachel, daughter of Urijah and Submit Cook, who was living in 1862. He died September 19, 1852, aged 71 years.

CHILDREN.

I. NATHANIEL WILLARD,[6] b. March 11, 1812.
II. POLLY ISABEL,[6] b. July 14, 1813; m. Johnston Laird.
III. NANCY FLEMING,[6] b. December 31, 1815; m. Samuel Christy, M.D.
IV. BENJAMIN STILLMAN,[6] b. January 5, 1822.
V. GEORGE JACOB,[6] b. February 24, 1824.
VI. JAMES COCHRAN,[6] b. May 12, 1827.

DANIEL W. RUSSELL,[6] eldest son of Daniel and Lucy, a farmer in Marion, Wayne Co., N. Y., married, June 17, 1824, Mary, daughter of Lewis Turner.

CHILDREN.

I. GILES B.,[7] b. April 17, 1825.
II. MILO T.,[7] b. October 29, 1826.

III. Cyrus H.,[7]   b. July 27, 1828.
IV. Lewis,[7]   b. October 3, 1830.
V. Avery P.,[7]   b. April 7, 1833.
VI. Whitney D.,[7]   b. January 27, 1836.
VII. Oscar F.,[7]   b. February 6, 1838.
VIII. Francis M.,[7] b. May 19, 1840.
IX. Edwin M.,[7]   b. November 20, 1842.

Judah R. Russell,[6] third son of Daniel and Lucy, removed to Tecumseh, Mich., in 1857, where he died in 1858; he married August 30, 1836, Prudence Prescott. She died June 19, 1851.

CHILDREN.

I. Ambrose,[7]   b. December 15, 1837.
II. Prescott B.,[7]   b. May 18, 1839.
III. Charlotte F.,[7] b. May 25, 1841 ; d. June 25, 1842.
IV. Lucy A.,[7]   b. 1843 ; d. March 16, 1846.

Benjamin Stillman Russell,[6] second son of Hamlin and Sarah, of Towanda, Penn., a banker in 1862; married May 20, 1827, Mary Gaskill from Philadelphia, Penn.

CHILDREN.

I. Sarah Norcross,[7]   b. May 7, 1848; d. July 12, 1848.
II. Edgar Fielding,[7]   b. September 5, 1849; d. March 31, 1851.
III. Hamlin,[7]   b. May 30, 1852.
IV. Edmund Gaskill,[7]   b. March 23, 1854.
V. Mary Elizabeth,[7]   b. September 18, 1856.
VI. Samuel Wagner,[7]   b. September 27, 1857.
VII. Benjamin Douglass,[7] b. April 8, 1861.
VIII. Rebecca Gaskill,[7] b. May 11, 1862.

George Jacob Russell,[6] third son of Hamlin and Sarah, a tanner at Mill Creek, Erie Co., Penn.; married January 26, 1854, Amanda J. Hayes, and had, in 1862, one

CHILD.

Minnie Myrtle,[7] b. October 20, 1856.

James Cochran Russell,[6] fourth son of Hamlin and Sarah, at Belle Valley, Erie Co., Penn., a farmer; married February 7, 1856, Octavene A. Chambers, by whom he had one

CHILD.

James Lewis,[7] b. October 15, 1860; d. October 2, 1862.

Benjamin Wheeler, Senior, probably came from Woodbury with his son, Benjamin Wheeler, Junior, in 1784. He died in Winsted, January 28, 1788.

BENJAMIN WHEELER, Junior, named of Woodbury, May 4, 1784, owned and occupied the farm late owned by Gideon Hall, Sen., deceased, until about 1814, when he removed to Mount Pleasant, Wayne Co., Pa. He built the house at the junction of South street with the Green Woods turnpike, now occupied by Mrs. G. Hall, in which he kept a tavern at the beginning of this century. He was postmaster of Winchester until about 1807, when the office was removed to West Winsted. He married, May 5, 1785, Lowly Mallory.

CHILDREN.

I. ZAYDE (dau.), b. March 13, 1786.
II. HEMAN, b. January 11, 1789; d. November 20, 1792.
III. FRANKLIN, b. February 25, 1791.

They had several younger children, whose names and births are not recorded, among them Heman, Jeduthan, and Lowly are remembered. All their children went with them to Mount Pleasant, and were settled around him at the time of his death.

1785.

OTHNIEL BRAINARD, Jr., named of Chatham, bought a lot now composing the south part of the O. W. Jopp farm, and lived in a log house on the east side of South street until 1795, when he sold to Ezra Woodruff, and left the town.

SEBA BRAINARD, WILLIAM CASE (of Barkhamsted), and NATHAN HOSKIN were temporary residents of Winsted, as appears by the tax list of this year.

JOHN JOPP, a native of "Sterderton, Scotland," and a probable descendant of Wallace's armor bearer—Jopp—who

" went on before,
And the great warrior's massy buckler bore,"

came to America in 1760, at 22 years old; lived in Boston one year; afterward went to Leicester, Mass., and married, April 7, 1763, Hannah Henshaw; thence removed to Glastonbury, Conn.; thence came to Winsted in June, 1785, and settled on the Henshaw tract, owned by his wife's brother. His house stood on or near the site of the Thomas Williams house, on the west side of South street. He died in Winsted, July 22, 1800. His widow removed to Butler, Wayne Co., N. Y., and died there in April, 1820, aged 77.

CHILDREN.

I. JOHN, b. March 6, 1765.
II. ELIZABETH, b. January 7, 1767.

III. HANNAH, b. August 25, 1769; d. November 25, 1857
IV. HULDAH, b. April 24, 1780.
V. BENJAMIN, b. September 21, 1782.

JOHN JOPP, Jr., came with his father to Winsted, and occupied, with him, the same premises. He built the Thomas Williams house, and occupied it until his death, November 4, 1829, aged 66. His wife, Jerusha, died December 22, 1844, aged 78.

CHILDREN.

I. RUSSELL, went west.
II. SAMUEL HENSHAW, died April 19, 1813, aged 19.
III. SALLY, m. Harris Brown.
IV. ORSON W., m. — Gilman; lives in Winsted.

NATHAN WHEELER, son of Benjamin, Senior, from Woodbury, this year bought the Potter farm, lately owned by the Holabird heirs, and occupied the old house on the east side of Still River, nearly opposite Nathan Champion's, until his death in 1800, at the age of 40, which was occasioned by falling from his hay-mow upon a pitchfork, which penetrated his bowels. His widow (Mary) resided in the house until her death, August 4, 1822, aged 55. He married March 23, 1786, Mary, daughter of Jesse Doolittle.

CHILDREN.

I. NANCY, b. Sept. 5, 1788; m. Reuben Baldwin; she d. Feb. 13, 1854, aged 67.
II. MINERVA, b. March 17, 1791; m. Seth Bishop, Jr.
III. PAMELA, b. Aug. 6, 1792; m. David Marble.
IV. HULDAH, b. March 3, 1794; m. Raymond Mather.
V. ANSON, b. Feb. 3, 1796; m. Flavia Barber of Canton, Conn.
VI. ALMA, b. July 17, 1798; m. Philo Hawley.

ANSON WHEELER, ESQ., son of Nathan, removed to Barkhamsted, not far from 1824, where he d. June 26, 1857, aged 61. He was m., but childless.

CAPT. ZEBINA SMITH came from Goshen to Winsted in 1784 or 1785. He lived and died on the farm, and in the house now owned by Geo. R. Doolittle, on the old North Road, near Colebrook line. He d. Feb. 4, 1842, aged 82. His widow, Martha, d. June 29, 1845, aged 87. He was a man of great amiability of character, and of sincere and earnest piety. He represented the town in the General Assembly in 1798 and 1802. He m., Norfolk, Aug. 1, 1780, Martha Benham.

CHILDREN.

I. Elisha,   b. March 28, 1785; m. Sally, dau. of John Fyler.
II. Orriel,   b. Oct. 7, 1790; m. Samuel E. Mills of Colebrook.
III. Miles Benham, b. 1795; d., unm., March 14, 1816.

Deacon Elisha Smith, son of Capt. Zebina, lived and d. on the farm, and in the house nearly opposite his father's, now owned by Solomon Sacket. He was a man of strong conservative mind and ardent temperament, who filled a prominent place in the community, as Deacon of the Congregational Church, a Major in the militia, an Assessor of taxes at various times, and in 1856, a representative of the town. He d. Jan. 29, 1860, aged 75. He m. Sally, dau. of John Fyler; she d. 1862.

CHILDREN.

I. Aurelia, b. Aug. 30, 1813; m. March, 1835, Alexander P. Cleveland.
II. Miles, b. July 6, 1817; m. Dec. 4, 1839, Matilda Baldwin.
III. Zebina, b. Aug. 9, 1820; d. Nov. 25, 1841, unm.
IV. Sarah, b. Dec. 11, 1825; m. Sept. 8, 1858, Rev. Henry A. Russell.

Miles Smith, m. Dec. 4, 1839, Matilda Baldwin; lived in the house previously occupied by his grandfather, Capt. Zebina Smith, and d. July 27, 1851, leaving a daughter, Martha Baldwin Smith, b. May 18, 1848; m. April 23, 1872, King T. Sheldon.

Aaron West, a minor, confessed judgment before Esquire Alvord, May 31, 1773, "for playing and laughing on ye Sabbath or Lord's Day," and was fined three shillings, and one shilling cost. His name next appears as grantee of the Lockwood Farm, on Spencer street, on which he lived until 1787, when he is named of New Hartford.

John Shaw, a Hessian soldier from Burgoyne's Army, captured at Saratoga, is on the tax list of this and several succeeding years. He was a currier and flaxdresser by trade, and after living in various parts of the town, retired to the Bourbon region, where he d. April 13, 1806, leaving a widow [Eunice], who rode a black and white pacing mare between Bourbon and Winsted, as late as 1815.

John Shaw, Jr., son of the Hessian, though a citizen of Barkhamsted, lived at frequent intervals in Winsted, grinding scythes through a long course of years, in defiance of the grinder's consumption, and dying at the allotted age of man, apparently uninjured by irregular habits. His sons, Levi and James, still dwell among us. He had other sons, Jehilamon, Addison, and Andrew Jackson, and one or more daughters.

CHARLES BARNES, son-in-law of John Shaw, Sr., lived at this period in a log-house on the Thomas Williams farm, and afterwards retired to Bourbon.

1786.

JOHN ALLEN'S name is on the tax list of this year, as the owner of the farm on Spencer street, recently owned, successively, by Nishus Kinney, Lucius L. Culver, and Luther G. Hinsdale. He built the large red house on the premises, in which he lived until 1798, when he sold out to his son-in-law, Elihu Rockwell, and removed, as is believed, to Oneida Co. N. Y.

JOHN ALLEN, JR., supposed to have been son of the above, bought land in 1797, immediately north of his father's farm, which he sold in 1798.

JESSE FILLEY'S name is on the list of this year as a resident of Winsted, and is not found elsewhere.

DAVID HOLMES, son of *Phebe* Holmes, afterwards second wife of *Chileab Smith*, of Goshen, served in the army at New York, in 1776, and came to Winsted in 1786. He owned and occupied the south part of the Rockwell farm, now owned by Mrs. J. R. Boyd, and built the old farm house now standing thereon. He sold out to Merritt Bull in 1805, and removed to Russell, Hampshire Co., Mass. He was brother of *Joseph Holmes*, step-brother of *Capt. Zebina Smith*, and half-brother of *Theodore Smith*, all of Winsted. He m. April 29, 1784, Chloe Strong.

CHILDREN.

I. WILLIAM,	b. Sept. 18, 1784.
II. CHARLOTTE,	b. Aug. 29, 1786.
III. ASENATH,	b. Dec. 6, 1788.
IV. CLARA,	b. Oct. 21, 1790.
V. CHLOE,	b. May 7, 1792.
VI. LYMAN,	b. March 7, 1794.
VII. SOPHIA,	b. Nov. 20, 1795; d. March 23, 1798, of small pox.
VIII. SALLY,	b. Jan. 26, 1798; d. March 13, 1798, of small pox.
IX. SOPHIA,	b. Dec. 30, 1799.
X. SALLY,	b. July 20, 1802.
XI. ASAHEL,	b. June 4, 1804.
XII. DAVID,	b. Russell, Mass., May 13, 1808.

ISAAC WHEELER, cousin of Benjamin and Nathan, in company with Levi Norton, bought the Deacon Hurlbut farm, east of Long Lake, in 1786. From 1788 to 1790, he lived on the south part of the farm between the lakes. In 1795 he bought the part of the West Village ground south of M. & C. J. Camp's line, and in 1798 built the old Higley tavern house next south of Camp's brick block, the first frame building erected on Main street between Col. Hinsdale's corner and Still River Bridge. In 1799, he sold out to Horace Higley and removed from town. He married, October 17, 1784, Mehitabel Williams, and had one son:

RILEY, b. Nov. 29, 1785.

HEZEKIAH WOODRUFF, Jr., named "of Southington," this year bought and occupied a part of the Amos Pierce farm, on Spencer street, and built his house on the summit of the hill a quarter of a mile east of Mr. Pierce's dwelling. An old orchard visible from the village indicates the place where his house stood. He sold out to Grinnell Spencer in 1791, and removed to Colebrook.

LUKE HART'S name is on the tax list of this year. In 1787 his wife, *Deborah*, became owner of a lot on the west side of Spencer street, nearly opposite Amos Pierce, on which they lived in a log house, and probably died there. They had three sons and one daughter, residents of Winsted, viz.: *Selah, Stephen, Samuel,* and ———, the wife of Hawley Oakley, and mother of Alva Oakley, now a resident of Winsted.

SELAH HART, son of Luke and Deborah, lived until about 1812 in a log house at the parting of the two Colebrook roads, a little west of Judson Wadsworth's, and about 1816 removed to Canaan Mountain, where he died. He was the tallest man in town, and one of the four tallest in the county, the other three being ——— Elmore of Torrington, father of Peleg, Hon. John Allen, M. C., of Litchfield, and Rev. Aaron Kinney of Winsted. When straightened up, his height was 6 feet 6½ inches. He worked at wall laying, was one of the fathers and pillars of the Methodist Church, a devout, kind-hearted, much-loved man. His children were: Deborah, wife of Zenas Alvord; Damy, wife of David Andrews, Sally, Phœbus Budd, and Newton. None of the family now reside in the town.

STEPHEN HART, son of Luke and Deborah, lived and died in the house nearest to Colebrook line, on the west side of the old Still er turnpike. He died September 17th, 1833, aged 66. His wife was rah Munson, from Middlebury, Connecticut. Among their children were Chester, Roseville, and Lovina, who married, March 1825, Zerah Doolittle. All of them removed to the West.

SAMUEL HART, son of Luke and Deborah, lived in various parts of the town as a tenant farmer. In his later years he owned and occupied a house that stood opposite the Uri Church bridge, on the east side of the

Green Woods turnpike, in which he died March 26, 1867, aged 70. He married a daughter of Elemuel Bassett.

CHILDREN.

I. WILLARD, who m Dec. 11, 1822, Rhoda M. Benedict; he m. (2d) Maria Andrews.
II. SYLVESTER,   m., June 23, 1822, Charlotte Walter.
III. WELLS.
IV. HAWLEY.
V. SYLVIA.
VI. SAMUEL,   m., Nov. 14, 1833, Laura Benedict.

Of their daughters, one was wife of Samuel Bandle, one of Levi Tuttle, and another of Edward Albro.

1787.

At the annual town meeting, November 12, 1787, in addition to routine business, it was voted "that the prayer of the memorial now lying in the General Assembly, for Winsted to be made a town, may be granted by the General Assembly, if they see fit to grant the same, without opposition from the First Society of Winchester, provided the west tier of lots in Winsted be not included in the proposed town of Winsted. This project, now agitated for the first time, was repeatedly revived in after years. The main reasons for seeking a division of the town were, the want of a central place for public meetings, and the separation of the two portions by Long Lake, and the mountain ridges along the south-westerly side of Mad River, rendering communication difficult. Added to this was an embittered local feeling growing out of the superior number and refinement of the people of the "Old Society," who had become organized and assimilated; while the sparse population of Winsted was as yet in a state of comparative poverty and barbarism. The projected town of Winsted was to embrace the eastern third part of Winchester, and the part of Barkhamsted west of Farmington River. Similar difficulties of communication, arising from the chain of mountains west of the river cutting off the dwellers along the Farmington valley, rendered the new organization so objectionable that all the applications to the assembly were unsuccessful; and the growth of the village of Winsted has put an end to all desire for a separation.

MOSES DARBE, named of Norfolk, this year bought the lot on South street, now owned by Jonathan Gilbert, on which he lived a short time. He is named of Norfolk in 1789.

BENJAMIN DE WOLF, "of Killingworth," this year bought jointly with his brother Daniel the lot on Spencer street, on which widow Lucy Coe now lives. About 1792 he bought and lived in a house now torn down on West Lake street, nearly opposite the John Stabell house, which he sold in 1805 to Benjamin Johnson. He lived in Winsted several years later, and worked in a wooden dish mill on the lake stream. He was a man of violent passions and a blistering tongue, sometimes very pious in profession, but always quarrelsome and mischievous. He married, May, 1786, Jerusha Carter.

CHILDREN.

I. JAMES (twin), b. Oct. 20, 1786.
II. CHARLOTTE (twin), b. Oct. 20, 1786.
III. MILLER, b. May 21, 1790.
IV. ALVAH, b. July 7, 1792.

They had several other children whose names are not recorded.

DANIEL DEWOLF, from Killingworth, lived with his brother Benjamin, on Spencer street, until 1793, when he bought and removed to a lot adjoining Colebrook line, opposite William E. Cowles, on which he lived until his removal to the northeast part of Colebrook. He was father and grandfather to the DeWolfs now at Colebrook River.

ELEAZER KELLOGG, from Barkhamsted, lived from 1787 to 1791, on the farm lately owned by Roswell Smith, in the northeast part of the town. Wife, Esther.

CHILDREN.

I. ELIJAH (twin), m. Oct. 23, 1794, Mabel Clement.
II. ELISHA " m. June 28, 1792, Persis Dunham.
III. ISAAC.
IV. ESTHER, b. Nov. 14, 1789.
V. CRUSA, (dau.) b. Aug. 13, 1791.

CALEB MUNSON, JR., from Waterbury, Middlebury Society, came to Winsted this year, and owned and occupied the David N. Beardsley farm, on the old hill road to Colebrook, living on the west side of the road in a house (now torn down) afterwards successively occupied by James Eggleston, Hine Clemons, Joseph Loomis, Stephen Hart, Cyrus Buttrick, and others. About 1800 he lived in a house, now torn down, on Lake street, near the "Old Factory house." About 1807, he migrated to Marcellus, N. Y. He m. April 20, 1790, Mabel Tuttle.

CHILDREN.

I. CALEB MILES, b. Jan. 15, 1792.
II. GLOVER STREET, b. May 14, 1794.
III. LEVE BENHAM (dau.), b. Jan. 13, 1797.
IV. AZUBAH, b. May 21, 1799; d. Oct. 17, 1799.

V. ALVIRA,   b. Nov. 24, 1800.
VI. JERRY,   b. March 25, 1803.
VII. LUCY,   b. March 8, 1806

NORTON WRIGHT, oldest son of Moses, and brother of Alvin of Colebrook, lived in the old deserted house on the east side of the Old Still River Turnpike, near Colebrook line, from this year until 1817, when he moved to Western or Northern New York. He m., July 7, 1781, Lucy Banning.

CHILDREN.

I.	SAMUEL,	b. Aug. 9, 1792.
II.	LUCY,	b. June 21, 1794.
III.	SARAH,	b. June 5, 1796.
IV.	ABIGAIL,	b. May 23, 1798.
V.	MOSES NORTON,	b. Sept. 1, 1800; d. 1803.
VI.	WEALTHY,	b. Oct. 2, 1802.
VII.	JONATHAN NORTON,	b. Oct. 31, 1805.
VIII.	MOSES,	b. Nov. 21, 1807.

1788.

DEACON SHUBAEL COOK and URIJAH COOK, of Winsted, hereinafter mentioned, were sons of DEACON JOHN COOK,[4] of Torrington, who was son of JOHN,[3] b. in Windsor in 1692, and d. May 25, 1751: grandson of JOHN,[2] b. Windsor, April 3, 1662; m. Nov. 26, 1686, Mary Downs, of Northampton; and great grand-son of NATHANIEL,[1] an early resident of Windsor, who m. June 29, 1649, Sarah Vare.

He, Deacon John[4], m. June 22, 1741, Rachel Wilson, of Windsor. They were among the constituent members of the First Church of Torrington, Oct. 21, 1741.

CHILDREN.

I.	RACHEL,[5]	b. May 2, 1742; m. David Soper.
II.	JOHN,[5]	b. Aug. 29, 1743; d. in Torrington, aged 80.
III.	EUNICE,[5]	b. March 5, 1746; m. Ensign Jonathan Coe, of Winchester.
IV.	FRANCES,[5]	b. Sept. 18, 1747; d. Dec. 23, 1750.
V.	DEA. SHUBAEL,[5]	b. April 21, 1749.
VI.	SARAH,[5]	b. Oct. 31, 1750; m. Hurlbut.
VII.	EDE,[5]	b. Nov. 28, 1752; d. in early life.
VIII.	URIJAH,[5]	b. Sept., 1754.
IX.	LUCY,[5]	b. Oct. 3, 1756; m. Moses Loomis.
X.	HANNAH,[5]	b. March 13, 1758; m. Simeon More.
XI.	ELIHU,[5]	b. March 18, 1760; d. July 20, 1760.
XII.	ELIHU,[5]	b. March 29, 1761; d. in Torrington.
XIII.	MARY,[5]	b. Nov. 10, 1764; d. in early life.

DEACON SHUBAEL COOK came to Winsted in 1792, and settled on the Daniel Tuttle farm, adjoining Torringford line on South street. His house, long since torn down, was on the west side of the road, a little north of the Daniel Tuttle house. About 1815 he removed to a house on the south side of Green Woods turnpike, in which he died, Dec. 27, 1824, aged 75 years. His wife died in 1827, aged 79. In 1802, he was chosen Deacon of the Congregational Church, which office he filled with great fidelity and acceptance, until his death. Deacon Cook was a man of warm and cheerful piety, poor in this world's goods, but rich in Christian attainments, and in the love of his brethren. He m. Sept. 17, 1773, Sarah Bassett Gillett.

CHILDREN.

I. ROSINDA,[6] b. 1776; m. Asher Loomis of Windsor, where she d. in 1855.
II. REUBEN,[6] b.   d. young, scalded.
III. EDE,[6]   b. 1783; d. single, Feb. 1, 1818, aged 35.
IV. REUBEN,[6] b. Sept. 10, 1786.

URIJAH COOK,[5] came to Winsted in 1788, and settled on the east side of Spencer street. He built and lived in the Lockwood House, at the top of the hill, in sight of the West Village. In 1819, he sold out and removed to Barkhamsted (Wallen's Hill), where he died June 28, 1832, aged 73. His wife (Submit) d. Dec. 16, 1844, aged 88. In addition to farming, he carried on brick making in a swale at the east end of his farm, in the early part of this century. He was a man of ardent temperament, a zealous Federalist, and equally zealous theologian of the Hamiltonian and Hopkinsian schools, — not over tolerant of opposing views, either in politics or religion. In his old age, Christian charity predominated over party and sectarian zeal, and he died in peace and love with all men. He m. Feb. 8, 1779, Submit Tuttle.

CHILDREN.

I. ANSON,[6]   b. in Torrington, Oct. 4, 1779.
II. LOIS,[6]   b.   "   March 25, 1781 ; m. Giles Russell.
III. SALLY,[6]   b.   "   March 28, 1782; d. unm.
IV. RHODA,[6] (twin), b. Winsted, Jan. 7, 1790; d. April 29, 1807.
V. RACHEL,[6] "   b. Jan. 7, 1790; m. Hamlin Russell.
VI. HULDAH,[6]   b. Feb. 9, 1795.
VII. PHILO,[6]   b. Sept. 28, 1798; m. a dau. of Capt. William Swift, of Colebrook, moved with his father to Barkhamsted, where he d. about 1858, s. p.

REUBEN COOK,[6] son of Dea. Shubael,[5] came to Winsted with his father, — was clerk for S. Rockwell & Brothers, and soon after coming of age, went into the manufacture of bar iron in the works erected by him on Still River, recently owned by the Cook Axle Co. He lived in the house on North Main street, nearly opposite the bridge leading to his works, until a recent period. He m. April 15, 1811, Ruth Shepard. She d. Jan. 8, 1841. He d. March 16, 1872.

CHILDREN.

    I. JERUSHA,[7]   b. March 17, 1812; m. Jan. 1856, Daniel Spring.
   II. SARAH,[7]   b. June 9, 1813; m. Shepard S. Wheeler; d. Feb. 8, 1855.
 III. CHARLES,[7]   b. Oct. 15, 1815; m. Sept., 1837, Mary Jane Lewis, of Suffield.

CHILDREN.

    1. Jane Elizabeth,[8] b. 1838; d. June, 1842; 2. Rollin Hillyer,[8] b. Aug. 24, 1844, m. June —, 1866, Minnie Graves, of New Milford; she d. Oct. 20, 1868, leaving children, Minnie Graves,[9] b. June, 1867, and Eliza Jane,[9] b. Sept. 30, 1868.

 IV. HARRIET,[7]   b. May 29, 1818; m. Sept. 7, 1853, Eli R. Miller.
  V. JULIA,[7]   b. Dec. 1, 1820; d. Jan. 22, 1837.
 VI. JOHN R.,[7]   b. Feb. 18, 1823; m. Oct. 15, 1845, Marietta A. Phelps, of Norfolk; she d. Jan. 21, 1861; and he m. (2d) Sept. 29, 1863, Jane M. Dickinson, of New Britain.

CHILDREN.

    1. John Phelps,[8] b. Jan. 25, 1849; 2. Eliza Phelps,[8] b Feb. 15, 1851; 3. Marietta,[8] b. June 5, 1861, d. at Chicago, July 12, 1864.

ANSON COOK,[6] son of Urijah, came with his father to Winsted. He was by trade a millwright, and lived for several years in the west village, and afterward in a house on the north side of the Wallen's Hill road, a little east of the clock shop, until a few years before his death, when he removed to the house in the east village immediately south of the Episcopal Church, in which he died December 17, 1860, aged 81. His wife, Amelia, died May 15, 1851, aged 70. He was an industrious, quiet, upright man, and sincere Christian. He married, December 31, 1806, Amelia Hinsdale, sister of Colonel Hosea. She died May 15, 1851, aged 70.

CHILDREN.

    I. JAMES,[7]   b. March 9, 1809.
   II. RHODA A[7]., b. December 16, 1810.
 III. SHERMAN TUTTLE,[7] b. March 22, 1813; m. November 27, 1839, Cornelia Emeline Jacqua, b. Canaan, October 16, 1817. She died by a railroad accident about 1858, and he married, 2d, Mrs. Lucia (Stillman) Cross.

CHILDREN.

    1. Edward Sherman, b. December 20, 1841.
    2. Frederick Monroe, b. March 28, 1843.
    3. Cornelia Elvira, b. September 15, 1850.
    4. Emma Amelia, b. October 3, 1853.

 IV. ANSON BISSELL,[7]   b. December 12, 1814.
  V. LAURA,[7]   b. May 24, 1818.

LIEUTENANT JONATHAN DUNHAM, named of Colchester, this year bought a part of the Moses M. Camp farm on South street, on which he lived until 1790, when he moved to the highest point of Wallen's Hill, and lived until 1800 in the house afterward occupied successively by Reuben Palmer and George Treal, and now torn down, when he removed to Whitestown, Oneida Co., N. Y. His children are not on our records. The following may be only an incomplete list of them :—

Jonathan Dunham, Junior, married, November 24, 1791, Susanna Kellogg.
Elias Dunham married, March 10, 1791, Jerusha Lewis.
Mehitabel Dunham, married Asher Rowley.
Hazael Dunham, married Abigail Rowley ; lived in Utica, N. Y.
William Dunham, settled between Erie and Ashtabula, O.

DEACON MICHAEL GRINNELL'S name is on the tax list of this year. He was born in Saybrook, Conn., March 20, 1752; removed with his parents to Salisbury, Conn., at the beginning of the Revolution, and about 1788 came to Winsted. He first owned land on the east side of Long Lake. In 1793 he bought the Wedge lot at the northeast corner of the town, lately owned by Joel Mead, on which he lived (in the Partridge House) until 1823, when he removed to Clinton, Wayne Co., Penn., where he resided until his death, on the 12th day of February, 1858, aged one hundred and six years. He served in the Revolutionary Army, and witnessed the tearing down of the leaden statute of George III. at the Bowling Green in New York. His hearing almost entirely failed during the last thirty years of his life, while his sight continued nearly unimpaired until past his hundredth year. He was a deacon of the Baptist Church in this town, and was always in his place in the stated meetings of the Church, until more than one hundred years old. He married in 1777, Susanna Balcom, perhaps daughter of John ; she died in August, 1825, aged 70 years. Of their six children only two births are recorded in this town.

CHILDREN.

I. RUFUS, b. in Salisbury; lived in this town on the old North road, nearly opposite Riley Smith's, from 1805 to 1810, and afterward removed to Clinton, Penn. His second wife was Harriet, daughter of Grinnell Spencer, and widow of Sheldon Norton.
II. BEULAH, b. December 31, 1787.
III. MICHAEL, b. May 28, 1790 ; m. Susan Hurlbut, b. Goshen, Conn., March 26, 1788, daughter of Gideon and Anna (Beach) Hurlbut. They had two sons and two daughters. He d. November 30, 1857. She was living in 1858, and so were Sally and Sibyl, her sisters, who were born at the same birth with her.

SALMON TREAT came from Wethersfield, when a boy, with Deacon Josiah Smith, from whom he this year received a deed of the farm on Wallen's Hill, now owned and occupied by his son Sylvester, on which he lived during the remainder of his long life. He died March 30, 1858, aged 91. He married November 2, 1794, Esther, daughter of Elisha Mallory, who died August 21, 1853, aged 79. They had sons, George, Syra, Asa, Sylvester, Luke, Luther, and a daughter Betsey, who married, April 17, 1831, Asahel Castle of Harwinton. No record of their births is found.

WILLIAM WATERMAN, Jr., lived, it is believed, on the premises east of the Still River turnpike, near the Halsey Burr place. There is a tradition of his being routed out of the town, in consequence of the quarters, hide and horns of an ox belonging to his neighbor Captain Whitford being found ingeniously hid under a pile of lumber near his house. There appears to have been also a William Waterman, Senior. There is a quit claim in 1793 of the interest by inheritance or otherwise in the same land by Walter, Zebulon, Lucy, John, and Fanny Waterman of Barkhamsted.

1789.

DANIEL EGGLESTON, Jr., from Colebrook, bought land in the town this year, and his name also appears on the tax list as a resident. His farm on the old road adjoining Colebrook line is now owned by William E. Cowles. He died on this farm about 1820. Wife, Anne.

CHILDREN.

I. ERASTUS.
II. CHAUNCEY, m. Chloe Coe.
III. NANCY.
IV. ANNE, b. Winsted, July 17, 1792.
V. SIDNEY.

DANIEL EGGLESTON, Senior, was of Winchester in March, 1779, and by wife Sarah had daughter Sarah, born September 17, 1779. He was from Windsor, and removed to Colebrook as early as 1785. None of the family remain in town.

LEWIS MILLER, probably from Torrington, is on the list of this year. He lived from 1796 to about 1803 or 1804 in a small house that stood on north side of West Lake street, in front of the Sherman T. Cook house. He had a wooden dish mill on or near the site of the Beardsley Scythe Co.'s grinding works. He went to parts unknown not far from 1803, leaving behind him a wife and

CHILDREN.

I. BELINDA, the first wife of James C. Cleveland; she died December 26, 1819, aged 27.
II. SHELDON, b. November 10, 1799.
III. AURELIA, d. young.
IV. GEORGE.

SHELDON MILLER married, October 31, 1822, Jerusha Ann Starkweather.

CHILDREN.

I. LEWIS ALLEN, b. Nov. 3, 1823; m. in Lee, Mass., April 8, 1846, Phebe Ann Sheffield, b. Stonington, Jan. 21, 1822. Children: Frances Amelia, b. Lee, Aug. 11, 1847; Edward Lewis (twin), b. Lee, April 2, 1851; Eunice Louisa (twin), b. Lee, April 2, 1851.
II. GEORGE HUDSON, b. June 24, 1825; m. in Canaan, N. Y., October 16, 1848, Eusebia N. Herrick. Children: Emma Jane, b. West Stockbridge, Nov. 9, 1849; d. July 13, 1850; Eva Maria, b. West Stockbridge, June 6, 1857.
III. HENRY ELIJAH, b. April 18, 1830; m., Nov. 29, 1853, Caroline Moore.
IV. LAURA ANN, b. Aug. 29, 1832; m. May 7, 1851, Henry McCullock. Children: 1. Agnes Marilla, b. April 9, 1852; 2. Albert Henry, b. April 5, 1853, d. Aug. 28, 1853; 3. Lila Ann, b. May 1, 1855, d. March 8, 1857; 4. Charles Sheldon, b. April 8, 1857.
V. MARY MARIA, b. Dec. 6, 1841; d. March 23, 1842.
VI. MARY JERUSHA, b. Jan. 13, 1844.

DANIEL MARSHALL, son of Eliakim of Windsor, first appears on the list of this year as a resident. He built a fulling mill on the lake stream below the works of the Henry Spring Co., and a clothier shop where Lake street now runs above the stone tenement house of E. Beardsley. He resided until his death in a dwelling house which stood adjoining his clothier shop. He died in 1804, and was buried in the old burying ground above the clock shop. His monument is the only one now standing in that ground. Wife Sarah.

CHILDREN.

I. ABRAHAM, b. April 11, 1789.
II. LUCY, b. July 6, 1790.
III. DANIEL, b. June 12, 1792.
IV. GARRISON, b. July 20, 1794.

1790.

JOHN BURTON, supposed from Middlebury, this year bought the farm on the hill road to Colebrook, now owned by David N. Beardsley, on which he lived until about 1810, and then removed from the town. He married, May 7, 1787, Phebe Wooster. She died February 15, 1807; he married (2d) Hannah, daughter of George Miller.

CHILDREN.

I. SALLY,   b. March 10, 1789; m. Spencer Shattuck.
II. SILAS,   b. March 15, 1781; m. Lucia, daughter of Asahel Miller.
III. DAVID, b. Feb. 18, 1793.
IV. POLLY,   b. May 12, 1795.

THADDEUS FAY'S name is on the list of this year. He owned the part of the Augustus Perkins farm lying west of the brook, and lived in a log house on the original road from Old Winchester to Colebrook, which has been discontinued since about 1800. He died September 1, 1798, aged about 30 years. He married, October 7, 1793, Esther Lucas.

CHILDREN.

I. LUCY,   b. May 1, 1794.
II. ELECTA,   b. Feb. 5, 1796; d. Feb. 8, 1796.
III. SALLY,   b. March 20, 1797; d. June 25, 1797.
IV. THADDEUS, b. Nov. 11, 1798; d. next day.

EZRA GRIFFIN, from Barkhamsted, owned land lying east of the Winsted Manufacturing Company's Works from 1788 to 1794, and is on the list as a resident this year only. He is named of Barkhamsted in 1794. Wife Margery.

CHILDREN.

I. ABIGAIL,   b. Dec. 12, 1785.
II. ELIZABETH, b. Nov. 17, 1788.
III. SEVILLA, b. October 6, 1790; d. Aug. 11, 1792.

THEODORE HOSKIN, son of Joseph,[1] who removed from Torrington to Old Winchester in 1771, this year came to Winsted and settled on the old Colebrook road, and built the house now occupied by his son-in-law, Alvah Oakley, in which he resided until his death, December 18, 1839, aged 74. Eunice, his wife, died June 4, 1849, aged 83. The names and births of his children are given in connection with the family of Joseph Hoskin. He wore, as did others in his day, a cue which hung down his back some fifteen inches. He persisted in wearing it after most of his cotemporaries had abandoned their "caudal appendages," and would probably have carried it with him to the grave had not the doctor ordered it to be "exscinded" while he was confined to his bed with sickness.

ROSWELL HOSKIN, brother of Theodore, came with him to Winsted, and was joint owner with him of the farm, which he quit-claimed to Theodore in 1792. He afterward removed to Vernon, N. Y.

SOLOMON PALMER, son of Enoch, a shoemaker, this year bought land on Wallen's Hill, and lived in a log-house on the highway at the east line of the town, between Harris Brown's and the Wallen's Hill school house. He is named in 1795 of Barkhamsted. He married, October 14, 1787, Hannah De Wolf.

CHILDREN.

I. STEPHEN DE WOLF, b. April 3, 1788.
II. LAMENTINE, (dau.)   b. Jan. 7, 1791.

JONATHAN ROGERS, from Lynn, a blacksmith, and brother of Simeon, already named, owned the land on which the houses of John Camp and Edward Whiting stand, and extending from the east side of Still River westerly to the second tier line. His house and shop stood on the road then running along the east side of the river. He sold out in 1794, and is named of New Marlborough, Mass., in 1798. Wife Ruhama.

CHILDREN.

I. WILLIAM PECK,   b. June 1, 1790.
II. JOSEPH (twin),   b. Nov. 17, 1792.
III. BENJAMIN (twin),   b. Nov. 17, 1792.

JOSEPH LOOMIS, from Torrington, this year bought of John Burton, a part of the D. N. Beardsley farm, on the hill road to Colebrook, and sold the same to Asahel Miller in 1800. He is named of New Hartford in 1806, in a joint deed of himself and his wife Mary, who is described as daughter of David Crissey.

1791.

JONATHAN COE, 3d, son of Ensign Jonathan, of Winchester, this year came to Winsted, and built the rear wing of the red house on the Colebrook road, one mile northerly from West Winsted, now owned by Judson Wadsworth. The upright part of the house was built soon after 1800. In this house he lived until about 1830, when he built and moved into the brick house, on the west side of the same road, now owned by his son Jehiel Coe, in which he died May 31, 1849, aged 79. He was a tall, reverend-looking man, slow of speech, a man of great shrewdness and moderation, an early Methodist and a Jeffersonian Democrat; steadfast in the support of his sect, yet catholic in spirit: zealous in politics, yet incapable of changing his principles to square with the changing ideas of party expediency. When it became democratic to ignore the manhood of the African race and deny the right of petition and free speech in its behalf, he cheerfully accepted the offensive epithet of Abolitionist, and stood in the front rank of the little band that battled for the right and prevailed. He died with his armor on, while the conflict seemed doubtful to men of feeble faith. In him there was no doubt, no fear, nor trembling. When the minister refused to read from the pulpit the notices of prayer meetings for the slave, he would rise from his pew and give the announcement. His house was one of the stations of the "Underground Railroad" from Dixie to Canada, where the panting fugitive was fed, clothed, and speeded on his journey. His influence in the town during his middle age probably transcended that of any other man. He held at different times nearly every town office, and represented the town in the Assembly in four sessions between 1822 and 1828. His family record has already been given on page 53.

CHAPTER XXIII.

WINSTED IMMIGRANTS AND FAMILY RECORDS CONTINUED.

FROM 1791 TO 1801.

1792.

JENKINS & BOYD, the pioneer manufacturers of Winsted, came into the Society this year, and erected the first scythe factory in the state and the third in the country, on the site of the Winsted Manufacturing Company's East Village Works. About 1795, in company with Thomas Spencer, Jr., they erected the first forge for making bar iron in the town, on the lake stream, opposite the grinding shop of the Winsted Manufacturing Company. In 1802 they erected another scythe factory on the site of the Winsted Hoe Company's shop, near the corner of Lake and Meadow streets.

BENJAMIN JENKINS, of the above firm, was born October 15th, 1765, at Scituate, Mass., and learned the scythe maker's trade of Colonel Robert Orr of Bridgewater, Mass., who was the first manufacturer of scythes by water-power in this country. From Bridgewater he went to New Windsor, adjoining Newburg, N. Y., as foreman of the scythe works erected by Colonel Robert Boyd, where he married, September 10, 1791, Elizabeth, daughter of Samuel Boyd of Little Britain, soon after which he removed to Torrington, and thence in 1792 to Winsted. In company with Mr. Boyd he built, in 1795, the double house afterward owned and occupied by Rev. James Beach, in which he lived until about 1806, when he built and moved into the original building of the Winsted Hotel. In 1812, he built a scythe shop on the site of the Strong Manufacturing Company's Works, which he carried on until about 1816. In 1818 he removed with his family to Wayne County, Penn., and began the world anew, in the then unbroken forest, on the Lackawaxen, four miles west of Honesdale. Here he cleared up a new home, built a scythe shop and saw mill before the first explorers of the Hudson and Delaware Canal and Rail Road route visited that region, and before Honesdale existed. The rail road was located through his farm, and the pleasant village of Prompton grew up around him, and principally on the land which he had first cleared. Here he lived to a good old age, the pioneer and revered patriarch of a region which he had first entered at the age of fifty-two. He died January 18, 1853, aged 87 years, 4 months and 26 days. His wife, with whom he had lived more than sixty years, died April 25, 1851, aged 81.

Mr. Jenkins was a man of fine personal appearance, and pleasing address — genial and kind-hearted — liberal and public-spirited — energetic and honorable — a good husband and kind parent.

He represented the town in the general assembly in 1803 and 1804.

CHILDREN.

I. ELIZABETH,   b October 5, 1792 ; m. Horace Kent of Boston ; d. October 24, 1820.
II. SUSAN,   b. April 25, 1794 ; m. Doctor Henry Noble ; d. 1814.
III. BENJAMIN, Jr., b. December 6, 1796 ; m. October 4, 1820, Mary Kent.
IV. SAMUEL,   b. December 4, 1798 ; m. 1st, Elizabeth Buckland ; 2d, Mary Jane Buckland.
V. LIONEL,   b. 1799 ; d. May 18, 1807.
VI. LOUISA,   b. 1801 ; m. 1st, Arah Bartlett ; 2d, Jacob S. Davis.
VII. EDWARD,   b. 1804 ; d. 1854, unmarried.
VIII. MARIA,   b. 1806 ; m. Ralph Case.
IX. JOHN,   b. 1808 ; m. Jane Greeley.
X. HENRIETTA,   b. 1810 ; m. Luman Hubbell.
XI. MARIETTA,   b. 1812 ; m. Benjamin Jenkins 3d ; she d. 1842.

JAMES BOYD[3] came to Winsted with his brother-in-law and partner, Benjamin Jenkins, in 1792, having previously learned from him the scythe maker's trade at New Windsor, his native place. He first lived in a small house that stood on the west side of North Main street, nearly opposite the parsonage house of Rev. James Beach, which was built by him and his partner in 1795, and jointly occupied by them until 1802. He then built and moved into the house on the east side of Main street, west village, opposite Munro street, now owned by John T. Rockwell, where he spent his remaining life, and died February 1, 1849, aged 78 years. In 1803 he dissolved partnership with Mr. Jenkins, taking for his share the joint property of the firm in the west village. In 1808 he built a forge and saw mill on the water-power opposite the Clarke House, now owned by the New England Pin Company. In 1822 he built a drafting and forging shop in rear of the Beardsley House, and in 1828 he rebuilt the "Upper Forge," on the lake stream, above Hulbert's present iron works. He also built, in 1816, the old iron store on Main street, next north of Dudley's brick block.

He was a man of indomitable energy. Few men ever did more hard work, and more thoroughly managed a large business than he, until past the prime of life. Frugal and temperate in all his habits, and retiring in his disposition, he was also public-spirited and benevolent. No wandering outcast, however degraded, ever turned away from his door without food, and lodging if needed. With a good common school education, he possessed a strong, discriminating mind and studious habits. His range of reading extended from "Tristram Shandy" through general history to "Edward's on the Will," and other abstruse theology. Trained in the faith of the Scotch seceders, he made the Bible his constant study, and deduced from it his own independent belief, matured by careful study, and reverently cherished. With an erect figure and rapid gait, he had a sternness of aspect and an immovable decision which repelled familiarity; yet, he had a strength of affection and tenderness of heart little realized by those who superficially knew him. Perfect integrity was a dominant trait of his character.

The Little Britain branch of the Boyd family, to which he belonged, was of the Kilmarnock stock, originating in Ayrshire, Scotland, transferred to County Down in the North of Ireland, from whence four brothers, SAMUEL, ROBERT, JAMES, and NATHANIEL BOYD migrated to America.

SAMUEL BOYD, the oldest of the brothers, may have been the one among the so-named North of Ireland men who came over to found the Londonderry settlement in New Hampshire about 1720, many of whom finally went to other places. He settled in the City of New York about that period, accumulated a large estate, and died a bachelor. By his aid and counsel, his three brothers, before named, and a sister Mary, who married — Wargh, came over from County Down, and settled in the town of New Windsor, Orange Co., N. Y.

ROBERT BOYD, above-named, settled at New Windsor, near the mouth of the creek which empties into the Hudson a mile below Newburgh. He had a son Robert,[2] and a daughter Mary,[2] who married — Harris.

COLONEL ROBERT BOYD[2] erected iron and scythe works on the creek before mentioned. He inherited the estate of his bachelor uncle, and removed to the City of New York early in this century, and there held the office of sheriff of the county. He died Oct. 29, 1804, aged 70, as appears on his monument in Little Britain Church-yard. He married — Smith, and had

CHILDREN.

I. SAMUEL,   a Counsellor-at-law in the City of New York.
II. JOHN,   of Ogdensburg, Sheriff of St. Lawrence Co., N. Y.
III. JENNETT,   wife of Rev. James Schrimgeozir.
IV. AGNES,   wife of Dr. Baltus Van Kleek.
V. ELIAS,   died a bachelor.
VI. GEORGE,   Episcopal clergyman, Philadelphia.

NATHANIEL BOYD, the fourth brother, lived in Little Britain Parish, New Windsor, and had sixteen children by his first and second wives.

BY MARGARET BECK.

I. JANE, w. of — Butler.
II. JOHN, of Amenia, N. Y.
III. SAMUEL.
IV. JAMES S.
V. MARY, w. of William Bradner.
VI. NATHANIEL.[2]
VII. MARTHA, w. of — Homan.

BY MARTHA MONSEL.

VIII. JANE.[2]
IX. ELIZABETH.[2]
X. NATHANIEL.[2]
XI. MARY,[2] w. of — Thompson of Esopus.
XII. CHARLES.[2]
XIII. HANNAH,[2] w. of — Alexander.
XIV. JANE.[2]
XV. ROBERT W.[2]
XVI. NATHANIEL.[2]

JAMES BOYD,[1] the third brother, sailed from Belfast, Ireland, August 9, 1756, with his second wife and children, whose names and date of birth are recorded in his family bible, as follows :—

BY SARAH, HIS FIRST WIFE.

I. SAMUEL,[2] b.   1734.
II. SARAH,[2]   b. August 13, 1738.
III. ROBERT,[2] b. January 10, 1740.
IV. MARY,[2]   b. March 28, 1742, married and settled in Scotland.
V. JEAN,[2]   b. January 20, 1749; m. — Soper of Esopus, N. Y.

BY MARY, SECOND WIFE.

VI. SEABORN AGNES,[2] born on the voyage, September 23, 1756; m. Richard Hudson of Newburg.
VII. JAMES[2] (date of birth torn off).
VIII. ELIZABETH,[2] b. February (torn off); m. — Belknap of Newburgh, N. Y.
IX. DAVID,[2] b. December   , of Phelps, Ontario Co., N. Y.
X. NATHANIEL,[2] b.
XI. ALICE,[2]   b.; m. John Wood.

SAMUEL BOYD,[2] oldest son of James,[1] visited America four years earlier than his father, and returned to Ireland, whence he came back as a permanent settler in 1756, and thereafter resided in Little Britain Parish until his death, May 27, 1801, in his sixty-seventh year. He served in the French Canadian War, and furnished a substitute in the Revolution. He m. (1st) Elizabeth, dau. of Mathew McDoel, of New Windsor, who d. Aug. 25, 1775, and (2d) Mary Lyon, who d. in 1812, s. p.

CHILDREN BY FIRST WIFE.

I. ELIZABETH,[3] b. at Little Britain, N. Y., 1769; m. Benjamin Jenkins.
II. JAMES,[3] b. L. B., Nov. 15, 1770.
III. MATHEW,[3] b. d. young.
IV. JOHN,[3] b. d. young.

JAMES BOYD,[3] son of Samuel,[2] settled in Winsted as already stated. He m. at Torringford, Conn., Dec. 23, 1795, Mary Munro, b. Boston, Mass., March 10, 1771, dau. of Alexander and —— (McIntosh) Munro, from Inverness, Scotland. She d., Winsted, Sept. 2, 1821; and he m. (2d) June 27, 1822, Jane Munro, b. at Bridgewater, Mass., June 8, 1788, dau. of Alexander and —— (Hutchinson) Munro, and half-sister of his first wife. She d., Winsted, Dec. 29, 1852.

CHILDREN.

I. NANCY,[4] b. May 27, 1797; m. 1820, Lucius Clarke.
II. JOHN[4] (twin), b. March 17, 1799.
III. JAMES MUNRO[4] (twin), b. March 17, 1799; d. Aug. 28, 1826.
IV. ELIZA,[4] b. March 18, 1801; d. April 1, 1801.
V. SAMUEL,[4] b. June 24, 1802.
VI. ELIZA,[4] b. June 25, 1804; d. Sept. 10, 1821.
VII. MARY,[4] b. Aug. 11, 1807; d. Aug. 30, 1821.
VIII. JANE MUNRO,[4] b. Dec. 10, 1812; m. Luman Hubbell.
IX. SUSAN,[4] b. March 19, 1815; m. Sept. 7, 1836, Elijah Phelps Grant, b. Norfolk, Conn., Aug. 23, 1808, son of Dea. Elijah and Elizabeth (Phelps) Grant. He graduated Yale College, 1830; lives at Canton, Ohio; a lawyer and banker. Children, all born in Canton, Ohio: 1. Elizabeth, b. May 21, 1838; m. May 18, 1858, Thomas J. Hurford, of Omaha, Neb.; 2. Susan, b. Jan. 8, 1841; d. July 19, 1841; 3. Mary, b. Sept. 12, 1842; m. ; 4. Charles Fourier, b. Aug. 12, 1844; d. May 25, 1845; 5. Jane, b. Nov. 27, 1846; 6. Martha A., b. April 30, 1849; d. June 27, 1859; 7. James Boyd, b. Nov. 10, 1853.
X. ALEXANDER MUNRO,[4] b. July 2, 1823; d. June 12, 1824.
XI. JENNETT,[4] b. May 16, 1825; d. April 14, 1827.
XII. ELIZABETH,[4] b. Oct. 23, 1827; m. June 1, 1859, Stephen A. Hubbard, b. Sunderland, Mass.
XIII. ROBERT LEWIS,[4] b. Aug. 15, 1831; commenced and carried on the manufacture of planter's hoes, in Winsted, from 1852 to 1860; then went to New York, where he now resides. He m. Nov. 6, 1862, Helen A. Peck, dau. of Edward B. and Mary Ann Peck, of Fairfield Co., Conn., b. April 18, 1840. Her name changed, by adoption, to Helen Annette Wooster, in which name she was married.

CHILDREN.

1. Anna, b. N. Y. city, June 30, 1864; d. July 2, 1864.
2. A son, still born, in Brooklyn, July 6, 1865.

3. Ralph Booth, b. Brooklyn, June 4, 1866.
4. Louis Roland, b. Brooklyn, Dec. 10, 1867; d. Aug. 13, 1868.
5. James Hubbell, b. in B., Nov. 13, 1869; d. Aug. 17, 1870.

JOHN BOYD,[4] m., New Haven, May 17, 1831, Emily Webster Beers, b. N. H., March, 1805, dau. of Elias and Jerusha (Fitch) Beers. She d. Nov. 25, 1842; and he m. (2d) Dec. 10, 1843, Mrs. Jerusha (Rockwell) Hinsdale, widow of Theodore Hinsdale, and dau. of Solomon and Sarah (McEwen) Rockwell. He grad. Yale Coll. 1821; admitted to the bar of New Haven Co., 1825; Rep. General Assembly, 1830 and 1835; County Commissioner, 1840, 1849, and 1850. Town Clerk, 1829–33, 1837–41, and from 1855, to the present time, Judge of Probate for fifteen years, till disqualified by age, in 1869; State Senator, 1854; Secretary of State of Conn., 1859, 1860, and 1861; a manufacturer of the firm of J. Boyd & Son, 1827 to 1850, afterwards to 1853, alone.

CHILDREN.

I. ELLEN WRIGHT,[5]   b. Sept. 3, 1833.
II. JAMES ALEXANDER,[5]   b. Nov. 12, 1835; d. Oct. 5, 1837.
III. EMILY BEERS,[5]   b. June 23, 1842; d. Oct. 16, 1852.

JAMES MUNRO BOYD,[4] was trained to business as an iron manufacturer and trader, under his father, which he followed with decided ability and energy until his death. He was an extensive reader, social, warm-hearted and upright. He died unmarried, Aug. 28, 1826, beloved and lamented.

SAMUEL BOYD,[4] m. Sept. 20, 1825, Sylvia Coe, b. Aug. 12, 1806, dau. of Jonathan and Charlotte (Spencer) Coe. He was a trader and manufacturer in Winsted, till 1833; Custom House Appraiser in New Orleans, till 1850; Commission Hardware in New York, till 1860; Appraiser in Custom House, in N. Y. to the present time.

CHILDREN.

I. JAMES MUNRO,[5]   b. Winsted, Sept. 28, 1826; was drowned in Mad River, June 10, 1829.
II. MARIANNE,[5]   b. W., July 31, 1828; m. Aug. 28, 1850, Henry Bascom Keen, a merchant and banker, of New York; b. Pittsburg, Penn., July 18, 1825, son of Robert Lewis and Phebe A. (Page) Keen. He d. Dec., 1868.

CHILDREN.

1. Robert Lewis,[6] b. Brooklyn, N. Y., Aug. 23, 1851; 2. Henry Boyd,[6] b. B., Jan. 9, 1854; 3. James Munro, b. B., July 16, 1856.

III. SARAH JANE,[5]   b. W., June 10, 1831; m. Brooklyn, N. Y., Sept. 30, 1853, Thomas Howe Bird, b. Boston, Mass.

IV. ROBERT MUNRO,[5]   b. W., Aug. 12, 1834; m. Nov. 10, 1859, Kate Baldwin Crane, b. Bloomfield, N. J., Dec. —, 1838, dau. of Matthias and Susan (Baldwin) Crane. He is a merchant of New York; resides at Mont Clair, N. J. Children: 1. Susie; 2. Robert M.; 3. Bertha.
V. ALICE ISABEL,[5]   b. New Orleans, La., June 26, 1845; m. May 11, 1869, Rev. Nelson Millard. Child: Ernest Boyd, b. Dec. 11, 1870.

CYRUS CURTIS, of Colebrook, bought land adjoining Colebrook line, and lived thereon in a house on the west side of the road above Wm. E. Cowles' dwelling, and probably left town the next year.

DEACON JOHN LEE this year bought the Fyler farm, on South street, and lived in the Albro Fyler house, recently burned down, until about 1799. He was chosen Deacon of the Congregational Church in 1795.

EPHRAIM SCOVILL and REUBEN SCOVILL, father and son, from Colchester, this year bought the farm on South street, now occupied by Goodloe H. Camp, which they occupied during their remaining lives. Ephraim quit-claimed his half of the farm to Reuben in 1801, and lived not many years after.

REUBEN SCOVILL died August 5, 1821, aged 55. He had a daughter Deborah who married John Maltbie; a son, Truman, who married a daughter of David Talmadge and continued to occupy the homestead until about 1837, when he removed to Granville, Mass.; and a daughter Lydia who married, January 17, 1821, Miles Marsh, of New Hartford.

CAPT. ABIJAH WILSON,[2] from Torrington, this year bought land at the crossing of the old North Country road and the old Still River turnpike, and soon after built the house at that point now owned and occupied by his youngest son, Daniel B. Wilson, which he occupied until his death, March 24, 1833, aged 86. He was a representative of the town in 1798 and 1802. He was born in Torrington, December 18, 1746, son of Noah[1] and Ann Wilson; married, October 5, 1767, Margaret Beach, of Torrington. She died 1794, aged 47, and he married (2d), Hannah Bushnell, of Hartland; she died June 16, 1844, aged 81.

CHILDREN BY FIRST WIFE, BORN IN TORRINGTON.
I. ZENAS,[3]   b. Jan. 22, 1768; d. April 15, 1769.
II. ZENAS,[3]   b. April 11, 1769; m. Polly, daughter of Daniel Coe Hudson, of Torrington.
III. SOLOMON,[3]   b. Feb. 8, 1772; d. Nov. 26, 1775.
IV. REYNOLD,[3]   b. June 18, 1774.
V. ORREL,[3]   b. Jan. 5, 1777; m., 1795, Nathaniel Bacon, of Fabius, N. Y.

VI. ABIJAH,[3] b. June 8, 1779; m. Lucy, daughter of Freedom Wright, of Winsted.
VII. LOVISA,[3] d. unmarried, Dec. 16, 1806, aged 20.

CHILDREN BY HIS SECOND WIFE, BORN IN WINSTED.

VIII. MARGARET,[3] m. Edgar West, of Chardon, Lake Co., Ohio.
IX. AMANDA,[3] m. Henry Munson, of Mentor, Ohio.
X. DANIEL[3] b. Nov. 27, 1800; m., April, 1825, Adeline, daughter of Lyman Doolittle.

CAPT. ZENAS WILSON[3] lived on the old North Country road, on the farm, and in the house recently sold by Henry Dowd to Allen N. Hitchcock, until his removal, about 1821, to Fabius, N. Y., whence he afterward removed to Concord, Lake Co., O., where he died in 1847. His wife died in 1843.

CHILDREN.

I. ANSEL[4] had children, George[5] and Hiram.[5]
II. ORRIN[4] (twin) had children, Zenas[5] and Hudson.[5]
III. ORSON[4] (twin) had children, Henry,[5] Eliza,[5] and Jane.[5]

REYNOLD WILSON[3] lived until his removal to Fabius, N. Y., about 1815, on the farm on Wallen's Hill recently owned by Lorrin Smith. He married Chloe, daughter of Elisha Mallory. He died 1835.

ABIJAH WILSON, Jr.,[3] lived on and owned until his death the Stephen Rowley farm on the Old Country road west of Still River. He died April 17, 1813, aged 34. He married Lucy, daughter of Freedom Wright. He died April 17, 1813; she died November 15, 1817.

CHILDREN.

I. NELSON WRIGHT,[4] b. Feb. 13, 1799; m., May 10, 1820, Wealthy Coe, daughter of Jonathan and Charlotte (Spencer) Coe; she d. at Sudbury, Vt., Feb. 2, 1845; he d. Nov. 21, 1851. Children: 1. George Coe,[5] b. Dec. 13, 1821; m., Lenox, Mass., Oct. 19, 1843, Caroline Miles, b. Lenox, Nov. 26, 1822, daughter of Richard and Rhoda (Porter) Miles. He d. March 4, 1854. Children: 1. Franklin Henry,[6] b. Jan. 4, 1845; d. Jan. 6, 1845; 2. James H.,[6] b. Jan. 27, 1846; 3. Alice,[6] b. July 28, 1847; 4. Ida,[6] b. June 2, 1849, d. Sept. 7, 1849; 5. Charles,[6] b. Sept. 17, 1850. 2. Charles Horton,[5] b. May 22, 1826; d. May 18, 1847. 3. Harriet Elizabeth,[5] b. April 23, 1831; m. Feb. 6, 1850, Alexander Charles Thompson, b. Martinsburgh, N. Y., July 20, 1822, son of Enoch and Betsey (Murdock) Thompson. She d. Jan. 7, 1855, s.p., and he m. (2d) May 31, 1856, Mrs. Caroline (Miles) Wilson, widow of George Coe Wilson. He d. July 14, 1866. 4. Henry,[5] b. Oct. 20, 1833; d. Oct. 19, 1836.
II. HARRIET E.,[4] m., May 22, 1825, Charles W. Horton, M.D.; had children Jane E.,[5] and Rollin C.[5]
III. HIRAM A.,[4] b. Dec. 19, 1812; m., May 12, 1841, Hannah Bosworth; graduate of Wesleyan University, Middletown, Conn.; late principal of Janes-

ville Academy, N. Y. Now resident of Saratoga, N. Y. Children:
1. A son,[5] b. October, 1844, d. young; 2. Laura,[5] b. July 20, 1846, d. Sept. 15, 1847; 3. Hiram B.,[5] b. April 17, 1848, d. Feb 2, 1849; 4. Mary Lenita,[5] b. March 5, 1850.

DANIEL B. WILSON[3] has owned and occupied the homestead of his father since his death. He married, April 25, 1827, Adeline, daughter of Lyman Doolittle.

CHILDREN.

I. ELVIRA J.,[4] m., Nov. 25, 1846, Allen M. Hitchcock.
II. JOHN,[4]
III. MARGARET,[4]
IV. JANE,[4]
V. ROLLIN,[4]
VI. EMORETT,[4]
VII. ADELAIDE,[4]
VIII. HENRY,[4]
IX. ISABEL.[4]

1793.

LEVI ACKLEY, from Chatham, owned and lived on a farm on the east side of Long Lake, now owned by John T. Rockwell. He sold out to John Westlake, in 1807, and removed to Tyringham, Mass., and died there November 10, 1817, aged 52. He married January 6, 1795, Lois Alvord, daughter of Eliphaz. She died April 20, 1841, aged 70.

JEHIEL ACKLEY BURR, son of Jehiel Burr of Torrington and adopted son of Levi and Lois Ackley, born June 25, 1795, and died November 24, 1814.

EPAPHRODITUS BLIGH this year bought a lot "on the brow of Dish Mill Hill," with a potashery, tannery and dwelling house thereon, supposed to be the tannery and dwelling on Still River turnpike, near Daniel B. Wilson's, now owned by Frederick Woodruff. He sold out to Asher Loomis in 1795.

ISRAEL DOUGLASS this year bought the portion of West Winsted village lying south of M. and C. I. Camp's store and dwellings. He sold to Isaac Wheeler in 1795, and bought the Nisus Kinney farm, on Spencer street, and lived in a log house nearly opposite Amos Pierce until after 1804, when he removed to Leyden, Lewis Co., N. Y. Wife Ruth.

CHILDREN.

I. RUTH, b. Oct. 29, 1794.
II. ANSELM, b. April 28, 1796.
III. ANNA, b. March 10, 1798.
IV. ELIZABETH, b. April 16, 1800.

BENJAMIN WHITING, Jr., (see his father's record under 1779). this year bought and settled on the farm on Colebrook road lately owned by Silas

Hoskin. He lived in what is now the rear part of Mr. Hoskin's house until his removal to Austinburg, Ashtabula Co., Ohio, in 1811. He married, May 24, 1791, Rebecca Swift.

CHILDREN.

I. MYRON, b. Jan. 3, 1795.
II. MILO,   b. Feb. 26, 1798.
III. BENJAMIN, b. Dec. 30, 1801.
IV. MELISSA, b.

GUERNSEY GOFF, this year bought a lot at the outlet of Long Lake, on which the Beardsley saw-mill stands, which he sold out in 1794 to Ananias Dearthick.

ENOCH GOFF, from Colchester, this year bought the Deacon Hurlbut farm on the east side of Long Lake, — and sold out to Levi Norton in 1796.

WILLIAM MERRIAM, a joiner, this year bought the farm on Wallen's hill, now owned by Florin Parsons, near the school house, on which he lived until 1797, when he sold out to Samuel and Moses Camp. He married, Aug. 8, 1793, Lydia Wright.

CHILDREN.

I. WILLIAM,   b. Sept 14, 1794.
II. SALLY WRIGHT, b. Aug. 12, 1796.
III. SOPHRONIA,   b. Aug. 26, 1798.

JOSEPH MITCHELL, a wheelwright, from Chatham, first lived on the west side of South street, a little south of the Ebenezer Rowley house. About 1805 he built a house, recently torn down, at the east corner of Main and Walnut streets, in which he lived until his death April 28, 1847, at the age of 81. No record is preserved of his family. His children, as far as recollected, were Selden, who built and occupied until 1822 the Sheldon Kinney house, on the south side of Main street, and died in Granville, Mass., — Diademia, wife of Henry S. Brown, of Winsted, — Hubbard, who died in Granville, Mass., — Huldah, wife of Zenas Cady, and Cordelia, wife of Harmon Cady.

ANDREW PRATT, from Saybrook, this year bought of Martin Hurlbut, his subsequent homestead on the hill, three quarters of a mile southerly from the railroad depot, now occupied by his grand-son, James W. Ward. He was a very shy, retiring man, rarely seen away from his farm, who acquired a large estate of timber land, which he carefully preserved during his life. He died May 2, 1849, aged 83. His wife died April 18, 1835, aged 64. He married March 7, 1796, Sarah Miller of Torrington.

CHILDREN.

I. SALLY,   b. Oct. 7, 1797; m. Oct. 19, 1820, Harry Ward, of Torrington; had one child, James W. Ward, of Winsted; she d. 1858.
II. PHEBE,   b. Feb. 22, 1800; d. single.
III. ORREL,   b. Dec. 18, 1802; d. single.
IV. ANDREW,   b.   ; d.   1810.
V. NEWELL,   b.   ; m. Esther Ann Barnes; and lived on part of his father's farm until 1850, then moved to Norfolk, and from there to Illinois.

1794.

THOMAS BOYD, from Amenia, New York, is on the tax list of this year. He married, Jan. 1, 1794, Huldah, daughter of David and Huldah Mills, born Oct. 19, 1776. He soon after returned to Amenia, New York, where he died, leaving children, — one of whom, a son, became a resident of Alabama.

ANANIAS DEARTHICK, a Baptist preacher, this year bought ten acres of land on which now stand the Second Congregational Church, the Winsted Bank, S. W. Coe's store, and the residences of Doctor Welch, Moses Camp, and Caleb J. Camp. He also owned the Beardsley saw-mill site and lands adjoining on the west, and lived in a log house thereon. He sold out before 1797; in which year he is named of Warren, in a writ before Justice Alvord.

JAMES FRISBIE is on the tax list of Winsted this year, with ten acres of land set to his name, of which the records say nothing.

GODFREY JONES, "of Winchester," this year bought land on the hill road to Colebrook, between the Everitt C. Holmes and the Elihu Rockwell farms, which he sold soon after. In a court record of 1796, he is named as "late of Hartland, Conn., and now of Burke, in the State of Vermont."

JOEL LUCAS this year bought the Clothiers' works, dwelling house and the land on the south side of Lake street from the top of the hill to Lake street bridge, previously owned by Daniel Marshall, which he sold in 1795. His name is on the tax lists of 1795 and 1796; and he lived in Sandisfield, Mass., in 1797.

ZACHEUS MUNSILL, this year bought of Ananias Dearthick, the land in West Winsted on which stand the Second Congregational Church and other buildings. In 1798, he built and occupied the old house recently torn down on the north side of West Lake street, opposite the Stabells

41

brick house. He conveyed this property in 1801 to Preserved Crissey by a deed in which he is named "of Westmoreland, Oneida County, N. Y." He married, December 10, 1796, Lovisa, daughter of Stephen Spencer.

CHILDREN.

I. STEPHEN,   b. June 12, 1796.
II. LUCY,   b. Oct. 27, 1800.

WILLIAM A. STONE, "of Winchester," this year bought thirteen acres of land near the west end of the Everitt Holmes farm, which he conveyed away in 1795 by deed, in which he is named of Goshen.

The names of DANIEL BROWN and ABSALOM GRIFFIN are on the tax list of this year as residents of Winsted, and are not found elsewhere.

TIMOTHY CANNON'S name is on the list of 1795. His wife Lucy was received into the Church in 1794 by letter from Southwick, Mass. They probably lived on South street. He died soon after 1800. They had children, Benjamin, Nathaniel, Elijah, and Tracy, who lived in Winsted after 1800.

DAVID COLLINS is on the list of this year as a resident. From 1797 to 1799 he owned land on the east side of the road, north of David N. Beardsley, adjoining the Everitt Holmes farm. In 1799 he is named of Colebrook.

SAMUEL CUMMINS, and his wife Margaret, from Torrington, this year bought the farm on Spencer street now owned by Edward Manchester, which they sold to Ensign Jonathan Coe in 1796, and then moved out of the town.

JOSIAH CURTIS, and his wife Emma, named of Sheffield, Mass., this year bought a house and land on the west side of South street, near Torrington line, which they conveyed to Ulysses Fyler in 1798.

JAMES EGGLESTON, and Jemima, his wife, this year bought a house and lot on the east side of the road, north of David N. Beardsley, which they sold in 1798, to Hine Clemmons, and left the town.

HORACE HIGLEY, from Windsor, this year, jointly with Daniel Phelps, bought the Artemas Rowley farm, south of the burying ground in the old society. In 1799, he bought of Isaac Wheeler, the tavern property on Main street, south of Camp's Block, and all the land on Main street from M. & C. J. Camp's south line to the Clifton Mill Bridge, and including High, Elm, Center and Willow streets, most of which was then a forest, without an inhabited tenement thereon. The tavern buildings were erected the year before in anticipation of the opening of the Green Woods Turnpike, a new and shorter avenue of travel, which was to supercede the Old North road, on the route from Hartford to Albany. Mr. Higley was a model farmer and tavern keeper of the old school. His lands were thoroughly cleared and skilfully tilled. No tippler ever haunted his bar-room. His table fare was suited to the taste of an epicure; his beds were ever clean and well aired; and his guests found him a social, dignified, and gentlemanly host. The travel on the new road was so abundant that he could choose his guests; and his choice of customers gave him an aristocratic reputation, which was by no means lessened by a sight of the unchained lion on his sign-board, indicative of his strong federal propensities. He was a public-spirited and influential man in the community, largely employed in public business,—was Postmaster from 1806 to 1830, and six times a representative of the town in the General Assembly. In 1828, he retired from the tavern, and built and occupied the house on the flat, now owned by A. N. Beach. In 1838 he moved to Painesville, O., where he died Jan. 5, 1842, aged 77. His wife d. at Painesville, Aug. 17, 1849, aged 82. He was son of Nathan and Anna (Barret) Higby, of Windsor, was b. East Windsor, 1765, and m. Eleanor Loomis.

CHILDREN.

I. HORACE LOOMIS, b. Windsor, Dec. 29, 1794; lived at Pensacola and Mobile; d. Mobile, Aug. 20, 1856, leaving a family.
II. HOMER, b. Winchester, Dec. 30, 1796; m. Amelia, dau. of Raphael Marshall, Tor.; moved to Painesville, O., in 1829, where he d. in 1862.
III. PETER, b. Feb. 10, 1802; d. Sept. 17, 1813.
IV. MARY, b. May 18, 1804; d. in Painesvile, O., Aug. 10, 1841; unmarried.
V. CHARLES, b. Nov. 14, 1806; d. at Satartia, Miss., Aug. 19, 1835; unmarried.
VI. WILLIAM, b. April 3, 1809; m. Sept., 1831, —— Beach of Sandisfield, Mass.; d. at Springfield, Mass., in 1863.

ASHER LOOMIS, a tanner and shoemaker, from Windsor, this year bought the Widow Hawley place on Dishmill Hill, immediately west of Daniel B. Wilson's, where he lived until about 1800, after which he lived on South street, near the Salmon Burr place, until about 1808, when he returned to Windsor. He m. in 1796, Rosinda, dau. of Deacon Shubael Cook, and had sons and daughters born in this town. One of his daughters was second wife of Riley Smith, of Winsted.

SETH LUCAS, from Torrington, this year bought a farm now composing part of the Gillett and Fosket farms, and lived in a house now torn down, on the discontinued road north of Gillett's. He sold out to Theodore Smith, in 1803, and removed to Colebrook.

TRUMAN SEYMOUR, from Colebrook, a blacksmith, came from Colebrook and resided in Winsted two years,—after which he lived in Colebrook, until 1807, when he returned to Winsted and lived in the gambrel-roofed house on Lake street, near the bridge, until 1815, when he removed to Oneida Co., N. Y. He was an ingenious mechanic, and much esteemed for his social qualities and obliging disposition. He had a large family of children, among them three sons, George, Chauncey, and Arah, and three daughters, Ann, Sophia, and Parnel. There were younger children, whose names are not remembered.

AMOS TOLLES, from Durham, Green Co., N. Y., owned the farm on Coe street, late owned by Anson Fosket, and built the house thereon, in which he lived until 1837, when he went to live with a son-in-law and daughter in Barkhamsted. He d. July 18, 1845, aged 80. His wife d. June 2, 1838, aged 64. He m. Marian Baldwin, b. Goshen, Conn., Nov. 29, 1773, dau. of Bruin Baldwin.

CHILDREN.

I. HANNAH, b. about 1793; m. Daniel Sage, of Colebrook.
II. ELISHA, b. about 1794; m. Harriet Frisbie; d. at Cincinnati, July 13, 1849.
III. RILEY, b. 1796; d. at the South, unmarried.
IV. LUCIA, b. 1798; m. Amasa Mallory, Jr ; d. Dec. 17, 1834.
V. SYLVIA, b. m. May, 1826, William S. Boyd.
VI. MARY ANN, b. m. Amasa Mallory, Jr.

CHILDREN OF ELISHA AND HARRIET (FRISBIE) TOLLES.

I. HELEN MARIA, b. March, 1820; m. Augustus B. Clark, of New Britain.
II. ROBERT BRUCE.
III. HIRAM FRISBIE.
IV. MARY AUGUSTA, m. May 16, 1830, Elder Miles Grant.
V. HARRIET FRISBIE.

ELISHA LEWIS, from Goshen, this year built a gambrel-roofed house, that stood on the site of Moses Camp's dwelling, on Main street, opposite Lake street bridge, in which, in company with Moses Lyman and Elihu Lewis, of Goshen, he kept a store until 1798, when he returned to Goshen.

1796.

LEVI BARNES, from Torrington, owned a lot with a house and barn thereon, now owned by Jonathan Gilbert, on the east side of South street, until 1799, and continued to reside in the town until 1802.

JEHIEL BURR, from Torrington, lived first on the east side of South street, below Jonathan Gilbert's, and afterwards in a house on same street, next south of Whiting J. Miner's. He and his wife, Mabel, d. about 1800. They had three sons, who resided in the town.

CHILDREN.

I. ERASTUS, m. Polly West; moved to Western N. Y., about 1812.
II. ROSWELL, m. Nancy West; moved to Ohio about 1830.
III. HELSEY. d. in Winsted, Jan. 25, 1861, aged 71.

ELI FOX, probably from Chatham, this year bought the Roswell Pond lot on North Main street, and became a pauper, as appears by a vote of the town in 1802, directing a suit to be brought against the town of Chatham for his support.

LEVI FOX is on the tax list of this year. In 1797 he bought the Ha'sey Burr place, and sold it the following year. In 1798, he bought the Roswell Pond place, above mentioned, and sold it in 1802.

DOCTOR AARON MOORE is on the tax list of this year as a resident of Winsted. In 1802 he bought the Roswell Pond lot, and during his remaining life resided in the house now torn down, about eight rods east of the road. He was a physician of some note in his day, being the only practitioner in the society until 1810, and the teacher of many doctors who have recently gone off the stage, among whom were Doctors Luman Wakefield, and T. S. Wetmore, of this town. He died February 16, 1813, aged 40, of putrid pleurisy, which prevailed at that period. The doctor of the beginning of this century was a more marked personage than his successor of the present day. Doctor Moore, mounted on his Narraganset pacer, with his capacious saddle-bags crammed with physic enough to doctor a cavalry regiment, horses and riders, projecting beyond and above the sides of the animal, making a safe seat for the rider, with stirrups so shortened as to bring his knees to a right angle, was a sight next in solemnity to that of his cotemporary, Parson Kinney, with his gaunt six-and-a-half-foot length of figure, surmounted with a cocked hat and white flowing wig. He married Polly Fyler, sister of Ulysses. She died May 26, 1807.

CHILDREN.

I. CULLEN, drowned in Georgia; unm.
II. ERASMUS DARWIN, b. September 30, 1802; a clergyman.
III. OSTA (daughter), b. March 12, 1805; d. Nov. 30, 1806.
IV. JEREMIAH MARKHAM, b. May 9, 1806; d. Nov. 16, 1806.

GIDEON HALL came from Litchfield a young man, and had charge of a store near Wallen's Hill school-house, owned by Arthur Emmons. In 1803 he bought the Moses M. Camp farm, on South street, and there resided until 1814, when he bought of Benjamin Wheeler the farm at the parting of South street from the Green Woods turnpike, which he occupied, with an interval of a few years of tavern keeping in the East Village hotel, until his death, February 23, 1850, aged 75. He was a shrewd, uncultivated man of indomitable energy, but without system or method in his business transactions. He was largely employed in public affairs, and in settling the estates of insolvent and deceased persons. As a selectman he managed the affairs of the town with economy, but could render no intelligible account of his doings. As sheriff's officer, in which capacity he acted for many years, his success was wonderful in escaping the consequences of his bungling mode of serving and returning legal process. As a politician, he could pull the strings and manage the wires of a canvass with great adroitness. As a neighbor he was kind and useful in ways of his own. His religious profession was zealous and sincere, but spasmodic. He filled a large place in the doings of the community, worked hard during the day, and spent the night in serving writs, canvassing votes, and attending political or religious meetings. He accumulated a handsome estate, and enjoyed the good will of the community. He married, in 1797, Polly, daughter of Samuel Hayden, Esq. She died March 16, 1830, aged 53. He married (2d), October 4, 1835, Lavinia, daughter of Daniel White, who survives him.

CHILDREN BY FIRST WIFE.

I. SAMUEL HAYDEN, b. April 9, 1801; d. October, 1820.
II. ABIGAIL, b. Oct. 17, 1804; d. Sept. 12, 1823.
III. GIDEON, Jr., b. May 1, 1808, m. Lydia Foskett; graduated at Litchfield Law School and admitted to the Litchfield county bar 1829. He practised law with success in Winsted until 1866, when he was appointed a Judge of the Superior Court, which office he held until his death, Dec. 8, 1867. He was representative of the town in 1838, 1846, and 1854; a state senator in 1847, and Judge of Probate from 1839 to 1841, and from 1844 to 1848.
IV. WILLIAM SMITH, b. June 26, 1817; d. Feb., 1819.

CHILD BY SECOND WIFE.

V. JANE CATHARINE, b. Oct. 20, 1845; m. May 9, 1871, Samuel A. Wetmore, of New Haven; had a son, b. Sept. 18, 1872.

NATHAN ROSE, when a child, was brought away from Wyoming to Woodbury by his mother, after the British and Indian massacre, of which his father was a victim. He came from Woodbury to Winsted this year, married a daughter of William Davis, lived in a log house on Pratt street, afterwards owned successively by Aaron Marshall, and Joseph Cook, until his removal to Bridgewater, Herkimer Co., N. Y., in 1798.

SAMUEL WESTLAKE, an iron refiner from Orange or Rockland Co., N. Y., came into the employ of Jenkins & Boyd this or the preceding year, and lived in a house long since torn down, which stood near Timothy Hulbert's office. He died October 13, 1818, aged 75. His wife died June 7, 1815, aged 64.

CHILDREN.

I. SARAH, b. March 31, 1770; m. —— Timpson.
II. MARY, b. Dec. 17, 1777; m. —— Blakeslee.
III. WILLIAM, b. March 18, 1780.
IV. SAMUEL, b. March 24, 1782.
V. ABIGAIL, b. Jan. 9, 1785; m. Andrew Walter.
VI. JOHN, b. April 26, 1787.
VII. THOMAS, b. Nov. 20, 1789.
VIII. NANCY, b. March 12, 1792; m. Daniel Albro.

SAMUEL WESTLAKE, Jr., removed, soon after his first marriage, to Wolcottville, where he died. He married (1st) Clarissa, daughter of Christopher Whiting, by whom he had a daughter.

WILLIAM WESTLAKE resided in one of the two houses recently removed from the Connecticut Western Railroad track to the bank of Mad River, near the pin factory, from 1809 to the time of his death on January 7, 1848, and worked in the forge of James Boyd, opposite the Clark House. He married Laura Peet, of Sheffield, Mass.

CHILDREN.

I. JOHN, who d. young.
II. GEORGE, d. unmarried.
III. FANNY, m. Franklin Wolcott.
IV. MARY, m. Wm. Barker.
V. WILLIAM.
VI. LAURA ANN, m. —— Woodward.
VII. JAMES.
VIII. JANE, m. —— Martin.
IX. SAMUEL, d. young.
X. LOUISA.

JOHN WESTLAKE came into the town with his father and was esteemed the best iron refiner in the place. He first lived in a house adjoining his brother William's residence, near the pin factory, for several years. About 1831 he bought the Philo G. Sheldon place on Main street, where he lived until his removal to Utica, N. Y., in 1841. Returning to Winsted in 1848, he soon after built the house at the east corner of High and Union streets, where he lived a few years, and then moved to the Old Society of Winchester, where he died Nov. 9, 1860, aged 74 years. He was a kind-hearted man, of genial humor and unblemished character, respected and loved for his many virtues. He married, in 1809, Flora, daughter of Ebenezer Rowley, of W.

CHILDREN.

I. RILEY, who d. unmarried.
II. JULIA, m. Edwin R. White.
III. FLORANIA, m. Lem'l Hurlbut, Jr.
IV. AMANDA, m. Thomas Senior.

THOMAS WESTLAKE became a permanent resident of Winsted about 1816. He first lived southward of the pin factory, and afterward, until his death, in the house of his son-in-law, Philo G. Sheldon, on Main street. He was an industrious, well-informed man, and good citizen.

He married, in 1816, Sophia Goodwin of New Hartford. He died July 11, 1858, aged 68 years. She died June 11, 1864, aged 69.

CHILDREN.

I. MATILDA, b. January 1, 1817; m. August 18, 1835, Philo G. Sheldon.
II. RUTH, b. November 20, 1825; m. October 22, 1845, Upson Bunnell.
III. HORACE, b. February 9, 1828; m. at Hillsdale, N. Y., in April, 1851, Henrietta Foster. He was licensed as a physician in 1850, and has since practised at Hillsdale to the present time.

RANDALL SHATTUCK "of Middletown," owned a dish mill near Meadow street bridge, on the lake stream, from 1797 to 1803. He is said to have lived in a log house on the site of the Beardsley House. He removed to Torrington in 1803, and had a son, Randall Shattuck, Jr., who is now living.

OLIVER WHITE is on the tax list of Winsted for 1796 and 1797, and lived in the Lazarus Palmer house, near the Wallen's Hill schoolhouse, whence he moved over the line into Barkhamsted, and thence to Dyberry, Wayne Co., Penn., where he died about 1855, aged 82. He married Lucy Wood.

CHILDREN.

I. OLIVER, b. November 12, 1796.
II. RALPH, b. 1803; d. December 27, 1809.
III. DANIEL.
IV. LUCY, m. Halsey Burr.
V. CHARLOTTE.
VI. MARIA, m. November 25, 1838, Alonzo R. Bishop.
VII. RIETTA, m. March 8, 1837, William Weaver.
VIII. ELIZA, m. Jonas Stanton.

OLIVER WHITE, Jr., as early as 1825 began to manufacture farming implements, between the Clock Factory and the Cook Axle Factory, on the road east of Still River, where he still resides. He married, July 6, 1817, Pamelia Bacon of Barkhamsted.

CHILDREN.

I. JAMES, b. April 9, 1818; m. Charlotte Greene.
II. LUMAN, b. July 19, 1819; m. Sarepta Reynolds.
III. ORRIN WASHINGTON, b. April 5, 1821; a clergyman.
IV. WILSON B., b. January 24, 1823; m. Harriet Leach.
V. GEORGE, b. June 4, 1825; representative in 1861; m. Ellen M. Kelsey; she d. December 24, 1864, and he m. (2d) Mrs. Emily M. Putnam.
VI. JULIA A., b. May 29, 1827; m. Charles H. Wattles.
VII. AURELIA A., b. July 18, 1830; m. Grove Stannard.
VIII. SUSAN P., b. May 11, 1832; m. Hiram J. Norton.

1796.

ASAHEL MILLER from Torrington, owned and lived from 1797 to about 1810 on the farm lately owned by Anson Fosket, on the old hill road to Colebrook, in a house that stood nearly opposite that of D. N. Beardsley. About 1811, he built the house on the easterly side of Main street, next above the Dudley Tannery, and in company with James Shepard built the original tannery at that point. In 1815 he sold out to Abiel Loomis, and removed to Tyringham, Mass. He was a carpenter; an intelligent, industrious man, and much respected. He was born at Torrington, October 24, 1760, son of George and Sarah Miller. Married, October 26, 1788, Lovina, daughter of Ensign Jonathan Coe of Winchester. They died in Erie, Penn.

CHILDREN.

I. JOEL, b. Tor., June 26, 1790.   V. WILLARD.
II. LUCIA, m. Silas Burton.   VI. KIRBY.
III. LAURA, m. John W. Sweet.   VII. SARAH.
IV. ARVIN.

JOEL MILLER, oldest son of Asahel, an ingenious mechanic and deeply religious man, married a daughter of Grove Pinney of Colebrook, and resided in Winsted, dying childless before middle life.

TIMOTHY and WILLIAM SOPER, father and son, from Windsor, lived from 1797 to 1800, on the Roswell Smith farm, on Wallen's Hill, and returned to Windsor.

DANIEL WILCOX from Berlin, this year bought the clothier's shop and fulling mill on Lake street, and lived in the "Old Factory house," at the easterly corner of Lake and Rockwell streets, until 1813, when he sold out to S. Rockwell & Brothers, and removed to Great Barrington,

Mass. He was a man of iron constitution, energetic, social and hospitable. He married, September 7, 1797, Mehitabel Wright.

CHILDREN.

I. PATTY, b. August 31, 1799; m. — Beckwith of Great Barrington.
II. MAURICE, b. May 15, 1801.
III. MERCY, b. June 29, 1803.
IV. EMILY, b. December 11, 1805.
V. JULIETTE, b. April 30, 1808.

FREDERICK EGGLESTON from Colebrook is on the list of this year. In 1799 he bought the house that stood on the site of George Dudley's dwelling on Main street, which he sold in 1801 to David West, and then returned to Colebrook. He again lived in Winsted from 1810 to 1814, working for S. & M. Rockwell as a blacksmith, after which he returned to Colebrook.

SAMUEL and MOSES CAMP, sons of Moses Camp of Norfolk, and grandsons of Abraham Camp of New Milford, this year bought the Florin Parsons farm, near the Wallen's Hill schoolhouse, where they carried on the hatter's trade until 1804, when they bought the Stephen Knowlton farm on south street, next south of the Ebenezer Rowley farm, and lived in a house, now torn down, on the east side of the road.

Samuel Camp continued his residence here until his removal in 1824, to the farm now owned by Hiram Burnham, in Barkhamsted, where he died May 10, 1850, aged 77, a pious and highly respected man. He was born in Norfolk, March 4, 1773; married July 10, 1799, Mercy Sheldon of New Marlboro, Mass. She died August 21, 1854.

CHILDREN.

I. SAMUEL SHELDON, b. December 13, 1800; m. Elizabeth, daughter of Amasa Mallory.
II. MOSES, b. October 5, 1803; m. Miranda Goodwin of Goshen. She died April 7, 1865, aged 57 years, s. p. He m. (2d) February 12, 1867, Amelia S. Humphrey of Guilford, N. Y. He has been town clerk, representative in general assembly, and president of the Winsted Savings Bank.
III. ELECTA, b. November 27, 1806; m. April 28, 1831, George Dudley, b. Bloomfield, September 17, 1803, son of Levi and Abigail (Hitchcock) Dudley. He was a manufacturer of bookbinders' leather; president of the Winsted Bank for many years; postmaster, state senator, and presidential elector, at General Grant's election.

CHILDREN.

1. Jane Mehitabel, b. June 28, 1833; d. October 6, 1851.
2. Emily Sheldon, b. July 17, 1838.
3. Mary Beach, b. May 21, 1840.

AND FAMILY RECORDS. 331

4. Alice Mercy, b. April 6, 1842; m. June 11, 1868, Theodore
F. Vaill, editor of *The Winsted Herald*, and Adjutant of the
Second Connecticut Heavy Artillery.
5. George, b. July 1, 1844.

IV. EDWARD, b. April 25, 1809; m. September 29, 1831, Maria Norton, daughter of Deacon Lewis M. Norton of Goshen; she d. October 6, 1848, and he m. (2d) December 18, 1850, Desiah Knapp, daughter of Bushnell Knapp of Norfolk; she d. November 29, 1856, s. p., and he m. (3d) January 20, 1858, Louisa A. Williams of Natick, R. I. He represented the town of Barkhamsted in 1848; has been selectman of Winchester, and burgess of the Borough of Winsted; has one child, Frances Maria, b. July 28, 1844.

V. BEULAH, b. June 20, 1811; m. September 29, 1845, George Kellogg.

VI. MEHITABEL, b. May 9, 1813; m. October 22, 1840, George Kellogg; she died at Columbus, O., June 13, 1842.

VII. CALEB JACKSON, b. June 12, 1815; m. May 22, 1839, Mary, daughter of Rev. James Beach; was associated with his brothers, though, being a minor, his name did not appear in the mercantile firm of M. & E. Camp, organized March 1, 1835; in the firm of M. & C. J. Camp, which succeeded it, March 1, 1839, and that of M. &. C. J. Camp and Co., formed March 1, 1854, he has long been the principal manager.

CHILDREN.

1. Mary Mehitabel, b. March 4, 1842; m. October 23, 1866, Herman E. Curtis of N. Y.; settled in Winona, Minnesota, where her son, Clinton James, was born August 21, 1870.
2. Augusta, b. April 3, 1845; m. October 17, 1871, Franklin A. Rising of N. Y.
3. James Beach, b. October 15, 1846; d. November 13, 1849.
4. Anna Beach, b. August 2, 1850; d. March 24, 1852.
5. Ellen Baldwin, b. August 16, 1855.

MOSES CAMP, SR., in 1814, bought the farm on the South street, now owned and occupied by his son, Moses M. Camp, where he died March 6, 1852, aged 78. He was a man of strong mind and decided principles, highly esteemed and respected. He married Deidamia Knowlton, daughter of Stephen.

CHILDREN.

I. JOHN, the able and efficient manager of the Winsted Manufacturing Company from May, 1835, till his death Aug. 16, 1862, aged 56 years. He was Representative, Selectman, and Judge of Probate. He m. Ursula Whiting, who d. s. p.; and he m. (2d), Julia Root; had

CHILDREN.

1. Julia, d.   4. Alice.
2. Electa, d. Jan. 16, 1866, aged 17.   5. Lewis L.
3. John K.   6. William.

II. HARRIET,   m. Henry Dutton of New Hartford.
III. MARY,   m. Sept. 4, 1833, Elijah B. White.
IV. ADELINE,   m. James J. Preston.

V. GOODLOE H., m. Tuttle.
VI. MOSES M., m. Worthington.
VII. EMELINE, m. Lewis E. Loomis.
VIII. GEORGE G., m. Sept. 19, 1850, Sarah A. Hart.

AARON MARSHALL, from Torrington, this year bought a farm, with a log house thereon, on the east side of Pratt street, three quarters of a mile south of the depot. He died Sept. 7, 1807, aged 74, leaving two incompetent daughters, Chloe and Asenath, both of them now deceased and unmarried.

DANIEL WHITE is on the tax list of this year as a resident. He afterward lived for many years over the Barkhamstead line on Wallen's hill, where he raised a family of children. In his latter years, he resided with his daughter, Mrs. Hall, where he died Dec. 28, 1859, aged 85. His wife, Clarissa (Cleveland), died June 12, 1822, aged 40.

CHILDREN.

I. EMILY, b. Feb. 9, 1801; m. Hezekiah G. Butler.
II. LAVINIA, b. Aug. 20, 1803; m. Gideon Hall of Winsted.
III. MARY CLEVELAND, b. Jan. 31, 1805; m. Edward A. Rugg.
IV. HARRIET, b. Jan. 28, 1807; m. Oren Kellogg.
V. HORACE CLEVELAND, b. Feb. 22, 1809; m. Susan A. Wolcott.
VI. URANIA CLARISSA, b. July 20, 1811; d. near Lake Superior, Aug. 5, 1839.
VII. PHILENDA MILLER, b. June 11, 1814; m. Elizur G. Perry.
VIII. JENNETT, b. April 6, 1816; d. July 26, 1816.
IX. PEMBROKE, b. Sept. 18, 1819; went to Iowa. See Allyn S. Kellogg's *White Memorials*, p. 179.

1798.

MERRITT BULL, came from Harwinton to Winsted and served his apprenticeship as a scythe maker. He is first on the tax list as an inhabitant this year. He first lived in the house on Spencer street, now owned by Sarah Loomis, and carried on blacksmithing in a shop that then stood on the house lot of Samuel W. Coe. In 1802 or 1803, he built a scythe hop where the stone shop of the Winsted Hoe Company now stands, on Meadow street, which he carried on until his death. In 1809 he bought, and thereafter occupied, the gambrel-roofed house which stood on the site of Moses Camp's dwelling, opposite Lake street. He was instantly killed by falling among the gears of his grinding works, May 28, 1824, at the age of 49. He was an amiable and industrious man, who failed of success in business by attempting more than he could accomplish. He represented the town in the General Assembly of 1827. He married, Nov. 26, 1801, Hannah, daughter of Aaron Cook, of Winchester; born January 20, 1775.

CHILDREN.

I. ELIZA MIRIAM, b. Sept. 20, 1802.
II. NELSON, b. Feb. 6, 1804; d. April 17, 1817.
III. SIDNEY, b. " 18, 1806.
IV. TRUMBULL, b. Dec. 2, 1807.
V. HENRY BOGUE, b. Feb. 2, 1810.
VI. WOLCOTT, b. Nov. 2, 1812; d. May 7, 1815.
VII. DELIA, b. May 29, 1815.

CYRUS BUTRICK, a blacksmith, is on the tax list of this year as a resident of Winsted. In 1801 he bought the house that stood where Lake street now runs, at the turning of the hill a little east of the works of the Henry Spring Company, and worked in a shop that stood on the west side of Lake street, opposite the old mill house. In 1803 he removed to the old hill road to Colebrook, above the D. N. Beardsley place. He left the town about 1805. He married, Oct. 18, 1798, Phebe, daughter of Rev. John Sweet.

CHILDREN.

I. POLLY, b. Dec. 16, 1799. II. PHEBE, b. Feb. 21, 1802.

JOSEPH COOK, son of Aaron and Lydia, and a native of the town, is on the list of this year as a resident of the Old Society. In 1809 he bought the Aaron Marshall place, on the Pratt road, where he afterward dwelt until his death Oct. 11, 1814, aged 39. He left a son and two daughters. One of the latter is wife of Allen Roberts, of this town. He married, July —, 1803, Amelia Davis, who, after his death, married Sylvester Roberts.

JONATHAN DOUGLASS, brother of Israel, owned from 1798 to 1801, a part of the Kinney farm, on Spencer street road, and lived on the west side of the road, not far from Amos Pierce's residence.

CAPT. GEORGE FRASIER, a Scotchman, is on the tax list of this year as a resident of Winsted. He was a trader near the Wallen's Hill school-house for a few years, and probably for the most part resided over the line in Barkhamsted.

LEVI NORTON, 2d, from Norfolk, lived in the northernmost of the two contiguous houses recently owned by Halsey Burr, deceased, on the west side of the old Still River turnpike until after 1817. In 1822, he is named "of Hartland," in a deed on record. His wife was Rhoda, daughter of Enoch Palmer; the land records give the names of five of their children, viz:

CHILDREN.

EDEN, of Benson, Vt., in 1822.
ISAAC A., of Cornwall, in 1821.
FANNY, wife of Asa Mallory.
JEMIMA,
SOLOMON.

ELIHU ROCKWELL, youngest son of Joseph, and descended in the fifth generation from Deacon William Rockwell, a first planter of Dorchester, Mass., and Windsor, Conn., came this year from Torrington to Winsted, and purchased from his father-in-law, John Allen, the farm on Spencer street recently successively owned by Nisus Kinney and Luther G. Hinsdale. He lived on this farm until his removal to Euclid, Cuyahoga Co., Ohio, in 1825. He was a man of marked character and influence, entertaining political and religious sentiments not in harmony with those of his Puritan ancestors. No record is found of his family. His daughter, Lydia, by his first wife, married Clarke H. Roberts, late of Colebrook, deceased. He also had by his second wife a son and daughter who removed with him to Ohio.

REUBEN ROWLEY, oldest son of Ebenezer, and a native of the town, is on the list of this year. In 1801 he became owner of the portion of the East Village bordered by the Holabird property on the north, Still river east, Main street south, and Oak street west, which he exchanged in 1802 for a farm in the northeast corner of the town, recently owned by Joel Mead, now deceased, on which he lived until his removal to Hitchcockville in 1847, where he died May 2, 1851, aged 74.

CHILDREN.

I. ORPHA, m., Oct. 23, 1823, Isaac Brown; she d. Sept. 26, 1827, aged 23.
II. SOPHRONIA, m., Aug. 29, 1832, Allen Bacon; she d. about 1855.
III. GAD.

JOEL WRIGHT lived on the road to Colebrook above David N. Beardsley's until his death, March 16, 1813. He was a hard-working, faithful man, much employed as a farm laborer and teamster. His wife died February 21, 1813, aged 40. They had children, Sally, Joel, Flora, and Artemas. Flora married, February 7, 1821, Alexander Baldwin.

JOSEPH HOLMES, brother of David, named in 1786, while living in Torrington, owned land in this society as early as 1796, but his name first appears on the list as a resident in 1798. He owned and occupied the farm on the Spencer street road, near Colebrook line, afterward occupied by his son Willard, and now by Everett E. Holmes, son of Willard. He represented the town in six sessions of the Assembly between 1807 and 1815, and was in all respects an exemplary man and citizen. He died September 1, 1826, aged 68. His wife died October 31, 1820, aged 68. He married, at Torrington, Conn., Sept. 9, 1788, Lydia Curtis, born in Torrington, Dec. 29, 1751.

CHILDREN.

I. DAVID, b. April 27, 1779; d. at the age of 9 years.
II. RUFUS, b. April 29, 1781.
III. JERUSHA, b. April 25, 1783; m. Jan. 27, 1807, Henry Bass, of Colebrook.
IV. ROXANA, b. Sept. 21, 1785; m. David Collins, Blanford, Mass.
V. PHEBE, b.   1787; m. Daniel Deming, Colebrook.
VI. POLLY, b.   d. aged 2½ years.
VII. WILLARD, b. Nov. 14, 1792.

RUFUS HOLMES, second son of Joseph, lived after his first marriage in Colebrook, adjoining Winchester line, until 1850, when he bought of Henry E. Rockwell the Seminary building near High street in Winsted, in which he and his son, Lucius L., afterwards resided until their death. He was a thrifty farmer, an upright, public-spirited, and highly respected man, and a sincere Christian. He married (1st), Esther Eno, of Colebrook. She died August 18, 1831. He married (2d), July 1, 1835, Belinda, daughter of Nathan Bass, of Colebrook. He died June 26, 1855, aged 74 years. She died October 6, 1855, aged 60.

CHILDREN BY FIRST WIFE.

I. LUCIUS LORENZO, b. Colebrook, Nov. 7, 1811; m., March 20, 1833, Mary A. Gaylord, b. Nov. 7, 1810. He d. at Winsted May 14, 1854. She d. at Winsted Nov. 26, 1854.
II. SUSAN JENNETT, b. Colebrook, Dec. 6, 1816; m. Rollin S. Beecher.

CHILD BY SECOND WIFE.

III. RUFUS (EDWARD), b. Colebrook, May 4, 1857. He m., Dec. 24, 1857, Lucy, daughter of Nelson D. Coe, b. Winchester, Nov. 18, 1834. He was cashier of the Hurlbut bank from June 3, 1857, to Dec. 7, 1863; cashier of the Winsted bank from Dec. 7, 1863 to Aug. 27, 1864; and president of the Hurlbut bank from the last date to the present time. Children: 1. Anna Louisa, b. Sept. 17, 1860; 2. Susan Beecher, b. Oct. 27, 1862; 3. Rufus, b. April 4, 1865, d. March 16, 1866; 4. Edward Rufus, b. March 7, 1867; 5. Ralph Winthrop, b. Oct. 6, 1869.

CHILDREN OF LUCIUS L. AND MARY G. HOLMES.

I. An infant b. Jan., 1834; d. Feb., 1854.
II. SUSAN JANE, b. Colebrook, March 26, 1835; m. Dec. 10, 1854, Edward Clarke, b. Winsted.
III. LUCIUS LORENZO, b. April 12, 1840; m., Dec. 25, 1861.
IV. CHARLES BEECHER, b. Jan. 25, 1846; m. Abby, daughter of Amos Pierce.

WILLARD HOLMES, youngest child of Joseph and Lydia (Curtis) Holmes, resided from birth to death in his father's homestead. On the night of Feb. 22, 1857, he was awakened by finding his house in flames. He and his wife, the sole occcupants, having escaped to the open air, he re-entered the burning building to secure his papers and valuables, when suffocation ensued, and he was burned in the ruins. He was a well-educated, thoughtful man, of strong convictions and independent actions; a friend of the slave, the opponent of every wrong, and a humble Christian. He married at Norfolk, Oct., 1819, Miranda, daughter of David and Mary (Everett) Frisbie.

CHILDREN.

I. LUTHER WILLARD, b. Sept., 1820; m.
II. EVERETT CURTIS, b. April 28, 1821; m., Nov. 1, 1848, Laura Pease, b. April 22, 1824.
III. LYDIA, b. 1823; d. August, 1833.
IV. MARY MELISSA, b.

CHILDREN OF EVERETT C. AND LAURA (PEASE) HOLMES.

I. EDWARD E., b. Dec. 27, 1849.
II. ELIZABETH S., b. Sept. 1, 1852, adopted Nov. 1, 1854.
III. WILLARD P., b. Aug. 22, 1857.
IV. LUMAS H., b. Nov. 4, 1864.
V. MARY ISABEL, b. July 25, 1867.

1799.

ISAAC AND MARY BELLOWS owned land on the Colebrook road, and lived above D. N. Beardsley's. They sold out in 1800, — and afterwards lived until 1814, on Colebrook line on the site of the house recently built by Birdsey Gibbs.

ROSWELL MARSHALL, from Torrington, this year lived in the De-Wolf house on the west side of Colebrook road, adjoining Colebrook line, above the house of W. E. Cowles. He removed, in 1800, to his adjoining farm in Colebrook.

CHARLES OSBORN is on the Winsted list of this year, and owned land west of the D. N. Beardsley road, near Colebrook line. Charles and William owned land on east side of Green Woods Turnpike, opposite the Uri Church bridge, from 1801 to 1805, and probably occupied the house thereon, which has been recently torn down.

NATHANIEL PARKS, probably from Bristol, this year lived in a "pest house" that stood on East Lake street, near the great spring. He afterwards owned and lived on land on the Still River Turnpike, south of

Roswell Pond's, which he conveyed to the town of Bristol in 1801. He was a miller, and had charge of the Doolittle Mill, opposite the Clock Factory. His wife was a woman of weight, who pressed her cheese by sitting on the driver of the hoop while knitting her stockings, thereby dispensing with a cheese press. Their son, Jonathan, became a showman of pictures, through a magnifying glass; — and when moving from house to house, with his show box on his back, appeared as majestic as a castellated elephant. His drawling, snuffling, yankee twang, in describing his pictorial views, was inimitably and irresistibly ludicrous. He outgrew his maternal fatness, and became a Daniel Lambert. While on a visit here, about 1812, his pants were surreptitiously obtained from a tailor, with whom he had left them to be mended; and three full grown men invested themselves within their ample folds, adjusting their right and left legs in the corresponding legs of the garment — and after some practice in the lock step, were able to march around the east village green, to the great entertainment of the public. The fit of the garment, however, to the triple nondescript, was not perfect, — there being room within the girth for another legless body.

Jonathan was self-important, and affected sanctimony. He gave up the show business, and took to distributing tracts and begging for gingerbread and other sweet food, — was advertised as an impostor, and died in a poor house. Byron may have had his epitaph in view when he wrote,

"'Tis Greece, but living Greece no more."

THEODORE SMITH, from Goshen, first lived on Brooks street, in the Danbury quarter, south of, and adjoining the Asaph Brooks farm. In 1803, he removed to Winsted, and lived until 1815, in the house now torn down on the discontinued part of the old Colebrook road, between Junius Gillett, and Anson Fosket's. He removed thence to Tolland, Mass. He was son of Chileab, of Goshen, and half-brother of Capt. Zebina, of Winsted. His wife's name was Rhoda. They had sons, Erastus, late of Colebrook; Riley, who d. June 4, 1865, in Winsted, on the Old Country road, west of Daniel B. Wilson's, leaving two sons, who live at Riverton. Roswell living on Wallen's Hill, and Lorrain living over the line in Barkhamsted.

HENRY SANFORD, from Barkhamsted, lived first on South street, and after 1801, in a log house on Hinsdale street, on land lately owned by Nathan Champion. He left the town about 1805. His son, William Sanford, kept the Tavern and Livery Stable, south of Camp's Block, for several years before his death, which occurred Jan. 20, 1859, at the age of 53 years. He m. (1st) Sophronia, dau. of Stephen Fyler, who d. May 7, 1832, aged 32; (2d), Harriet Wade, now living. By first wife he had daughter, Jane, now wife of George M. Wentworth. By second wife, he had a son, William.

1800.

The new comers of this year were Bissell Hinsdale, Philemon Kirkham, Josiah Apley, Elijah Benedict, Nathaniel Smith, Solomon Lemley, Jacob Lemley, William Davis, and Gedeliah Chase.

BISSELL HINSDALE, a native of Windsor, began mercantile business on the old North Country road in Colebrook, near the Rowley Pond, whence he this year removed to Winsted, and built the store which was removed about 1848, to make room for the brick block, at the corner of Main and Lake streets. Here he carried on a large and for many years a prosperous business, — selling goods, buying and slaughtering cattle for the West India trade, making potash and buying cheese for the New York and Southern markets. He bought the gambrel-roofed house, built by Mr. Kirkham on the site of Weed's brick block, where he lived until 1814, when he built and occupied the house removed by Doctor Welch from the ground now occupied by the Second Congregational Church. In 1826 he became involved in the failure of his brothers, J. & D. Hinsdale, of Middletown, on whose paper he was indorser to a large amount, and thereby his business was broken up, and his property swept away. He continued to reside in Winsted until about 1842, when, after the death of his son, Theodore Hinsdale, he removed to Rochester, N. Y., where his two daughters resided, and where he carried on a commission business for several years. He died at Rochester, in February, 1866, aged ninety-one years, and his remains were buried in Winsted. Mr. Hinsdale was a thoroughly trained merchant of the old school, — large of frame, dignified and reserved in manner — diligent in business, a stern but indulgent parent, a firm supporter of good order and good morals. He made a profession of religion at middle age, which he sustained by a consistent life, and verified by a steady growth in Christian graces to the close of life. He was liberal in the support of education and religion, kind to the poor, and firm for the right. If there were those who considered him overbearing in his prosperous days, their hostility was disarmed by his patience in adversity, his cheerful acquiescence in his altered circumstances, and his blameless life. For many years after removing to Rochester he annually visited his family friends in Winsted, and was greeted with reverent regard by all who had known him in his earlier years. The infirmities of age abated not his loving trust in his Saviour. He was gathered to his fathers as a shock of corn fully ripe.

AND FAMILY RECORDS.

The following line of families shows his descent from an early settler of New England:—

ROBERT HINSDALE[1] was one of the founders of the church at Dedham, Mass., November 8, 1638, freeman of Mass., March 13, 1639; member of the Artillery Company, 1645; had wife Ann; removed to Medfield, Mass., where he aided in forming the church; thence, as early as 1672, to Hadley, Mass., where he lived several years, and married (2d) Elizabeth, widow of John Hawks; removed to Deerfield, Mass., where he was gathering his harvest in the cornfield, and was killed, with his sons, Barnabas, John, and Samuel, when Captain Lathrop, with the flower of Essex, fell at Bloody Brook, surprised by the Indians, Sept. 18, 1675. His widow married (3d) Thomas Dibble.

CHILDREN.

I. ELIZABETH,[2] m. July 7, 1657, James Rising of Boston.
II. BARNABAS,[2] b. November 13, 1639; bap. November 17, 1639.
III. SAMUEL,[2] birth record not found; m. Mehitabel Johnson, and had six children before he was killed by the Indians.
IV. GAMALIEL,[2] (supposed by Savage to be a mistake for Samuel), b. March 5, 1642; bap. March 13, 1642.
V. MARY,[2] b. February 14, 1644; bap. February 25, 1644.
VI. EXPERIENCE,[2] b. January 23, 1646; bap. February 8, 1646.
VII. JOHN,[2] b. January 27, 1648; bap. April 16, 1648.
VIII. EPHRAIM,[2] b. September 26, 1650; bap. October 27, 1650.

BARNABAS HINSDALE,[2] of Hatfield, Mass., married October 15, 1666, Sarah (White) Taylor, daughter of John and Mary White, and widow of Stephen Taylor. He was slain by the Indians, September 18, 1675.

CHILDREN.

I. BARNABAS,[3] b. Hatfield, February 20, 1668.
II. SARAH,[3] b. —; m. January 8, 1691, Deacon Samuel Hall of East Middletown, now Chatham, Conn.
III. ELIZABETH,[3] b. October 29, 1671; d. March 8, 1672.
IV. ISAAC,[3] b. September 15, 1673.
V. MARY,[3] b. March 27, 1677.

BARNABAS HINSDALE[3] was admitted an inhabitant of Hartford, Conn., in 1693, and died there January 25, 1725, aged 57. He married, November 9, 1693, Martha Smith of Hartford, who died December —, 1738, aged 68.

CHILDREN.

I. BARNABAS,[4] b. August 28, 1694; settled in Tolland, Conn.
II. MARTHA,[4] b. February 17, 1696; m. November 9, 1736, Thomas Bull of Harwinton, Conn., and d. April 15, 1761.
III. JACOB,[4] b. July 14, 1698.

IV. SARAH,[4] b. July 22, 1700; m. Nathaniel White [see "White Memorials," pp. 32–3, and 49].
V. ELIZABETH,[4] b. January 9, 1702; m. April 4, 1728, Jacob Benton of Harwinton.
VI. MARY,[4] b. July 13, 1704; m. March 30, 1738, James Skinner, Jr.
VII. JOHN,[4] b. August 13, 1706.
VIII. DANIEL,[4] b. May 15, 1708; m. August 21, 1737, Catharine Curtis of Wethersfield, who was buried April 12, 1788, aged 68. He was a deacon; lived in Hartford; buried September 13, 1781, aged 73.
IX. AMOS,[4] b. August 24, 1710; m. Experience —, who d. May 4, 1781, aged 61.

CAPTAIN JOHN HINSDALE[4] married, November 8, 1733, Elizabeth Cole, born March 18, 1711; she died July 1, 1784, aged 73. He lived in Kensington, now Berlin, Conn., and died December 2, 1792, aged 86.

CHILDREN.

I. JOHN,[5] b. August 19, 1734; d. October 13, 1743.
II. ELIZABETH,[5] b. June 29, 1736; m. David Atkins of Middletown.
III. THEODORE,[5] b. November 25, 1738.
IV. LUCY,[5] b. July 16, 1741; m. Samuel Plumb of Middletown; d. Feb. —, 1791.
V. ELIJAH,[5] b. April 1, 1744; m. Ruth Bidwell; had a daughter Elizabeth, who was the mother of Elijah Hinsdale Burritt, the astronomer, and of Elihu Burritt, "the learned blacksmith."
VI. LYDIA,[5] b. August 11, 1747; m. Samuel Hart of Berlin, and was the mother of Mrs. Emma Willard, and of Mrs. Almira-Lincoln Phelps, each of them widely known as an instructress and authoress.
VII. JOHN,[5] b. August 21, 1749.

THEODORE HINSDALE[5] graduated Yale College, 1762; was ordained pastor of the church at North Windsor, April 30, 1766; married July 14, 1768, Anna Bissell, born March 11, 1748. They removed to Hinsdale, Mass., which town was named in his honor, where she died, March 14, 1817, in her 69th year. He died December 29, 1818, aged 80 years.

CHILDREN.

I. ANNE (Nancy)[6], b. April 16, 1769; d. Troy, N. Y., May 16, 1851.
II. LUCY,[6] b. December 31, 1770; d. March 21, 1792.
III. THEODORE,[6] b. November 12, 1772; d. October 14, 1855.
IV. JOSIAH BISSELL,[6] b. November 15, 1774; he discarded the first name "Josiah," and was always known as Bissell.
V. JAMES,[6] b. September 28, 1776; d. September 28, 1777.
VI. JOHN,[6] b. November 10, 1778; d. Brooklyn, N. Y., March 13, 1856.
VII. LEVI,[6] b. November 29, 1780; d. February 19, 1830.
VIII. ALTAMIRA,[6] b. November 8, 1782; m. — Emmons; she d. at Princeton, N. J., November 11, 1836.

IX. DANIEL,⁶ b. March 22, 1785; d. at Rising Sun, Ia., May 4, 1837.
X. HORATIO,⁶ b. November 3, 1787; d. April 9, 1813.
XI. WILLIAM,⁶ b. March 5, 1790.

JOHN HINSDALE⁵ married Philomela Hurlbut, daughter of Dr. James Harvey, and — (Hart) Hurlbut. She died in 1790, aged 36 years. He died at Berlin, Conn., December 9, 1795.

CHILDREN.

I. HOSEA,⁶ b. Berlin, Conn., February 15, 1775. [See 1802.]
II. ABIGAIL,⁶ b. —; m. Wm. Benham; settled in West Hartford.
III. ESTHER,⁶ b. —; m. Amos Hills of Farmington; d. at Cabot, Vt.
IV. AMELIA,⁶ b. —; m. Anson Cook; had five children.
V. NANCY,⁶ b. —; m. Norman Spencer; lived in Winchester, and in Ypsilanti, Mich.; had seven children.

BISSELL HINSDALE⁶ married Temperance Pitkin, born May 3, 1772, daughter of Rev. Timothy and Temperance (Clap) Pitkin. She died August 13, 1817. He died at Rochester, N. Y., February 6, 1866.

CHILDREN.

I. THEODORE,⁷ b. Colebrook, Conn., December 27, 1800.
II. ANN,⁷ b. W., Oct. 16, 1802; m. September 12, 1825, Fred. Whittlesey of Rochester.
III. MARY PITKIN,⁷ b. January 10, 1806; m. September 21, 1829, Selah Matthews of Rochester.
IV. TIMOTHY PITKIN,⁷ b. May 5, 1809; d. February 5, 1810.
V. CHARLES,⁷ b. May 23, 1812; d. March 1, 1814.

THEODORE HINSDALE, ESQ., son of Bissell, graduated at Yale College in 1821, read law for a brief period with Seth P. Staples, Esq., of New Haven, and afterwards studied at Andover for one or two years; and in 1827 went into manufacturing business with his father-in-law, in the firm name of Rockwell & Hinsdale, successors of the Rockwell Brothers, who for nearly fifty years had conducted the same business. After the death of Mr. Rockwell in 1837, he was associated in the same business with the late Elliot Beardsley, deceased, in the firm name of Hinsdale & Beardsley until his death.

As a business man, he manifested great energy and executive ability; while as a citizen he was prominent and influential in advocating every good cause, and leading others by his activity and ardor. Gifted with a commanding person, a fascinating manner, and a native oratory, he became widely known and admired, and was sought as presiding officer or prominent speaker in the largest public gatherings in the county and State.

In the meridian of his manhood, with a career of distinguished usefulness and honor in prospect, he was struck down by typhoid fever, and died Nov. 27, 1841, in the fortieth year of his age.

He married, April 26, 1826, Jerusha Rockwell, born March 28, 1803, daughter of Solomon and Sarah (McEwen) Rockwell. After his death she married (2d), Dec. 10, 1843, John Boyd.

CHILDREN.

I. SARAH McEWEN,[8] b. April 2, 1827; d. in New London, Aug. 17, 1833.
II. MARY PITKIN,[8] b. Dec. 11, 1828.
III. SOLOMON ROCKWELL,[8] b. Aug. 25, 1835; m. in Baltimore, Md., Jan. 26, 1864, Julia Merritt Jackson; b. in N. Y., Aug. 4, 1840, daughter of Samuel and Julia Ann (Brown) Jackson. He has a son, Theodore Rockwell,[9] b. in Ellenville, Prince Georges County, Md., Jan. 31, 1865.

PHILEMON KIRKUM, ESQ., attorney at law, came from Norfolk to Winsted in 1800, and built a house on the site of Weed's Block, which was burned down March 25, 1853. He soon sold this house to Bissell Hinsdale, and in 1807 he built the original house on the lot next north of the Congregational Chapel, which was taken down by Dr. Welch to make room for his present dwelling. In this house he lived until his removal to Norton, Ohio, in 1814. He was a native of Guilford, Conn.,— served for four or five years in the revolutionary war, afterwards studied law with Augustus Pettibone, Esq., of Norfolk, and was in due course admitted to the Litchfield bar.

Tall of stature, erect of form, imposing in manner, fluent of speech, imaginative and impetuous, a Jeffersonian of the first water, he was a man of note in Northern Litchfield County. As a lawyer, he was well read, ingenious in argument, and oratorial in manner. The drawback to his professional success, and the blemish of his life, was an excitable and uncontrollable temper, mounting at times to frenzy. His competitors at the bar, when unable to cope with him in argument, not unfrequently contrived to arouse his passions, thereby upsetting his argumentative faculties and destroying his self-control. He eventually withdrew from the bar, and limited his practice to Justice Courts.

He was the sole representative of the Democratic party in the village during its early growth. His neighbors were straight-haired Federalists. He was thoroughly indoctrinated and saturated with the principles of liberty and equality. The Democratic farmers, on the surrounding hills, looked to him as the advocate and defender of their political faith, and the organizer of their party. It was deemed necessary that a Democratic store should be got up in opposition to the Federal store of Mr. Hinsdale. Some twenty of his friends furnished the capital and made Mr.

Kirkum the managing partner. The Federals owned or controlled every foot of ground on Main street from George Dudley's down to Clifton Mill bridge, and would not, for love or money, allow the new store to be built on the street — consequently the gambrel-roofed building west of the Lake street bridge was erected and stocked with goods. A large, fanciful sign-board on the eastern gable, announced that "Philemon Kirkum & Co.," were prepared to sell goods to their friends and the world at large. It was the first sign-board ever erected in Winsted, and it made a sensation. The twenty partners, as they had spare time, were in attendance, to see the working of the new institution, and to discuss the political issues of the day. Crowds of customers and idlers were attracted to the "free and easy" establishment, and captivated by the principles there inculcated. It was soon decided to expand the business, and the building in the East village, now occupied by Mr. Bird, was erected for a branch store.

A business so auspiciously inaugurated did not fulfill its promise. Clouds began to obscure its horizon. The partners began to perceive that a free and equal distribution of worldly goods, to customers unable or unwilling to pay for them, brought no percentage of profit, and an inadequate return for meeting the bills payable, and revoked his agency. Mr. Kirkum was found to be too imaginative and unsystematic for a country merchant; but his integrity was unimpeached. He resumed practice as a lawyer in a small way — talked philosophy, wrote poetry, made political speeches, and rode his old white horse as if he were charging the ranks of Cornwallis at Yorktown. His tall, erect figure and soldierly gait, combined with fluency of speech, rising at times to real eloquence, made him a man to be noted among thousands. In 1814, as before stated, he left our village, with his wife and son and worldly goods, in a covered wagon drawn by a pair of oxen, and wended his weary way to the Western Reserve, where he invested the small avails of his Winsted property in an uncleared but now valuable farm, located in Norton, Ohio, which he occupied and improved during his remaining life, and left to his worthy grandson, Charles Coe, Esq., who was his stay and comfort in his declining years. A change of residence and associations essentially modified his peculiarities and smoothed down his sharp angularity of character. He diversified his farm labor with occasional law practice, and in his later years became a most popular "stump speaker" in the Harrison and subsequent campaigns. Mr. Kirkum failed to square his sharp cut principles of Democracy with slavery propagandism. He saw with loathing the political ascendency of the South and the knuckling of the North, and would none of it. He watched the progress of events with deep sorrow, and predicted the bloody issue which he did not live to see. He died in 1855 at the age of 91 years. Age had not bent his erect form, nor scattered his flowing gray locks, which he wore in a revolutionary cue or club until the last years of his life. His teeth, with one exception, continued sound and white as long as he lived. His wife was a Mills, of East Windsor, who died before him. They had a daughter Eliza who married Eben Coe, son of Jonathan[2] in the Coe Genealogy; and a son George who became a highly esteemed member of the bar in Cuyahoga county, Ohio, and died not far from 1860, leaving one or more children.

JOSIAH APLEY, from Torrington, this year bought a house and land on the hill road to Colebrook, north of Nelson Beardsley, where he lived until his return to Torrington in 1804. He married, Feb. 4, 1795, Elizabeth, daughter of Chauncey Mills.

ELIJAH BENEDICT, a blacksmith, came in this year, and worked in a shop on the west side of Lake street, opposite the old lean-to-house, in which he resided. After two or three years he moved out of the town. He returned about 1810, and after remaining about five years, removed to the West.

His first wife died during his second residence here, and he married (2d) Lovina, dau. of Simeon Moore. He had children by his first wife, GERSHOM, HEPZIBAH, and KETURA, and perhaps others.

NATHANIEL SMITH is found on the tax list of this year, and in 1801 he purchased land in the vicinity of Everett C. Holmes, on which he lived until his sale of the same in 1806 to Zebina Smith.

SOLOMON LEMLY, a forgeman, came from Colebrook this year, and lived in a house, now torn down, on Lake street, above the parting of the new Winchester road, until about 1815, when he moved to Salisbury. He had a brother, Jacob Lemly, who came here the following year, and lived in a house now torn down, adjacent to Hurlbut's forge dam, until his death, about 1815. They were of Low Dutch extraction, and each had a large family of children, most of whom were named in pairs, — distinguished from each other by taking their patronynim Christian name as a surname. There was a John Solomon and John Jacob, Hannah Solomon and a Hannah Jacob, a Sol. Sol. and a Jake Jake, and a like duplication of Sally and Polly. No descendants of either family remain in the town.

WILLIAM DAVIS first appears on the list of this year. He lived on West Lake street, in a small house then standing in front of the first house west of the lake outlet, until his death in 1805.

His wife was a Hancock, from Southwick, Mass. They had two dau., Lucy and Sally, who m. Timothy and Alpheus Persons, — and a son.

Lyman, who went to Clayville, N. Y., about 1820, and probably died there.

GEDELIAH CHASE, a miller, came from New Hartford to Winsted in 1799 or 1800, and took charge of the Austin Mill, living in the old lean-to Mill House on Lake street, near the lake outlet, until his removal to Old Winchester about 1807, where he afterwards resided most of his remaining life. He was b. Nov. 28, 1761, and d. July 4, 1832. He m. Nov. 11, 1790, Rebecca ——, b. July 14, 1768.

CHILDREN.

I. GEORGE, b. Ap. 18, 1792. V. REUBEN, b. March 28, 1800.
II. CHARLOTTE, b. Aug. 15, 1794. VI. HARRIET, b. May 8, 1804.
III. DUDLEY, b. Aug. 30, 1796. VII. JERUSHA, b. June 20, 1810.
IV. BETSEY, b. May 22, 1798. VIII. HORACE, b. Oct. 24, 1812.

CHAPTER XXIV.

ANCIENT AND MODERN WINSTED.—ECCLESIASTICAL HISTORY.

In tracing the settlement of the Winsted section of the town, we have thus far made no mention of the Ecclesiastical Society of Winsted as an organized body. Its religious services up to this period were mainly held beyond the eastern border of the town. Its first meeting-house was there erected, and the first minister there ordained and settled. Its original members were residents along the old North Country road and its vicinity, a larger portion of them in Winchester and a considerable number in Barkhamsted.

To modern Winsted, its origin and growth, its struggles and dissensions prior to 1801, would seem a myth, did not its quaint old records avouch the reality of its history. These records begin with a society meeting lawfully warned and held March 17, 1778, at the dwelling-house of John Balcom, by a warrant granted by Matthew Gillett, justice of the peace, dated seven days earlier. Of this meeting John Wright was chosen moderator, and Eleazer Kellogg clerk; and Isaac Kellogg, Josiah Smith and John Balcom were appointed committee men; and it was voted that the annual meetings of the society should be holden on the second Monday of December annually, and that warnings therefor should be set up at Austin's Mill, Abram Callers' shop, and at the crotch of the road that goes from John Wright's to Lemuel Walters, twelve days before such meeting. Another meeting, held September 15 of the same year, voted that the money paid to Mr. Porter and to Mr. Ausbon for preaching, and also the money due Mr. Balcom for boarding Mr. Ausbon, should be paid out of a tax when collected. At the annual meeting of this year it was voted "that a meeting be warned to see if this society are a mind to be made a distinct town." The same subject was brought up at various subsequent meetings, but no definite action appears to have resulted.

At the annual meeting in 1780 the matter of locating and building a meeting-house seems to have been first agitated: and it was voted "that we will git the original plans of Winchester and Barkhamsted, and apply to Cornal Shelding to find the middle of this society, and if he cant by them give us the senter, then to measure the bounds of this society, the said

Shelding to measure, and that this society will pay the cost to Cornal Shelding for doing the business for said society, and that Lieut. John Wright to see the Bisness done." The subject was resumed May 24, 1782, when it was voted " that we do try to agree to pitch a stake for a meeting-house," and " that we apply to the next county court for a committee to pitch a stake for our meeting-house," and that we nominate Esq. Asaph Hall of Goshen, Major Jiles Pettibone of Norfolk, and Esq. Ensign of Hartland." In December, 1792, Col. Sheldon was substituted for Esq. Ensign on this committee, and at a meeting, August 25, 1783, it was voted " to establish the stake for our meeting-house where it now stands pitched by Col. Shelding, Major Pettibone and Esq. Hall, and that Ensign Jesse Doolittle shall go and make returns to the Honorable County Court of our voting the establishment of our meeting-house stake."

This looked like an auspicious beginning of the constructive work of the society, but the appearance was deceptive. A meeting was called, Dec. 22, 1783, " to see if the society will go on to bild our meeting-house where the stake now stands," and the question was decided in the negative. On the 2d of February, 1784, it was voted " that we chuse a comitte to go and view the society and se if we can't pitch a stake for ourselves ; " and December, 1784, it was voted " to go on and build a meting-house at the stake pitched by the committee " the house to be 45 by 35 feet and a suitable height for galleries ; and a tax of sixpence on the pound was laid for defraying expenses. This again looked hopeful ; but at a meeting in January, 1785, the hopeful project was knocked in the head by a vote " that all the bisness voated" in the previous meeting " be holy set aside consarning bilding a meeting house in this society."

On the 9th of May, 1786, another committee, consisting of Capt. Josiah Smith, Nathaniel Russell, Ensign Jesse Doolittle, Othniel Brainart, Capt. Robert Whitford, and Sergt. Reuben Sweet pitched a stake at the West end of Jonathan Sweet's lot, where it was voted by more than two-thirds to build the house. In June following it was decided to build a house 50 by 40 feet with height in proportion, and that an agent be sent to the county court to get the stake established. Again the project was nullified by a vote of Sept. 4, 1786, " that we will not send an agent to the County Court."

Another stake-pitching committee was appointed Sept. 25, 1786, which seems to have performed its duty. In October following it was voted " that this meeting be adjourned to the place where the committee have prefixed for to build a meeting-house ; " and it was there " voted, by more than two-thirds, that we will bild a meeting house where the comitte have pitched the stake." Although this vote of more than two-thirds was solemnly taken on the very ground " prefixed by the committe, yet subsequent records show that the stake would not yet stay pitched. But, before tracing these measures to a final result, it is fitting to advert to other occurrences in the history of the Society.

Up to 1786, preaching was had at irregular intervals, and no money raised by taxation for its support. Individuals seem to have advanced money, and to have found difficulty in getting it refunded. The Society, in 1780, voted "to make up the sink of money due individuals for advancements, according to Congress scale." In 1782, May 14, it was voted to hire preaching, and "that the committe do advise where to apply for a candidate," and that Lieut. Josiah Smith be appointed to read the Psalm on Sabbath days, and that Eleaser Kellogg read the Psalms when Lieut. Smith is absent.

In 1783 it was voted to have preaching in the summer, and in the fall a tax of seven pounds was voted "to be applied for the youse of supporting singing." A committee was also chosen "to regulate the singing in this society on the Sabbath-day, and to introduce such tunes as they shall think proper to be sung on Sabbath days;" and it was also voted that preaching should continue during the winter.

It might be inferred, that with preaching summer and winter, and the support and regulation of singing under the supervision of three choristers and a committee to introduce tunes proper to be sung on the Sabbath, harmony and concert of action might have been promoted: but stakes could not be pitched and voted on so often without moral friction. Heartburning and dissensions prevailed to such a degree that in October, 1785, a mutual council consisting of Rev. Messrs. Taylor of New Milford, Canfield of Roxbury, Huntington of Middlebury, Belden of Newington and Smalley of New Britain, was called to advise with the church and society in regard to the subsisting difficulties. The records fail to show the result, if any was reached. Harmony, in any event, was not restored. Meetings were frequent, and contradictory in action. Votes passed at one stage of a meeting were not infrequently voted down before adjournment, and the doings of one meeting were undone by another. The meetings were often protracted into the night, and unfair advantages taken in carrying measures at a late hour, that could not be accomplished in a full meeting. To correct some of these irregularities a standing rule was adopted about this time, "that no vote should be put after sunset for the futer, except the business so drive them that they find it necessary, and passed a vote to continue the same before sunset." Another vote required "that all accounts against the society shall be brought to the annual meeting yearly, or shall be forfeit for the futer, except it be made to appear that it could not be done."

The following votes illustrate the way of doing business in committee of the whole, under the new rule, and show an example of thoroughness worthy of all imitation:

Voted, Elkana Phelps, £1, 11s., 4d. for boarding Mr. Fowler eleven sabbaths.

Voted, Eleanor Kellogg, £9, 6s., 0d. for the youse of his house.

Voted, Enoch Palmer for boarding ministers and house room for holding meetings sabbath days, £1, 9s.

Voted, Elisha Mallory for boarding Mr. Beach 1 week, 4 days, 12s.

Voted, Capt. Josiah Smith, for boarding Mr. Hitchcock and other ministers $3\frac{1}{2}$ weeks, and keeping their horses, £1, 6s. 3d.

Voted, Ensign Doolittle for going to Torringford to get Mr. Edmund Mills to preach hear, 3s.

Voted, Samuel Hayden for holding meetings in his house for 28 Sabbaths, £2, 2s.

Voted, That those that board ministers in the summer season, and keep their horses for the futer, be allowed 7s. 6d. a week.

The pitching of stakes for a meeting house having been played out in 1786, it was thought best to defer the building of a meeting house, and to settle a minister; and accordingly, at the annual meeting of the year, it was "voted, by more than two-thirds, that we give Mr. Parsons a call, in order to a settlement." It was also voted to give him a salary of forty pounds a year, and the use of two hundred pounds as a Settlement. A committee was also appointed to purchase a place or settlement for the use of the minister of the value of about £200, to be holden as the property of the society.

The church having united with the society in a call to Rev. Stephen Parsons to settle with them in the gospel ministry, his reply was laid before the society on the 12th of March, 1787; whereupon it was voted to settle Mr. Parsons agreeable to his Ritten Answer, which is as follows, viz:

March yᵉ 11th, 1787.

To the Church and Society of Winsted, wishing grace, mercy and peace to be multiplied unto you.

Having taken into consideration the call you gave me to settle with you in the work of the Gospel Ministry, as it appears to me a matter of great importance that I am lead by the Spirit of God in the right way to promote the general cause of God in the world. I thought it my duty to give you some idea of my present profession and principles, respecting Christian fellowship and connection with churches.

As to my profession it is what is called, in this state, a strict congregationalist; and my connexions are with the ministers and churches of that denomination, which appears to me the nearest to the rule given in God's word, of any within the compass of my acquaintance,—on which account I can by no means renounce my connection with them. Yet I could heartily wish the wall of partition between the different denominations was broken down, that all the true friends of Christ were united in one army, under the glorious captain of our salvation, against the kingdom of Satan, the prince of darkness. Wherefore, I think it my duty to maintain and cultivate liberal sentiments, and hold fellowship with all those who appear to practice and love the truth; and if I was to receive an ordination, I should choose to apply to a number of ministers of different denominations, not exceeding that of my own.

If the church and society in this place can receive me on these principles, and there is a prospect of their being united so that I may be useful in this part of the vineyard of Christ, and at the same time promote the general good of mankind, it appears to be my duty to comply with your call. Otherwise, I have no desire to be received, by giving up my principles, or renouncing my connections. I close with subscribing myself, yours to serve in the Gospel of our Lord and Saviour, Jesus Christ.

STEPHEN PARSONS.

Why this acceptance of the call did not result in the settlement of Mr. Parsons, does not appear. It may have been frustrated by a conflict of views between the candidate and the consociation, in regard to church order and fellowship. It only appears on record that the church and society, on the 18th of April, 1787, voted "to continue the call to Mr. Parsons to settle with us in the Gospel Ministry."

The Parsonage Lot, which, a few years after, became a subject of fatal contention, was purchased at this time, and a tax was laid to provide the first payment therefor, and a parsonage house was soon after erected thereon, and so far finished as to serve as a place of worship until a meeting house should be located and erected. It stood east of Barkhamsted line, at the intersection of road from the clock factory, with the Old Country road, was occupied successively, by Rev. Mr. Woodworth, Moses Haydon, Isaac Brown and others, and was torn down many years ago.

The location of a meeting house site was again attempted this year [1787]. A stake was pitched; and the society voted that they "be agreed to build," etc., but no building was built, and no further steps were taken in that direction until 1791.

The records during this interval show the progress of events and the nature of the business transacted. A better knowledge of the law of stake-pitching and other ecclesiastical matters, was provided for by the purchase of a Society Law Book, and a quire of paper "to keep accompts on." The Law Book was ordered to be kept two months at David Anstus', two months at Nathan Wheeler's, two months at Othniel Brainard's, two months at Sergt. Jonas Weed's, two months at Enoch Palmer's, and two months at Zebina Smith's; and other regulations were adopted for a general diffusion of legal knowledge. An application to the Assembly was voted for a Land Tax "to better enable us to pay for the Parsonage Lot, and to build a Meeting House,"—and then a vote was passed "that we will build a meeting house if we can be agreed on a place."

In August, 1791, Rev. Ezra Woodworth preached in the society as a candidate, and a sharp negotiation soon followed, with reference to his settlement. No little diplomatic skill was found requisite to adjust the terms. Mr. Woodworth wanted an absolute conveyance to himself of the Parsonage Lot as a part of the bargain. A large portion of the society, on the other hand, were strenuously opposed to alienating the property to a minister, whose long stay with them would be very precarious. The minister carried his point, and on the 7th of November the society decided to make the conveyance in accordance with his demand, and the compact was completed. On the 15th December a committee was chosen to proceed with the ordination, and the 18th of January, 1792, was assigned for the ill-omened ceremony.

In the mean time, deep trouble in regard to the hard bargain of Mr. Woodworth with the society, was daily becoming more manifest. Six days before the ordination a meeting was called, and a committee appointed "to go and see if Mr. Woodworth will make any alterations as to his settlement or not," and another committee was appointed "to appear before the Ordaining Council, and oppose the opposition, if any there be, against his ordination." Four days after, another meeting was called "to see if the society will make any alterations as to giving our Society Farm as a settlement to Mr. Woodworth," and a committee of six was appointed to converse with him, and agree on some different plan of settlement.

The interview resulted in the following change of terms, committed to writing:

"*Whereas*, there is a dissatisfaction in some persons' minds in the proposals made to Mr. Woodworth in respect to his settlement, and in order to form a better union, propose to exchange the terms of the same as follows, viz; to except of the yuse of said farm as a Parsonage with the house and barn, said farm to be appraised by indifferent men when he receives the same, and also when he resigns the same, and the betterments, if any there be to be allowed to him or his heirs, and the property to be kept good, to be as a settlement in the room of receiving the property of said farm as in the former plan: the vallew of said former proposals of settlement being made equal thereto, to be determined by the judgment of indifferent men, to be paid in neat cattle in the spring, or fat cattle in the fall, as agreed on, and the salary to remain as in the former proposals.

Dated Winsted, Jan. ye 16th, 1792.

Ezra Woodworth,
Nath. Crowe,
Elkena Phelps,
William Moore.

This agreement removed all hindrance to the ordination, which took place on the day appointed. Had the agreement been adhered to in good faith, it is more than probable that harmony would have been restored; and that the faithful ministrations of a pastor valuing the souls of his flock more than their fleeces, would have strengthened the walls and enlarged the borders of this feeble Zion.

Mr. Woodworth, now invested with the pastoral office, had a field for eminent usefulness. An inviolate adherence to the terms of adjustment effected two days before his ordination, was a dictate alike of policy and duty: but he and his adherents seem to have thought otherwise. A meeting of the society was called, April 6, 1792, which voted to reconsider the prior vote of Jan. 16, by which the tenure of the society parsonage lot was changed, and that Mr. Woodworth should be put into possession of the same according to the terms first agreed on.

The society, though hitherto divided as to the location of their meeting-house, seems to have acted harmoniously in other matters; and nearly all were of the standing order: but this breach of faith on the part of the minister and his adherents produced irremediable discord. Certificates of withdrawal began to be handed in by seceding members, most of whom connected themselves with the infant Methodist and Baptist churches in the vicinity. Endeavors were made to recall members already withdrawn, and to prevent others from withdrawing, by an offer of the minister to relinquish a portion of his salary for the five coming years, but without avail. Secession went on until many of the best and ablest members of the church and society had identified themselves with other denominations.

Notwithstanding this debilitated and distracted condition of the society, the adhering members resumed the project of locating and building a meeting-house, as the only means of sustaining their position. They voted, Sept. 14, 1792, not to build at the stake established by law, whereever that might have been, and "to see if the sosiaty will Be willing to Bild a meeting-house at the senter of the land of the sosiaty, allowing those things that ought to be considered to draw from the same its due and proper weight;" then followed a vote to build on "a certain nole of land at the West end of Mr. Woodworth's land, as near the town line as the ground will admit of;" and then a committee of nine men was appointed to pitch a stake and apply to the Assembly to establish the same. The committee thus appointed reported to an adjourned meeting, October 2, as follows:

"*To the Inhabitants of the Society of Winsted, convened at the usual place by us, the 2d day of October,* 1792:

"*Whereas,* we, the subscribers, being appointed a Com. at the last special meting, to fix a Stake on a Sertain Spot of Ground near the town line, so called, on the Rev. Mr. Woodworth's lot, at the most convenient spot to erect a meating-house for the inhabitants of said society near the town line, in consequence of our appointment, we, on the above said 2d day of October, repaired to said place, and after taking into the moste mature and Deliberate consideration, all those matters and circumstances that ought to be considered according to the best information gained and our ability, we are of opinion that the Sartain spot of ground is situated near the heighth of said nole upon said lot, or near the south end to Beach Stake and Stones cast up, to be the most convenient and commodious place for the same, and have fixed the above said stake and stones, and marked the same on the particular spot of ground which we have established for said purpose, the day and date above certifyed by us, the day and date above."

This lucid report was, by vote, "excepted," and measures were taken to get the place established by the Assembly. Measures were also taken to ascertain the size and length of timber required, and to see how cheap they could get some man to build the house, and a tax of a shilling on the pound was laid.

The Beach Stake, now planted, marked, reported, and accepted, was destined to stand. A day was fixed for the people to meet for the purpose of finding stone and laying the under-pinning. It was also voted that the people will find cake and cheese by free donation for refreshment at raising the meeting-house.

At this stage of the proceedings, another attempt was made to conciliate "those of the society that think themselves agreaved as to giving away the society's farm," &c., by submitting the matters of grievance to arbitration, but no conclusion was reached. The meeting house was raised, covered in and floored in season for the Annual Meeting, Nov. 25, 1793. It stood on the south border of a grove near the east and west road, between the late residence of Harris Brown, deceased, and the old country road. It was 50 feet long, 40 feet broad, and two stories high, without tower or steeple, a very unpretending and short-lived sanctuary. No traces of it now remain except a large stone horse-block. It was sold and taken down, when the present house of worship was first erected. Some of its timbers were worked into the original building of the East Village Hotel.

The doings of the Society have now been brought down to 1793, a period of fifteen years. It took twelve years of controversy to locate a meeting house, and it might have required a dozen years more had not the intervening contest about the settlement of a minister led to the withdrawal of some twenty members. The unfinished church opened its doors to a congregation, small in numbers, disheartened by long dissentions, and unable to sustain the burdens they had assumed. The records of the following seven years indicate the quiet of exhaustion rather than the prevalence of Christian graces. Taxes were more easily laid than collected. New names from time to time appear on the records, but the accessions brought no element of strength to the Society as then constituted and located, for the new comers were mainly from the Still River valley, now filling up with settlers interested in a transfer of the meeting house to their vicinity.

Patient endurance of the burden of supporting a grasping minister had its limit. At the annual meeting in 1797 it was voted "to choose a committee of five to treat with Rev. Mr. Woodworth, to see what measures can be come into on account of the burthen the Society is under as to paying his salary, and whether he is willing for a dismission or not." This vote was followed by another in December following, "to choose a committee, with power to agree with Rev. Mr. Woodworth on his dismission, and that said committee allow him no more than the Society's former contracts." This committee arranged with the pastor that the existing connection should be dissolved at the expiration of the year, and that the Society should pay and confirm all contracts with Mr. Woodworth, and what should be found due him to be paid or secured by notes of hand on demand. It was also voted to call a dismissing council on the 9th of January, 1798. The result of this council is not recorded, but the dismission took place at or near the date specified. Mr. Woodworth was afterwards settled at Whitestown, near Utica, N. Y., for several years. His subsequent history is unknown.

In January, 1799, Rev. Salmon King, after preaching as a candidate for settlement, received a call, which he declined, and in October following a call was voted to Rev. Noah Simons, but was not accepted.

About this time Rev. Aaron Kinney was employed and continued to supply the pulpit for four or five years.

Hitherto the old north road had been the great thoroughfare of travel for the adjoining region, and a large portion of our inhabitants had settled along its borders, on Wallen's Hill, and northwestward to Colebrook line, and the location of the meeting house best suited their convenience. But near the close of the century the water power of the Still River and Mad River valleys began to attract manufacturers to those secluded and comparatively inaccessible regions. The Green Woods turnpike, a shorter and far more level line of travel than the old road over the hills, was opened in 1799. It at once diverted all the long travel from the hill road and opened a direct access to the valleys. Hamlets grew up around the Doolittle and Austin Mills. The Wallen's Hill meeting house ceased to be central, and it became apparent that the young and energetic new comers of the valleys were soon to assume the lead, and take the direction of Society affairs out of the hands of the dispirited and exhausted champions on the Old Country road.

In July, 1799, a vote was carried for building a new meeting house by subscription, in one year from the first of October then next, where Captain Charles Wright and others had that day pitched a stake, and on the 7th of October following, Colonel Hezekiah Hopkins of Harwinton, Esq. Elisha Smith of Torrington, and Major Jeremiah Phelps of Norfolk, were appointed to advise as to the location, and at the annual meeting following it was decided to build the house where this committee had put a stake and stones, if the county court should establish the same.

These brief votes embrace all the preparatory measures recorded in reference to building the present house of worship in the east village of Winsted, and the virtual extinction of the ancient regime on Wallen's Hill. New men, not identified with old controversies, took the lead, and effected an entire renovation of the Society.

The new meeting house, particularly described in the following chapter, was raised, covered in, and floored in 1800, and in this condition was used for worship until its final completion in 1805; the funds originally subscribed and contributed not being adequate for its completion, application was made to the legislature for a lottery in aid of the enterprise. There were at the same time two other like applications from the societies of Preston in New London County, and Canterbury in Windham County, and a joint lottery was granted to the three societies. They were jointly represented in the management of this gambling scheme, and the details were so arranged that the two drawings were allowed by the Winsted Society to be made in Preston and Canterbury, in consideration of some equivalent advantages conceded to Winsted. As a result of these arrangements, the two eastern societies failed to realize any profit, while Winsted secured about six hundred dollars. With this sum, and additional subscriptions, the interior of the house was finished and the building painted in 1805.

The pulpit of the new meeting house was first supplied by Rev. Aaron Kinney, who had been for a few years previous the minister in charge at the first meeting house on Wallen's Hill. He continued his labors two or three years, and then removed to Alford, Berkshire Co., Mass. Several candidates were then successively employed for brief periods, the last of whom was Rev. James Beach, who received a pastoral call, and was ordained on the 1st day of January, 1806, with a salary of $350 a year, and an advance of funds to purchase a dwelling, repayable in installments from year to year. His pastorate continued until his dismission in 1842. His ministerial character and labors, as well as those of Rev. Mr. Kinney, are referred to in personal notices of them in their order as incoming citizens of the Society.

Mr. Beach was succeeded by Rev. Timothy M. Dwight, who, after supplying the pulpit until February, 1844, received a call for settlement, which he declined; soon after which Rev. Augustus Pomeroy, after supplying the pulpit for two or three months, received a nearly unanimous call to the pastorate, and was presented to the consociation for approval and installation in June following. After a long and searching examination on the question of approval, it was found that there was a majority of one in the united body sustaining his examination, but on analyzing the vote, it appeared that there was a majority of two of the lay delegates sustaining, and a majority of one of the clerical members of the body non-sustaining the examination. By one of the rules of the body, in case of non-concurrence of either, the clerical or lay delegates — although there should be a majority of the whole — in case of a call for the application of this rule, the candidate should be rejected. The call was made by a lay member, and the synodal body refused to install the candidate.

Mr. Pomeroy continued to supply the pulpit for about a year after this result; near the end of which the church dissolved its connection with the Consociation; and the call for his settlement was renewed on the 19th of November, 1844; but the majority in his favor being essentially reduced, he declined acceptance, and withdrew to another field of labor. We state the facts of this case in the briefest possible form, without note or commentary, save that the grounds of objection to Mr. Pomeroy were doctrinal rather than personal, and that his Christian character was unquestioned.

After Mr. Pomeroy, several other candidates filled the pulpit, — the most prominent of whom, and the longest incumbent, was Rev. John D. Baldwin, — afterwards member of Congress from the Worcester District, Mass. After his departure, Rev. Ira Pettibone, from York Mills, N. Y., was employed, called and settled early in 1846. He continued his pastorate until measures were taken for the formation of a Second Congregational Church in the West Village, when he resigned, and engaged in teaching at Cornwall. His resignation was not occasioned by discontent or dissention in the Congregation.

In 1853, fifty-one members of the church, residing in the West Village, were regularly dismissed in order to form themselves into a new church. They were immediately thereafter organized as "The Second Congregational Church of Winsted."

In February, 1854, Rev. Henry A. Russell, a graduate of Yale Theological Seminary, was called and ordained to the pastorate of the first church, and continued his ministrations until his resignation and dismissal, Aug. 25, 1858.

On the 30th December, 1859, Rev. James B. Pierson was called; and the call was unanimously renewed in May, 1860, and he was ordained Nov. 14, following. His ministrations continued until his dismission in March, 1862.

Rev. M. McG. Dana, now pastor of the First Cong. Church, Norwich, supplied the pulpit from May 11, 1862, until Dec. 25, 1864; and during the intermediate time a call for settlement was tendered him, which he declined.

In January, 1867, a call to the pastorate was tendered Rev. — Walker, and accepted by him, but was not consummated by installation. He supplied the pulpit until April, 1869. Rev. H. E. Cooley afterwards supplied the pulpit for one year, ending Sept. 1, 1870.

On the 15th of October, 1870, Rev. Thomas M. Miles, the present worthy incumbent was called, and on the 10th of November, following, was installed as pastor.

The centennial of the First Congregational Church of Winsted will occur on the 17th day of March, 1878; when it is to be hoped that its birth will be suitably commemorated, and its interior workings, its periods of depressions and revival, — its diminutions and accessions of membership, — the merits and demerits of its pastors, office-bearers, and members, will be set forth in due order by a clerical hand.

CHAPTER XXV.

VILLAGES OF WINSTED.—EARLY ASPECT AND GROWTH.

UNTIL 1799, the territory now within the Borough lines of Winsted was mainly a wilderness, with fifteen to twenty families along its northern border. A road had been brought down from Old Winchester to Austin's Mill, near the outlet of the lake stream, and thence down the hill to the new forge immediately below. Around these establishments a small hamlet had arisen. From the east, another road came down to Doolittle's mill, on Still River, immediately south of the stone-arched bridge.

A bridle-path was opened near the close of the Revolutionary War running eastward down the hill from Austin's Mill to the depot grounds of the Connecticut Western Railroad, thence crossing the Lake stream near Meadow Street Bridge, and Mad River, where the Rockwell tannery now stands, then following the line of Hinsdale street easterly to Still River, and then following its west bank northerly to Doolittle's Mill. Subsequently the traveled road diverged from the bridle path at the depot grounds, and crossed the river at the present Lake Street bridge, and thence, following the line of Main street northerly some fifty rods, turned northeasterly, crossing over the site of John T. Rockwell's house, and rejoined the original bridle path near the old school house of the Fourth District, and then followed its line to the Doolittle mill.

The school-house of the Fourth, or West Winsted, District was a central point where the Spencer Street road, then populated with nearly twice as many families as at present, joined the Hinsdale Street road. The Coe Street road, then largely populated, came down along the line of Indian Meadow Brook and Mad River to near the residence of Mrs. Samuel W. Coe, where it turned easterly, and passing below the house of Sarah Loomis, joined the Spencer Street road near the school house. From the Doolittle Mill a road ran southerly, east of Still river, towards Torringford, on which the Potters, Rogers, Wheelers, Rowleys, Porters, Knowltons, Brainards and others had settled. In 1799 the old Higley tavern, still standing, immediately south of Camp's brick block, and a gambrel-roofed house on the site of Moses Camp's residence, were the only buildings on the line of Main street between the bridge crossing Indian Meadow brook, and the Green Woods turnpike bridge crossing Still river. With these exceptions, the whole area of the borough lying south of Hinsdale street, and bordered by Mad river and Still river, was without a habitation and without a road, except the part of Main street between John T. Rockwell's and the old tavern above mentioned. The only way of reaching Hartford or any of the other Eastern towns, from the Winsted valley, was up Wallen's Hill, by way of the Doolittle Mill, and then by the Old North Road. There were no light wagons or carriages in those days; and if there had been any, the roads were too rough for their use. Whitewood lumber and white-ash oars and sweeps, nearly the only marketable products of the forests, were carried to Hartford, Windsor, and Wethersfield, on ox carts and sleds. Fat beeves and hogs for the West India market went on foot to tide water to be butchered and packed. Every farmer went to the Connecticut river in shad time, with a strong empty bed tick, in which to stow away his year's supply of fish, and bring them home loaded across his horse's back. From Old Winchester to the north end of New Hartford was a good day's journey. With a good horse, good weather, and good luck. the shad fisheries could be reached in another day. If the shad could be bought for a copper a-piece, and the journey accomplished in five days, the venture was considered a prosperous one.

In this state of things, the opening of the Talcott Mountain and Green Woods turnpikes was an event as auspicious to our fathers, as was the opening of the Naugatuck Railroad to their children, or as is the majestic march of the Connecticut Western Railroad trains up the Norfolk hills, to our present community.

The Old North Road avoided the water-courses, and sought the hill tops. It crossed the streams at the foot of one steep hill and forthwith began the ascent of another, sometimes by a zig-zag path. The turnpike, on the other hand, followed the line of the Farmington and its Pleasant Valley tributary, then up the line of Mad river to Norfolk and onward towards Albany by comparatively easy grades and a smooth well rounded roadway. Entering the Borough at the Still River bridge in the southeast, it penetrated the tangled forest of hemlocks and ivies* along the bank of Mad river northwesterly, and gave easy access to the present centre of business and population.

From the Doolittle Mill another road was at once extended west of Still river down to the turnpike; and these two roads, now known as Main street and North Main street, made a natural connection of the two hamlets, and formed the nucleus of our consolidated village. The level area at the joining of the two roads made a natural and convenient centre of population for the renovated church and society, and an eligible parade ground. The original highway was laid six rods wide through the centre of the present Green Woods Park, and the new meeting-house lot was

---

* The misapplied term "ivy," has so long been used to designate the "calmia" that this most splendid of our flowering shrubs is almost unknown by its true botanical name.

located on the west side of the highway, extending westerly to the west border of the Park, and southerly to the turnpike. The house fronted on the highway and extended back to Woodruff's confectionery store. It was built, floored and covered in 1800, a year after the opening of the turnpike; and was, for the period when it was built, the best proportioned and finished church edifice in the region. The interior was completed five years afterward, in a style of the then modern composite architecture.

For its day, it was a sightly, well-proportioned building, with tower and cupola at the east end. Its inner furnishing and adornment was picturesque. The body of the audience room was occupied by three aisles, with high-paneled, square pews of unpainted pine. The pulpit was an eight-square tub, supported by a single pillar, standing about ten feet high, and resembling an immense goblet. Narrow, rectangular stairs, with elaborate railings, ascended from each end of the altar to half the height of the structure, and then turned toward each other, and met at a two and-a-half-foot platform in rear of the tub, from which a door opened to receive the preacher, and on being closed a seat was turned down for him to sit on, and affording scant room for a companion to sit by his side. The crowning appendage of this unique structure was an eight-square wooden sounding board, suspended by a half inch square iron rod fastened in the arched ceiling. It resembled a woolen tassel attached to a frail cord incapable of sustaining it. It vibrated sensibly with every motion of the air, and fearfully when the windows were open, and a thunder storm impending. This feature gave to the concern an element of the sublime, which modified its fantastical character, especially in the eyes of the youthful worshippers, whose fears of the demolition of the minister by the breaking of the imaginary string were not altogether unreasonable.

A row of columns, arranged in an ox-bow line, supported the gallery, the curve at the east end of the room being opposite the pulpit at the west end. A single row of singer's seats went around the entire front line of the gallery, so that every singer could see the majestic swing of the chief chorister's arm as he beat the time from the center of the arched line, though they at the extreme ends could but faintly hear the pitch-pipe. A narrow, elevated alley ran in the rear of the singer's seats; and in the rear of this, on the sides of the house, were still more elevated pews, furnishing admirable places of concealed retirement for the boys and girls who chose to worship in a more cheerful way than their parents below would have approved.

In rear of the chorister's seat, and falling back into the tower of the building were two commodious pews, one appropriated to the class of young men who brushed and greased their upper hair into a high pyramid over the forehead, and tied that which descended behind into a pipe-stem cue, who wore wide projecting ruffles at the bosom, and Suwarrow boots, with pendant silk tassels at the knees, and magnified their strut by anchoring their thumbs in the arm-holes of their waistcoats; and the other appropriated to the young women who wore gunboat-bonnets, well-displayed bosoms and street-sweeping skirts or trails. By what rule of selection the parties were dignified to these high places, was never made known to the compiler; but according to his best recollection, they were mainly composed of clerks and schoolmasters, tailoresses and schoolmarms. Into these pews, compeers of their occupants from neighboring parishes were ushered, in stately form.

As the congregation increased in numbers, the two gallery pews before appropriated to worshippers of the colored persuasion were needed by their white brethren and sisters, and two corner pews were erected over the gallery stairs, for the special use of the colored worshippers. The position of these pews was lofty, but the access was so difficult, and the honor of occupancy so dubious, that the prayers and praises of the sanctuary ceased to be participated in by the African race.

The parishioners were seated in the lower pews by an annually appointed committee, who were required to take into consideration the combined elements of age, wealth, and official position in assigning seats of honor or mediocrity. This heart-burning method of seating the congregation grew out of the system of supporting the gospel by taxation, and ceased when the funds were raised by annual sales of the pews by auction, about 1820. In Norfolk, and perhaps some other neighboring parishes, the old system is believed to be still retained.

The interior of the house retained its pristine form and adornments until 1828, when the pulpit, sounding-board and all, was taken down, and a less pretentious, but more convenient one, was placed at the east end of the audience room, the floor was laid on an inclined plane, raising it some four feet above a level at the west end, and modern slips were put thereon which faced eastward. In the gallery the aristocratic front pews, and the devil-possessed side pews were removed. Rising tiers of seats for singers occupied the place of the former, and open seats along the walls, without high screens to hide the unruly boys and girls from the view of their parents below, were erected. The untenanted cock loft negro pews over the stairs were left intact. In 1848, the house was removed to its present site, and so entirely remodeled, without and within, that only the frame of the original building remains. The interior is tast... and conveniently arranged and furnished. A fine toned organ has r... been purchased, at a cost of $2,000, and placed in the choir, ind... ng the prosperity and liberal spirit of the congregation.

The six-rod highway being insufficient for a parade ground, the society purchased, in December, 1802, a strip of land five rods wide, extending northerly on the east line of the highway, to near the Episcopal Church, "to be forever kept for a public parade." About the same time a strip of land was purchased, by individuals, on the west side of the six-rod highway, extending north from the north line of the meeting-house, a distance of nine rods, and with a width of fifty-four feet, for the purpose of erecting horse-sheds thereon. The sheds were eventually built in the rear of this land, opening on its west line and leaving the land open to the public. A strip of the same width was some years after thrown open to the public, extending north to the Holabird premises, thus making a parade ground about fourteen rods wide from east to west, and twenty-five to thirty roods long.

From the Rock House, westerly, to the Old Tavern in the West Village, the turnpike, when opened, ran through a nearly unbroken forest. There was one small opening on the flat, where some unknown person had once built a log shanty, which had then been abandoned; and another a little north of High street, and a little east of Elizur B. Parsons house, where a log house once stood, of unknown origin. We have referred to the two hamlets around the two mills at the lake outlet, and the stone bridge on Still River. The first of these extended down the hill to, and along the turnpike at Lake street bridge. The other extended south along the new road to the parade ground or green, and the contiguous Turnpike. These sections, under the designations of West street and East street, became separate and rival villages, whose bitter and frequent contentions about Post Office location, road improvements, and business enterprises, have given to our community an unenviable notoriety, and to the Post Office Department a constant annoyance.

The extension of the Naugatuck Railroad to Winsted, with its terminus intermediate between the two villages, gave rise to another distinct village on "the Flat," which has expanded in each direction, so as to unite with both of the rival sections. It would seem a natural result of this physical consolidation, that sectional feelings and interests would have died away, but as yet, old animosities and new causes of contention have prevented this most desirable consummation.

CHAPTER XXVI.

SETTLERS—FAMILY RECORDS—SCHOOL HOUSES AND SCHOOLS—STATISTICS.

1801 TO 1811.

THE Rockwell Brothers — Solomon, Reuben, Alpha, and Martin — were engaged in the iron business in Colebrook, at the close of the last century. Their works were on the stream flowing out of the meadows at the center, which were submerged by their dam, making an extensive pond of shallow water; and a nuisance was generated thereby which caused the death of several residents of the vicinity by fever. It consequently became necessary to lower their dam and drain the meadows in order to disinfect the atmosphere. This rendered the water power insufficient for their works, and obliged them to change their locality. In 1799 they bought the Austin Mill and water power from the lake outlet to Meadow street bridge, except the Jenkins & Boyd interest in the upper forge, and in 1802 removed one of their Colebrook forges to the site of Timothy Hulbert's present Iron Works, and a few years after, built another forge on the site of Lathrop & Barton's Lake Stream Cutlery Works.

SOLOMON ROCKWELL, Esq., came to Winsted this year, and took up his abode in the house built by David Austin, Jr., near the lake outlet, and continued his residence there until the completion of the homestead of his after life, now owned by his daughter, Mrs. Jerusha R. Boyd.

No one of the founders of our village made a deeper impress on its institutions and moral character, or did more to increase its business and stimulate public improvements than Mr. Rockwell. He was the first justice of the peace in the Society, and was the foremost in all measures of public and benevolent enterprise. The following sketch of his character was drawn in substance by another hand, soon after his death:

"As a business man he possessed great energy, and a good degree of prudence and sound discretion. He successfully accomplished most of his business projects, and although in his early career some of his enterprises were attended with disasters which would have crushed an ordinary man, he was never disheartened. If one project failed he tried another. Experience taught him prudence, without in any degree diminishing his energetic and sanguine temperament. He was a man of integrity, constitutionally and from principle, and was liberal and generous, without a narrow or contracted streak in his character. He practised hospitality, without stint or grudging. His unwearied cheerfulness, his genial humor, and exhaustless fund of anecdote made him the favorite of old and young, wise and simple. He was a true gentleman of the old school, a puritan of the puritans, yet liberal and catholic in his religious views.

"His profession of faith in the Redeemer was made after his fiftieth year, and his subsequent life gave witness of a good profession. His faith rested not in abstractions, but was manifested in works of love and mercy. After the prostration of his body and mind by paralysis his faith knew no abatement, but shone clear and tranquil to the closing scene of life."

In May 1835, while present at a fire which consumed his woolen factory, he was struck down by paralysis, which for some time rendered him helpless and speechless. After a partial recovery, a second attack in 1838, followed in a few weeks by a third, so impaired his bodily and mental powers that death was a messenger of mercy rather than of judgment. He died August 1, 1838, aged seventy-four and a half years.

1801.

DEACON ALPHA ROCKWELL, younger brother of Solomon, was the first male child born in Colebrook, as indicated by his baptismal name. He came to Winsted in 1801, and during the same year erected his homestead on the corner of Main and Lake streets, where the Beardsley House now stands. His health was impaired in childhood by whooping cough, which permanently affected his lungs and terminated in death by consumption, in the fifty-first year of his age.

Associated in business with his more versatile and sanguine brother, Solomon, his vigilance and method, and his skill as an accountant and financier imparted to the firm the qualities essential to success in its varied and complicated transactions. No two brothers ever acted more in accord with each other, or were bound together by more sincere affection.

As a member of society he was active in promoting education and good morals. As a father, husband, and brother he was affectionate and loving beyond most men. As a Christian he was eminent for piety, and zealously efficient in furthering the interests of the church of which he was a member and office-bearer. He died in the triumph of Christian faith, June 1, 1818, aged 50 years.

Though only two of the Rockwell brothers moved to Winsted, yet descendants of four of them are now, or have been, residents here, while the fifth died childless.

DEACON WILLIAM ROCKWELL,[1] from England, came to Dorchester, Mass., in 1630, thence with the early planters to Windsor, Conn., where he died May 15, 1640. He married in England, Susanna Chapin, born April 5, 1602, who married (2d) May 29, 1645, Mathew Grant, and died November 14, 1666.

CHILDREN.

I.	JOAN,[2]	b. England, April 25, 1625; m. Jeffrey Baker.
II.	JOHN,[2]	b. England, July 18, 1627.
III.	MARY,[2]	probably died young; not named in Mathew Grant's record.
IV.	SAMUEL,[2]	b. Dorchester, Mass., March 28, 1631.
V.	RUTH,[2]	b. Dorchester, August —, 1633; m. October 7, 1652, Christopher Huntington, and among her descendants is General Ulysses S. Grant, the President of the United States.
VI.	JOSEPH,[2]	date of birth not known; d. young.
VII.	SARAH,[2]	b. Windsor, Conn., July 24, 1638; m. Walter Gaylord.

SAMUEL ROCKWELL[2] married, April 7, 1660, Mary Norton of Saybrook, daughter of Thomas and Grace (Wells) Norton of Guilford, Conn.

CHILDREN, ALL BORN IN WINDSOR.

I.	MARY,[3]	b. Jan. 18, 1662; m., Oct. 23, 1683, Josiah Loomis.
II.	ABIGAIL,[3]	b. Aug. 23, 1664; d. May 3, 1665.
III.	SAMUEL,[3]	b. Oct. 19, 1667; m., Jan. 10, 1694, Elizabeth Gaylord.
IV.	JOSEPH,[3]	b. May 22, 1670; m. Elizabeth Drake.
V.	JOHN,[3]	b. May 31, 1673; m. Anne Skinner.
VI.	ABIGAIL,[3]	b. April 11, 1676; m. John Smith.
VII.	JOSIAH,[3]	b. March 15, 1678; m., Dec. 14, 1713, Rebecca Loomis, of Lebanon.

JOSEPH ROCKWELL,[3] "sarjant," m. Elizabeth Drake, born Nov. 4, 1675, daughter of Job and Elizabeth (Alvord) Drake. He d. June 26, 1733, aged 63 years.

CHILDREN, ALL BORN IN WINDSOR.

I.	JOSEPH,[4]	b. Nov. 23, 1695; m. Hannah Huntington.
II.	ELIZABETH,[4]	b. Dec. 12, 1698.
III.	BENJAMIN,[4]	b. Oct. 26, 1700; m. Margaret Drake.
IV.	JAMES,[4]	b. June 3, 1704; m., Nov. 7, 1728, Abigail Loomis.
V.	JOB,[4]	b. April 13, 1709; m., Jan. 20, 1736-7, Miriam Hayden.
VI.	ELIZABETH,[4]	b. July 24, 1713; m. Jonathan Huntington.

JOSEPH ROCKWELL[4] married Hannah Huntington, born Norwich, Conn., March 25, 1693-4, daughter of John and Abigail (Lathrop) Huntington, and grand-daughter of Christopher and Ruth[2] (Rockwell)

Huntington. He died Oct. 16, 1746, aged 51. She died of small-pox Jan. 18, 1761, aged 67 years.

CHILDREN, ALL BORN IN WINDSOR.

I. JOSEPH,⁵ b. March 15, 1715-16; m. Anna Dodd.
II. HANNAH,⁵ b. Dec. 25, 1717.
III. A SON⁵ (twin), b. June 5, 1720; d. same day.
IV. JERUSHA⁵ (twin), b. June 5, 1720.
V. JONATHAN,⁵ b. May 2, 1723.
VI. SAMUEL,⁵ b. March 9, 1725-6; d. young.
VII. SAMUEL,⁵ b. Jan. 19, 1728; m. Hepzibah Pratt.

JOSEPH ROCKWELL⁵ married Anna Dodd. He died ——— —, 1775. aged 60.

CHILDREN, ALL BORN IN EAST WINDSOR.

I. ANNA,⁶ m. Nathan Bass.
II. JOHN.⁶
III. ELIJAH,⁶ b. Nov. 14, 1744, O. S.; m. Lucy Wright.
IV. MARY,⁶ m. William Goodwin.
V. JERUSHA.⁶
VI. ELIZABETH.⁶
VII. GURDON.⁶
VIII. JOSEPH.⁶
IX. ELIHU,⁶ lived in Winchester.

SAMUEL ROCKWELL⁵ married Hepzibah Pratt, born in East Hartford (date unknown), daughter of Jonathan and Mary (Benton) Pratt, grand daughter of John and Hepzibah Pratt, and great-grand-daughter of John Pratt, one of the original members of Mr. Hooker's Cambridge Church, and an early settler of Hartford, where he died July 15, 1655, leaving a widow Elizabeth, and sons John and Daniel. He died at Colebrook Sept. 7, 1794, aged 66. She died   , 1814.

CHILDREN.

I. SAMUEL,⁶ b. East Windsor, Feb. 18, 1759.
II. TIMOTHY,⁶ m., 1793, Mary Burrall, of Canaan. He d. Sept. 4, 1794, aged 34 years, s. p.
III. SOLOMON,⁶ bap. East Windsor, Oct. 3, 1762; d. young.
IV. SOLOMON,⁶ b. East Windsor, Jan. 20, 1764; bap. Jan. 22, 1764.
V. REUBEN,⁶ b. East Windsor, Oct. 1, 1765; bap. Oct. 6, 1765.
VI. ALPHA,⁶ b. Colebrook, Sept. 21, 1767, the first child born in the town; hence his name.
VII. MARTIN,⁶ b. C. 1772.
VIII. LUMAN,⁶ b. C. d. Nov., 1777.
IX. HEBZIBAH,⁶ b. C. d. Nov., 1777.

ELIJAH ROCKWELL⁶ married, Jan. 19, 1775, Lucy Wright, born in Goshen, Conn., Oct. 7, 1756, daughter of Capt. John Wright. He was the first justice of the peace, and the life-long town clerk of Colebrook. She died at Colebrook, May 24, 1830, in her 74th year. He died August 2, 1841.

CHILDREN.

I. LUCY,[7] b. June 8, 1776; d. April 2, 1778.
II. ELIJAH,[7] b. Nov. 9, 1777; m. Sophia Ensign, daughter of John.
III. LUCY,[7] b. Jan. 8, 1779; m. Aaron Case of Norfolk.
IV. THERON,[7] b. June 5, 1782.
V. ANNE,[7] b. Oct. 9, 1783; m. Joseph P. Hurlbut.
VI. BETSEY,[7] b. Feb. 18, 1789; m. Dr. Luman Wakefield.

SAMUEL ROCKWELL,[6] a physician, settled in Salisbury, Conn.; afterward removed to Sharon, where he died June 24, 1836. He married 1788, Eunice Canfield. She died and he married (2d) 1798, Hannah Reed.

CHILDREN BY FIRST WIFE.

I. HEPZIBAH,[7] m. Nathaniel B. Gaylord.
II. JOHN CANFIELD,[7] d. at Colebrook, unm.

CHILDREN BY SECOND WIFE.

III. MARY ANN,[7] b. Salisbury, June 2, 1800; m. Aaron Hawley.
IV. WILLIAM,[7] grad. Yale College Law School; lawyer in Brooklyn, N. Y.; Judge of Superior Court of Kings county at the time of his death: m. Susan Prince of Brooklyn.

SOLOMON ROCKWELL[6] married, July 2, 1800, Sarah McEwen, born March 2, 1775, daughter of Robert and Jerusha (Doolittle) McEwen. She died March 15, 1837; he died Aug. 1, 1838.

CHILD.

I. JERUSHA,[7] b. March 28, 1803; m. Theodore Hinsdale; and (2d) John Boyd.

REUBEN ROCKWELL,[6] of Colebrook, born in East Windsor Oct. 1, 1766, married Rebecca, daughter of Col. Bezaleel Beebe of Litchfield.

CHILDREN.

I. JULIUS,[7] grad. Yale College; lawyer at Pittsfield, Mass.; representative and senator from Mass. in Congress; and now judge of supreme court, Massachusetts.
II. LOUISA,[7] m. Giles H. Bass, of Colebrook.
III. BEZALEEL BEEBE,[7] of Winsted, b. Oct. 28, 1809; m. April 23, 1834, Caroline, daughter of Col. Hosea Hinsdale. CHILDREN: 1. Elizabeth,[8] b. Jan. 8, 1836; 2. Julia,[8] b. Oct. 13, 1838; 3. Caroline Rebecca,[8] b. June 1, 1840; 4. Mary Pitkin Hinsdale,[8] b. Sept. 10, 1844; 5. John Hinsdale,[8] b. Sept. 27, 1847; d. April 10, 1848; 6. Kate Louisa,[8] b. June 29, 1850; 7. Lilian,[8] b. Feb. 22, 1854. He resides in Winsted, holds the office of assistant assessor of U. S. Internal Revenue.

IV. ELIZABETH,[7] living in Colebrook.
V. REUBEN,[7] of Colebrook, m. Amelia L. Eno; representative and senator of Connecticut legislature, and now holds the office of collector U. S. Internal Revenue, Fourth District of Connecticut.

ALPHA ROCKWELL,[6] married, May 20, 1800, Rhoda Ensign, born in Salisbury, ———— —, 1775, daughter of John and Rhoda (Lee) Ensign. She died Feb. 25, 1817; he died May 31, 1818.

CHILDREN.

I. EDWARD,[7] b. Colebrook, June 30, 1801.
II. SAMUEL,[7] b. Winchester, April 18, 1803.
III. CAROLINE,[7] b. Dec. 27, 1804; m. William Lawrence, of Norfolk, who d. at Northampton, Mass., Feb. 22, 1867, s. p.
IV. CORNELIA,[7] b. March 23, 1808; m., Oct. —, 1838, Osmyn Baker, of Amherst, Mass., and d. Feb. 12, 1840, leaving one child, William Lawrence,[8] b. Oct. 5, 1839; "grad. Dartmouth College, 1858; made the tour of Europe, 1860; was commissioned second lieutenant of artillery in the regular army, August, 1861; was promoted to first lieutenant, November, 1861; was in the battles of Winchester, Port Republic, Manassas Heights, Chantilly, South Mountain, and was killed at Antietam, Sept. 17, 1862, aged 23 years."
V. DELIA ELLEN,[7] b. Jan. 16, 1811; m. March 28, 1838, Dea. Elliot Beardsley, b. Monroe, Conn., Dec. 26, 1801, son of Elliot and Abigail (Patterson) Beardsley. He moved from South Britain to Winsted in 1840, and engaged in business, in company with Theodore Hinsdale; and after the death of the latter became sole owner of one of the largest manufacturing establishments in the Society, and managed it with consummate ability during his remaining active life. Reticent and deliberate by nature and habit, he minded his own business entirely, yet had an eye on all that was going on around him, and participated influentially, though quietly, in public affairs. No man in the town was more looked to for advising and giving a direction to all measures for public interest; and none more respected for purity of life, religious example, and earnest patriotism; he was one of the first office bearers of the Second Congregational Church; a Director and President of the Winsted Bank; a Representative of the town and Senator of the 15th District in the State Legislature, and held various other offices. The war of the rebellion opened near the close of his active life; — and no citizen of the town exceeded him in energetic and persistent efforts to aid the Union Cause. A slow decay of his physical faculties, and eventually of his mental powers, clouded the last years of his life, which terminated Jan. 19, 1871. Mr. Beardsley, by a former wife, —— (Johnson), had a daughter, Martha E., b. in South Britain, Feb. 13, 1856, now living.

CHILDREN BY SECOND WIFE.

i. Edward Rockwell,[8] b. Jan. 10, 1839; grad. Yale College, 1859; m. Jan. 10, 1867, Emma Adelaide Watson, b. in New Hartford, Jan. 30, 1840; has twin sons, Elliot Gay,[9] and Edward Watson,[9] b. June 4, 1868.

E. Beardsley

AND FAMILY RECORDS. 369

2. Cornelia,[8] b. July 27, 1840; m. Oct. 23, 1867, Rev. Samuel Baker Forbes, b. in Westborough, Mass., Aug. 1, 1826, son of Nahum and Polly (Davis) Forbes; he grad. Williams College, 1855 ; East Windsor Theological Seminary, 1857 ; licensed by Hartford Fourth Association, 1856 ; ordained at Manchester, Conn., Oct. 20, 1857 ; dismissed April, 1859 ; resides in West Winsted; his one child, Henry Stuart,[9] b. June 16, 1871.
3. Sarah Hinsdale,[8] b. Jan. 9, 1842; m. Oct. 13, 1868, Eugene Potter; she d. April —, 1871, at Lexington, Mich., leaving a son, Lawrence William, b. April 4, 1871.
4. Elliot,[8] b. Nov. 17, 1843 ; d. June 12, 1862.
5. Julia Plummer,[8] b. Oct. 1, 1845 ; m. May 28, 1867, George F. Barton ; lives at W. Winsted; has children, Elizabeth Nichols,[9] b. April 4, 1869, and George Elliot,[9] b. Dec. 19, 1870.
6. Theodore Hinsdale,[8] b. April 13, 1851 ; m. June 15, 1870, Alura Francis Harrison, b. in New Milford, Conn., Feb. 7, 1850; has one daughter, Sarah Harrison,[9] b. May 11, 1871.

VI. RHODA,[7] b. Feb. 22, 1817; m. May 2, 1838, Rev. Clement Long, b. in Hopkinton, N. H., Dec. 31, 1807, son of Samuel and Mary (Clement) Long; Prof. of Int. and Moral Philosophy in Wes. Res. Coll., O., 1834–1852 ; Prof. of Christian Theology in Auburn Theol. Sem., 1852–1854 ; Prof. of Int. and Moral Phil. in Dart. Coll., from 1854 till his death, at Hanover, N. H., Oct. 14, 1861.

CHILDREN.

1. Mary,[8]   b. in Hudson, O., June 8, 1839.
2. Samuel Rockwell,[8]   b. H., April 25, 1841 ; d. Aug. 3, 1842.
3. Caroline Rockwell,[8] b. H., Oct. 24, 1844.
4. Julia Russell,[8]   b. H., April 6, 1851.
5. Cornelia Baker,[8]   b. in Auburn, N. Y., Dec. 5, 1853.

MARTIN ROCKWELL,[6] of Colebrook, married (1st), Mary (Burrall) Rockwell, widow of his brother, Timothy Rockwell, deceased, and by her had

CHILDREN.

I. ELIZA,[7] who m. Rev. Ralph Emerson, D. D.
II. TIMOTHY,[7] who lived in Winsted until 1827, and thence removed to Painesville, O., where he still resides. He m. Helen Maria, daughter of Seth Marshall, Esq.
III. MARY,[7] living (1872) in Colebrook.
IV. SUSAN,[7] m. Rev. George E. Pierce, D. D., minister at Harwinton, Conn., and afterwards President of Western Reserve College, Hudson, O.
V. WILLIAM,[7] m. Maria Roberts; d. at Honesdale, Penn.
VI. CHARLES,[7] grad. Yale College ; Chaplain U. S. Navy ; clergyman.
VII. CHARLOTTE,[7] living (1872) in Colebrook.

He married (2d), Lucy (Beebe) Robins, who survived him ; he died Dec. 8, 1851.

THERON ROCKWELL,[7] married, September 6, 1814, Clarissa Treat, born in Hartland, Conn., September 6, 1788, daughter of John Treat. They settled in Colebrook, where he died January 30, 1848.

CHILDREN.

I. JAMES SIDNEY,[8] b. Oct. 2, 1817; m. Nov. 11, 1844, Catharine A. Corley; lives in Brooklyn, N. Y.

CHILDREN.

   1. Clara,[9] b. 1847; d. 1851.
   2. Fanny,[9] b. April 17, 1850; m. Nov. 16, 1870, James Dunham Carhart.

II. HENRY EDWARDS,[8] b. Feb. 12, 1824; d. May 20, 1825.
III. JOHN TREAT,[8] b. Jan. 21, 1827.
IV. ANNIE CLARISSA,[8] b. Sept. 29, 1832; m. Sept. 28, 1854, Frederick Michael Shepard, b. in Norfolk, Sept. 24, 1827; lives in the city of New York.

CHILDREN.

   1. Annie Rockwell,[9] b. June 7, 1856.
   2. Frederick Michael,[9] b. June 8, 1858.
   3. Clara Margaret,[9] b. Oct. 12, 1862.
   4. Joseph Minot,[9] b. Aug. 31, 1864.
   5. John Andrus,[9] b. March 15, 1869.

EDWARD ROCKWELL,[7] graduated at Yale College in 1821; admitted to the bar at New Haven in 1825; removed to Ohio, and was Secretary of Cleveland and Pittsburg Railroad Company till 1867, when he resigned and moved to New York. He married Matilda du Plessis Salter, of New Haven.

CHILDREN.

I. SARAH,[8] b.   m. John M. Isaacs, Cleveland, O.
II. MATILDA,[8] b.   m. George E. Kent, N. Y.
III. CLEVELAND,[8] b.   Engineer U. S. Navy.
IV. EDWARD,[8] b.   d. young.

SAMUEL ROCKWELL[7] graduated at Yale College in 1825; admitted to the ministry in 1828; ordained pastor at Plainfield, April 11, 1832; dismissed April —, 1841; installed pastor of South Church, New Britain, January 4, 1843; resigned his pastorate June 20, 1858; elected Representative to the Legislature of Connecticut in 1862 and 1869, and Senator in 1865; Judge of Probate, Berlin District, since July 4, 1864; Treasurer of Savings Bank of New Britain, from its incorporation in 1862. He married, June 6, 1833, Julia Ann Plummer, who died April —, 1838; and he married (2d) May 5, 1840, Elizabeth Eaton, of Plainfield. She died, and he married (3d) July 29, 1844, Mrs. Charlotte (North) Stanley.

CHILD BY FIRST WIFE.

I. GEORGE PLUMMER,[8] b. May 9, 1834.

CHILD BY SECOND WIFE.

II. ELIZABETH EATON,[8] b. April 9, 1843; d. March 11, 1866.

JOHN TREAT ROCKWELL,[8] married, December 14, 1853, Harriette Ann Burt, born April 19, 1830, daughter of Miles C. and Ann (Mallory)

Burt. She died Oct. 24, 1855; and he married (2d), Feb. 26, 1857, Mary Ann Hawley, born in Sharon, Conn., June 22, 1827, daughter of Aaron and Mary Ann (Rockwell) Hawley; she died June 5, 1859, and he married (3d), April 18, 1861, Jane Elizabeth Arcularius, born in New York, May 14, 1828, daughter of Andrew Merrill and Eliza Lucretia (Saltonstall) Arcularius.

CHILDREN.

I. ANNIE MALLORY,[9] b. March 14, 1855.
II. THERON,[9] b. July 18, 1863.
III. ELIZA SALTONSTALL,[9] b. Jan. 2, 1867.
IV. JAMES SIDNEY,[9] b. July 18, 1868.

EZRA ROCKWELL, this year bought and occupied the house on South street, near Torringford line, previously owned by Jehiel and Mabel Burr, which he sold in 1803. He lived in the town some years later.

JACOB CHAMBERLIN, from Colebrook, this year bought the Israel Crissey farm, adjoining Colebrook line, and now a part of the William E. Cowles farm, which he occupied until 1805, and then returned to Colebrook.

AARON LOOMIS owned and occupied land on South street, near Torrington line, from 1801 to 1806, or later. He was b. May 25, 1766, son of Ephraim and Jane (Campbell) Loomis. He m. Feb. 12, 1789, Anne Drake, of Windsor. Their children were probably b. in Torrington.

CHILDREN.

I. AARON, b. May 16, 1790.
II. JANE, b. March 11, 1792.
III. LAURA, b. Feb. 17, 1794; m. Jan. 5, 1809, Erastus Hodges.
IV. ANNES, b. June 23, 1797.
V. ALVAN, b. Dec. 22, 1800.   [*Loomis Genealogy*, p. 111.]

1802.

COL. HOSEA HINSDALE,[6] [see Genealogy under 1799,] from Berlin, came to Winsted in the spring of this year, and resided in the gambrel-roofed house that stood on the site of Moses Camp's present dwelling. He was a tanner by trade, and had made arrangements to begin the world in Western New York; but the discovery at that time made, of the tanning properties of hemlock bark, changed his plans, and he came here to avail himself of the abundance of this material found in our forests. In company with his brother-in-law, Major James Shepard, afterwards of Norfolk, he built the tannery at the corner of Spencer and Hinsdale streets, the last vestiges of which have this year (1871) been obliterated, by the excavation of Mr. J. T. Rockwell's skating pond, where he did a leading business for some thirty years. In 1810, Major Shepard withdrew from the concern, and it was conducted solely by Col. Hinsdale until about 1845.

Colonel Hinsdale, in addition to the tanning business, was largely engaged in public affairs, "swinging around the circle" of town offices, and trying his hand as grand juror, constable, selectman, assessor, justice of the peace, and representative, and of military affairs from private to colonel of cavalry. He was also for several years a deputy, under Sheriff Landon, who prided himself on his selection of a staff of not only able but portly and fine looking assistants, thereby sustaining the dignity of the county magistracy. He closed his public life with the presidency of the Litchfield County Temperance Society, which he filled with punctuality and ardent zeal for seven or eight years.

His social qualities were of a high order. His acquaintance with men of the county and state was extensive, and his memory of events accurate in a remarkable degree. At ninety he could recall an acquaintance or event of early days with the readiness of a young man. Like most of his neighbors he was a reading man, well posted in all current events. In person and manner dignified, fluent and attractive in conversation; he was the chronicler and patriarch of the village, the last of the generation of men who laid the foundations and controlled the destinies of our community. He married, March 2, 1798, Elizabeth Shepard, born at Hartland, September 2, 1777, daughter of Eldad and Rebecca (Seymour) Shepard. She died January 25, 1861. He died October 21, 1866.

CHILDREN.

I. ELIZABETH,[7] b. December 17, 1798; d. December 4, 1804.
II. HARRIET,[7] b. September 25, 1801; d. December 10, 1804.
III. JULIA,[7] b. November 14, 1805.
IV. HENRY,[7] b. August 31, 1807.
V. CAROLINE,[7] b. July 19, 1811; m. April 23, 1835, Bezaleel Beebe Rockwell.
VI. HARRIET,[7] b. December 6, 1813; d. October 7, 1816.
VII. JOHN,[7] b. May 10, 1817.

HENRY HINSDALE,[7] married October 13, 1834, Jane Coe, born August 14, 1812, daughter of Jonathan Coe. She died October 5, 1839; he died October 14, 1846.

CHILD.

I. HARRIET AMELIA,[8] b. October 22, 1835; d. June 1, 1842.

JOHN HINSDALE,[7] married August 31, 1841, Amanda Malvina Alvord, born August 20, 1821, daughter of Deacon James H. Alvord.

CHILDREN.

I. MARY ELIZABETH,[8] b. March 18, 1848; m. June 19, 1867, Robert R. Noble, b. September 27, 1840; had, 1. Susie Alvord,[9] b. April 9, 1868; d. March 1, 1869; 2. twins, John Hinsdale and Robert Chamberlin, b. Oct. 3, 1872.
II. JOHN ALVORD,[8] b. October 22, 1858.

COLONEL JAMES SHEPARD from New Hartford, came to Winsted with, or soon after, Colonel Hinsdale, his brother-in-law, and in 1803 built the house at the parting of Main and Spencer streets, afterwards the life-long homestead of Colonel Hinsdale, with whom he was associated in the tanning business until 1810, when, in company with Asahel Miller, he built the original tannery on the site of the present establishment of George Dudley & Son.

In 1815 he removed to Norfolk, where he resumed the tanning business for a few years, and afterwards became a highly respected tavern keeper and stage owner. He married Abigail Andrus, and had

CHILDREN.

I. JOHN ANDRUS, b. July 15, 1802.
II. LAURA SEYMOUR, b. March 19, 1804.
III. JAMES HUTCHINS, b. August 11, 1806.
IV. JERUSHA TREAT, b. September 27, 1808 ; m. A. E. Dennis.
V. SAMUEL, b. December 10, 1812 ; m. — Dennis; kept the Beardsley House for several years ; d. Norfolk, January 14, 1872.

JESSE CLARK became a resident of Winchester this year. He owned and lived until 1837, on the farm on Wallen's Hill, which he then sold to Elisha Kilbourn, and moved into Barkhamsted, where he died December 17, 1853, aged 76. His wife died December 11, 1849, aged 72. His parents were Paul Clark, born August 29, 1750 ; died March 1, 1804, and Sarah Wheeler, born March 28, 1754 ; died August 14, 1829.

He married, November 26, 1801, Lydia, daughter of Elisha and Esther Mallory.

CHILDREN.

I. NATHAN WHEELER, b. April 25, 1803.
II. ORLANDO MALLORY, b. March 11, 1805 ; d. November 7, 1807.
III. ESTHER, b. March 9, 1807.
IV. AMASA, b. March 24, 1809 ; d. December 8, 1809.
V. ZAYDA, b. October 18, 1810.
VI. BETSEY, b. December 24, 1812 ; m. October 5, 1848, George E. Shelton ; d. March 17, 1850.
VII. SARAH ANN, b. April 8, 1815 ; d. October 16, 1817.
VIII. ORLANDO, b. December 25, 1820.
IX. JOHN BENJAMIN, b. April 20, 1820 ; d. March 20, 1842.

NATHAN WHEELER CLARK, oldest child of Jesse and Lydia, a resident of the town from birth, resides on Wallen's Hill, near his father's old residence. He married, June 5, 1830, Rebecca Cordelia Dickinson, born November 7, 1805.

CHILDREN.

I. LUCIUS WADSWORTH, b. September 19, 1831.
II. JOHN BENJAMIN, b. April 14, 1834.

III. EMMA HARRIET, b. March 22, 1836.
IV. BURTON MALLORY, b. October 11, 1838; d. December 7, 1840.
V. MARY BETSEY, b. December 2, 1840.

ORLANDO CLARK, eighth child of Jesse and Lydia, removed with his father to Barkhamsted, where he still resides. He married, November 30, 1852, Melissa Race, born June 25, 1821.

CHILDREN.

I. ALBERT MALLORY, b. October 12, 1843.
II. SARAH ANN, b. December 21, 1844.
III. GEORGE ORLANDO, b. August 17, 1848.
IV. GEORGIANA MELISSA, b. August 17, 1848.
V. MILES BELDEN, b. July 31, 1851; d. September 5, 1853.

SALMON BURR from Torrington, this year came to Winsted, where he built and occupied the brick dwelling on the west side of South street, now owned by Hilamon Fyler, until his death, December 19, 1851, at the age of 77; a man of retiring manner and sterling worth. He married Mary Ensign, born September 8, 1776; died December 29, 1846.

CHILDREN.

I. MARIA, b. February 17, 1799; m. November 29, 1820, Ansel Shattuck; d. July 29, 1840.
II. RUFUS, b. December 17, 1800; m. May 10, 1828, , daughter of Barzillai Hudson of Tor.
III. SAMUEL, b. September 22, 1802; m. February 22, 1831, Louisa Flowers.
IV. WILSON, b. April 11, 1804; m. May 5, 1829, Morinda Cadwell.
V. MARY, b. June 12, 1806; m. May 11, 1827, Porter Gibbs; d. November 23, 1835.
VI. RHODA, b. January 11, 1808; m. George Ransom.
VII. SARAH, b. March 2, 1810; m. February 22, 1831, Anson H. Stuart.
VIII. WILLARD, b. February 8, 1812; m. September 1, 1843, Sarah, daughter of George Burr.
IX. HULDAH, b. May 21, 1814; m. October 5, 1834, Luman Smith.
X. HARMON ENSIGN, b. November 13, 1818; m. May 1, 1849, Ann Squire.
XI. CHARLOTTE, b. October 3, 1820; m. June 29, 1839, Erasmus N. Ransom.

JACOB SEYMOUR, a carpenter and joiner, this year bought the land around the new meeting house, now constituting the larger portion of the east village, and lived in a dwelling that stood on the site of Normand Adams' store. He sold out his purchase in a few years, and subsequently lived in the old hemlock building then standing at the north corner of Hinsdale and North Main streets. He left the town about 1810. The first gravestone in the central burying ground was erected by him over the remains of a deceased child.

JOHN SEYMOUR, brother of Jacob, also lived in the Society for a few years at this period, and became part owner of the east village property.

JOHN PHILLIPS, an iron refiner, of Welsh extraction, came into the employ of the Rockwell Brothers this year, or earlier, and lived in the rear wing of the house on Lake street, adjoining the carriage entrance to Mrs. J. R. Boyd's premises. He had a son, WILLIAM, who lived in the same dwelling until his death, February 26, 1817, leaving a son, WILLIAM S., born December 22, 1816, who lived in this Society from 1846 to the time of his death, aged 41 years. He was trained to business in Sandisfield, Mass., where his widowed mother resided until her death, and came here as a partner-in-trade with his brother-in-law, David A. Rood, now of Hartford. He built the house now occupied by his widow, at the head of Spring street, where he died of dysentery, August 19, 1860. He was a retiring, exemplary, kind-hearted, Christian man, highly esteemed, and sincerely lamented. He married June 10, 1844, Frances Slocum Hamilton, born in Tolland, Mass., February 2, 1822, daughter of Henry and Maria (Slocum) Hamilton. She in died Otis Mass., May 13, 1845 (leaving a son, William Henry, born March 30, 1845, who died January 14, 1846). He married (2d) October 18, 1847, Harriette J. Rood; she died Winsted, July 31, 1848, aged 23 years, *s. p.*, and he married (3d) March 18, 1850, Ellen Amanda Griswold, daughter of Roswell and Jerusha (Grant) Griswold.

CHILDREN.

I. WILLIAM BANISTER, b. February 16, 1853.
II. MARY LOUISE, b. April 29, 1857.

The other children of William Phillips were Aurelia, who died unmarried, Semantha, born February 11, 1805, now living in Winsted unmarried, Emeline, wife and widow of Lemuel K. Strickland, Esq., late of Sandisfield, deceased, and Clarissa, wife of Carlton Hayden.

THOMAS R. BULL is on the list of this year. He worked with his brother, Merritt Bull, in a blacksmith shop, afterwards burned down, that stood near the premises of G. W. Gaston on Main street. He afterwards moved to Colebrook, from whence he returned in 1810, and bought the old Jenkins & Boyd Scythe Works, and lived in the house on the top of the knoll east of the parsonage house of Mr. Beach. In 1816 he bought an interest in the Cook forge, which proved an unfortunate investment, bringing him to poverty, in spite of his untiring industry and frugal habits. He died November 6, 1829, aged 49.

He married, April 3, 1806, Diantha, daughter of Ebenezer Rowley, by whom he had

CHILDREN.

I. CELESTIA, a deaf mute, who m. Isaac Davis.
II. MARY, m. Lucius Phelps.
III. CLORINDA, m. Lemuel Munson
IV. JANE, m. James Gilman.
V. CATHARINE M., m. — Clapp.
VI. THOMAS.

TIMOTHY PERSONS came into the town this year, and continued a resident until about 1807, when he moved to Colebrook river, where he carried on a tannery until his death, a hard-working, honest man. He married Lucy Davis of Winsted.

ALPHEUS PERSONS, brother of Timothy, came here about the same time with his brother, and left the town with him, moving to North Colebrook, and carrying on a tannery there during his remaining life. He died in August, 1858, aged 72. His wife died in 1821, aged 32.

He married in 1810, Sally Davis, sister of Lucy aforesaid. Their son, WING PERSONS, came to Winsted in 1851, and has since resided here, living on the north side of Hinsdale street, adjoining the graded school building. He married, in August, 1843, Flavilla, daughter of Travis Phillips of Colebrook.

CHILDREN.

1. BENJAMIN FRANKLIN, b. January 8, 1844.
2. GRACE, b. July 6, 1851.
3. CHARLES, b. June, 1865.

1803.

With the year 1803 the personal reminiscences of the compiler begin. The Green Woods turnpike then, as now, ran along the easterly and northerly border of Mad River, from Coe street to Chestnut street. The green, or east village park, and the road northward, now constituting North Main street. had been recently laid out, and was cleared in its whole extent. At the south end of the park was a gravel knoll of eight or ten feet elevation, and to the west of it, about opposite Woodruff's confectionery store, was a sink hole or frog pond, depressed to the level of the river channel, which was soon after partially filled with flood-wood logs from the river, which were covered over at successive "spells" by plowing the knoll and spreading the gravel on them, until the depression and elevation were graded to one level.

The level land north of the lake stream, through which Meadow street now runs, was an unbroken forest; so also was the westerly and southerly border of Mad River from near Lake street to Still River, the meadow land south of the east village being an impenetrable morass covered with timber, where the flood-wood of Mad River had lodged and accumulated to such a degree that in time of winter and spring floods the road above the creek bridge would be submerged and covered by broken ice, not unfrequently to a depth of six feet, rendering it impassable until the water subsided, and the cakes of ice could be removed from the road path. The hill lands, encircled on three sides by Main and North Main streets, and bordering Hinsdale street, were an unbroken forest, save at points where houses had been erected. A part of the flat had been cleared, but the aboriginal stumps remained, only partially decayed.

On Lake street stood nearest the lake outlet the one and a half story house built by David Austin, Jr., and then occupied by Solomon Rockwell and his recently married wife. Next northerly on the east side of the street was the two-story lean-to house built by Deacon David Austin and then occupied by the miller and one or two other families. Next northerly stood the Daniel Wilcox house, immediately west of which Rockwell street now runs. The Lake street road then ran directly down the hill in front of this house, and has since been swung around to the north for ease of grade.

The lake stream was then conducted by a canal easterly across the street opposite the lean-to house and then on the east border, to near the Wilcox house where it again crossed back, and poured its waters on the wheels of the old Austin Mill, which stood where the road now runs, a little below the Henry Spring Company's works. On the westerly side of the road, immediately below the first canal crossing, stood a blacksmith shop and dish mill, and below the corn mill, a clothier's shop, fulling mill and carding mill. A dwelling house, soon after this period burned down, stood below and adjoining the clothier's shop. There was another dish mill where the Beardsley company's grinding shop now stands. Below this stood the old original forge where the Winsted Company's grinding works now stand, and "the middle forge" then recently erected by the Rockwells and now rebuilt and owned by Timothy Hulbert. Around these forges were three tenements for workmen, and two others stood on Lake street.

On the depot grounds of the Connecticut Western Railroad Company stood the oldest store building within the borough limits, built before 1800 by Thomas Spencer, Jr., and Hewitt Hills. Below the middle forge stood a saw mill, on the site of which "the lower forge" was built a few years after by the Rockwell Brothers. On the next privilege stood the scythe works of Meritt Bull, this year completed, where the stone shop of the Winsted Hoe Co., adjoining Meadow Street bridge, now stands. Below this on the northerly side of Lake street, immediately east of Meadow street, was James Boyd's scythe works; and nearly opposite them stood and now stands the gambrel-roofed store-building, that year erected by Mr. Kirkum.

On the turnpike, or Main street, there stood an old house on the site of George Dudley's residence, occupied by David West. The next house was erected and afterwards occupied during his life by James Boyd, and now owned by John T. Rockwell. The next house was built in 1802 by Deacon Alpha Rockwell on the site of the Beardsley House. The Lyman & Lewis store-building stood on the site of Moses Camp's dwelling until taken down and re-erected about 1842 on Prospect street and now owned by Benjamin Lawrence. On the south corner of Main and Lake streets stood the small gambrel-roofed store built two years earlier by Bissell Hinsdale. Next south of this stood, and still stands, the old Higby tavern; and beyond this, on the site of Weed's block, the gambrel-roofed Kirkum dwelling. From this point to the new meeting-house in the east village, not a single building had been erected on either side of the road, except the store now occupied by T. Baird. There had been a log house on the flat and another on High Street hill, but both had disappeared.

In the East Village the original hotel building had been raised and covered, and a small dwelling or shop, stood on or near the Normand Adams store site, and a coarse hemlock covered dwelling, built by one of the Potters, stood behind the ancient elm tree at the corner of North Main and Hinsdale streets. There was a small opening in the woods through which Hinsdale street ran, near the residence of John G. Wetmore, on which stood a small log-house occupied by a shoemaker named Henry Sanford. Around the Doolittle mill, on the east wing of the clock-factory dam, stood the Jesse Doolittle dwelling, afterwards owned by Asaph Pease, and now removed, nearly in front of the new James G. Woodruff house, on the west side of the North Main Street road, as it then ran. North of this, on the same side of the road, stood a small house occupied by the miller; and still further north another small house, which was afterwards removed to the top of the high knoll, beneath which it before stood. Opposite this house, on the east side of the street, stood, and still stands, the double house of Jenkins & Boyd, afterwards the parsonage house of the late Rev. James Beach, in which the compiler was born.

The district school-house of the West District was a building of dubious age and color on the site of the long one-story school-house standing west of the newly erected Graded school edifice. The Coe Street road, Spencer Street road, and Hinsdale Street road concentrated at that point; and it was reached from Lake street by way of the new turnpike.

On the now discontinued road on the east side of Still River stood, and now stands, in a ruinous condition, the Nathan Wheeler house, with a floating foot bridge crossing the river, and two other houses near the

Turnpike bridge, which have since disappeared. The Widow Hall house at the parting of the turnpike and the Torringford road, had been recently built for a tavern by Benjamin Wheeler, who kept the only post-office in the town.

The elms around the East Village Park were set out this year and were probably the first transplanted shade trees in the society, with the exception of an occasional willow. Most unfortunately for New England, the spiky Lombardy poplar was first imported about this period, and gained a most unaccountable popularity. Its easy propagation by slips, of rapid growth, and its singular though graceless form, gave to it almost universal favor. It had a run of a whole generation to the almost entire exclusion of our beautiful native shade trees. Fortunate indeed were the older villages which had reared their wide branching, majestic elms before this graceless and short-lived tree gained a footing among us.

On the subsidence of the Lombardy poplar mania, the rock-maple found general favor by reason of its cleanliness and depth of shade, rather than the grace and majesty of its matured form. The elm, though somewhat later in its introduction, has proved itself a more rapid grower and a more hardy tree. None of ours away from the East Park have yet attained the maturity of size which developes their full grace and majesty; yet the large number now in process of healthy growth, give assured promise of a beautiful town in the future, in spite of its ill proportioned and comfortless residences.

For the edification of the antiquary of nineteen hundred and three, — in the event of a copy of these annals reaching his hands — we here note the date of transplantation of some of the trees now standing on Main and Lake streets, as follows:

The elms around the East village Park, as already stated, in 1803; — and those in the vicinity on Main street perhaps a year later; — the maples around the Solomon Rockwell place on Lake street, and in front of the Congregational Church, about 1818. The elms in front of the E. S. Woodford place about 1825, and those fronting Moses Camp's place about 1830; those in front of the Winsted Savings Bank and the S. W. Coe store, in 1832.

Of the seedling elms along the bank of Mad River, which may be known by their irregular positions, probably not one had sprung up before the opening of the Green Woods turnpike, in 1799.

In recalling Winsted as it was in its infancy, memories of the West village school house and its occupants crowd upon us. It was there that we this year began to ascend the hill of science, seated on one of the slab benches, supported by four rough-hewn legs, — without backs, — and a little too high for our feet to touch the floor. The building was erected in the last century,— how early no one now living can tell, and no record informs. It was of mature age,— had once been painted red, but then had a dirty, brindle look, neither venerable nor picturesque. It had a large stone fire-place at the north end, with the entry from the outer doors on one side and " the dungeon,"— a dark closet,— on the other.

A smaller fire-place and chimney of later construction stood at the south end. Writing desks, fronting inwards, stood near the east and west walls. In front of these were the hemlock slabs in two tiers for tormenting the young children,— and teaching them at the outset, the ruggedness of the path of learning they were to ascend. The teacher's table, a small platform of boards, fastened on top of an over-grown saw-horse, and a splint bottom chair, were the only other articles of furniture or adornment, save that sundry hieroglyphics and portraits were frescoed on the walls, by using the end of a tallow dip for a pencil or brush, and bringing out the figures in relief by the vigorous application of a black felt hat. New inscriptions and new pictures would from time to time appear, as some new genius in the school developed his talents.

In the rear of the school house ran a little brook, well stocked with striped dace, on whom the sporting boys tried their first experiments with a crooked pin attached to a linen thread, and baited with a grub.

It is hard to realize, that before there were half a dozen dwellings along the Mad River, this school house was filled to overflowing with strapping boys and girls from the surrounding hills. There were the Spencers, the Loomises, the Cooks, the Douglasses, the Harts, the Walters, Millers, Burtons, Osborns, Apleys, Butrixes, and Wrights, from Spencer street; the Sweets, Coes, Whitings, Hoskins, and Russells, from Coe street; the Chases, Holmeses, Elwells, DeWolfs, Westlakes, Phillipses, Lemleys, Munsons, and Davises, from the upper part of Lake street.

The butternut coats of the larger boys were all too small of girth to button round their bodies, and leather straps, from three to six inches long, with button holes at each end, were used to hold them together. High peaked, woolen caps of mitre shape, made of alternate perpendicular stripes of " white, red, and blue," or other fancy colors, were in general vogue for winter wear. Long leggins, of mixed sheep's wool, tied close to the cowskin shoes with tow-strings, were chiefly used instead of boot-legs to keep out the snow from the feet. The girls had winter dresses of cam-wood colored cloth, or red flannel, for winter wear, and calico or home-made gingham petticoats and short gowns for summer, with pockets, fastened outside, around the waist.

There were no puny children in those days. The big boys were bullies, and the small ones game-cocks. One strapping girl I remember who could flax out any boy in school. She was called " Bonaparte's wife." There was a big boy, Miles Munson by name, who was proud of his strength and prowess, and had curious ways of showing himself off to the smaller boys. One day he laid himself down on the descending ground between a large, half rotten saw-mill log and the brook, and told the boys they might roll the log over him, — not dreaming that the little imps could move it. They laid hold of the log with a will, and it yielded to their united strength. Before Miles could get out of the way it had flattened him down and gone over him, into the brook. Strange to say, it didn't kill him, nor break his bones. It was pitiable and laughable to see the poor fellow gather up his scattered senses and limbs, and straighten himself up; — and to hear him with mouth full of dirt, streaming eyes and flattened drooling nose, pour forth, with Yankee drawl, his emphatic " Gaul darn you, boys! what on airth did you du that for?"

Snow-balling was a science in those days; and so was sliding down the hill above the school house. A dozen boys would come down on their sleds at locomotive speed. Another dozen would form a gauntlet near the foot of the hill, with each a pole to place before the sled runners, and overturn the rider. The boy who could run the whole gauntlet, right side up, was a trump. One of the indoor games was gambling for pins. Two boys would each place a pin parallel to that of his opponent on the crown of a hat. One would strike the side of the hat with his hand so as to jostle the pins, and then the other would follow, until one of them had thrown one of the pins across the other, when the two became his, and then a new stake commenced. The most successful gamblers in this line were distinguished by the long rows of pins displayed on their coats sleeves. This game gave rise to a brisk manufacture of pin-boxes, by pealing the bark from an elder stick, punching out the pith, fitting a plug into one end and a stopper at the other. The price of these varied from two to six pins, according to quality.

The school-masters and "school-marms" of this model school come up before us. The good Deacon Lorrin Loomis, lately gone to heaven at nearly a hundred years old, first appears on the vista of memory, — a kind, loving, cheerful-spirited man, — who impressed his Christ-like character on more of the children of Winchester than any other, — priest or layman. Then comes the hated vision of Doctor Pratt, — a tyrant of the hyena sort, who brought in his whips from the woods by the armful, — ran them through the hot embers to make them tough and supple, and was never without one in his hand. His amateur diversion was to switch the small boys into a bolt upright position on their slabs, and to wallop the bigger ones with or without cause, until his savage nature was soothed into complacency. The classes were marshaled for reading or spelling with the whip. Its hissing sound, as he swung it around his head at the door of the school house, was the signal to come in from play; and woe to the urchin who was among the last half of the in-gathering procession. A worthy resident of the Western Reserve, who went from this seminary with his parents to the West, remarked in mature life that he was at peace with all the world except Dr. Pratt; and that if he should ever see him again he would thrash him if he died for it.

Next come the two Haydens, Seth and Moses. Seth was a mild, kind-hearted man, who ruled by love more effectually than any tyrant of the rod could do by force.

Moses was a crack teacher, a good disciplinarian, and skilled in showing off his school to the visitors at the end of his term. We remember on one of these occasions his calling up his youngest geography class, remarking that time would only permit of his asking each of them a single question. He then began with the question, "What is geography?" to the first; to the second, "How is the earth divided?"; to the third, "What portion of the earth is land?" and so on. The third question had been previously given out to our sister, and she had learned to answer, "About three fists (fifths) of the whole," and this was her whole stock of geographical knowledge. Each of the other members of the class had been drilled in the same way to one question and answer, and knew nothing more of the science. The pitiful farce worked to a charm, and added a new laurel to the brow of the pedagogue.

Giles Russell was a flippant, sarcastic teacher, who could work considerable learning into a blockhead in the course of a winter.

Our first teacher in this school wore a female garb, but possessed masculine powers. Miss Roxy F—— was the name of this semiramis. She was large-boned, corpulent, loud and sharp-voiced, choleric, and at the meridian of single blessedness. She had a ferule that she carried in her capacious pocket, something like a watchman's billy, only that it had a round head two and a half inches in diameter, beveled down on one side, so as to make a flat surface, fitting the palm of an urchin's hand. This was freely applied, *secundum artem*, to the hands of delinquents within her reach, and thrown with unerring aim at any disorderly boy in a distant part of the room, who brought it back for application to his own hand. Miss F. had her predilections and antipathies. She hated the itch, and rapturously kissed the children that came to school with a strong smell of brimstone.

In striking contrast with this virago was Miss Sally Sherman, afterwards wife of Joseph Miller, Esq., a young lady of exquisite refinement and cultivated intellect, adorned with grace of manner and a loving heart. No unkind word ever escaped her lips. If she ever used a ferule, it was so mildly applied as to give no pain, and to escape remembrance. The tired and sleepy child on the hemlock slabs, instead of having its ears cuffed for falling to the floor in pure exhaustion, was gently laid on a blanket in the center of the room and allowed to sleep away its fatigue and petulance. It was not uncommon for half a dozen of these wearied sleepers to occupy the blanket during a warm afternoon.

Other teachers, male and female, might be named—some of them loveable and some of them hateful—but the specimens given must suffice. The punishments of those days inflicted on such of the children as inherited dispositions too sprightly for puritanic decorum were various. The birch was in use to some extent, but the beech was the more favored implement, as being tougher and more durable. The "dungeon" in the old school house was a dark, unwholesome cell, unventilated and unlighted. It was the imaginary habitation of she bears, snakes, and vermin, and cruel was the shock to children of sensitive natures consigned to its darkness. Various amateur punishments would be introduced by different teachers. One master would make the delinquents crawl under and between the cross legs of the school table; another would fasten a split stick to their tongues; another would make them stoop over with unbent knees, and place the forefinger of the right hand on a nail head in the floor.

The saturnian "school marms" were generally powerful with the ferule, and effective in the cuffing of ears, and some of them in pulling hair. Fine sewing, working muslin, and especially making "samplers" of block lettering, were an important part of the teaching of the female scholars in the summer months.

The catechism tasks, and the reading of the New Testament as a school book, in all the drawling tones and halting utterances of unsophisticated Yankee children, were ill calculated to impress the mind with a favorable view of Calvinistic doctrines, or of the divine teachings of the Saviour.

1803.

SAMUEL and LUTHER HOADLEY (brothers) from Waterbury, became residents of the town during this or the preceding year. The Doolittle mill had been swept away previously, and they became the owners of the dam, water privilege, and the land adjoining on both sides of the river. They built a saw mill on the old corn mill site, and soon after erected a new grist mill on the east side of the stream, on the site of the brick clock factory, recently burned down. They also built for the town the wooden bridge crossing the chasm where the stone arched-bridge has been, within a few years, erected. The original bridge crossed the river above the dam, nearly opposite the Rollin L. Beecher's late residence, and was abandoned on the erection of the wooden bridge before mentioned. About 1807 they erected a small wooden clock factory adjoining the east wing of the bridge on the south side of the road, in which they did a large and prosperous business in connection with Riley Whiting, who married their sister.

They were for ten years prominent and highly esteemed business men, and by their ingenuity and enterprise contributed largely to the growth and prosperity of the village.*

SAMUEL HOADLEY retired from business on his appointment as Major of Volunteers in the war of 1812. He was promoted to a colonelcy, and served through the war, mainly at New London. He continued his residence in Winsted until his removal to Ohio about 1825. He built and resided in the two story house west of and nearly opposite the stone bridge. He married, about 1801, Content Barnes, from near New Haven.

CHILDREN.

I. SARAH ANNA, b. January 1, 1802; m. Bennett Blakeslee of Medina, Ohio.
II. AMELIA, b. October 25, 1803; m. Dr. Deming of Ashland, O., and (2d) — Du Bois.
III. HARRIET, b. August 6, 1805; d. November 27, 1817.
IV. SOPHRONIA, b. May 2, 1808; m. Wm. P. McCrary of Paris, O.
V. SAMUEL BUCKLEY, b. April 20, 1810; m. Jemima Hickox.
VI. JULIETTE, b. March 3, 1812.
VII. CHARLOTTE, b.
VIII. LUCIUS, (twin).
IX. LUCIEN, (twin).
X. CHARLES, died when six years old.

LUTHER HOADLEY, son of Lemuel and brother of Samuel, built and lived in the first house south of the Wallen's Hill road, near the clock factory. In 1813 he went to New London as captain of drafted militia, and died there Sept. 8, 1813, aged 31 years. He married, in 1810, Sophia Dexter of Windsor.

CHILDREN.

I. SOPHIA DEXTER, b. Feb. 1, 1812; m., at Harwinton, —— Cone, of Peoria, Ill.
II. LUTHER J., b. March 6, 1814; after his father's decease, m. (1st), at Harwinton, Jane, daughter of Truman Kellogg, Esq.; (2d), Hannah Wood; (3d), Hannah Abby Wood. He settled at Brownsville, Nebraska.

---

* They were sons of Lemuel and Urania (Mallory) Hoadley, whose children were as follows:—

I. MARY, m. Asahel Osborne, Esq., of Columbia, Lorrain Co., O.
II. DAVID, the builder of many churches in Conn.
III. SALLY, m. Zaphni Potter of Columbia, O.
IV. CALVIN, settled and died in Columbia, O.
V. SAMUEL, see text.
VI. LUTHER, see text.
VII. URANIA, b. May 5, 1788; m. February 9, 1806, Riley Whiting. She m. (2d) December —, 1841, Erasmus Darwin Calloway.
VIII. LEMUEL, d. Olmsted, or Concord, Ohio.
IX. MARSHALL, was drowned when about twelve years old.

HAWLEY OAKLEY, lived on West branch of Spencer street above Nelson Beardsley's from this date for five or six years, and then moved to Canaan, Conn. He married Lydia, daughter of Luke Hart, and had

CHILDREN.

I. ALVA, b. Hartland, Oct. 13, 1799, now a resident of Winsted, and WILLIAM, now of Norfolk, and may have had other children.

ALVA OAKLEY, son of Hawley above named, came from Canaan to Winsted, not far from 1830, and has since resided in the Hoskin homestead on Coe street. He married, May 25, 1826, Roxana, daughter of Theodore Hoskin.

CHILDREN.

I. HENRY, b. Canaan, April 13, 1827; d. W., Oct. 27, 1846.
II. HELEN, b. C., April 13, 1827; m. Thomas Atkins.
III. JUNIUS SILAS, b. C., June 12, 1829; m. Mary A. Atkins.
IV. MARIA ELIZABETH, b. C., April 23, 1831; d. W., Sept. 6, 1834.
V. JENNETT ALMA, b. W., Jan. 18, 1833; d.
VI. SARAH ELIZABETH, b. Jan. 1, 1839.

1804.

ERASTUS BURR, son of Jehiel and Mabel, appears on the list of this year. He learned the scythe maker's trade of Jenkins & Boyd, and in 1806 bought their original scythe works of Mr. Jenkins, which he operated until 1810 when he sold out to Thos. R. Bull, and soon after moved to Western New York. He married, about 1806, Polly, daughter of Judah West of Winchester.

ROSWELL BURR, younger brother of Erastus above, lived on the east side of North Main street, half a mile north of the Woodruff tannery until 1833, when he moved to Ohio. He married ——— Nancy, daughter of Judah West, and had a son DAVID, who married a daughter of Reuben Rowley, and lived in the same house with his father until his removal to Ohio in 1846; and had other children, Luther, Halsey, and Roswell.

HALSEY BURR, younger brother of Erastus and Roswell, learned scythe making of Benjamin Jenkins, and in 1814 built a scythe shop on North Main street, which he operated until about 1853, when he sold his shop to B. & E. Woodall, who erected the long factory building now standing on the premises. He lived on the West side of the road, opposite the shop, until his death, Jan. 15, 1861. He married Lucy, daughter of Oliver White, Sen., by whom he had

CHILDREN.

I. ELIZA, b. July 19, 1819.
II. DUNCY, b. April 10, 1821; d. May 26, 1848.
III. MATILDA, b. July 28, 1822.

IV. JEHIEL,	b. Aug. 24, 1824.
V. LUCY,	b. July 5, 1827.
VI. MARY,	b. June 13, 1829.
VII. JANE A.,	b. June 27, 1831.
VIII. NANCY,	b. July 7, 1833.
IX. GEORGE H.,	b. Aug. 7, 1837.
X. ABBY M.,	b. June 2, 1839.
XI. CARLOS,	b. Dec. 29, 1841.

LUKE HAYDEN, from Torringford, this year bought the John Wright farm, on the Old Country road near Rowley pond, on which he lived until his removal to Hartland, in 1814.

1805.

REUBEN BALDWIN, from Derby, a joiner, came to Winsted this or the preceding year, and superintended the finishing of the meeting-house in the east village. He continued his residence in the Society until his death, Dec. 15, 1855, at the age of 71. His residence was in the one-and-a-half-story house near the Lake outlet. He married, July 13, 1807, Nancy, daughter of Nathan Wheeler. She died Feb. 7, 1854, aged 65.

CHILDREN.

I. EMELINE, b. Sept. 20, 1808; m. Sept. 27, 1832, William F. Hatch; d. Sept. 22, 1870.
II. LYMAN, b. March 12, 1810; m., Nov. 30, 1837, Rebecca C. Mather, of Middletown: CHILD: Sarah Gray, b. July 16, 1852.
III. MATILDA, b. Feb. 15, 1816; m., Dec. 3, 1839, Miles Smith, who d. July 27, 1851. CHILD: Martha Benham, b. May, 1848; m., April 23, 1872, King T. Sheldon.

ELIAB BUNNELL this year bought the lot east of the Park, on which the James T. Norton house now stands. In company with Reuben Baldwin, he built thereon, for a work shop, the house since owned by Chester Soper, and afterwards removed to the south side of Main street, east of Hiram Perkins, in which they made patent washing machines until about 1810, when Mr. Bunnell removed to Vernon, N. Y.

ANDREW WALTER, son of John, of Winchester, this year returned from Vermont, and spent his remaining life in the town. He was born Dec. 5, 1779; married, ———— —, ————, Abigail, daughter of Samuel Westlake, of W., and had several children, of whom Charlotte, the oldest, married Sylvester Hart, of W.

1806.

REV. JAMES BEACH was ordained pastor of the First Congregational Church on the first of January of this year. He was a native of the town, but resided from infancy to early manhood in Torrington. He was graduated with honor at Williams College, studied divinity with Rev.

Asahel Hooker, D. D., of Goshen, and after a brief candidacy, was called to and settled over this church on a cash salary of $350 a year, with an advance of funds to purchase a dwelling, repayable in yearly installments. No record is found of the ordaining exercises.

He was sound, dignified, and conservative; faithful in his parochial duties, — especially in his pastoral visits and his supervision of the schools. The faithfulness of his ministry was attested by repeated revivals and the exemplary lives of most of the converts. He was dismissed from his charge, at his own request, January 26, 1842, but continued his residence until his death on the 10th day of June, 1850, at the age of 70 years.

His character and standing in the ministry is happily portrayed in the following sketch by Rev. Doctor Eldridge of Norfolk.

"Rev. Mr. Beach had been settled in the ministry at Winsted many years when I came to reside in Norfolk. I immediately formed his acquaintance, and soon came to look to him with filial affection and confidence, feelings that I continued to entertain towards him to the end of his life.

"Mr. Beach was endowed with strong intellectual powers. His bias was more towards the practical than the merely speculative. This tendency, combined with a calm temperament, fitted him to be a wise counselor, and a most useful member of our ecclesiastical associations.

"His disposition was social and genial. He was a pleasant man to meet. He had a considerate regard for his ministerial brethren, in respect to their feelings and reputations; rejoiced in their success and in their usefulness. I never saw him out of temper, never heard him utter a harsh or censorious remark; he never thrust himself forward, was more disposed to stand back and make room for others.

"I heard him preach but a few times. His sermons were full of truth, clearly and plainly expressed. In their delivery he was earnest, but never impassioned; — perhaps more of emotion would have improved them. His prayers in public, especially those on special occasions, such as ordinations and the like, were very remarkable for their ease, their felicitous adaptation in all respects to the circumstances of the case, and the happy introduction of scriptural quotations; and at the same time remarkable for their exemption from everything of the nature of effort at display, and for their simple tone and humble earnestness.

"My recollection of Father Beach, as I used to call him, are very dear to me. I loved him in life, and lamented him in death, and feel that I owe it to his kindness and his encouragement and advice in no small degree, that I have so long remained where I am."

He married, Oct. 28, 1806, Hannah Clarissa Baldwin, born in Goshen,

Conn., March 10, 1784, daughter of Isaac and Lucy (Lewis) Baldwin. He died June 10, 1850; she died May 7, 1752.

CHILDREN.

I. LUCY BALDWIN,[2] b. Aug. 20, 1807; m. Dec. 16, 1830, Henry Hazen Hyde, b. in Catskill, N. Y., July 1, 1805, son of Wilkes and Sarah Hazen Hyde. She d. Feb. 7, 1846; and he m. (2d), Feb. 14, 1856, Sarah B. Shepard, of Boston.

CHILDREN.

1. James Beach,[3] b. Nov. 14, 1831; d. Jan. 8, 1850, while in College, an undergraduate.
2. Henry Baldwin,[3] b. Feb. 15, 1834; m. March 20, 1864, Annie Fitch, of New York; is Vice-President of the Equitable Life Assurance Company of New York; has children: 1. Annie Baldwin,[4] b. Jan. 15, 1865; d. Sept. 2, 1865. 2. Mary Baldwin,[4] b. Nov. 9, 1867.
3. Mary,[3] b. Sept. 4, 1839; d. Jan. 4, 1840.
4. Lucy Baldwin,[3] b. Aug. 20, 1841.

II. HANNAH CLARISSA,[2] b. March 20, 1809; d. Oct. 26, 1815.

III. MARY,[2] b. Dec. 16, 1814; m. Caleb J. Camp. (Their children noted in connection with the family record of Samuel Camp.)

CAPTAIN EZEKIEL WOODFORD, from Avon or Bloomfield, this year purchased of John Sweet the house and land at the corner of Main and Coe streets, and there resided during his remaining life. During most of this period he kept a tavern, and managed a saw-mill nearly opposite his house. He died May 10, 1820, aged 71; his wife, Anne (Bishop), died December 23, 1831, aged 77.

CHILDREN.

I. LUCY, m. Wadsworth of West Hartford.
II. ERASTUS, late of Winsted.
III. JEREMIAH, late of Bloomfield.
IV. NANCY,
V. ROMANTA,
VI. EZEKIEL, late of Winsted, b. June 30, 1790.
VII. MARY,
VIII. HARRIET, m. Shepard.
IX. LESTER, b. June 19, 1797.

ERASTUS WOODFORD, son of Ezekiel, came to Winsted soon after his father, and owned and occupied the Green Woods Hotel property, on the Green Woods turnpike, near Colebrook line, until soon after 1820, when he removed to his father's late homestead, where he resided until his death, April 20, 1855, at the age of 74. He was Town Clerk from October 1826, to October 1829, and filled other town offices from time to time. He married, November 14, 1805, Ruth Barber, born October 27, 1780, daughter of Benjamin and Ruth (Bolles) Barber.

CHILDREN.

I. BENJAMIN BARBER, b. Jan. 22, 1807.
II. ERASTUS STERLING, b. Sept. 20, 1808.
III. JULIA ANN, b. Feb. 14, 1811; m. Willard S. Wetmore.
IV. LUCIUS JONAH, b. May 16, 1814.
V. CORDELIA RUTHY, b. June 2, 1818; m. James H. Tuttle.

ROMANTA WOODFORD, son of Ezekiel, came into the town a few years after his father, and built and occupied the house on Main street, next his father's homestead, carrying on the tinning business until his removal to Bennington, Greene County, New York, in 1818.

EZEKIEL WOODFORD, son of Ezekiel, sen., came into the town with his father in his minority. He bought his brother Romanta's Homestead in Dec., 1817, and there resided until his removal to Windsor in 1832. Returning to Winsted in 1857, he lived in the house on the north side of Hinsdale street, next east of the graded school house, until his death, August 14, 1859, at the age of 69. He was born June 30, 1790; m. Sept. 7, 1825, Roxana Lyman, b. June 18, 1797; died Dec. 26, 1871.

CHILDREN.

I. ANDREW D., b. June 15, 1826; d. Dec. 9, 1826.
II. GEORGE L., b. Dec. 29, 1827.
III. JOHN, b. March 4, 1831.

LESTER WOODFORD, youngest son of Capt. Ezekiel, came with his father to Winsted while a minor. In 1823, in company with N. Kinney, he bought the Elihu Rockwell farm on the Spencer Street road north of Amos Pierce, and resided there until his removal to the Russell homestead on the Coe street, now owned by Junius Gillett, where he afterwards resided until his removal to ——— in 1867. He married, Dec. 10, 1823, at W., Rosanna, daughter of Luke Case, late of Winchester, deceased.

CHILDREN.

I. LYMAN CASE, b. June 15, 1826, d. Feb. 10, 1835.
II. CAROLINE ELIZABETH, b. April 28, 1832, d. May 21, 1836.
III. CHARLES BISHOP, b. Feb. 10, 1837.
IV. MARIANNE, b. Oct. 16, 1839.
V. WILLIAM STERLING, b. Sept. 3, 1842.

BENJAMIN BARBER WOODFORD, oldest son of Erastus, lived in the Green Woods Hotel, his father's early residence, from his first marriage to about 1848, when he built a small brick house on High street, which he occupied until his removal to Derby about 1851. He now lives in Springfield, Mass. He married Polly Ann Hills, and has one daughter, Mary C., his only child.

ERASTUS STERLING WOODFORD, second son of Erastus, became a partner with Samuel W. Coe and Luman Hubbell, under the firm name of Coe, Hubbell & Co., about 1830, and continued with them in mercantile business until 1842, when he withdrew from the firm, and did business in his individual name until about 1849, when he went to California, whence he returned some three or four years later, and engaged for a few years in the manufacture of pins, and was subsequently engaged in Insurance business until his death. He was a man of refined literary culture and modest deportment, kind-hearted and public spirited; as a neighbor, obliging; as a citizen, liberal, not only in his contributions to public objects, but indefatigable in his personal labors for their advancement. He married, October 13, 1834, Huldah Coe, born April 6, 1809, daughter of Jonathan and Charlotte (Spencer) Coe. She died of consumption, April 18, 1859. He married (2d), June 26, 1862, Anna J. Coe, daughter of Asahel M. Coe. He died Sept. 26, 1870.

CHILDREN.
I. FRANK MUNRO, b. August 10, 1843; d. Dec. 25, 1848.
II. LOUISE HALE, b. June 6, 1863.

LUCIUS J. WOODFORD, third son of Erastus, lived as a farmer on the old Waterbury turnpike, near Colebrook line, from his first marriage, until his removal to the Daniel Tuttle farm on South street near Torringford line, in 1845. It is painful to refer to the long protracted and bitter controversy between him and his brother-in-law, resulting in the death of the latter by a gun-shot wound inflicted by the former, and the conviction of Mr. W. of murder in the first degree, for which he was sentenced to state prison for life by the superior court for Litchfield county in 1866. On his application for pardon in 1869, evidence was introduced before the legislative committee, which made a report recommending his pardon, and in accordance with the recommendation, he was by the Assembly pardoned and liberated. He married Catharine, daughter of Daniel G. Tuttle, by whom he had a son, George E., born ——— —, ———, who married, Nov. 27, 1864, Rosa A., daughter of John S. Fyler.

CHILD.
FRANK, b. Feb. —, 1868.

GEORGE WOODFORD, oldest son of Ezekiel,[2] learned the joiner's trade, and resides in this town. He married, Sept. 15, 1856, Helen J. Watson, born June 5, 1833.

CHILDREN.
I. ELLA LOUISA,   b. Jan. 18, 1859; d. Nov. 23, 1860.
II. CORA ISABELLE,   b. Jan. 19, 1862.
III. DE WITT CLINTON,   b. May 16, 1863.
IV. FREDERICK EZEKIEL, b. Oct. 5, 1865; d. Sept. 5, 1869.

S. S. Woodford

JOHN WOODFORD, second son of Ezekiel,[2] served his time as clerk in the mercantile firm of M. & C. J. Camp, and was received into and continues a partner in the concern. He married, May 24, 1860, Laura C., daughter of Hiram and Irene (Sanford) Burnham, born March 6, 1840.

CHILDREN.

I. ARTHUR BURNHAM, b. Oct. 7, 1861.
II. FRANK CLARKE, b. Nov. 24, 1867; d. Nov. 17, 1868.
III. FANNIE LOUISE, b. Jan. 18, 1870.

1806.

JOSEPH T. CUMMING this year came from Kinderhook, N. Y., and, in company with Benjamin Jenkins, went into trade in the store building on Main street, east village, now occupied by Theophilus Baird, and lived in the Ezra Baldwin house adjoining. In 1809 he moved to Otis, Mass., where for several years he kept a store and tavern.

SAMUEL ROWLEY, Jr., from Torrington, this year bought the homestead on the Old North road, adjoining Colebrook line, now occupied by his son Edwin Rowley, which he occupied until his death in 1854.

No record is found of his family. His widow died several years after him. They had

CHILDREN.

I. CALVIN, who died a resident of Illinois.
II. ELIZA, wife of Orrin Freeman of Winchester.
III. LUCIA J., of Colebrook, in 1858; d. in Illinois about 1869.
IV. EDWARD (twin).
V. EDWIN (twin), of Colebrook.
VI. MARY, (twin), m. — Miller.
VII. MARIAH (twin), m. Darwin Smith.

BENJAMIN JOHNSON, a cabinet maker, owned and lived in a house, now torn down, on the north side of West Lake street, nearly opposite the brick house built by John C. Stabell, from 1806 to 1812, when he moved to Ohio. Among other children he had one daughter, who married Dr. Steese of Massilon, O.

BEMSLEY CARPENTER, a singing master, is on the list of this year. From 1807 to 1816 he lived on the Jonathan Gilbert farm, on South street. He had one or more sons and two daughters — Eunice, now living (1872) here, and Emily, who married, August 24, 1834, James B. Phelps, from Leicester, Mass., and resided here until his death, March 25, 1857. She died in 1870.

ELIZUR HINSDALE came from Torrington in 1805. He this year

built, and afterwards occupied, the house on north side of Main street, now owned by Philo G. Sheldon, and a trip-hammer shop on the site of the Foundry & Machine Co.'s Works, in which he manufactured axes until his removal to Leroy, N. Y. His first wife, Olive, died October 28, 1816, aged 30. He married (2d) Mrs. — Everett of New Milford, in 1817.

CHILDREN.

I. MARY ELIZABETH, baptized June 7, 1807.
II. MORRIS.
III. CHARLOTTE MARIA, bap. October 16, 1814.
IV. A DAUGHTER, bap.   , 1819.

ELAM ROCKWELL appears on the list as a resident this year. From 1812 to 1814 he owned and lived on Mad River, near the Danbury schoolhouse.

DANIEL BURNHAM, from 1806 to 1814, owned and lived in a house nearly opposite and west of the stone bridge over Still River, and carried on a chair factory in the upper part of Hoadley's Mill. In 1826 he bought the Lemuel Clarke place on Wallen's Hill, which he occupied until his death, May 19, 1836, at the age of 54. His wife, Clarissa C., died February 22, 1855, aged 74. The names of their deceased children, as found in their burial lot, are—

I. DANIEL C., d. January 19, 1810, aged 6.
II. LUTHER, d. August 23, 1837, aged 26.
III. ERWIN, d. February 12, 1812, aged 19.
IV. HENRY S., d. July 5, 1818, aged 2.
V. SALLY A., m. December 9, 1830, Rufus Cleveland; d. April 17, 1854, aged 51. They had another daughter, CLARISSA, who m., September 13, 1831, Milo Hall of New Marlboro, Mass.

JOSEPH MILLER, Esq., attorney-at-law, commenced practice in Winsted this year. In 1807 he built the house on the north side of Main street, now owned by Mrs. Parke, in which he lived until his removal to Kalamazoo Co., Michigan.

He was a graduate of Williams' College, and of the Litchfield Law School; a man of literary tastes and sound legal acquirements; a kind, generous-hearted man, genial and upright; a good neighbor and citizen.

As a lawyer, he was able in argument, and honorable in practice. An inborn principle of uprightness unfitted him for resort to professional tricks, and his moral sense revolted at whatever was mean or treacherous. By the court and bar he was highly respected.

In 1834, with a view to the advancement of a large family, he removed to Richland, then a sparsely-settled region, where he devoted himself to clearing and cultivating his new homestead, and limitedly to law practice. His children grew up around him, prospered and respected.

While a resident of Winsted, he was chosen a delegate to the convention which framed the constitution of Connecticut in 1818, and was subsequently a representative of the town in the general assembly.

In Michigan he was also a delegate of his county to the constitutional convention of that state, and held other public offices.

He married, in June, 1808, Sarah Sherman, who died December 30, 1816; married (2d) October 1, 1817, Elizabeth, daughter of Eli Richards, who died July 17, 1858, aged 73.

CHILDREN BY FIRST WIFE.

I. SHERMAN, b. April 29, 1809; lost on the steamer Pulaski, on the Carolina coast, in June, 1838, unmarried.
II. SARAH ANN, b. January 28, 1811; m. Ira Peake; d. at Richland, Mich., January 27, 1859; left six children.
III. JANE, b. December 23, 1812; m. Doctor E. Stetson of Neponset, Ill.
IV. LYDIA M., b. Apr. 5, 1825; m. Enos Northrup, Richland, Mich.
V. JOSEPH, b. December 13, 1816, studied law with his father and was admitted to the bar of Kalamazoo county. Prosecuting attorney of said county for several years; U. S. Attorney, District of Michigan, from 1857 to 1861; an able and upright lawyer, a public-spirited and influential citizen. "Thoroughly identified, both by early associations and matured intimacy with the people among whom he lived, his genial nature, his ripened and unerring judgment, his high legal attainments, and above all, his pure and unsullied integrity and entire truthfulness of thought and expression, won the heart and secured the attachment of all who approached him." At the session of the U. S. District Court, holden at the time of his decease, the district attorney, in announcing his death, remarked, "The period of our deceased brother's connection with the officers and bar of this court is so recent that it is unnecessary to call to mind the ability, the courtesy, the clear intellect, and the warm heart which characterized him in the manifold relations of his official and professional life. He was endowed by nature with a mind of high order, and with sympathies unusually tender, which drew around him troops of friends, whom his talents enabled him to serve. A handsome competency, and the best practice of his section of the state, was the fruit of his diligence and ability." He m. Charlotte B. Brown.

CHILDREN BY SECOND WIFE.

VI. ELI RICHARDS, b. Oct. 12, 1818; m., 1st, Artheusa Mills; 2d, Harriet Cook.
VII. JAMES, b. Feb. 11, 1838; m. Mary Ada Smith.

1807.

BENJAMIN SKINNER, from East Hartford, a miller, came to Winsted this year and had charge of Rockwell's mill during his remaining life, and lived in the old lean-to house on Lake street. He was a man of most industrious habits and sincere piety, training and educating his large family, and discharging the duties of a Christian citizen with exemplary fidelity. He died Feb. 5, 1814, aged 48. His wife Nabby (Spencer) died Dec. 2, 1830, aged 59.

CHILDREN.

I. JAMES, b.   m.,   , Harriet Spencer, of Hartford; d. in Hartford. CHILDREN: 1. Edward, d. young; 2. James, m. Harriet Spencer.

II. BENJAMIN, b. 1794; m.   d. Sept., 1854, aged 60; has one son (Henry) now m. and living in Ohio.

III. ABIGAIL, b. 1797; d. unmd. June 16, 1842, aged 45.

IV. RHODA, b. d. unmd. Feb. 17, 1864.

V. HORACE, b. m. (1st) Charity Sage, (2d) Sarah Clark. CHILDREN BY FIRST WIFE: 1. Charles; 2. Horace; 3. Sarah. BY SECOND WIFE: 4. Abby; 5. Mary; 6. Belle; 7. Sarah Beach. Had seven children, all dead in 1872.

VI. HENRY.

VII. TIMOTHY PHELPS, b. Sept. 11, 1807; m., March —, 1840, Mary T. Jaques.

VIII. FREDERICK.

IX. LUCIUS, b. m., June 20, 1836, Lucy Champion; was drowned in Naugatuck river by railroad disaster at Plymouth, Conn. CHILDREN: 1. Ellen Maria, b. May 22, 1838; 2. Hannah Clark, b. May 10, 1840, d. ; 3. Lucius Spencer, b. March 28, 1843; 4. Frank Bevins, b. April 23, 1850.

CAPT. LEMUEL CLARKE, from Whately, Mass., came to Winsted this year, and bought the David Mills farm, afterwards owned by Daniel Burnham, on Wallen's Hill, on which he resided until 1826. He served as a sergeant in the Continental army in the Revolutionary War; was in the battle of Bunker Hill and other engagements, and retired from the service with a certificate of honorable discharge signed by Washington. He was born at ———, Mass., March 24, 1755; married at Sunderland, Mass., by Rev. Mr. Ashley, in October, 1779, to Kezia Hubbard: he died Aug. 22, 1840; she died March 22, 1843.

CHILDREN.

I. LUCIUS, b. July 14, 1780, d. March 9, 1782.

II. LEVI HUBBARD, b. Sept. 22, 1782; grad. Yale College, 1802; states attorney Middlesex Co., Conn., 1807-8; judge of Monroe Co. court, N. Y., in 1818; judge of seventh and tenth ward court, N. Y., in 1835; assistant editor of New York American, 1821-4, and New York Commercial Advertiser 1833-5. He m. Nov. —, 1809, Mary Ann, daughter of John Griswold, of Lyme, Conn., eldest son of Gov. Matthew Griswold. She d. Jan. 30, 1812, aged 26.

CHILD.

ELIZABETH BRAINARD, m. Sept. 14, 1844, Bushnell White, Esq., a lawyer of Cleveland, Ohio. CHILD; John Griswold White, b. August 10, 1845, at Cleveland, Ohio, and now practising law in that city.

III. CAROLINE,   b. Feb. 6, 1785, d. May 11, 1790.
IV. KEZIA,   b. Dec. 21, 1787; m., —— ——, William Moore, d. December, 1824.
V. LUCIUS,   b. Whately, Mass., Aug. 22, 1790, d. Dec. 28, 1863.
VI. ERASTUS LEMUEL, b. May 21, 1793; m.   ; d. Oct. 27, 1835.
VII. AUGUSTUS,   b. Sept. 8, 1796; d. Aug. 9, 1803.
VIII. GEORGE HUBBARD, b. Dec. 27, 1799; d. Feb. 22, 1852; m. (1)

LUCIUS CLARKE, son of Capt. Lemuel, married, Jan. —, 1819, Nancy, daughter of James Boyd, of Winchester.

CHILDREN.

I. CAROLINE,   b. Rochester, N. Y., May 4, 1822; d.   1822.
II. FREDERICK BOYD, b. Rochester, N. Y., Dec. 11, 1823; d.   1825.
III. LUCIUS HUBBARD, b. Winsted, Sept. 25, 1825; d. s. p.
IV. MARY MUNRO,   b. Winsted, May 4, 1827; m. H. B. Alvord.
V. THOMAS MONTAGUE, b. Winsted, Jan. 4, 1830; m., May 6, 1839, Julia Catlin, daughter of Dr. Orrin B. Freeman, Canton, Conn.; CHILDREN: 1. Carrie, d. in infancy; 2. Lucius F., d. in infancy; 3. Harry Catlin; 4. Caroline Freeman; 5. Boyd; 6. Munro, d. in infancy; 7. Thomas M., d. in infancy; 8. Fanny; 9. Jessie.
VI. EDWARD,   b. April 15, 1832; m. Susan Holmes.
VII. MARTHA,   b. Springfield, Mass., 1834; d.
VIII. SUSAN,   b. Feeding Hills, Mass., July 10, 1838; m. Rev. Malcolm McGregor Dana, minister of First Congregational Church, Norwich. CHILDREN: 1.

JASPER GRINNELL appears on this year's list. He built a house on the south side of the Wallen's Hill road, a little east of the ancient burying ground near the clock factory, in which he resided until his death, Feb. 24, 1832. Of his family we have no record except his marriage to Lucy Filley, Sept., 1811, and the grave stones of two

CHILDREN.

LYDIA E., d. March 28, 1809, aged 8.
EDWIN D., d. Feb. 10, 1814, aged 2.

DAVID TALLMADGE is on the assessment list of this and many succeeding years. He was not a land owner, and had no permanent residence. He raised a family of children, of whom the wife of Truman Scovill was one.

EBEN COE, son of Ensign Jonathan, married, Dec. 1, 1806, Eliza, daughter of Philemon Kirkum, and after living with his father, built and occupied the Jesse Williams house, on Spencer street, until near the date of his death. He died Sept. 10, 1813, aged 33, soon after which his widow and children moved to Ohio. (See COE Record.)

DEACON ELISHA SMITH is on the list of this year. He is noticed, and his family record given in connection with the record of his father, Capt. Zebina Smith.

1808.

Dr. Lyman Strong, from Southampton, Mass., this year began practice in Winsted as a physician, and in 1809 became principal of the grammar school or Academy then first opened there, and continued to teach and practice until his removal to Guilford in 1810, where he practiced until 1816, when he moved to Hartford and opened a boarding and day school for young ladies. In 1821 he moved to Beaufort, S. C., and officiated as president of a college in that place. Here he was licensed to preach by the Presbytery of Charleston, S. C., he having, before coming to Winsted, studied theology with Rev. Asahel Hooker, of Goshen. Returning to New England, he was, in 1825, settled in Hebron, Conn., and in 1830, at Colchester, Conn., where he spent his remaining life, and died Dec. 31, 1861, aged 80. He graduated at Williams' College in 1802, and was tutor for one year; studied medicine with Dr. Sumner, of Westfield, Mass. He was a man of fine appearance and address, and a teacher of high order — a Puritan of the Puritans; "an industrious, earnest, cheerful man, full of joy in his life of active service to God and mankind."

He was born Sept. 12, 1781; married, March 12, 1808, Clarissa Morse, daughter of Jacob Morse, of Westfield; she died at Colchester, Dec. 20, 1821, aged 49; and he married (2d) at Middletown, Conn., Widow Rhoda Matson, daughter of Israel Newton. She died Dec. 18, 1843, aged 58; and he married (3d) widow Olivia (Bridges) Brooks, b. March 24, 1808.

CHILDREN BY FIRST WIFE.

I. Clarissa Morse, b. at Winsted, June 24, 1809; m., May 4, 1837, Rev. Jason Atwater, a grad. of Yale in 1825, and pastor at Middlebury, Conn., where she d. Feb. 13, 1844.
II. Elizabeth, b. June 5, and d. June 8, 1812.
III. Lyman, b. in Guilford, Feb. 20, and d. July 21, 1815.

Hermon Munson, from Middlebury, Conn., is on the list of this, and several following years. He moved into Barkhamsted, after his marriage, and lived on the Green Woods turnpike, about half a mile east of the town line, until his death, April 7, 1854, aged 72. He married, Jan. 1, 1810, Polly, daughter of Benoni Bronson of Winchester. She died May 9, 1849, aged 60, and he married (2d), Mrs. Smith. He had

CHILDREN BY HIS FIRST WIFE.

I. Mary, who d. unmarried, Jan. 30, 1831, aged 21.
II. Sidney, of Minnesota.
III. Emerett, m., Nov. —, 1837, Henry E. Rockwell; d. Aug. 22, 1852, aged 36.
IV Abigail, of Minnesota.

1809.

Deacon James H. Alvord* moved from East Hampton, Conn., this year, and soon after built the house at the north corner of North Main street and the lane leading west of the center burying-ground, where he lived the remainder of his days a quiet, industrious, and exemplary life, devoted to the wise training and educating of a large family, and the upbuilding of the Church, of which he was an office bearer from 1836 to his death. He was born in Chatham, Conn., Aug. 8, 1781; married Oct. 11, 1804, Lucy Cook, born Aug. 7, 1784. He died July 29, 1868. She died Sept. 11, 1850.

CHILDREN.

I. Clarissa Pitkin, b. Aug. 7, 1805; resides in Winsted.
II. John Watson, b. April 18, 1807; began life as a merchant's clerk in Hartford, Ct., in 1828, and during the next year becoming convinced that he must preach the gospel, declined an offer of partnership, and in 1830 began his preparation, studying at Oneida Institute, Lane Seminary, and Oberlin, where he graduated in 1836, and was ordained the same year. He preached one year at Maumee City, O., and since that has preached at Barkhamsted, and Stamford, Conn., and at South Boston, Mass.; has been District Secretary of American Tract Society, Boston; Inspector of Schools and Finances for the Freedmen, under Maj. Gen. Howard; and since 1869, Pres. of the Freedmen's Savings Bank and Trust Company at Washington, where he now resides.

He m. June 3, 1845, Myrtilla Mead Peck, b. Greenwich, Conn., Oct. 11, 1819, daughter of Obadiah and Lisette (Mead) Peck.

CHILDREN.

1. Mary Anna, b. Granville, Ct., July 21, 1846; d. Boston, Mass. Aug. 18, 1847.
2. Julia Mead, b. Boston, Aug. 8, 1847; m. in Washington, D. C., Dec. 15, 1870, John L. Cole, and has a son, Dorr Edward, b. Dec. 29, 1871.

---

*His father, Ruel Alvord, son of Seth and Elizabeth (Spencer) Alvord, was cousin to Deacon Eliphaz Alvord, who has already been noticed. He married, Nov. 15, 1774, Hannah Hall. He settled in Chatham, Conn., where he died, March 27, 1810, in his 60th year. She died, Aug. 3, 1830, aged 77 years.

CHILDREN.

I. John, b. Chatham, Oct. 14, 1775; d. at sea, Nov. 11, 1800.
II. Sibyl, b. " May 30, 1777; m. Parmenas Watson.
III. Mary, b. " March 14, 1779; m. March 14, 1802, Elisha Rowley, b. C., March 14, 1780; they settled in Winchester in 1805.
IV. James Hall, b. Chatham, Aug. 8, 1781.
V. Lucy, b. Durham, Conn., May 14, 1785; m. Sept. 30, 1806, Chauncey Brooks; settled in Winchester, where she d. Sept. 1, 1831.
VI. Esther, b. Chatham, July 18, 1789; d. Aug. 28, 1835, unmarried.
VII. Jabez, b. " Sept. 27, 1792; d. Feb. 28, 1828, "
VIII. Hannah, b. " March 1, 1795; d. Aug. 17, 1832, "

  3. Charles Stewart, b. Boston, March 3, 1849; d. Boston, Jan. 3, 1853.
  4 John Watson, b. Boston, Nov. 20, 1852; d. Greenwich, Conn., May 8, 1853.
  5. George Lewis, b. Groton, Mass., Aug. 2, 1854; d. Groton, Oct. 21, 1855.
  6. Samuel, b. Newton Centre, Mass., Feb. 23, 1857.
  7. James Hall, b. Newton Centre, Mass., April 23, 1858; d. Newton Centre, March 19, 1861.
  8. John Watson, b. Newton Centre, Jan. 25, 1861.
III. MARY COOK, b. W., Feb. 26, 1809; d. Feb. 12, 1830.
IV. SUSAN B., b. Feb. 12, 1811; m. May 30, 1838, Asahel M. Rice, of W., has one daughter, Harriet M., b. March 24, 1848.
V. RICHARD, b. March 8, 1813; d. Dec. 1, 1818.
VI. CATHARINE, b. Feb. 12, 1815.
VII. JAMES, b. " 10, 1817; d. March 17, 1820.
VIII. CHARLES, b. Aug. 16, 1819; m. June 5, 1844, his cousin, Melissa Watson, b. Jan. 4, 1818, daughter of Parmenas and Sibyl (Alvord) Watson; has

CHILDREN.

  1. Lucy Cook, b. June 5, 1846.
  2. Theodore Watson, b. April 11, 1848.
  3. Clara Melissa, b. July 25, 1850.
  4. Jabez, b. " 15, 1858.
IX. AMANDA MALVINA, b. Aug. 20, 1821; m. Aug. 31, 1841, John Hinsdale.
X. JAMES RICHARD, b. Oct. 7, 1823; m. Dec. 3, 1849, Mary Eliza Landon, b. in Poultney, Vt., Sept. 12, 1824, daughter of Rev. Seymour and Phebe (Thompson) Landon.

CHILDREN.

  1. Louise Landon, b. Sept. 5, 1852; d. Jan. 4, 1870.
  2. Charles, b. March 20, 1854.
  3. Seymour Landon, b. Aug. 6, 1856.
  4. Elliot Beardsley, b. Aug. 2, 1859; d. Aug. 19, 1859.
  5. James Richard, b. April 3, 1860; d. 1865.
XI. GEORGE, b. Aug. 23, 1825; m. June 1, 1863, Elizabeth Peck Hubbard, b. Sunderland, Mass., May 19, 1830, daughter of Ashley and Betsey (Dole) Hubbard; has been clerk in the Navy Department, Washington; Cashier of Hurlbut Bank, West Winsted; is now in the printing business in Winsted; no children.
XII. JABEZ, b. Feb. 3, 1828; a machinist; a soldier of the w of 1861, and Postmaster of Winsted; unmarried.

1810.

  JESSE BYINGTON came to Winsted this year, and in the following year built the Evert Bevins house, on the west side of North Main street. He also built a nail factory on the water privilege of the Winsted Manufacturing Company (long since burned down), in which the nails were cut, and another shop, opposite his house, where the nails were headed by hand-blows. He employed a large number of hands, and did a prosperous business until about 1815, when he abandoned the business. He died Sept. 12, 1831, aged 46. He married about the time of his coming to Winsted, and had two daughters, JANE and FINETTE. Jane was of Torrington, and Finette of New Haven, in 1839.

WILLIAM GOUCHER, an iron refiner, lived in Winsted from 1809 to about 1825. He had among other children, Samuel, who went to Enfield and died there; Polly, married, Jan. 13, 1833, Legrand Hubbell, who was killed in October, 1838, by the bursting of a grindstone, aged 32, and Hiram, now (1872) living, a bachelor, in Winsted. His wife died December, 1833.

JOSHUA HEWITT came to Winsted in his boyhood, and came of age this year. He worked as a shoemaker a few years, and then became an iron refiner, which trade he pursued until about 1835. He built the house on Spencer street, at the foot of Cobble Hill, in 1850, in which he afterwards lived until his death, April 13, 1864, aged 73. He married, April 24, 1808, Polly Williams. She died April 14, 1842, aged 55.

CHILDREN.

I. SALLY, b. July 8, 1809; m. Squire Sackett.
II. HOMER, b. January 14, 1811; d. November 2, 1831, unmarried.
III. MARIA, b. ; m. August 23, 1837, Francis Brown. Child: Sarah, b. ; m. Charles Perry.
IV. ABIGAIL, b. ; m. Daniel Brown.
V. LUCIA, b. ; m. August 16, 1838, Justin Hodge, Captain of Volunteers in Mexican War, and Colonel of Volunteers in War of the Rebellion. Child: Thadeus Kosciusko.
VI. HARRIET, d. January 24, 1821, aged one year.
VII. JULIA ANN, d. December 3, 1821, aged one year.
VIII. HENRY HIRAM, b. September 24, 1822; m. (1st), October 24, 1848, Marietta T. Coe. She d. August 14, 1851. Child: Marietta, b. Aug. 12, 1851; (2d), October 12, 1852, Amanda M. Coe. Child: Henrietta, b. December 14, 1853.
IX. SYLVIA, b. May —, 1824; m. August 5, 1844, John B. Bishop.
X. EDWARD (twin), b. May —, 1826; m. Laura Andrews; m. (2d), Mary Wheeler.
XI. EDWIN (twin), b. May —, 1826; m. Charlotte Wilbraham.
XII. CHARLOTTE, d. January 31, 1830.

ISAAC JOHNSON from Rhode Island, lived in an old barrack house at the north corner of North Main and Hinsdale streets. He died November 6, 1829, aged 50, leaving sons and daughters — among them —

ISAAC, now of Barkhamsted.
The wife of Jonas Le Roy of W.
LODOISKA, wife of — Scovill of Litchfield.

Selden Mitchell, son of Joseph, is on the list of this year. He built, and occupied until after 1820, the house on the south side of Main street, now (1872) owned by Sheldon Kinney, Sen., and had a wagon maker's shop in the rear basement. He moved to Colebrook River about 1821. No record of his family is found.

William Murray, son of David, an early settler, lived in Winchester from this year to about 1840. He married Ann Hewitt, sister of Joshua, was by trade a shoemaker, and afterwards a carpenter. No record is found of his family.

John Rohrabacher, an iron refiner, came from Ancram, N. Y., this year, and lived on the north side of Lake street, immediately above the Connecticut Western Railroad bridge, until his removal to Cortland Co., N. Y., about 1820.

CHILDREN.

I. Electa, m. Andrew Brusie of Virgil, N. Y.
II. Betsey, d. August 10, 1817, aged 13.
III. Isaac, and others.

John Storer, a joiner, married, January 7, 1808, Eunice, daughter of John Church, and had by her,

CHILDREN.

I. Simeon, b. September 30, 1808, now an inhabitant of this town.
II. David, b. December 3, 1810.
III. Eliza, b. November 4, 1812; m. July 3, 1834, Samuel D. Sheldon.

About 1820 Mr. Storer joined the Shaker community, at Tyringham, Mass.

Riley Whiting, son of Christopher, an early settler of the town, this or the preceding year became a resident of Winsted. He is noticed and his family record given in connection with his father, under date of 1799.

1801 to 1821.

We compile a summary of buildings erected, roads opened, and institutions established within the limits of the borough of Winsted from 1800 to 1811, as follows :—

1800.

The original store of Bissell Hinsdale, on the site of Camp's brick block, enlarged about 1812, and removed about 1848. It now constitutes two tenant houses on the west side of Main street, next south of Monroe street bridge.

1802.

The dwelling house of Deacon Alpha Rockwell was built on the site of the Beardsley house, and was taken down and re-erected on the east corner of High and Union streets, in 1849, by John Westlake. The scythe establishment of James Boyd, near the corner of Lake and Meadow streets, was erected in 1802, rebuilt about 1833, and in 1853 was converted by Louis R. Boyd into a manufactory of planters' hoes.

1803.

The dwelling house on Main street, now owned and occupied by John T. Rockwell, was erected by James Boyd, and occupied by him and his widow until 1853.

The Woodford homestead, at the corner of Main and Coe streets, was erected by John Sweet.

The Hosea Hinsdale homestead, at the corner of Main and Spencer streets, erected by James Shepard.

The original tavern building, on the site of Hicks' Hotel, east corner of Main and North Main streets, erected by Benjamin Jenkins.

Merritt Bull erected a scythe establishment on the pond stream adjoining Meadow street bridge, which was rebuilt by Rockwell and Hinsdale about 1832, and has recently been purchased by the Winsted Hoe Company for plating of hoes and forging chisels.

Hosea Hinsdale and James Shepard erected a tannery on the site of the fish pond recently excavated by John T. Rockwell, near the parting of Main and Spencer streets. The original building ceased to be used as a tannery about 1851, and was torn down about 1870.

The gambrel-roofed store on Main street, occupied by T. Baird, near the corner of North Main street, was erected by Philemon Kirkum in 1804.

1805.

Joseph Mitchell built a one-story house on or near the site of Joseph H. Norton's dwelling, on the north side of Main street, which was torn down by Henry B. Crowe about 1851.

In the same year, the two-story house on the west side of North Main street, nearly opposite the west wing of the clock factory dam, was built by Samuel Hoadley.

1806.

The house on the north side of Main street, now owned and occupied by Ezra Baldwin, was built by Joseph T. Cummings and Benjamin Jenkins.

1807.

Philemon Kirkum built a small house on the east side of Main street, which was torn down by Dr. James Welch to make room for his present residence.

The late homestead of Reuben Cook, on North Main street, was built by Benjamin Hoadley.

The original west village district school was burned down at the close of 1806, and a new one was erected this year on the same ground, and with slight improvement on its predecessor. It continued in use as a school house until about 1840, when it was removed to make room for the long and unsightly building erected in its place, which has recently been superseded by the new graded school edifice on Hinsdale street.

James Boyd and Horace Higley erected a saw mill on the site of the New England Pin Company's Works, near the Naugatuck Depot, and also the bridge communicating therewith from Main street; and in 1808 they erected an iron forge on Main street, directly opposite the Clarke house. It was kept up as long as the manufacture of refined bar iron continued remunerative, and was sold in 1845 to parties who erected the Pin Company's building.

1808.

The first Methodist meeting house was built on the east side of Spencer street, immediately north of the school house, and, within a few years, has been converted into a double tenement house. Prior to the building of this house, the Methodists had worshiped in the adjoining school-house. Their number, though limited, included a highly respectable class of our inhabitants.

In those days, the Methodist and Congregational religionists had little more sympathy or intercourse with each other than the old Jews and Samaritans. The circuit-rider came on his rounds and declaimed against steeple meeting houses, pitch-pipe singing, and the doctrine of Election. The membership kneeled on the floor in prayer, and gave vent to their devotional feelings by the loud "Amens," or the Gloria Patri. The women eschewed ribbons, curled hair, and gay dresses. The old men — and some of the young ones — wore straight-bodied coats; — and both sexes wore a vinegar aspect.

The "Presbyterians," — as they were termed, — on the other hand looked on the Methodists as interlopers and fanatics, who had come in to disturb the peace of the Standing Order as by Saybrook platform established. The Methodists were all Democrats; the Standing Order were mainly high-toned Federalists of Pharisaical tendencies. The two had apparently no mutual sympathies, and never inter-communed with each other.

Time and circumstances have worn away the prejudices and softened the asperities of the two denominations. Intermarriages have led to mutual forbearance. The temperance movement brought the best men and women of the two orders into co-operation; and the anti-slavery movement, fearlessly advocated by the living Christianity of both churches, was the death blow to sectarianism.

1809.

Joseph Miller, Esq., erected his dwelling-house on the northerly side of Main street, now owned and occupied by Mrs. Parke; and Solomon Rockwell and Brothers erected an iron store on the lot next north of the Beardsley House, which was torn down about 1860.

The Rockwell Brothers erected an iron forge on the site of the table cutlery works on the lake stream, immediately below Hulbert's iron works. It was discontinued as a forge about 1850, and converted into a cutlery establishment by the Eagle Cutlery Company.

1811.

Reuben Cook, of Winsted, Russell Bunn & Co., and Charles Seymour, of Hartford, erected an iron forge on Still River, below the Winsted Manufacturing Company's Scythe Works, which subsequently became the sole property of Mr. Cook, and was carried on until the organization of the Cook Axle Company about 1850, where the present brick factory on the premises was erected.

After the burning down of the west village district school-house in 1807, there was a general desire to erect a new building of sufficient capacity for a graded school, to meet the growing wants of the community. Plans were proposed and debated;—jealousies arose, and the project fell through. The house erected was contracted and shabby. The new villagers, with limited outside aid, set about providing better facilities for the education of their growing families, and this year erected the building on Main street, next north of Forbes' furniture establishment, for a grammar school. It was arranged with an upper room for the advanced scholars and a lower room for the younger class; and was opened by Doctor Lyman Strong as principal, and his sister-in-law, Miss Eliza Morse, as assistant teacher. The enterprise was a decided success. The teachers not only attracted the scholars of the village but numbers from adjoining towns. Doctor Strong removed to Guilford in 1810, and was succeeded by Curtis Warner, a graduate of Yale, who continued his faithful and acceptable labors until his sickness, which terminated in death in 1813. He was succeeded by our late fellow citizen, Nathaniel B. Gaylord, who taught one or two seasons with eminent success.

Other teachers followed, of varied qualifications, until the children of most of the projectors of the school had completed their academic education, and several of them had entered college. From 1817 to 1835 the sessions of the school became irregular, and the attendance so limited, that the school was abandoned and the building appropriated to other uses.

Great as were the benefits of this school to those who attended it, the cause of general education would have been far more effectually promoted by combining the energies of the whole community in the organization and support of such a graded school as had been projected and defeated.

The failure of that project at so early a day is not to be wondered at when it is considered that, with the clearer light thrown on the subject by modern educators, and the universal attention directed to it, repeated efforts at reform have, during the past fifteen years, been frustrated; and that effective measures of improvement have only been initiated during the last five years.

In 1808 the homestead of the late James H. Alvord, deceased, on the west side of the East village park, was erected, and was finished the following year.

Elizur Hinsdale erected the original house on the north side of Main street, now owned by Philo G. Sheldon, which he afterwards enlarged to its present dimensions, and occupied until about 1820.

1809.

In 1809, Selden Mitchell built the house on the south side of Main street, now owned and occupied by Sheldon Kinney, senior, and during the same or following year, Jesse Byington built, on the west side of North Main street, the house subsequently owned by Evart Bevins and Edward G. Whiting, and now the homestead of George B. Owen.

In 1810, Asahel Miller built the house now owned by Thomas F. Davis, on the east side of Main street, above George Dudley's tannery; and Riley Whiting built, on the east side of Still River, the house recently owned and occupied by Rollin L. Beecher.

The Pratt street road was laid out and opened in 1810. As laid out, it crossed Mad River immediately east of the Foundry and Machine Company's Works, and extended about one mile southward to its present termination, but when made it was found best to cross the river by the depot bridge, then recently erected by Mr. Boyd for the convenience of his iron works, and to run by an easier grade to where the surveyed line crossed Prospect street.

Nearly cotemporaneous with the opening of Pratt street road, the ancient road along the line of Hinsdale street was discontinued, it being considered no longer of public convenience and necessity after the opening of the Green Woods turnpike, and the diversion of travel from the Old Country road over Wallen's Hill. The wisdom of this measure proved short-sighted, for about 1835 it was relaid and opened at a heavy expense to the town.

The assessment list of 1810 comprises the following items:

103	Polls between 21 and 70,	at	$60.00
11	" " 18 " 21,	"	30.00
119	Oxen,	"	10.00
388	Neat Cattle,	"	7.00
102	"	"	3.34
78	Horses,	"	10.00
5	"	"	7.00
2	"	"	3.34
298	Acres Land,	"	1.67
1046	" "	"	1.34
51	" "	"	.84
2226	" "	"	.34
2123	" "	"	.17
1782	" "	"	.09
2	Chaises,	"	30.00
6	"	"	20.00
13	Silver Watches,	"	10.00
2	Brass Clocks,	"	20.00
36	Wooden "	"	7.00
4	Fire-places,	"	5.00
18	"	"	3.75
64	"	"	2.50
69	"	"	1.25
2	Stores,		
	Money at interest,		275.00
	Assessments on trades,		1417.00

Net amount after deducting abatements,	13,474.03
Net amount of Old Society,	17,398.32
Total amount of whole town,	$30,872.35
Highway tax, 3 per cent. in labor,	$ 906.17
Town tax, 5 " " cash,	1544.72

CHAPTER XXVII.

NEW COMERS.—FAMILY RECORDS.—WAR OF 1812; ITS EFFECT ON BUSINESS, &c.

1811 to 1821.

WE note among the new comers of the year 1811 as follows:

ANDREW BRUSIE, an iron refiner from Ancram, N. Y., first appears on the tax list of this year. He resided in the West Village until his removal to Virgil, Cortland Co., N. Y., about 1830, where he erected and carried on an iron forge for several years, and is believed to be still living. He married Electa, daughter of John Roherbacher, and had children.

RUSSELL PAGE, a tailor from Cheshire, this year bought the house that stood on the site of James T. Norton's present residence where he lived and worked at his trade until 1814. He had a wife but no children.

CHARLES C. CAUL, an iron refiner, this year came from Ancram, N. Y., and worked mainly for the Rockwell Brothers until his death, about 1830. He had a wife, and children—Aaron, Hiram, Amelia, Andrew, and Nelson. Aaron became a physician and formerly practised in Cortland Co., N. Y. Amelia married a Schermerhorn.

ELEAZER HAWLEY, from Norfolk, a clock-maker, is first on the list of this year. He lived and raised a family in a now-abandoned house at the top of the hill, above the Woodruff tannery, near the crossing of the Old Country and North Main Street roads. He died April 1, 1839, aged 47, leaving, among other children, Romulus and George, none of whom remain in the town.

JOHN MALTBIE came into the society a single man, and married, in 1812, Deborah, daughter of Reuben Scovill, and had children whose names are not ascertained. He bought, in 1814, the place, as is believed, now owned by Jonathan Gilbert, on South Street, where he died Aug. 17, 1827, aged 42.

DARIUS TURRELL, a clock maker, lived in the Stephen Rowley house on North Main street until about 1840. He had daughters, Betsey A. and Ann, and may have had other children. His first wife died in March, 1828, aged 30.

SAMUEL WILLIAMS, a forge man from Ancram, N. Y., lived in Winsted, near Hulbert's forge, from 1811 until about 1840, and raised a family of children, among them two sons, Samuel and John. He served in the war of 1812.

1812.

DANIEL ALBRO learned the tanner's trade in Winsted, and came of age this year. He lived in the town until about 1836. He married in February, 1811, Nancy Westlake, and had several children—among them, Edward and Henry. He was living at Windsor Locks in 1871.

NATHAN CHAMPION came from Middlesex County this year, and began casting clock bells, to which he afterwards added other castings, and was the only iron founder in the town until after 1833. He owned and occupied during his later life, the dwelling on North Main street, next north of the new graded school building. He died at a good old age, early in 1868, after a blameless and exemplary life.

His wife, Mary, died August 28, 1843, aged 60. They had a son, HENRY S., now living in Bridgeport; and daughters, SARAH C., who married September 24, 1840, William R. Richardson of Bristol; JULIA, who died October 18, 1826; LUCY A., who married, January 20, 1836, Lucius Skinner, and LUCINDA, recently married.

WILLIAM GREEN from Salisbury, a forgeman, came to Winsted this year, and worked during most of his after life in Cook's Iron Works, in the east village. He raised a family, some of whom now reside here, and died in the town.

CHRISTOPHER LYON, a joiner, became a resident this year. He built and occupied until his death, the house on North Main street now occupied by Roswell Pond. He married Clarissa, daughter of Theodore Hoskin. He died August 5, 1844, aged 56, and she died February 22, 1867, aged 77. They had a daughter, ROXANA, married, October 19, 1824, Aaron W. Crane, and another daughter, EUNICE, married October 2, 1839, Benjamin Johnson.

GEORGE SAGE, a mason, this year became an inhabitant of the Society, and lived, until his removal to the west about 1828, on the east side of South street, now Torrington line. No record of his family is found.

1813.

WILLIAM CAUL, an iron refiner, from Ancram, N. Y., came to Winsted this year, and worked in the different forges most of the intervening time, until his death, at the Insane Retreat, Hartford, in June, 1828.

He married — Culver, and had children: JAMES M., WILLIAM, ANN E., who married, June 2, 1847, Frederick Murray, and another daughter, who married Hervey V. Blake.

DAVID MARBLE, from Sutton, Mass., a mason, came here this year. In 1816 he built the Wm. S. Holabird house, at the north end of the east village park, and there resided some five years, when he deserted his wife, and went to Louisiana, and probably died there. He married, December 15, 1814, Pamela Wheeler, who is now (1872) living. They raised no children.

JOSEPH W. HURLBUT, son of Martin of Winchester, appears on this year's list. He inherited the farm of his father, on the east side of Long Lake, on which he still resides; has been an honored deacon of the Congregational Church since 1836. He married, April 25, 1817, Sarah, daughter of Stephen Merrill of Barkhamsted. She died Oct., 1864.

CHILDREN.

I. JAMES MARTIN, b. January 5, 1818; d. August 14, 1847, unm.
II. JOSEPH MERRILL, b. September 28, 1824; m. June 2, 1869, Anna Augusta Field.
III. WARREN PHINEAS, b. January 4, 1827; resident of Winsted.
IV. WILLIAM FLOWERS, b. January 27, 1835; a member of the Litchfield County bar, and now resident in Winsted.

DOCTOR HENRY NOBLE from Vermont, a physician, came here this or the preceding year, as a practitioner. He married the same year, Susan, daughter of Benjamin Jenkins, who died January 14, 1815, aged 22, when he left the state. By his wife he had one son, JAMES DWIGHT, baptized November 6, 1814; supposed to be still living.

GEORGE ROBERTS from Torringford, became a resident this year. He lived during his later years on the east side of the Still River, in the first house north of Green Woods turnpike bridge, where he died in 1867 or 1868, when past seventy years of age. He married — Judd, who died before him. They had a son, EDWARD J., and two or three daughters.

HORACE REYNOLDS, a blacksmith, came here this year, and resided, with his family, mainly in the east village, until his removal to Illinois about 1835. He was for some years a partner with Thomas R. Bull in the old Jenkins Scythe Works, on the site of the Winsted Manufacturing Co.'s Works, and then owned and occupied the Byington house on North Main street. He had a wife and children, of whom we find no record.

1814.

SAMUEL BARTLETT, a native of Cohassett, Mass., came from Malone,

N. Y., to Winsted, and built and occupied until his removal from the town, the Widow Marble house, on the east side of the east village park. He removed, with his family, to Wayne County, Pennsylvania. His wife was sister to Benjamin Jenkins. His children, resident with him here, were his son, ARAH, and his daughters, RHODA, AMANDA, and others whose names are not remembered.

JAMES C. CLEVELAND, son of Rufus of Barkhamsted, first appears on this year's list. He was for many years a clockmaker in the employ of Riley Whiting. In 1816 he built the house on the east side of the east village park, which he has continued to occupy to the present time (1872). He married (1st), Belinda Miller, by whom he had a son, CHARLES, who died unmarried; (2d), Sally Taylor, who died childless, December 27, 1819, aged 28; (3d), Lucy Northrup, still living (1872), by whom he had JANE, born July 21, 1821, who married, May 11, 1842, Charles H. Blake.

LEWIS MCDONALD from Waterbury, a shoemaker, lived in Winsted from 1813 to 1818, when he moved westward, and in 1871 was living in Illinois. He married, about 1817, Betsey, daughter of Asher Rowley.

JOEL MILLER, son of Asahel of Winchester, an ingenious mechanic, and an exemplary and earnest Christian, lived in Winsted until his death, about 1820. He married a daughter of Grove Pinney, Esq., of Colebrook; had no children.

DR. LUMAN WAKEFIELD, born in Colebrook, August 29, 1787, studied medicine with Dr. Aaron Moore, and this or the preceding year commenced practice with his teacher in Winsted. Dr. Moore dying in 1813, he succeeded to an extensive practice, which he retained and enlarged until he became disabled for active professional duties by a slow palsy which terminated his life, March 20, 1850, at the age of 63. He owned and lived in a house on the site of Charles B. Hallett's present residence, on the east side of the east village park, which was burned down shortly after his decease. He was a man of equable temperament, and a thorough knowledge of human nature, which gave him a controlling influence in the community, and secured to him the strong attachment of many friends. As a successful practitioner, he was aided by sound judgment and close observation, more than by high scientific attainments. He was a supporter of good order, a decided friend and advocate of the temperance reform, and in later life became a consistent member of the Congregational church. He was born at Colebrook, Aug. 29, 1787; m. Betsy, daughter of Elijah Rockwell, Esq., of Colebrook, born Feb. 18, 1789. She died Oct. 23, 1831.

CHILDREN.

I. JULIA W., b. Oct. 1, 1815; m., May 23, 1839, Eli T. Wilder, Esq.
II. ELIZABETH A., b.   m., Oct. 1, 1831, Normand Adams.
III. LUCY C., b. March 24, 1820; m., May 28, 1840, Wm. H. Phelps.
IV. JOHN LUMAN, b. May 25, 1823; grad. M. D. Yale College, 1847.
V. JAMES BEACH, b. March 21, 1825; grad. A. B. Trinity College, Hartford. A judge of supreme court in Minnesota.
VI. MARY H, b. Sept. 7, 1827; m., Sept. 21, 1852, Richard H. Yale; d. at New Orleans, La., Sept. 22, 1858.

He married (2d), March 12, 1840, Ann (Tolbert), widow of Ambrose Fyler; she d. Sept. 24, 1867, aged 75.

LUCIUS CLARKE, son of Captain Lemuel, came with his father from Whately, Mass., in 1807, and appears on this year's tax list. In 1813 or 1814, he formed a partnership with Nathaniel B. Gaylord in mercantile business, which was continued until his removal to Monroe Co., N. Y., about 1818, where he went into trade, first at Carthage, at the foot of the Genesee Falls, and then in the village of Rochester. He returned to Winsted in 1824, and in company with Samuel Boyd, opened a new store on the site of Woodford's Block in the West Village. In 1827, he bought the Hinsdale store, on the site of Camp's Block, in which he traded until his removal to Massachusetts, in 1834; whence he returned in 1841, and purchased of the widow of Riley Whiting the clock factory in the East Village with which he was connected in business until 1845, when he purchased real estate on the flat, between the East and West Villages, and thereafter contributed more largely than any other person to the building up of that section of the now consolidated borough. He was the prime mover and one of the most efficient promoters of the measures which secured the extension of the Naugatuck Railroad from Waterbury to Winsted. He was an upright and correct man of business, energetic and hard-working, but versatile to a degree that impeded the complete success of some of his enterprises. As a citizen, he was right minded, public spirited, and deservedly popular. He served as state senator in 1846, and died Dec. 29, 1863, aged 73. His family record is given in connection with that of his father, Capt. Lemuel Clarke.

ALPHA ROWLEY, son of Ebenezer of Winchester, appears on the list of this year. He became the owner of his father's farm on South street in 1835, and there resided until his removal to western New York in 1838. He studied law for a time, but was never called to the bar except as a defendant. He died in September, 1872, while an inmate of the Utica Insane Hospital.

1815.

HALSEY BAILEY, a blacksmith from Barkhamsted, lived in Winsted from 1814 to 1829, when he moved to central New York. He married, —————, ————, Mira, daughter of Ebenezer Rowley.

SILAS BURTON, son of John of Winchester, first appears on the list of this year. He married Lucia, daughter of Asahel Miller, and lived here until 1818, when he removed to Erie, Pa.

ORRIN CLEVELAND, son of Rufus of Barkhamsted, a school-master, lived in the town, mainly in Winsted, from 1815 to about 1830. He had a wife and family of children, one of whom became the second wife of the late Grant Thorburn.

SHUBAEL CROWE, from New Hartford, this year built, in company with Horatio G. Hale, of Burlington, a carriage maker's shop on the site of John T. Rockwell's tannery, which they carried on about two years, when he left the town.

REUBEN HALL, a shoemaker from New Haven, came to Winsted this year. In company with David Edwards, he built, and for several years occupied the house nearly opposite the old Methodist meeting-house building. He removed to Fayetteville, N. C., about 1825, returning in 1831, and continued his residence here until his removal to Ohio in 1835. If living he now resides in Illinois. He was a man of kindly nature, a pillar and class leader of the Methodist Church, a neighbor of the Good Samaritan order. No record of his family is found. His wife was a Ward from Cornwall. They had a son, Truman B., who married, May 21, 1836, Fanny M. Wood; and one or more daughters.

DAVID MUNSON, from Colebrook, removed to the farm bordering on Colebrook line, lately owned by George A. Marvin, deceased, and occupied it until his removal to the West, about 1830.

ANSEL SHATTUCK, about this time, built a small house on the west side of South street, in which he lived until 1829. No record of his family is found.

1816.

SHELDON KINNEY, from Washington, Conn., this year, or earlier, came to Winsted, and carried on the tailoring trade for ten or fifteen years. He built and occupied, until 1825, the house next north of the East Village meeting-house, after which he removed to Colebrook for a few years; and on his return bought the house on the south side of Main street in which he now (1872) resides. He has sons, Francis, Sheldon, Jr., of Windsor, and George W., who married, Dec. 4, 1849, Betsey C. Brown; and a daughter, Charlotte M., who married, May 19, 1856, Charles H. Knapp.

CAPT. STEPHEN FYLER, son of Stephen of Torrington, this year bought the farm on South street recently owned in part by his son, Albro Fyler, on which he lived until his death on the 21st of April, 1853, at the age of seventy-three. He was descended, in the sixth generation, from Lieut. Walter Fyler, who came from England to Dorchester on the ship Mary and John, in 1630, through his son Zerubabel,[2] born Windsor, Dec. 23, 1644, and his son Zerubabel,[3] born Windsor, Dec. 25, 1674, and his son Silas,[4] born Windsor, ——— ——, 1710, and his son Stephen,[5] born May 27, 1755. He (Stephen, Jr.) was born Torrington, March 6, 1780; married, October, 1803, Armira Wilson, of Torrington; he died April 21, 1853; she died Dec. 27, 1866, aged 87.

CHILDREN.

I. HILEMON, b. Aug. 8, 1804; m., April 23, 1850, Charlotte Hamilton.
II. SOPHRONIA, b. Oct. 9, 1806; m., July, 1832, William Sanford, who died Nov. 7, 1838. CHILD: Jane, m., Oct. 15, 1860, George M. Wentworth. CHILDREN: 1. George S., b. Feb. 20, 1864; 2. Frank L., b. Sept. 20, 1866; 3. Minnie, b. Aug. 12, 1868, d. Sept. 2, 1868; 4. Arthur M., b. Sept. 22, 1869, d. Aug. 9, 1870; 5. Alice M., b. Jan. 29, 1871.
III. ALBRO, b.   m., June 23, 1850, Jane E. Kinney.
IV. MASON WILSON, b. Oct. 7, 1810; m.,   Munson.

HARRY BISHOP, LEVERITT BISHOP, and SETH BISHOP, brothers, from Litchfield, came to Winsted this season. Harry owned a place on Wallen's Hill, in which he lived until about 1830, and afterwards moved to Colebrook. Leveritt died here August 1, 1852, aged 67. He had two sons, EDWARD and WILLIAM, formerly residing here, and perhaps other children.

SETH BISHOP married, ——— ——, ——, Minerva, daughter of Nathan Wheeler, by whom he had a son, SETH, Jr., now (1872) living at Collinsville, and a daughter, MINERVA W., who married, April 22, 1841, William S. Bunnel, now residing in Winsted. Minerva, wife of Seth, Sen., died July 1, 1826, aged 35. He now (1872) resides in Barkhamsted.

JEHIAL COE, son of Jonathan,[2] came of age this year and first lived on Spencer Hill for a few years, and has since lived on his father's farm on Coe street to the present time (1872). His family record is already given in connection with that of his forefathers.

WILLARD HOLMES, son of Joseph, is on the list of this year. He resided with his father (on Spencer street) until his death, and continued to occupy the paternal homestead until the morning of Feb. 22, 1857, when he was burned up with his house while attempting to save his papers from the flames.

He was a man of superior culture, of strong mind and sincere piety. He formed his opinions deliberately and independently, and carried them out with unswerving rectitude. Modest and retiring in his disposition, he would hardly have been known beyond the circle of his immediate neighbors, but for his early advocacy of the cause of the slave, and his fearless persistency amid reproach and contumely, in asserting the radical principles of liberty and duty. His family record is given in connection with that of his father.

HENRY B. CROWE, from New Hartford, succeeded his brother Shubael in the part ownership of the carriage shop in the West Village, and after some years became owner of the Joseph Mitchell place in the East Village, where he died after 1856. He married, ———— —, ————, Nancy, daughter of Amasa Mallory, Sr., and had a highly respected family of children, of whom we have no record except the baptism of HENRY, LUTHER, JANE, and JAMES on the 4th of July, 1828.

1817.

CHESTER SOPER, from Windsor, a clothier, this year came to Winsted and bought the clothier's works in the East Village, erected by Ansel Wilson, and the house that then stood on the site of James T. Norton's present residence. He converted the clothier's works into a Woolen Mill, which he carried on until about 1838: soon after which he removed to Windsor, and has since died. His wife was a Welles from Wethersfield. They had no children.

1818.

WHEELOCK THAYER came from Vermont this year and commenced work as a scythe maker in the West Village. In 1820, he became connected with James Boyd in the scythe business, under the firm name of Boyd & Thayer, which was continued until 1832, when he built the scythe works on Mad river now owned by his daughter, Mrs. Julia A. Bachellor, which he continued to operate until a few years before his death. He bought the "Deacon Rockwell house," then on the site of the Beardsley house in 1830, in which he resided until his purchase of the house now owned by his daughter, Mrs. Julia A. Bachellor, in which he resided until his death. He was a man of sanguine temperament and indomitable energy. By industry, frugality, and judicious investments, he rapidly accumulated a large estate. Democratic in politics and a universalist in doctrine, he advocated the faith that was in him with untiring zeal, and exerted a powerful influence in the community: an influence that favored the temperance reform and recognized the colored man as a human being endowed with the rights of "life, liberty, and the pursuit of happiness."

With failing health he retired from active business in 1854, and died Sept. 23, 1857, aged 67.

He was born in Northbridge, Mass., May 10, 1790, and married, Nov. 28, 1816, Clarissa Fuller, born at Brookfield, Mass., May 9, 1795, who died Feb. 16, 1829.

CHILDREN.

I. JULIA ANN, b. at Weston, Mass., Aug. 17, 1817; m. Aug. 3, 1835, William G. Bachellor, who d. Dec. 15, 1844, aged 33. Children: 1. Wheelock Thayer; 2. William G.
II. CHARLOTTE, b. July 22, 1819; d. July 28, 1821.
III. HARRIET, b. July 22, 1822; m. Sept. 10, 1840, Seth L. Wilder; d. childless Sept. 10, 1840.

He died June 23, 1857. He married 2d, Nancy Joslin, who died childless, February 26, 1855, aged 71.

DANIEL G. TUTTLE, from Torringford, this year built the house on South street, bordering on Torrington line, lately owned by his son-in-law, Lucius J. Woodford, — which he occupied until his death, March 4, 1844, at the age of 58. He married, Clarissa, daughter of Daniel C. Hudson of Torrington.

CHILDREN.

I. FANNY M., m. Dec. 31, 1835, Charles Seldon.
II. CATHARINE, m. Lucius J. Woodford; d. Jan. 5, 1872.
III. GEORGE H.
IV. LAMPHIER B., m. Sept. 14, 1841, Charlotte, daughter of Jehiel Coe.
V. JAMES H., m. May 26, 1841, Cordelia, daughter of Erastus Woodford.
VI. RUTH O., d. Nov. 4, 1859, aged 36.

JESSE WILLIAMS, from Colebrook, resided here some three years of his minority, and appears on the list of this year. He purchased the Eben Coe house, on Spencer street, in which he now resides. It may safely be said that no man in the town has exceeded him in hard and difficult labor. If there was an ugly job to be done, he was the man to do it effectually, with a calculating head and a giant's strength. Labor seemed never to weary him, nor age to impair his physical powers, until partial blindness within the past three years has compelled him to hold up and look back on a life well spent, in the enjoyment of health, and a competency of worldly goods. As a Constable and Sheriff's Deputy he was prepared for every emergency. For some forty years he has been, and continues to be, the honored Tyler of St. Andrew's Lodge.

He married (1st), Sept. 14, 1825, Roxana Hurlbut, who died Sept. 9, 1832, aged 37. He married (2d), May 4, 1833, Mabel Wright, of Cornwall.

CHILDREN BY FIRST WIFE.

I. HENRY, b. Dec. 25, 1826.
II. SYLVIA, b. Jan. 28, 1829; m. Rev. Wm. B. Osborn.
III. ANNIE R., b. Jan. —, 1831; m. Lyman J. Parsons.

AND FAMILY RECORDS. 415

CHILD BY SECOND WIFE.

IV. JANE, b. April —, 1835; m. Henry Case.

1818.

NISUS KINNEY, a native of Colebrook, was brought up in the family of Grinnell Spencer. He appears on the list of this year and still resides in the town. He built the house on the west side of Spencer street, a little north of Amos Pierce, from which he moved after a few years to the old Elihu Rockwell house, still further north, where he resided until about 1860. He lived in Torrington from 1864 to 1868, and has since resided here.

He married Sally, daughter of Adin Wakefield, of Colebrook, who died Sept. 28, 1856, aged 57. They had a son, Andrew; and daughters, Sarah J., who died July 22, 1848, aged 17. Jane E., who married, June 23, 1850, Albro Fyler; Harriet, who married, Jan. 14, 1851, Lucius L. Culver; and Susan W., married, Dec. 25, 1861, Luther G. Hinsdale; and they may have had other children.

1819.

SILAS HOSKIN, son of Theodore, appears on the list of this year. He owned and occupied, from 1824 to his death, Sept. 9, 1870, at the age of 72, the Benjamin Whiting place on Coe street. He married, Oct. 13, 1823, Priscilla, daughter of Ransford Bailey, of Groton, Conn.

CHILDREN.

I. RANSFORD BAILEY, b. June 24, 1825; d. Oct. 17, 1828.
II. TRUMAN SILAS, b. March 23, 1827.
III. THEODORE BAILEY, b. April 26, 1829.
IV. THOMAS COE, b. March 15, 1831.
V. ERASTUS, b. April 9, 1833.
VI. CHAS. SHERMAN, b. Feb. 4, 1835.
VII. GEORGE, b. " 5, 1837.

ELIAS ROWLEY, son of Asher, is on the list of this year. He first occupied his father's homestead on South street, and about 1845 erected his present residence on the Wolcottville road, south of the burying-ground. (See his family record in connection with that of his father.)

NELSON WILSON, son of Abijah, Jr., appears on the list of this year, After marriage he lived until 1830 on Spencer street, and thereafter, while he remained in the State, on Coe street, adjoining the Colebrook line. After 1845 he removed to Saratoga County, N. Y., where he died Nov. 21, 1851. He married, Wealthy, daughter of Jonathan Coe, Esq., by whom he had

CHILDREN.

I. GEORGE C., m. Caroline Miles; d. March 8, 1854, aged 33.
II. CHARLES C., d. May 20, 1847.
III. HARRIET E., m. Alexander C. Thompson; d. Jan. 7, 1855, aged 23, childless.
IV. HENRY W., d. Oct 19, 1836.

NORMAN SPENCER, from New Hartford, served his apprenticeship as a tanner with Col. Hosea Hinsdale, and thereafter owned and carried on the tannery built by Horace Ranney, near the Cook Forge, on North Main street, until 1834, when he removed to Michigan, and died there.

He married, about 1820, Nancy Hinsdale, sister of Col. Hosea, by whom he had several children, — among them Richard, who returned to Winsted after his father's removal, and resided here until about 1855.

During this decade our second war with England occurred. The dominant sentiment of our people was opposed to the war, though it had many and ardent supporters among us. Party spirit raged with a bitterness never exceeded in subsequent periods. Singularly enough, the Federalists were the states'-rights party of that period. They loved the English and hated the French. They found unconstitutional encroachments in almost every measure of the national administration. They discouraged enlistments into the army, and insisted on the entire control of the drafted militia by state officers, and in order to sustain this asserted right, the governor of this state went to New London when the militia were called to the defence of that place in order to out-rank, as captain-general, the United States officer then and there in command.

The state flag was then the supreme object of Federal worship. Liberty poles, bearing aloft the stars and stripes, were repeatedly cut down by unknown parties. On a training day in 1814, on the east village green, the national flag was unexpectedly hoisted on a newly-erected liberty pole during the parade of a company of recently-organized state troops, and an infantry and a cavalry company of militia. The captains of the three companies ordered the flag to be taken down. The sturdy Democrats rallied around it, with the revived and concentrated spirit of '76. The three companies were formed in line, and marched up to the pole to disperse its defenders. A melee was brought on by one of the defenders, Eli Marshall by name, seizing with the grip of a bull dog the throat of the axman who was about to cut down the pole. It took some minutes to detach the democratic fingers from the federal throat, and at this crisis, the fence passing near the foot of the pole, and loaded with lookers-on, came down with a crash that induced a momentary panic of the contending parties, and a partial breaking of the military ranks. Though no one was hurt by this catastrophe, the white feather became manifest, and the military force becoming essentially disorganized, was marched off without the honors of war, and the star-spangled banner continued to wave until sunset.

A review of the dissensions of that period, and the results growing out of them, is highly instructive.

The war, though perhaps unwisely declared, and feebly carried on, until the latest campaigns, was successfully closed. Our navy acquired immortal honor, and our army, long mismanaged and badly officered, finally retrieved its credit. The final disaster fell on the party which, though perhaps rightly opposed to the declaration of war, not only failed to stand by the government in carrying it on, but arrayed itself against all its measures, and almost paralyzed its energies. It bore a load of popular odium that in a few years so utterly broke it down that no "departure" could retrieve it. The lesson is an instructive one to modern politicians.

The number of soldiers recruited in this town for the regular army was very limited. Most of them entered a regiment that served, without a battle or skirmish, at New London through the whole war. The only two officers commissioned from this town, Colonel Samuel Hoadley and Captain Riley Sweet, belonged to this regiment.*

A few Winsted soldiers were enlisted into the 25th U. S. Regiment, that was cut to pieces on the Niagara frontier, and but few, if any of them, ever returned.

Detachments of militia were from time to time drafted to serve at New London, and Captain Luther Hoadly was called out to command one of the detached companies, and died in the service. One of the ten companies of state troops, as they were called, organized by the state legislature, and composed of about equal numbers of Winchester, Barkhamsted, and New Hartford men, was also called out for service at New London.

Prior to the war, our manufacturing interests were in a healthy and prosperous condition, and the growth of our two villages, though slow, was healthy. The war stimulated manufacturing to a high degree of activity by its high tariff of duties, and the almost entire exclusion of British manufactured goods. Old establishments were enlarged, and pushed to their utmost capacity, and many new manufacturing enter-

---

* The late General Edmund Kirby of the U. S. Army received his Ensign's commission while a clerk in Winsted, and served on the Canada frontier with distinguished honor. He belonged in Litchfield.

prises were started and pushed forward without experience or economy. Prices of farm products and manufactured articles were enormously inflated by the suspension of specie payments, and the enormous issues of bank bills. Our community shared largely in the apparent prosperity induced by these causes, and suffered proportionally by the collapse induced by the return of peace, attended as it was by the contraction of bank issues preparatory to a return to specie payments, the paying off of improvident indebtedness, and the flooding of the country with British fabrics, at prices below the cost of the raw materials used by our own infant establishments.

The results, though less ruinous to Winsted than to many other manufacturing communities, were seriously felt for many succeeding years. The wire factory in the east village, employing a large number of hands, was at once and forever abandoned. Two establishments for making hand and machine cards soon followed. The cut-nail factory of Mr. Byington, then employing more men than any other establishment in town, soon after went down. The woollen factory of the Rockwell Brothers continued to run, though at a heavy loss, through long years of depression. Only two of the scythe establishments moved forward. The iron works, then the heaviest interest in the place, were saved from utter prostration by a limited sale to the government of iron for gun-making at the Springfield Armory. Cheese, the staple farm product, went down from ten to five cents per pound, and other articles in the same proportion. One "breathing hole of hell," in the form of a whisky distillery, of fungous growth, had just begun its polluting career on the slope of Wallen's Hill, above the clock factory, which, by the mercy of God, was so utterly prostrated that not a trace of its existence is left.

"The cold summer" of 1816 added to the gloom of this period. The spring was cold and backward, and the summer cold and dry. Frosts prevailed in every month of the year. The mowing lands yielded less than half an average crop. Scarcely an ear of corn in the town came to maturity. Potatoes were few and small, and dairy products were as scant in quantity as low in price. Much apprehension prevailed of a famine winter, which was measurably averted by a provident planting of turnips, when it was perceived that other crops were to fail. This crop was large, and thereby the lack of hay was partly made good in wintering such stock as was not killed or sold off in the preceding fall.

This cause, combined with the prostration of our manufacturing interest, drove large numbers of farmers and artisans to seek means of support in the new settlements of the west. Not until 1820 did business begin to assume a lively aspect, and prosperous growth become manifest.

The dwellings and other buildings erected within the borough limits during this decade were as follows :—

1811.

The iron forge of Reuben Cook & Co., on the site of the present works of Charles and John R. Cook, together with two or three forgemen's houses.

The scythe shop built by Mr. Jenkins on the site of the Strong Manufacturing Co.'s Works, east village.

A clothier's shop on the site of the Winsted Carriage Company's buildings, recently burned down.

The Wakefield homestead (burned down), on the site of C. B. Hallett's present residence.

1812.

The Luther Hoadley dwelling, north of the R. L. Beecher house, and nearly opposite the clock factory.

The Jesse Williams homestead, on Spencer street, built by Eben Coe.

1813.

The Bissell Hinsdale house, built on the site of the Second Congregational Church, and about 1855 moved by Dr. James Welch to the adjoining lot on the north.

The Rockwell grist mill and woollen factory buildings on Lake street, burned up in 1835, and not rebuilt.

The grammar schoolhouse on Main street, next north of Forbes' furniture store.

A wire factory was erected by Samuel and Luther Hoadley and James Boyd, on the west wing of the clock factory dam, one of the first in the United States wherein the wire was broken down from the rod, and reduced to the finest fibre. While the war with England continued it prospered, but it had to be abandoned when peace was restored, and foreign wire began to be again imported.

1814.

The Solomon Rockwell house, corner of Lake and Prospect streets.

The widow Marble house, on east side of east village park, built by Samuel Bartlett.

The Hulsey Burr scythe shop, on the site of works on North Main street, now owned by Frederick Woodruff.

The Oliver Loomis house on Main street, built by Romanta Woodford.

The oil mill on Mad River, near the south wing of Clifton mill dam, torn down about 1830.

1815.

The James C. Cleveland house, on east side of east village park, built by Mr. Cleveland and Arah Bartlett.

A carriage works, on the site of John T. Rockwell's tannery, built by Shubael Crowe, and converted into a store by Coe & Hubbell, about 1830, and since removed.

The Widow David Coe house, on Spencer street, nearly opposite the old Methodist meeting-house, built by Reuben Hall.

The James Boyd & Son iron store, on Main street, now remodeled as a furniture store, occupied by S. B. Forbes & Co.

A whisky distillery, on Wallen's Hill road, some eighty rods east of the clock factory.

1816.

The "Holabird House," opposite the Episcopal Church, now owned by Henry Bills, was built by David Marble.

The house of A. L. Weirs, next north of the east village Congregational meeting-house, was built by Sheldon Kinney, sen.

By the return of peace, the reduction of tariff duties, and the renewed importation of foreign fabrics, almost every branch of domestic manufacture was prostrated; and as a consequence, building operations in a great measure ceased during the remainder of this decade. The only building erected in the interval seems to have been a tannery erected by Horace Ranney at the south corner of North Main and Cook streets, which was abandoned as a tannery before 1860, since which the main building has been converted into a double tenement house.

The system of taxation having been radically changed in 1819, we compile for comparison abstracts of the Assessment Lists of 1810 and 1818, as follows:

ITEMS.		1810.		1820.	
		No.	Amount.	No.	Amount.
Polls between 21 and 70, at	$60.00	103		83	
" " 18 " 21 "	30.00	11		10	
Oxen, "	10.00	119		88	
Neat cattle, "	7.00	388		349	
" " "	3.34	102		38	
Horses, "	10.00	78		66	
" "	7.00	2		2	
Acres of land, "	1.67	298		388	
" " " "	1.34	1,046		1,164	
" " " "	84	51		63	
" " " "	34	2,226		2,716	
" " " "	17	2,123		2,016	
" " " "	09	1,782		1,718	

Chaises,	at		30.00	2		2	
"	"		20.00	6		6	
Silver watches,	"		10.00	13		2	
Brass clocks,	"		20.00	2		1	
Wooden clocks,	"		7.00	36		67	
Fire places, or smokes,	"		5.00	4		6	
" "	"		3.75	18		33	
.. "	"		2.50	64		81	
" "	"		1.25	69		151	
Stores,	"		20.00	2		3	
"	"		10.00	0		1	
Money at interest,					$ 275.00	250	$ 250.00
Assessments of trades,					1,417.00		1,860.00
Bank stock,							2,500.00
Net amount after deducting abatements,					13,474.03		16,292.68
Net Amount of Old Society,					17,398.32		18,057.64
					$30,272.35		$34,350.28
Highway tax (in labor), 3 per cent.,					926.17		1,030.51
Town tax (current expenses), 5 per cent.,					1,543.62		1,717.51
					$2,469.79		$2,748.02

CHAPTER XVIII.

NEW COMERS—FAMILY RECORDS—GRAMMAR SCHOOL.

1821 TO 1831.

The year 1821 opened with renewed activity, indicating a decided renovation of prosperous business. Debts had been liquidated; the banks had resumed specie payments, and expanded their issues; and such branches of manufacturing as could be made remunerative, in competition with foreign fabrics, were resumed and actively prosecuted.

From this time forward our increasing population was largely made up of individuals and families holding only temporary residences among us, while the ranks of leading business men were largely filled by the descendants of our pioneers. To enumerate all the new men coming on the stage will no longer be attempted; and our notices will be confined to those who became permanent or long continued residents.

STEPHEN ROWLEY, farmer and land surveyor, a native of Torrington, this year came to Winsted from Colebrook, and owned the Abijah Wilson, Jr., farm, on the old North road, until 1842, when he bought and occupied until his death, in 1856, a house on the east side of North Main street, next south of Lucius Griswold's. He died, childless, leaving a widow, Roxy (Whiting), now (1872) living.

HORACE W. HOUSE, from Windsor, came to Winsted in 1821, and engaged in trade and manufacturing with N. B. Gaylord. He built the brick house on Main street, now owned by Normand Adams, in 1823, which he occupied until his removal back to Windsor in 1828, where he died, childless, about 1870.

1822.

ELISHA A. MORGAN, from New London County, bought in 1822, the William E. Cowles farm, on Colebrook line, which he exchanged for the Higley Tavern in the West village, in 1827, and lived there until his removal out of the State in 1829. He had a wife, but no children.

RILEY SMITH, son of Theodore and Rhoda, this year bought his homestead on the old north road, above the Woodruff tannery, on which he resided until his death, June 5, 1865, aged 70. He married, Nov. 9, 1826, Emily Cadwell, of W., by whom he had two sons, James R., and Hiram C., now (1872) resident in Riverton. She died Sept. 15, 1855, aged 54, and he married (2d), Dec. 25, 1865, Sarah Loomis, of Windsor, who died childless, Dec. 25, 1865. He died June 14, 1865, aged 68.

1823.

SAMUEL BOYD, son of James and Mary, of Winchester, in 1823 erected the original store on the site of Woodford's brick block, and entered into trade in company with his brother-in-law, Lucius Clarke, under the firm name of Clark & Boyd. In 1824 he built the E. S. Woodford homestead. In 1827, Mr. Clarke withdrew, and soon after Samuel W. Coe was associated with him for two or three years, after which E. W. Bronson came into the concern, which turned its attention to the manufacture of hoes, shovels, and other tools. The business was wound up in 1833, and Mr. Boyd removed to New Orleans, where he resided until 1850; soon after which he went into the hardware business in New York, and subsequently became an Appraiser in the Custom-House, which office he still holds. His family record is given in connection with that of his father.

1824.

ASAPH PEASE, originally from Sandisfield, came to Winsted from Colebrook in 1824, and owned and occupied until 1848 the old Doolittle house, on the east side of North Main street, opposite the clock factory dam, and which was subsequently taken down and re-erected on a new street turning westerly from North Main street. In the latter year he moved to New Britain, where he died Dec. 12, 1856, aged 80, his wife surviving him. He married, Feb. 4, 1805, Clotilda Hoyt, born June 1, 1777.

CHILDREN.

I. LEUMAS, b. Colebrook, May 9, 1806; d. aged 2 years.
II. MARY CLOTILDA, b. " Nov. 15, 1808.
III. LEUMAS HOYT, b. " Jan. 20, 1811; graduate of Williams College, 1835; minister of the gospel, now (1872) located at New Orleans as Chaplain of Seamen's Friend Society; unmarried.

IV. Julius Walter, b. Colebrook, May 19, 1814; m. April 1, 1849, Mary Hotchkiss. Has

CHILDREN.

1. Leumas Hoyt, b. Jan. 20, 1845.
2. Martha Francis, b. Nov. 28, 1845.
3. Julius Hotchkiss, b. July 7, 1849; d. Sept. 13, 1847.
4. Julius Hotchkiss, b. Nov. 22, 1848.
5. William Walter, b. Nov. 3, 1850.
6. Mary Emily, b. Dec. 24, 1854; d. Aug. 28, 1855.
7. Clarence, b. Feb. 24, 1857; d. Jan. 6, 1858.
8. Charles Wiard, b. June 18, 1859; d. Sept. 28, 1859.

V. Lucy Jemima, b. April 10, 1817.

VI. Laura Persis, b. April 22, 1824; m. Everett C. Holmes.

Hon. William S. Holabird, a native of Canaan, Conn., studied law with Hon. W. M. Burrall, attended the law lectures of Judge Gould at Litchfield, was admitted to the bar about 1820, and soon after commenced practice at Colebrook, Conn., — whence he moved to Winsted in 1824, and soon after secured a large practice and high standing at the bar.

He held the appointment of District Attorney for four years under President Jackson, and was Lieutenant Governor of the State in 1842 and 1844; besides which he held the offices of Postmaster and Assignee in Bankruptcy.

He was a man of commanding person and pleasing address; as a lawyer he was adroit rather than learned—thorough in preparing his cases, quick to discern the weak points of his adversary, and energetic beyond most men in carrying forward his cases to a final issue. The same qualities were prominent in his political career, but his success as a lawyer was more decided than as politician. About 1850 he withdrew from legal practice and devoted himself to financiering with decided success. He died May 22, 1855, at the age of 61. He married, in 1826, Adaline, daughter of Abijah Catlin, of Harwinton, who died Nov. 10, 1859, aged 59. They had

CHILDREN.

I. John Catlin, who graduated at Wesleyan University, Middletown, and d. in California unmd., May 28, 1853, aged 24 years 4 months.
II. Adaline, m. Henry B. Horton; d. April 3, 1856, aged 24 years 3 months, leaving one child, William Holabird.
III. Edward, m., Dec. 16, 1860, Sarah A. M. Howe; d. May 26, 1862, aged 28.
IV. Anne, d. July 27, 1859, single, aged 22.
V. Louise, d. July 8, 1842, aged 2 years and 9 months.
VI. William Swift, m. May 6, 1863, Mary I. Bell. He d. Oct. 23, 1866, aged 24. She d. May 5, 1871, aged 28. Child. William Swift.
VII. Louise, m. Oct. 14, 1868, aged 23, Henry C. Wicker, of Chicago.

William O. Talcott, M. D., from Killingworth, came here as a medical practitioner in 1825, and resided in the widow Marble house, on the

east side of the East Village park until his death, Oct. 26, 1831, at the age of 37. He was a skillful and faithful physician of pleasing manners, social nature and high-toned character. His death, by hemorrhage of the lungs, was sudden, and deeply lamented. He married Elizabeth M. ——, by whom he had a daughter, Elizabeth Olmsted, baptized Nov. 6, 1831.

OLIVER LOOMIS, from Torrington, purchased. in 1827, the farm between the two lakes, on which he lived until 1844, when he removed to his recent homestead on Main street, above Dudley's tannery, where he died childless, Feb. 7, 1872, aged 85 years, leaving a property of nearly ten thousand dollars to the use of the Methodist Episcopal Church, of which he was a zealous and exemplary member.

ALANSON LOOMIS, son of Abiel,[1] of Winchester, in 1827 bought the tannery and house adjoining it on the west, which had been previously owned by his father, which he occupied until his sale of the same to George Dudley in 1832, when he moved to Sandisfield, Mass., for a few years, and then returned to Winsted and bought and occupied the Ebenezer Rowley farm in 1845, soon after which he removed to Fulton, Oswego Co., N. Y., where he now (1872) resides. His family record is given in connection with that of his father, Abiel Loomis, Sen.

HENRY L. GAYLORD, originally from Torrington, came here in 1828, and was first associated in trading and hardware manufacturing with his brother, Nathaniel B. Gaylord, and afterwards with Chester Soper in woollen manufacturing. He owned and occupied the brick house on Main street, East Village, now owned by Normand Adams. He removed to Cleveland, Ohio, in 1837, where he died not far from 1850, leaving a widow and one son, now living. He was a man of high-toned character and sterling worth.

LUMAN HUBBELL, son of Silliman, of Winchester, a dyer by trade, and for several years a resident of Massachusetts, purchased in 1828, the tavern property between Camp's block and the Woodford block, and became a permanent resident. He first engaged in the manufacture of dyestuffs; and in 1831, in company with Samuel W. Coe, he went into the country store and produce business in a building then standing on a part of the site of J. T. Rockwell's tannery on Main street. Here they prosecuted a large business until, in 1845, they erected the building known as the Coe store, on Main street, opposite the Beardsley house. The building was nearly completed when Mr. Hubbell was suddenly taken sick and died within a week, on the day that had been fixed for removing their goods and opening their business therein.

Mr. Hubbell was a man of great promptitude and activity, a kind neighbor and sympathizing friend, who visited the sick and bereaved, and aided the destitute and unfortunate. In all measures of public improvement, he was among the foremost. His family record is given in connection with that of his father.

The following dwellings and other buildings were erected in Winsted during the decade from 1821 to 1831.

1821.

The Frederick Woodruff tannery on North Main street was erected by Horace Ranney, and was successively owned from 1824 to 1831 by Caleb Lewis, and then by Eli Foster, Ichabod Wood, Miles C. Burt and James Arault, who, in 1841, sold it to Mr. Woodruff, who, in 1869, sold it to George Dudley & Son, the present owners.

A forging and drafting shop was erected by James and James M. Boyd, in 1822, on Lake street, at the joining of the Lake stream and Mad river, which was taken down, and the present brick machine shop was erected on its site by John Boyd in 1853.

1822.

The Normand Adams house was built by Horace W. House.

1823.

A bark mill and tannery was built by Hosea Hinsdale on the site of John T. Rockwell's tannery.

1824.

The brick house on North Main street recently owned by the widow and legatees of Stephen Rowley, deceased, was erected by Joseph B. Lewis, and was occupied by him until he left the town in 1834.

The brick basement wooden house next south of the above was built the same or the following year by Darius Turrill and occupied by him until his removal from the town about 1840.

1825.

The E. S. Woodford house at the corner of Main and High streets was built by Samuel Boyd and occupied by him until his removal to New York in 1834.

Wheelock Thayer built the small brick tenement next south of the Woodford place now occupied by Martin Bradford.

The small brick tenement in front of J. T. Rockwell's tannery on Main street was built by Hosea Hinsdale and Ichabod Loomis, and was occupied in part by Col. Hinsdale as a leather store, and in part by Mr. Loomis as a liquor grocery, the first of these establishments in the town. It was burned out in 1827, leaving the walls so little injured, notwithstanding the explosion of a keg of powder, that it was rebuilt without taking down the walls.

The house near the outlet of the lake, recently owned by Benjamin F. Perry, was built by William Dexter, who occupied it until his removal to Illinois in 1836.

1827.

The "Upper Forge," on the site of the Winsted Manufacturing Company's Lake street grinding works, after running thirty-three years, was re built in 1827 by James Boyd & Son, and operated until about 1855, when the manufacture of bar iron ceased to be remunerative in the old way of working.

The original house on the site of Edward R. Beardsley's residence on Main street, was built for a tenant house, and now stands within the same enclosure, it having been removed by the late Seth L. Wilder to its present site.

1828.

Samuel Boyd erected the tenant house on Main street, between the residences of Mrs. Parke and Mrs. Eleazer Andrews.

1829.

Horace Higley built the house on the north side of Main street, now owned by Albert N. Beach, which he occupied until his removal to Painesville, Ohio, in 1837. This was the second dwelling erected on the section known as the "Flat" which then intervened between the east and west villages, and is now occupied by nearly a hundred stores and dwellings.

1830.

A wooden dwelling and brick blacksmith shop on the south side of Main street, nearly opposite Walnut street, were erected by Martin Denslow. The blacksmith shop has since been converted into a dwelling; and next east of the wooden dwelling a brick dwelling was erected the same year by Horace Skinner.

The dwelling house on the north side of Main street, and now owned by George Taylor, was erected in 1830 by William Benham; and the next dwelling on the west, was erected the same year by Daniel D. Lamb.

The Samuel Smith house, on the north side of Main street, was also erected in 1830 by Orentus Bronson, who, in succeeding years, although a cripple, erected about twenty dwellings in various parts of the village, almost unaided by any assistant help.

The Congregational Church in the East village was remodeled in 1828 by removing the high tub-like pulpit and its pendulous sounding-board, and substituting modern slips for the ancient square, pen-like pews, with high paneled sides. The new pulpit was placed at the east end of the audience room, and the floor had an ascending grade from the east to the west end. The building retained its original position on the green until 1848, when it was removed to its present site, and so remodeled, without and within, as not to retain a single feature of its original construction.

In 1828 the brick store on the corner of Main and North Main streets, now occupied by L. R. Norton & Company, was erected by an association of some fifteen individuals for an Academic School, which was first opened therein by Rev. Sardis B. Morley, a graduate of Williams College, assisted by Miss ——— Treat, of Hartford, who afterwards became his wife. The school was continued as a public academy, under a succession of teachers, until 1830, when the building was purchased by Mr. Henry E. Rockwell, who continued the school as a private enterprise until 1847, when he erected a new and more commodious building on Seminary Hill, north of High street, now occupied as a double dwelling, and recently owned by W. K. Peck, Esq.

Mr. Rockwell discontinued his school in 1850, and soon after removed to Massachusetts, and subsequently engaged in phonetic reporting and various educational pursuits.

He is gratefully remembered by a large portion of our middle-aged business men as a faithful and earnest teacher, and by the whole community as a quiet, public spirited citizen. His George Washington head was as cordially greeted as that of any other of the returning pilgrims to our late Centennial Commemoration.

In connection with Mr. Rockwell it is fitting to notice his cotemporary, Elder Miles Grant, who for some four or five years taught the west village district school, with an ability and success never excelled in our annals. To the sincere regret of parents and scholars, and of the whole community, a sense of duty constrained him to leave a calling for which he was eminently fitted, and to devote himself to the Master's service in another sphere of labor. Highly esteemed and loved as a minister of the Gospel, he has no more cordial friends than his Winsted pupils, now in the active stage of life, who owe to him a training far beyond what is ordinarily secured in a district school.

In 1830, GEORGE TAYLOR took a lease from JAMES BOYD of the land and water power on which the Elizur Hinsdale Axe Factory had stood, and erected a small machine shop, now constituting a part of the present Foundry & Machine Company's building. Mr. Taylor has been connected with the establishment in all its changes, up to the present time. Under the firm of Taylor & Whiting, woollen machinery of superior quality, and in large quantities, was manufactured. The foundry was erected about 1850.

We compile abstracts of the polls and taxable property of the Society on the lists of 1820 and 1830, showing the increase or decrease in the respective items during the decade as follows:—

	1820.		1830.	
	No.	Amount.	No.	Amount.
Houses and two-acre lots,	105	54,524	118	48,264
Acres of land,	8153	149,739	7696	108,266
Manufactories,	10	5,625	18	15,600
Grist mills and saw mills,	5	3,475	4	1,650
Stores,	4	2,400	7	2,750
Clocks and watches,	76	361	142	578
Horses,	64	2,695	118	4,395
Neat cattle,	648	8,825	862	10,319
Riding carriages,	13	470	5	210
Bank stocks,		2,800		300
Turnpike stock.		424		424
Money at interest,		3,040		8,034
Sheep,	863	1,120		
Polls taxable,	108		192	

These abstracts are rendered nearly useless for comparison by the arbitrary changes in the valuation of houses, lands, neat stock, &c., from year to year, according to the wisdom or caprice of the assessors.

In the item of dwelling houses, while the number is increased by the erection of some twenty new buildings, the total amount of assessment is reduced $6,260; whereas, if the standard of valuation had been uniform, the totals would have shown an increase of $6,751. So also in the valuation of lands, if the standard had been kept up, and the same number of acres assessed at the beginning and end of the decade, the aggregate would have been the same in the first and last years, instead of showing a diminution of $41,473. So also in the valuation of neat stock, the reduction of the value of cows from $13 to $11, and of other cattle in the same proportion made an aggregate reduction of $1,578.

With these equalizations of the two lists, we shall find an increase of the taxable property of the society of $15,925, while the increased number of polls, when brought up to the valuation of 1820, would have added to the list of 1830 an increase of $27,932, thus making the whole increase of the decade $43,897, or an increase of $4,390 per year.

CHAPTER XXIX.

GROWTH OF VILLAGES.—BOROUGH OF CLIFTON.—POST-OFFICES.—NEW BUILDINGS AND FACTORIES.

1831 to 1841.

We have thus far traced the early growth of Winsted with a minuteness of detail, the further prosecution of which would be equally tiresome to compiler and reader; and have reached a period when the public records cease to furnish family statistics in an available form for compiling, owing to the neglect of the old, and the imperfection of the new system of registration. We propose, therefore, in the further prosecution of our Annals, to allude only to the origin and growth of public institutions and private enterprises of special public interest.

Up to 1832, the Green Woods turnpike along Mad river, the road along the west side of Still river, and the road along the Lake stream, now respectively known as Main street, North Main street, and Lake street, furnished nearly all the building ground as yet required, and would have supplied the demand for another decade, had the land owners been disposed to meet the requirements of the increasing population.

The first movement for expanding our borders was made by an association of young men, who, in 1832, purchased a line of fifteen building lots and the land for a highway in front of them, from Lake street to Pratt street, which they named Prospect street. After making and opening the road at their own expense, they applied to the town authorities to accept it as a public highway. It was an unprecedented case. Conservatism became alarmed. It required some finessing to induce the town to accept the gift; and when accepted, the enterprise had so much fogyism to encounter, that it proved a poor investment. At the end of three years, only three houses had been erected on the street, and it was ten years before the unoccupied lots could be sold at first cost.

During the same year Wheelock Thayer erected the scythe works on Mad river now owned by his daughter, Mrs. Bacheller, and operated by the Thayer Scythe Company; and Samuel Boyd erected the Clifton Mill works, now owned by the Winsted Hoe Company, in which he manufactured shovels, hoes, and carpenters' tools for two or three years, and was succeeded by the Clifton Mill Company, who converted the original building into a flouring mill and erected the three-story building for the manufacture of bolts and nuts. The establishment was sold in 1870 to the Winsted Hoe Company, and is now used for making planters' hoes and carpenters' tools.

In 1833, on application of inhabitants of the West Village, the General Assembly granted a borough charter to comprehend the part of the borough of Winsted lying west of the second tier line. Conservatism again took the alarm, and at the first meeting for choice of officers, a ticket was elected not favorable to the objects contemplated by the charter. A small tax was laid for purchasing a fire engine and organizing a fire company. Payment of the tax was refused by some of the tax payers, and there was not found sufficient vitality in the corporate body to enforce the payment. The bantling had a paralyzed existence of two or three years, and then expired. Its primary object was, to secure an efficient fire organization; but, behind this there was a plan for securing a second post-office in place of the original office, which had been recently transferred to the East Village, the two villages being then distinct communities separated from each other by a wide space of land not then obtainable for building purposes.

In this connection a sketch of post-office changes and the almost perpetual dissensions growing out of them, which have given to our community an evil fame, seems appropriate as an element of our history. Indeed, to ignore them would be like performing the play of Hamlet with Hamlet himself left out.

There was a time, strange as it may seem to the present generation, when the post-office department was conducted without reference to party politics; when the post master general was not a cabinet officer; when the ruling question in the appointment of a deputy post-master was—is he honest, capable, and acceptable to the community; when the best interests of the public and of the department were the sole considerations applied to questions of location of offices. These principles were recognized and acted on not only in the days of Washington and Jefferson, but onward through the administrations of Monroe and the second Adams.

About 1806, the only post-office in Winchester was held by a zealous Democrat in the Widow Hall house, on the turnpike beyond the eastern border of the present borough of Winsted. The West Village had then become a business centre, and also more central to the whole town than any other point on the mail route. On a representation of these and other considerations to Post-master General Granger, a removal of the office to the West Village was ordered, and a high-toned Federalist was appointed to the place of his democratic predecessor.

It is a rule with scarcely an exception, that when rival villages exist in close vicinity to each other, a feeling of jealous rivalry grows with their growth; and if they are both within the same post-office delivery, this feeling is liable to become highly intensified. To this rule Winsted has been no exception. Prior to and during the War of 1812, the Federal element predominated in the West Village, and the democratic in the East. Efforts were made from time to time to change the politics of the postmaster and the location of the office, without avail, until the resignation of the Federal incumbent in 1830, when, on an ex-parte hearing of an application from the East Village, an unexpected appointment was made, and the location of the office transferred to that section. A second-class earthquake could scarcely have produced a greater sensation. The West Village at once sent a deputation to Washington, accompanied by a Hartford Times editor, and on a second ex-parte hearing, the department ordered the office to be re opened in the West Village; but it couldn't be made to stay there. Within six months, on another ex-parte hearing, the department ordered it back to the East Village. Remonstrances flowed in so thickly, that in about a year an oily-tongued official, rejoicing in the name of Barnabas Bates, was sent to investigate the case. Nearly three days were devoted by him to a public hearing of the contending parties. He reported to the department, in substance, that both parties ought to have it; but as they couldn't, it had better be located at an intermediate point, half a mile distant from each village centre, where next to nobody then wanted it, and, as a consequence, it rested in the East Village until after the Harrison campaign, when, under a new post-master, it again returned to the West Village, leaving a branch office for receiving and delivering letters in the East. Two years after, under Capt. Tyler's accidental reign, the office went back to the East Village, and the branch office to the West, and so continued through the administration of President Polk.

By this time the nomination of postmasters within a congressional district had, by usage, become the unquestioned prerogative—not to say perquisite—of the sitting members. Our member acted honestly and wisely by obtaining the establishment of a new office in the West Village, and leaving the old office where it then happened to be, and appointing two new postmasters. With this arrangement the land had rest for some years; but, in the mean time, each village had encroached on the intermediate vacant space. The Naugatuck Railroad was opened in 1849, and the two villages became one. But this one village had three sections instead of two—the East, the West, and the Flat. The Flat, being the central point and the railroad terminus, naturally looked to a speedy preponderance over the other sections. A consolidated post-office seemed easy of attainment. Senator Dixon, like Barkis, "was willing" and ready to help by "ways that are dark and tricks that are vain," and representative Hubbard was befogged; and like a thunder clap in a clear sky the announcement came that the West office was defunct, and the East office was transferred to the Flat! Fearful was the indignation of the outlying East and West enders. Their reciprocal heart burnings, the growth of a half century, dissolved into thin air. The whilom combatants became loving friends and turned their combined batteries upon the new victor. The Department, finding itself in a quandary, sent another political seer, named Nehemiah D. Sperry, to look into the matter, and see what was expedient to be done in the premises. Nehemiah heard the parties publicly and privately, by daylight and with a dark lantern. He too got into a quandary, and betook himself to secret negotiations and quack nostrums. The result was, a restoration of the two offices, a very imperfect healing of the new sore, and a general impression that Nehemiah was a wonderful negotiator. The two offices remained as they were until a new muddle grew out of the manipulations of a defeated candidate for congress in the fourth district, who got the Republican nomination, but could not get votes enough to elect him. His successful Republican colleagues, sorrowing for his defeat, conceded to him the bestowment of the post-offices in the district. Our people were not suited with his nominations for the twin post-offices, and some twenty-five or thirty of them went to Washington, and had a boisterous hearing before the gentlemanly P. M. G. Cresswell, who appointed two meritorious soldiers to the places, which they now hold.

It would be a wrong conclusion to draw from this detail of sectional squabbles, that our community is wholly given up to them, or that the feelings engendered are very deep or bitter. The question at issue once settled, general good feeling is soon restored, and the combatants return to their business, and with accustomed energy and cordiality unite in promoting unsectional measures of improvement or benevolence.

In 1833 the old Jenkins & Boyd scythe shop was torn down, and a new establishment was erected by parties, soon after incorporated as the Winsted Manufacturing Company. This concern, under the able and efficient agency of the late John Camp, Esq., until his death in 1862, has prosecuted the business of scythe-making to the present time with uninterrupted success, making large dividends and sustaining a high reputation for good workmanship and upright dealing. Mr. Camp died of a hemorrhage of the lungs, August 19, 1862, aged sixty-one years, leaving a name honored for integrity, public spirit, and private benevolence.

GEORGE DUDLEY, a native of Bloomfield, after a residence of several years in the east part of Winsted, purchased the Loomis tannery on Main street in 1832, and soon after went into tanning skivers or split sheep skins, imported from England, and prepared for book-binding and other purposes, a branch of the business which has proved highly remunerative to those prosecuting it with skill and energy. Mr. Dudley, after various enlargements of his works, erected his present main building about 1856, having, two or three years earlier, put up his two large drying houses on Meadow street.

The present Methodist Episcopal church on Main street was erected in 1833, under the supervision of nine trustees, of better capacity for managing dairy farms than for contracting and supervising the building of a church edifice. Many repairs and improvements of the building have, from time to time, been made, the last of which was the taking down of the insignificant spire, and replacing it with one of symmetrical proportions, creditable to the society, to the village, and to Rev. Mr. Simonson, who supervised the work.

During the latter part of this decade, from 1837 to 1840, one of our periodic business revulsions occurred, which, in a great measure, checked the growth of the place for the time being. The accession of inhabitants and of new dwellings had been rapid during the five preceding years.

Among the more permanent inhabitants of the society not already named, who came in during this decade, were Orentus Bronson, James Birdsall, Elliot Beardsley, George Taylor, Doctor James Welch, James Humphrey, Asa Parke, Alvin Gilbert, Ambrose Whiting, Horatio L. Wetmore, Anson Foskett, David N. Beardsley, Elisha Kilborn, William G. Batcheller, Caleb J. Camp, Seth L. Wilder, Normand Adams, Willard S. Wetmore, John G. Wetmore, and Chester Wentworth.

The assessment list of 1840 comprises the following items:

176	Houses,	$79,850
	Land,	127,026
19	Factories,	24,500
4	Grist and Saw Mills,	3,425
7	Stoves,	3,600
	Clocks and Watches,	1,134
104	Horses,	4,869
838	Neat Cattle,	11,392
4	Carriages,	325
	Bank Stock,	2,500
	Money at interest,	14,053
152	Taxable Polls,	3,040
	Total,	275,714

CHAPTER XXX.

NEW STREETS AND FACTORIES—WINSTED BANK—HURLBUT BANK—NAUGATUCK RAILROAD—EPISCOPAL CHURCH—NEW BURYING-GROUND.

1841 TO 1851.

In the year 1840 the meadow land between the two villages, north of Mad River, and the upland around the Naugatuck Railroad station and eastward, came into the hands of a new owner, and was opened to sale for building purposes. On the meadow between the west line of the Clarke house property and the tier line near Clifton Mill Bridge, and extending northward so as to embrace Elm street, High street, Wheeler street, most of the Green Woods Agricultural Park, the whole of Center street, and the part of Main street between the points first indicated, was used solely for farming purposes, with only one dwelling on the whole area. On the south side of the river, a road, since named Willow street, turned easterly, along the rear of the Clifton Mill property, and joined the Burrville road, on which but three houses had, as yet, been erected. Opposite the Clarke house, between the road and river, stood an ancient forge with its large coal houses, and a small forgeman's house, and across the river, a dilapidated saw-mill and three forgemen's houses on and near the site of the New England Pin Company's factory.

The lots on the north side of Main street were laid out and mainly taken up in 1841 and soon after built upon by new comers, who here found eligible openings, not before obtainable, at moderate prices. A new life and energy became apparent. New enterprises were projected and prosecuted, and old ones were stimulated to new vigor. Old indebtednesses were paid off, and the system of doing business with accommodation paper discounted at the Hartford banks and renewed at maturity, which had long prevailed, was gradually abandoned.

About 1845 the Methodist parsonage and the house now owned by Rufus E. Holmes were erected by Charles B. Weed, on the north line of High street. The line of the street had been agreed on by the proprietors of the lands through which it ran, but no action was had by the town until August 22, 1846, when, on report of the Selectmen, a survey of the proposed road along the line of High street to Elm street, and thence southerly to Main street at the Clarke House, was accepted and approved by the town; but on the 26th of October following the town voted to discontinue it, and a resort to the County Court became necessary to establish it. The lots were speedily taken up, and it has proved a favorite section of the borough.

In 1845 the new burying-ground, south of the east village, was purchased and opened. It had been laid out in lots some years earlier. The grave of a daughter of Harmon Munson, who died June 28, 1831, was the first that was opened in it. It was enlarged to its present dimensions in 1871.

In 1846 " the Home Company," a joint stock concern, now extinct, erected the factory building now owned by the New England Pin Company and went into the manufacture of doeskin cloths. The company had no previous experience in this line of manufacture; their successive foremen proved incompetent, and the enterprise shared the fate of all previous attempts at woolen manufacture in Winsted. The property was subsequently purchased by Anson G. Phelps, who, in 1855, sold it to the New England Pin Company, its present owners.

The Winsted Bank, with a capital of $100,000, was chartered in 1848. The bill for its charter was in the first instance rejected by the Assembly at the instance of the Hartford bankers; but it was at once discovered that the rejection was operating a change of views of Litchfield County members on the Air Line Bridge question, then before the Asssembly; the Hartford members obtained a reconsideration of the adverse vote; and in six hours after its rejection the charter had passed both houses.

The location and control of this institution was a matter of deep interest to the two outside sections of Winsted. Plotting and counter-plotting were resorted to. The commissioners distributed the stock in the interest of the east section, which secured five of the directors and allowed to the west section only two. Then came the presidential question. Unfortunately, the dominant party were not agreed as to which of their directors should control the institution. One of them controlled directly or indirectly six hundred out of the one thousand shares of the stock, yet he failed of an election by reason of two eastern votes being cast for a western candidate. This result was followed in a few days by the transfer of six hundred shares of stock to western parties, and soon afterwards by other transfers, which vacated the seats of two of the eastern directors, whose places were filled by directors in the western interest.

Soon after this, the banking office was opened in a room of the Beardsley House, with George Dudley as President, and E. S. Hamilton as Cashier.

The banking house, now the property of the Winsted Savings Bank, was erected in 1851. The profits of the first six months' business were swallowed up by the failure of one customer residing out of the State. By experience and caution, the bank thereafter in a great measure escaped similar losses, and did a prosperous business until Nov. 9, 1861, when its vault was broken open by burglars, who carried off cash assets to the amount of $60,100, only about $18,000 of which were finally recovered, at a cost of over $2,000. This calamity, by impairing its capital, prevented its reception as a National Bank; in consequence of which, and the heavy tax on circulation of State banks, its business was thereafter prosecuted at great disadvantage, and it was closed and the charter surrendered Sept. 1, 1867.

Notwithstanding this loss, and disadvantage, the institution had been so carefully and judiciously managed that the stock-holders received on the final liquidation $113 on each $100 of their stock.*

The Hurlbut Bank was organized in June, 1857, under the provisions of the General Banking Law of 1852, and under the presidency of William H. Phelps, Esq., its organizer, who controlled its operations until his death on the 25th day of August, 1864, at the age of about 46.

The directors of the bank, by vote on record, Resolved " that we are fully sensible of the loss to this institution of an able financier, whose faithfulness and diligence in managing the affairs of the bank are fully apparent in its success, and the character it has sustained at home and abroad for its soundness and prosperity. We also feel deeply his loss in common with this community, as an honest and capable adviser, a genial companion, and highly esteemed citizen."

The bank was organized with a capital of $130,000, which was increased in 1854 to $200,000; to which has since been added a subscription of stock to the amount of $5,000 by the American Deaf and Dumb Asylum.

It was reorganized as a National Bank immediately after the passage by Congress of the National Banking Law; and since the death of Mr. Phelps has been successfully and profitably managed by officers trained by him.

The Naugatuck Railroad, from Derby to Plymouth, was chartered in 1845. In 1847 the company was allowed an extension of one year for commencing its road and expending thereon the sum of fifty thousand dollars; and were authorized to extend its line to Winsted. Prior to the awarding of the contracts and extending the line to Winsted, it had been transferred to Alfred Bishop, of Bridgeport, and his associates, who in

---

* It should have been noted that the capital stock of the bank was enlarged in 1854 to $300,000.

consideration of a bonus of thirty thousand dollars and payment of the land damages along its line to Waterbury, by the citizens interested in its completion, contracted to build the road and open it to that point in 1849. Soon after the extension to Winsted was authorized, Mr. Bishop proposed to so extend it, on being secured another cash bonus of $30,000, and a right of way from Waterbury northward. The proposition was unlooked for, but was promptly responded to. A meeting of citizens interested along the line was immediately called, and a division of responsibility was agreed upon, by which the citizens of Winsted assumed half the bonus and the securing the whole right of way and depot grounds within the town of Winchester; and the citizens of Wolcottville and Plymouth agreed to assume the other half of the bonus and the whole expense of the remaining land title.

A spirit of liberality, before unprecedented, prevailed. Men gave their thousands who had never before given a hundred for any public object. The subscription was speedily filled up,— when the chronic sectional disease of our community broke out on the question of locating the terminus,— whether it should be on the East village green, on the Flat, or in the West village. There was a backing down of a portion of subscriptions, which rendered a new subscription necessary on the basis of locating the terminus on the Flat where the depot now stands. A reassessment of the adhering subscribers was proposed and speedily adopted. About five thousand dollars was assumed by adhering subscribers to make good the withdrawn subscriptions, and the contract with Mr. Bishop was thereupon perfected.

The iron horse paid his first visit to the Winsted depot, Sept. 21, 1849. The first passenger train came up on Saturday the 22d, and returned on the following Monday. The population of the whole town at that period was less than 2,100. In 1860 it was 3,550. As the population of the Old Society remained stationary, or decreased during the intervening period, we may safely estimate the increase of Winsted population during the eleven years after the opening of the railroad at 1450,— or 65 per cent.

The number of taxable polls in the town in 1849 was, - - 438
In 1860, it had increased to - - - - - 853
Showing a gain in eleven years of 94¾ per cent.

This increased value of property is not to be wholly assigned to Winsted Society, as it results partly from the greatly increased valuation of wood lands throughout the whole town.

Mr. Bishop, the projector and builder of the road, died before its completion. He was a man of far seeing and comprehensive views,— of quiet energy, and liberal spirit. He looked to ultimate results rather than to immediate gains, and believed in a policy of promoting the growth of manufacturing and commercial business along the whole line of the road, to be affected by low freights on raw materials going from tide-water to the interior, and thereby increasing the return freights of manufactured articles. His successors entertained more conservative views. They looked to immediate results, not by fostering the interests of the business sections remote from tide-water, but by imposing high fares and indiscriminating tariffs of freights, — so high as to discourage new manufacturing enterprises. This policy was peculiarly unfavorable to Winsted by reason of her manufactures being mainly of heavy iron hardware, requiring iron, steel, coal, grind-stones, etc., to be brought from tide-water.

The result was, for several years, a most unsatisfactory income to the company from the northern section of the road. The main cause of this did not so impress itself upon the comprehension of the directors of the road as to induce any change of policy. Nevertheless, our business, though sadly retarded, could not but be benefited by a small reduction of freights and fares below the cost of transportation by teams to and from Hartford on the east, and the Housatonic Railroad on the west.

The unprofitableness of the road until a recent period, grew in part out of its cheap original construction. A large portion of the stone masonry and bridges have required rebuilding not only once, but in not a few cases, oftener. The track has had to be raised or changed in many places, and no inconsiderable damages have been paid for accidents growing out of imperfect construction and repairs. To the stockholders, it has eventually become a profitable pecuniary investment; — whether more or less so by reason of its enormous freight charges and penurious management, is a question on which there may be a diversity of opinion.

The first stated worship of the Protestant Episcopal Church in Winsted was begun in 1847, by Rev. H. Frisbie, and some funds were then raised for a church edifice. During the following year arrangements were made for building a church and a location was agreed on. The present Episcopal Church was soon after contracted for and was completed in October, 1848; and on the 27th day of that month the parish of St. James was legally organized by choice of Rev. Jonathan Coe, Jr., Rector, James R. Coe and Uriel Spencer, Jr., Wardens; and Dr. John L. Wakefield, Hon. Wm. S. Holabird, and Alexander Durgin, Vestrymen. The church was consecrated the same autumn. Rev. Jonathan Coe, Jr., was succeeded in 1854 by Rev. James W. Coe, who officiated for one year. In 1856 Rev. James R. Coe, brother of the first Rector, was chosen Rector, and officiated as such until 1860, when he was succeeded by Rev. David H. Short, who remained about two years, after which the parish was for some time supplied by Rev. J. D. Berry, D.D., of Litchfield. In 1866 Rev. Wm. H. Williams was chosen Rector, and served two years; and was succeeded by Rev. Wm. H. Lewis, Jr., who remained until May, 1870, when Rev. D. P. Sanford, the present Rector, took charge of the parish. The location of the church, influenced by the liberal subscriptions of individuals in its immediate vicinity, has been deemed ill-judged, and is supposed to have essentially retarded its growth. Endeavors have been made to obtain its removal to a more central point, intermediate between the east and west sections, but as yet without success.

Meadow street was laid out in the fall of 1849 by Col. Hosea Hinsdale and Samuel Boyd, who owned the adjoining lands and laid them out in building lots of five rods front and eight rods depth. The northern portion of the land had been the home meadow of Col. Hinsdale, and the southern, the home meadow of James Boyd, then recently deceased. Buildings began at once to be erected on these lots, and they were nearly all taken up and improved within five years. Monroe street was also laid out and opened by Mr. Boyd the same year.

We note, among our prominent citizens who died during this decade, the following:

 Capt. Zebina Smith, February 4, 1842, aged 82.
 Capt. Grinnell Spencer, March 5, 1843, aged 74.
 Theodore Hinsdale, Esq., Nov. 27, 1841, aged 40.
 Rev. Daniel Coe, Jan. 12, 1847, aged 64.
 James Boyd, Feb. 28, 1849, aged 78.
 Rev. James Beach, June 10, 1850, aged 70.
 Jonathan Coe, May 31, 1849, aged 79.
 Luman Hubbell, Oct. 1846.
 Gideon Hall, Sr., Feb. 23, 1850, aged 75.
 Dr. Luman Wakefield, March 20, 1850, aged 63.
 Nath. B. Gaylord,   1849.

We compile abstracts of the Assessment Lists of 1840 and 1850, showing the increased quantity and amount of property during the decade as follows:

	List of 1840.		List of 1850.		Increase.	
Dwelling houses,	176	$79,850	311	$161,880	135	82,030
Acres of land,	8,168	127,026	8,477	184,103	309	57,077
Mills, factories, and stores,	30	31,525	39	65,605	9	34,080
Horses,	104	4,869	177	9,135	73	4,266
Neat cattle,	838	11,392	1,201	15,397	363	4,005
Investments in trade and manufactures,		8,225		76,790		68,565
Bank stocks,		2,500		71,430		68,930
Railroad bonds,				5,400		5,400
Money at interest,		14,053		74,294		60,241
Taxable polls,	152		383		231	
Total amount of taxable property on the two assessment lists,		459,649		669,999		209,350
Population of town,		1,667		2,179		512

It will be seen by the foregoing abstracts that the dwellings had nearly doubled in number, and more than doubled in value during the ten years; — that the value of factories, stores, etc., had more than doubled; that the bank stocks had increased more than twenty-fold, and money at interest more than five-fold.

The population of the Old Society remained stationary or decreased during the decade, so that the gain was altogether in Winsted.

CHAPTER XXXI.

1841 TO 1851.

MECHANICS AND LABORERS.—ROMAN CATHOLIC CHURCH.—SAVINGS AND BUILDING ASSOCIATION.—NEW STREETS.

The elements of the steady and prosperous growth of Winsted have been, first of all, business men not only of energy, but of sound moral and religious principle; second, the manufacture of such articles of prime necessity as require skillful and hard-working artizans; third, a variety of moderately-sized establishments, conducted by actual resident owners; fourth, a mutual sympathy of employers and employed, combined with a desire on all hands for the moral improvement of the community.

The original iron workers—forgemen, as they were termed—came from Ancram, N. Y., and from the Jerseys. They were mainly of Low Dutch descent, working hard at irregular hours, blowing up their fires at from two to four o'clock in the morning, completing their day's work soon after noon, and spending the rest of the day in fishing and drinking. This was the general characteristic, but there were some of them who broke loose from these habits, and became thrifty men and good citizens.

The iron masters discovered the evils of rum selling and rum drinking years before the general temperance movement began, and applied the remedy in part, abandoning the sale of liquors, and getting rid of their most intemperate workmen.

The early scythe makers were mainly Down Easters, of industrious, thrifty habits, and good morals. Their successors have maintained their characteristics, and constitute a large class of our most respectable citizens and property owners. The same qualities characterize our tanners, clockmakers, hoemakers, machinists, and other handicraftsmen. In no other manufacturing place in the state are as large a portion of the mechanics owners of comfortable homesteads, to say nothing of savings bank deposits and ten per cent. bonds, as in Winsted. We are most fortunately exempt from overshadowing cotton mills, print works, paper mills, and other establishments mainly sustained by the bone and muscle of poor children, imported—with their degraded parents—in box cars from the cities, and uncared for by their absentee employer, save in securing from them the largest amount of labor, at the lowest cost.

The diversity of our manufactures is a special source of prosperity. The depression of one or two branches does not paralyze the community nor crowd the poor house.

Prior to the opening of the Naugatuck Railroad, the number of residents of foreign birth was very limited. Some of the railroad laborers remained after the road was finished, and their friends and relations joined them. Others followed them by the new channel of access to this before secluded region. All of them found ready employment in a sober and temperate community, as yet uncontaminated by a vicious class.

It is a prevailing habit to carp about the faults and vices of our foreign laborers and domestics. The first question is, what could we have done without them in our rapidly enlarging community, in which every native born robust man could have found better employment than precarious day labor, and every healthy intelligent girl could go into a school or factory, where higher wages could be earned, and better dresses worn than at domestic service. Better, it doubtless might have been, that the good old time had continued, when a trade required from five to seven years apprenticeship, instead of six months as at present; when the young farmer's son worked out by the month to earn his first investment in land, and the smart farmer's daughter, besides doing the household drudgery, spun her two runs of yarn each day, and went to conference or singing school at night, on a stipend of four-and-sixpence a week; but those times had been played out long before the advent of Patrick and Bridget. It was Patrick, with his unreasoning muscle, who brought the railroad to our doors, and then cheerfully, though unskillfully, took up and carried forward the lost art of hard drudgery, which the discontented and fretful employer, not owning a gang of fat healthy negroes, could obtain from no other earthly quarter. It was Bridget who became the angel of the kitchen — an imperfect angel to be sure — but considerably more charming than the slatternly home-raised hired help; the remnant of her race, who, in later times, shirked the hardest drudgery of the kitchen on her careworn mistress, and combed out her carroty locks in the parlor in presence of the mistress's guests.

There is a prevailing tendency to berate the Irish beyond reason. Glaring faults they have, as a result of grinding oppression and cruelty to which they and their fathers have been subjected for centuries. They have also virtues, which are to be developed only by patience and considerate kindness. They are ignorant, and must be enlightened by education and moral culture. They are among us and of us, and they bid fair to outnumber us in half a century, unless the Yankee race becomes more prolific in the future than in the present era of barrenness among native women.

Roman Catholic worship was first instituted in Winsted in 1851, by Rev. James Lynch, from Birmingham, in the schoolhouse of the west district, which was attended by about forty Catholics. Land for a church lot was secured the same year, and in 1852 Rev. Thomas Quinn entered on his pastoral duties, and commenced the erection of St. Joseph's Catholic Church. Until its completion mass was celebrated on the sabbath in Camp's Hall. Rev. Philip Gilleck succeeded Father Quinn in 1853, and supervised the completion of the church so far as to render it suitable for divine worship. The Rev. Thomas Henricken, now Bishop of the Diocese of Rhode Island, succeeded Father Gilleck in 1854, and in 1855 was transferred to Waterbury, when Rev. Richard O'Gorman succeeded him in the pastorate. He was succeeded in 1856 by Rev. Lawrence Mangan, and he in 1860 by Rev. Daniel Mullen, who was soon after transferred to the chaplaincy of the 9th Regiment, Connecticut Volunteers. He was succeeded in 1861 by Rev. Philip Sheriden, who remained in the pastorate until 1864, when Rev. Father Leo da Saracena, of the Order of St. Francis d'Assissi, who had succeeded Father Mullen in the chaplaincy of the 9th Connecticut Volunteers, was appointed to the pastorate by Bishop McFarland of Hartford.

Under his energetic supervision, the parish was thoroughly organized, and additional lands were purchased, with buildings thereon for a parish school, and a residence for the sisters of the third order of St. Francis, by whom the school was organized, and has been successfully conducted, the number of children in attendance being from fifty to sixty. In 1866 he secured the purchase of other adjoining lands for the institutions of his order, on which he proceeded to erect the brick monastery standing immediately west of the church, the church itself having been donated to the order by Bishop McFarland in November, 1866. In January, 1867, other land and buildings were purchased and fitted up for the Academy of St. Margaret of Cortonia, an institution for educating young ladies in the higher branches. A fine grove in the rear of the church and monastery has also been purchased, in which it is designed to erect a future residence of the sisters of the order.

The buildings stand on a hill sloping down to Main street on the south, so elevated as to command a splendid view of the surrounding village and valley.

The institution was incorporated in 1866, under the name of "The St. Francis Literary and Theological Seminary," and is now (1872) conducted by the following officials:—

ST. JOSEPH'S R. C. CHURCH.

Pastor—Rev. Fra. Leo da Saracena, O.S.F.

ST. FRANCIS' R. C. LITERARY AND THEOLOGICAL SEMINARY.

President—Rev. Fra. Leo da Saracena, O.S.F.
Vice-President—Rev. Fra. Isaiah da Scanno, O.S.F.
Secretary—Rev. Fra. Diomedes, O.S.F.

ST. MARGARET'S R. C. ACADEMY FOR YOUNG LADIES.

Instructors—Sisters of St. Francis.

ST. FRANCIS R. C. PAROCHIAL SCHOOL.

Instructors—Sisters of St. Francis.

SISTERS OF ST. FRANCIS' CONVENT.

Rev. Mother Josephine Todd.*

John D. Howe and Willard S. Wetmore having, in 1850, purchased from the heirs of Luman Wakefield, deceased, two adjoining tracts of land on the west border of the east village, proceeded to lay out four streets thereon, and to divide the adjoining lands into quarter-acre lots. The streets laid out were — Grove street, running westerly from the east village park, Walnut street, Oak street, and Chestnut street, running parallel with each other, northerly from Main to Grove streets. They were accepted as highways by the town in 1851.

An epidemic building fever set in about this time, which expedited the rapid sale of these and other newly-opened lots. The source of this epidemic is traceable to an association of homeless men in New Haven, who sought to aid each other in providing homesteads by combining their limited resources, and loaning the same, as they accrued, to the members of the association offering the highest bonus, in addition to six per cent. interest therefor, and applying the loaned money to buildings to be erected on lots mortgaged to the association as security for the loans. Each associate on joining the institution took up any number of shares at his option, and contracted to pay in monthly installments of five per cent. until the stock taken was fully paid up. The amount monthly paid in was at once loaned to the stockholder who offered the highest bonus in addition to legal monthly interest, and the money borrowed, less the

---

* The foregoing details are gathered and condensed from materials furnished by Rev. Father Leo da Saracena.

bonus, was to be applied to building a house on a lot owned by the borrower, and mortgaged to the association for security of his loan. The theory was that each stockholder of a series was eventually to become a borrower of a sum equal to the amount of his stock. When this point was reached, or before, the whole capital of the series would be filled up, and the principal of each borrower's note be paid by a surrender of his fully paid stock, leaving the balance of profit, if any, to be divided to each of the series *pro rata.*

One series of stockholders being thus paid off and discharged, the same process of paying in and loaning out in due course of time discharged and paid off the next series, the third, and so on, as long as accessions of stockholders and borrowers could be secured. The whole thing looked rose-colored on paper. There were wise financiers who could mathematically demonstrate that however large the bonuses paid on loans, both the borrower and lender would be equally benefited.

On the promulgation of this financial discovery the General Assembly of 1850 gave it their blessing and sanction by authorizing the establishment of savings and building associations without limit of number or capital, and with a perfect abandon of prudential restraints and prohibitions. The principle of requiring each stockholder to become a borrower was discarded. The associations were allowed to receive deposits from outsiders, either on interest or without, and to make temporary or permanent loans of the same to outsiders or members, on personal or mortgage securities, and at any rate of premium added to interest they could extort from needy borrowers.

Institutions under this law were speedily organized all over the state. Our community, by reason of its chronic local jealousies, could not work together in one company, and so formed two: "The Winsted Saving and Building Association" in the East Village, and "The West Winsted Savings Bank and Building Association" in the West Village, which went into operation in May and July, 1852. The rich and the poor went into money making and homestead building with a rush. The rival companies stimulated each other. Our moneyed men, who had before loaned their funds on legal interest, found, in the workings of these institutions, a mine of legal extortion, of which they speedily availed themselves. They collected in their six per cent. loans, and made these institutions the dispensers of their funds. The banks had ceased to discount accommodation paper, and scrimped their business customers, in order to make western loans on protected circulation. The school fund had very limited incoming funds, and could loan them in New York state and elsewhere at 7 per cent. Honest, unsophisticated savings banks were mainly confined to the cities. The poor man and the man loaded with debt had no other resource but these disguised shaving mills. Their monthly loanings were competed for with blind desperation, and were taken at premiums of from 20 to 33 per cent. over and beyond legal interest, the premium being deducted from the principal in advance, and the interest made a monthly charge.

The stockholder was bound to pay in on the first of each month a five dollar installment on each thousand dollars of his stock. If a borrower, he bound himself to pay five dollars more on the thousand of the principal of his loan, and five more as interest thereon. He was told by those who ought to have known better — if they did not — that there was a talismanic working of the financial scheme, which would come out all right in the end, and make him the easy owner of a homestead. This system of grinding had some features of plausibility about it by which improvident men were encouraged to embark in the scheme, and induced to assume monthly liabilities which they could not discharge out of their monthly earnings without starving their families or running in debt for food and clothing.

But their charters permitted them to run another grinding mill without restraint or limitation. They could receive funds deposited at a legal rate of interest, and loan them out on short paper, secured by endorsers or collaterals, to the highest bidder, without limit of premium. The premiums discounted generally ranged from one to two per cent. a month, and in some cases higher, owing to the necessities of borrowing stockholders to meet their monthly dues.

The machines, at the outset, worked smoothly. There was a phrenzy of money making sentiment in their favor which silenced criticism, and put down all opposition. Series after series of stock were taken up. First series shares soon rose, not in value, but in estimation, based on apparent profits, to double the investments paid in. Men more far-seeing than avaricious began to sell their shares to their more sanguine associates; but still, little of friction was manifest. Borrowers still contrived, by hook or by crook, to pay up their monthly dues. This went on for two or three years before serious discontent became manifest. Some of the borrowers, to be sure, had already been driven to a forfeiture of their stock and a loss of what they had paid in, but their associates were slow to perceive that the same fate awaited their own ventures. At length discontent and alarm became general. Large numbers of borrowers ceased to pay their monthly dues, and defied the companies to collect them. Foreclosures were resorted to by the companies, and on trial of these the defendants raised questions as to the legality of the loans. The courts, impressed with the magnitude of the interests, and the nicety of the legal questions involved, were slow to decide, but finally sustained the legality of the loans; and the legislature passed an act affirming past illegal contracts, and limiting the extent of usurious robbery thereafter to an equivalent of twelve per cent.

By this time, the associates, much reduced in numbers, were ranged in two well-defined antagonistic classes, the rich speculators, who had retained their original stock, and bought in the stock of many of the smaller non-borrowing associates, and the rebellious borrowers who had not yet been ground to powder. There was, moreover, a small class of borrowers who heroically continued to pay their monthly dues. One after another of the borrowers made the best terms they could with the speculators and got rid of the concern, rather than waste their money in law suits. The persistent rebels were foreclosed. The surrendered and foreclosed homesteads were sold by auction, not to the public at large, but within the ring of surviving associates. The prices realized in these sales were uniformly below the cost of the buildings, and many of them did not pay half the pledged indebtedness; but they were mainly bid off by parties who could hold and rent them until, on a change of times, they could sell them at a large advance on the cost.

The legislature, in the meantime, had set about amending the organic law by enacting such provisions as should, at the outset, have protected the borrowers from the cruel extortions to which they were subjected. One of these provided that, in the future, no association should be formed unless all the stock should be owned and held by borrowers to an amount equal to their stock when fully paid in. Another act, in 1868, subjected the association to the scrutiny and supervision of the bank commissioners, and utterly abolished the system of bonuses on loans, and provided for an equitable liquidation of claims, and a winding up of such associations as were played out, and prohibited the formation of new ones under the law of 1850.

Some of the associations had a tenacity of life and sharp practice which defied extinguishment by previous enactments. These, by a law of that year, were required to pay into the state treasury one-fourth of one per cent. annually on their stocks and deposits; and by a law of 1860 they were prohibited from receiving deposits after 1861.

Whatever may have been the operations and results of these associations elsewhere — in Winsted they were oppressive and disastrous. The rich were made richer and the poor were made poorer. More than a hundred ill-contrived and poorly built dwellings were erected, in whole or in part, by means of funds from these associations, very few of which remain in the hands of the builders. Our two associations, so rich in promise, and so baleful in performance, breathed their last contemporaneously about 1860.

The following new streets, in addition to those already referred to, were laid out and accepted at the dates specified:—

Meadow street, from Lake to Main street, was laid out in 1850, and accepted by the town in 1851.

The west part of Willow street, which originally ran over the site of the Naugatuck passenger depot, was moved to its present line in 1849, and the three houses then standing on its south side were moved to the bank of the river.

Bridge street was laid out and accepted in 1856, and Elm street was extended northerly along the west border of the agricultural park the same year.

Center street and Case avenue were accepted in June, 1853.

Spring street, from Prospect street west to the residence of Mrs. Ellen A. Phillips, and the part of Rockwell street running thence south east to Pratt street, were accepted in October, 1853, but the latter had been graded and built on some two years earlier. The northerly section of Rockwell street, extending to Lake street, was graded and accepted in 1856. Each of these three highways, and the working of them, was granted to the town without claim for compensation.

Union street was opened and accepted as a highway in July, 1854.

The part of the new road from Winsted to Riverton, starting from near the east abutment of the Daniel B. Wilson bridge over Still River, and running northeasterly to Barkhamsted line, was laid out and accepted in August, 1858.

North Main street originally ran north and south through the center of the public green or parade ground in the east village. Preparatory to enclosing this ground as a park, the two streets now bordering the enclosure on the east and west sides were laid out and accepted by the town in 1858, and at the same time the central highway was discontinued. The area was enclosed and graded, and the trees and evergreens set out soon afterwards by voluntary subscriptions of citizens residing in the vicinity.

We compile from the assessment list of 1840 the items and amount of taxable property, and amount thereof in the Society of Winsted, as follows:—

No.	Real Estate.	Valuation.		
176	Dwelling houses,	$79,850	At 3 per cent.	
8,168	Acres land,	127,026		
19	Factories,	24,500		
7	Stores,	3,600		
4	Mills,	3,425	$238,401	$ 752.03
	Personal Estate.		At 6 per cent.	
838	Neat cattle,	11,392		
104	Horses,	4,869		
509	Sheep,	509		
4	Carriages,	325		
199	Clocks and watches,	1,137		
	Silver plate,	50		
	Money at interest,	14,053		
	Bank stock,	2,500		
	Turnpike stock,	400	$35,235	2,514.10
	Assessments of business,			247.00
152	Polls,			3,040.00
				$12,553.13
	Deduct for indebtedness,			407.67
				$12,145.46

CHAPTER XXXII.

FROM 1851 TO 1861.

1851.

PRIOR to 1851 only three churches existed in Winsted: the First Congregational, the Methodist, and the Episcopal. The Congregational house was located in the East Village, and was attended by members from all sections of the society. The Methodist house was located in the West Village, and was mainly attended by residents in the West section.

On the 14th of May, 1853, a meeting was called to consult in reference to the organization of a second Congregational church and society to be located in the West Village, and a committee was appointed to investigate the subject, and report to an adjourned meeting on the 21st. The committee reported on the 27th that the large increase of population, and the prospect of a more rapid accession in the future, rendered an increase of religious privileges and accommodations indispensable to the well-being of the community; and recommended an early organization of an Ecclesiastical society, and the location and building of a house of worship; and thereupon a society was duly organized under the corporate name of "The Second Congregational Society of Winsted." The original corporators were: James Humphrey, Timothy Hulbert, Phelps H. Parsons, James Cone, John Cone, Elizur B. Parsons, William S. Phillips, and Joel G. Griswold, not belonging to the first society, to whom were added, by certificate of withdrawal from the first society, John Boyd, John Hinsdale, Moses Camp, Wm. F. Hatch, Sherman T. Cooke, Geo. Dudley, Caleb J. Camp, James R. Alvord, John W. Bidwell, John T. Rockwell, Abram G. Kellogg, James Welch, Elliot Beardsley, James C. Smith, Charles C. Spencer, Joel J. Wilcox, Lyman Baldwin, Jenison J. Whiting, and James Birdsall.

The church with which the society was connected was made up mainly of members of the First Congregational Church regularly dismissed, and was organized with the advice of a council of neighboring churches. The first religious services were held in Camp's hall late in November, 1853, and conducted by Rev. C. H. A. Bulckley, of New York, who continued to supply the pulpit through the months of December and January following. On the 8th of February, 1854, a unanimous call of the church and society was extended to him to become the pastor, on a salary of one thousand dollars a year, which was accepted on the second of April following, and he was soon afterwards installed by an advisory council of neighboring churches.

The religious exercises of the church continued to be held in Camp's hall until 1857. In the meantime, the building of a church edifice was delayed by the difficulty of obtaining an eligible lot on which to erect it, until March, 1856, when the site of the present house was purchased, on which the house was built during the year following, and was dedicated September 16th, 1857.

Mr. Bulckley continued his pastorate of the church until May 7, 1859, when his resignation was accepted. During the same year the chapel immediately north of the church edifice was raised and covered in. Early in February, 1860, the steeple of the church was blown down, and nearly half of the roof was crushed in by its fall. It was rebuilt and the chapel finished the following season at a cost of five thousand dollars, which, when added to the previous cost of the buildings and ground, made up the sum of about twenty thousand dollars. As a token of the kindly feeling subsisting between the Congregational and Methodist churches, it is worthy of note that immediately after the disaster above mentioned the Methodist church cordially invited its unfortunate sister church to occupy their pulpit with its minister, either one-half of each Sabbath, or the whole of each alternate Sabbath, until its repairs should be completed. The First Congregational church in the East Village extended a similar invitation. These invitations were gratefully acknowledged, but declined in order that the Sabbath-school of the church might be kept up by meeting for worship in the old quarters at Camp's Hall.

In August, 1860, the church and society extended a call to Rev. Arthur T. Pierson to become their pastor, which was declined. On the 7th of September following an unanimous call of the church and society was extended to Rev. Hiram Eddy, which was accepted by him on Nov. 6, 1860, and he was soon afterwards installed. The repairs of the church were completed so as to re-open the services there early in January, 1861. Rev. Mr. Eddy having received from Governor Buckingham the appointment of Chaplain of the Second Regiment Connecticut Infantry, applied on June 16, 1861, for leave of absence for two months, which was granted, and provision made for the supply of his pulpit. He was taken prisoner by the rebels on the retreat from Bull Run, and went the round of rebel prisons, from Richmond to Columbia, S. C., thence to Charleston and back to Salisbury, N. C., where he was exchanged, after an imprisonment and the cruelest treatment for fourteen months, when he returned and resumed his parochial duties. In 1864 the organ now in use was purchased by individual subscriptions at a cost of two thousand dollars.

On the 16th of October, 1865, Mr. Eddy's resignation was presented to the church and society and accepted. On the 16th of May, 1866, Rev. Charles Wetherby, of North Cornwall, was called to the pastorate on a salary of $1500, and a free parsonage, which he accepted, and was installed soon afterward. He continued his pastorate until October 9, 1871, when he was dismissed at his own request.

On the organization of the Second Congregational church in 1853, Rev. Ira Pettibone, who had succeeded the Rev. James Beach in the pastorate of the First Congregational church, tendered his resignation, which was accepted, and the Rev. H. A. Russell, a licentiate from the Yale Theological Seminary, was called to fill his place, Feb. 11, 1854, and was soon afterwards ordained. He was dismissed Aug. 28, 1858, and was succeeded by Rev. James B. Pierson, who was called Dec. 30, 1859, and dismissed March 11, 1862, after which Rev. M. McG. Dana, a licentiate of Union Theological Seminary, supplied the pulpit about two years, until his call to the pastorate of the First Congregational church in Norwich, Connecticut, in December, 1864. The pulpit was supplied for several months by Rev. L. M. Dorman, afterwards settled at Manchester, then by Rev. Mr. Page from Durham, for about one year. Rev. J. B. R. Walker, then recently from Holyoke, Mass., supplied the pulpit from March, 1867, to April, 1869, and was succeeded, as a supply, by Rev. H. E. Cooky, from April, 1869, to April, 1870. Rev. Thomas M. Miles, the present pastor, on a unanimous call of the church and society, was installed on the 10th of November, 1870.

The two sections of Winsted having become united in one continuous village of as compact form as the conformation of the land would admit, many questions of police arose which could not be satisfactorily settled by the town authorities. Street lines needed regulating and a system of sidewalks to be established. Fire regulations were indispensable, and connected with them, a water supply and fire companies. Municipal regulations not required for town governments were needed.

An application for a borough charter was made to the Assembly in 1858, which was granted in June of that year, by which the defunct borough charter of Clifton, covering only the West section of the village, was repealed, and more enlarged powers conferred on the new body, which was organized by an election of the following officers on the second day of August of the same year:

WILLIAM H. PHELPS, *Warden.*

Rollin L. Beecher,
Edward Camp,
John T. Rockwell,
Charles Cook,
Charles B. Weed,
John G. Wetmore,
} *Burgesses.*

John Hinsdale, *Treasurer.*
Caleb P. Newman, *Bailiff.*

 The attention of the Warden and Burgesses was first directed to the improvement of streets, and the laying out and construction of sidewalks. A careful survey and plan of all the streets within the borough, as they then existed, was made, and sidewalks were ordered to be graded where immediately required.

 One of the earliest improvements ordered by the borough authorities was the closing of the road through the centre of the East Village Green and opening parallel streets on the east and west sides thereof, as already described. The intervening area was graded, enclosed with a stone and iron railing, and planted with maples, elms, and evergreens by private subscriptions at an expense of about two thousand dollars, receiving the corporate name of "Park Place."

 The first sidewalk surveyed was along the north and east side of Main street, from the corner of Main and North Main streets westerly and northerly to corner of Main and Spencer streets, a distance of one mile and twenty rods, which was ordered to be graded and rounded to a width of five feet. The portion of this walk east of Chestnut street was originally planked, and the remaining portion was flagged with North River stone. The portion originally planked was, at a later period, flagged with concrete. A plank walk was early ordered on the east side of North Main street, which, after a few years, was replaced by a concrete walk extending northward to the borough line. Another plank walk was laid on Main street from the corner of Spencer street to Dudley's tannery, of which the portions on the east side have been replaced by concrete. The flagged and concrete walks of the borough are believed to exceed a length of three miles, and are mainly from five to six feet wide, and in excellent condition.

 The organization of a fire department was delayed by reason of a general desire to obtain a supply of water for its use, by means of an aqueduct from the lake, distributing water to all parts of the borough. On the 30th of August, 1858, the warden and burgesses were instructed "to ascertain whether the borough has a right to draw water from Long Lake; whether the amount taken through a six-inch pipe would be prejudicial to the manufacturing interests of the borough, and if it probably would be so prejudicial, whether a reservoir of sufficient capacity to meet the wants of the borough might not be constantly filled by the waste water of the lake." On the 19th of August, 1859, on report of a committee of the warden and burgesses, a petition was brought to the assembly of 1860 for power to draw water from the lake on such terms and under such limitations as should be prescribed.

The Assembly, at its May Session in 1860, granted power to the warden and burgesses to take water from Long Lake or the Little Pond for fire and other purposes, and to raise the surface of the water in said lake or pond not exceeding four feet above the then existing high water mark, by suitable embankments where necessary, and such water to distribute by aqueducts, &c., throughout the borough for all purposes, with a proviso that the water should be so taken and distributed for fire purposes only, until the lake embankment should be made sufficiently high to raise the water of the lake at least three feet above the then existing waste-weir near the outlet of the lake, nor until the water shall have risen two feet above said waste-weir, and that the person controlling the outflow of water for manufacturing purposes shall not permit the water to be wasted thereafter in greater quantity than theretofore. Provision was also made for the appointment of water commissioners, with requisite powers to secure the right of flowage along the shores of the lake; to construct the necessary embankments, to lay and construct all necessary pipes and aqueducts, to regulate the distribution and use of the water, and establish and collect water rents therefor. The borough was authorized to raise by permanent loan a sum not exceeding $25,000, at six per cent. interest, to be applied to the cost and expenses of construction of the said water works, and for no other purpose whatever.

The powers granted as above by the assembly were accepted in a borough meeting, on the 1st of August, 1860, by a vote of 217 for, and 68 against the acceptance, and three water commissioners were appointed, who at once proceeded to carry out the necessary measures contemplated in their appointment. An imperfect embankment at the outlet of the lake was so far completed during the season, that on the 13th of March, 1861, a rise of water to twenty-four and a half inches above the previous high-water mark was duly certified. During the following three months the rise attained a level of fully four feet above the old high water mark, and so overflowed the frail embankment as imminently to threaten its destruction, and the consequent deluge of a large portion of the village. During the summer and fall the embankment was remodeled and thoroughly perfected, so that no danger of a crevasse has since been apprehended. The height of reserve water on the lake, when full, is about ten feet above the bottom of the gates through which it is drawn for manufacturing purposes.

During the making of the original embankment in 1860, a main pipe of sheet iron, lined within and without with water cement, having an interior diameter of nine inches, was carried from the lake, under Lake street, and thence under Main street; from the corner of Spencer street in a six-inch pipe of same materials, to the corner of North Main street, and thence in a four-inch pipe under North Main street to the corner of Wallen street, and from Lake street through Meadow street. In 1864 pipes were laid under Prospect street, and extensions made in other directions. Branches have been since laid from year to year, until nearly every street in the borough, sufficiently below the level of the lake, is now (1872) supplied with water for fire and family purposes, the whole length of pipe of all sizes amounting to about six and a half miles. The surface elevation of the lake is about 150 feet above the corner of Lake and Main streets, and over 200 feet above the terminus of pipe under North Main street. Experience has proved that with the free — not to say wasteful — use of the water thus far permitted, the size of the main pipe has become insufficient for fire purposes in the remote parts of the borough, and that the sheet iron and cement pipes are insufficient to sustain the pressure. This has become so apparent that measures have already been adopted, and partially carried out, for substituting a twelve-inch cast iron pipe from the Lake to Main street, with the expectation of being obliged, at no distant period, to substitute enlarged pipes of cast iron throughout the borough.

In November, 1862, the Fire Department was organized by dividing the borough into four fire districts, to be under the control of a fire warden, and an assistant fire warden, in each district, each district to be furnished with a hose cart, supplied with not less than 300 feet of hose, and other necessary apparatus, to be worked by a volunteer fire company of ten or more members. For the streets of the borough not supplied with available water, which could be thrown upon its buildings directly from the hydrants, only one fire engine has been provided, and this is rarely used.

In 1864 the assembly authorized the establishment of a police court, with power to determine all cases for violation of the by-laws or ordinances of the borough, and also to have the same powers and privileges within the borough as are exercised by justices of the peace within the town, and during the same or following year, a borough building, with a lockup in the basement, and accommodations for borough meetings and police courts, was erected near the corner of Main and Bridge streets.

The Winsted Gas Company, a private enterprise, was organized in 1861. with a capital inadequate to its successful operation and extension. Its operations are confined to the portion of Main street west of Chestnut street. The company greatly needs an increase of capital, and an entire renovation. Its entire extinction, and the organization of a new company, with greatly enlarged means and energetic direction, is exceedingly desirable.

The following manufacturing enterprises were organized or enlarged during this decade:—

James S. and John T. Rockwell erected the tannery on Main street, now owned by John T. Rockwell, in 1852.

The Eagle Works, a joint-stock company, for manufacturing table cutlery, erected a brick factory on the lake stream in 1852, and continued its operations until 1856, when the establishment was sold to Rice, Lathrop & Clary, and was thereafter operated by the successive firms of Rice & Lathrop, and Lathrop & Barton. The original building was burned down in 1860, and two wooden factory buildings were afterwards erected, which are now standing.

The brick factory on Mad River, adjoining Lake street bridge, was erected for a machine shop by John Boyd, in 1853.

The Winsted Auger Co., a joint-stock corporation, erected a factory in 1853, near the corner of Main and Coe streets, in which they manufactured augers until 1860, when it was sold to Rice & Lathrop, soon after which it was burned down and rebuilt. It is now operated as a table cutlery establishment by Wm. P. Lathrop.

In 1852, the Cook Axle Company erected a brick factory building on the site of the old Reuben Cook forge in the east village, which was operated by them until about 1864, after which it went into the hands of R. Cook & Sons, by whom it has since been carried on.

Benjamin and Edward Woodall erected, about 1853, a factory for making steel fire irons, on the site of Halsey Burr's abandoned scythe works on North Main street, which, in 1854, became the property of "The Winsted Shovel and Tongs Company," a short-lived joint-stock association, which ceased operations about 1857.

In 1854 The Clifton Lumber Company erected the factory building nearly opposite the Naugatuck Railroad depot on Willow street, now occupied by the Winsted Printing Company, which was operated as a planing mill and sash and blind factory, and propelled by the first steam engine employed in the borough. The business not proving satisfactory, the building was used for a brief period by the American Percussion Cap Company, and in 1863 was purchased by The Borden Condensed Milk Company, which used it in their manufacturing business until 1866.

In 1859 the Green Wood Agricultural Park Association was formed, and during the next year purchased the land for its park, graded the trotting course, and erected a building for agricultural exhibitions. Trotting courses were then at the spring tide of popularity, and country agricultural exhibitions had not been played out. More than one hundred subscribers from within and without the borough took stock in the concern, many of them believing it was to turn out a profitable investment. It has as yet made no dividends, and none are looked for.

The Empire Knife Company grew out of a small pocket cutlery concern, established by Thompson & Gascoigne, about 1853, and soon afterwards transferred to Beardsley & Alvord, who, in 1856, erected the factory buildings at the lake outlet, enlarged the business, and placed it on a permanent basis.

Before the middle of this decade the prosperity of Winsted was seriously retarded by one of the periodical revulsions of business which follows excessive stimulation. The banks, alarmed by their over-issues, checked the high speed of enterprise by a sudden application of the brakes, which prostrated some establishments and crippled many others, the severest calamities falling on the improvident borrowers from the savings and building associations, who were largely mechanics, dependent on daily and constant wages for meeting their monthly payments. Building of new houses entirely ceased, and large numbers of those already built came on a market destitute of buyers at any price. Many of our worthy mechanics sought in other places and in other pursuits to support their families and retrieve their losses. This state of things could not long continue in a community blessed with the recuperative power which has signally characterized our business interests. The lowest point of depression had been reached, and signs of returning prosperity had become apparent in 1860.

Notwithstanding the depression referred to, the proportional increase of population, buildings, manufactures, banking capital and moneyed investments was far greater than in any preceding decade. The opening of the Naugatuck Railroad made an outlet for our heavy manufactured articles never before enjoyed, and brought in a large number of new business men. The trading business of adjoining towns was largely attracted to this as the common center. Very little capital was brought in from abroad. Its rapid accumulation grew out of the profits of home business, stimulated by improved facilities.

The succeeding decade, though showing a substantial and healthy growth, will not exhibit as large a proportionate increase, owing to exorbitant freight charges, and the consequent superior facilities for the manufacture of heavy goods nearer to tide water.

We compile abstracts of taxable property and polls in Winsted on the lists of 1850 and 1860, as follows:—

Items.	1850.		1860.	
	No.	Amount.	No.	Amount.
Dwelling houses,	311	$161,180	494	$504,330
Acres of land,	2,278	180,103	8,864	188,880
Mills, stores, and factories,	48	66,320	82	196,505
Horses,	177	9,143	192	18,477
Neat cattle,	1,201	15,397	826	18,519
Sheep, swine, &c.,	0	—		294
Coaches and carriages,		5,389		8,320
Farming utensils,		2,957		25
Clocks and watches,		899		5,350
Pianos and Melodeons,		1,141		5,927
Household furniture,		57,810		4,225
Bank and insurance stocks,		79,073		211,130
Turnpike stocks,		—		225
Railroad bonds,		5,400		19,250
Investments in trade,		24,450		79,650
" in manufactures,		41,245		142,545
" in vessels,		520		200
Money at interest,		76,074		107,192
" on hand,		—		2,897
Taxable property,		18,555		825
Taxable polls,	383		743	

The population of the town had increased during this decade from 2,179 to 3,550, and Winchester Society having continued stationary, at about 500, the increase in Winsted was 1,371. It thus appears that in taxable property and population Winsted Society had more than doubled.

CHAPTER XXXIII.

WAR OF THE REBELLION.—VOLUNTEERS IN THE SERVICE.—CONTRIBUTIONS OF MONEY AND SUPPLIES.

1861 to 1871.

"PROCLAIM liberty throughout the land to all the inhabitants thereof" was the prophetic inscription on the bell which, on the fourth of July, 1776, announced the birth of our nation. Its tones were freighted with the solemn declaration "that all men are created equal, and endowed by their Creator with the inalienable rights of life, liberty, and the pursuit of happiness." On this fundamental principle our forefathers, appealing to the Supreme Judge of the world for the rectitude of their intentions, severed their connection with Britain, and fought to a triumphant end the Revolutionary War.

On the return of peace, a more perfect union of the states, in order to secure unity, justice, domestic tranquility, and the blessings of liberty, was found needful, and the convention of 1787 was assembled. A constitution was framed, nearly perfect in its distribution of political powers, but marred by compromising the first principle of the declaration of independence — the principle of universal liberty.

The bitter fruits of this compromise could not then be foreseen. Slave labor was then unprofitable in most of the states, and scarcely remunerative in any of them. The delusion that slavery, let alone, would die a natural death, was dotingly cherished as an opiate to tender consciences, made restive by this first desecration of the "Higher Law" of God and humanity. The mill of the gods ground slow, and was unheeded. The cotton gin was invented. The foundations of slavery were strengthened and enlarged. When it demanded an extension of its domain over the virgin soil of Missouri, before consecrated to freedom by a solemn ordinance, conscience was aroused, and resistance was made. The nation was convulsed as never before. The struggle was fearful, and was quieted by another unholy compromise, making the parallel of 36° 30' the dividing line between the law of God and the enactments of man.

Again all was peace and concord. The eloquent statesman of Kentucky was baptized "The Great Compromiser," and gloried in the title. One senator of freedom-loving Massachusetts pronounced the Declaration of Independence "a string of glittering generalities," and another — the very Jupiter Tonans of the North, the expounder *par excellence* of the constitution — eloquently adjured his constituents to conquer their prejudices and sustain the Fugitive Slave Law.

The mill of the gods, though the sound of its grinding had grown nearly inaudible, still ground on.

As early as 1830 voices crying here and there in the wilderness began to be heard protesting against the abominations of slavery and the subserviency in the North to the behests of slave owners. Such utterances were denounced by the pulpit, the press, and the pot-house; yet they found a lodgment in many thoughtful minds and tender consciences. The press began to teem with anti-slavery publications, and petitions for the abolition of slavery in the district of Columbia flowed into Congress. Joshua R. Giddings dared to advocate them in the Hall of Representatives, and old John Quincy Adams bravely sustained him. The South imperiously demanded that free speech and a free press should be put down, and the right of petition withheld. The northern pulpit uttered an uncertain sound. Orville Dewey, President Lord, and the Princeton Divines upheld the institution as not only patriarchal but divine. Castle Garden, backed by the mercantile community of New York, proscribed every trader who refused to sell his principles with his goods. Garrison was dragged through the streets of Baltimore and Boston with a halter around his neck. Lovejoy was shot down while defending his free press in Illinois; Sumner was brutally knocked down in the senate chamber, and old John Brown was hung in Virginia. The mill of the gods ground on with accelerating motion and fearful power. Lincoln was elected, and Sumpter bombarded.

Our last decade opens with this consummated crisis. It is our purpose not to dwell on the grand national results achieved, but to detail the humble though creditable contribution of moral force, men and means, made by this town to the common cause, and to commemorate the services of our noble boys who responded to their country's call and fought her battles.

Anti-slavery sentiment had become more pervasive and incisive in our town than in any other in Western Connecticut before the outbreak of the rebellion. At the organization of the Free Soil Party it commanded a decided plurality of all the votes in the town, but the unwise nomination of Van Buren for President paralyzed its power as a political organization. Large numbers, thoroughly imbued with anti-slavery sentiments, would not fight under such a vulpine leader. They fell back, mainly into the Whig party, and infused into it all the vitality that survived its dead issues. The party died, and its free soil element formed the germ of the Republican organization. There was also an infusion of free soil sentiment in the Democratic party, surviving the Van Buren fiasco, which fused with the Republican element, and consolidated the party that carried us safely through the mightiest civil convulsion recorded in history.

The bombardment of Sumpter flew over the telegraph wires on Saturday, April 4, 1861, and electrified the country to a degree not exceeded by the news of Bunker Hill. A nation educated for more than half a century to peace secured by successive compromises of moral principle, and so proficient in this teaching that the announcement of a Higher Law than the Constitution by a New York senator was denounced as traitorous by many of his compeers; a nation which had long worshipped money-bags as its gods, and served cotton as its king — was suddenly called to face the alternative of relentless slave domination for all future time or a war without parallel in the world's annals.

On Sunday the 5th, while yet the smoke of battle hung over Charleston Harbor, humble prayer was ascending to the God of Battles from a thousand sanctuaries throughout the Northern and Eastern states. Divine guidance was implored and granted. Patriotism, long dormant and seemingly dead, was revived and brought into vigorous power, as if by inspiration. The news was communicated to Rev. Mr. Eddy while finishing his sermon for the day. A new text was selected and a new sermon blocked out under the inspiration of the event, which electrified his hearers, and raised them to the plane of his own patriot ardor. The same spirit pervaded the other ministers and congregations. The key note was struck and the community marched to the inspiring music. A citizens' meeting was notified from the pulpits of three of our churches for that evening. The meeting was held in our largest hall, which was crowded to its utmost capacity. Party prejudices were dissipated; treasonable utterances were silenced; factious pretences were scattered to the winds. The fog of disloyalty rose with the smoke over Charleston Harbor, disclosing as clear a sky and as pure an atmosphere as was breathed by our Revolutionary fathers. The following address to Governor Buckingham was drafted, and immediately signed by nearly two hundred citizens.

"*To His Excellency, Wm. A. Buckingham, Governor of the State of Connecticut:*

SIR: Inasmuch as a spirit of unbridled license and treasonable disloyalty at the South, under a governmental policy too mild and passive, has now ripened into open rebellion threatening the dismemberment of the republic, and immediate and utter failure of the great American experiment of a people ruling itself—and inasmuch as events now transpiring in Charleston Harbor render it evident that the general government has entered upon a contest requiring the spontaneous and cordial co-operation of all loyal states and citizens,—

Therefore, we, the undersigned, feeling that Connecticut is called upon, now and at once, to proffer its aid to the General Government in defence of the Union, the Constitution and Laws, respectfully request Governor Buckingham to adopt such measures as shall afford this state an opportunity to place her resources at the disposal of the General Government."·

The call of Lincoln for volunteers speedily followed, and was promptly responded to. Enlistment papers were prepared and presented at a public meeting. Samuel B. Horne, an unassuming boy of scarce eighteen years, and in reduced circumstances, was the first to come forward and enroll his name. He served out his three months' term, and in October of the same year enlisted as a private in company E, Eleventh Infantry Volunteers; was chosen a sergeant, and rose by promotion to first lieutenant and captain; was in twenty-five battles and skirmishes — was three times wounded; and at the end of his three years term served as Provost Marshal of the Eighteenth Army Corps to the end of the war. On retiring from the service, he studied law, was admitted to the bar of Litchfield county and is now a practising lawyer at Grand Rapids, Michigan.

The following other Winchester recruits enrolled themselves in the squad that formed the nucleus of Infantry Company B, first organized in this town:—

Abram G. Kellogg, Caleb P. Newman, Francis T. Brown, Mason Atkins, Daniel Bellows, George Bellows, Jr., Henry Bradley, Frederick W. Daniels, Edward E. Day, Charles O. Dennen, Robert Dempsey, Fernando Gale, Westley Gale, Dennis Glynn, Charles Harris, Samuel B. Horne, George L. Leonard, James McCauley, Charles C. Potter, Charles Presber, Henry Roberts, William H. Strong, Joel G. Thorpe, Charles Vogel, Hubert A. Warner, and Henry Williams.

Two other squads of recruits having been now enrolled in New Hartford and Canton, together with six individuals from Norfolk, two from Barkhamsted, and one each from Colebrook, Salisbury, Woodbury, and Harwinton; they were all united with the Winchester squad, as company B of the Second Infantry, under Abram G. Kellogg, of Winchester, as Captain, and Charles W. Morse and Charles Warren, of New Hartford and Canton, as lieutenants.

We copy from the Winsted Herald of April 26, 1861, the following account of the departure of this company.

"On Sabbath (April 20, 1861) the company attended Mr. Eddy's church, where a powerful discourse was preached from 1st Samuel iv. 9. Orders were received on Sunday evening, instructing the company to proceed to the state rendezvous at New Haven the next day. We must be short with the proceedings of Monday — the suspension of business, the thronged streets, the banners and the martial strains, the procession of adventurous and patriotic youth through our streets to the depot — that prayer from the platform of the station, listened to as was never a prayer listened to before by this generation, the twice a thousand faces wet with tears which the manliest sought not to hide, the good-byes, short, but too long for choking voices fully to utter, the huzzas, and then as the train wound slowly around the hill, the oppressive stillness, broken by no rude word, but only sobs and low-toned syllables of consolation. There were whole chapters in these scenes, but we pass them. Every hamlet in the whole North, from Maine's wilderness to the Western Desert, is witness of the same. Northern blood is up, and history, faster than pen can write, is making."

"The trip of this company to New Haven," adds the Herald, " was not calculated to dispirit them. Word of their coming had gone down by the morning train, and receptions the most enthusiastic and soul-stirring awaited them at every depot on the route. Bands of music were playing, salutes firing, banners spanning the track, wherever the train halted. Patriotic speeches were made and responded to at the principal depots, and the whole trip was attended by the heartiest manifestations of sympathetic patriotism. At Wolcottville the reception was specially pleasing, and a banner with the words "We will soon follow you," attested the fact that her young men will not allow the victory to be won without assisting to achieve it. The boys were quartered at New Haven in a spacious hall near the depot. We saw them safely to bed and tucked in, with each his mattress and blanket, at a good seasonable hour — saw the ranks numbering ninety-seven lusty and hearty fellows at breakfast next morning, and afterwards on parade in front of the state house. They are a plucky crew, and if ever they get into action we shall be willing to stake the reputation of our section upon their good behavior."

The spirit of enlistment had hardly been aroused when Company B was transferred to New Haven. Simultaneous with its departure, the enrollment of another company was called for and opened, and was filled with the *élite* of our young men in a single week. The company was organized as Rifle Company E, 2d Connecticut Infantry, with the following rank and file: — From Winchester, Captain Sherman T. Cooke, 1st Lieutenant, Wheelock T. Batcheller; 2d Lieutenant, Charles E. Palmer; 1st Sergeant, Jeffrey Skinner; Sergeants, James N. Coe, Charles L. Hosford, Lucien B. Wheelock; Corporals, George L. Andrews, Alanson D. Bunnell, Edward Didsbury, Jacob T. Brown; musician, Hicks Seaman (?); privates, Antoine Albert, Hyppolite Bluet, Albert M. Beach, Edwin Beach, Ira C. Bailey, Decius C. Bancroft, Gustave

AND FAMILY RECORDS. 465

Bernhardt, James M. Burton, Victor Claudet, Chauncey D. Cleveland, Daniel S. Coe, David W. Coe, William S. Cooper, Samuel A. Cooper, William Couch, Chauncey S. Crittenden, John M. Dennan, James Dennan, Edgar V. Doughty, Burton B. Evitts, Philip D. Fisk, Daniel Fitzpatrick, Salmon A. Granger, Leonard S. Harris, William F. Hatch, Junior, Nelson Hodges, William S. Holabird, Benjamin F. Hosford, George Hoskin, Orson Howard, James N. Latham, Frank B. Marsh, Lorenzo Martin, Alexander McGuire, Milton T. Moore, Augustus Nevins, Leander Packard, George W. Pendleton, Charles H. Pond, Frederick H. Presber, James Price, Hiram C. Roberts, William E. Snediker, Orlo S. Smith, Charles H. Stewart, Platner S. Sweet, George M. Van Oustrom, Herbert L. Veber, Arthur Wadsworth, Joseph Watson, Thomas Welch, John P. Wilbur, Marcus J. Whitehead, John Wheeler, and James G. Woodruff.

The following members of this company came from adjoining towns:—
From Norfolk, Privates Samuel C. Barnum, Charles N. Decker, George J. Kermann, Samuel J. Mills, Calvin N. Sage, and John M. Walker.
From Torrington, Privates Henry G. Colt and George M. Evans.
From Mill River, Mass., Alonzo H. Conklin.

Company B was sent into camp at New Haven without uniforms or equipments, and was the last company of the regiment uniformed and equipped before being mustered into the United States service. Our patriotic male and female citizens determined that Company E should be promptly provided for. Cloth and trimmings of best quality were purchased, and measures adopted for working them into uniforms. On the arrival of the materials the master tailors of the town volunteered their aid in cutting and superintending the making up of the garments, without compensation, and all the sempstresses who could sew a strong seam went to work with a will on the same terms. The sewing machines from far and near were gathered at Camp's Hall, and the work went bravely on. Sunday came, and they had so crowded on the cutters that the latter had to work through the Sabbath to get ahead of them. Monday and Tuesday, and all the days of the week, the work went on with unabated ardor; those ladies who could not do the stronger work made up the shirts and other lighter garments. There were no idlers, and few inefficients. It was the women's battle week, and was bravely fought out on that line. Eighty-three uniform coats, pants, and vests made, and thoroughly made, were the product of that week's work, more than fifty of them made up by Winsted ladies, and the residue by ladies in adjoining towns. In addition to this contribution more than a hundred woollen shirts were made up prior to and during this battle week.*

---

* The following complimentary notice appeared in the *Winsted Herald* of May 17, 1861 :— "It is said, since our soldiers' uniforms are completed, that there are now,

Every man in both companies was also supplied with a rosette of white, red and blue, a "housewife" filled with thread, yarn, pins, needles, and buttons, and a pocket Testament. Innumerable other articles, including socks, wrappers, drawers, and medicines — more than the soldiers' knapsacks could hold — were furnished by individuals. A revolver was given to each Winchester man in Company B.

Company B departed for New Haven before enthusiasm had been wrought up to its highest strain. On the departure of Company E, on the 25th of April, its fullest intensity was manifested. Thousands assembled. Patriotic speeches were made by Rev. Messrs. Eddy, Loomis, and Pierson, of the Congregational and Methodist Churches; by Rev. Father Mullen, of the Catholic Church, and by several laymen.*

Company E, on its departure for New Haven on the 25th of April received an ovation in all respects similar to, but on a larger scale than that given to Company B on the 21st. It was emphatically a town company, while Company B was a contribution of three towns. More than half of them were mechanics, about one-fourth were farmers, and the remainder, in about equal proportions, were clerks and laborers. Germany had six representatives, Ireland three, and England one.

Both companies were thoroughly drilled, while at New Haven, by cadets from General Russell's Military School. On the 27th of May they were mustered into the government service, and on the evening of that day were embarked on the steamer Bienville for Washington, by way of Fortress Monroe and the Potomac River. On reaching their destination they were encamped and drilled on the height north of Washington for several weeks, after which they were marched to the neighborhood of Falls Church in Virginia, within some five miles of Fairfax Court House, which was occupied by a rebel force. Here they remained, except during the interval of their march to, and retreat from, Bull Run, until near the expiration of their term of service, when they were mustered out at New Haven. With the exception of Private James M. Burton, who died of diphtheria at New Haven Hospital, on the day

---

probably, not to exceed five girls in Winsted who cannot cut, baste, stitch, and make up to order any article of men's apparel, from the finest dress coat to the commonest mustn't-mention-ems, in a style, too, of unsurpassed neatness and excellence. Before the war there were probably not five girls within the same locality who could sew on a hat-band or a suspender button without double the labor in showing required to do the work in the first instance. So here is another good comes from the war."

* Among other ceremonies of this occasion, two Colts' revolvers were formally presented by Mrs. Julia Peck — one to Captain Cook, and the other to Private Boyd, the latter as a compliment to the oldest enrolled member of the company. After the refusal to muster in Mr. B. on account of his age, he gave his revolver to Chaplain Eddy, with instructions to present it at the end of the term of service to the private

after mustering in, not a death occurred in the company during its term of service.

While stationed at the Falls Church encampment, Captain A. G. Kellogg, of Company B., when on picket duty, a mile or more from camp, was captured by the rebels and hurried off to Richmond, and thence taken to Salisbury, N. C., whence, after nearly a year's captivity, he was sent to Potomac Creek and exchanged.

Rev. Hiram Eddy, pastor of the Second Congregational Church of Winsted, was appointed by Governor Buckingham chaplain of the Second Regiment, and on leave of absence from his pastoral charge, that he might be with the boys he had, by his patriotic eloquence, cheered "on [towards] Richmond," joined the regiment at Falls Church. At the rout of Bull Run he got separated from his comrades, and after wandering in uncertain ways for more than two days was captured by the rebels within a mile of the encampment at Falls Church, to which his regiment had retreated after the battle. His lofty stature and Daniel Websterian visage and mien deeply impressed his captors and guards. He was at once conducted to Richmond, and admitted to the hospitalities of the Tobacco Warehouse, after availing himself of which, to more than his heart's content, he was transferred to Columbia, S. C., and thence to Charleston, where he was treated to a course of yellow fever. The Hell of Andersonville had not yet been organized, else he would, doubtless, have been consigned to its torments. After grinding in these Philistine mills for more than a year he was exchanged, and welcomed back to his parochial charge with such an ovation as few ministers have enjoyed. During his captivity his clerical brethren of neighboring parishes, with the consent of their people, gratuitously supplied his pulpit, for the benefit of his family, for more than six months.

Private Samuel A. Cooper, of company E, was attached as an Orderly to the staff of General Tyler during the battle of Bull Run, and was captured by the rebels. He performed a tour of prison duty at nearly all the stations from Richmond to New Orleans, and thence back to North Carolina, where he was exchanged, and reached home a little before Mr. Eddy.

---

who should have proved the most meritorious soldier of the company. The weapon was lost at Bull Run, and consequently no award was made, but it was generally conceded that by right of merit it should have been awarded to Private Alonzo H. Conklin, of Mill River, Mass., who, on the march to Bull Run, found his feet so blistered by a pair of tight boots, that he threw them away near Centerville, and made a pair of moccasins out of the legs of his pants, in which he served through the day of battle and on the retreat without complaint or flinching.

A large portion of the officers and soldiers of these companies, from time to time, re-enlisted into other regiments, and were largely promoted to higher grades. Among them were the following:

Geo. L. Andrews, Corp. Co. E, 2d Infantry, to Sergt. Co. F, 28th Conn. Infantry.
Mason Adkins, Priv. Co. B, 2d Infantry, to 1st Sergt. Co. E, 2d Heavy Artillery.
Antoine Albert, Priv. Co. E, 2d Infantry, to Priv. and Veteran Co. G, 12th Infantry.
Wheelock T. Batcheller, 1st Lieut. Co. E, 2d Infantry, to Major 28th Infantry.
Jacob T. Brown, Corp. Co. E, 2d Infantry, to Corp. Co. B, 12th Infantry; killed at Cedar Creek.
Francis T. Brown, Sergt. Co. B, 2d Infantry, to Capt. Co. E, 11th Infantry.
Daniel Bellows, Priv. Co. B, 2d Infantry, to Corp. and Vet. Co. E, 7th Infantry.
Geo. Bellows, Jr., Priv. Co. B, 2d Infantry, to Priv. and Vet. Co. E, 7th Infantry; mortally wounded at Hampton, Va.
James N. Coe, Sergt. Co. E, 2d Infantry, to 1st Lieut. Co. I, and Capt. Co. H, 2d Heavy Artillery.
Daniel S. Coe, Priv. Co. E, 2d Infantry, to 2d Lieut. Co. E, 7th Infantry.
David W. Coe, Priv. Co. E, 2d Infantry, and detailed Clerk to Gen. Tyler and Major General Keys, U. S. A., enlisted on U. S. Frigate Sabine, and served as Executive Officers' Clerk.
Wm. S. Cooper, Priv. Co. E, 2d Infantry, to Corp. Co. E, 2d Heavy Artillery.
Frederick W. Daniels, Priv. Co. E, 2d Infantry, to Sergt. Co. E, 2d Heavy Artillery; killed at Cold Harbor, Va.
Robert Dempsey, Priv. Co. B, 2d Infantry, to 1st Lieut. Co. E, 7th Infantry; killed at Olustee, Fla.
Salmon A. Granger, Priv. Co. E, 2d Infantry, to 1st Lieut. Co. E, 2d Heavy Artillery.
Charles E. Hosford, Sergt. Co. E., 2d Infantry, to Capt. Co. D, 11th Infantry.
Benj. S. Hosford, Priv. Co. E, 2d Infantry, to Capt. Co. D, 2d Heavy Artillery; killed at Cedar Creek.
Geo. Hoskins, Priv. Co. E, 2d Infantry, to Priv. Co. F, 28th Infantry.
Orson Howard, Priv. Co. E, 2d Infantry, to Capt. 9th N. Y. Heavy Artillery; killed at Petersburg, Va.
Samuel B. Horne, Priv. Co. B, 2d Infantry, to Sergt., Lieut., and Capt. Co. F, 11th Infantry.
Geo. L. Leonard, Priv. Co. E, 2d Infantry, to Priv. Co. E, 2d Heavy Artillery.
Benj. F. Marsh, Priv. Co. E, 2d Infantry, to Corp. Co. F, 28th Infantry; lost an arm at Port Hudson.
Milton T. Moore, Priv. Co. E, 2d Infantry, to Sergt. Co. F, 28th Infantry.
Caleb P. Newman, 1st Sergt. Co. C, 2d Infantry, to 1st Lieut. Co. F, 28th Infantry.
Fred. O. Peck, Priv. Co. D, 2d Infantry, to Priv. 22d Mass. Infantry; twice wounded at Gaines' Mill, Va.
Charles E. Palmer, 2d Lieut. Co. E, 2d Infantry, to Capt. Co. E, 7th Infantry; died at Hilton Head, S. C.
Leander Packard, Priv. Co. E, 2d Infantry, to Priv. Co. E, 11th Infantry.
Hiram C. Roberts, Priv. Co. E, 2d Infantry, to Sergt. Co. E, 11th Infantry; killed at Sharpsburg, Md.
Henry L. Roberts, Priv. Co. B, 2d Infantry, to Sergt. Co. F, 28th Infantry.
Jeffrey Skinner, 1st Sergt. Co. E, 2d Infantry, to Capt. Co. E, 2d Heavy Artillery; promoted to Major and Lieut. Col. same regiment.
Orlo S. Smith, Priv. Co. E, 2d Infantry, to 1st Lieut. Co. I, 2d Heavy Artillery.
Lucien B. Wheelock, Sergt. Co. E, 2d Infantry, to Capt. Co. F, 28th Infantry.

Marcus J. Whitehead, Priv. Co. E, 2d Infantry, to Priv. Co. E, 2d Heavy Artillery.
John Wheeler, Priv. Co. E, 2d Infantry, to Sergt. Co. F, 1st and 2d Lieut. Co. G, 2d Heavy Artillery.

The first regiment of cavalry was originally a battalion consisting of four companies, recruited in the fall of 1861, and about a year after was increased to a full regiment of twelve companies.

The following Winchester men are found on its rolls:

In company A, Privates Frank Parkant and Geo. L. Leonard.
"   "   D,   "   Wm. C. Wakefield.
"   "   E,   "   James G. Ferris and Nelson Proper.
"   "   F,   "   Michael Finn and John Gloster.
"   "   K,   "   Burton B. Beach.
"   "   M,   "   John Rose.

Unassigned substitutes: Wm. Clancey, Michael Calahan, James Flynn, James H. Gannon, Hugh Gray, Wm. Garson, Charles Hull, John Harris, Charles Earne, Richard Mooney, John Schmidt, Julius Thorne, Thomas Daley, Peter Dunn, James Taylor, and Augustus Weiss.

Of these, Julius Thorne alone died in the service.

The Fifth Regiment Infantry was organized in June, 1861, and went into service July 29 following; fought at Winchester, Cedar Mountain, and Chancellorsville, Va.; Gettysburg, Pa.; Reseca, Dallas, Marietta, Beach Tree Creek, and Atlanta, Ga.; Chesterfield C. H., S. C.; and Silver Run, N. C.; and was mustered out with distinguished honor, July 19, 1865. On the rolls of this regiment, we find the following names of Winchester men:

> Harlan P. Rugg, Corporal in Co. I, wounded at Cedar Mountain, promoted to Captain, and mustered out July 19, 1865.
> Robert Arnold, killed at Cedar Mountain, August 9, 1862.
> Joseph Hermandy, mustered out July 19, 1865.
> William Murray, discharged Feb. 23, 1865.
> Robert St. Clair, mustered out July 19, 1865.

We also find the names of eleven deserters credited to Winchester, probably none of them residents, but recruits purchased by agents of the town.

During the month of September, 1861, a quota of sixteen Winchester men and about twenty men from other towns in the county of Litchfield were recruited under the auspices of Second Lieutenant Charles C. Palmer, late of company E, and on the 7th of September, 1861, were mustered into company E, 7th Infantry, commanded successively by Colonel Alfred H. Terry and Colonel Joseph R. Hawley. Of this company Lieutenant Palmer was appointed captain, and Robert Dempsey, late private of Company B, second lieutenant.

The regiment (1,018 men) left for Washington, September, 1861. It was the first to land on the soil of South Carolina. It was in the battle of Fort Pulaski, under Colonel Terry, April 10th and 11th, 1862, and in the battles of James Island, June 14th, under Colonel Hawley; was one of the first to enter the field, and the last to leave it. Under the same command it was in the battle of Pocataligo on the 22d of October, and was subsequently divided, five companies under Colonel Hawley remaining at Hilton Head, and the remaining companies, of which Company E was one, were moved to Fernandina, Florida, under Lieutenant-Colonel Gardiner, and participated in the battle of Olustee, in which Lieutenant Robert Dempsey was killed.

In May, 1864, the regiment was transferred to Bermuda Hundreds, Va., and participated in the battle of Chester Station, and repeated battles near Bermuda Hundreds. In August it fought the battles of Deep Run and Deep Bottom, Va.

After the promotion of Colonel Hawley to a brigadier in September, 1864, the regiment, under command of Lieutenant-Colonel Rodman, was engaged in the battle of Chapin's Farm, Va., on the 29th of September; on the 1st of October in the battle near Richmond; on the 7th of New Market Road; on the 13th at Darbytown Road, and on the 27th in the battle of Charles City Road, Va. Its battle record was closed at Fort Fisher, N. C., January 15th and 19th, 1865, and it was mustered out of service on the 20th of July, 1865. Few regiments in the service were engaged in more active and arduous service than the Seventh. It had 90 men killed in action, 44 died of wounds, and 179 of disease; total, 313.

The Winchester men in this regiment were Captain Charles E. Palmer, 1st Lieutenant Robert Dempsey, 2d Lieutenant Daniel S. Coe, Corporals Daniel Bellows and John G. Rowley, Privates George E. Andrews, John Biederman, Albert Burdick, George W. Daniels, Charles Gilbert, Charles L. Hewitt, Sterling D. Milliman, James A. Pease, Patrick Quigley, Henry H. Rowley, James Tencellent, all of Company E.

Captain Palmer, an unassuming young man of delicate training, developed in his first campaign the highest soldierly qualities by strict and cheerful performance of duty, and kind attention to the wants and comforts of his men. But it was not until he came into command of Company E that his endurance and bravery were fully tested. In the siege and capture of Fort Pulaski he commanded Battery Lincoln; and in the report of the bloody battle of Secessionville he was highly complimented for bravery and coolness. Soon after this hard fought but unsuccessful

battle he died from exposure and exhaustion. From Colonel Terry's letter to his parents, now bereaved of their last child, we quote as follows:

"At the time of the action on James Island he was so ill that, under ordinary circumstances, he would not have been in command of his company; but prompted by the devotion to duty, which always distinguished him, he led his company to the field, and gave to it and the regiment a splendid example of courage and firmness under most trying circumstances. The noble purity and uprightness of his nature and his eminently soldierly qualities had endeared him to us all, and had led us to look forward to a brilliant future for him; and we mourn his loss, not only as ours and yours, but as a loss to the country which he served so faithfully."

In answer to a letter to General Hawley from Palmer Post inviting him to the decoration ceremonies at Winsted, dated May 11th, 1872, he writes as follows:

"The name of your post awakens my recollections of that noble soldier and man, Captain Palmer. Never shall I forget that it was his extreme fidelity to duty that cost him his life. He ought to have gone to the hospital, but would not leave the field. Well I remember his countenance as I walked by the stretcher that carried him dying on board the steamer."

Lieutenant Dempsey was wounded in the shoulder June 1st, 1862, returned home on furlough while disabled, married Caroline W. Richardson, rejoined his regiment in the fall, and was killed at Olustee, Fla., February 24th, 1864. He was of Irish birth, well educated, and devotedly patriotic in the cause of his adopted country. His letters from the camp and field, published in the Winsted Herald, were highly appreciated.

Private Charles Gilbert, noted on the muster-rolls as from Canton, had his home residence in Winchester, where he was born and raised. Conscientious as well as patriotic motives induced him to enlist. His brothers had families, and he was single, and he felt it his duty to represent them in the service. He was a most worthy man and a good soldier; was wounded in the head and leg at Secessionville, S. C., taken prisoner on the field, and carried to Charleston, where he died of his wounds in the hospital, July 9th, 1862, aged 29. He was a son of Samuel D. Gilbert, deceased, late of Winchester.

Private George Bellows served in Company B, 2d Infantry, and after honorable discharge at the end of the term, enlisted in Company E, 7th Infantry, September 7th, 1861, and re-enlisted a veteran, December 22d, 1864, and died of wounds received at Hampton, Va., October 28th, 1864. He was son of George Bellows, Sr., of Winchester, and died unmarried.

Private Albert Burdick, Company E, died of fever at Beaufort, S. C., July 29th, 1862.

Private John Biederman re-enlisted a veteran, December 22d, 1863, and was killed October 13th, 1864.

All the other members of this company were honorably discharged or mustered out at the end of their terms.

In the 8th Regiment, recruited at Camp Buckingham, Hartford, which fought at Newbern, N. C., Fort Macon, N. C., Antietam, Md., Fredericksburg, Fort Huger, Walthall Junction, Fort Darling, Petersburg, and Fort Harrison, Va., we find the names of two Winchester men, Mathew Whiffler, private, Company A, and John C. Cooley, corporal, Company C, re-enlisted veteran, both mustered out at the end of their terms.

In the 9th (Irish) Regiment we find the name of Chaplain Daniel Mullen, at the time of his appointment pastor of St. Joseph's Catholic Church, Winsted, a young man of literary culture and earnest patriotism, who served at Baton Rouge, and Chackaloo Station, La., and Deep Bottom, Va. He was compelled, by ill-health, to resign on the 26th of August, 1862. He was succeeded as chaplain by Father Leo da Saracena, O.S.F., the present pastor of St. Joseph's Church, and President of St. Francis' Literary and Theological Seminary.

It is not to be inferred, from finding no other names of Winchester Irishmen on the rolls of this regiment, that our foreign citizens were wanting in patriotism, for the names of Winchester men in other regiments abundantly show that in proportion to our population Irishmen, Germans, and Englishmen are amply represented.

On the roll of the 10th Regiment the only name of a Winchester man is that of Colonel Ira W. Pettibone, who was commissioned as Major, served in the battles of Roanoke Island and Newbern, N. C., and was successively promoted to Lieutenant-Colonel and Colonel. The climate of North Carolina debilitated him to such a degree that he was compelled to resign, and he was honorably discharged in November, 1862.

The 12th Regiment of Volunteer Infantry was recruited at Camp Lyon, Hartford, under command of Colonel Henry C. Deming; was attached to Butler's Division, and sailed from New York for Ship Island, Mississippi Sound, February 24, 1862. It followed the naval armament, under Farragut, up the Mississippi, and witnessed the bombardment of Forts Jackson and St. Philip; followed the armament up to New Orleans, where it landed, and garrisoned the city on its forced surrender, Colonel Deming assuming the office of provisional mayor. It

was encamped for a time at Baton Rouge, and was afterwards engaged in active service in Louisiana. It bore a conspicuous part in the siege of Port Hudson, after which it returned to New Orleans, and in July, 1864, embarked for Fortress Monroe, and in August following joined Sheridan's army in the Shenandoah Valley, and participated in the battles of Opequan, Fisher's Hill, and Cedar Creek, after which, it having been reduced to a skeleton by losses in battle, and by disease, and by expiration of the term of service of a large portion of its men, it was reorganized under Lieutenant-Colonel Lewis, and continued to serve in Virginia until its muster out in August, 1865.

Only six Winchester men belonged to this regiment, as follows:—

Doctor John B. Welch, 2d assistant-surgeon, who died of scarlatina, on shipboard, at Ship Island, February 13, 1862. He was son of Dr. James and Mrs. Lavinia Welch of Winsted, born at W., September 14, 1838; studied in his father's office; graduated M.D. at Yale College in 1860; mustered 2d Assistant-surgeon of 12th Regiment, December 11, 1861; sailed with the regiment for Ship Island, Mississippi Sound, February 24, 1862, and on reaching there was unable to land with the troops, but not considered dangerously ill. He died off the Island, two days after the landing of the troops, separate from his comrades, and almost alone. His remains were sent home, and buried in the cemetery of his family, at Norfolk. His amiable character, and the circumstances of his death at the outset of his career, deeply affected the community with sorrow for his loss, and sympathy with his family in their affliction.

Dr. John R. Cumming, appointed 2d Assistant-surgeon in place of Assistant-surgeon Welch, was promoted to Surgeon, and was mustered out at Savannah, Ga., August 12, 1865.

Private Solomon R. Hinsdale, Company A, appointed Quartermaster-Sergeant, promoted 2d Lieutenant; resigned August 9, 1862, on his appointment as Assistant-paymaster in the Navy, after which he served on the Mississippi Flotilla above Vicksburg, until prostrated by fever, and compelled to resign by impaired health.

Sergeant Jacob T. Brown, Company C, killed at Fisher's Hill, Va., September 19, 1864. While giving water from his canteen to a wounded lieutenant of an Iowa Regiment, on the battlefield, he was shot in the abdomen by a rebel sharpshooter, and died three hours after. He was a model of physical manhood; a kind-hearted, unassuming man, and a consistent member of the Methodist Church, esteemed by his comrades as a conscientious Christian soldier.

Private George W. Eggleston, Company C, enlisted March 2, 1864, and mustered out at Savannah, August 12, 1865.

Private Wm. H. Pool, Company C, enlisted February 24, 1864; discharged at New Haven, April 29, 1865.

Private John W. Vaughn, Company C, enlisted February 24, 1864, mustered out at Savannah, Ga., August 12, 1865.

Second Lieutenant John W. Hurlbut, of Company G, resigned June 6, 1862.

A squad of ten Winchester men composed a part of the rank and file of Company D, 11th Regiment Infantry, consisting of Charles L. Hosford, 1st Lieutenant; Corporal Levi L. Dayton, Privates Frank S. Pease, Lewis Dayton, Edward S. Fleming, Charles Hull, George Kinney, Daniel Lotherington, William H. Slack, and Albert M. Tuttle; and another squad of twelve men composed a part of Company E of the same regiment, consisting of First-sergeant Francis T. Brown, Sergeants Samuel B. Horne, and Hiram C. Roberts; Corporals William T. Page, Jr., and John K. Twiss; Privates George Allen, William E. Cogswell, James Dudley, Erastus Eggleston and Rufus Eggleston (twins), Andrew M. Hurlbut, Leander Packard.

These companies were mustered into service at Camp Lincoln, in Hartford, December 16, 1861. The regiment was assigned to Burnside's Division, and fought its first battle at Newbern, N. C., March 14, 1862. In July, 1862, it was attached to the Army of the Potomac, and was in the battle of South Mountain, Md., September 14, 1862, and in the battle of Antietam, September 17th following. It was on the picket line at Fredericksburg, Va., during the battle of the 13th December, 1862, and was engaged in the defence of Suffolk, Va., during the siege from April 11 to May 3, 1863. In March, 1864, it returned from veteran furlough to Portsmouth, Va.; marched to and encamped at Williamsburg, where it constituted the force nearest to Richmond. On the 9th of May it was in the battle of Swift's Creek; it fought in the battle of Drury's Bluff, and on the 3d of June was engaged in the charge at Cold Harbor, Va. It was afterward in active service before Petersburg, from June 15 to August 27, and continued to serve in Virginia until mustered out of service December 21, 1865.

The following Winchester men of this regiment were killed or died in the service:—

Private Lewis Dayton, Company D, killed at Sharpsburg (Antietam), Maryland.

Private Wm. H. Slack, Company D, died of wounds (loss of an arm) received at Newbern, March 22, 1862.

Private Albert M. Tuttle, Company D, killed at Cold Harbor, Va., June 5, 1864.

Sergeant Hiram C. Roberts, killed at Antietam, September 17, 1862.

Corporal William T. Page, Jr., wounded at Antietam, September 17, and discharged for disability, October 25, 1862.

Corporal John K. Twiss, Company E, wounded and taken prisoner at Drury's Bluff; died of wounds at Richmond, May, 1864.

Private Wm. F. Cogswell, Company E, killed at Antietam, September 17, 1862.

The promotions of Winchester men in this regiment were as follows:—
Sergeant Francis T. Brown, Company E, promoted to captain.
Sergeant Samuel B. Horne, Company E, promoted to captain.
Lieutenant Charles L. Hosford, promoted to captain, and in command as senior officer of the regiment at the termination of the battle of Antietam.

On the rolls of the Thirteenth Regiment, organized at New Haven, Nov. 25, 1861, which participated in the engagements of Georgia Landing, Irish Bend, Port Hudson, Cane River, and Mansara, in Louisiana, and Winchester, Fisher's Hill, and Cedar Creek, in Virginia, the names of four Winchester men are found, viz: Second Assistant Surgeon Lucius W. Clark, Private George Losaw, of Co. D, who re-enlisted veteran, and was transferred to Co. B, from which he was mustered out April 25, 1866; Private Charles Daniels, of Co. F, who was promoted Second Lieutenant, and resigned Jan. 8, 1864; and Private Edward Skinner, of Co. G., who re-enlisted veteran, was transferred to Co. D, and mustered out April 25, 1866.

On the rolls of the Sixteenth Regiment is the name of Elliot Flemming, of Winchester, a private in Co. G, killed at Antietam, September 16, 1862.

The Nineteenth Infantry Regiment, afterwards reorganized as Second Regiment Heavy Artillery, was raised and organized as one of the five county regiments under the call of Lincoln, on the first of July, 1862, for three hundred thousand men. Its organization was initiated by the call of a mass county meeting at Litchfield on the 22d July, 1862, which was largely attended, and rather adroitly managed. Without a moment's notice, a colonel was nominated on individual responsibility, the question taken without opportunity for debate, and the sheriff of the county declared unanimously nominated. An executive committee was also appointed, consisting of four, three of them from Litchfield, who assumed the prerogative of nominating the other regimental officers. Not one of these was assigned to Winchester, the foremost town of the county in patriotic and efficient support of the war.

Company E of this regiment was recruited in Winchester and towns adjoining, under the auspices of Jeffrey Skinner, late First Sergeant of Co. E, Second Regiment, who was appointed Captain, and rose by promotion and desert to Lieutenant Colonel of the regiment.

The names of Winchester men in this company originally enlisted, amounting to sixty-two, are as follows; Capt. Jeffrey Skinner, 1st Lieut. Benj. F. Hosford, 2d Lieut. Chester D. Cleveland (of Winsted Society); Sergeants Orlow J. Smith, Salmon A. Granger, George White, Henry Skinner, Wm. S. Cooper, Stephen W. Sage, Mason Adkins, Frederick W. Daniels, Charles A. Reynolds; Musicians Wilson B. White, Myron Ferris; Wagoner Alfred G. Bliss; Privates James R. Baldwin, Edward Beach, Patrick T. Birmingham, Almeron Bunnell, Edward F. Carrington, Philip D. Carroll, Frederick M. Cook, Alfred Comins, Robert A. Cutler, Henry A. Dayton, Adam I. N. Dilley, Edwin Downs, Lewis Downs, Bernard W. Doyle, Birdsey Gibbs, George N. Gibbs, James A. Green, Manwaring Green, William Hall, Luther W. Hart, Timothy A. Hart, Willard Hart, Geo. W. Hurlbut, William S. Hurlbut, William R. Hubbard, Asa Humiston, Alonzo J. Hull, Henry C. Kent, Walter Martin, Herman P. Moore, Henry Overton, Joseph Pettit, Charles Henry Pine, Jerome Preston, Theodore Robbins, Edmund B. Sage, William Seymour, Lucius S. Skinner, John Smith, Prosper W. Smith, Philip Stabell, Darwin S. Starks, John M. Teeter, Hubert A. Warner, Marcus A. Whitehead, Warren M. Wood, Julius Woodford, Wallace M. Woodruff.

To these were added, by subsequent enlistment, the following Winchester men, who died in the service, or were honorably discharged or mustered out: Ernest A. Basney, Robert J. Balcroft, Samuel U. Brew, Henry Clarke, Wells Clark, Benjamin G. Carman, David Durand, Jared P. Evarts, Mathew Fitzgerald, Patrick Keegan, Jacob Le Roy, Julius Rogers, Henry J. Reynolds, William H. Rowe, Edward Rugg, Edward E. Rowe, Philip Shelley, Henry Van Duesen, William Warner, Erastus Woodworth, Henry Wenzell.

The regiment left Litchfield for Washington, Sept. 15, 1862, and was stationed at Alexandria, Va., until November 23, 1863, when it was changed from an infantry to an artillery organization, and was designated "The Second Connecticut Heavy Artillery." It was engaged in garrison and police duty in the defences of Washington, south of the Potomac, until May 21, 1864, and was there filled up to 1800 men, the maximum of an artillery regiment. On the 22d of May, 1864, it was assigned to the Sixth Army Corps, and was from that time continually on the march until June 1, 1864, when it received its first baptism by fire in the murderous charge at Cold Harbor, Va. It afterwards participated in battles at Hatcher's Run, Va., Feb. 6, 1865, near Petersburg, Va, March 25 and April 2, and at Sailor's Creek, Va., April 6, 1865; and was mustered out at Washington, D. C., August 18, 1865.

The promotions of Winchester men in this regiment were:

        Capt. Jeffrey Skinner to Lieut. Colonel.
        Lieut. Benjamin F. Hosford to Captain.

James E. Baldwin

Sergt. Orlow J. Smith to Captain.
Sergt. Salmon A. Granger to 2d Lieut.
Sergt. Henry Skinner to Captain.
Corp. Wm. S. Cooper to 2d Lieut.
Corp. Frederick W. Daniels to 2d Lieut.
Corp. Charles A. Reynolds to 2d Lieut.
Priv. Frederick M. Cook to 2d Lieut.

The killed and mortally wounded were as follows:

At Cold Harbor: Col. Elisha S. Kellogg, Sergt. Frederick W. Daniels, Musician Myron Ferris, Privates James R. Baldwin,* Alfred Comins, Lewis Downs, Birdsey Gibbs, James A. Green, Willard Hart, Alonzo J. Hull, Henry C. Kent,† Walter Martin, John M. Teeter, Jared P. Everts—14 of Co. E; to these add Albert M. Tuttle, Co. D, Eleventh Regiment—15.

At Cedar Creek, Capt. Benj. F. Hosford, whose remains were brought home for interment.

The following members of the regiment were wounded, but not mortally, in the service:

At Cold Harbor: Privates Edward Beach, Philip D. Carrol, William Seymour, Marcus A. Whitehead, Ernest Basney, Samuel N. Brew, Jacob Le Roy, Julius Woodford, Henry Wenzell:

At Cedar Creek: Major Jeffrey Skinner, Corp. Wm. S. Cooper.

The following named men (privates) died in the service:

Manwaring Green, Oct. 17, 1864, by railroad accident.
Geo. W. Hurlbut, at Fort Worth, Va., March 27, 1863.
Wm. S. Hurlbut, at Reg. Hospital, Oct. 25, 1863.
Wm. R. Hubbard, at Reg. Hospital, Aug. 4, 1864.
Jerome Preston, at Reg. Hospital, Oct. 24, 1863.

---

*Among the names on the foregoing list were James R. Baldwin and Henry C. Kent, who were in the assault at Cold Harbor, and were never seen afterwards. They were doubtless killed, and the remains buried during some of the following nights, by fatigue parties, who could carry no lights without drawing the fire of the rebel battery in close vicinity of the battle-field. Private Baldwin was son of Mr. Ezra Baldwin of Winsted; youthful and cheery—tenderly reared and religiously educated—beloved of his parents and comrades.

†Private Kent, son of an English cutler, at fifteen years old had never been to school, and was destitute of the first rudiments of education; was the oldest of a large family of children, and was kept at constant work in aid of their support. In this condition, he sought instruction from a benevolent lady during his winter evenings, and at the Sabbath school; made rapid progress, mastered thoroughly the ordinary branches of education, and made a consistent profession of religion. At twenty, he bought his time of his father, at once enlisted, and died in his first battle a Christian soldier.

Darwin S. Starks, at Reg. Hospital, Aug. 23, 1863.
Mathew Fitzgerald, prisoner of war at Salisbury, N. C., Jan. 6, 1865.
Julius Rogers, at Reg. Hospital, Sept. 21, 1864.
Edward E. Rowe, at Warren Station, Va., March 27, 1865.
Julius Woodford, at Reg. Hospital, Jan. 30, 1865.

The heroic Colonel Elisha S. Kellogg, who commanded the regiment at Cold Harbor, and there fell at the head of his men, though a resident of Derby on entering the service, subsequently removed his family to the society of Winsted, and his remains lie buried in the south cemetery under an appropriate monument.

The final contribution of Winchester men for the service was made to the 28th regiment of nine months infantry, consisting of the major of the regiment, a captain, two lieutenants, and fifty-nine enlisted men. The regiment encamped at New Haven until November 18th, 1862, when it embarked for Pensacola, Florida, and there remained inactive until ordered to join General Banks' army, and, after harassing marches in Louisiana, was actively engaged in the assault on Port Hudson, June 14th, 1863, sustaining a loss of fifty-nine killed, wounded, and missing. The regiment was mustered out of service at New Haven, Conn., August 28th, 1863.

The names of the Winchester men in the regiment were Wheelock T. Batcheller (late 1st lieutenant Company E, 2d three months Infantry), major; Lucien B. Wheelock (late sergeant Company E, 2d three months Infantry), captain of Company F; Caleb P. Newman (late 1st sergeant Company B, 2d three months Infantry), 1st lieutenant; Jabez Alvord, 2d lieutenant; sergeants, George L. Andrews, Silas H. McAlpine, Milton T. Moore, and Henry L. Roberts; corporals, B. Frank Marsh, William A. Wadsworth, William Couch, Charles H. Moore, and Joseph H. C. Batchelder; privates, Columbus C. Wright, Samuel C. Barber, George Bulcroft, Charles Baldwin, Edward Camsell, Henry P. Cook, Peter Coe, James Dugan, George N. Dewey, Henry Detert, Cornelius Dayton, Charles Decker, Lucius Eggleston, George W. Elmore, Paul Forcier, Correll T. French, Edward Finn, Mat. M. Fitzgerald, Claudius W. S. Foster, John E. Garrett, Ward Grant, Samuel E. Griffin, William Hague, Charles N. Hollister, George Hoskin, Edward B. Kinney, Ralph Lina, Charles Maddra, Harvey Moore, George R. Moore, Silas Moore, Elbert Manchester, Thomas Morris, James E. Maddra, James McDermott, William N. Pierce, George L. Pease, John Partridge, Elam E. Richardson, William H. Rowe, David R. Rankin, Stephen Scott, Frank S. Turner, Lyman Terrill, Cassius Watson, Howard S. Wheeler, William S. Woodford, Mark H. Wheeler, Henry C. White, and Michael Haggarty, of Company H.

The following deaths occurred in the service:

Private Columbus C. Wright died at Brashear City, La., May 23d, 1863.

Private Samuel C. Barber died on the Mississippi.

Private Charles Maddra died at Great Barrington, Mass., August 23d, 1863.

Private Cassius Watson died at Brashear City, La., May 23d, 1863.

Private Mark H. Wheeler, killed at Port Hudson, La., June 14th, 1863.

Private Howard S. Wheeler died soon after reaching home, of disease contracted in the service.

Private Michael Haggarty, of Company H, died of wounds received at Port Hudson, August 12th, 1863.

The following Winchester men served as officers of the 1st Regiment Louisiana Colored Engineers:

 Willard S. Wetmore, 1st lieutenant and quartermaster.

 Edward Hewitt, 1st lieutenant.

The following Winchester men served in the navy:

Marcus Baird, ensign and acting sailing-master, Gulf Squadron.

David W. Coe, executive officer's clerk, United States Frigate Sabine.

Solomon R. Hinsdale, assistant pay-master on the Mississippi Flotilla, above Vicksburg.

Henry Overton, transferred from 2d Heavy Artillery to the United States Navy.

Ansel Rowley.

We compile a connected list of soldiers of the town who died in the service, as follows:—

Robert Arnold, Corporal Company I, 5th Infantry, killed Cedar Mountain, August 9, 1862.

Jacob T. Brown, Sergeant, Company C, 12th Infantry, killed Fisher's Hill, September 19, 1864.

James M. Burton, Private, Company E, 2d Infantry, died in hospital, New Haven, May 13, 1861.

George Bellows, Jr., Private, Company E, 7th Infantry, mortally wounded Hampton, Va., October 19, 1864.

James R. Baldwin, Private, Company E, 2d Heavy Artillery, killed Cold Harbor, June 1, 1864.

Samuel C. Barber, Private, Company F, 28th Infantry, died of fever on Mississippi River.

Albert Burdick, Private, Company E, 7th Infantry, died at Beaufort, S. C., July 29, 1862.

John Biederman, Private, Company E, 7th Infantry, died October 13, 1864.

Alfred Comins, Private, Company E, 2d Heavy Artillery, killed Cold Harbor, June 1, 1864.

Wolcott Cook, Private, Company K, 2d Heavy Artillery, died City Point, Va., June 16, 1865.

Wm. F. Cogswell, Private, Company E, 11th Infantry, killed Sharpsburg, Md., September 17, 1862.

Frederick W. Daniels, Sergeant, Company E, 2d Heavy Artillery, killed Cold Harbor, June 1, 1864.

Robert Dempsey, Lieutenant, Company E, 7th Infantry, killed Olustee, Fla, February 20, 1865.

Lewis Downs, Private, Company E, 2d Heavy Artillery, killed Cold Harbor, June 1, 1864.

George C. Downs, Private, Company C, 13th Infantry, died on the Mississippi September 13, 1863.

Lewis Dayton, Private, Company D, 11th Infantry, killed at Sharpsburg, Md., September 17, 1862.

James Dolphin, Private, Company G, 14th R. I. Colored Artillery, died at Plaquemine, La., August 5, 1864.

Lucius B. Eggleston, Private, Company F, 28th Infantry, died at Memphis, Ten.

Jared P. Evarts, Private, Company E, 2d Heavy Artillery, killed at Cold Harbor, June 1, 1864.

Myron Ferris, Musician, Company E, 2d Heavy Artillery, killed at Cold Harbor, June 1, 1864.

Elliott Fleming, Private, Company G, 16th Infantry, killed at Sharpsburg, Md., September 17, 1862.

Mathew Fitzgerald, Private, Company E, 2d Heavy Artillery, died a prisoner at Salisbury, N. C.

Birdsey Gibbs, Private, Company E, 2d Heavy Artillery, killed at Cold Harbor, June 1, 1864.

James A. Green, Quartermaster-Sergeant, Company E, 2d Heavy Artillery, mortally wounded at Cold Harbor.

Manwaring Green, Private, Company E, 2d Heavy Artillery, killed by railroad accident, October 17, 1864.

Charles Gilbert, Private, Company E, 7th Infantry, died of wounds in Charleston, S. C., July 9, 1862.

Benjamin F. Hosford, Captain, Company D, 2d Heavy Artillery, killed at Cedar Creek, October 19, 1864.

Willard Hart, Private, Company E, 2d Heavy Artillery, killed at Cold Harbor, June 1, 1864.

George W. Hurlbut, Private, Company E, 2d Heavy Artillery, died at Alexandria, Va., March 27, 1863.

William S. Hurlbut, Private, Company E, 2d Heavy Artillery, died at Fort Worth, Va., October 25, 1863.

William R. Hubbard, Private, Company E, 2d Heavy Artillery, died at Fort Worth, February 28, 1864.

Asa Humiston, Private, Company E, 2d Heavy Artillery, mortally wounded at Opequan, Va., September 19, 1864; died September 21, 1864.

Alonzo J. Hull, Private, Company E, 2d Heavy Artillery, killed at Cold Harbor, June 1, 1864.

Lewis Hazzard, Private, Company G, 29th Colored Infantry, drowned at Plaquemine, La., October 5, 1865.

Michael Haggarty, Private, Company H, 28th Infantry, mortally wounded at Port Hudson, August 12, 1863.

Davis Hart, Private, Company A, Massachusetts Infantry, killed at Fredericksburg, Va.

Henry C. Kent, Private, Company E, 2d Heavy Artillery, killed at Cold Harbor, June 1, 1864.

Walter Martin, Private, Company E, 2d Heavy Artillery, killed at Cold Harbor, June 1, 1864.

Charles E. Palmer, Captain, Company E, 7th Infantry, died at James' Island, S. C., July 7, 1862.

Jerome Preston, Private, Company E, 2d Heavy Artillery, died at Alexandria, Va., October 24, 1863.

Hiram Roberts, Private, Company E, 11th Infantry, killed at Sharpsburg, Md., September 17, 1862.

Edward E. Rowe, Private, Company E, 2d Heavy Artillery, died at Petersburg, Va., March, 1865.

Julius Rogers, Private, Company E, 2d Heavy Artillery, died at Petersburg, Va., September 21, 1864.

William H. Slack, Private, Company D, 11th Infantry, mortally wounded at Newbern, N. C., March 22, 1862.

Darwin S. Starks, Private, Company E, 2d Heavy Artillery, died at Alexandria, Va., August 23, 1863.

John M. Teeter, Private, Company E, 2d Heavy Artillery, killed at Cold Harbor, June 1, 1864.

Albert M. Tuttle, Private, Company D, 11th Infantry, killed at Cold Harbor, June 3, 1864.

John K. Twiss, Sergeant, Company E, 11th Infantry, died at Richmond, Va., May 1, 1864.

Julius Thorne, Private, Company M, 1st Regiment of Cavalry, died at New Haven, December 14, 1864.

John B. Welch, Assistant-Surgeon, 12th Infantry, died at Ship Island, February 13, 1862.

Howard S. Wheeler, Private, Company F, 28th Infantry, died of scurvy at home after muster out.

Mark H. Wheeler, Private, Company F, 28th Infantry, killed at Port Hudson, La., June 14, 1863.

Julius Woodford, Private, Company E, 2d Heavy Artillery, died at Alexandria, Va., January 30, 1864.

William S. Watson, Private, Company K, 2d Heavy Artillery, died at Alexandria, Va., August 28, 1863.

Columbus C. Wright, Wagoner, Company F, 28th Infantry, died at Brashear City, La., May 23, 1863.

Cassius Watson, Private, Company F, 28th Infantry, died at Brashear City, La., May 23, 1863.

The enlistments by families is a notable feature of the volunteer force of this town. We find fourteen instances of two brothers in the service, nine instances of three members of the same family, two of four, and one of six connected in the relation of father, stepfather, sons and stepsons. We note the instances embracing three or more members of one family:—

    I. Sons of Caleb F. Daniels—

        1. Frederick W., private Company D, 2d Infantry, and sergeant Company E, 2d Heavy Artillery, killed at Cold Harbor, Va.

        2. George, private Company E, 7th Infantry.

3. Charles, private Company G, 13th Infantry, promoted t 2d Lieutenant.

II. Sons of Isaac Downs—
1. Edwin E., private Company E, 2d Heavy Artillery; discharged for disability.
2. Lewis, private Company E, 2d Heavy Artillery; killed at Cold Harbor, Va.
3. George C., private Company C, 13th Infantry; died of swamp fever.

III. Sons of Rufus M. Eggleston—
1. Gustavus, private Company B, 1st squadron cavalry.
2. Erastus, } twins, privates Company E, 11th Infantry; dis-
3. Rufus, } charged for disability.
4. Lucius, private Company H, 28th Infantry; died of swamp fever on Mississippi.

IV. Sons of Arad Hosford—
1. Charles L., sergeant Company E, 2d Infantry, captain Company D, 11th Infantry.
2. Benjamin F., private Company E, captain 2d Heavy Artillery, killed at Cedar Creek.
3. William A., 1st lieutenant Company E, 2d Heavy Artillery.

V. Sons of Sylvester Hurlbut—
1. George W., private Company E, 2d Heavy Artillery, died at Alexandria, Va.
2. William S., private company E, 2d Heavy Artillery, died at Fort Worth, Va.
3. Andrew M., private Company E, 11th Infantry, re-enlisted a veteran.

VI. Sons of Anthony Horne—
1. Samuel B., private Company C, 2d Infantry, captain Company F, 11th Infantry, provost-marshal 18th Army Corps.
2. Robert, drummer Company F, 11th Infantry, wounded at Petersburg, Va.
3. John J., private Company F, 15th N. Y. Heavy Artillery.

VII. Sons of Newton Hart—
1. Davis, private Company A, 10th Massachusetts Infantry, killed at Spotsylvania, Va.
2. Geo. L., private Company A, 10th Massachusetts Infantry.
3. Timothy A., sergeant Company E, 2d Heavy Artillery.

AND FAMILY RECORDS. 483

VIII. Sons of Sylvanus Pease—
  1. Byron W., assistant surgeon United States Colored Engineers, La.
  2. Frank S., musician Company D, 11th Infantry.
  3. Robert, musician Company I, 5th Infantry.
  4. James A., private Company E, 7th Infantry.

IX. William H. Rowe, (father,) musician 1st Heavy Artillery, private Company F, 28th Infantry.
  1. Edward E., (son,) private Company E, 2d Heavy Artillery, died in the service.
  2. Charles H., (son,) private Company E, 2d Heavy Artillery.

X. Sons of Elias Rowley—
  1. Henry H., private Company E, 7th Infantry.
  2. John G., private Company E, 7th Infantry.
  3. Warren, private, Cavalry.
  4. Ansel, private, Navy.

XI. Sons of John Skinner—
  1. Jeffrey, 1st sergeant Company E, 2d Infantry, captain, major, and lieutenant-colonel, 2d Heavy Artillery.
  2. Henry, sergeant Company E, 2d Heavy Artillery, lieutenant Companies E and G, captain Company B, same regiment.
  3. Edward, corporal Company G, 13th Infantry.

We note, in closing this list, a mixed family, all of them residents of this town, before, during, or immediately after the war. Francis H. Kinney was father of two sons, and Margaret, his second wife, was mother, by a former husband, (Miller,) of three sons, all of whom served in different regiments, as follows:

1. Francis H. Kinney, (father,) private Company H, 15th Infantry; discharged for disability.

2. Horace Kinney, (son,) private Company E, 11th Infantry, and veteran.

3. George Kinney, (son,) private Company D, 11th Infantry, transferred to 20th United States Cavalry.

4. David Miller, (step-son,) color-bearer, Company D, 1st Infantry, corporal Company E, 2d Heavy Artillery, wounded at Cold Harbor.

5. John B. Miller, (step-son,) private Company E., 11th Infantry; veteran; promoted to lieutenant; wounded at Cold Harbor, Va.

6. Frank Miller, (step-son,) private Company A, 8th Infantry; wounded at Cold Harbor.

The three Millers belonged to three distinct regiments, all present at Cold Harbor; were all wounded successively on the 1st, 2d, and 3d days of June, 1864, and were successively brought to the hospital at Alexandria on the 5th, 6th, and 7th days of the same month.

Frank, the youngest of the three Millers, was fourteen years old when he enlisted. He was wounded at Cold Harbor by a rifle ball in the shoulder. Chloroform was twice administered to him preparatory to amputation of his arm at the shoulder joint, but it was deferred, through fear of a fatal result. He lived to become a strong, hearty man.

From the foregoing data we gather, as the effective force of Winchester men, regularly mustered and engaged in the military and naval service, and honorably discharged therefrom, three hundred and fifty-two efficient men, thirty-four of whom re-enlisted for second terms of service, early in the war, and twelve or more re-enlisted as veterans, after three years of service.

To these are to be added not less than seventy-five substitutes, purchased by the town authorities in the bounty-jumping shambles, who never resided in the town, and whose names it would be superfluous to give. Of this class full forty deserted—most of them immediately after receiving their bounty; twenty were unassigned or not taken up on the rolls; and a small number were killed, or honorably discharged at the end of their terms of service, and are named among the effective men.

SUMMARY.

Whole number of effective men,	352
Men enlisting and serving second terms,	46
Deserters, bounty-jumpers, and "dead beats,"	75
	473

Probably no army in the world's history was made up of better material in the aggregate (Cromwell's Ironsides excepted) than the volunteer force of the United States in the War of the Rebellion; better in physical power, moral training, intelligence and social standing, but unused, at the outset, to discipline and subordination. There was enough of religious zeal and patriotic ardor to call into the field thoughtful and high-principled men, rather than those of a debased order. East and West this element predominated. In the West the volunteers were mostly farmers; in the East they were more largely intelligent mechanics, inferior in bone and sinew, but excelling in elasticity and endurance. Our men, to a large extent, were made up of the latter class, and of young men tenderly reared, and apparently unfitted to endure hardship and privation; yet an examination of the foregoing statistics will show that far the largest proportion of discharges for disability and deaths by disease occurred among the agricultural class.

Among the evil forebodings at the beginning of the conflict, none seemed better warranted than that a whole generation of young men would be demoralized by the debaucheries of army life. Experience of other wars had taught this lesson; but it signally failed in its application to the younger or older volunteers of this town. It is very doubtful whether, among our soldier boys, an instance can be found where a young man, entering the service with good moral and temperate habits, has returned to civil life with those habits essentially deteriorated. Almost without exception, they at once resumed their accustomed occupations in the factory, on the farm, and at the counter, or embarked in new fields of enterprise suggested by their enlarged experience and observation.

Another foreboding of the early days of the war took the form of assurance that every branch of manufacturing and mercantile business was to be prostrated, that farms would be uncultivated, that the rich would become poor, and that the poor must fight or starve. An all-wise Providence has averted these evils. Our citizens in nearly every branch of industry and business have been prospered during the ten years ending in 1871, as in no earlier decade; and this prosperity has resulted from no direct government patronage in the way of army contracts or war speculations.

The pecuniary outlay of the town in bounties, expenses of filling quotas and aid of soldiers' families, as appears by the accounts of the selectmen, was as follows:

1861.	Paid volunteers and their families,	-	-	-	$	851.63
1862.	" expenses of filling quotas,	-	-	-		492.59
	" bounties on enlistments,	-	-	-		6,500.00
1863.	" bounties and expenses of filling quotas,		-	-		16,110.00
1864.	" " " "		-	-		16,481.05
1865.	" " " "	-	-	-		14,233.45
1866.	" " " "		-	-		300.00
1867.	" " " "	-	-	-		8.53

$54,977.25

The individual contributions, as far as ascertained, were as follows:

Balance of cash raised in 1861 by citizens for purchase of materials for soldiers' uniforms, and for support of their families, and not refunded by the state, - - - - -	$	676.14
Cash paid by individuals for filling quota in 1864, - -		664.42
Bounties of $10 each to 100 men by Elliot Beardsley, - -		1,000.00
Bounties paid by other citizens (estimated), - -		2,000.00

$4,340.56

A large amount of hospital stores, clothing, bedding, provisions, and cash were furnished by female societies, only a portion of which can be ascertained, by reason of the imperfect records made of the same. We compile from such records and memoranda as have been preserved, the following items:

Making up 103 uniforms from materials paid for by the state,	$412.00
" 112 shirts (cloth furnished),	84.00
200 linen havelocks,	100.00
Sent to *Christian Commission*, 16 boxes and barrels of clothing, bedding and hospital stores, valued at	688.18
Cash, proceeds of tableaux exhibition,	252.50
To *Sanitary Commission*, hospital articles and stores,	476.39
To Mrs. Harris, *Supt. of Hospitals, Phila.*, hospital articles and stores,	370.71
To *Freedmen's and Refugee Aid Societies*,	1550.50
To *Soldiers' Aid Society*,	31.70
To *Soldiers in Connecticut Regiments*, 96 barrels and 15 boxes vegetables, provisions, and stores,	635.00
	$4,600.98

The above articles, estimated below their value, and comprising an infinite variety of articles, were mainly furnished by one of our two female organizations. Of the number and value of articles supplied by the other society, we have obtained no statement, but may safely estimate them at $2,081.21; and so estimating them, we have the following summary of town expense.

Town expenses,	$48,977.25
Cash items by citizens of the town,	4,340.56
Clothing, bedding, hospital stores, provisions and cash from West Winsted Soldiers' Aid Society,	4,600.98
Similar articles furnished by other societies and individuals (estimated),	2,081.21
Grand Total,	$60,000.00

The contributions furnished by the female society above named, are specified with great particularity and precision, and are largely made up of the most valuable and indispensable articles of clothing and bedding, the cost of materials worked up and paid for in cash, making a large part of their estimated value.

One item of hospital stores, nowhere enumerated, was the product of ninety-five bushels of blackberries, which were gathered in one day, mostly by females, on a proposition of Gail Borden, Esq., that he would convert into jam all the blackberries so gathered in one day, at the condensed milk factory owned in part by him, the sugar and cans being paid for.

NOTE.—The compiler has learned, since this chapter went to press, that our worthy neighbor, Caleb P. Newman, First Sergeant of Company B, 2d Infantry, and 1st Lieutenant of Company F, 28th Infantry, had signed an enlistment paper before the meeting at which Captain Horne enrolled his name.

CHAPTER XXXIV.

BUSINESS OPERATIONS AS AFFECTED BY THE REBELLION—BUILDING OPERATIONS—INCREASE OF TAXABLE PROPERTY—CONNECTICUT WESTERN RAILROAD—TEMPERANCE REFORM AND DECADENCE—MASONIC SOCIETIES.

1861 TO 1872.

AMID the enthusiasm and firm resolve of the loyal masses of the North, at the outbreak of the rebellion, there was among intelligent men a consciousness of a mighty struggle impending, and a belief that it would be attended with ruin to all our business interests. The merchant encouraged his clerks to volunteer, by assurances that their places should be kept open for their occupancy on their return from military service, and by pecuniary bounties. The manufacturers held out like inducements to their operatives.

The struggle was mightier and longer than was apprehended; but business interests were only partially affected or deranged. In our community the only business entirely suspended was the manufacture of planters' hoes for the southern market. The business employed a large number of men, who were represented in most of the battle fields of the Atlantic States.* Other manufacturing establishments for a time reduced their business, but soon found it enlarged in amount and profit. The evil day of collapse and ruin apprehended at the beginning of the war was not realized, but was foreboded at its end. At the end of seven years, after the return of peace — thanks to the wise management of the financial affairs of the nation — no business revulsion has occurred. Nearly four hundred millions of national debt — to say nothing of state and town debts approaching an equal amount — have been paid off, and the business affairs of the country were seldom more prosperous. Very few new dwellings or factories were erected during that period, but nearly all the dwellings previously built with funds borrowed from savings and building associations, and afterwards sold to speculating capitalists, found purchasers at largely advanced prices, and came into the hands of substantial resident owners. Population rapidly increased

---

* We have, in the preceding chapter, noticed six members of one family who served in various regiments, all of whom — with perhaps one exception — had been employed in this branch of business.

from year to year, though the increase has hardly been noticeable by reason of the crowding to a large extent of two or more families in buildings previously occupied by only one.

Owing to the great increase of taxation, falling more largely on real estate than on personal property on the one hand, and on the other hand the inducements held out to investors by ten per cent. mortgages, railroad bonds and stocks, but few tenant houses have been erected in the borough since 1860 by capitalist or manufacturer.

During the twelve years since 1860, the following public buildings, factory buildings, and stores have been erected.

The graded school building in west district was built in 1867, at a cost of $19,400.

Number of scholars on the roll November, 1872, - - 310
Number of teachers, - - - - - - 5
Aggregate amount of salaries, - - - - - $4,600

The graded school building in the east section was built in 1870, at a cost of $15,000.

Number of scholars enrolled November, 1872, - - 160
Number of teachers, - - - - - 4
Aggregate amount of salaries, - - - - $2,302

The monastery building of St. Francis' Literary and Theological Seminary was erected in 1867. Connected with the seminary is a parish school, with from fifty to seventy-five scholars, under charge of Sisters of the third Order of St. Francis; and also the Academy of St. Margaret of Cortona, for tuition of young ladies in the higher branches.

The borough building and lock-up was erected in 1861.

The Woodford four-story brick block, containing a store, banking office, and masonic hall, was finished in 1861.

Dudley's three story brick block, containing four store tenements, was erected in 1861.

Moore's south three-story wooden block, containing fish market, smith shop, and stove warehouse, was erected in 1866.

Moore's north three story wooden block, containing clothing store and feed store, erected 1869.

Phelps' three-story wooden block, containing millinery and drug stores, erected in 1868.

Gilman & Hallett's three-story wooden block, containing two store tenements, erected in 1872.

Hicks' three-story Hotel, corner of Main and Park streets, erected in 1870 on the site of the old Stevens' House.

Gilbert Clock Company's brick factory on north side of Wallen street, built on site of factory burned in 1871, erected in 1871.

Gilbert Clock Co.'s brick factory, south of Wallen street, erected in 1872.

Strong Manufacturing Company's building erected in 1866.

Gilman Carriage Company's building erected in 1866.

The four-story brick block, north of the Beardsley House, on Main street, containing two store tenements and a banking office, erected by the Beardsley family in 1872.

The Music Hall building, erected in 1872 by a joint-stock company, a brick and iron structure, fronting fifty-six feet on Main and 126 feet on Elm street, is three stories above the basement floor, and surmounted by a Mansard roof, contains a public hall 54 by 92 feet, and three store tenements on the first floor. Adjoining it on the east, and in the same style and material, is a block of 48 feet front, containing a banking office and a store tenement, erected by John G. Wetmore.

The Connecticut Western Railroad Depot, on Lake street, was erected in 1872, in part by funds appropriated by the railroad company, and in part by contributions of George Dudley and other citizens.

The dwelling houses erected by resident owners, though limited in number, have been of a superior order in style, architectural proportions, and conveniences. Among them we note the following, with their locations and date of erection:—

Dwelling of Thomas M. Clarke, on Elm street, in 1864.
" John G. Wetmore, on Hinsdale street, in 1867.
" James R. Alvord, on Meadow street, in 1867.
" David Strong, on Walnut street, in 1869.
" E. R. Beardsley (built by Seth L. Wilder, deceased), on Main street, in 1862.
" George F. Barton, on Prospect street, in 1869.
" Edward Clarke, on Hinsdale street, in 1870.
" James G. Woodruff, on North Main street, in 1870.
" William C. Phelps, on High street, in 1870.
" T. M. V. Doughty, on Union street, in 1862.
" William McAlpine, on Hinsdale street, in 1871.
" James Cone, " " in 1872.
" Wm. L. Camp, " " in 1872.
" F. L. Pond, " " in 1872.
" Wm. C. Welch, on Main street, in 1871.
" Julius Gregory, Beach street, in 1870.
" Patrick Reidy, Elm street, 1870.
" Charles J. York, " 1871.
" Jos. W. Parsons, Beach street, 1871.
" Charles L. Norton, Elm street, 1871.

We compile from the lists of 1861 and 1871 abstracts of taxable property in Winsted, and also whole amount of assessments of the whole town :—

Description of Property.	1861.		1871.	
	No.	Valuation.	No.	Valuation.
Dwelling houses,	502	$514,450	555	770,225
Acres of land,	8,800	186,884		217,426
Factories, mills, and stores,	77	201,500	93	279,150
Horses,	219	17,780	285	33,745
Neat catttle,	758	14,847	872	19,941
Sheep and swine,		259		289
Carriages, &c.,		9,201		23,150
Farming utensils,				125
Clocks and watches,		6,354		14,281
Musical instruments,		6,020		13,875
Extra furniture,		5,550		14,935
Bank stocks,		204,344		186,556
State stocks,				2,100
Railroad bonds,		21,188		328,585
Invested in merchandize,		90,350		140,415
" manufacturing,		113,900		191,200
" steamboats,				9,500
Money at interest,		79,443		216,767
Money on hand,		3,428		16,150
Taxable property,		270		8,075
		$1,475,768		$2,486,490

We omit the taxable polls on account of changes in valuation from time to time, and the variation of numbers exempted for various reasons.

The whole number of unexempt polls in 1861 was, - - 645
While in 1871 the number was reduced to - - - - 451

In 1840 the taxable property of the whole town was, $ 477,865
In 1851 " " " 1,023,875
In 1861 " " " 1,750,921
In 1871 " " " 2,759,943
Polls not included.

The population of the town, at the periods specified, was as follows:—

By census of 1756, - - - - - 24
" " 1774, - - - - - 339
" " 1781, - - - - - 688
" " 1800, - - - - 1,368
" " 1810, - - - - - 1,466
" " 1820, - - - - 1,601

By census of 1830, - - - - - - 1,766
" " 1840, - - - - - 1,667
" " 1850, - - - - - - 2,179
" " 1860, - - - - - 3,550
" " 1870, - - - - - - 4,102

After the opening of the Naugatuck Railroad in 1850, the necessity of a railroad communication eastward to the Connecticut River, and westward to the Hudson, became more and more apparent, but until recently seemed impracticable, by reason of the high grades and circuitous lines required in running roads easterly and westerly over the mountain ranges between the Hudson and Connecticut rivers.

The steady growth of Collinsville, New Hartford, and Winsted, and the great enlargement of the iron interests of Salisbury and Canaan, stimulated the desire to overcome difficulties in the way of the enterprise, which had seemed to the communities interested to be insuperable.

Public attention was first called to the practicability of the enterprise by E. T. Butler, Esq., of Norfolk, in 1865, and mainly through his instrumentality, experimental surveys were made during that year; and in 1866 a charter was granted to "The Connecticut Western Railroad Company," with power to construct a road from Collinsville, Conn., to the Massachusetts state line on the border of North Canaan. Strenuous efforts were made by Mr. Butler and others to interest capitalists in the scheme. The Boston and Erie Railroad Company were vainly solicited to make the route a part of their line. Hartford and Springfield capitalists were appealed to in vain. The Canal Railroad Company would have nothing to do with it. The Harlem, Housatonic, and Naugatuck Companies, with which it was to form connections, gave it a cold shoulder.

At this nearly hopeless stage of the enterprise, the Dutchess and Columbia Railroad Company, under the auspices of George H. Brown, Esq., of Washington Valley, N. Y., had completed their road from Fishkill, on the Hudson, opposite Newburg, to near Pine Plains in Dutchess County, N. Y., and were seeking an eastern connection. The existence of the Connecticut Western Charter was made known to Mr. Brown, who, with characteristic energy, at once embarked with Mr. Butler and others in the enterprise. A new charter was obtained from the Legislature of 1868, granting power to extend the road from the City of Hartford to Collinsville; thence to follow the line of the charter of 1866 through New Hartford, Winsted, and Norfolk; and thence to diverge westerly through North Canaan and Salisbury, in the direction of Millerton, on the Harlem Railroad, so as to connect with the Dutchess and Columbia Railroad at the state line. The charter authorized towns along the line of the road, in their corporate capacity, to subscribe and pay for stock in the road to an amount not exceeding five per cent. of their grand lists last made up, on being empowered so to do by a two-third vote of the inhabitants of such towns at meetings duly called and notified for that purpose.

The town of Winchester, on the 22d of August, 1868, by a ballot of 366 to 66, voted a subscription of five per cent. on its list, amounting to $116,000, to the stock of the company, and individual citizens of the town made further subscriptions to the amount of $74,900. Winchester was the first town on the line to vote on this test question, the result of which was to determine whether the road should be carried through. Subscriptions of other towns along the line were soon afterwards voted as follows:—

Salisbury, by town,	$50,000	By citizens,	$103,090*
Canaan,	"	34,000	"	16,000
Norfolk,	"	41,500	"	10,800
Canton,	"	40,000	"	0,000
Simsbury,	"	50,000	"	20,100
Bloomfield,	"	42,300	"	25,900
Hartford,	"	750,000	"	64,000
Add Winchester,	"	116,000	"	74,900

The surveys, estimates, and location of the road were completed in 1870, and the whole line was put under contract immediately afterward. The first passenger train passed over the road from Hartford to Millerton, N. Y., on the 21st December, 1871, and returned the same day, and since then the communication has been uninterrupted. Its connections with other roads along its line, and at its termini, will make it a trunk line of equal importance with the other east and west roads of New England. Its connections with roads already completed, are with three roads at Hartford, with the Canal Road at Simsbury, its branch at Collinsville, the Naugatuck at Winsted, the Housatonic at Canaan, the Pokeepsie and Eastern, and the Dutchess & Columbia at state line, and the Harlem at Millerton. Other connections are shortly to be completed with the Connecticut River and Boston & Albany roads at Springfield, the Collinsville & New Britain branch at Collinsville, the Farmington River Road from Lee to New Hartford, or Winsted, and the road from Rhinebeck on the Hudson to the state line, the three latter now in process of construction.

With these new avenues of intercourse with every portion of New England, and especially with direct access to the coal fields of Pennsylvania, and the wheat and lumber regions of the great West, a rapid

---

* This amount of private subscriptions is supposed to include a subscription of $50,000 by Mr. Brown of the Dutchess and Columbia Railroad.

growth in the population and wealth of Winsted is confidently anticipated.

In the regular course of our annals, the great temperance movement, which has contributed largely to the prosperity and moral improvement of our community, and which has been largely promoted by our citizens, has found no place.

As early as 1825 the Temperance Reform, by organized associations, began to be agitated in this vicinity. Able lecturers from time to time appeared among us, setting forth the evils of intemperate drinking, its almost universal prevalence, and the remedy to be found in total abstinence from spirituous liquors, and associated action in enlightening the public mind, and aiding the intemperate in their endeavors to abandon their evil habits. It was then thought that abstinence from distilled liquors would remove the giant evil of the country, and the original societies were organized on a pledge thus limited.

We have before us the records of the Winsted Temperance Society, organized August 16, 1829, as an auxiliary of the Litchfield County Society, and based on the following pledge:—

"The members of this society, believing that the use of intoxicating liquors for persons in health is not only unnecessary but hurtful, and that the practice is the cause of forming intemperate appetites and habits, and that while it continues the evils of intemperance can never be prevented, do therefore agree that we will abstain from the use of distilled spirits, except as medicines in case of bodily hurt or sickness; that we will not allow the use of it in our families, nor provide it for the entertainment of our friends or persons in our employ, and that in all suitable ways we will discountenance the use of it in the community."

This and other societies at that period formed in nearly every town in the county and state, was organized for active work, and fulfilled its mission. The county society, composed of delegates from its auxiliaries, assembled monthly with some one of these, received reports of the state of the work in all the towns, consulted on measures promotive of the cause, and heard addresses from its ablest advocates. The subordinate societies were stimulated to activity by reports from their delegates, and guided in their course of action by the combined wisdom and experience of the parent society.

For several years the county meetings were crowded by delegates and friends of the cause. The work went bravely on. The auxiliary societies at every meeting called for signers of the pledge, and appointed frequent committees to go from house to house circulating temperance tracts, and soliciting new recruits. Lecturing agents were employed to address the children in the school districts, and enroll them in temperance bands.

The original members of the Winsted Society were: Rev. James Beach, Solomon Rockwell, Asaph Pease, Willard Holmes, Salmon Burr, Austin Crane, Norman Palmer, William S. Holabird, Anson Cook, James H. Alvord, Lyman Case, Sidney Munson, Horace E. Rockwell, Erastus Woodford, Josiah Smith, Leumas H. Pease, and Eleazer Andrews. Accessions of members were rapidly made from month to month, until, in 1836, there were enrolled 297 males and 268 females. At the outset, it was a mooted question whether females had any temperance rights the lords of the creation were bound to recognize by admitting them to membership in the society. The question was speedily decided affirmatively, and their efficient co-operation in the cause was secured.

The active laborers in the temperance field at this day can but faintly realize the obstacles encountered, and the prejudices overcome by the pioneers of this movement. At the outset, the Methodist body, which eventually furnished many of the noblest and most persistent workers in the common cause, conceived that their churches were strict temperance bodies, competent to carry on the cause by enforcement of their discipline. This exclusiveness, however, was short-lived, and was followed by a hearty co-operation of the membership in the general work. There were also religionists of diverse persuasions who prated and canted about the sin of rejecting any good creature of God, and of covenanting with associates without the pale of the church. This class of opposers were in high favor with the drinking masses, who felt assured of their competency to take care of themselves, and who scorned to sign away their own liberty.

Nevertheless, the doctrine of abstinence gained ground rapidly, and to short-sighted observers seemed to promise a speedy renovation of society. Distilling of spirits by Christian men was generally abandoned. Respectable traders and taverners ceased to sell the villainous compounds. Farmers and manufacturers, to a large extent, ceased furnishing them to their workmen. But a radical defect in the pledge of abstinence soon became apparent. It embraced only distilled spirits in its prohibition; and by implication sanctioned the use of fermented drinks, as harmless. The consequence was, that habitual and intemperate drinkers, the classes to be arrested in their downward course, naturally and almost inevitably resorted to fermented drinks to satisfy and perpetuate their craving appetites. The poor inebriate substituted hard cider for cider brandy, and ale for whisky; while the richer one found in highly-drugged wine a solace for abstinence from cogniac brandy. It was not pleasant nor edifying to hear half-boozy guzzlers of wine, ale, and cider, expatiating on the benefits of abstinence from rot-gut in a distilled form. It sometimes seemed better that they should speedily terminate their drunken career by use of the concentrated poisons than to dishonor a noble cause by their advocacy and example.

Nevertheless, very many who signed the limited pledge, carried out the principles on which it was based by abstaining from every form of alcoholic drinks; and thus the original organization was productive of incalculable good.

The transition from the first to the second stage of temperance reform was gradual in the Winsted Society. Earnest and conscientious members, from time to time, affixed the letters T. T. A. to their names, subscribed to the original pledge, thereby binding themselves to total abstinence from all intoxicating drinks. A new life and activity became apparent as these cabalistic letters were appended to the names of members. By the close of 1836, every active member of the society had become a radical Tee Totaller, while many partially reformed members had fallen by the way side and many other once zealous members had become neutral or hostile to the cause.

At or near this period the original society was re-organized; or rather, it was left in the hands of the abstinents from ardent spirits only, and forthwith died of inanition; and a new society was organized under the name of "The Winsted Total Abstinence Society." Every live member of the old organization who had super-added to his name the total, or "tee-total," abstinence initials, joined the new society. Its members were active and earnest, and accessions of new members were made at every monthly meeting. Nearly every business man, and every trader in the town became an active member of the society, or an outspoken advocate of its principles. Every store-keeper in town ceased to buy or sell intoxicating liquors. We had few, if any, saloons in those days, and no apothecaries. Taverners, on applying for liquor licenses, were steadfastly refused by the civil authorities. Respectable farmers were ashamed to bring into the village their barrels of cider for sale to the topers. Not a few of them cut down their ungrafted apple trees, and many others fed their apples to their stock. The cider mills rotted down or were torn down, and the buildings were appropriated to better uses. We speak advisedly when we say that public opinion and public action had reached this stage in our community years before the advent of the great Washingtonian temperance movement.

Our limits permit only a brief allusion to the first legislative acts giving to towns the right to prohibit the sale of liquors within their borders. Winchester first voted for prohibition; a second meeting was called and voted for licensing the traffic; a third meeting, and a fourth, voted as the first had done, and the contest was abandoned. In these meetings, the principles of Total Abstinence were thoroughly ventilated in the presence of men who had never attended a temperance meeting. Arguments long before worn trite and threadbare in temperance meetings, found a lodgment in the consciences of many who had never before heard them. The law which had given occasion for these municipal debating societies was repealed by an adverse legislature, but the results were abiding. The moral suasion movement went onward.

In 1840 or 1841, the Washingtonian movement was initiated by an association of intemperate mechanics in Baltimore, who banded together for mutual aid in freeing themselves from the slavery of intemperance, by a pledge of abstinence from all intoxicating liquors. Large numbers of intemperate men flocked to their standard. Their delegates went abroad and organized associate bands in many of the neighboring cities. John Hawkins, the ablest of the pioneers in this movement, came to Hartford during the legislative session in 1842. His public addresses made a profound impression on the members of the legislature and every class of citizens. A Washingtonian society, embracing a large portion of the intemperate men of Hartford, was at once formed. Every member was an apostle of faith and good works in advancing the cause.

Delegates from this society came to Winsted in the summer of 1842, and were cordially received. They related their personal experiences, their emancipation from the slavery of intemperate drinking, their improved condition, the happiness and comfort of their families, and their own conscious manhood. They were listened to by crowded and thoughtful audiences; but they departed without obtaining a signature to the new pledge. On the day after their departure, however, the fruits of their labor of love became manifest. Some twelve to fifteen men, most of them habitual drinkers, who had ever before kept aloof from the temperance movement, came in a body to the Secretary of the Total Abstinence Society and enrolled their names on the pledge. Others speedily followed their example; and in ten days nearly every habitual drinker in the place had signed the pledge.

The new converts soon embodied themselves in a distinctive Washingtonian Society, which was also joined largely by members of the old Total Abstinence Society, which thereafter became dormant, leaving the temperance work in the hands of the more popular and zealous organization.

The principle of total abstinence, after an agitation of near fifteen years, had now become an article of faith and practice in this community. Its positions were unassailed and unassailable. The old west village tavern, the last stronghold of the rumselling interest, had finally succumbed to the power of moral and legal suasion. Not a haunt, above or below ground, existed where liquors could be obtained in large or small quantities, without extreme privacy. We were in advance of any other town in the county.

The new organization, formed in the midst of excitement, and controlled by recent, though earnest converts to the temperance cause, lacked the steadfastness of its predecessor. Its action was spasmodic rather than persistent. Some of its most zealous members fell away within the first year of its life; others followed in the downward road; the cause was dishonored, and the organization paralyzed. Yet, the vital principle had become deeply rooted and widely pervading. Without combined effort advancing progress ceased, though retrogression was hardly perceptible until the opening of the Naugatuck Railroad in 1849, and the consequent influx of new inhabitants not trained to temperance principles and habits. A more free intercourse with the outside world, and a rapid increase of population and wealth, tended to a relaxation of moral sentiment, and an acquiescence in fashionable customs and indulgences. Moral suasion had signally reformed our community up to the time of the Washingtonian movement, but it lost its power over men recreant to their solemn pledges, and over both the fashionable and degraded classes of new comers.

The advocacy of severe prohibitory laws indicated decadence rather than advance in the reformatory movement. Such laws became a necessity, growing out of a relaxation of persuasive efforts.

In 1854 a legislature favorable to entire prohibition was chosen, and the Maine Law was enacted. Public sentiment was in accord with its stringent provisions. It carried terror to the hearts of conscienceless rum sellers, and filled the prohibitionists with rejoicing. For a time it worked like a charm. The open traffic in liquors was in a great measure abandoned. Drunken men were arrested and fined, and prosecutions were instituted against open and secret traffickers. It was easy to convict and fine the poor inebriates, but to bring to justice the shrewd and unscrupulous panderers to their vitiated appetites was a far more arduous undertaking. It was found, as a general and almost invariable rule, that vitiated customers refused to betray the sellers of intoxicating liquors, and the proof of guilt in most cases could not be substantiated without their testimony. With this hindrance in the way, if the prosecutor succeeded in making out a case before a justice court, an appeal could be taken to the higher court, where a jury trial could be had, and juries are very uncertain dispensers of justice. In almost every jury impaneled more than one juror proves to be in sympathy with the rumseller, and his conviction is frustrated. As a consequence, the law, when applied to the arch promoters of intemperance and its kindred pollutions, became a dead letter.

Yet the Maine Law has not proved an utter failure, else foul-breathed and red-nosed demagogues had ceased to rail against it. Its terrors have restrained in a great measure the tempting exhibition of liquor bottles, and the barefaced sale of their contents in open day. It has confiscated thousands of barrels of vile decoctions more dangerous to life and health than gunpowder or glycerine. Even the staggering graduates of the pot-house have learned to avoid public exhibitions of their accomplishments. During the long years of its neglected enforcement, it has retained a reserved force that could be, and often has been, applied to the effectual suppression of outrageous haunts of drunkenness.

Much more good might have grown out of the Maine Law, had not the delusive idea prevailed among temperance men that legal enactments possess an inherent power to do the work of reform, which can be done only by stiff-backed, straight forward workers, by means of their instrumentality. To this infatuation, as much as to inherent defects of the law, is the decadence of temperance principles and habits to be ascribed.

Those of the surviving temperance men who labored in the field from 1830 to 1850 — who fought the early battles, and achieved the early victories — have retired from active life, and another generation of workers, now in the field, struggling manfully to stem the overflowing torrent of intemperance, have an arduous but not a hopeless work before them. They have not, as their predecessors had, to contend with professedly good and pious men in settling the first principles of total abstinence and prohibition. Doctors of divinity have ceased to denounce the movement as heretical. Political demagogues no longer exhaust their spread-eagle eloquence in asserting the inherent right of every American citizen to get drunk, and to make drunkards. The question of to-day is rather one of expediency than of moral or religious principle.

A "tidal wave" broke over the Legislature of 1872, and swept away, for the time being we trust, the fundamental principle of the Maine Law, and again legalized the traffic under a license system. Stump orators now tell us of the amount of money that is to flow into our town treasuries for licensing, and thereby clothing our rumsellers with the robe of legal respectability. When the disciples of Mrs. Woodhull shall apply for a law to legalize adultery, and license prostitution, they will find the principle of expediency already established, and the argument of license money flowing into the treasury already promulgated and irrefutably established.

It is bad enough in all conscience to allow every person who wills to sell liquors in violation of law, but it is infinitely worse to remedy the evil by giving the traffic a legal sanction. The talk of licensing only respectable and conscientious men to deal out the villainous decoctions, is the merest twaddle. Where is the board of selectmen who will recommend for license the palatial hotel proprietor and the aboveground saloon-keeper and apothecary, and dare to refuse the subterranean restaurant, be he Yankee, Paddy, or Dutchman?

The temperance reformers of this era must work with an indomitable will to achieve the lost ground, combining moral and legal suasion wisely and persistently. Many excellent provisions of the Maine Law continue unrepealed. The passage of the new license law was a blunder of legislation, not in accord with the views of the legislators who permitted it to be enacted, nor of their constituents. Let its crude provisions and evil tendencies be thoroughly ventilated; let its repeal be made a test question to candidates for legislative honors, and it will sooner or later be repealed, and the traffic in intoxicating drinks again be outlawed.

There are in all communities numbers of men of owl-like wisdom, who assert as an unquestionable fact that more tippling prevails, and that the yearly crop of drunkards is greater in these years, than in the years before concerted temperance movements began. Such Jeremiahs, in order to speak with authority, should have been on the stage more than forty years ago, when there was a cider mill and a cider-brandy still in every school district; when there were two or three taverns to every one now existing, each of them sustained more by neighborhood tipplers than by traveling customers; when every store-keeper bought and sold four-fold more rum and whisky than molasses; when bleared eyes, rubicund noses, and pot-bellies infested all public gatherings, and even put in their appearance around the communion table. Such men, if any there be, may rejoice at the prospect of our soon getting back to the "good old times" of free rum, improved by town treasuries overflowing with license money.

The temperance bands now on the stage of action have arduous duties to perform, but not more arduous than those performed by the pioneers in the cause some forty years ago. They have in the last few years earnestly labored in stemming the flood of intemperance, amid reproach and discouragements. Let them continue steadfast and immovable; let them "trust in the Lord, and keep their powder dry," and they will in the end become as invincible as Cromwell's Ironsides.

St. Andrew's Lodge of Free and Accepted Masons, No. 64, was chartered in the Spring of 1823, and was installed in June or July following by a deputation from the Grand Lodge, consisting of Jeremy L. Cross, William H. Jones, and Laban Smith, of New Haven; George Putnam, of Hartford, and others. The officers installed were:—

    Josiah Smith, W. M.
    Hosea Hinsdale, S. W.
    Wheelock Thayer, J. W.
    Elisha Smith, Treasurer.
    James M. Boyd, Secretary.

The first lodge room was fitted up in the old academy building, now a tenant house, immediately north of Forbes' cabinet establishment, on Main street, west village. About 1829 the lodge was removed to the hotel in the east village, and about 1830 was removed to the old Higley Tavern in the west village.

The anti-masonic excitement growing out of the disappearance and probable death of Morgan, extended to this state in 1829, and paralyzed the masonic order for several years. St. Andrews, in common with most of the other lodges of the state, became dormant, and surrendered its charter to the Grand Lodge about 1835.

In 1853, on application to the Grand Lodge of members of St. Andrew's Lodge, its charter was restored, new officers were appointed, and work was resumed in Woodford's original brick block, which was burned down, March 25, 1853, and the lodge was removed to the Clark and Wetmore store, then standing on the site of the Clarke House. This store was burned down in 1856, and the furniture, jewels, regalia, and all the records of the lodge were consumed. The lodge was reopened in Chamberlin's store, now owned by James A. Bushnell, and thence in the same year was removed to Weed's brick block, and thence to Woodford's new block, in which a new and spacious hall for its occupancy has been fitted up under the new Mansard roof recently erected on the building.

Meridian Chapter, No. 15, of Royal Arch Masons was early located at Canaan, and its charter was revoked by the Grand Chapter in 1839. It was reinstated at New Hartford in May, 1848, but not reorganized. It was transferred and reorganized at Winsted in May, 1857, occupying the same halls with St. Andrew's Lodge.

In 1858 Tyrian Council of Royal Masters, No. 31, was chartered and installed, and has occupied the same hall with the preceding orders.

Prior to the reorganization of St. Andrew's Lodge in 1853, Orion Lodge of the Independent Order of Odd Fellows was chartered, installed, and located in Clarke & Wetmore's store. A dissension among its members resulted in the charter of Union Lodge of I. O. O. F., which was located in Woodford's block. On the burning of the Clarke & Wetmore store, Orion Lodge became dormant, and has never been revived. Union Lodge has also become extinct.

Of the early and later public libraries in Winchester, only a meagre account can be given. In the "Old Society" a library of standard works was in existence early in the century, and continued until about 1845, when the books were sold or distributed among the shareholders.

In the early reading days of the compiler, there was a library of unknown origin kept in the office of Solomon Rockwell & Brothers, between the east abutment of Lake Street bridge and Camp's brick block. What was the character of the more solid works we have no knowledge; but from the lighter class we obtained our first reading of The Fool of Quality, Tom Jones, Pamelia, and Tristram Shandy. This library was broken up, and sold or distributed as early as 1810.

As early as 1808, under the auspices of Joel Miller and other scholars of the West District School, a youth's library was organized and located at the house of Asahel Miller, then standing nearly opposite the house of David N. Beardsley, on Spencer Street road. Strange as it may seem, this location was then central to the largest portion of the scholars of the district. The collection consisted mainly of paper-covered volumes, then termed chap-books, which constituted a part of the stock in trade of the trunk peddlers of that period. Among the books were Robinson Crusoe, Baron Trenck, Stephen Burroughs, The Ring, Count de Lovinski, and other similar works, by the careful reading of which we were precociously trained to a love of sensational works of a higher order. This library was of short continuance, and would be unworthy of mention otherwise than as illustrative of the craving for literary food by the boys and girls of that day, and of the kind of provender provided for them before the age of model children who were too faultless to live in this sinful world.

The next library was got up about 1810 by members of the Congregational society, and was named "The Winsted Historical and Theological Library," and was kept in the study of the pastor. In the Theological department were, Edwards on the Will and on the Affections, Gilles' Church History, Witherspoon's Sermons, Griffin on the Atonement, and Kinney on the Prophecies. In history it contained Smollet's England, Marshall's Washington, and Trumbull's Connecticut. In its miscellaneous department were two strictly religious novels—Thornton Abbey, and Cœlebs in Search of a Wife. The most readable, and most read book of all, was Silliman's Journal of Travels in England, Scotland, and Holland, then just published. This library, after some five to ten years, was purchased by the pastor, for whose use it was mainly instituted.

About 1812, another library was organized in the West Village, and located at the house of Colonel Hosea Hinsdale. The books selected were such as the people wanted to read rather than such as a severe moralist would have said they ought to read. Russell's Modern Europe was the most ponderous, and Knickerbocker's New York the most popular work in the collection. Butler's Hudibras and Peter Pindar were highly appreciated. As a whole it was a well selected library, and well managed; but, like its predecessors, the society was dissolved, and the books were sold after five or six years.

The next library was got up by a set of young men about 1820, and was located in the East Village. The books were suited to the taste of its founders. They consisted of poetry, novels, plays, and a modicum of history. The life of this institution was brief. The books were sold and scattered in four or five years.

The last and longest-lived library was founded by parties in connection with the Methodist Episcopal Church. With a view to its permanency, provision was made in its articles of association for its being holden by the Trustees of the Methodist Society in trust for the use of its share holders. Its books were to be religious and historical, and all fictitious works were to be excluded. No books were, under any circumstances, to be sold; any attempt to break up the library, or otherwise to dispose of it was to divest the trustees of their right to control it, and the trust was to be transferred to the town of Winchester. Though denominational in its character, it was not sectarian in an exclusive sense. The Life and Sermons of John Wesley, The Life of Adam Clarke and his Commentary, and divers other standard Methodist works constituted the nucleus of the collection, but beyond this the selection of books was suited to all classes of religionists and to every cultivated taste. A majority of the committee of selection were not Methodists in name or religious preferences. Historical and biographical works were largely selected. Boswell's Johnson and Irving's Conquest of Grenada had a place on the shelves, although the latter was objected to as a fiction; but on a suggestion that Fra de Savedra was not the author of the chronicles, but the warrior who effected the conquest, and that Irving was the historian of the campaign, the scruples of the objector were removed, and the book enjoyed a high degree of popularity.

The funds for renovating the library by purchasing new books were raised by occasional taxes levied on the shareholders, and by competitive bids on drawing out books. This library furnished largely the reading of the community for nearly twenty years; but as the first projectors, one after another, withdrew from its direction, a looseness of management prevailed. Books seldom called for were sold in violation of a fundamental article of the association. The taxes laid were largely unpaid, and the shares forfeited. Competitive bidding ceased; drawings of books diminished from year to year; valuable books disappeared; and finally, about 1860, on investigating the affairs of the concern, it was found that only six shareholders remained who had not forfeited their shares by nonpayment of taxes. It was found, also, that the library was reduced to a mere skeleton of such books as no one had considered worth appropriating to private use; and in this predicament a once valuable and highly valued institution has become the shadow of a shade.

And such is essentially the history of innumerable libraries throughout the state, organized without a liberal fund from the income of which new books, as they are required, may be provided. Most of the cases where valuable libraries have been preserved from one generation to another are those where some benevolent founder or founders have provided an endowment fund for a liberal supply of new works suited to the changing times and tastes of successive readers.

The changed circumstances of modern times render the support of public libraries far more precarious than it was when family libraries were limited for the most part to a Bible, Hymn book, Catechism, Pilgrim's Progress, a yearly almanac, and one or two devotional or biographical works — when the cost of miscellaneous works exceeded the means of individual readers. In those times a public library was a blessing of priceless value to a community. In these times circumstances are changed. The press teems with thousands of new books every year; the weekly newspaper, of four-fold the size of the old-time papers, is crowded with every variety of miscellaneous reading; and the daily paper, once confined to the cities, now finds its way to the remotest sections of the country. Almost every family in comfortable circumstances takes a monthly magazine; and very few of them are so remote or obscure as to escape the visits of canvassers without number seeking subscribers for new and valuable works.

Instead of permanent libraries, the tendency in these days is, to form book clubs of limited membership, each member contributing two, three, or five dollars, as the case may be, for the purchase of approved modern publications, which successively pass through the hands of each member with the privilege of a fortnight's use; each member, at the end of his fortnight, passing his successive books to the next reader on the list, so that each book makes a complete circuit and returns to the librarian. At the end of the year the books are sold to the highest bidding members of the club, and the avails are distributed equally among the members. This process being completed, the club is dissolved or reorganized for another year.

There are now two or more such clubs in our community, the oldest of which has existed for ten or more years. The machinery is very simple, and easily adjusted, and if the directing committee are competent and faithful in their selection of authors, the influence of such associations cannot but be highly beneficial.

Another invaluable substitute for the libraries of olden times, is the system of free Sunday-school libraries of the various religious denominations. Renovated from year to year by careful selections of new volumes and by withdrawing those that are found to be unreadable, or of evil tendency, they furnish a supply of pure and instructive reading, not only for the scholars, but for the families to which they belong.

Times are changed, and we are changed with them. Had we at this day a richly endowed library, crowded with all the treasures of ancient theology, history, science, and poetry, and replenished with modern views of doctrinal theology, newly broached emendations of history, rapid advances of science and art, and a poetry that appeals more to the heart than to the ear — we might well be proud of such an institution, but it is very doubtful whether the people, as a mass, would be benefited thereby to the same extent as they are by the unpretentious modern Sunday-school libraries.

CHAPTER XXXV.

RISE AND PROGRESS OF MANUFACTURES.

The predominating element of growth in all interior New England towns is the introduction and enlargement of machinery in aid of handicraft operations, inaptly termed manufacturing. The handicraftsman, comprehending the smith, carpenter, shoemaker, and tailor, comes into every new town as an indispensable accessory of the farmer. He combines his skilled labor with that of the soil tiller in sustaining the life of a civilized community. The minister, school-master, doctor, and tradesman follow as essential elements of its existence. These are mutual aids to each other. They are all primarily dependent on the product of the soil; and as this is naturally fertile or otherwise, well tilled, or exhausted by bad husbandry, the community grows or declines.

The manufacturer who utilizes the water-fall by making it the motive power of ingenious machinery, brings in a new element of growth and prosperity, without which most of our sterile towns decline with the exhaustion of their virgin soil, and with which they are sustained and enriched.

Winchester, without its factories, would have culminated in 1800 and have declined in productiveness and population every succeeding year; and Winsted would have remained through all time a "Hard Scrabble" region.

We propose very briefly to trace the rise and progress of manufacturing in the town, beginning with

Wooden Ware.

The saw-mill was, of course, the first utilization of water power in this, as in most other primitive communities. The location of the earliest of these has already been noted. Besides supplying the home demand for lumber, they early turned out a limited supply of white-wood boards and clap-boards, which were sledded over winter snows to Hartford and other distant towns. White-ash sweeps, oars, and materials for ship-blocks were also got out and carried to Hartford and Wethersfield for up and down river navigation of the Connecticut.

Dish mills for making wooden bowls, trenchers, and mortars, followed as accessories to the saw mills. They used up the slabs from the saw-mill logs, by cutting them into disks which were centered and turned in coarse lathes to the convex surface of the outer dish. With a curved turning tool, the outer dish was separated from the disk, and then smaller ones were turned off successively until the disk was exhausted. The slabs from which these disks were made were wider and thicker than were taken from logs when lumber increased in value. The trenchers and mortars were turned by a similar process. The maker or peddler of these articles packed them into a strong bed tick, in which they were carried on the back of a horse, along the narrow bridle-paths to the earlier settled towns, where they were bartered for "store pay." At least four of these mills were located along the lake stream, and as many others in various parts of the town in the last century, two of which — one at the Meadow Street crossing of the lake stream, and the other opposite the old lean-to mill house on Lake street, were in operation as late as 1805.

Cheese Boxes, Scale Boards.

Early in this century, John McAlpine erected and carried on a shop on the stream at the foot of the burying ground hill in Old Winchester for making scale-boards used for separating cheeses from each other, when packed in casks for distant markets. As he enjoyed a monopoly of the manufacture in the centre of the dairy region of Connecticut, the demand for his article was extensive until the practice of packing each cheese in a separate box was adopted. This change necessitated the manufacture of round boxes, with covers, of sizes fitted to the various diameters and thicknesses of the cheese. This mode of packing went into vogue between 1820 and 1830 and was universally adopted as early as the latter year. One of the earliest manufacturers of this article in Winchester was Silas H. McAlpine, whose shop on the Naugatuck Branch is believed to be still in operation. Another establishment on Hall Meadow, now owned by the Ford Brothers, has been and is still in operation. Another establishment was carried on in Winsted by Cook & Bacon, from 1842 to about 1846, in a shop adjoining the lake stream saw mill.

Grist Mills.

The two early grist mills of the town have been already noted. The first, built by David Austin in 1771, near the Lake outlet, is described on page 42; the second, supposed to have been originally built by Elias Balcomb about 1776 (see page 266), stood on the west side of Still river, immediately south of the stone bridge. It was owned and operated for many years by Ensign Jesse Doolittle, and was carried off by a flood about 1800; and was rebuilt by Samuel and Luther Hoadley about 1844 (see page 383).

Both these mills had three run of stones and were carried by permanent water power. The Austin mill was rebuilt by the Rockwell Brothers about 1810, and was finally burned down and abandoned in 1835. The Hoadley mill was abandoned by Riley Whiting about 1825 and the Brick clock factory (burned down in 1870) was erected on its site.

The Clifton mill was erected by Case, Gilbert & Co., about 1836, and was operated as a grist mill until about 1869.

Three or more feed mills have come into existence within a few years; one owned by Eugene Munson, opposite the Clarke house, another owned by Persons & Hewitt, on the Lake stream, adjoining the Connecticut Western Depot grounds, and a third, owned by Frederick Woodruff on North Main street, all of which are now in operation.

Scythe Works.

Until the closing part of the last century, the scythe was, in this country, strictly a hand-made tool, wrought out in smiths' shops by sledge and hammer, and ground on a stone turned by a hand crank, or hung on the shaft of a flutter wheel, without gearing or other appliances. The Harris family of Pine Plains and Salisbury learned the trade of a negro slave purchased by their immediate progenitor from a former master who had taught him the trade.

The first establishment in the country for welding, drawing, and plating the scythe under trip-hammers by water power and grinding it on a geared stone, was erected by Robert Orr, of Bridgewater, Mass., during or after the Revolution. The second establishment of this nature was erected by Col. Robert Boyd, near the west bank of the Hudson, between New Windsor Landing and Newburg before 1790. Benjamin Jenkins, from Bridgewater, was foreman, and James Boyd, of New Windsor, was an apprentice in these works. They became brothers-in law, and in 1792 came to Winsted and erected the third establishment in the country on the site of the Winsted Manufacturing Company's present works on Still river. In 1802 they built another establishment on the site of the Winsted Hoe Company's plating shop on Lake street, and soon after separated, Mr. Jenkins taking the original works on Still river—from whom they have passed by successive conveyances to the present owners—and Mr. Boyd taking the Lake Street works and carrying them on, individually or with partners, until near the close of his life in 1849.

Merritt Bull, an early apprentice of Jenkins & Boyd, erected a scythe shop in 1802 or 1803, on the site of the present stone shop, at the crossing of the Lake stream by Meadow street, which he managed until his death in 1824, when the works went into the hands of S. & M. Rockwell, and formed the starting point of the large and prosperous establishment built up and managed by the successive firms of Rockwell & Hinsdale, Hinsdale & Beardsley, Elliot Beardsley, and the Beardsley Scythe Company.

Halsey Burr, an apprentice of Mr. Jenkins, built a scythe shop in 1814, near the site of Woodruff's feed mill, on North Main street, which he carried on in a small way until a few years before his death.

In 1831, Wheelock Thayer, previously a partner and acting manager in the scythe business of James Boyd & Son, erected the scythe works on Mad River, now owned by his daughter, and carried on by the Thayer Scythe Company.

The process of manufacturing scythes has been from time to time greatly improved by the invention of new machinery. The first of these in date and importance, was a spring die with attachments to the triphammer for holding the back and setting down and smoothing the web of the scythe, — a very slow and laborious process when performed with the hand-hammer. The next improvement was, by a series of light tilt-hammers to shape and finish the point: — the next was a machine for turning and finishing the heel: — another was for spinning the straw rope for binding up the scythes in dozen packages, by a machine similar to the Dutch wheel and flyer for spinning linen. Most of these improvements have originated in Winsted.

Scythe making was — with the exception of wooden ware — the earliest factory work carried on in Winsted; and has been uninterruptedly prosecuted to the present day, little impeded or accelerated by protective tariffs. The three establishments now in operation, have a capacity for making 250,000 scythes per annum, and rarely fail of turning out that number. Within a few years, fears have been entertained that the newly invented mowers and reapers would entirely supersede the use of the primitive implements. The same fears were not many years ago entertained, that the iron horse would so far supersede the much abused domestic animal, as to diminish his value and the demand for his services. Experience proves that these fears in both cases are equally groundless.

Bar Iron and Blistered Steel.

Bar iron had been made directly from the Brown Hematite ores of Salisbury, Kent, and Amenia, from time immemorial. In Litchfield county bloomary forges stood on most of the available water courses in nearly all the western towns. They furnished iron for three rolling and slitting mills, one in Canaan, another in Litchfield, and the third in Washington, where the iron was rolled and slit into rods for nail making. These mills worked up only a small portion of the iron manufactured. Besides domestic uses of all kinds, it was largely made into anchors, which were sent to the seaboard.

Nearly all of these bloomaries, and all of the slitting mills, have long since disappeared; and their sites would mostly be forgotten, did not the cinder heaps and imperishable charcoal brays indicate their location.

The old Salisbury, or Lakeville Blast Furnace, was erected in 1762. In 1768 it became the property of Richard Smith, an Englishman, who initiated the process of making refined iron of the best quality, not from the ore, but from pig metal. For some inscrutable reason he erected his first refining forge at Robertsville, in the southeast corner of Colebrook, at a distance of nearly thirty miles from his furnace, in a region then nearly destitute of settlers.* Mr. Smith went back to England on the breaking out of the Revolutionary war, and the forge was continued in operation successively by Jacob Ogden, Theodore Burr, Elisha Beeman, and David Squire; and was abandoned as an iron works by the latter person before 1810.

Two other refining forges were erected at Colebrook Center, by the Rockwell family, during, or soon after the Revolution, one of which was removed to Winsted in 1802, and the other abandoned the same or following year, for causes detailed on page 363.

In 1795, Jenkins & Boyd, in company with Thomas Spencer, Jr., erected the first forge in Winsted, on the water power of the Lake street grinding works of the Winsted Mfg. Co. (See page 311.)

In 1803, the Rockwell Brothers removed and put up their Colebrook forge on the site of Timothy Hulbert's present iron works on the Lake stream.

In 1808, James Boyd erected another forge on Mad River, immediately opposite the Clarke House; and on that or the following year the Rockwell Brothers built another forge on the Lake stream, below and adjoining the Conn. Western Depot grounds.

In 1811, Reuben Cook, in company with Russell Bunce and Charles Seymour of Hartford, built the old Cook forge, on Still River, where the Axle works of Charles and James R. Cook now stand.

All of these forges manufactured refined bar iron from the best quality of Old Salisbury Ore Hill pig iron, for the supply of the U. S. Armory at Springfield, which required the best iron the country could produce. If there was the slightest defect in the quality, the finished gunbarrel

---

* One reason traditionally assigned for this location was, that he apprehended a scarcity of charcoal in the Salisbury region for the furnace, in the event of his enlarging the consumption by running additional iron works there.

There is another vague tradition that this forge was first erected on the Farmington River at Collinsville: and that not being able to sustain his dam, he removed the establishment to Colebrook. There was in ancient times a forge where the first of the Collins Company buildings was afterwards erected, known as the "Humphrey Forge," but its existence seems to have continued later than the erection of the "Old Forge" at Colebrook.

would reveal it by defective polish or failure to stand the proof of a double test charge. Only a limited portion of the iron made could be brought up to these crucial tests by the best skilled workmen. Iron of a slightly inferior grade was required for scythes, wire rods, and fine machinery. A still lower grade answered for the ordinary uses of country blacksmiths.

In the process of refining, the cinders drawn off through the tent plate retained a percentage of iron nearly equal to the ordinary hematite ores. This was worked over in a chafery or bloomary fire, and produced a strong coarse iron, which was worked into tires, axle and crow-bar patterns, and plow molds, or into heavy shafting, saw-mill cranks, &c. Each forge had in connection with it a drafting shop with lighter hammers to draw down the bars into rods and shapes of all kinds in demand, and especially to work up the refuse iron by welding to each piece an equal layer of blistered steel, and drawing the united masses into sleigh-shoes.

The iron and scythe business constituted the staple manufacturing business of Winsted until near 1840, when the Government had settled its policy of importing its gun iron from Norway; the English had introduced better and cheaper iron of every form and size than theretofore; when the puddling process of iron making had grown up in more favored localities; when wood and charcoal had advanced in price, while transportation of raw material and manufactured articles—always a heavy burden—could no longer be endured. Under all these discouragements the iron manufacture rapidly died out. The lower Rockwell forge on the Lake stream was converted into a scythe shop about 1845. The Boyd forge opposite the Clarke house breathed its last about the same time. The upper forge on the lake stream lingered on until about 1850. The middle forge on the Lake stream was sold by Eliot Beardsley to Timothy Hulbert in 1853, and was changed into a forge for puddling scrap iron, and is still in success-ful operation. The Cook forge, on Still river, about 1850 confined its operations to working scrap iron into axle drafts for finishing in the Cook Axle Company's works, of which the forge became a component part.

The consumption of bar iron in Winsted, instead of decreasing with the decadence of its home manufacture, has steadily increased. The new brands of Norway iron were found cheaper and better for scythes, hoes, and other articles than the costly home-made refined iron, and came into general use in our hardware manufactures. The scythe manufacture increased. The hoe manufacture was introduced and soon consumed more iron than the whole scythe interest had required in 1830; and other new hardware manufactures took the place of the iron forge.

BLISTERED STEEL.

The first cementing steel furnace in Western Connecticut was erected before 1800 in Colebrook by the Rockwell Brothers, under the supervision of Mr. Jencks, an ingenious iron and steel worker from Taunton, Mass., which has been perpetuated to the present time, though rarely operated of late years. It was found that the Salisbury iron was deficient in the ingredient, whatever it is, that produces an edge-tool quality in steel. The steel produced has an elastic quality fitting it for carriage springs, hay and manure forks and similar articles, and before 1850 was largely used for these manufactures, and likewise for sleigh shoes and for general blacksmith work. Since 1850 the steels made from Swedish and Russian irons have nearly superseded the domestic irons except those recently made from Spathic ores.

The second steel furnace in this region was put up early in this century by Col. Abram Burt, in Canaan, Conn., and continued in operation but a few years. The third was erected in Winsted by James Boyd & Son, in 1832, on the site of Thompson's Bakery, south side of Monroe Street, adjoining the bridge. It was designed for converting their own iron into steel, which they were then largely supplying to fork manufacturers; but was soon abandoned by reason of inducements held out by the Colebrook concern, making it more advantageous to have their iron converted there than to do it themselves.

Cut Nails.

Shingle nails were cut from old hoops and headed by hand for the First Congregational Meeting House in 1800. The cutting machine is supposed to have been worked by hand. Another machine for cutting shingle nails from hammered strips of iron, by water power, was started by James Boyd about 1808, and soon abandoned.

In 1810 Jesse Byington rented water power from the old Jenkins scythe shop proprietors, and erected a nail factory a little south of the Winsted Manufacturing Company's scythe works, in which he used a newly invented machine for cutting nails more accurate and uniform in size than by the old hand machines, but without heading them. Before and during the war of 1812 he employed more men as cutters and headers than were employed in any other branch of business in the place. After the return of peace in 1815, and the introduction of the combined cutting and heading machine, Mr. Byington's business broke down, and has never since been resumed in any form.

Axes.

Axe-making as a trade, distinct from other smith work, was introduced here by Elizur Hinsdale in 1804 or 1805. He first had his shop on Lake street, near the lake outlet, and in 1806 erected a shop on the site of the Foundry and Machine Company's works, which he subsequently enlarged to a trip hammer and grinding works adapted specially to his business, which he prosecuted until near the close of 1819, when he failed, and the business was abandoned.

About 1828, after the Collins axe factory went into operation at Collinsville, Nathaniel B. Gaylord, then owner of the old Jenkins scythe works, entered into the business of axe-making under the supervision of Marcus Morgan, an original worker in the Collins establishment. Mr. Morgan soon after purchased the works and prosecuted the business until 1832, when he sold out to Reuben Cook, Luman Wakefield, John Camp, and others, who, with a view to continuing and enlarging the business, tore down the old building and built a stone dam and commodious factory building, before the completion of which they decided to change the business to scythe making; and in 1835 obtained a corporate charter, under the name of the Winsted Manufacturing Company, which has for thirty-seven years had a prosperous career, with good promise of long continuance.

Iron Wire.

In 1812 Samuel and Luther Hoadley and James Boyd erected a wire factory on the west wing of the clock factory dam; the first, or one of the first, erected in the country for breaking down iron wire from the rod and drawing it down to any size from a half inch to a hair's diameter. The rods, of the very best Salisbury iron, were hammered down to a half inch square, and then rounded by trip-hammer swaging dies, and then, after successive annealings were drawn down by "rippers," as they were called, to a size whence they could be further reduced by a continuous drawing around an upright block. It was the ripping operation, by self-acting pincers seizing the point of the wire at the plate, drawing it about eighteen inches, then letting go and sliding back and taking a new hold at the plate, and drawing another length, which was then new in this country. At that period there were few, if any, rolling mills in the country that rolled out round rods suitable for wire drawing.

The business was profitable, and was vigorously prosecuted until the close of the war, when foreign competition paralyzed it, and compelled its abandonment.

Leather.

In the last century, the regular shoemaker — as distinguished from the cobbler and cat-whipper — was also a tanner. He had his vats, under cover, in or out of doors, in which he tanned his own and his neighbor's skins, and made them into boots and shoes on the same premises with his tan vats. Of these tanneries there were in the last century three or more in Old Winchester, to which the traveling currier periodically resorted, and curried, or smoothed and softened the sides of leather when taken from the vats. The oak bark then solely used for tanning

MANUFACTURES. 513

had its outer surface shaved off, and was then pounded, or crushed under a heavy circular stone attached to a ten-foot shaft, stationary at one end, and rolled round a circle by a draft horse,—the bark being distributed along the circular track, and kept there by a man or boy with a rake. Two of these, owned respectively by the Wade and Blake families, continued in operation, by water power and modern improvements, until about 1850. Both are now abandoned. There was a like establishment in Winsted, erected and owned by Elias Loomis, at the close of the last century, at the foot of "Dish Mill Hill," where the Woodruff tannery now stands, which was abandoned many years before the present works were erected.

About 1800 it was practically ascertained by trial that hemlock bark possessed the astringent and other properties requisite for tanning; and in consequence the business was thenceforward conducted on a larger scale in the Green Woods region.

Colonel Hosea Hinsdale and Col. James Shepard came to Winsted in 1802, and erected a large tannery on Spencer street, where the fish pond of John T. Rockwell has lately been excavated. The business was successfully prosecuted here by Col. Hinsdale until 1851, when he sold out to J. S. and J. T. Rockwell.

In 1807 Col. Shepard sold out his interest to Col. Hinsdale, and in company with Asahel Miller, erected the original tannery, on the site of the present tannery of George Dudley & Son. This establishment was owned and managed successively by Shepard & Miller, Abiel Loomis, and Alanson Loomis, until purchased by George Dudley in 1832.

In 1820, another tannery was erected by Horace Ranney, at the corner of North Main street and the Cook bridge, taking its water power from the west wing of Cook's dam, which was successively owned and managed by Ranney & Hawley, Norman Spencer, Jonathan K. Richards, Charles B. Hallett, and others, and was abandoned as a tannery in 1857.

In 1821, Horace Ranney erected another tannery, on the site of the present Woodruff tannery, on North Main street, now owned by George Dudley & Son, which was successively managed by Lewis & Foster until 1834, by James A. Ayrault until 1841; since which it has been owned and managed by Frederick Woodruff until his recent sale to Dudley & Son; it having during his ownership been carried away by a flood, and afterwards rebuilt and enlarged.

The tannery business of Winsted has, since 1850, been confined to preparing sheep and calf skins for book-binding and similar purposes, and has become one of the prominent branches of our manufactures. The skins are imported from England, after having been split into two or more thicknesses, salted and packed in hogsheads, ready for the vat. The bark is finely ground in a mill in the second story of the building, and passed to a large receiving vat, where it is soaked in water until the tanning principle is extracted, when the liquor, or tea, as it is termed, is drawn off into a line of receiving vats, and the exhausted bark is thrown out. A paddle, or flutter wheel is fixed over each vat and connected by gears with a line of shafting propelled by water power. A sufficient number of vats are filled with the hemlock tea; the right number of skins are thrown into each vat, and the flutter wheels are set in motion and operate on the surface of the liquid, creating a current which keeps the skins in constant movement, and perfects the tanning process without hand labor. The tanned skins are then smoothed, trimmed, assorted, and packed for market; the whole process requiring less than three weeks' time.

This branch of business was originated in Winsted by George Dudley, before 1850, in the works he purchased from Alanson Loomis in 1832. In 1853 he rebuilt and enlarged his works, and added two three-story buildings for dying the skins when tanned. In company with his son he has recently purchased and now carries on the Woodruff tannery on North Main street. During the present year, 1872, they have consumed in both tanneries 6,000 tons of bark, and have turned out 432,000 skins.

In 1851, J. S. & J. T. Rockwell, previously engaged in this branch of tanning in Colebrook, erected the four-story tannery on the site of the Hinsdale premises. These works, now owned by John T. Rockwell, are believed to turn out nearly the same amount of work with the larger tannery of the Dudleys.

Woolen Cloths.

Joseph Platt is believed to have been the first clothier in the town. He built a clothier's shop and fulling mill in the Danbury Quarter, between 1783 and 1787. The establishment had a brief existence. It is not mentioned in any deed on record, and its precise locality is unknown.

The first clothier in Winsted was Daniel Marshall, (see p. 307,) whose shop stood on Lake street as it then ran, nearly opposite the house at the corner of Lake and Rockwell streets, and the fulling mill in the rear on the Lake stream. Mr. Marshall died in 1794, and Daniel Wilcox became the owner until his sale of the premises to the Rockwell Brothers in 1813. A carding machine was added to the establishment about 1804. The Rockwell Brothers, in 1813, erected additional buildings and began the manufacture of broadcloths and satinets. The business was enlarged and vigorously prosecuted during the continuance of the war of 1812, and moderately thereafter until 1830, in the hope of making it a paying business, but with doubtful success. In 1835 the works were burned down, and never rebuilt.

About 1816 another clothier's works was erected by Ansel Wilson, on the site of the Strong Manufacturing Company's new factory. Chester Soper purchased this establishment about 1830, and a few years after erected a woolen mill on the premises, in which he manufactured broadcloths until about 1838. The works were afterwards carried on by John Thornton and others until 1845, when the woollen business was abandoned and the building afterwards used for making joiners' tools.

Another clothier's works, built about 1814 on the Naugatuck branch in Old Winchester, and carried on by Alva Nash and others until 1828, when it was converted into a woolen mill for making broadcloths and satinets by John M. Galagher, who failed within a few years and was succeeded by Isaac Bird, who continued the making of satinets, until the establishment went into the hands of the Winchester Center Mfg. Co., in 1854. This Company confined its operations to making woollen knitting yarn until the establishment was burned down about 1860, and was never rebuilt.

The Home Manufacturing Company, a joint-stock concern, was organized in 1846, and the same year erected the factory building on Mad River now occupied by the New England Pin Co., and went into the manufacture of broad cloths and doeskins. It labored under the disadvantage of having no stockholders acquainted with the business, and was unfortunate in selecting overseers of the manufacturing department. No profits were realized; and in 1850 the concern was wound up. The establishment was sold to Anson G. Phelps, who operated it in connection with his woolen mills at Wolcottville until 1852, when it was purchased by the Hartford Pin Co.

Not one of the foregoing enterprises proved successful, and most of them ended disastrously.

CLOCKS.

Samuel and Luther Hoadley, and Riley Whiting began the manufacture of wooden clocks about 1807, in a small factory building immediately south of the east wing of the stone bridge on Still River. The machinery was carried by a tin wheel on an upright iron shaft. The cog-wheels were of cherry, the pinion was of ivy, or calmia, and the face of white-wood — all home products. These, with a little wire, a very little steel, brass, tin, and cordage, made up the staple of material in the old one-day shelf clock which they produced and scattered all over the United States and Canada.

The Hoadleys retired from the business — Luther dying in 1813, and Samuel, the same year, going into the army. Riley Whiting, the remaining partner, prosecuted the business with energy and final success. In 1825, he tore down the old grist-mill on the north wing of the bridge and built the brick factory, recently burned down, and engaged in making eight-day brass clocks. Mr. Whiting died in 1835, and in 1841 the concern was purchased by Lucius Clarke, and has since been conducted by Clarke, Gilbert & Co., W. L. Gilbert, The Gilbert Manufacturing Company, and "The William L. Gilbert Clock Company," incorporated by the Legislature of 1871. In 1870, the brick building erected by Mr. Whiting, and a large wooden one adjoining, was burned down; on the site of which the company erected a spacious three story brick factory building, and in 1872 a similar building on the south side of the road, where the original wooden clock factory building stood; the two making the largest manufacturing establishment in the borough.

CARDS.

At the beginning of the war of 1812, two establishments for making hand and machine cards were started, one by Coe, Miller & Co., in the Shepard & Miller Tannery, and the other by the Hoadley Brothers in their grist-mill. Both companies used one set of machines for cutting and bending the teeth, and another set for pricking the leather, and the teeth were inserted in the leather by children at their homes. Other machines shaped and turned the handles on which the hand card leathers were fastened by tacks. Two causes put an end to this branch of manufacture; one, the return of peace in 1815, and the influx of cheaper cards from England, — and the other, the invention by Mr. Levi Lincoln, of a combined machine which, in one operation, pricked the leather, cut and bent the teeth, and stuck them through the pricked leather.

WAGONS AND CARRIAGES.

There were, doubtless, wheelwrights and wagon-makers in Old Winchester at an early day, but the compiler has no knowledge of them Randall Covey had a wagon-maker's shop at the Centre from 1817 to 1821.

Joseph Mitchell was probably the first wheelwright in Winsted. His house and shop, now torn down, were directly opposite the residence of Sheldon Kinney on Main street. He made cart wheels and bodies from the beginning of the century, or earlier, to about 1830.

Selden Mitchell, son of Joseph, above, made light wagons in the basement in rear of the Kinney house above mentioned from 1809 to about 1820.

In 1813, Shubael Crow and Ebenezer R. Hale erected a carriage-maker's shop on the site of John T. Rockwell's tannery, in which wagons and chaises were made until after 1830 by Crowe & Hale, Crowe & Bandle, Henderson & Ball, and others, — the premises having been used from 1823 to 1826 for manufacturing pails, tubs, and keelers by Hinsdale & Dimock.

Wagon making was subsequently carried on in Winsted by James Hermance from 1838 to his death in 1840, and by G. W. Gaston from 1849 onward to 1872.

MANUFACTURES.

In 1851, Walter & Son erected a large carriage shop on the corner of Elm and Center streets, which has since been managed successively by Erwin M. Walter, Uriah S. Walter, W. H. Stickney, and others, and is now owned and managed by Franklin Lincoln.

In 1856 the Winsted (Joint Stock) Carriage Company was organized and carried on a large business in Southern wagons and buggies until the opening of the War of the Rebellion, occupying the old Soper woolen factory. In 1866 the company was re-organized with a reduced capital, and Marcus Baird, Walter Stickney, Wm. S. Holabird, and others, as stockholders, and was wound up in 1867.

The Gilman Carriage Company was organized with a capital of $25,000 in 1867, and purchased the factory property of the Winsted Carriage Company; and soon after, on the burning down of the factory building, erected a spacious establishment on the same site with facilities for a large business. This establishment was burned down in 1870, and the operations of the company were thereby suspended.

Another carriage establishment was erected on Case Avenue in 1870 by Walter Stickney, Bennet Palmer, and Wilbur F. Green, with capacity for a large amount of work.

WHISKEY.

A company of grain speculators, at the close of the War of 1812, found themselves loaded with several thousand bushels of rye, bought at a high price, in the hope of selling it at a still higher, if not extortionate, rate, to needy consumers of the article. The price in market fell with the return of peace. Nobody wanted to buy; the article was growing musty on their hands, and they,—shrewdly, as they thought—resolved to turn it into a commodity that never lacked consumers. So they built a whiskey distillery half way up Wallen's hill, east of the clock factory, and a sty for forty or fifty swine to be fattened on the de-alcoholized mash. The rye was ground at the mill where it was stored; the breathing hole of hell vomited its pestilent smoke, the whiskey trickled from the undying worm of the still, and the swine bloated and fattened on the mash, until the frowzy grain was converted into vile whiskey and viler pork. The most bloated drunkards around home wouldn't drink the foul whiskey, and so it was sent away to markets where sots with less delicate stomachs could be found; and the pork, not being relished at home, was salted, packed, and shipped for negro consumption in the Carolina market. On the voyage to Charleston, it became so tainted and offensive that it was thrown overboard to prevent a pestilence on the vessel. On stating the profit and loss of the whole transaction, the profit was found to be a minus quantity, and the loss positive and total of the whole investment. The distillery building and hog sty were taken down and removed, and not a trace of their location remains.

Linseed Oil.

An Oil Mill was erected by Bissell Hinsdale, on Mad River, a little west of the Clifton Mill works, about 1816, which was worked only a few years, and was removed before 1830.

Hay and Manure Forks.

The Spring Steel Hay and Manure Forks were introduced as a substitute for the coarse and clumsy articles previously in use, soon after the war of 1812. They were made here in numerous small shops by handicraftsmen, no machinery, save the sledge and hand hammer, propelled by muscular arms, being used. Large quantities were made, not only for supplying the country stores, but for the New York and Philadelphia markets. The three Browns, Orrin, Harris and Isaac, Oliver White, Julius Weaver, and others, were engaged in this business. Establishments grew up in other places in which the tilt-hammer came into use for drawing out the tines, which made the hand labor operation unremunerative; and the business was, in a great measure, abandoned here about 1850.

Foundries.

The casting of iron clock bells was begun in Winsted by the Hoadley Brothers, about 1810, as a secret process in a detached building, from which outsiders were rigidly excluded. The skilled founder of the establishment ran away after some two years service. In 1812 Nathan Champion commenced the same business in the Jenkins scythe shop that stood on the Strong Manufacturing Co.'s premises, and afterwards built a shop near the Winsted Manufacturing Co.'s works, in which he made other small castings.

In 1834 Nathaniel B. Gaylord erected a foundry on the site of the Strong Manufacturing Co.'s works for casting stoves, plows, gears, and general custom work, which he operated until 1846, after which it was carried on a short time by Calvin Butler, of Canaan, and was then abandoned.

In 1847 Taylor & Whiting erected a foundry in connection with their machine shop now owned and operated by the Foundry and Machine Company, which is now the only establishment in the borough.

In 1853, John Boyd erected another foundry for large castings in connection with his machine shop adjoining Lake Street bridge on Mad River, which was discontinued in 1854.

Machine Shops.

In 1831, George Taylor erected the original building of the present Foundry and Machine Company's establishment on Main street for making woolen machinery as a specialty and doing general job work in that line. Two years later he associated with Ambrose Whiting as a partner in the name of Taylor & Whiting. They did a large business in carding machines and spinning jacks for some twenty years. After the retirement of Mr. Whiting in 1857, the concern was organized as a joint stock company with the name of The Winsted Foundry and Machine Company, by which the business is still carried on.

In 1823 James Boyd and James M. Boyd began making saw-mill cranks, mill spindles, and various other branches of heavy forging in a shop then built on the west side of Mad river, in rear of the Beardsley house. To this business James Boyd & Son added in 1830 the making of finished coach axles and mill screws. In 1851, after the death of Mr. James Boyd, the junior partner erected the present machine shop on the site of the old shop, for the purpose of enlarging the mill-iron and axle business of the old firm; and in 1853 built the foundry last referred to as an appendage to the establishment. The works were purchased by the Clifton Mill Co. in 1857, and were a few years after employed in the manufacture of monkey wrenches. They are at present idle.

About 1840, Reuben Cook & Sons went into the manufacture of finished axles at their iron works, and in 1852 organized "The Cook Axle Co.," which enlarged the business and erected the brick factory building on the site of the old Cook forge, for this manufacture.

In 1864 the company was dissolved and the business resumed by R. Cook & Sons, and is now continued by Charles and John R. Cook.

Hoes, Shovels, and Carpenters' Tools.

About 1828 Samuel Boyd engaged in the manufacture of steel hoes and shovels, and erected the original buildings of the Clifton Mill Company works on the south side of Mad river. He also manufactured in these buildings nail hammers, socket chisels, and draw shaves until 1833, when the business was discontinued.

In 1852 John Boyd, Louis R. Boyd, and Daniel B. Wheelock began to manufacture planters' hoes for the Southern market in the brick scythe works at the corner of Lake and Meadow streets. It was a new business, and encountered serious difficulties, one of them being the anti-slavery proclivities of the first and third partners, of which the Southern customers were duly notified by competing manufacturers. The obnoxious partners withdrew from the concern, and it became a decided success under the name of "The American Hoe Co." The hoes became the leading article in the market. They were sent to England and duplicated as to the style and finish by English manufacturers, but their work proved inferior in working quality.

The establishment was enlarged by the erection of grinding and polishing works on two other water powers, and in 1855 employed more hands than any other concern in the borough. In 1868 the establishment was purchased by Horace and Ralph W. Booth, and was continued in operation by L. R. Boyd, until paralyzed by the slave-holders' rebellion. It remained idle during and after the war until 1866, when it was purchased and resuscitated by the Winsted Hoe Company, which has also purchased the Clifton Mill works, and added to hoe-making the manufacture of socket chisels, draw shaves, and wrenches.

Bolts and Nuts.

The Clifton Mill Company, soon after the purchase of Samuel Boyd's works on the south side of Mad river, engaged in the manufacture of nuts and washers, and about 1855 added carriage bolts and nuts to its other manufactured articles, adding for that purpose the three story building on their premises, and also the Boyd machine shop at the foot of Lake street. On the purchase of their works by the Winsted Hoe Co., the nut and bolt manufacture was discontinued.

Another carriage bolt manufacture was started on the premises of R. Cook & Sons by Franklin Moore and Edward Clarke about 1867, which is still in active and successful operation, under the ownership and management of Mr. Moore.

Table Cutlery.

In 1852 the "Eagle" works, a joint stock company with a capital of $25,000, was organized and put in operation under the supervision of Albert Bradshaw, an English cutler, in a brick factory building on the Lake stream adjoining the Connecticut Western depot grounds. The business not proving successful, operations were suspended about 1854, and in 1856, the establishment was purchased by Rice, Lathrop & Clary, under whose ownership the brick factory building was burned down, and a smaller wooden building was erected on its site; and soon afterward the auger factory building on Mad river, near the corner of Main and Coe streets, was purchased. This building was burned down and rebuilt about 1866. Mr. Clary died in 1861, and Mr. Rice retired from the concern in 1862. George F. Barton came in as a partner with Mr. Lathrop in 1864, and retired from the partnership in 1872, leaving Mr. Lathrop the present sole owner. The concern has been impeded and crippled by two successive fires, but is still carried on with a reduced business.

Pocket Cutlery.

In 1853 Thompson & Gascoigne (Englishmen) carried on a small pocket cutlery business in the factory of the Eagle Co., which was soon after taken up by Beardsley & Alvord, and gradually enlarged and made profitable. In 1856, they built their cutlery works at the Lake outlet, and have since transacted a large and prosperous business in the name of "The Empire Knife Company."

In 1854, C. F. Clark, an Englishman, started a pocket cutlery concern in the attic of the Cook axle factory, which was taken up by Horace Phelps, and after a trial of one or two years, was abandoned.

AUGERS.

The Winsted (Joint Stock) Auger Company was organized in 1853 with a capital stock of $10,000, and immediately after erected the factory on Mad river near the corner of Coe and Main streets, at a cost beyond their capital. It was managed inefficiently by men unacquainted with the business, and was wound up before 1860.

STEEL FIRE IRONS.

Benjamin & Edward Woodall (Englishmen) began making, of highly polished steel, shovels and tongs and other fire irons, about 1850; and in 1854 organized the "Winsted Shovel and Tongs Co.," under the agency of Justus R. Loomis, they bought the Halsey Burr scythe shop and water power, and erected the factory building now used as a feed-grinding mill by Frederick Woodruff, on North Main street. The concern lacked capital, energy, and business skill, and was closed up about 1857.

PINS.

In 1852 Erastus S. Woodford, J. B. Terry and others organized "The Hartford Pin Co." (Joint Stock), and purchased of Anson G. Phelps the woolen factory building on Bridge street, opposite the Naugatuck Railroad depot grounds, and began making pins the same year. The company at once came into conflict with the Howe Pin Co. of Birmingham, in respect to a patented sticking machine for sticking the pins on paper, which impeded operations until the question of infringement was settled by litigation in the U. S. Circuit Court. In 1857 the factory property and machinery of the company became the property of James R. Keeler, who conveyed the same to "The New England Pin Co.," organized in May of the same year, and composed of said Keeler, Hector Armstrong, C. O. Crosby, and John G. Wetmore, stockholders, and with a capital of 100,000 dollars.

Under this organization the business has been vigorously and prosperously conducted to the present time and bids fair to continue one of the leading manufacturing interests of the place. The company also manufactured percussion caps for a few years, and afterwards shoe laces and braids.

Joiners' Tools.

The Winsted Plane Company, organized in 1851, entered on the manufacture of Joiners' tools in the old Soper woolen factory building, and continued until about 1856, when it became insolvent and was wound up.

Lumber.

The Clifton Lumber Co. was organized in 1854, and erected the building near the Naugatuck depot, now occupied by the Winsted Printing Co., for planing lumber and manufacturing doors, sashes, and blinds by steam power. The concern was wound up in 1857.

Plated Ware and Coffin Trimmings.

The Strong Manufacturing Co. was organized in 1866 by David Strong, Clark Strong, and others, for manufacturing plated handles and other coffin trimmings as a specialty. They erected their factory buildings on the site of the Gaylord foundry, and have since prosecuted the business largely and successfully, their wares being sold to every section of the country. They have recently purchased the water power of the Gilman Carriage Co., and are now (December, 1872) laying foundations for an additional factory building of capacity for more than doubling their work.

The business promises to be large, successful, and permanent.

Another company or partnership, consisting of Ralph H. Moore, Franklin Moore, and others, has this year (1872) erected a factory on Case Avenue for making plated spoons and other plated articles.

Condensed Milk.

The Borden Condensed Milk Co., consisting of Gail Borden, Theron Bronson, and Elhanan W. Tyler, was organized in 1863, and purchased the factory building near the Naugatuck depot, now occupied by the Winsted Printing Co., in which they condensed milk until 1866, when, not finding the location favorable for the business, the concern was wound up.

Carriage Springs.

The Henry Spring Co. was organized at New Haven in 1869, and its location was transferred to Winsted in April, 1870, and the grinding shop on Lake street, erected by the American Hoe Co., was purchased by the Spring Co., and its machinery placed therein. The business has been vigorously prosecuted to the present time (1872), with a promise of becoming large and permanent. The company has this season erected an additional building for enlarging their working power. The Spring made by them is a patented article combining equal strength and elasticity with springs of other manufacture of a third more weight, and are in constantly increasing demand for light buggies and carriages.

A tendency has prevailed here for the last thirty years among moneyed men, to "try all things and hold fast that which is good" in the way of manufacturing. This accounts for the large number of joint stock companies of brief existence and unsuccessful ending herein recapitulated. They have been slow to learn that manufacturing operations, organized and conducted by men not specially qualified and experienced in the branch of manufacture undertaken, are almost inevitable failures. Notwithstanding these drawbacks, profitable manufacturing operations have steadily increased, have never been more profitable than at the present time, and have never given surer promise of permanence and enlargement.

CENTENNIAL EXERCISES

COMMEMORATIVE OF THE ORGANIZATION

OF THE

TOWN OF WINCHESTER,

CONNECTICUT,

AND OF THE

First Ecclesiastical Society of said Town.

AUGUST 16TH AND 17TH, 1871.

REPORTED BY

HENRY E. ROCKWELL, ESQ., *PHONOGRAPHER.*

PRELIMINARY.

The following article appeared in the *Winsted Herald* of April 21st, 1871 :—

"We are desired to say that the organization of Winchester as a corporate town occurred on the 22d of July, 1771: and those citizens desirous of commemorating the event are requested to meet at the Lecture Room of the Second Congregational Church, West Winsted, on Monday evening, April 24, 1871, at seven o'clock, to consider and adopt preliminary measures. A prompt attendance of all persons interested is earnestly desired, the time for action being brief, and the preparations to be made important."

Pursuant to the foregoing call, a meeting was held at the time and place therein designated, and a committee, representing the several sections of the town, was appointed to consider and report to an adjourned meeting as to the desirableness of a commemorative celebration, and as to the time, place, and manner of arranging the same, and the following committee was appointed :—

Theron Bronson,	Thomas M. Clarke,
Abel S. Wetmore,	Charles H. Blake,
Ira W. Pettibone,	Samuel L. Andrews,
Isaac A. Bronson,	Rollin L. Beecher,
Benjamin W. Pettibone,	Charles Cook,
Samuel Hurlbut,	James R. Alvord,
James L. Bragg,	John T. Rockwell,
John Boyd,	George M. Carrington,
William G. Coe,	Hiram Perkins,
Normand Adams,	Elias E. Gilman,
Timothy Hulbert,	Moses Camp.

This committee, after mature consultation, published in the *Winsted Herald*, and in printed notices, circulated throughout the town the following call for an adjourned meeting, to be held on the 6th of May, 1871 :—

"The town of Winchester was organized, and the first town meeting held, in July, 1771. It is proposed that we celebrate that birth-day of a hundred years ago: that we call home the wanderers from the old town and their descendants, wherever scattered, spread a tent, bring together history, reminiscences, and cheerful story; and as a big family reunited, talk over the old times. Shall we do it? The undertaking requires the enthusiastic aid of every man and woman.

"Citizens of Winsted, and of the whole town, are requested to meet at the Second Congregational Church this week, Saturday evening, May 6th, at half-past seven, to decide the matter. Ladies are especially invited, and men modestly entreated, to attend and say the celebration shall go ahead. Such preparations are already made that this meeting can act decisively and effect a prompt and efficient organization if it will. If the community is indifferent to the project, neglect to attend this meeting will effectually kill it.

"THERON BRONSON,
"Chairman of Committee."

Pursuant to the above call, a meeting was held at the time and place therein named, and was called to order by Theron Bronson, Esq., chairman of the advisory committee. Rollin L. Beecher was appointed chairman, and George M. Carrington, clerk.

After remarks by Wm. G. Coe, John Boyd, M. P. Hubbell, and others, those in favor of a celebration were called on to manifest it by rising; carried by a nearly unanimous vote. The time of holding the celebration was fixed for the last two weeks in August, the exact time to be named by a supervisory committee afterwards appointed.

The organization of the first Ecclesiastical Society of Winchester having occurred during the same year with the town organization, it was decided that the celebration should occupy two successive days, the first to be commemorative of the Ecclesiastical Society, the services to be held at Winchester Center, and managed by citizens of that society, and in the evening a reunion of a social character to be held in Winsted; and the second day's exercises to be specially connected with the town organization, and to be held in Winsted.

The following committees were then appointed:—

General Supervisory Committee.—William G. Coe, John T. Rockwell, James A. Bushnell, Samuel Hurlbut, Theron Bronson, James L. Bragg.

Finance.—Henry Gay, Charles H. Blake, James H. Welch, Rufus E. Holmes, McPherson Hubbell, Silas Hurlbut, John McAlpine, Samuel M. Munsill, David Le Roy.

Invitations.—Rev. Frederick Marsh, Abel S. Wetmore, Alva Nash, John Boyd, Ira W. Pettibone, George M. Carrington, Theron Bronson,

CENTENNIAL CELEBRATION. 529

John Hinsdale, William C. Phelps, B. B. Rockwell, Mrs. Norris Coe, Mrs. Leonard B. Hurlbut, Miss Mary P. Hinsdale, Mrs. Harvey L. Roberts.

Exercises and Ceremonies.—Samuel B. Forbes, Roland Hitchcock, Thomas M. Clarke, Rev. Arthur Goodenough, Ira W. Pettibone, Isaac A. Bronson, Abel S. Wetmore, Mrs. Ellen A. Phillips, Miss Julia E. Rockwell.

Tents and Audience Rooms.—David W. Coe, Rollin L. Beecher, Edward R. Beardsley, Hiram Perkins, Samuel L. Andrews, Isaac A. Bronson, Frank L. Whiting, Frederick L. Loomis, John J. Fanning, George Tibbals, Worthy B. Bray.

Reception and Entertainment of Guests.—Charles Cook, Caleb J. Camp, James R. Alvord, John G. Wetmore, Aug. M. Perkins, Wm. P. Lathrop, Lucius Griswold, Normand Adams, James L. Bragg, Edward H. Bronson, Lorenzo S. Nash and wife, William W. Waugh, Samuel Hurlbut 2d, Mrs. Harvey Andrews.

Collations.—Winsted, Jabez Alvord, George W. Kinney, Jenison J. Whiting, George White, Caleb P. Newman, Mrs. Lyman Case, Mrs. Henry A. Bills, Mrs. Charles Cook, Mrs. William G. Coe, Charles B. Hallett, Robert R. Noble; Winchester Society, Joseph M. Marsh, Samuel M. Munsill and wife, Dudley Chase and wife, Isaac Dayton, Samuel W. Starks, William Johnson, Luman Munsill and wife, Martin Drake, Newton Phelps, David Le Roy, Harvey Andrews and wife, Orrin Tuller and wife, Benjamin F. Waugh, Alonzo T. Parsels and wife, Frederick M. Baldwin and wife, William L. Munsill and wife, Trumbull H. Brooks, Mrs. William W. Waugh, Mrs. Catherine M. Carrington, Mrs. George W. Beach, Miss Mariette Whiting, Mrs. Sally Drake, Mrs. Theron Bronson, Mrs. George Tibbals, Mrs. Frank L. Whiting, Mrs. Worthy B. Bray, Mrs. Abel S. Wetmore, Miss Sarepta Munsill, Elizabeth Tibbals.

Decorations and Antiquities.—Wm. L. Camp, Clarke Strong, David W. Coe, Miss Elizabeth Kilbourn, Mrs. Isaac B. Woodruff, Miss Phebe A. Brazie, McPherson Hubbell and wife, Horace Humphrey, Mrs. Le-Roy W. Wetmore, Miss Ellen Chase, Miss Kate Murray, Miss Louisa M. Carrington, Mrs. Clara Turner.

Music.—Edward Clarke, Rufus E. Holmes, John F. Peck, George Dudley, junior, Joseph H. Vaill, Eugene W. Meafoy, Harvey Andrews, Frederick Murray, Mrs. Luman Munsill.

Registration.—Harvey L. Roberts, Rollin H. Cook, Hubert P. Wetmore, Wilbur M. Bronson, Le Roy W. Wetmore.

Bonfires and Illuminations.—Lamphier B. Tuttle, George E. Woodford, Homer W. Whiting, Spencer G. Pierce, Wilbur F. Coe, Marshall G. Wheeler, Solomon R. Hinsdale, Edward E. Dayton, George

Tibbals 2d, Lyman Tibbals, Chester Dayton, George E. Andrews, James F. Beach.

Processions and Bands.—Winsted, Colonel William T. Batcheller, Colonel Jeffrey Skinner, William F. Hurlbut, Florimond D. Fyler, Salmon A. Granger, Eugene W. Meafoy; Winchester Society, Frederick Murray, Henry Drake, Nelson D. Ford, Elias T. Hatch, Nelson Brooks, Washington Hatch.

Corresponding Secretary.—George M. Carrington.

Recording Secretary.—Henry Drake 2d.

Marshals.—Colonel Ira W. Pettibone, Colonel Wm. T. Batcheller.

The supervisory committee having fixed on the 16th and 17th days of August for the commemoration, the following circular was issued, and distributed by mail to all known former residents of the town, or their descendants, residing out of the County of Litchfield:—

Winchester Centennial!

It is proposed to commemorate the year of the organization of the Town and of the First Church of Winchester, Conn., by a

Centennial Celebration,

ON THE

16th and 17th Days of AUGUST, 1871.

Arrangements are in progress for appropriate Ceremonies and Services.

The Centennial of the Church will be celebrated in the Old Society of Winchester—where the first church was organised—on the 16th, forenoon and afternoon. In the evening a Reunion of a social character will be held in Winsted. The Centennial of the Town will be celebrated in Winsted on the 17th.

You to whom this Circular is sent, whether allied to us by birth, wedlock, a sometime residence, or in whatever manner, are cordially invited to attend this proposed Reunion of the Sons and Daughters—children by adoption are children all the same—of Winchester, and thus contribute to animate and make memorable an occasion which can occur but once in a lifetime. Come, bringing your sheaves with you, and let's have a grand harvesting of the crops whose seeds wind and wave have been this hundred years scattering.

Provision will be made for the reception and entertainment of those who may signify to the Committee their intention to be present—notice of such intention to be addressed, as early as convenient, to Geo. M. Carrington, West Winsted, Ct.

FREDERICK MARSH,	MRS. HARVEY L. ROBERTS,
JOHN BOYD,	MRS. LEONARD B. HURLBUT,
ABEL S. WETMORE,	JOHN HINSDALE,
GEO. M. CARRINGTON,	IRA W. PETTIBONE,
THERON BRONSON,	WILLIAM C. PHELPS,
MARY P. HINSDALE,	ALVA NASH,
MRS. NORRIS COE,	B. B. ROCKWELL,

Committee of Invitation.

P. S.—You are requested to invite any descendants or former residents of Winchester not specially invited, through accident, or want of knowledge, to be present as guests of the town.

AUGUST 16, 1871.

The town was filled with sons and daughters of "Old Winchester," gathered from every section of the country. The exercises of the day were at Winchester, in commemoration of the institution of the first Congregational Church.

"The arrangements were admirable. A large pavilion tent on the Green, in front of the Meeting House, accommodated a large concourse of people, the porch serving as a platform and speaker's stand. Theron Bronson, Esq., presided, and Colonel Ira W. Pettibone officiated as Marshal, with Edward H. Bronson and Henry F. Marsh, assistants. Harvey Andrews, musical conductor." The church front was decorated with evergreens, and bore the names of Pastors Knapp, Bogue, Bassett, Marsh, Dill, Pettibone, and Goodenough.

Rev. Frederick Marsh, ninety-one years old, was present, and took part in the exercises.

The exercises were opened with reading by Deacon Abel S. Wetmore of the following hymn, composed by the reader, which was sung to the tune of "Auld Lang Syne":—

CENTENNIAL HYMN.

[Written by request.]

God of our life, our fathers' trust,
  Thy blessing now we crave;
Deep in the ocean of thy love
  May our glad spirits lave.

Unite our hearts, and tune each voice
  Inspire our lips to sing,
A loud Hosanna to thy name;
  A heart-felt off'ring bring.

This festive day, one hundred years
  Since Winchester was named,
We welcome friends, from far, and near,
  And sing with loud acclaim.

One hundred years, since our grand-sires
  Adopted *this* their *home*,
When fierce wild beasts, and savage men
  The wilderness did roam.

With pious hearts, and robust forms,
  Our fathers hither came,
A rustic temple reared to God,
  In which to praise his name.

This church at once was organized,
  A pastor soon ordained;
And we, this day, commemorate
  Our blessings thus obtained.

Seven Pastors here have been installed,
  To teach, and guide the flock;
Knapp, Bogue, and Bassett, and F. Marsh,
  Of Puritanic stock;

And next came Dill, then Pettibone,
  The fifth, and sixth in turn;
We now rejoice in Goodenough,
  Wise lessons may we learn.

Well may we mingle joys, and tears,
  As we recount the past,
A century!—a hundred years!
  Can old Time always last?

Ah, no! and when life's toils are o'er,
  And we are called away,
May each, enwrapped in Christ's embrace
  Spend an eternal day.

The president announced that owing to the illness of Rev. Ira Pettibone he would call on their pastor, Rev. Arthur Goodenough, who read the 67th psalm, and invoked the blessing of the Deity as follows:—

PRAYER.

Most merciful and ever blessed God; Thou who art the God of our fathers, and art still the same to-day, merciful and gracious and forbearing toward the descendants of them that believed on thy name, that loved thee; shewing thy kindness even unto the third and fourth generation; oh, our Heavenly Father, wilt thou be with us and bless us on this day of commemoration. May we indeed feel that thou art present, inspiring our thoughts and affections, raising our desires heavenward, making us to rejoice in Thee, and to rejoice in what Thou didst for those who have gone before us, and for us who have entered into possession of that which they have left. Our Heavenly Father, wilt thou make us all to rejoice in Thee, and grant that harmony of feeling may prevail among all those who gather here to celebrate this day.

Give thy blessing to all who shall take part in these exercises, that they may have thy grace resting upon them, and be able to discharge the duties that devolve upon them; and may all present feel that they are instructed and benefited; and may thy children be strengthened in faith; and may the influence of the memory of thy dealings with our fathers, and the history of their lives as it is recorded and made known to us to-day, be such as shall enable us to see thy favor to them, and lead us back to the God of our fathers and to the old land-marks of piety, faith, and love, by which they were guided. Oh, our Father, wilt thou be near to us, and make us to rejoice in Thee, as thine own children; and more and more, as we are permitted to live in the world, may we feel that Thou art the guide of all our steps; and may we commit our ways to Thee, that Thou mayest direct in all our paths. Guide us and give us thy grace, and save us for Christ's sake, amen.

The following original hymn was then sung:

HYMN.

WRITTEN FOR THE WINCHESTER CENTENNIAL BY DR. W. J. WETMORE.

Tune—*America.*

Here in this sacred fane,
Let us in joyful strain
Praise Thee above;
Dear ones here seem to stand,
A consecrated band
From memories' hallowed land,
Hearts that we love.

Then let our thanks arise,
Like incense to the skies,
   In songs divine;
Our gratitude to show
To those who here below,
A hundred years ago
   Reared Faith's pure shrine.

Their names are sacred yet,
Nor shall we e'er forget
   Friends passed away
On Jordan's peaceful shore,
Life's toil and trouble o'er,
They sleep forevermore—
   Dear hallowed clay.

Father, on Thee we call,
Thou art our hope, our all,
   Our faith and love;
Here on each bended knee,
May we Thy glory see,
And dwell at last with Thee,
   In Heaven above.

ADDRESS BY REV. HENRY B. BLAKE.

The following historical address was then given by Rev. Henry B. Blake, a native of Winchester, but now a resident of Wilmington, N. C.

Psalm 50 : 2.—Out of Zion, the perfection of beauty, God hath shined.

BRETHREN AND FRIENDS: We meet here to-day for a holy purpose; we gather from varied wanderings at the old home. The old hills greet us on every side. The houses in which we were born open their doors to us. We drink water out of the old wells, from their deep fountains. The streams into which we cast our first fishing lines murmur their gladness. Trees that were set since some of us were children whisper welcome to us.

We renew to-day the memories and affections of other, and perhaps distant, years. We enjoy again the pleasures and learn the lessons of our youth. The rocks around which we played in our childhood are in their old places, and many of the faces of those with whom we played then are here to-day. Should we know them if we saw them in a land of strangers? The by-gone years ask leave to pass in review before us and show their life. Without disturbing their repose, we shall call up the dead that we may see their forms and hear their voices, giving them a resurrection in our hearts. We would enshrine the influences and memories of these fading years before they pass into oblivion.

We who are the children of those years meet each other with glad welcomes to-day. We looked into the same faces, sat on the same benches, roamed over the same fields and heard the same benignant tones in Sabbath worship, and we have never forgotten our birth-place. We recount gratefully the loving Providence that has been over all our life and grown young again in the memory of our early years.

A hundred years ago and these hills and valleys, covered, through immemorial time, with the silence of the unbroken forest, taking on the soft verdure of spring, the sere and yellow leaf of autumn, the crystal glory of winter, rearing and giving to decay their mighty monarchs through uncounted centuries, disturbed by no sound but the voices of nature and the stealthy footstep of the savage, had heard, for a few years, the sound of the woodman's axe, and felt the heat of the woodman's fire. Clearings were seen here and there, and the early dwellings of the pioneer. Paths were cut through the forests and the signs of civilization began to appear.

It is one of the evidences of our immortality that we are ever seeking for something better. Men are ever looking after a paradise somewhere, and so the dwellers in the lower lands on our Southern shores, had come up here to make homes for themselves and their children. There was a divine hand in it.

True to the instincts of their puritan origin, these settlers early made provision for Christian institutions, and on the 30th of October, 1771, Rev. Ammi R. Robbins of Norfolk, and Rev. Nathan Roberts of Farmington, constituted Mary Loomis, Hannah Averit, Dinah Filley, wife of William, John Hills, Seth Hills, Adam Mott, Abiah Mott, Lent Mott, Abram Filley, Robert Macune, Joseph Preston, Mary Preston, Amy, wife of Joel Beach, and Elizabeth Agard the first Church in Winchester. I suppose the constitution of the Church was in the first meeting house which was built probably in 1769. It stood half a mile south of the present site, about twenty rods to the right of the present road on the brow of the hill. It was a rude unfinished building, 24 by 30, resting on chestnut logs, and having rough seats of planks or slabs.

Imagine the settlers on a crisp October morning, the hills just swept of their autumnal glories, gathering in such a structure, for such a purpose. The smoke is rising from the log houses in the clearings here and there among the hills. There is not a wheeled vehicle in the town, there are no roads, only paths. These two pioneer ministers come in from their distant homes. The people are in homespun, and the place is rude. But the occasion is momentous, the beginning of a Church of Christ, the home of Christian influences, the center of all that is worth any thing in this human life, and the source of all our hopes in the eternal future.

Credentials are examined, and with psalm and prayer, and the word of God, these fourteen believers solemnly assent to the great doctrines of the puritan faith, and enter into solemn covenant with God and with each other. Then five more, on the same confession, are added to their number, and, with psalm and benediction, the services are closed, and the infant church begins its course.

The society was constituted before the church, in 1768. There were several candidates for the ministry. Among them we find the names of Mills, Starr, Johnson, Potter, and Brooks. Father Mills preached a considerable time. In the old parish book, we find these entries:

Voted, if Mr. Mills cannot come to try Mr. Johnson.

Voted, if Mr. Johnson cannot come to apply to the Association for advice.

Voted, That Mr. Bellamy hire a candidate for us.

Voted, That Mr. Robbins assist Mr. Bellamy.

Voted, David Austin to read the psalm.

Voted, That Beriah Hills shall assist in reading the psalm.

Voted, That John Hills and Abram Filley shall set the psalm.

The first pastor of this church was Rev. Joshua Knapp, a native of Danbury, a graduate of Yale College in 1770. He was ordained here November 11, 1772. The Council consisted of Rev. Messrs. Bellamy of Bethlem, Roberts of Torrington, Lee of Salisbury, Brinsmaid of Washington, Farrand of Canaan, Canfield of New Milford, Newell of Goshen, Benedict of Woodbury, Day of New Preston, Robbins of Norfolk, Hart of North Canaan, and Starr of Warren, with their delegates. Mr. Robbins preached the sermon, which was published and of which some copies remain. Mr. Farrand offered the ordaining prayer, and Dr. Bellamy gave the charge.

Mr. Knapp is spoken of as a man of fluent and ready gifts, not studious, and somewhat careless in worldly matters. He was sound in the faith and a strenuous opposer of the half-way covenant, and by his influence the church was established. Mr. Knapp was dismissed October 13, 1789. He preached afterwards in New Hartford, North Canaan, and Milton in this county, and Hamilton, N. Y., and ended his days with his son-in-law, Dea. Abel Hinsdale, in Torrington, March 23, 1816. His grave is here with his first people.

In 1783 and 1784, there was a revival of religion here and eighty-four persons were admitted to the church during the ministry of Mr. Knapp.

The first deacon in the church was Seth Hills, born Sept. 13, 1736; chosen deacon Dec. 15, 1772; died at Vernon, N. Y., June 3, 1826. He was the son of Benoni Hills, who was a native of Northampton, and came here from Torrington, and died at the age of 93. His children were numerous.

The selection of Deacon Hills is evidence enough of his supposed eminent fitness for his office; his life, I am told, justified their estimate. He removed to Vernon, N. Y., in 1798. His son, Deacon Ira Hills, of that place, is with us to-day. His sister, Mary Hills, was the mother of Deacon Loomis The second deacon was Samuel Wetmore, chosen in 1777; died March 2, 1809.

Deacon Wetmore, if we may judge of him from tradition as well as from what we know of his descendants, known to so many of us, and so many of whom are here to-day, was a man of marked ability, and we are assured of his eminent piety and usefulness. The farm which he subdued is supposed to be the only land in the town which has been in the possession of the same family a hundred years. It is now the home of his great-grandson, Deacon Abel S. Wetmore.

On the 16th of March, 1773, Samuel Wetmore leased to Seth Hills, Wareham Gibbs, Oliver Coe, and the rest of the inhabitants of the society, for nine hundred and ninety-nine years, a piece of ground for a burying place. You know where it is with its enlargements. There are but few of us who have not trodden the paths to it with sorrowing feet. There our dead wait the trump of the archangel and the resurrection morning. Let it be the joy as it is the duty of those who dwell here to keep it as becomes the receptacle of such precious treasures till He whose eye is ever on the sleep of his beloved comes to call his own.

The second church edifice was built in 1786, and was 54 feet by 40. Many of us remember it, as it stood alone in unadorned grandeur on the Green, with its high pulpit and sounding-board, its high pews and narrow singers' seat, and its tything-men. We remember too the preaching we heard in it, even when we were so young our friends supposed it made no impression on us, and we shall remember it

"While life and thought and being lasts,
And immortality endures."

Rev. Publius V. Bogue, the second pastor of this church, was ordained Jan. 26, 1791. He was the son of a minister in Avon, and was born March 30, 1764. His father died when he was two years old, and his early education was limited. For a time he was in the army of the Revolution. He was converted at 18 and graduated at Yale College in 1787. He was licensed by the Hampshire Association at Feeding Hills, Mass. Mr. Bogue was a man of fine personal appearance and address, and an able and useful preacher. He was dismissed on the 20th of March, 1809, much to the regret of his people, and his wife said that he used to say in after years that he had never been sorry he left Winchester but once, and that was always. He finished the house in which I was born, long occupied by Dr. Wetmore, and now by Leonard B. Hurlbut.

After leaving Winchester, Mr. Bogue preached at Vernon, N. Y., at Georgia, Vt., at Paris, N. Y., and his ministry was greatly successful. He died suddenly at his house in Clinton, N. Y., in the 73d year of his age and the forty-fifth of his ministry. "The memory of the just is blessed."

A general revival of religion occurred near the close of Mr. Bogue's ministry. Its fruits were lasting and blessed. He received fifty-one members to the church.

Eliphaz Alvord was chosen Deacon June 19, 1799, and died April 15, 1825, aged 83. He was eminent for many years in the church and in civil affairs. The history of the town cannot be given without an extended notice of him. He began at his house the Thursday evening prayer meeting, which was continued, almost without interruption, in the eastern part of the parish for forty years.

Robert McEwen—Macune—descended from the Scotch Covenanters, came from New Stratford at 22 years of age in 1766 or '67, took up four hundred acres of land, cleared the forest with his own hands, and built his house. He married, about the time of the organization of the church, Jerusha Doolittle, of Stratford. He brought his bride, who was seventeen years of age, to their new home on a pillion, making the journey, forty miles, in a single day. She endured the ride bravely till it was dark, and they were coming up through the dense hemlock forest below the hill when she exclaimed, "Where are we going?" "We are almost there," he replied, and soon they came out into the cheerful clearing.

For two or three years, while Mr. McEwen was hewing down the forest, he often attended public worship in Norfolk. In a leaf of a diary of his which I have seen is this entry. "July ye 17 in yr 1770. Heard ye famous Mr. Whitfield preach at Norfolk from John ye 5 : 25, which i hope was a word in season to me." Perhaps this was the day of his conversion.

When the church was organized he was chosen Moderator and Clerk, and the early records show that the meetings were often holden at his house. The house he built, now owned by Deacon Munsill, is, I judge, one of the oldest in the town. He was chosen Deacon July 12, 1799, and died November 16, 1816. Of him and his family you will hear more as these exercises go on. His son was that eminent minister of the gospel, Abel McEwen, for fifty years pastor of the church in New London, a fine scholar, a courtly gentleman, a genial friend, a builder of the wastes in Eastern Connecticut, a leader of his generation, a man of whom it might have been said when he was seventy years of age, that though he had never lived in his native county since his majority, he knew more of its history, more of the life of its men, than any man who had always had his home in it.

His son, Rev. Robert McEwen, is now living at New London. Of him I may say, after a long and thorough acquaintance, he is one of the most complete Christian men I have ever known. Though laid aside from a very useful ministry, his life is a blessing wherever it is.

The second daughter of Dea. McEwen was married to James Beebe, who came from Litchfield, succeeded to the farm, and was in my boyhood a leading man in the church, and in the town. "Squire Beebe" he was always called. If the pastor was sick or away, he read the sermons in the sabbath service. He was moderator of parish and town meetings, a Christian magistrate, a representative and a senator in our general assembly. He had a large and intelligent family, none of whom remain in the town. He died at a very advanced age only a few years since in Ohio. When he was very aged, Dr. McEwen made him a visit, and he said it was worth a journey to Ohio to see the look of joy that came in Bro. Beebe's face when he recognized him.

It belongs to another to sketch the families prominent here in the last generation. I may be allowed, on the score of filial piety, a brief notice of two men who came here before 1800.

Adna Beach came from Goshen. He was a grandson of John Beach, one of the first settlers of Goshen, whose descendants are almost numberless and found in all departments of life. He first settled a mile west of the meeting-house, but removed north into the forest, which he cleared and there he built his house. His wife was Mary Stanley. One of the earliest things I remember is the funeral of my grandfather, which occurred in April, 1820, before I was three years old. He had nine children, and they all lived till the eldest was seventy years of age. Twenty of his grandsons and nearly as many of his granddaughters are now in active life. Three of his grandsons are in service in the ministry, and others are successful and useful in other pursuits. He and his wife and several of his children and grandchildren were members of the church.

Elijah Blake came here in 1798 from Torringford, where his sons in their boyhood were the playmates of Samuel J. Mills. He was a descendant of one of the early settlers of Dorchester, Mass. He was not a member of the church but always maintained family prayer and a consistent life. He died in 1833. His wife was Sarah Hamlin. She died in 1811. Father Mills attended her funeral and said in testimony of her worth, that his mind went back to Joppa when the widows stood weeping around the dead body of Dorcas, showing the coats and garments she had made. You may find a large number of the names of the children and grandchildren of this family on the rolls of the church. One son and one grandson have held the office of Deacon. One great-grandson fills a popular Unitarian pulpit in Boston, and another has a large law practice in New York.

The third minister of this people was Rev. Archibald Bassett. He was a native of Derby, and graduated at Yale College in 1796. He was ordained here May 20, 1801. He was a fine scholar and an able writer and preacher, but his ministry here was short. He was dismissed Aug.

27, 1806. He afterwards settled at Walton, N. Y., where he died at an advanced age. Thirteen were received to the church during the ministry of Mr. Bassett, and eleven before his settlement after the dismission of Mr. Bogue.

And what shall I say of the fourth pastor of this church? We thank God that, after a life of more than sixty years among his people, and past the age of ninety, he is with us, to-day, linking us to the earlier life we commemorate. The companion of those ancient men, as we look into his face, some of us after the lapse of years, the tide of time rolls back, our fathers and mothers, the venerable men and women of our early years, gather around him and we stand in the midst of our departed ones.

Of the man who married my father and mother, and baptized all these children, and gathered almost every one of us into the church, and buried those who died early, who was with us when we gathered at the golden wedding around the old altar, and who when the time of their departure in peace and triumph came, was with us, as we laid our dead away to rest till the coming of Christ, from whom I received gratuitous instruction by which I gained admission to college, whose constant friendship has been a joy in our family for sixty years, whose life has been a benediction in this community, I *must* speak though he is with us.

Frederick Marsh was born in New Hartford, September 18, 1780. His youth was under the ministry of Dr. Griffin, in the midst of those remarkable revivals of religion whose influence he has felt and extended in all his life. He fitted for college with the Rev. Mr. Robbins, of Norfolk, graduated at Yale College in 1805, studied Theology with the Rev. Mr. Hooker, of Goshen, was licensed at Salisbury in 1806, and ordained here February 1st, 1809. He relinquished his salary and asked for a colleague Feb. 1, 1846, and was dismissed Oct. 2, 1851. Of the ability and faithfulness, the earnestness and zeal of this ministry, and the simplicity, purity and benevolence of this life, I shall not speak at length. The record is in our hearts and on high. Early in the ministry of Mr. Marsh there came to the parsonage, one September evening about nine o'clock, a young lady who was teaching the school in Danbury Quarter. She had ridden on horseback, with Sarah Benedict, over the hills to Deacon Alvord's to attend the conference meeting, and had come from that meeting to tell the young pastor that she was in great anxiety about her soul. After the interview, which added to her distress, they mounted their horse and rode up through the dark woods to Danbury Quarter. In the morning she resumed her school and soon became a happy Christian. I need not tell what Polly Grant has done in her generation. She was the first convert, so far as he knows, under the ministry of Mr. Marsh.

I cannot speak at length of the revivals that occurred during this period. Their history is a part of the history of our New England. How pungent their convictions of guilt were, how keen was the anguish of those experiences, some of you know. What sources of heroic life and glorious death they were, the world knows. How they peopled the mansions of the Father's house, how they swelled the songs of heaven, will be known in the day of the manifestation of the sons of God. No other such scenes of solemnity and joy does this earth witness. They were in 1813, 1815 and '16, 1820 and '21, 1826, 1831, and 1842. Two hundred and three persons were added to the church in this ministry. Since his dismission Mr. Marsh has done a good deal of pastoral work among his people, and received many tokens of their kindness. On the 11th of March, 1860, Mrs. Marsh left her family and this world, and entered into rest. A native of the same town, the fitting companion of such a man, Parnal Merrill was married to Mr. Marsh on the 22d of May, 1809. The patient, untiring, and efficient helper of her husband in all his work, the faithful and loving mother of her children, the courteous, hospitable mistress of her home, the kind friend of all who came within the sphere of her life, she deserves an honored and loving remembrance, now that we are trying to gather up the treasures of our past, and put them for safe-keeping into the casket of the future.

Their children were eight, of whom five still live. The same house has been the home of the family, and largely the home of the whole people, for more than sixty years.

If it please God may this life be continued a little longer, for it seems to us the sunlight and shadow will fall more lovingly on these hill-sides, and we *know* that the affections of many a wanderer will cluster more sweetly around the old spot, while it lasts; and when it passes it will be to hear sweeter welcomes and to greet a goodlier company than surround our venerated Father to-day, and that heavenly voice, "Servant of God, well done."

Deacon Lorrain Loomis was chosen to his office Feb. 28, 1812. He was born in Torrington Jan. 9, 1764. He became a Christian, as he supposed, when he was a little more than 18 years of age. I have often thought that if I were asked to make a list of the most eminent Christians I have ever known, nearly first, if not first, would be the name of Deacon Loomis. He is said to have said early to a young friend, "Jesse, the world are living on the failings of Christians; let us starve them to death." That was the key-note of his life. For thirty years he was an instructor of youth, and my friend, the historian of the town, says he was the only district school-master he ever loved. He once taught a school in Albany and had occasion to punish a boy, the son of a Dutchman. The father came to him in great wrath and threatened to spit in his face. "You can if you wish," was the reply, "I can wipe it off." He was so near his Master that when he was reviled, he reviled not again. His heart was full of love to all men. He furnished, at his own expense, the first stove ever put in the old meeting house. Those of us who remember the intense suffering from cold in that house must bless his memory. It was just like him. The only accusation ever brought against him was, he gives too much. Blessed is the man of whom a carping world can say nothing worse.

The secret of the Lord is with them that fear him. Deacon Loomis sometimes said to his intimate friends that he was just as sure of the coming of a revival of religion before there were any outward signs of it, as in the midst of its glories. It has passed into our current literature how Lorrain Loomis, Micajah Hoyt, and Stephen Wade, in a coal cabin on our northwestern hills, entered into a solemn covenant to pray for the conversion of Lemuel Hurlbut till he should be converted, or he or they should pass away from earth. They desired the conversion of Mr. Hurlbut because of their high regard for him, and his great influence in the community. I do not know that it ever has been told how, when his associates had long been dead, and he was more than ninety years of age, Deacon Loomis and Mr. Hurlbut met to rejoice together over that for which the three had prayed so long.

I remember well a prayer meeting on a cold winter's night at Squire Beebe's. I suppose it must have been in January, 1834. Deacon Loomis was present, though not living in town. He had just reached the end of his seventieth year. I think it was his birthday. How tenderly he spoke of his great unworthiness, of the shortness of his life, and his expectation of dying soon. How modestly he spoke of his hopes of Heaven! How meltingly he exhorted us to holy living and preparation for death. Yet, he lived after that almost twenty-five years. For several years he was steward and accountant at the Foreign Mission School at Cornwall, a position of great usefulness. He lost his property in middle life, and he worked many months after he was seventy years of age, at twelve dollars a month, to get money to pay obligations assumed for others long before. I thank God that this earth has been consecrated by the lives of such men. Their feet have trodden it; their tears have baptized it. Its air is holy with the perfume of their saintly lives. God made good to him his promise to the liberal soul, in abundant provision for his old age. He died July 7, 1857, aged ninety-three and a half years. "They that be wise shall shine as the brightness of the firmament, and they that turn many to righteousness, as the stars for ever and ever."

Benjamin Benedict was chosen deacon in 1812, July 9. He is spoken of as an excellent man. He emigrated early to Coventry, Chenango County, N. Y., where he died July 22, 1850, aged 83.

Levi Platt was chosen deacon in 1819, April 30. No two men could well be more unlike in form and temperament than Deacon Loomis and Deacon Platt. Deacon Platt was gigantic in form, of stern stuff, a patriarch, a puritan. Deacon Loomis was slender and loving as a child, a very lamb for gentleness. Yet these men wrought together in most loving partnership all the long years of their connection with the church, and I do not believe any pastor ever trusted more implicitly in any two men than Mr. Marsh, who was the junior of both, trusted these two men. They were the Aaron and Hur that stayed the hands of our leader to the promised land.

My most vivid recollections of Deacon Platt, as a church officer, are in the prayer meetings holden in the old school-house south of Hurlbut's store, in the Sabbath intermissions of the summer of 1831. In these meetings he prayed, and talked, and *wept*, as though he believed that men must speedily submit to God or be lost in eternal perdition. He did believe it.

Deacon Platt died August 14, 1856, aged 90 years, eight months, having been a member of the church more than seventy years — a venerable and holy man. "The righteous shall be in everlasting remembrance." He was a son-in-law of Deacon Alvord.

Stephen Wheadon was chosen deacon, May 30, 1823. He was a man of strong character, and gave promise of eminent usefulness, but he died suddenly December 2, 1824, aged 40, "And devout men carried Stephen to his burial, and made great lamentation over him."

Micajah Hoyt was chosen deacon, December 2, 1825. He was eminently a man of prayer. He emigrated to Barton, N. Y., where he died April 14, 1848, aged 77.

David Bird was chosen in 1835, and served the church faithfully till his removal in 1857. He died in 1863, aged 59 years.

Allen Blake was chosen in 1835, and served faithfully till his death in 1850, at the age of 58.

Of the eleven deacons of this church who have died, three were more than ninety years of age, three more were more than eighty-three, two more averaged seventy-five, and the whole average is more than seventy-five. "Length of days is in her right hand, and in her left hand riches and honor."

The living men who have held the office of deacon are Abel S. Wetmore, chosen in 1835, Marcus Munsill, chosen in 1858, Elijah F. Blake, chosen in 1858, and Isaac A. Bronson, chosen in 1865. The church has had fifteen deacons.

Mr. James H. Dill was ordained colleague with Mr. Marsh, August 26, 1846. Mr. Dill, like all his predecessors, was a graduate of Yale. He came here in his youth, and labored earnestly a few years, and was dismissed October 2, 1851. He afterward had a successful ministry in

Spencerport, N. Y., and in Chicago. His name is on that long roll of honor which the nation saved, will ever keep bright. He was a chaplain in the army, and died in his work.

After the dismission of Mr. Dill, Rev. John Cunningham preached several months, and accepted a call, but the consociation refused to settle him.

Rev. Ira Pettibone was installed here in October, 1857, and left his pastorate in 1866. Mr. Pettibone is now pastor of the church in West Hartford. In his life he has given a good deal of time to the cause of education. While here he founded and conducted the Winchester Institute. That beautiful building is one of the marks he made here. Members of the church gave their money to assist in its erection, and others have since given their money to put it into the hands of trustees as a perpetual gift to the community. Of these last, Mrs. Jonathan Blake and her daughter, Mrs. Mitchell, are worthy of special mention, they having given $4,500 for this purpose, which is the largest sum any one family has placed in this enterprise. It is now in the care of Colonel Ira W. Pettibone, and if the people of Winchester are wise they will cherish it, for besides its incalculable advantages to your children, nothing draws a good population like a good school, and there is a growing demand for places of education away from the vicious influences of our large towns. Seventy-two persons were added to the church here during the ministry of Mr. Pettibone. Mrs. Pettibone, whose death occurred here April, 1865, was Louisa Welch, of Norfolk. She was an early teacher of mine. I have always felt the stimulus of her instructions, and had pleasant memories of her. I believe she was universally beloved.

Rev. Wm. M. Gay supplied the place of a pastor for two or three years.

Rev. Arthur Goodenough, the present pastor of the church, was installed Dec. 28, 1870. He is a native of Jefferson, N. Y., and a graduate of Yale College.

The church has had five hundred and twenty-three members. If it has not grown larger the population has not increased around it. It has given largely to other churches, as to the church in Vernon, N. Y., a majority of her first members. We rejoice that the town has steadily increased and that other churches strong in numbers and influence, occupy the ground where the population is largest. May the Divine life grow in them all.

The present church edifice was raised Aug. 26, 1841, and dedicated June 30, 1842. It has recently been thoroughly repaired and speaks for itself.

Honorable mention should be made of those who supported with a liberal hand the institutions of religion even while they were not members of the church. Messrs. S. & L. Hurlbut, for a long course of years, paid one-quarter of the salary of Mr. Marsh, and supplemented the salary with large gifts which they continued as long as they lived. They also paid at least one-third of the cost of the present house of worship. The late Isaac Bronson and his brothers were liberal supporters of the society in the early years, as his children have been in the more recent, and there have been many others.

It is hardly possible to touch anything in the history of the last hundred years without dwelling on the changes in the life of the world. Our presence here and the journeys we have come are significant of these changes. The steamboat, the railway, and the telegraph have made possible the wide dispersion of this family, and this pleasant re-union. In this hundred years these agencies have come into use, and are the instruments by which freedom, knowledge, and Christianity are doing the mighty work of regenerating the world.

When the fathers began here they were a part of some feeble colonies of Great Britain planted along the Atlantic coast of this wilderness continent. We are a part of the mightiest nation on the face of the earth. I speak advisedly when I say the mightiest nation. I do not estimate the might of a nation simply by the number of her people, her wealth, or her armies. I take in the character of her people and the power of her principles, and I say that a nation that has a domain from ocean to ocean, and from tropic seas to polar ice, capable of sustaining a thousand millions of people; that has spanned a continent with a great highway of the nations, bringing London within forty days of Canton; that established a system of popular education that has become a necessity and an inevitable destiny for the civilized world; that has made chattel slavery henceforth impossible anywhere; that has shaken by the simple power of her principles every throne in Europe; that has made a republic certain in Great Britain at no distant day; that is giving a home under her free institutions to the natives of every land, and gathering under her tutelage representatives of every nation and sending them forth with her stamp on them to give her life to the world — may claim without arrogance to be the mightiest nation on the face of the earth. I say that no other nation has so much power in the life of this world to-day as these United States of America.

A hundred years ago and there was but little general education in the world, save in these N. E. colonies. Within this century the boundaries of knowledge have had a marvelous enlargement. The stars have been measured and the mighty movements of the firmament have been discovered. Matter and life have given up their secrets till sometimes it seems as though the gates of the mysterious were to swing wide open and reveal all their treasures to the vision of man.

Now, the mightiest states enforce the education of all their people, the essential equality of all men is seen, and what is known to our highest civilization is soon to be known everywhere.

A hundred years ago despotism prevailed in the world. Chattel slavery, with all its abominations, existed under all governments, and the labor and life of the people were sacrificed to the aggrandizement and luxury of kings and nobles. The young giant of freedom now stalking over the earth and shaking thrones was in the birth throes.

Now slavery is virtually abolished everywhere. The mightiest governments are free, and kings hold only a barren scepter. The people are rising in their majesty with the rising tides of intelligence to their true place.

A hundred years ago and Christianity was confined within narrow limits. Darkness covered the earth, and gross darkness the people. Now the outposts of the church are in all lands, the Bible is known in all human languages, and the onward march of time is pregnant with prophetic voices, saying, "Now is come salvation and strength, and the kingdom of our God, and the power of his Christ."

To come back to our text. How much have this church, and others like it, done in the line of these changes? "Out of Zion the perfection of beauty God hath shined." How much have they done for popular education? General Garfield, in a speech at Williams College at the last commencement, said he was at the Paris Exposition in 1867, and one morning a friend called him out of the building to show him something. Going outside he saw a farmer's house, a cottage, framed in our west, taken across the water, and set up there, and beside it a school-house, and the crowned kings and representatives of the nations were looking at it. It needed but one thing more to represent the trinity of our American life — the *home*, the *church*, the *school-house*. Our fathers built their rude homes, then the church of God, then the school-house, and their children, as they have created new states, have followed their example, only often the school-house has come before the church and served the double purpose.

Popular education is an outgrowth and a necessity of our congregationism. A democratic church, as well as a democratic state, must have an intelligent constituency, and the New England Church inaugurated popular education for the world.

How much have these churches done for freedom? A few weeks since, in the first flush of this summer's verdure, I stood in one of those cities of our patriot dead that are here and there in the South. It was on the bank of a running stream, and was well enclosed, with graded drives and walks, and more than two thousand graves. A thousand flags waved from the head boards, the skies were bright and peaceful, and as the procession filed in, marshaled by the colored police of the city, lately slaves, and a colored band playing the dirges, followed by hundreds of colored citizens, and the children of the schools singing patriotic songs, and scattering with their dusky fingers floral offerings on the graves of the heroes; the scene was both touching and significant. New England first lighted the fires of freedom. New England said the virgin soil of the continent should be free. The place was holy with the dust of the sons and grandsons of New England. New England sent the men and women who opened the mysteries of knowledge to these dark souls, from whose hands New England bravery had wrenched the manacles. And these are but the vanguard of a mighty host, redeemed themselves, and ministers of redemption to a mighty continent soon to stretch out her hands unto God.

The congregational church, arising out of the fires of persecution a free church, gave type to the civil government—*created* the Republic. The leaven of freedom that was in her beginning is fast leavening our humanity. New England saved the Republic in the day of her mortal peril. No thoughtful man who was in the Northwest in the great Rebellion could fail to see that New England principles vitalized those great states, kept them true to loyalty, and sent their armies into the battle fields, over which our flag of victory finally waved in triumph.

How much have these churches done for Christianity? There is a germ of infidelity in every human heart. "The fool hath said in his heart, there is no God." There are two things that are ever alive in the world as antidotes to this: the providential government of God and the church. When I see one who has spent life in the service of an unseen God, trusting in him, when his days of active service are over receiving in ways as unexpected and supernatural as though it had dropped from heaven, the supply of daily want, I cannot be an infidel. Sodom in her day, Jerusalem in her day, Rome in her day, Paris in her day, have proclaimed through the centuries the presence in human affairs of an unseen almighty and all-avenging God.

Men may reason as they please. Darwin, Huxley, Herbert Spencer, Renan. We who have felt the influence of the ministry of Frederick Marsh, and heard Lorrain Loomis and Levi Platt pray, and seen how they lived, and the holy men and women that were around them fifty years ago, cannot be infidels. John Randolph said he should have "been an infidel but for the remembrance of the hour when his mother laid her hand on his head and taught him to say 'Our Father who art in heaven.'" How many of us have felt the same influences. A church with such mothers as we had is impregnable against all the assaults of infidelity. How much have these churches done for missions for the regeneration of the world? I know of no spot where this question could be better answered than in this hill country of Connecticut. Six miles from this spot, eighty-eight years ago, there was born a son to the pastor of a sister church. Grown to manhood, he became the subject of a remarkable religious experience. In one of the most beautiful valleys on the face of the earth, among the majestic hills of Northern Berkshire, in sight of one of our honored colleges, is a park of twenty acres, and a grove and a marble monument, marking the spot where that young man gathered his companions for prayer, and where one day, when they were sheltered from a passing shower by a hay-stack, he first proposed to them to go on a mission to the heathen. He stimulated a missionary spirit everywhere. Samuel John Mills is known through the earth as the father of that mighty missionary movement of modern times which has its home in this country. He it was who said to a friend, "You and I are very little beings, but we can make our influence felt to the ends of the earth," and he did, whether you measure space or time.

Fifty-two years ago, in sight of this ground, two young men were ordained to the missionary work. They were the actors in that marvelous drama of modern times, the creation of a Christian state in those volcanic islands in the Pacific, once peopled by savages. Why were they ordained here? Because this was historic ground. Here Mills was born. Here was the first auxiliary of the American Board. Here was the Foreign Mission School which grew out of the romantic history of the landing of Henry Obookiah on our shores. Here was a group of pastors who were fanning the missionary spirit into a flame, whose glorious brightness fills the land.

The first pastor of this church had a grandson, born just over our border, near the spot where the first settler of the town made his home, who ended a devoted and brilliant, but brief, life as a missionary in Persia.

Has this church done her part in the mighty changes of the century in which her sisters have had so potent an agency. If she has not, her centennial year is not worth celebrating. Samuel J. Mills was not born here. The first missionaries to the Sandwich Islands were ordained at Goshen. The Foreign Mission School was at Cornwall. I do not know that this church has ever sent any of her members to the heathen, though Mr. Daniel H. Austin, who was born here, was a missionary to the Osage Indians, but I do not believe that any pastor ever did more to foster a missionary spirit among his people than Mr. Marsh. I do not believe that any member of any of our churches, that did not go or send a child to the field, ever did more for missions than Deacon Loomis or Deacon Platt. I know that this church has had many members that have been mighty in prayer for the extension of the Kingdom of Christ. I know that she has had a great many sowers and reapers in the great field of the world. A considerable number of ministers have grown up here for come rom families who have emigrated from here. I mention Rev. Noble Everitt of the early days, Rev. David Goodwin, Rev. Eliphaz A. Platt, Rev. George Baldwin, Rev. James R. Coe, of the Episcopal Church.

This church has not been behind in the reformatory movements of the age. When Mr. Marsh came here he found the usual drinking customs, but after the attempt to accept the proffered hospitalities of his people for one or two whole days of pastoral visitation, he told them they need never more offer him any alcoholic drinks, and when the temperance reformation began, he and the leading men, and the great body of the church, came promptly into it, and there they have remained.

If the church did not come into the anti-slavery movement as soon as some others, she was true to freedom and loyalty in our great struggle, and gave of her life for the life of the nation.

I know not how it was with the early pastors of the church, but I know that Mr. Marsh always supervised the schools, as he did every thing else, thoroughly and well, and the church fostered education.

We have sent forth a great many teachers of the young. Fifty years since there was a quiet, silent young man here, who did a great deal to stimulate culture and prepare teachers in all the surrounding country. He fired many a young heart with his own love of learning, and sent many with his own stamp on them to every corner of the land. Only when we fully comprehend that mysterious spiritual thing we call influence, which grows broader and deeper, like the rivers as they near the sea, and lasts through the centuries as the forests that grow from the scattered seed, will it be known what Silas H. McAlpine did for the world. The same influences have been at work since, are at work now here, and I know of no spot more favorable for the training of the young.

And what shall I say of the work of the church in these hundred years in our sainted ones and in ourselves? How many struggling with imperfection and sin have been made meet for heaven? How many have crowned a Christian living with a Christian dying? This air seems to me to be astir with the breath of lives that have been transferred to immortal scenes, and yet are immortal here. Our fathers and mothers, though dead, yet speak. Our dead! Their life was far away from the scenes of excitement that consume us. Engaged in the same round of toil day by day, and year by year, they found their pleasure in their religious life. The Sabbath was to them a day of benedictions. They delighted in prayer. From youth to hoary age they walked with God, and when they came to die, though we saw it not, they saw in the golden sunlight the chariot and horses of fire, and the cloud of glory on which the spirit went up to its home.

We who know something what we owe to a mother's prayers, and who cherish her memory in our heart of hearts, know that she received the secret of her power and drew the inspiration of her life in the church. If there is a God, Infinite, Almighty, and full of love, He has been in the church. If there is a home of goodness, glorious above all description, she has been furnishing residents for it. If you would measure her work you must measure eternity. If you would compute her work you must compute the bliss of heaven.

Let our dead, whom the years one by one have been carrying away to their rest, from their high seats as they wait in their songs to greet us to-day, tell what the church has done. Let the children and grandchildren of the church scattered over the earth, working for our humanity, give in their testimony. Let the unfolding future, the better ages that are coming, reveal it. We commit the question to that eternity which alone can show the boundless wealth of good there is in a true church of the living God!

How shall we greet the new century of our organized life? Will it see as many changes as the buried years? Will it see as many holy lives and as many triumphant deaths as the old? Will it send forth as many sons and daughters to help in the final battles and final victories of truth and righteousness in the world? There have been times when it has seemed that the new agencies would depopulate the hills, and cause some of these old churches to become extinct. Now I have a fancy that the same agencies, bringing these hills with their health-bearing breezes and their summer beauty near the great centers of life, may soon repopulate them, covering them with new homes of beauty and a better culture, making them radiant with new life. May it be as good as the old, and better! The church, fragrant with the memory of our sainted ones, enshrined in the perpetual life of those who have entered into rest, will live and God will live in her. The coming years will take us from this earthly scene. May they take us to the departed, the general assembly and church of the first born!

Let us be glad and rejoice! This world has been waiting long for its king. He who died once is to reign forever, and the mightiest changes are to go on till He comes. The children of men are not always to sit in the region and shadow of death. Poverty, enforced and unrequited toil, ignorance and vice, pestilence and famine, are not to curse the earth forever. Not forever are the nations to seek glory in the destruction of each other. Not forever shall the earth groan beneath the battle of the warrior with confused noise and garments rolled in blood.

> Down the dark future, through long generations,
> The echoing sounds grow fainter and then cease;
> And like a bell with solemn sweet vibrations,
> I hear once more the voice of Christ say peace.

> Peace! and no longer from its brazen portals,
> The blast of war's great organ shakes the skies,
> But beautiful as songs of the Immortals
> The holy melodies of love arise.

The choir then sang the hymn, " Oh, for a thousand tongues to sing," &c.

ADDRESS OF WELCOME BY THERON BRONSON, Esq., PRESIDENT OF THE DAY.

LADIES AND GENTLEMEN:—In assuming the duties assigned me I have but a word to say.

I rejoice at seeing so many familiar faces before me of half a century ago. It calls to mind most vividly many pleasing scenes of our early childhood; and I rejoice at the privilege of tendering to you to-day a most joyous welcome.

Welcome in our hearts; welcome to our homes; enjoy with us this social gathering. And to all the friends who this day honor us with your presence, we bid you a hearty welcome; doubly welcome to the humble entertainment which it is our privilege to offer you.

And to my venerable friend on my right (Deacon Ira Hills), from the State of New York, in behalf of our Reverend Father (Rev. Frederick Marsh), permit me, sir, to extend to you a most joyous greeting; and to you, venerable fathers, whose years reach back almost to the period we this day commemorate, who, under a kind Providence, have stood for so long a period of years as beacon lights, thus uniting the past with the present—and may we not hope with the future, by the *divine permission*, to the completion of a full century — may your *last days* be your *best days;* and as your setting sun shall wane, may your remaining days be as calm, as peaceful, and as joyous as your former ones have been prosperous and victorious; and beyond life's pilgrimage may a glorious immortality be yours.

And now to the young before me :— Permit me to ask where are the fathers and the mothers, that little band of *fourteen*, for the commemoration of whose noble acts of a hundred years ago we are this day assembled? For an answer, go to yonder grave-yard; see there inscribed the names of that immortal band, upon the most unpretending, humble tablets, and that apparently almost by nature's hand. And the question recurs to us, where, at the next centennial, will be every person here assembled to-day? The history of our fathers but too plainly answers. We stand here to-day as did our fathers, occupying the front ranks in the history of the next century. Let me say to these youth, remember that little band; emulate their example; cherish their memory; live lives devoted to usefulness, that unborn generations, whose privilege it shall be to celebrate the next centennial, shall rise up and call you blessed. I doubt not the recollections of to-day will be with you until these hearts shall cease to beat.

The formal exercises of the forenoon were then closed with a benediction by Rev. Frederick Marsh, as follows: May the grace of our Lord Jesus Christ, the love of God the Father, and the communion of the Holy Spirit, be and abide with us now and forever, Amen.

A procession was then formed to visit the locality of the first church, and after returning to the scene of the previous exercises, upon the green in front of the church, a most bountiful collation was partaken, the divine blessing having been first invoked by Rev. Joseph Eldridge, D. D., of Norfolk:

INVOCATION.

Our Father in Heaven, we thank Thee for Thy providential government over the world and for the establishment and preservation of Thy church among men. We thank Thee that Thou didst extend Thy care over those that came to this land and those who have descended from them. We thank Thee for all Thy favor to those who, one hundred years ago, dwelt here; and for all the prosperity and all the blessings conferred upon them and their descendants, and that in circumstances of so much favor we may meet on this beautiful day; and that this day we have been permitted to commemorate their history and derive lessons from their experience and their service, and enter into the blessings that, through Thy grace, they have transmitted to us. We thank Thee for all the blessings of the past and of this occasion. May we deliver the blessings granted to us unimpaired to those who shall come after us, so that when a hundred years have passed away, our descendants may look back towards us as we now look towards those who dwelt here a hundred years ago; through Jesus Christ our Redeemer, Amen.

The collation occupied nearly an hour, and was everywhere praised for its richness and abundance.

AFTERNOON EXERCISES.

The assembly having been called to order by the President of the Day, Rev. Samuel T. Seelye, D. D., of Easthampton, Mass., was introduced, who spoke briefly as follows:

ADDRESS OF Rev. SAMUEL T. SEELYE, D. D., of Easthampton, Mass.

Mr President, Ladies, and Gentlemen :—I have had the pleasure of looking over your programme, and I see you have a very large and rich entertainment provided for the afternoon. I will not, therefore, venture to trespass upon your time, allotted to those who have specially prepared themselves to entertain you. But it requires an effort on this occasion, with so much to inspire one, not to indulge in the luxury of making a speech for I fully enter into sympathy with this occasion, and am glad to see Old Winchester to-day in all her glory. As I was for twenty-five years the minister in an adjoining town, and used to come here occasionally to see you, I am glad to find so many here to-day whom I did not expect to see. High as my opinion was of the good people of Winchester, I must say I did not know you could do as well as you have done to-day; and I am glad to be here. I can say this with special unction and force after the grand collation you have provided. And if everybody, and more too, is not satisfied, it is not the fault of the good people of Winchester; and what the speakers are to do after having eaten so much just now, I do not know.

While I rejoice to be here on this grand occasion, and feel the inspiration which stirs all your hearts, I am especially glad to see here my honored Father Marsh; and in fact I came to Winchester expressly to see him and take him by the hand. I never shall forget him; for although my relations with my brethren with whom I associated in Litchfield county were always pleasant and profitable, no man did so much for my good, by his example and teaching, and the influence which I felt coming from him, as Father Marsh. I shall never forget his kindness at my examination, when theological controversies were more in vogue than to-day, and how Father Marsh poured oil upon the waters; and he has always been a peace-maker, not given to strife. I have honored him for the way in which he has lived, for the example he has set his brethren in the ministry; and I am sorry, for one, that I have come so far short. But that is not his fault; his light has been shining steadily all the time.

One thing I know of him that perhaps many of you do not, and which has been of great service to me. You know what Father Marsh's estate has been; how many acres of land; how large an income he has had. He said to me years ago, that notwithstanding his wants might be ever so pressing, he always had the Lord's drawer in which was something, though not very much, which he consecrated to the Lord, and which he used for benevolent purposes. He said that more than twenty years ago. That has remained in my heart and influenced me as much as any one thing I ever heard. And I bless God for that example, and for that evidence of the consecration of property and all that he had to God and His service. And I have tried to do my duty better and be more liberal and more generous, because of my reverend father.

But Father Marsh is not perfect. There was one thing that I heard long ago that was a comfort, one thing that showed he had our weak, human nature; and to a man who is as great a sinner as I am, that is a comfort. But I never heard that Father Marsh came short and came to a dead halt, and lost his faith in his Christian principles but once. A good lady in Wolcottville related this, and said she never knew but one bad thing of Father Marsh; that on one occasion, when his good wife presented him with a pair of twins, the good man was overcome. (Laughter.) That was the only time when his faith was staggered. (Renewed laughter.) But that did not last long: he soon got over that. I told the lady, my informant, that probably the tears shed, if any, were tears of joy, because the blessings God sent him were so much more abundant than he expected. (Continued laughter.)

I could say much more to show my appreciation of Father Marsh, but I can simply express the hope that God may keep him to his hundredth year and more to bless us and our children, if we are so fortunate as to have children. (Applause.)

ADDRESS BY REV. ARTHUR GOODENOUGH.

It is thought proper that I should say a few words on this occasion, not because it was thought I have anything to say to this audience that may be especially interesting, but to show that the church in Winchester has a pastor, and I come forward on this occasion to make that announcement.

Our chairman has already extended to you a cordial welcome here, and in the words that he has used I have no doubt he expressed the sentiments of this entire community. I can but repeat that we are glad to see you here to-day, that we sincerely hope that nothing has occurred or will occur to mar the joy of this occasion.

As we recall the events of our local history for the past hundred years, we value that history not alone for the fathers' sake, not alone for the sacred influence which it throws around our homes to-day, we value it for the bond by which it unites so many loving hearts, separated so far and wide, with a common love of these old memories. The fact that I, a stranger to most of you, assume to welcome you on this occasion, shows to many of you undoubtedly that your childhood's home is not in all respects what you once knew it; that changes are taking place. I myself have known something of the sadness that comes from a consciousness of a past, that will not and cannot join hands with the present, and I sincerely hope that none of you will experience changes to-day that will cause sadness as you visit these old familiar places. Surely the rocks, and the hills, and lakes are ready to welcome you with a glad smile of recognition, and if many well known faces have passed away, and others have changed almost beyond the power of recognition, yet we believe that the spirit of the elder times has not departed, even the spirit of the fathers. The spirit that wrought in and with the fathers abides to-day where they dwelt, and will not let us forget them, but pointing to their foot-marks will say to generations yet unborn, "This is the way, walk ye in it."

And now that myself and others enter into your places, we do not come so much to be agents of change as we come to learn the lessons which these grand hills, with their hallowed memories, may teach, and to enter into possession of the influences which the lives of good men and women in the past have established here.

It is not right that I should intrude myself too long upon your attention, or interrupt the greetings more appropriate to this occasion. We have the evidence before us, not merely in historical statements of what has been here, but in the living examples, in the institutions, the church, the schools, the homes, and the scenes which the Great Creator calls upon us to admire, that these have not been in vain. Poets are born here ; they learn to think here. They may go away from us to the crowded city, to the din and hum of busy life; but they are born here. Such men cannot be born in the great Babylons, and we are thankful that they delight to return to us and lay their garlands of triumph before our feet. I do not intend to try to prove it by any arguments of mine, but we shall prove it in a better way, and I shall now introduce to you the poet of the day, Dr. W. J. Wetmore. But I would not have you think we bring forward all our poets to-day. Those of you who know the place know something of what we can do in this direction. I know it was said of an old Greek who had a house to dispose of, that since he could not carry around the house to show he took a brick of the same material as that with which the house was constructed as a specimen, and desired the people to look at it. We bring you now our chosen poet, only as a specimen brick. (Laughter and applause.)

CENTENNIAL CELEBRATION.

POEM BY WM. J. WETMORE, M. D., New York City.

Kindred and friends, why are we met together
Within this tent this lovely summer weather?
Why gather here on this delightful day,
To pass a few reflective hours away?
'Tis not to boast of martial conquest here,
Bought at the price of blood that costs so dear,
But 'tis the song of peace that floats around,
And where we stand seems consecrated ground.
Here did our fathers their first altar raise,
Where hearts sincere could join in prayer and praise;
Here they first met, their pious zeal to show,
Their trust in God a hundred years ago.

A hundred years ago! from thence we date
The birth of this old town, so fixed by fate,
When law and order over chaos reigned,
And with increasing age new vigor gained.
Young hearts, strong arms, here strove with fresh delight,
When rising beauties cheered the welcome sight;
Bright dwellings rose to glad the traveler's way,
Though Winter frowned, or smiled the flowery May.

A hundred years ago! like swallows on the wing
Come floating back loved scenes of boyhood's Spring;
And forms and faces seem to gather here,
Long since departed, but forever dear;
Here on these rugged hills, with artless grace,
Our fathers lived and toiled, a sturdy race;
They tilled the soil so rough in its repose,
And made the fields to blossom like the rose.
Among the many well-tilled farms I see,
With rock and hillside, meadow, brook, and tree;
One with its fond associations well I know,
My grandsire's home a hundred years ago:
Though somewhat changed with steady lapse of time,
'Tis much the same as when in early prime;
The old domain, some buildings yet the same,
And dearer still, my old ancestral name.
These still remain a pleasure and a joy,
And make me almost feel again a boy;
These add a priceless value to the place
Of one's own birth, his kindred and his race.

The church our fathers reared beneath the hill,
The first, though humble, had its comforts still:
From summer's heat and winter's piercing cold,
It shielded both the shepherd and his fold:
And though the tempest scowled along the sky,
O'er those true hearts the storm swept harmless by:
But soon that little church proved far too small,

To hold the crowd within its narrow hall,
When farther north a better site was found,
To rear a shrine where faith might more abound:
Our ancient fathers planned with cunning skill,
Another church with zealous hands and will,
When soon a beauteous temple rose to view,
Where faith might light her vestal flame anew:
There oft the faithful worshipers repaired,
And all its blessings, all its comforts shared.
The saintly Knapp there ministered awhile,
And Bogue with pleasant voice and winning smile;
Then Marsh new courage, new existence gave
To fainting hearts, and made the thoughtless grave.
To him a debt of gratitude I owe,
For favors past, for kindness long ago:
With him I studied first the poet's art,
When Virgil's lines I scanned and learned by heart;
And as the days sped happily along,
I loved the teacher and the poet's song.

But time rolls on and other change takes place,
That church is gone, and strange seems every face;
The dear old congregation is no more,
The sweet old songs that pleased so well are o'er;
And those we knew and met from day to day,
Are now in other lands far, far away,
Or down on Burial Hill, cold, slumbering clay!
Sleep on, belovèd dust! till that blest morn arise,
To waft your souls, redeemed, beyond the skies:
Where kindred spirits in reunion sweet,
In bliss immortal shall each other greet:
May none be lost, but all through grace and love,
Meet their kind Father God, in realms above!

But, dear old town! you've had your joys and cares,
Your men severe, your wit that never spares:
And as we feared the one, we loved the other,
And laughed to hear their jokes of one another.
One man I knew, whose heart seemed e'er inclined
To call men fools or ignorantly blind,
Who dared to say this globe did not stand still,
And sun and moon rolled through the sky at will;
For, if the world turned over, on his head
He sure must stand or tumble out of bed:
Long Lake, alas! its oozy bed must leave,
And thirsty turtles for lost waters grieve;
The perch and pickerel mourn the absent flood,
And eels and bullheads flounder in the mud,
But this was only one particular CASE,
The last, if I mistake not, of his race.

Another, skilled in mythologic lore,
Brought spirits forth at will, from Stygean shore;
Old Pluto's realms he studied well, by heart,
And knew each god and goddess on the chart;
And while he read and learned their wondrous power,
He sought the graces in their native bower;
But oft like Orpheus mourned with unfeigned woe,
His fair Eurydice in shades below.
The planets, too, that glittered in the sky,
Their names he called as each one met his eye:
And in their course astrology sublime
Rang on his heart its planetary chime.
His home was humble, but his heart sincere,
And what he lacked in wealth made up in cheer:
Indeed, the Dugway would have been forgot,
But Alvord's name immortalized the spot.

O'er these old hills my footsteps oft have strayed,
Where I, with youthful friends, delighted played;
Their names on memory's tablet brightly shine,
And fleeting time but makes them more divine:
Oh Beebe! how I loved your generous heart,
Devoid of guile or hypocritic art:
But ever true and faithful to defend
From envy's spite misfortune or a friend.
And other names I dearly, fondly trace,
With joy recall each pleasant, smiling face;
The Blakes, the Hubbells, and the Coits appear,
With Hurlbuts, Marshes, and McAlpines dear;
Wade, Nash, and Bronson in our circle shine,
While Platt and Hoyt to sanctity incline;
Chase, Goodwin, Murray put the blues to flight,
While Hills and Benedict gave fresh delight;
Miner and Clarke, as ancient dates will show,
Here pitched their tents a hundred years ago.
Everitt and Brooks in youth we often met,
Nor can we ancient Chamberlain forget!
Who built his home upon the coldest hill,—
(I wonder if that *old* house stands there still!)
Andrews and Loomis, kindly and sincere,
Like Hatch and Adams, left their impress here;
Humphrey and Riggs, both noblemen and peers,
Their names shall live along the flight of years.
But why recall the varied names of old,
Their life's career is briefly, quickly told;
Stern in their duty—honesty their pride,
They lived respected, and lamented died.
These were the good old times, when virtue shone,
And men had merits honestly their own;
Though Joel Beach and Lent Mott wake a smile,
Blue street without them would been bluer still:

So many a visage with expression droll,
Provokes a smile we scarcely can control:
Even now we see them dance before the eyes,
A motley crowd of every form and guise:
The Prestons, Jacklins, Ellwells now appear,
With Gurdon Root, the pundit and the seer;
While Church and Tucker gave peculiar grace
To every spot where'er they showed their face:
Around the Little Pond the chattering jays
Made Rattling Valley vocal with their lays;
While Beckley whistled as he trudged along,
And charmed the wood nymphs with his rustic song.
But let us not forget one hero brave,
Who fought and bled, his country's life to save;
His name was Leach — his fame we all well know
As warlike scars he proudly loved to show:
Gained, as he said, on bloody fields of strife,
Where many times he died — then came to life,
To fight again till legions ran away,
And left him victor, hero of the day:
But spare the muse — this record nobly won,
Was blasting rocks from morn till set of sun;
Blown out of wells and hurled from many a rock,
He fell, at last, reduced by nature's shock:
Brave soldier, let him rest, life's toils are o'er,
He'll blast out rocks, and battles fight no more.

But what a change! few spirits yet remain,
Few living links in memory's golden chain;
Loved scenes and places change as time rolls on,
Men tread life's stage, the actors soon are gone;
But here again they pass in swift review,
And smiles and tears alternate rise anew:
And though again these scenes theatric glow,
Time's curtain soon will fall on all below,
Death soon will bring life's drama to a close,
The final exit to earth's joys and woes.
Change comes to every circle here on earth,
And fond affection mourns departed worth;
That dear old home so cherished in my youth,
Still calls me back in tenderness and truth:
For there my father, mother lived and died,—
They watched my youth with all a parent's pride:
But now the town to me deserted seems,
And pleasures past appear but idle dreams.
My playmates scattered, once a numerous band,
While here, returned, almost alone I stand,
Reviewing days and years forever past,
Too bright for earth, too beautiful to last.

CENTENNIAL CELEBRATION. 559

Life is a dream, the story of a day,
A flower that blooms to perish and decay,
But as our friendship on love's altar burns,
Youth with its pictured memories returns:
And as we view each well-remembered place,
We see reflected many a welcome face,
That brings up joys and pleasures once so dear,
That had remained forgotten many a year.

The Lake where summer days I loved to float
With friends delighted in our uncouth boat,
I now recall, while youth and pleasure beam,
The brightest jewels in a poet's dream.
O, lovely lake! no fairer waters shine,
No wave reflects a brighter sheen than thine;
No other lake a purer wave can show,
No brighter skies above their waters glow.
Although unsung, still round thy rocky shore,
Those old-time songs seem sounding evermore:
On every breeze they fondly, sweetly swell,
The dear old songs we loved in youth so well;
They tell of days departed, hopes and fears,
That floated off with swiftly fleeting years;
But now return on echo's airy wing,
Like Heaven's own doves that bring perennial Spring.
The heart seems touched as by some magic spell,
A pensive charm that makes the bosom swell
With fond emotion as those scenes appear
With spirits of the past now gathered here;
Not e'en the gondolettas of Italian seas
Charm with a cadence half so sweet as these.
They 're deathless as the music of thy waves,
That seems to rise from out thy hidden caves;
Far down beneath the watery depths below,
Where Naiads dwell and glittering jewels glow,
Where elfins gather—then at evening glide,
In songs and dances o'er thy rippling tide.

Turn from this picture in antique repose,
Another still upon the canvass glows;
O! Winsted, 'tis of thee I fondly sing,
And to thy shrine my humble offering bring;
A few short years have scarcely rolled away,
Since dwellings plain along Mad River lay;
A humble village one would scarcely note,
A hamlet, far from busy life remote;
But now a city rears its strength so great,
It wields a telling power throughout the State;
There toil and labor their best trophies bring,
While listening ears hear numerous anvils ring;
Sloth cannot find a single foot-hold there,
But every soul its bounteous wealth can share;

Though mountains darkly frown on either side,
And brawling streamlets through the meadows glide ;
There strength and beauty hand in hand repair,
And each their several burdens freely bear.
The church with open doors invites to peace,
And bids our worldly cares and sorrows cease ;
There law in justice's scales impartial weighs
The felon's crimes — the penalty he pays ;
And to the mind diseased or body frail,
There Esculapean skill should never fail.
The Press, that source of intellectual light,
The news of nations spreads before the sight ;
It comes from North and South, from East and West,
The "WINSTED HERALD" proves a welcome guest ;
Such, such is Winsted now, and still apace,
It grows and thrives in every art and grace:
Its schools well taught, its teachers full of zeal,
Fit men for business and the public weal ;
Indeed, in every part, on every hand,
It seems the smiling Auburn of our land.

Who cannot call to mind the crazy mill,
Hard by Long Lake that overtopped the hill ;
Where grain was taken and where grists were ground,
And with revolving wheels the jest went round ?
There Skinner reigned, the genius of the place,
And honest merit marked his genial face ;
Down that steep hill I've journeyed many a time,
And stopped to hear the distant belfrey's chime.
I scarcely dreamed that at some distant day,
The men so oft I met could pass away,
So noble, generous, and so good were they.
That Rockwell, Hinsdale, Wakefield, Boyd, and Coe,
Could join the army of a hundred years ago,
But still those old and honored names remain,
To show those pioneers lived not in vain.

But Winchester, thou'rt like a parent old,
Whose strength has failed, whose heart seems dull and cold ;
Who grieves that sturdy manhood cannot last,
And now sits mourning over glories past.

But such is life — in youth we're filled with mirth
And scarcely feel how much our being's worth :
But time rolls on — old landmarks pass away,
And joys, like short-lived blossoms, soon decay ;
We could not dream in youth it could be so,
Of change so great since fifty years ago :
But when around these dear old hills I roam,
I stop and ask — " Where is my dear old home ? "
The pleasant faces that I used to meet,
And talk and chat in accents fondly sweet ;

They're gone forever—every well-known face,
And desolation marks each favorite place;
Still, few I greet, as friends I knew of yore,
But seldom seen,—perhaps to see no more!
But when our days are ended here below,
And eyes that shone have lost their cheerful glow;
Though through life's struggle souls seem tempest-tost,
May all a haven reach, no spirit lost;
But all redeemed, and through a Savior's love,
Meet with our dearest friends in realms above;
Where every heart a record pure can show,
To join our fathers of a hundred years ago;
And when another hundred years shall glide,
Down time's swift current, time's returnless tide,
And other lips shall talk of dear ones fled,
Oh! may they pay one tribute to the dead:
Breathe one short prayer for those who've gone before,
And now lie sleeping on death's silent shore:
Remember those in life from far and near,
The friends and kindred loved now gathered here;
And while our hearts with grateful memory's swell,
To one and all I bid a kind farewell.

The reading of the poem was followed by singing by the choir, "Blow ye the trumpet, blow," &c.

Rev. Arthur Goodenough.—We have been talking a good deal about ourselves to-day. I suppose it is proper for the most modest people to be guilty once in a while of a little glorification of themselves. I have not heard anything about our family to-day. But in the changes of these hundred years we have had a little daughter; at least she seems to be a little daughter, now growing up and settled down in a little obscure valley, out of the way, in a place we call Winsted. After being prosperous there a little while she had another daughter, that seems to be coming up a lively sort of a girl, and has come and settled a little nearer to her old grandmother. We think they are rather promising girls, and we want to give them a chance to talk a little while now. They cannot tell much; they have not lived long enough. Perhaps they think they know almost as much as this grandmother. But I hope they will be wiser, and grow in grace. But we will not talk much about them; they are able to speak for themselves.

RESPONSE BY DEACON ELIAS E GILMAN, of the First Congregational Church, Winsted.

As allusion has been made by the last speaker to having a daughter residing in an adjacent valley, and as the pastor of the church residing in that village is absent for his vacation, it becomes me, as senior deacon of that church, to respond.

I am happy, in behalf of that church, to return our thanks to the parent church for the kindness and sympathy which they have this day and ever before exhibited towards that daughter, planted in that "obscure" village. But I will just say that the church formed from this parent stock was organized in 1784, as the records show.

The first member was John Balcom, senior. Eight hundred and thirty-six (836) additions have been made to the church. At the present time there are about one hundred and eighty (180) members belonging to it. And we think, as young people are apt to think at the present day, that our grandsires did not know but a little; but still we look upon the parent church with interest and affection, and think they are what they have always manifested themselves towards us, our faithful friends, and when Father Marsh comes over to speak to us we hear him with rejoicing hearts, and we look back to-day with thankfulness that he has been spared so long, and is now permitted to participate in this centennial celebration. If our church is spared to see its hundredth year, we hope Father Marsh may also be spared to celebrate it with us.

RESPONSE BY REV. CHARLES WETHERBY, Pastor of the Second Congregational Church, West Winsted.

I was married to this granddaughter of this church some five years ago, and she has made me on the whole, with a little trouble now and then, a pretty good wife. I have passed a great many pleasant days with her, and hope to a great many more. But, as the representative of the Second Congregational Church in Winsted, I come here before this grandmother to stand before this church that has carried my own in her heart's love, with something of the feeling of the college boy when returning from college days and college scenes, he comes to the old farmhouse and homestead. As I look upon the brain and brawn that have given strength and nerve and energy to the boy, so do I feel that the virtue, and power, and strength of the Winsted Churches is the result of the culture, influence, and power that has been bestowed upon them from these old hills.

I come here to the grandmother church to preach once in a while, and as I listen to her praises to-day, and have done before, I feel that there is a great power in these old churches; their influence has been a great power. And we send back greetings from Winsted to this old church on the hill for the piety she has endeavored to stamp upon the heart of her descendants. We send back greetings to the old church for the loving care with which she has watched over our tender years; we send back greetings for all the New England purity and New England principle that she has sent out all over the land. I have seen men here to-day from the west, from New York, and from many places abroad. I have taken hold of the hands of those who have passed from you and taken up their abode in far off states, and they come back here, and I see as I look in your faces that the faces of the ladies are all beautiful, and those of the men all full of strength and power, and the recollection crowds upon me that such as these have planted New England institutions, and the New England churches, and I am thankful to God, who cares for all and watches over all, that he has reared up here on these hills such a power and such an influence to go abroad into all the land.

I suppose it is true, as the speaker who introduced us said, that the grandmother thinks she knows a little more than we do who live in the humble valley. She has reason to think so, for in the first place she is up the highest in the world; I think she is eight or nine hundred feet above us, and that is a great deal we find when we come up here to pay her a visit. I know a little boy who stood up by the side of his father to measure his height, and he said, "Papa, I shall be bigger than you are by and bye." But we never expect, grandmother, that we shall be able to lift ourselves up to be high as you are. You are nine hundred feet above us, and you always will be. (Laughter).

I was thinking this morning, as I listened to that excellent address, how much of the history of these towns never will be told. After all the eloquent account we had to-day, the real struggles, the real triumphs, and real conquests of the fathers and the mothers who planted themselves a hundred years ago along these hills will never be told. But when those men came from Hartford to settle Winchester, and when the men from Winchester went forth to settle other places, they all carried the church and the school with them; they carried sobriety of character, temperance, a sabbath-keeping spirit, a home spirit, a law-abiding spirit; they carried a large-hearted, sanctified spirit wherever they went. When we hear about new settlements in the west now, we expect to hear a good deal about whiskey saloons, about riotous proceedings generally, about western roughness; a great deal about law-breaking, and a great deal about those activities and sentiments that are not brought under the restraint of principle and duty. And the question by contrast comes back, why do we not expect to hear of such things in the old New England settlements? It is because every New England town, when it planted itself on these high hills, where the free air is playing ever, and where the sun is shining brightly ever, planted also the church; and the sound of the sabbath bell, the sabbath song, and sabbath prayer went forth, reminding men of immortality.

Oh, friends, let us thank God to-day, on this centennial occasion, for the fathers' prayers, the fathers' faith, and the fathers' hope; and God grant that the churches you have planted down in the valley of Winsted, down where the streams are flowing, and where the workmen are so busy; where the sound of the hammer is heard all day long. Oh, may God grant that as those churches grow strong — as they are growing strong in numbers — they shall have all the love, all the purity, all that moral power, and all that sublime devotion to principle and duty which sustained the fathers when they planted, on this free New England soil, "a church without a bishop, and a state without a king," but a land governed by God.

Music by the band.

Rev. Joseph Eldridge, D.D., of Norfolk, was then introduced, and spoke substantially as follows:—

ADDRESS OF REV. JOSEPH ELDRIDGE, D.D.

Mr. President, I should not presume to appear before such an audience as this without more preparation than it has been in my power to make, were not the circumstances such as they are. I arrived home last evening, and received a notice of this meeting, and found my name down on the programme. But I am very happy to learn that it has been removed. Still, I have been called upon to say something, and I present myself before you, somewhat as the pastor of this church said he did, merely to go through with the motions of appearing before you.

If I recollect what the programme calls for, I am to speak somewhat in reference to the pastors of this church. My memory does not go back of the ministry of our venerable father, whose presence cheers us this day. Forty years ago, the 25th of next April, was the day on which I first saw Reverend Frederick Marsh. He was then present, and took part in my examination, and in my ordination and installation over the parish where I have remained since that day. And, perhaps, as my recollection goes back to this period, it might be interesting for you to know something about the ministers at that time in this region, and the state of feeling that existed during that period on various subjects.

We are sometimes disposed, and especially men who have reached my time of life, to look back and think that every thing that is past is preferable to any thing now in existence. There was a state of things just about that time, in reference to points of doctrine, that was exceedingly exciting. It was in the midst of one of the most bitter theological controversies that has existed in this state when I was settled. And after my settlement, when ministers met for the purpose of examining a candidate, the great point was to ascertain not how much he knew on subjects in general, but what were his particular ideas on special points which were then in discussion, and as Mr.

Marsh comes in somewhat in that matter in a particular way that will strike you as an illustration of the state of feeling, I will relate an anecdote in regard to an event in which I took a part.

At that time it was not unfrequent that ministers had what they called Four Days Meetings, during which they invited the neighboring clergymen to assist them, as the case might seem to require. One of the ministers in one of these churches had had such a series of meetings on a certain occasion, and invited me to come and preach a sermon. It was in the spring of the year, and the mud was very deep, and I was a little late in reaching the place. I was to be there to preach in the afternoon. When I reached the church, the exercises of a preliminary nature had been gone through with, and the clergyman was just about to give out the hymn before the sermon, so that I had only an opportunity of showing him what sermons I had, of mentioning their texts, and giving a sort of statement of the points in each of them. I asked him, knowing as he did the state of the congregation, to mention that which he thought would be most appropriate. Just at that time the door opened, and our reverend friend, Mr. Marsh, entered, and walked, in his meek, humble way up the aisle, and took his seat in one of the pews. Then the clergyman said to me, selecting a particular sermon, "preach that; that will cut up Brother Marsh." (Laughter). That man twisted up his Taylorism so strongly that it fairly kinked.

On another occasion—to show you to what extremes he had carried his views—I had been with him two days, preaching in a parish near by, and it so happened that he was to preach the final sermon. It was one of those parishes that did not entirely sympathise with him in his peculiar ideas on the subjects then in controversy. But the pastor of that church was a magnanimous man, and although he attached some importance to these points of difference, he still was willing to have his brethren around him supply his place occasionally. There was some feeling in the congregation, as the result of the two days' service which we had previously had. My brother, who was my colleague, and was to preach the last sermon, chose for his text, "Make yourselves a new heart," and his doctrine was, the duty of man to regenerate himself, a result that could only be applied to those who are self-made. Though the thoughts presented were to a certain extent true, yet the idea of a man regenerating himself could apply only to the man who could make himself. I bring up these cases to show the extremes to which the feelings were carried at that time. Happily, I think, without any relinquishment of sound views on that and kindred topics, that state of feeling has passed away; and although I have lived to see a great many generations of ministers all around me, and to regret the removal of those who have preceded me, by death or otherwise, yet I am delighted with the class of young ministers that now surround me. I love them; but while I love them well, I do not forget the old ministers. I do not forget Father Beach; I do not forget Mr. Prentice, Mr. Perry, and Dr. Lathrop; I do not forget any of that class of men who have passed away. They were good men.

But we had great times in those days as to our incomes. I think, if I recollect right, my reverend friend (Mr. Marsh) during the whole of his ministry never received more than $430 per annum. Whatever he has done for this church, whatever he has done for this community, whatever he has done for the world, he has received as a pecuniary compensation for it, while he did receive anything, $430 per annum! I think my brother Beach, in that flourishing village, received $500. But one of my parishioners said they meant to have me have a fat salary, and that should be $650, and it was that for a long series of years. So we had great times in those days as to tmaking money and getting rich!

But there is one thing that I ought to notice. A great deal has been said, and justly said, with which I entirely sympathise, in commendation of my venerable and

long-tried friend, Mr. Marsh. His influence over his brethren, as one of them has already testified, has been silent, modest, not obtrusive; not so much that of great intellectual power as of sincerity, truth, self-sacrifice, and unfeigned devotion. No jealousy in his mind of his brethren if they had gifts; no jealousy of their reputation if they acquired it; no jealousy of their influence, but delighted by it, wherever it was manifesting itself.

One other thing I may notice, unless I exceed my time. It is said, and I do not know but it is true, for I never have had any experience of the kind myself, that an ex-minister, residing in the place where he has been a pastor, is likely to be — and often proves — one of the most uncomfortable of parishioners that it is possible to find. My venerable friend has been an ex-minister longer and sooner perhaps than he ought to have been, but I will not insist on that. But in all that time he has never in any instance exerted a disturbing influence on the congregation. He never has been otherwise than willing to become small and to retire, while his successor came forward and occupied the place that he had filled so long. I think this is a great test of character, for if we have had influence in a community it is with difficulty that we consent to relinquish our position.

But I fear if I proceed further on this theme I shall exceed my time and abuse your patience. I wish simply to say that I also feel that the influence of our venerable friend has been good over me, and I thank God that He has lengthened his days for this very purpose, that he might exhibit these beautiful traits as the fruits of that gospel which he has preached so long and so successfully. I love him, and he loves me, and we cheer each other; but, as I said, I love all the young ministers too. I feel almost as though I was young, although they begin to tell me that I am old.

The choir then sang the hymn, "All hail the power of Jesus' name," &c.

Mr. Coridon A. Alvord, of Hartford, was next introduced, and spoke as follows :—

Mr. Chairman :—I did not expect this honor, and am therefore quite unprepared to respond satisfactorily; and yet the occasion, the old friends I see before me, and the feeling of love for the dear old town, ever active in my mind, combine and impel me to say a few words. Forty years ago I was a Printer's Devil,—a harmless Imp, I trust, but still a Devil. While in that form, C. W. Everest, having some knowledge of the Typographic Art, labored a few hours every day in the regions where I was Imp, for the purpose of obtaining means wherewith to pay his board while obtaining an education, for verily, like every other genius, he was poor. C. W. E. was fond of music, was a Poet, and a candidate for the ministry, and with all these inspirations in his soul, he often encouraged our "Quartette Club," which never existed except when "P. C." was out of the office, ("P. C." was our master,) to sing sentimental songs. Eventually our store became exhausted, and we produced the only one we had left, the air of which pleased him very much, but he was not satisfied with the words. The next morning he took from his pocket an original manuscript which he had composed the previous evening, and requested us to sing it to the old air he loved so well; and as it seems so fitting to the present occasion, I will recite it, for we subsequently sang it to him so frequently that I shall never forget it.

The friends we loved in childhood,
  Oh whither have they fled?
Beneath the village church yard
  They slumber with the dead.
In peace they rest beneath the sod,
  Their earthly labors o'er;
The friends we loved in early youth
  We meet on earth no more.

The friends we loved in childhood,
  When life was young and gay,
How blithesome were their footsteps
  Throughout the joyous day;
And lightly tripped their merry feet
  Across the flowery plain,
But the friends we loved in early youth
  We ne'er shall meet again.

The friends we loved in childhood,
  How fond their memory seems;
They haunt us in our slumbers,
  They whisper in our dreams;
And then we wake with saddened heart
  To find our bliss but vain,
For the friends we loved in early youth
  We ne'er shall meet again.

The friends we loved in childhood,
  Oh peaceful be their rest;
And green may be the willow
  That sighs above their breast,
And when in death we lowly sleep,
  Secure from all our pain,
Oh the friends we loved in early youth
  May we meet in peace again.

Most good landscape paintings have their shades, shadows, and perspective,—their high lights, and their deep shadows. I have given you the shady part first. It may not be agreeable, but it is full of rich color, and is an excellent study. Now, look this way and see how beautifully the light breaks in upon it from beyond McAlpine's hill, and there we see several of those nice little girls who, not *very* long ago, tripped merrily with us "across the flowery plain," over the hills, and through the woods, in pursuit of blackberries, partridge berries, chestnuts, pleasure, and health, in all the simplicity of innocence and co fidence; studied the dreaded lessons with us at school, rode down the steep hills with us on our hand sleds, and husked corn with us at the evening gathering in the well filled old brown barn, and were not afraid to laugh when a red ear came to their hand, though they fully understood its tremendous consequences. They are here in goodly numbers; a little more mature, indeed, but still essentially the same. And here again is a motley group of those barefooted, earnest looking little boys, fresh from the pasture, the field and the garden, who never liked to rake after the cart when father or the hired man wielded the pitchfork, especially if hurried by the approach of a shower, and somehow or other father always seemed to fancy that there *was* a shower coming up when we were getting in hay. But those boys did like to get their task finished and then go down to the brook, or over to the pond, and catch a good string of fish. The Sunday School is prominent here in the foreground, and just there to the left is the Singing School, with the Pitch Pipe in the hand of a very short, pleasant looking man, and a reasonable sized violoncello in front of a still pleasanter and younger man, who strikingly resembles a prominent musical one upon the present stage. It seems to me that I can see in that smoke a pleasant afternoon tea party of old ladies, with their bright knitting needles snapping away in an animated style, and we can almost hear them gossiping, but not really slandering anybody very much; and there is surely an accidental evening gathering of men at a neighbor's house, with the ever-present dish of apples and pitcher of cider upon the table, and we can imagine them discussing politics, breaking roads, and giving the Minister a "spell."

Far back in the dim distance we can discern men riding to meeting on horseback, each with a woman behind him on a pillion, for wagons are scarce, the roads are rough, and go straight from point to point over the tops of the highest hills, with thick forests on every hand, and occasionally a black bear and a brown Indian from the thicket glare at them as they pass quietly along, but do not molest them, for these are days of wonderful advancement and civilization as compared with the wilder ones immediately preceding. That is one hundred years ago, and a choice and cherished few present have been *almost* to the threshold of that enchanted castle, but not one can really say that he saw it, though he remembers many who resided within its walls; yet we all contribute ourselves and our lives to make up portions of this plain picture of the past.

And now turn we to the right, and just square before us opens another picture, more brilliant, more beautiful, and much more agreeable to contemplate, because so much of it is illumined with the high lights of the hopeful future. See how broad and even all the roads are, and with what graceful curves and easy grades they wind around those beautiful elevations, which in the other picture seemed such ugly hills, because presenting so sharp an obstacle to progress. See those open, airy, gorgeous carriages, each containing from six to ten persons, as elegantly dressed as their carriages are ornamented, and unconcernedly moving on over this once rough country, at the comfortable rate of sixty miles an hour, impelled by that element once so much feared and so little understood, but now the faithful, powerful, humble servant of enlightened man, electricity. Those are all our own descendants, and I believe they are going to the renowned city of Winsted, to celebrate the bi-centennial of their native town, and rehearse, with occasional touches of affectionate derision the stupid customs of their savage ancestors, when none but men made the laws, while women cooked the food and took special care of the young, and, absurd as it may seem, many will believe it.

I believe my time has expired, and I will take my seat.

Music by the band.

DEACON ABEL S. WETMORE then briefly related a few anecdotes illustrative of the character and habits of the people of the earlier days of the town, and began by a reference to two former deacons of the church, who were spoken of in the address of the morning as being very pious and godly men—namely, Deacon Seth Hills and Deacon Samuel Wetmore, who were said to occupy together the front seat before the pulpit, and to love each other very much. But on one occasion they had such a dispute about the sawing of some logs, at the mill of Deacon Wetmore, as to prove they still had a little human nature about them; but after some sharp words they retired to a thicket near the mill, and doubtless became completely reconciled by mutual confession and forgiveness, as they came out with shining faces, and never gave any occasion in the future for doubt as to their genuine regard for each other.

The real origin of the name of Blue street was from a sort of agreement made among the settlers in that street, amounting to a regular code of laws. One rule was that every man must have his wood pile cut out by such a day in Spring, and every man must have his grain threshed out by a certain date. One man by the name of Beach failed to come up in this respect to the rule, and one very dark night the rest of the neighbors got into the barn and took positions on the floor so that they would not beat each other, and began threshing the grain with all their might. They waked up the old gentleman and his wife, and after some hesitation the two started for the barn to see what was going on there. The old gentleman took his lantern, but the men in the barn being in the dark, when they saw the light shining through the cracks of the barn became still as mice, except to keep the threshing going. This so frightened the old man that he went back and told his wife he believed there was "some evil design if not evil spirits out there."

There was a man living in the centre by the name of Theodore Goodwin, a very benevolent man to all the poor, though not a professor of religion. Uncle Jed. Coe lived about three-fourths of a mile north. He was in moderate circumstances, and was preparing to move to Vermont. Mr. Goodwin took it into his head to collect some money to help neighbor Coe. He went down to Mr. Beach to get some money, and took another man to go in with him to see how he succeeded in getting a subscription. On going in Mr. Goodwin said, " How do you do, Mr. Beach ?" " Pretty well ; how do you do, Mr. Goodwin ?" Said he, " This gentleman and I have had a little discussion about a certain passage in Scripture. The passage is, ' Cast thy bread upon the waters, and thou shalt find it after many days.' What does that mean ?" Says Uncle Joel (Mr. Beach) : " I am pretty ignorant, but I suppose it means that if you don't give when any body wants help you will be a covetous old hunk." Says Uncle Theodore Goodwin, 'I vow that's just as I thought, exactly. I am doing something for Mr. Coe, and I came in to see what you would do for him ! " Mr. Beach drew out a quarter of a dollar and said, " Mr. Goodwin, I wish you would be good enough to hand that to Mr. Coe."

REV. F. A. SPENCER, of Vernon, N. Y., was next called upon. He did not know why he was invited to speak, as he was not a native of the town. His father and mother moved away a little too quick. His grandfather, however, was buried here. He came to the town about ninety-nine years ago. His grave is by that of the Rev. Mr. Knapp, whose gravestone is in three pieces.

The Spencers came to this country about 245 years ago with old Parson Hooker of the First Church of Hartford, and I hold in my hand the cane that my grandfather walked through Winchester with a hundred years ago, and notwithstanding the changes of the fashion, it is still in the fashion of to-day. It is 250 years old at least. I have also another specimen that appertains to Winchester. It is my grandfather's account book. Here are the names of the old men whom Mr. Blake mentioned in his address this morning. These charges were made almost a century ago, in 1774—

In october 1774 Cap. Alvord Debter to horse				
to torrington twice	00	02	00	0
to soling your shoes	00	1	2	0
to washing your shirt sundry times	00	3		
to spining your wool	00	1	8	0
to nitten mitten	00	1	4	00
to nitten stokens,	00	1	6	

My grandfather was a farmer, and he lived on the farm which Mr. Eggleston now owns. The old house, I am told, is torn down, but when I came here, eighteen years ago, I went to see it, then standing, and found myself in the room where Uncle Jonathan Coe said all the courting was done, for there were seven or eight daughters.

In regard to the cane, my English ancestor gave it to his son Thomas, because he bore his name. It has upon it still the initials, T. S. My grandfather died before I was born. He loved his minister, and lies buried by his side. My parents were married by the Rev. Mr. Bogue.

Mr. JOHN R. PITKIN was the next speaker, who said that though Colebrook was his native town he came to Winchester when fourteen years of age, and remained here for some time. He said he was at eight o'clock this morning in the city of New York, and he had made all possible haste to be present to attend this meeting. He then went on to relate some incidents that he was familiar with when a boy in that part of Winchester called Millbrook. One man lived there who always kept his word. He was in company at one time with six young ladies, and fell in love with the whole of them. He finally said he would marry the one that spoke first, agreeing to it. One accepted him at once, and they were married, and lived happily. That man was Reuben Hungerford. Mr. Hungerford was a farmer, and he measured his hay so that he knew exactly how much to give out every day of the year. He cut his pork into a certain number of pieces, so as to have a piece for each day. He had about an acre of grass cut down at one time, and nearly ready to be put in the barn, but he said to himself, "I will turn it out once more before I go to dinner." He commenced but there came up a heavy thunder shower while he was at work. I happened to stand in front of the field, and saw him keep on during the shower, turning his hay, first one way and then another. After the shower he came up and laid his hand on the fence, and said, "I don't know but you think it odd to see me turning hay in the rain, but I said I would do it, and I thought I would finish it."

Other incidents were related, showing the same characteristic trait in Mr. Hungerford, and the speaker then proceeded to tell of his own experiences: first in Torrington, where he taught a rather disorderly school, and brought it to a good condition without the use of the rod, so fashionable in those days; then going back, he spoke of his boyhood at Millbrook, and of his working there for Mr. Erastus Woodford for $5 a month, and closed by a short sketch of his future life.

The Benediction was then pronounced by Rev. Mr. Marsh, and the meeting was adjourned till 7½ o'clock at the Second Congregational Church in Winsted.

EVENING MEETING AT THE SECOND CONGREGATIONAL CHURCH, WEST WINSTED.

B. B. ROCKWELL, PRESIDENT.

The meeting was promptly called to order at half past seven o'clock, at which time the church was filled to overflowing.

WELCOME BY THE PRESIDENT.

OLD FRIENDS AND ACQUAINTANCES:—I have been thinking, since I sat here this evening, about the familiar scenes that used to transpire at our home, where father and mother sat around the fire, and the children began to come in from their play and the men from their work; neighbors began to drop in and the circle widened all around the room, and there was a kind greeting for all. I believe that we who are the present residents of Winsted feel pretty much so when we see our friends come back as you have done on this occasion. We bid you welcome; we are glad to see you. We have had to-day sermon and song and excellent entertainment at the other Society; to-night we meet in a more informal manner. The names of several gentlemen have been handed me, and I shall, perhaps, call on some others whom I have met. There are many here whom we shall be glad to hear from.

The first gentleman called upon was JAMES MILLER, ESQ., of Grand Rapids, Michigan, a native of Winsted.

He commenced by a reference to his profession, that of a lawyer, and thought it time that lawyers were oftener invited to participate in meetings of this character; that clergymen should not enjoy all the front seats, as they have done since the landing of the Mayflower. His father was the first lawyer who settled in Winsted, and practiced here more than twenty-five years, having settled in town about 1806, and having acquired the name here, although he was a lawyer, of honest Jo. Miller.

Many things recollected by the speaker as having occurred here in his boyhood were recited. He was only eleven years old when his father's family removed to Michigan; and it was in part because his father thought it not a good place in which to bring up his sons, that he removed West. In fact, the older boys had been drawn into some rude scenes that troubled their father's spirit, one of which was a sort of calithumpian concert on the occasion of the marriage of a spinster named Candace Scoville. On one occasion, his father, returning from Litchfield where he had been attending court, brought home some boys' hats that did not please the older brothers, for whom they were intended; and so, to be rid of them, they put them on, one Independence day, and wore them to the place where the cannon was being fired, and as it was loaded, they clapped one hat into the other, and both over the muzzle of the gun, when, as the word fire was given by Joseph, the elder boy, the hats disappeared in the smoke; but two hatless boys had a flogging that evening as a part of the day's celebration. Several other reminiscences of his early days were recalled, bearing upon the habits of certain individuals then residing here, as they appeared to the eyes of a child; among others, the names of his early teachers were mentioned, particularly that of Mr. Huntington, teacher of the Academy, and those of his playmates. As one of the experiments in chemistry and physiology, Mr. Huntington had a trial of laughing gas. Among others who took this gas, was George Gaylord, who was not much affected by it at first, but after a time he "made a straight wake for a young lady by the name of Champion, and put his arms around her neck and kissed her, which, on her part, did not seem to be considered much out of the way."

"When I think of the changes," said he, "which have occurred in New England in the past forty years, when I see what I have seen during the past week or two in traveling through this section, and that it is a country of the most surpassing loveliness that ever met the eye of man; and when I see how much man has done to beautify it, I wonder that my father ever emigrated to the West, and why those who have gone out on the prairies do not come back to this land of loveliness. New England, to-day, I believe to be the very centre of the planet, so far as it relates to everything that is worthy of human aspiration and human desire. I may not look upon it with impartial eyes, but it seems to me that here is a return to the rejuvenated paradise." (Applause.)

The President. I find here the name of a man who was so unfortunate as not to be born here; but he did the next best thing, he came here and married a wife — REV. DR. SEELYE, of Easthampton.

CENTENNIAL CELEBRATION. 571

REMARKS OF REV. SAM'L T. SEELYE, D. D., of Easthampton, Mass.

MR. PRESIDENT, LADIES, AND GENTLEMEN : — I am sorry for several things, but glad of many more. I am sorry there is not a platform here instead of a pulpit; I am sorry there are not more lawyers to relieve the ministers from the necessity of addressing you this evening. It is such a luxury for ministers to keep still, it is always a pleasure to listen to others. I am glad we have had one lawyer to address us. I am sorry to be in the pulpit and to be compelled to take up a new subject so that I cannot take a text, and consequently cannot turn the barrel over for an old sermon; for I was requested to say something about the ladies. What shall I say? Most of us express the honest sentiments of our hearts in the question, what could we do without them? Now and then I hear a man say, what can we do with them? (Laughter.) But I am satisfied that the first class are largely in the majority here; and I am happy to say a word for them, and to express here in this public manner my indebtedness to them. I believe no man enters into this celebration with a more joyous heart than I do; that no man, even if he be a lawyer, and had the good fortune to be born in Winsted, has a better right to speak to you on this occasion than I have to-day; because I don't think that all of these gentlemen who were born here in Winsted — I don't think one of them — appreciates the privileges he has enjoyed as I appreciate those which have been given to me. I found my wife here. She was born in the town of Winchester and borough of Winsted. And, my friends, it is a thing I have never told before, even privately; but it was in the town of Winchester, twenty-three years ago, that I, with that tremor which some of you have felt, I am sure, and that sinking of heart, plead with a Winchester girl to take pity upon me. (Laughter.) And she, blushing sweetly, here in the town of Winchester, with great diffidence, consented to share the trials and the joys of a poor minister's life. She has been by my side through these twenty-three years, an unfailing and blessed help-meet, making every day brighter by her sunny presence. To her I owe everything; all the happiness with which my life, for these twenty-three years, has been filled.

And I am glad to say this to you to-night, and to give you this reason for the joy that fills my whole heart on this glad occasion, this Centennial Celebration. Now, who of you rejoices as I do on this occasion? There are some of you who have been blessed as I have, and can share my joys; but these men that were simply born here, they have no right to this platform to-night, I am very sure!

Now I owe to the ladies what I owe to Winchester, and I shall express my obligation to them all. But I hardly know where to begin when I am obliged to do this in ten minutes. When boys have been sitting near the clock while I was speaking, I have known them to stop it; but I know those young ladies in the gallery this evening will not do it. There is one contrast in their favor.

When my brother was giving the contrast between the state of society a hundred years ago and now, he said nothing about the ladies, and it seemed to me that if we could have a picture before us of the young lady of a century ago, by the side of a young lady of to-day, we should see what changes had come over this world of ours more clearly than we do see them by the representations of the material progress in other directions, to which our attention is commonly turned. Now that shows to me the changes wrought in a hundred years better than the railroads and telegraphs, and all the inventions in which we pride ourselves.

I remember my grandmother, who was a young lady nearly a hundred years ago, dressed in her short gown and flannel petticoat. (Laughter). Some of you have seen such a dress. There she was, at the expense of a dollar and fifty cents, well dressed, with a dress fit for all the demands of her household and her farm. What was her house-keeping? She has told me many a time how she used to put the pot on the fire in the morning, and the logs were big enough in the fire-place to keep burning all the forenoon, and at this season of the year she used to go out and help her husband in the harvest and hay field, and when they came in at dinner time it was all ready, all that was wanted was to put it on the table. There was little ceremony, but they ate as heartily and with as much satisfaction as we eat to-day. What a change! Dress up a young lady now in a short gown, not over a yard and a-half, and a flannel petticoat, and put her by the side of the young ladies of to-day. (Laughter.) Why, I could not begin to mention the articles in my ten minutes that go to make up a lady's dress of to-day, and then the expense of it all! A dollar and a half? What do they charge for making a dress? I have occasion to know, for my wife asks me for the money. Why, Mrs. Flint of Boston, you know, charged $1,500 for making a single dress! What a contrast! And what a glorious change! (Laughter.) As the picture comes to my eye, see what an advance has been made in our civilization. (Great Laughter.) Who would wish to go back to those days? Why, my wife, much as I love her — to see her dressed in a short gown and a flannel petticoat — why, we could not get used to it, and I could not love her as well as now.

What taste they manifest in arranging the colors; what a vast amount of material they require; how much time they spend in shaping; how improving to their minds; what a means of mental and moral improvement; how expanding to the intellect. (Laughter.) Why, what taste there is exhibited in a little bonnet, little as it is, so small that you can cover it with the palm of the hand! Who would wish to go back?

Why, I rather have such a young lady than my grandmother. (Great laughter.) Who would not? Now, here is an evidence of the advancement made in the last one hundred years. Don't talk about the Atlantic cable, and flashing your thoughts over the ocean or under it in an instant, and reading the news of Europe to-day at your breakfast table to-morrow morning. Don't talk about that! Just think of your grandmother; there you have the whole thing right before you in an instant. (Renewed merriment.)

Well, my friends, in another respect there has been a great change. My grandmother used to sew, and make my grandfather's clothes. She took the wool and carded and spun it, and then she wove it into cloth. And my grandfather was a good-looking man, appeared admirably, as you might imagine, and dressed in his homespun suit, every bit of it made by my grandmother. Then my grandmother helped him in the field, and rode behind him on a pillion. The lady then acknowledged the husband as the head of the house; his word was law. But this lady of the present day; whose word is law to her? Now the gentleman has to put his hat under his arm and stand as a humble servant. What a wonderful change, and what an improvement! (Laughter.) How much better fitted to guide the world. Put a young lady of to-day by the side of my grandfather, splendid man as he was, and how much better fitted to tell him what the men ought to do than my grandmother was!

But I want to say of the grand old celebration up in Winchester, the thing that delighted me as much as any thing was to find — as the razor-strop man used to say — a few more left, like my wife. There are ladies like her, young gentlemen, and I hope you will profit by my example. By the way, speaking of the razor-strop man reminds me of one way in which I got the better of my wife; about the only time. When we began life we were bored by having agents of all sorts who wanted to come and stop with us. That was because they found my wife was a good cook, and they liked to come and stay a good while, till I got tired of it. My temper is not so sweet as hers, and I could not endure their crowding upon us as well as she did. There was one codger came at one time and brought a paper showing that he was a member of the New Haven North Consociation, and said he had a claim on me. I did not see how that was. It was in the forenoon; I was busy writing my sermon. He said, "I have nine children." I said, "You have?" and kept on with my writing. I did not want to be bothered by him, and let him go. When he had gone out, my wife thought I was too bad, and so I rushed to the door and said, "Brother Butts, if you cannot find any place for dinner, come here to dinner." That was the most cordial invitation I gave him. He did not come to dinner, but he came to tea, and stayed over a week, peddling books throughout Wolcottville. One night I went to bed early, and he did not get in. The next evening he asked me, "Brother Seelye, when do you go to bed?" I said, "When nobody is in." After that he came in every evening early. (Laughter.) One day a German Jew came along peddling, and wanted to trade. "No," I said, "clear out." Said he, "Don't you want a razor for twenty-five cents?" "Yes," I said, "I do." All those chaps would borrow my razor, and dull it, and it struck me that that was just the thing I wanted for them. Next week a brother came along, announcing himself as Brother Simmons. He has gone now, I trust, to Heaven, though I am anxious about him. (Laughter.) He came to stay with me, of course, and my wife's influence was sufficient for that. The next morning while I was dressing he came down, with an enormous black beard, and looked as though he had not shaved for a week. He wanted to borrow my razor. So I let him have the new one that had never seen a hone, and I gave him soap and a brush, and he went back, and I was happy for half an hour. At the end of that time Brother Simmons came down, with just as much hair on his face as when he went up. (Laughter.) Said he, "I want to ask one question. Did you ever shave you with that razor?" "No, sir, I got it for just such chaps as you." He never came again, and that is where I got the better of my wife.

Now I come back to my subject, the ladies. There was a lady in my first parish who was of the old school, for she lived nearly a century ago, and she managed her household, for a wonder, as a premonition of what was to be at this time. I was invited there to tea, and when we had seated ourselves at the table, I supposed, as her minister, and the only pastor present, she was going to invite me to ask a blessing. She said, "Mr. Seelye, I would like to ask you a question." I looked up. Said she, "I would like to enquire whether you ask a blessing at the beginning, and return thanks at the close, or do you do it all up under one?" I said, "I usually do it up under one." Said she, "Then please to do it." (Laughter and applause.)

Singing by the Choir.

Rev. Samuel Rockwell, of New Britain, Connecticut, was then introduced.

I am requested, Mr. President, to speak of the pioneers of this town, and of their work. It would give me great pleasure to speak, for the short time allowed me, in recalling to mind some of my own cotemporaries of sixty years ago, as they appeared to my youthful eyes. I would like, if there were time, to single out the individuals and give their characteristics as they presented themselves to me; to speak of your Coes, your Cooks, Boyds, Hinsdales, and many other honored names, who bore no mean part in laying the foundations of the social structure of this now populous and thriving town. I would like to pay my respects to that honored lady and teacher who taught our village school. She kept a trundle bed in her school room for the benefit of those little urchins who were weary even with their listless want of occupation, and became drowsy on the warm summer days. It was the great aspiration of many who attended that school to occupy a place in the trundle bed.

I recollect many honored names of the past generation, from the Old Society, as they came over the hills to this then growing village. One of this class I recollect, who came over one stormy winter's day when the wind was whistling and the snow flying. He remarked that when he got to Winsted, he felt as if he had got into Abraham's bosom. Whether those who now come here from the Old Society feel precisely in that way, I leave them to determine.

I might recall the name of the daring innovator upon the customs of society and the church, who, it was feared, was far in advance of the age, when he advocated the introduction of the bass-viol into the village choir. Some of you may remember the strong and bitter controversy which arose on that occasion in regard to that innovation. But there were at that period many such scenes of scandal in different parts of the country. They did not proceed so far here as in one place of which you may have heard, where the clergyman, after exhausting his arguments against the introduction of instrumental music into the choir in vain, determined to try ridicule; and in order to make the practice appear as incongruous as possible, as he rose to read the morning hymn, he said, with as much gravity as he could assume, "Let us fiddle and sing to the praise of God the 119th Psalm, fourth part, long metre." (Laughter.)

The men of that period, as I recall them, were men of laborious toil, and they had a hard soil to cultivate. It is said that a traveler, passing through the north part of Winchester, going towards Colebrook, in those early days, meeting a person, inquired, "Can you tell me where I am, and where I am going?" "You are in Winchester, and you are going to hell," was the reply. "Well," responded the traveler, "I thought, from the looks of the country and the inhabitants, I could not be very far distant." (Laughter.)

I rejoice, Mr. President, in such a celebration as this, for various reasons. It brings together a great number of those who have formerly been acquainted, and it recalls many very interesting reminiscences of the early history of our New England towns; and it also establishes many important facts of history which will be found of great value at some future period. These facts of history, which we now esteem of so little importance, will hereafter be regarded as of the greatest consequence, as they stand connected with the progress and advancement of the country. And for this do I rejoice in such celebrations as recount the virtues of the settlers of the New England towns, because they laid broad and deep the foundations of public virtue in private Christian lives, in the church and in the cultivation of all those graces which adorn humanity, which strengthen the cause of good order among men, and which prove to be at the very basis of all civil government and all true advancement in Society.

I find in the organization of these New England towns, based as they are upon broad and liberal Christian principles, the solution of one of the most difficult and one of the most important problems which now agitates the various nations of the world, as it bears upon the true source of political power, and the most effective means of promoting true social advancement and high intellectual culture. Sir, these towns are the aggregate of the Christian families. States and empires, where well organized, are the aggregates of towns and municipal corporations; but these towns and municipal corporations are but the aggregate of well-ordered families; and I find in these New England families, built up upon Christian principles, the very germs of all our social order and public virtue, of all that constitute the elements of greatness in the community.

I rejoice in it therefore, and would gladly recall the names and the labors of those men, who have taken even the humblest part in this great work of laying the foundations of our social structure thus broad and deep, so that future generations may rise and call them blessed.

It is sometimes charged against us as a people, by foreigners and even our own citizens who have traveled abroad, that we have here no public monuments. We look around in vain for those stupendous columns of marble or brass which are erected to commemorate some splendid event in war. They are not here. But a year ago my daily walk in Paris took me under the shadow of that majestic column in the Place Vendome, where, but a few months later, the brainless mob vented their spite and hate against the man whose image crowned its summit by bringing all the resources of their engineering art to level it with the dust. You may go through Europe and find everywhere a veneration for antiquity, and in every city some splendid monument of the past, something that has existed for a thousand years or more. The whole people take a pride in these noble monuments. But when foreigners or our own citizens tell us we have no public monuments, I reply, we have something better; we have founded and built institutions, which extend their benign influence over all classes of society, which carry their blessings to every fireside and every individual, which define, protect, and sacredly guard individual rights as the very germ of all social advancement. It is a glaring shame upon the men of any nation, that, whatever may have been the monument that they so hated, they should prostrate it in the dust; but it is a deeper dishonor for any man who exerts an influence in society to scatter around him a corrupt example, thus attacking at the very basis all public virtue, and upturning from their deep foundations those institutions, so noble and beneficent, which our fathers took such pains to build. The men who found institutions upon the Bible are doing a nobler work than the erection of monuments of brass or marble; and those who are living for the future, who are exerting an influence of purity, intelligence, and virtue, worthy of that society which shall reach to future generations, are doing a nobler work than those who built Karnac or Palmyra. Then all honor to the men who built their homes on these hill tops and in these valleys; who cultivated these slopes and even subdued the ridges of the granite hills, to leave to us this heritage.

THE PRESIDENT. I have a long list of names here of persons on whom I wish to call this evening, but I fear if long speeches are made there will not be time for all to be heard. I want now to ask Deacon Ira Hills, who is a native of this town, to let us hear from him.

DEACON HILLS not being present, HON. JOHN BOYD stated that he had himself expected to see that gentleman present; but he would say that Deacon Hills was probably the oldest Winchester-born man living, and would be known to many in the audience as the able correspondent of the Winsted Herald. He is a son of Deacon Seth Hills, the first deacon of Winchester, who went into the woods of Vernon, New York, and cut down the first trees in that town, and was the deacon of the first church there; and our guest, Deacon Ira Hills, is now, or has been, one of his successors.

It is proper to state, that I think there were over forty Winchester families, who in that great exodus found their way into that town, as soon as they could get through the Dutch settlements; and they made there one of the best towns in New York. Deacon Hills also wishes me to state that he comes here in behalf of himself and townsmen, but was especially delegated to represent Mrs. Rebecca Church, the eldest daughter of the elder Samuel Hurlbut. I think she is 93 or 95 years old, and wished to be especially remembered on this occasion.

SAMUEL BOYD, ESQ., of New York, was next called upon, who disclaimed any recognition of the right of the President to present his name as one of the speakers. He, however, proceeded to say:

I was born in this town, and married my wife here, and lived here until about 1834. I used to be about here considerably subsequently; but I am now among entire strangers. I do not know you. Previous to 1834 I knew every man, woman, and child within ten miles of this place. I have resided since I went away from here, nearly half the time, in an extreme southern state, and a part of the time in New York. I have not come back to you a worse man than when I left you; I am a better man. I do not know that I have any vice, as it can be called, about me. I have no speech to make, but I am glad to see you, my old friends and young friends. It is, to be sure, somewhat mortifying to come back and find myself among strangers, where formerly I have known every man, woman, and child. About 45 years ago I was an ambitious young man, in a store directly across the street here. I started the first opposition store that was built in this town, and which was the only one, I believe, for many years. There was a Democratic store started some years ago in opposition to the Federalists. But I started the store which I have referred to, and afterwards carried on a large manufacturing business. I come back now a comparative stranger. I have met a great many men in the Old Society, who had gone out of my mind. I have made the acquaintance of thousands and thousands since I went away. I have lived in a southern city fifteen years, and have seen hundreds and thousands die; have taken care of the sick in that terrible disease, the yellow fever. "I have seen the elephant;" and am thankful that I am spared, and that my children, who were most of them born here, are all doing well.

The choir then sang the following:—

BEAUTIFUL DAYS.

CENTENNIAL ODE, BY DR. W. J. WETMORE, OF NEW YORK.

  Beautiful days of the past,
   How your bright visions return:
  Bringing back faces and forms
   Long buried in love's hallowed urn;
  Voices seem heard on the air,
   Echoes that tenderly sigh;
  Oh! what delight to recall
   Past friendships that never can die.
    CHORUS.—Beautiful days of the past.

  Memory, sweet memory, restore
   Loved ones long, long ago fled,
  Who would not see them again,
   Our cherished and favorite dead?
  But they can never return,
   Memory's bells mournfully chime:
  Years are fast floating away,
   Down the dark river of Time.
    CHORUS.—Beautiful days, &c.

CENTENNIAL CELEBRATION. 577

> Hark! how the melodies float
>   Out from the grave of the past;
> Bringing back memories of old,—
>   Sweet memories that ever will last.
> Round us bright spirits appear,
>   Breathing their lessons of love;
> Oh! may we join them at last,
>   To praise Thee in mansions above.
>   CHORUS.—Beautiful days, &c.

DR. D. WILLIAMS PATTERSON, of Newark Valley, N. York, was then introduced. He said,

MY FRIENDS:—I suppose you remember the fellow, who, on being asked to speak, while pleading the suddenness of the call (though he had privately had three weeks' notice) and lamenting his consequent lack of preparation, coolly drew from his pocket, and began to read his fully written speech. I am here to-night to fill his place. My notice was ample, under ordinary circumstances, but such were the difficulties for me to overcome before starting for this place, that I had scarcely time to pack my extra shirt before the whistle blew for the starting train.

Perhaps the only reason your committee can give for calling on me, is, that as I, for nearly twenty years, took my bread out of the mouths of this community, I must, of course, be filled with good things, and should be required to open my mouth in return. This may all seem very fair, but pay-day is not always pleasant to the debtor; nor, in case of his failure, to the creditor.

Now, as you find me thus unprepared, I must put in practice the parting injunction of the Irish law-professor to his student, as he sent him into the world to begin his practice, which was this; "when you have nothing to say, say *something else*."

I have for more than ten years looked forward to this celebration, though during the last half of the time I have scarcely hoped to be present. Thus far my enjoyment has been far beyond my brightest hopes, but never in my life have I been so forcibly reminded of the constant procession of humanity from the cradle to the grave; and much more forcibly must that be felt by many of you, whose knowledge of this place covers, not like mine, only a quarter of the century whose lapse we now commemorate; but a much larger part, running from fifty to ninety years of the time; and how short are the centuries made to seem when we meet and take by the hand our venerable friends, Deacon Ira Hills, of Vernon, N. Y., and the Rev. Frederick Marsh; the first a native, the other a resident, of the "Old Society," whose lives have covered more than nine-tenths of the time occupied by the history of this town.

If life endures so well among the natives and residents of that part of the town, the oft repeated threat of our old friend, Luke C. Coe, that he would "get set off to the Old Society," might well be put in practice by some of us who desire a long life, though the chances still seem good in Winsted, for I have to-day seen my old friend, uncle Peter Tatro, now eighty-eight years old, showing his age scarcely more than at sixty.

Of those whom I have known in active life, many are no longer to be seen. Among them I recall the names of the venerable Deacon James H. Alvord, whom all remember with affection and respect; my excellent neighbor, Deacon Elliot Beardsley; and the Rev James Beach, whose long and consistent ministry, in the First Church in Winsted, did so much to develope and make permanent the religious faith of the people. The venerable James Boyd, one of the pioneer scythe-makers of the place, whose large heart, good will and loving kindness to his fellow men, would never let him accept the whole creed taught by the parish minister.

The Rev. Daniel Coe, who in his earnest zeal in the temperance cause, allowed himself to be outwitted by mine host Fyler, formerly of the old tavern here, whom he persuaded to promise that he would sell no more rum; which promise did not prevent the sale of other liquors as abundantly as before; Fyler using the word rum in its specific sense, while our reverend friend used it in the generic. His son Nelson D. Coe, and others of the name; good old Uncle Jonathan Coe; Samuel Ward Coe, the merchant; and Norris Coe, who for so many years carried the mail between Winsted and the "Old Society," scarcely ever losing a trip, till tripped by death, who seemed to care nothing for the penalty threatened by "Uncle Sam." for stopping the mail; and I think death has never been arrested for the offence, though he is yet lying in wait for Coe's successor on the route.

Nathan Champion, who long acted as the oldest mason here, bearing the Holy Scriptures in their processions.

Lucius Clarke, whose dream of cementing in common brotherhood the rival parts of the town, "East Street" and "West Street," by building between them a village so large as to swallow them both, and blot out the famous "Creek Bridge," may yet be realized by his successors.

The forcible and energetic Gideon Hall, who, to use his own words, long "lived on borrowed time;" and his son of the same name, who, with less than his father's force of character, and more than his polish, rested his weary frame on the bench of the Superior Court of Connecticut.

Lieutenant Governor William S. Holabird, whose pious zeal did so much to fix St. James' Church in its present location.

The brothers, Samuel and Lemuel Hurlbut, the successful merchants and stockbreeders of the "Old Society," who, by their enterprise, did so much to improve the cattle of their town and state, and build up their own fortunes.

The genial Colonel Hosea Hinsdale; Rufus Holmes; and James Humphrey, whose honest independence everybody liked.

William H. Phelps, the successful founder of the Hurlbut Bank.

William S. Phillips, the merchant, whose excellent qualities made all who knew him wish his life far longer, and his fortune great.

Lucius Skinner, whose violent and untimely death, met in the discharge of his duty, every one deplores.

William Sanford, the popular landlord of the old hotel.

Captain Wheelock Thayer, the successful manufacturer and earnest free-soiler; and his son-in-law and successor, Seth L. Wilder, who offered, one bright first-of-April, to take several of his friends in partnership in a new manufacturing enterprise, which, after a somewhat elaborate consideration, proved to be for the production of gigantic bull-frogs in India-rubber, and forever silenced the jokes, which he for years had borne, over the mammoth frog of Columbia County.

The brothers John and Thomas Westlake, whose social qualities none have forgotten.

Charles B. Weed, who did so much to mend your ways; and last, but not the least, my excellent and lamented friend, ERASTUS STERLING WOODFORD, whose sterling qualities of heart and brain endeared him more and more, not only to those who knew and loved him well, but to the public generally, and whose place, I know, the people have never had harder work to fill, than during the preparation and execution of the plan of this centennial commemorative feast.

But the world is full of compensations; and while we drop a tear to the memory of those who are gone, we rejoice at the evidence of the continued prosperity of the town under their successors. I rejoice in your graded school, which has grown up, mainly since I left here, the present standing of which I believe to be largely due to the energy of our friend William G. Coe, who, when chosen school committee in 1864, allowed himself to be convinced that, although the districts had twice voted not to have a graded school, he yet had power to establish one, and, acting on that conviction, did so at once, and put it in successful operation. I feel proud of your water-works, and possibly not the less, for having penned in 1853, a little paragraph for George B. Cook's *Winsted Advertiser*, the first paper printed in town; which, so far as I know, was the first article ever printed in favor of the project.

And now, while I must candidly admit that in my theological examination a year ago I failed to get a license, and so have no right to preach to you, yet I must beg leave, in behalf of those who, like myself, have left the good old town, to offer a word of exhortation to you who yet remain, to guard well its reputation in all respects.

We, by our removal, have not lost our pride in that good name, but our ability to keep it up is greatly lessened. Remember that the past history of the town is not alone to be considered; its future history is to be made, and we charge you to see that it be so made that neither you nor we shall feel shame for it.

Let your churches, while they maintain the best reputation for sound doctrine, practice the largest toleration, that the greatest number may be brought within their influence. Let your schools deserve the name of keeping the best and most accomplished teachers, and of sending out the most ripe and liberal scholars. Let your merchants maintain their reputation for honest, fair, and liberal dealing; let your manufacturers keep up and improve the good name of their productions; let your scythes have the stiffest backs, the brightest blades, and the keenest edges; your pins, the firmest shafts, the smoothest heads, and the sharpest points; let your railways be the safest, surest, and most successful, and your telegraphs the most reliable that ever distanced lightning.

Two of my children were born here, and the third first saw the light in another state, and I earnestly hope that he may never have a chance to cast upon his elder brother and sister the reproach of an unworthy birth-place.

The choir then sang the old hymn, " The New Jerusalem ;" " From the third heaven, where God resides," &c.

During an earlier period in the evening, his Excellency the Governor, MARSHALL JEWELL, had come in, and been received with applause. At this point the president took the liberty to call on him for an address. He said :—

MR. CHAIRMAN, LADIES, AND GENTLEMEN—I think if any body can plead immunity from speaking here to-night, I certainly ought to be permitted to do so; for, sir, when I was invited, two or three days since, to come here on this occasion, and it was intimated that I might be called upon to " stand and deliver," I did not suppose the demand would be made to-night. I perfectly well recollect that on one occasion, when President Lincoln was situated somewhat as I am, he expecting to be called on to address some soldiers on the following day, was visited the evening before by a number of them, who wanted a speech. Said he, " Boys, how do you suppose I can speak to you to morrow if you draw it all out of me to-night?"

I am not a native of Winsted. From some things I have heard here to-night I could wish I were; but it is a very difficult feat, I know, for the boys to catch up with the fathers. I used to hear, in my boyhood days, of the prominent men of this section, and I thought that John Boyd, and the old brass-mounted abolitionists about here, and Methusaleh were among the oldest men known; but when I come out here now I seem to be almost as old as John Boyd.

I know there are many here who wish to speak to-night, and I will not occupy your time. I want just to say, in the name of the state and of New England, and of all that is valuable, that it is just such occasions as this that make the community. This New England has no second in the elements of national strength, and when we come together on an occasion like this, and see what the past generations have done, we see what we ought to do; we take the best position we can in a republic like ours, and learn to drop the bad examples of the past, and go on to make the future better. And if Winchester can do any better in the future than she has done, I hope I may be Governor of Connecticut a hundred years hence, and meet her boys here to celebrate the next centennial. (Applause.)

Dr. Patterson, in his seat, responding—It is pretty early to electioneer for that, Governor.

The next speaker was Rev. C. H. A. Bulkley, of Malone, New York, a former pastor of the 2d Congregational Church, whose name, as announced by the president, was greeted with applause. He said :—

As I came up these steps the chairman said to me, "You can have the pulpit." I think if any one can claim this privilege it should be myself, because when this church was erected the only two privileges that I asked of the architect were, that I might have the direction of the ventilation of the church, and the construction of the pulpit. And my idea was to make it as much of a platform as of a pulpit.

I am not a native of Winchester. I was born in Charleston, South Carolina, a fire eater, and all the good sense I have, if I have any, comes from my paternal ancestor, who was from the State of Connecticut. But to-night I find myself a sort of patriarch, as the founder of this West Winsted Church, and it is of this church that I can speak better, perhaps, than any one else not a resident here. I found that to-day every thing said with respect to the past was of the most agreeable kind, and every thing unpleasant was left entirely out of view. So, in my reminiscences of the past history of this church I shall leave out every thing that might be unpleasant to you or me in the recollection.

I remember very well when I was asked to come up here to Winsted. I was met in the city of New York by my good brother N. H. Eggleston, who said he had got into a dilemma, having a call to West Winsted, and another to Chicago, and he did not wish to come here and have the people become interested in him, as he preferred to go to Chicago. So he asked me to come here and take his place, as he had agreed to come and preach on the next Sabbath. I came here late Saturday, and I was directed to the house of my good friend, George Dudley, where I introduced myself and told him I was not Mr. Eggleston. You know how he has a way of shrugging up his shoulders. He washed his hands in invisible water, and rather hesitating said, it had been advertised that Rev. Mr. Eggleston was to preach. I told him I would go on and preach, and he need not say any thing more than that the minister had come, until it was all over, and then he could tell the people that the minister was not Mr. Eggleston. I must confess that coming from New York, where the soil was so fertile and the fields so beautiful, I felt a little shrinking at the idea of coming to settle here. I remember, when coming in the stage coach, of meeting my good brother, Dr. Eldridge, and he related the story then new to me, of a man who when riding somewhere in this vicinity inquired where they found the stones for the stone walls that were so plenty, and on being assured that they were taken from the adjoining fields expressed his doubts, as he could not perceive that any were missing from the fields.

The question was asked by a friend whether I would accept a call to this church, which was not then a church, not having been formed. I replied that I thought I could not, for I did not think the people could give the salary I thought I ought to have. "Why, how much do you suppose they will offer?" I said I thought that they would probably offer about $600; and I said I thought I could not stay for less than $1,000. A few days after a committee called on me to be the prospective pastor of the church at a salary of $1,000. I was, therefore, in a measure committed; but I accepted the call, at $1,000, provided they would build me a church within a year. They gave a kind of provisional pledge, and after some little time I accepted the call, and came here just after there had been one of those damaging freshets in Mad River, and the roads were washed away and gullied out, and everything looked desolate and forlorn. I must confess my heart sank within me; and my family especially thought they had come to a pretty dreary sort of country.

But it did not prove so in the end; for the blessing of God came, and the spirit of God was outpoured, and there were some pleasant conversions; and when, about that time, I met with an accident, my good friend Mr. Winslow came to my assistance. But the great work done was in the revival of 1857-58. I remember very well that little school-house that stood on the promontory near the mill-pond. There was my study, in that little school-house; and the Methodist minister came to me and said, "The Lord is with us, and we want you to come and help us." I had been brought up under influences that made me think but little of the Methodists—I am ashamed to say—and I gave him the cold shoulder. But I finally went, and I saw that the Spirit of God was at work, and young men were bowing at the altar. This church was not then built, and we were worshiping in the hall. We had no place where we could meet except in private rooms; and so we co-operated there at the Methodist church. The result was, to draw these two denominations more closely together. This church was organized, I think, in the Spring of 1854; and the number that joined with us by profession of faith or by letter, was fifty-eight. I think there were one hundred and fifty-seven names on the roll of this church when I left.

I recollect a number of ladies got up an "old folks' kitchen," and they had a dance. Just think of it; that the Congregational church should have done such a thing! There was a man came in with bag-pipes, with legs exceedingly thin, that looked like pipe stems; and some lady of middle age got up and began to dance with him, but not very well. And old Mrs. Thayer, who had been on her bed for five weeks with rheumatism, had been taken out to see the old folks' kitchen; and when she saw that the lady did not dance very well, Mrs. Thayer was quite indignant, and she took her dress in her hand and danced most vigorously with the gentleman; and they had a real old-fashioned jig. The next Sunday the old gentleman came into church, and I saw his legs just as I saw them while he was dancing the jig; and I had to put my face in my hands and laugh; I was afraid I should laugh out in meeting.

The catechism class was a pleasant feature of my work. I used to catechise the children, and have an annual exhibition, and I was astonished at the close of the second exhibition by a presentation of a gold-headed cane by a young lady.

It was my great privilege to stand here, after this church was built, as the first minister who ever entered this pulpit. In the providence of God, I have been permitted to labor elsewhere; but have come back with a heart that is warm and full of Christian feeling towards all here. When here a few weeks ago, collecting some material for my poem, I was asked by a gentleman if I found anything to awaken poetry here, and I replied, "Oh, yes, the faces of my friends do that." My heart has been most tenderly affected since I have been here now, as it was during that visit. I then had a deep sense of God's goodness; and it came through the manifestations of affection by this people towards me. And so, I have felt that to-night the words that I should speak must be with gratitude to God and thankfulness to these friends who have ever shown to me so much sympathy and love. (Applause.)

The choir then sang, to the tune Mear, the hymn, "Let children hear the mighty deeds," &c.

THE PRESIDENT then said: Ladies and Gentlemen, we are very much obliged to you for your patient attention this evening. We have detained you longer than our usual wont. We have a hard day's work before us to-morrow, and we will now close.

The Benediction was pronounced by REV. HENRY B. BLAKE, and the meeting adjourned till to-morrow morning.

WINSTED, THURSDAY MORNING, AUG. 17TH, 1871.

This morning the town wore a festive appearance. The streets were thronged with thousands of people, and flags were flung to the breeze on every hand. There were many happy reunions. People who had not met for years greeted each other joyfully, and happiness beamed on every countenance. The oldest living native of Winchester, Deacon Ira Hills of Vernon, New York, was present, hale and hearty, at the age of 88 years. And there were hundreds of the old residents from all over the country. The doors of the citizens were thrown hospitably open, and never was a more happy family gathered than that of old "Mother Winchester" to-day.

The procession formed at half-past 8, a. m., in front of Rockwell's Tannery, in the following order:

Marshal—Col. Wheelock T. Batcheller.
Aids—Col. Jeffrey Skinner and Porter S. Burrall.
Gilbert Cornet Band.
St. Andrew's Lodge, No. 64, A. F. & A. M.
Historian, Poet, His Excellency the Governor, and other speakers.
Warden and Burgesses of the Borough of Winsted.
Union Hose Co., No. 1.

When the procession moved down Main street, it was joined at the Clark House, by

Palmer Post G. A. R.
Monitor Lodge I. O. G. T.
Bushnell Cornet Band of New Hartford.
Deluge Hose Co. No. 2.

At Oak street, by

St. Patrick's Benevolent Society.
St. Francis' T. A. B. Society.

And at Park Place, by
> Niagara Hose Co. No. 3.
> Cascade Hose Co. No. 4.
> Citizens on horseback.
> Citizens on foot.

And marched around the Park, thence up Main to Meadow, down Meadow to Monroe, through Monroe to Main, down Main to the front of the Methodist Church, where there was a stand erected, and thousands of people were assembled, the sheltering trees affording a sufficient canopy to protect them from the August sun. An arch over the street bore the motto, "Winchester welcomes her children." The welcome was cordial indeed.

The officers of the day were—

William G. Coe, *President.*

Reuben Cook,
Jehiel Coe,
Rev. Frederick Marsh, } *Vice Presidents.*
Beebe B. Rockwell,
George Dudley,
Oliver White,

The President having called the vast assembly to order, delivered in an eloquent manner the following

ADDRESS OF WELCOME.

The first duty assigned me, is to greet you, Sons and Daughters of Winchester, with cordial welcome. It is painful to be able to command only common-place and stereotyped words to express the kindly emotions which your presence awakens. Be assured, however, that the occupants of the old homestead are joyous and happy over the return of the absent ones, and bid you all a sincere and heartfelt welcome.

Time, here as elsewhere, supplemented by no little enterprise and public spirit, has wrought its changes, and many of you will find few landmarks to lead you back to scenes fast fading and soon to be past recall. Here and there you will meet some of the older children of the family, now aged and venerable, but without exception honored and esteemed, who may prompt and refresh your memories.

Our rugged old hill-sides, now perhaps more stern and forbidding than when you clambered over them, will to some of you be convincing witnesses of the wisdom which led you hence.

An occasional old homestead, dwarfed in its proportions from childhood's estimate, and much less cheery and inviting, may still be found.

The old red school-house, dreary and uncomfortable, is replaced by one of ampler proportions and luxurious appointments. And of the old church, naught but its stately pulpit, in the barn-yard museum of our venerable townsman, Jesse Williams, exists.

Our forests have disappeared at the beck of the manufacturer, and our waters are utilized and controlled by the same power.

To view these changes, to re-visit old scenes, renew old friendships, to collate and preserve the early history of Winchester, to recall the memories and deeds of its settlers, to quicken our appreciation of their virtues, to join in social pleasures, to gather up and re-unite the broken threads of friendship and consanguinity, to link the past of the old township to the present, we have bid you meet us to-day. And when these public exercises shall have closed, a fraternal greeting will await you at our homes and firesides.

Rev. Asahel C. Eggleston, of Hartford, was then introduced to conduct the devotional exercises, remarking to the audience, that it was an old-time custom to open all exercises of our congregations with prayer, the audience rising. Let us rise and give God thanks.

PRAYER.

Oh, our God, Thou hast been our dwelling place in all generations. From everlasting to everlasting Thou art God. A thousand years in Thy sight are but as yesterday when it is past. We humble ourselves this day beneath Thine exalted hand as we are gathered here on this centennial occasion. Thou art the living God; Thou wast our father's God; Thou art our God. This day do we acknowledge Thee. This day would we praise and laud and magnify Thy holy name. We bless Thee for Thy mercies shown towards our fathers; we thank Thee for the history of the past; we thank Thee that Thou leddest them through the great sea, and that Thou didst establish them in this land, driving out the inhabitants thereof before them, and making their enemies to be at peace with them, and giving them prosperity until a little one has become a great nation. We bless Thee for the holy memories that come to us this day. We thank Thee for the goodly heritage of our fathers; we bless Thee for the grace given to them, as manifested by their humble faith and trust in Thy Holy Word, for their keeping of Thy Sabbath, for their regard for Thy worship, for their faithful lives of righteousness, equity, justice, and judgment.

Blessed be Thy name, oh God, for this heritage, which has thus come down to us; and we bless Thy name for the excellent institutions of our country which have come to us from our fathers, and which make our land the desire of all the earth. We humble ourselves before Thee, for we fear we have not loved Thee as did our fathers. We have not always exhibited the same integrity; we have not so honored Thy Sabbaths, we fear; we have not so regarded Thy worship and Thy holy altars.

We thank Thee, oh Lord our God, for Thy mercies towards us; pardon us now as we humble ourselves before Thee, seeking that pardon in the name of Jesus Christ, our Lord. Let Thy blessing, O Lord, be upon us in all these centennial exercises; and grant unto us Thy grace; for well we know that, although we rejoice in the blessings of the past, and indulge bright hopes of the future, these hopes will not end in fruition unless the blessing of the Lord our God be upon us. And we pray for Thy blessing upon this whole community and all our citizens. May we all learn to love righteousness, to love Thy holy law, to keep Thy Sabbaths, that in all things we may regard Thee and follow Thy commands.

Bless all the citizens in this community in all their industrial pursuits, in all business arrangements, in all commercial enterprises. Let them enjoy length of days, with a goodly heritage, and with freedom from great and unusual calamities, as individuals; let Thy grace turn all our hearts from sin and lead us to righteousness and unfeigned faith in our Lord Jesus Christ.

Again we thank Thee for this occasion, for this bright and beautiful day, for the joyful remembrances of the past and the brighter hopes of the future, while we invoke Thy continued blessings upon us through Jesus Christ our Lord. Amen.

THE PRESIDENT.—The only person living who can write the history of Winchester is John Boyd. For his unwearied research and effort in this direction, it is proper that every native of Winchester should pay him the debt of gratitude they owe. It is my pleasure to present him to you to-day as our historian.

HON. JOHN BOYD.—Mr. President, I disclaim the merits attributed to me, and beg leave to say that neither power of voice nor my physical condition will enable me to make myself heard, even by the smallest part of this audience, and I therefore ask the privilege of appearing before you this day by proxy. I have therefore requested my friend, Mr. Forbes, to read my address, assisted by Mr. Hubbard. I ask attention to the reading of the first part by Mr. Forbes.

REV. S. B. FORBES.—Ladies and Gentlemen: It is proper that I should say, in behalf of the writer of this address, that if it seems broken, it is because its great length forbids that only fragments should be read to-day.

Mr. Forbes then commenced the reading of the portion of the address assigned for the day, and Mr. Stephen A. Hubbard, of the Hartford Courant, read the concluding portion.

The address, which occupied an hour and a quarter in reading, is not here printed, for the reason that it is a digest of the author's history of the town, and would involve a repetition of what is herewith published as the main part of this book.

After a chorus by a choir selected for the day, the exercises of the forenoon were closed, and an hour was spent in partaking of an excellent collation, and in more direct personal and social interviews and greetings among old friends, who had not, in some cases, met for years. It was a happy hour.

AFTERNOON EXERCISES.

After the audience was called to order again by the President, and after music by the band, the Poet of the occasion, Rev. C. H. A. Bulkley, of Malone, N. Y., was introduced, who remarked that he was largely indebted to the historical notes of Hon. John Boyd for the material of his poem; and proceeded to deliver, in a clear voice and with much energy of manner, the following

POEM.

A RHYME OF WINCHESTER.

Why all this crowd and pinch and stir
In our old town of Winchester?
Why speech and song and heart-true chime
Here, in the hot mid-summer time?
Why ripple laughs and shouts, like rills,
Amid these rock-ribbed Litchfield hills?
Why come these sons and daughters far
From homes of peace or fields of war,
From prairies or Pacific slopes,
With planter's gains or miner's hopes,
From Southern plains or Northern mounts?
From commerce marts or wisdom founts?
With grasping hand and greeting word,
Why are their hearts so deeply stirred,
Their eyes so tearful, yet so bright,
Their lips so trembling at the sight
Of once smooth cheeks by Time's hand wrinkled,
And brows with locks of silver sprinkled?

To-day, swift steeds of memory travel back
A hundred miles of fruitful years,
Faster than steam car on the iron track,
To bring the thoughts, the hopes, the fears,
The joys and griefs that heap the piers
Of that far time, the precious freight
Of lives long passed beyond death's gate,
That now on our remembrance wait.

A hundred years! battalion strong
Of veterans, on our hearts they throng,
Marshaled in ancient, homespun uniform,
After the end of life's hard strife and storm,
To tell of toils, of victories and defeats,
A century through; when either war's fierce heats
Or arts of rugged peace dropped grain or grime
From off the changing pendulum of time.
What changes, in those years of five score span,
Have marked the face of nature and of man!
Here, the rude region, ere their steps began,

Lay a huge giant, with his granite arms
Clad in the verdure of the forest's charms,
The pine and hemlock, chestnut, oak and beech,
'Mid which the Indian waked the panther's screech,
Chased frighted deer, the wildcat and the bear,
With their warm fur to fight the frosty air.
No meadows rich, no uplands smooth and fair,
No prairies wide gave grain with little care;
The rocks, where sheep could but bill noses ply,
Said to the emigrant, "Root, hog, or die!"

Bold, sturdy men and women were they,
Who felt that life was no time for play,
   When they braved this rocky region,
They delved 'mid dangers without dismay,
They sweetly slept on brush or hay,
   Though their troubles counted legion;
They lived on mush from Indian maize,
And scared off wolves with hemlock blaze,
And kept hearts strong with godly praise,
   Sustained by their religion.

In homespun style they cured their pork,
And ate it without silver fork;
They shaved their shingles, split their laths,
Cut timber from their forest paths,
Built their rude kilns, made their own lime,
And raised their log house in due time.
Their wives, because sometimes so fat,
Were their own cheese-press, when they sat;
Their children were well-spanked and rocked,
Their boys well-breeched, their girls well frocked
From wool, all carded, spun and wove
By their own hands with hearts of love.

They talked not then of "women's rights,"
From pulpit-desks or platform-heights;
They were more proud to make a coat
Or pair of pants than shave a note;
To overcast, than cast a vote;
Their candles, soap, and flaxen cloth,
Their woolen garments, kept from moth,
They deemed more worthy man's true praise,
Than soft soap speech or flaxing phrase;
They never dreamed of "*free love*" things,
Nor thought to break their marriage strings,
But loved their husbands and obeyed
God's law, in giving birth to aid
The nation by a sturdy race,
Not having learned the modern grace
To shirk the mother's care and cheat
The nurse and doctor of their meat.

They were a race prolific; many a Cook,
Who boiled his beans beside the babbling brook;
A Handee, handy at the hoe or plough,
A Steele, who dared not steal his neighbor's cow,
A Burr, who stuck to labor, friends, and life,
A Hart, who bore all heart-felt cares and strife;
A Rogers, who could use, not make a knife,
A Batcheller, who yet could boast a wife;
A Holmes, who had no homes that he could spare,
A Barnes, whose barns were yet unraised in air;
And there were Bulls that never lifted horn;
Their babes, no calves, save when of cows, were born;
And Rockwells, cool as wells within a rock;
Masons, who built no brick and mortar block,
Cases, that doctored many a sickly case,
Parsons, who never preached with godly grace;
Shepherds, whose flocks were not all sheep of price,
Smiths, who at no anvil wrought, or vise;
Arnolds, who turned not traitors to the land,
Potters, who worked no clay with wheel and band;
Hinsdales, who in dales or on rocks could roam,
Hills, who on hill-tops found a fitting home;
Wakefields, all wakeful on the field of death,
Clarkes ne'er responsive to a prelate's breath;
Mills that went not by water or by steam;
And Holabirds who gave no hollow scream.

Time fails for all the names to come to light,
Of Wrights who were not always in the right;
Doolittles, busy every shining hour,
Or Sweets, sometimes a very little sour;
How many to our day, not least, but last,
Have through the changing generations passed;
The Beardsleys, Alvords, Gilberts, Phelps, and Camps,
Who, history says, were neither saints nor scamps,
But men, who o'er life's way in toilsome tramps,
Like us, felt Heaven's warm rays or earth's chill damps;
Welches, hereditary doctors, who
Though quick to physic, slowly come to you,
Whose doses on their patients' stomachs sit
Not quite so pleasing as a "Welsh rarebit."
Oh! that I could each Coe and Boyd and Hall
Out of their resting places loudly call,
And bid them stand, a "goodlie companie,"
In all their primal power and purity;
How then to them most reverently we'd bow,
Those spirits of the just made perfect now,
Those sires whose sons are here together met,
Their virtues to recall, their faults forget.

    Why were they brave and strong?
    What made them true and pure?

How dared they thus the throng
  Of life's hard ills endure?

Lo! there the answer see!
  Where by the village-green,
  The School and Church agree
  To shed on them Truth's sheen.

There stands the meeting-house with low steeped roof,
From which no sceptic soul dare keep aloof;
Upon the hill-side, like a beacon-light,
It rises sacredly in human sight,
Built on great chestnut logs instead of stones,
With rough plank seats that pain the nether bones;
The gallery, reached by ladder, opes its floor,
Through whose great gap the Parson's thunders pour;
No paint, or plaster, ceiling, organ-loft,
No carpet, curtain, cushion, rich and soft,
Tempts the stern sense of zealous Puritan;
No heating stove kindles his angry ban;
His zeal is all-sufficient fire to warm
His body and his soul from wintry storm,
He needs no carnal coals to melt the form
Of sin or snow while hell-fire fears up-swarm.
Sound doctrines furnish fuel, always strong;
His orthodoxy bars out ill and wrong;
Only the weakly women, more in sin,
There footstoves bring and lay beneath the shin,
To warm the inner heart and outer skin.—

  But in due time, as cash increases,
From all their harvests and their fleeces,
Another meeting-house arises,
Bringing to all some dreadful crises.
They meet, they talk;—alas! what fightings,
What bitter words, what sad backbitings,
What rousings of their saintly mettle,
What pullings here and there to settle
The question grand of Church-erection;
Almost to schism and defection,
Those sires, so orthodox, are hitching,
Where they the church-stake sh'd be pitching;
Now here 'tis down, now there uptaken,
To-day, their spirits calm are shaken,
Now stubborn, silent, now discussing,
Now praying and now almost '*cussin*'
Over the stake that keeps on walking
From point to point while they keep talking.
A martyr-stake well nigh becoming
Amid such strife, so soul-benumbing.
At last,—in some more happy hour,
The stake is fixed, by sovereign power.

Then in the forests ply the axes,
Then from the pockets pours the taxes,
Then lotteries with their funds are streaming,
And workmen in their sweat are steaming.
The structure grandly grows and towers,
'Mid hopes of future gracious showers.—
Within are high-backed pews to keep
The worshipers from sinful sleep.
The pulpit, on a pillar placed,
Eight-square and ten feet tall, is braced
By cork-screw stair-ways on each side;
While high o'er all, in sacred pride,
With threatening look, the sounding board,
Hangs stern, like Damoclesian sword,
Filling the sinner oft with dread
Of holy Justice, on his head,
Though wicked urchins sometimes prate
Of hopes 'twould crush the parson's pate!
Above, the gallery, ox-bowed, bends,
Whence nasal strains the singer sends,
When, deaconed out by drawling tongue,
The hymn in old fugue tune is sung,
The key-note sounded, clear and good,
By Leader from pitch-pipe of wood.—

'Tis Sabbath-time; begun last eve,
When happy boys were made to grieve
That Saturday was o'er, and shades
Crept up the hill-sides. Swiftly fades
The play-time light; five stars are out;
Now all must leave the bat and bout,
Shoes must be blacked and laid in row,
Washings be made from head to toe,
Clothes brushed and hairy knots combed out,
To save the nails of scratching lout.

Now dawns the sacred day; the sire
And matron, filled with holy fire,
Gather their tribe at morning prayer,
Bid them nor lie nor steal nor swear,
Their psalm and catechism hear;—
For meeting now they all prepare,
In ox-cart or on foot repair,
While "PA" and "MA," upon the mare,
On saddle and on pillion ride,
As erst they did when groom and bride,
Each one, to meet his waking need,
Bearing a bunch of fennel-seed.—

The meeting house is filled with sober faces,
The older taking all the forward places,
The younger, in the back or gallery sitting,
Kept by the tithing man from talk and spitting.

Oh! what a terror he, whose hand is itching
To give some urchin wild a birch-rod switching,
Who well deserves the keenest kind of whacking,
For cracking nuts, and other sorts of cracking.

The Parson comes! the church-yard throng
Opens for him to pass along;
Loud whispers sound—"Hats off, ye boys,
Girls, 'show your manners, stop your noise.'"
They bow and curtesy low to him,
Great bugbear to each Satan's limb.
A wide, shad-bellied coat he wears,
His head, a broad brimmed cocked-hat bears,
'Neath which a white wig flows full down,
As if a sheep's back were his crown;
His small clothes, like his coat, are brown
From butternut, like good-wife's gown;
With silver buckles, stripéd hose,
And top-boots to contain his toes,
He mounts the pulpit, like a pope,
Inspires with dread, yet talks of hope,
Prays as if God were far away,
Yet calls him father of our clay.
Doctrines as sound and hard as rock,
He hurls with logic on his flock,
Who, by the hour-glass patient sit,
With nods approve the heaviest hit,
And smile, as they the meeting quit,
That sinners *were* sent to the pit,
And saints but scarcely saved from it.

Yet justice bids that I should say,
Not thus they all did preach and pray
Though each his faults and graces had,
Who, like us all, mixed good and bad.
There were WOODWORTH and KINNEY and wordful KNAPP,
Whose sermons came forth with an eloquent snap,
That gave his dull hearers a wakening rap;
There was BOOGE, tall and handsome and straight as a pillar,
And BASSETT, full sound, though in love with the "*siller*,"
And BEACH the rue father whose children find CAMPS
That honor his graces and gather the stamps,
And he whom we welcome to-day, Parson MARSH,
Ever true, ever good, oft severe, but ne'er harsh,
And PETTIBONE, not of a *petty bone* frame,
With back bone enough for a martyr's name,
Who cared not for tongues and feared not the flame
Of hate, for the love of the good Pastor's fame.

I might be personal to speak of others
Who were my compeers and dear brothers,
So let us back again to those old days,

And learn still more their quaintly ways.
The meeting done, the crowd outpours,
They stand in knots, by tens and scores,
Or gather in the Sabbath-house,
To eat their lunch, but ne'er carouse,
Talking their politics and doctrines o'er,
Counting their crops and live stock store,
Amid discussions oft irate,
Of foredoom, faith, free-will, and fate.

The second session o'er, they go
As came they there, thoughtful and slow,
Homeward to finish Sabbath-work,
To dine on cold baked beans and pork,
Till sundown comes, when Sabbath ends,
And boys are glad, and thought unbends;
When spruced up lover quickly wends
His way to her with whom he spends,
Till midnight hour, the sparking time,
In talk that tells the heart's true chime.
Oh! days of primal, purest love!
When, simple as the mated dove,
Uncursed by Fashion's foolish ways,
Young hearts rejoiced, in homely phrase
To speak of marriage without shame;
Sought not for gold, or style, or fame,
And gladly heard their coupled name,
Published from pulpit, when 'twas said,
On such a day they would be wed.

Oh! happy time, when cakes and beer,
And "apple-sass," made nuptial cheer,
When earthen ware and pewter spoons,
And frying pans sang home's sweet tunes,
When wash-tubs were a woman's shrines,
Her pride the clean clothes on the lines,
Her sheets and bed-quilts, near a score,
On closet-shelves kept well in store!

Alas! the lover now must bring
The maid's left hand a diamond ring,
And weddings, secret long as may,
Must show their gold and silver tray
Full of rich gifts from "BALL and BLACK;"
When groom and bride must take the track,
And ride to Canada and back,
Ere settling down, nor ever lack
The coach and team with hoofs so quick,
And liveried driver dressed so slick,
And house of brownstone or of brick,
Unless they wish it said aloud
That they are of the common crowd.

In those days scarce was silver in their tills,
Worthless were all their Continental bills,
Their specie was in rye and corn and lard,
In pork and beans; the parson's pay came hard
In tallow, suet, beef and wool and flax,
From every househould brought by stated tax,
For which he must well flax his flock for sin,
And they in turn might flax his heart within.

It was a question though, as to the whether,
His or the school-master's were toughest leather;
Who, hapless wretch, for dull and heart-sore teaching,
Was boarded round by folks sometimes o'erreaching,
Was hounded much by urchins full of evil,
Whose nether ends seemed hung upon a swivel.

Poor little devils! Ah! 'tis not much wonder
They could not sit still at his voice of thunder;
Since such hard seats, such air to lungs defiling,
Such winsome girls before them sweetly smiling,
Made them, in spite of all their wills, so frisky,
E'en though to stir they knew was dreadful risky;
For, Oh! those nine-tails made of knotted leather,
Would then come down upon their tender nether!
Relieved from study, how upon the green,
Barefooted, hatless, rushing are they seen,
Playing at leap-frog, base-ball, snap-the-whip,
The girls at mulberry bush and hop and skip.

Oh! days of that far childhood, who'd not give,
The wealth of Ind, in such a time to live,
When bliss it was to roll in new-mown hay,
When butter-cups were gems of purest ray,
When daisies drove away the darkest gloom,
And sweetest perfume breathed from clover-bloom;
What joy was theirs when training day came round,
When fife and drum made stirring martial sound;
The village green from fences then was cleared,
Full tables in the orchard near appeared,
And ladies, in their lute-strings lovely stood,
To serve the "*sojers*" with their cakes so good;
The "Kurnel" on his prancing charger came,
With ostrich-plume borrowed from stylish dame,
His coat of blue all decked with golden lace,
And big brass buttons shining like his face;
His cocked hat nodding o'er his sword and sash,
As thro' the hollow-square he made a dash,
'Mid veterans who could give the war salute,
Play Indian with his whoop, and shoot
The bow or musket, with an equal skill,
To face the foe, but no one ever kill.
What sham-fights then were seen when guns went off,

And swords were flashed with tongues, as if in scoff,
And sweat ran freely in the stead of blood;
When cider flowed for thirst, in yellow flood,
And old metheglin toddy made a muddle
Amid the ranks, because some brains 'twould fuddle.

As grand a time they had when came
"The glorious Fourth" with Freedom's name,
When Captain Bunnell's big train-band
Their four-pound field-piece drew by hand,
At dawn, at noon, at evening fired,
Till patriot hearts were full inspired.

The grand procession, with each guest,
Poet and Orator to do his best,
With President, and all the rest,
Moves to the meeting-house; each head,
Uncovered, bows when prayers are said;
Hearts gladden at each patriot-word,
And when the old fugue tunes are heard.

The feast of fat things comes thereafter,
With ready speech and ringing laughter,
While rich baked meats, without sharp mustard,
With Indian puddings, pies of custard,
Are eat with eager gusto greater
Than ever comes with luxuries later;
All which proceedings, histories warrant,
Were printed in the *Hartford Courant*.

Those voices, ending with the sun,
Were echoed by that ancient gun,
Which, since the century's evolution,
In French war or the Revolution,
From Cobble Hill has poured its thunder;
The dread of girls, of boys the wonder,
The foe of many an ancient maiden,
Who by its tones with nerves were laden,
And hid it in their little garden,
Where found, it came forth as the warden
Of Freedom 'gainst all Federal brewing,
Lest they should pull her pole to ruin.
That ancient gun! how oft 'twas crammed,
With powder to its muzzle rammed,
When Democrats or Whigs were found
To give *"darned"* Radicals the fits,
And scare their abolition-wits.

Why burst it not to atoms then,
When crammed and rammed by hateful men?
Oh! 'twas the nation's type of life,
Which no foul play or venom-strife,

No fullest charge of ill could break;
Its heaviest thunder could but wake
The love of freedom till it rolls
In fullest tones o'er patriot-souls.

For, in the century's early time
They heard her call to blood and grime,
And deemed it but a duty-chime;
They answered her at Lexington,
They were of troops who victory won
At Saratoga, o'er Burgoyne,
Who fought for king and British coin,
Whose troops, defeated, o'er these ways
Were marched by men we love to praise.

Since then, heroic souls, like them were found,
When sadly came the South's rebellion sound,
They poured from Winchester with shout and song;
A brave battalion, full three hundred strong;
By Skinner led, by Eddy prayed for well,
Sworn ne'er to hear their country's funeral knell;
They fought, they bled, alas, too many fell;—
Freedom's true sons, they rest where then they died;
Or in yon grave-yard, honored, side by side;
Sad memory weeps for them; sweet flowers we strew,
To thank them for *our* joys, they never knew;
Their names are sacred; in our heart's deep place
We walk with them in friendship face to face.
Lo! ARNOLD comes, soon as the nation calls,
No traitor,—he, at Cedar Mountain, falls.
BROWN, who to meet his comrade's thirsting quest
Receives the rebel bullet in his breast,
A Christian soldier, glad for life's war done,
If dying he may see the victory won;
BELLOWS, who perished at the Hampton fight,
BALDWIN, who, e'er struck down, could calmly write,
"Soon, at Cold Harbor, into strife we go,
If shot, 't will be with faces to the foe!"*
That son of Afric, DOLPHIN, shows the fire
Most worthy of his Revolution-sire;
HOSFORD at Cedar Creek;—at Sharpsburg too,
COGSWELL and DAYTON perish, brave and true;
DOWNS, FERRIS, GIBBS, and GREEN;—the list they swel
With PALMER, COMMINS, DANIELS, all who fell
Upon the field. Not less heroic they
Who sadly pined in hospital away;
BENTON and BARBER, and a score beside,
The gentle SURGEON WELCH, who early died.
We honor them, proud of their hero-fame,
We gladly speak each soldier's worthy name;

---

* Written, in substance, to his mother, on the day before the battle of Cold Harbor.

Not less we honor those who live to-day,
Here with us met, or from us far away.
Ye sons of Freedom, hearts of patriot-power,
We greet you here, we crown you in this hour;
We give you thanks for toils and wounds endured,
By which the nation's weal was well secured ;
With ancient worthies we your names unite,
And on the scroll of fame your record write.

Like them, with souls that feared no terror-shape,
You met the rebels' sword, and gun, and grape;
You flung fair Freedom's red-barred banner out,
Starred from the sky amid the angel's shout,
And to our sons, an heir-loom rich and grand,
Gave it to wave it o'er a ransomed land
Alas! that men, along the Southern sand,
A reckless crew, a wild, rebellious band,
Should thus have striven, by Slavery's brazen hand,
Basely to *un*wind Liberty's strong strand,
And rend in twain her banner and her land!
From mountain top, and citadel, and fort,
From village-belfry, and from ocean-port,
They tore it down with passion's wildest gust,
And trailed its tattered fragments in the dust.

But, roused to wrath, you, sons of Northern sires,
Marshaled your hosts and built your battle-fires,
Trampled on traitors in their march of power,
Made ranks of hate before your courage cower,
And smote the hands that forged the bondman's chain,
Till Freedom's songs, as erst, were sung again,
And every link of wrong, o'er hell's dark brink,
Was hurled forever in its depths to sink,
While up and high that blazing banner went,
Blood-stained, yet beautiful, though bullet-rent,
To win new star-beams from the azure sky,
And drink fresh hues from Freedom's sun-dipped dye.

Float on forever! Oh thou flag of God!
O'er paths these hero-feet have boldly trod,
O'er homes where martyr-souls have bled and wept,
While for the dead their vigils long were kept,
O'er graves that cluster countless on the fields
Where to the brave, love all her homage yields.

Float on forever, in thy might and pride,
The glory-shroud for those who 'neath thee died,
The flag to which the living all things gave,
To make thy stripes.—O banner of the brave,
The flush and fairness of perpetual youth,
Thy stars all blended in one Star of Truth.

Grim war, gray Time, and Art's deft hand,
Have stamped deep changes on the land;
Mansions of elegance and mark,
Stand where was raised the roof of bark;
Churches of cost lift lofty spires,
And breathe with warmth from furnace fires,
Where meeting-houses, rude and old,
Through gaping cracks let in the cold;
The organ's deep tones sound the stave
Where pitch-pipes erst the key-note gave;
The cushioned seats invite to sleep,
The parson makes few sinners weep;
In varnished carriages these ride
To church and back again in pride,
Decked with fine silks and broadcloth rich,
Made by the strong machine's swift stitch;
A thousand spindles, in great rooms,
Weave fabrics fine from scores of looms; —
The blacksmith's shop, which every boy
Peeped into with a wondering joy,
To mills and foundries huge gives place,
And factories line the lengthened race,
Where chisels, scythes, and knives outpour
To cut and carve the wide world o'er,
Where ploughs and clocks come forth from grime,
To till the soil and tell the time.

Poor lunatics for board and bed,
Once auctioned off so much a head,
Are cared for in asylum halls;
The whipping post no more appals;
The only "*Stocks*" that now hold men
Are issued from some Wall-street den;
State prisons stand with walls of stone,
To make the lawless fear and groan;
Turnpikes are turned to railroad tracks,
That tear our front yards into racks;
In cars and not on horses' backs,
Men mostly ride, and women find
No fun on pillions placed behind,
But rather run the risk of smash,
Than fail to make the swiftest dash,
And fond of blowing up their own,
Oft find themselves by steam upblown.

The Doctor, in those days of old,
On Narragansett steed behold!
His leathern saddle-bags he fills
With plasters, powders, and with pills,
All made in doses big enough
A corps of cavalry to stuff,
His stirrups short bring up his knees

At angles with his saddle trees,
And thus he rides, by night and day,
To kill or cure, and get his pay
In cheese or pumpkins, corn or hay.

The modern Doctor in his gig,
With team and harness, best of rig,
Dispenses finer, smaller pills,
And sends in oft the biggest bills,
To be all paid in good greenbacks,
Unless we choose the cheaper quacks.

The Lawyer, politic or proud,
Still oracle to all the crowd,
Looks out with hawk-eye for his prey,
To get from clients richer pay;
E'en parsons preach and pray full well,
When salaries fat their pockets swell,
And worshipers in peace are bent,
If they for cash get twelve per cent!

The old economy of life
When, as 'twas said, to kiss his wife
On Sabbath-day a man was fined,
Is somewhat changed; men now scarce mind
Week days to kiss their wives enough;
But more delight in other stuff,
And oftener kiss some lawless lips,
Or make a few frail "free-love" slips;
Wives get divorce, through lawyers bold,
From husbands who refuse them gold,
Fortunes are made by hook or crook,
Seldom by rules of Heaven's own Book;
And Sabbaths are not strictly kept,
As when, if e'er we played or slept,
Into hay-mows or nut-trees crept,
We felt the rod and sorely wept;
When, as 'tis said, barrels were whipt
For working beer in cellar crypt,
Whipt now that they may work the more,
And fuller make the beer outpour.

The Parson comes, no demi god of fright,
With name to silence children in the night;
He questions not with catechism dread
To pound sound doctrine in the urchin's head;
His frown gives not the sinner Sinai-quakes,
His hand the sword of justice seldom shakes;
With white cravat and ivory-headed cane,
He moves no more, of youthful joys the bane,
Less pope and ruler; more the equal friend,
He teaches how those joys with Heaven's to blend,
And thither pleasantly our footsteps bend.

Not yet forgot are old " Thanksgiving-days,"
Though spent with more of guzzling than of praise;
The sermon finds its hearers, few and dull,
But turkeys lack no eaters to the full;
Our children's stomachs, like those of our sires,
Need to be greased and stretched at kitchen fires;
And night-mares horrible disturb our rest,
With giant chicken-pies upon our breast,
Oysters and lobsters ope their shelly jaws,
Snapping at us for breaking Nature's laws.

But conscience makes things equal now we think,
For gin-slings, toddies, and each fuddling drink
Curse not the festive board or burn the brain,
And thus our age hath made some social gain.
Oh! that from low saloon and tavern-room,
Such evil spirits might be hurled to gloom,
Or only used when mixed with poison lead,
To kill the bugs that blight the traveler's bed.

The land is free; it feels no curse of Cain,
Free let it be from vice and sordid gain,
Free from the rule of rascals and of rum,
Free from the martial din of fife and drum,
Free from the bands of party-power and strife,
From bigot hands with persecution rife,
From trucklings low of office-men of note,
Who throw a sop to Cerberus for his vote;
Why should not we make all these hill-tops ring
With Freedom's fullest music while we sing?

Freely the sweet lark springs from earth,
To sing his matin song of mirth,
And plays amid the gathered dew
That white clouds hold in th' ether blue;
Freely the cool drops fall to earth,
O'er fonts where first they gushed to birth;
That like the tinkling feet of fay,
In shades and moonbeams chainless play.

Freely the light of sun and star
Through myriad worlds of space from far,
Journeys along the paths of God,
Alone by angel footsteps trod;
Freely the sea's white surges pour,
O'er sandy beach and rocky shore,
Where in its depths of skiey blue,
The dolphin plays with changing hue.

Freely through woods or over waves,
The zephyr breathes or storm-wind raves,
Each quivering leaf a pulse of life,
Or every tree a foe in strife;

Freely the heart within us beats,
The ear sweet tones of nature greets,
The eye, all beauteous things beholds,
The memory every joy unfolds.

Freely all things of being seem
To bring the end of life's sweet dream;
Why should not we, with all things be
In body and in spirit free?
Oh! may the high, benignant God,
Ordain to break each tyrant rod,
And teach our souls for aye to hate
The abject lot and servile state!

The free-born voter yet may go
With ballot to the polls, e'en though
Election sermons, balls, and cake,
No thoughts of old and young awake;
These ancient ways leave us to find
Joys other than theirs left behind.
The four horse stage-coach comes no more,
"OLD LINE AND NEW,"—to many a score
Of gaping villagers a thing of pride,
In which to take a wedding ride
Was bliss indeed for rustic bride,
Whom Hartford merchants could but bless,
In selling her a marriage-dress.
The driver's horn, with shrilling toot,
The urchins hanging to the boot,
The letters, bundles, papers, all
For which each eager lip would call,
Are of the past; and in their place
The locomotive runs its race,
With mail-car and the express-train,
And crowds, for pleasure or for gain;
The steam-pipes shriek, the smoke, and rush,
The start, and sometimes fearful crush;
The hurry, scurry, flurry, here
And there, of throngs from far and near,—
Oh! how unlike are all these ways
To those that charmed our boyhood's days;
They wake sensations wild and bold,
But bring not half the bliss of old!

Oh! the huskings and the quiltings,
And the bussings and the jiltings,
And the huggings and the hidings
In the hay-loft, and the bidings
By the gate in evenings starry,
Where 'twas bliss with one to tarry
Near to midnight,—whom to marry
Was we thought, a life-long blessing
Made up only of caressing,

With no ills for our confessing,
Needing not the law's redressing.

Loving lips that trembled greeting,
Finger-tips that tingled meeting,
Horseback trips with maiden rider,
Autumn straws for sucking cider,
Nutting days and squirrel chasing,
Blind man's buff with warm embracing,
Feats of fun and youthful daring,
Talking times of apple-paring,
Sharp snow-balling, and the boasting
Over sleds the swiftest coasting;—
These for us the years are bearing
To the past, always unsparing!

Over yon grave-yard, where each tomb
A marble record gives of gloom,
We wander sadly, reading names
Of those with whom we cherished aims
Of future good and glorious fames,
Or talked our boyish mischiefs o'er,
And shared the orchard's stolen store;
Oh! as we think of them, the waves
Of memory surge up o'er their graves,
And from each heart this sad lament
Tells of a love as yet unspent.

 Ye days of blessed boyhood!
  The better time of life!
 Now lost amid the whirlpool
  Of earth's absorbing strife!
 Ah! never more returning,
  Its halcyon moments come,
 For toward old age a pilgrim,
  'Tis journeying from its home!

 Far fled art thou, my boyhood!
  I miss your morning sheen,
 With eyes all dim and tearful,
  Though fruitlessly I ween;
 For gone with years departed,
  Are all its joys and hopes,
 Since life has changed to manhood,
  And thro' dark caverns gropes.

 I grieve o'er thee, my boyhood!
  I want your bounding heart,
 Your shout of gleeful music
  That made old bosoms start;
 I want your step elastic,
  Your buoyancy of hope,
 Your oft unrivaled vigor,
  That with each arm could cope.

Oh! I am lone, my boyhood!
  Where are my playmate friends,
Who with me blithely sported
  O'er all these hills and glens?
Where is the bird-like echo
  Of all their uttered joys?
Where are their jocund faces?
  Where are those happy boys?

Oh! many friends of boyhood
  Far from these homes have gone;
Some tread earth's devious pathways,
  And some life's task have done;
Some sleep in caves of ocean,
  Some bleach upon its shore,
Some rest on fields of battle,
  Who weltered in their gore!

Where art thou gone, my boyhood?
  Why come my friends no more
To share the joys so guileless,
  That filled my bosom's core?
Ah! some look on me coldly
  From Alpine heights of pride,
Some pass me by despairing,
  Since all their hopes have died.

I mourn, I mourn my boyhood,
  Because my heart's dear ones
Are not now round me moving,
  Nor on me shine like suns;
That in earth's burial places
  All silently they sleep,
Here never more to bless me,
  Or o'er my follies weep.

Yet soothed am I, my boyhood,
  For hope hath not all died,
E'en though your days have perished
  Your font will be supplied;
For from the crystal river
  That flows in yonder Heaven
I'll drink new youth immortal,
  In draughts exhaustless given!

Oh, then, thou deathless boyhood,
  There in thy new-born days,
I'll meet the dear departed,
  And with them join in praise.
Oh! it will be all blissful
  Around God's throne to move,
And chant in hymns celestial
  With them of Jesus' love!

Though changed the times and faces, yet each hill
Is high and green, tree-clad and rocky still,
The laurel, clover, butter-cup all bloom
On them with beauty, shedding sweet perfume.
The myriad stone-heaps in the fields yet rest,
We miss but few from off their rugged breast;
Each lake spreads out its bosom bright and clear,
And sends its currents downward to the mere;
Its pike and pickerel, perch and bass and eels,
Oft tempt the fisher's skill to test his reels;
The brooks shine as of old in summer sheen,
Though trout in them are few and far between.
Through chasms long-time cut, Mad River flows
When swelled by showers or spring-time melted snows,
Flooding its banks, its bridges sweeping off,
And covering plains, of human skill in scoff,
Upon whose ruin-rush and wildering trend,
These lines, one time, a bilious poet penned:

"Mad River, glad river, leaping 'mid mountains,
   Gathering the echoes that roll from their caves,
Mingling the owl-hoots with song of the fountains,
   In the weird music that peals with thy waves.

"Mad River, sad river, moaning the losses
   Of the grand forests that shaded thy sides,
Floated away to the rock-realms where tosses
   Ghost-foam of ocean's wild storm-haunted tides.

"Mad River, bad river, fierce in thy pleasure,
   Over the toiler's dear homes and rich fields,
Sweeping away to the deep every treasure,
   Never to him a new harvest that yields.

"Mad River, glad river, sad river, bad river,
   Thou art the type of each tide changing soul,
Either with joy or with grief made to quiver,
   Ever as tides, good or ill, in us roll."

Yet in the time of drought or further flow
Down to the eastern meadows miles below,
Mildly "Mad River" smiles o'er happy homes,
Becomes "Still River" as it southward roams,
Turns mighty wheels of mills that make men's bread,
Moistens the sods that cover up the dead,
And tells the living how that youth's wild rage
May bring the work of art or calm of age.

As nature is—our hearts, are they the same?
Or are *we* changed, in life, and deed, and name?
Our fathers had their faults;—these do we keep
And leave their goodness in the past to sleep?
They had their fierce ecclesiastic fights,
Their orthodox discussions, and their flights

Of eagle logic to celestial heights;
Parson and parish equal were in sin,
When half-way covenants let church-members in,
Or when disputing loud of Adam's fall,
They proved that in him they had sinnéd all;
Oft by Hopkinsians with the doctrine crammed
That to be saved you *must* wish to be damned!
Their Federal and their Democratic speech
Caused in their households many a widening breach,
When party spirit and New England rum
Made their lot doubtful in "*The kingdom come.*"
Their hard-earned means and economic thrift,
Oft made them chary of a lavish gift;
Yet were they just and honest, true and pure,
Patient and hopeful, trained well to endure
The hard rubs of the world and break the wiles
Of evil, coming e'en with angel-smiles.

Such roughness, toughness, toil and carking care,
Nature and Time do not to us now bear;
With strong machines we pull out stumps of trees,
We clear our fields from rocks that blast with ease;
The scythe and sickle we in scorn ignore,
And cut our meadows with a patent mower;
No tall well-sweeps their burdened buckets bring,
To us come now, we go not to the spring;
The telegraph our message swiftly sends;
By lightning flash we gain our money ends.
Volumes are writ and grand ideas we catch
By pregnant words in one concise despatch.

In self-conceit we boast that we all are
Than our good fathers, keener, richer far,
More quick at bargains, sharper at a note,
With bigger barns ashore or ships afloat;—
No wonder wealth and wisdom here are found,
"*Barkhamsted Lighthouse*" shines on all around!

Are we so strong of thought? On Faith's great wing,
Up to the heights of Truth soar we and sing?
With earnest spirits dive we down so deep,
Where pearls divine of wisdom darkly sleep?
Or have our ease and luxury made us weak,
The things of God with throes of soul to seek?
Are we as bold to grapple with great themes,
To them so real—to us more like past dreams?
Are we in love with sacrifice of self,
Or, chained to earth, in love with petty pelf?
Shall Darwin prove a monkey *was* our sire,
Or Huxley mix us in material mire?

What moral progress parallel with these
Inventions of our day that so much please,

Do we now make? What loftier stand of good
Do we now take, as Duty bids we should?
Higher and truer, purer, nobler, we,
Than were our Fathers, in our life, must be.

Oh! as we onward sweep, by spark and steam,
To the blest heights of some Eutopian dream,
Where temporal ill, and human strife shall cease,
Where nations may from bondage find release,
So let us mount, by footsteps all divine,
And on the hills celestial brighter shine,
The noble sons of fathers noble-born,
Beholders of a better generation's morn,
The grander offspring of the grand old times,
Who hear the music of millennial chimes
Come floating o'er the far off Future's sea,
And to the rhythm of their crystal wave
March forth in power, humanity to save,
Along the ways our strong-souled fathers trod
To wield the force—the enginery of God,
The culture, treasure, wisdom of the age,
In full accord with Revelation's page,
To launch the world upon that truth-lit sea,
To float the nation, great, and true, and free,
On to the shores where bliss and glory wait
To usher souls through Heaven's love-guarded gate,
And bring them, star-bright, to their thrones on high,
Amid the God-crowned circles of the sky!

The reading of the Poem was often greeted with cheers and laughter, as the telling points impressed themselves upon the eagerly listening audience. This was followed by an Anthem by the Choir.

THE PRESIDENT. Ladies and gentlemen, we have placed in the vestry of the church before us our mementos of the past and our curious works of art, for your inspection; but we have placed upon this platform our Jewell, His Excellency, the Governor of Connecticut,—God bless him. (Long continued applause.)

Thus introduced and thus welcomed, His Excellency proceeded to respond, as follows:

ADDRESS OF GOVERNOR JEWELL.

MR. PRESIDENT, LADIES, AND GENTLEMEN:—When I accepted the invitation of my honored friend, the historian of the day, to be present at this centennial celebration, I knew I should derive both pleasure and profit by so doing, but to what extent I did not, could not anticipate. It is far beyond my most sanguine expectations. It is always a pleasure for me to mingle with my fellow-citizens, either in a public or private capacity, and it is particularly so on occasions like this.

When in a community like this, renowned alike for its intelligence, its thrift, its devotion to those fundamental principles of equality and justice which underlie the republic, and insure its success; when in such a community, an epoch has been reached, or a period has been marked on the great cycle of time, and the people meet together to compare notes, and to give as it were an account of their stewardship; when this happens, as in the present instance, it is the best of all times to see what real, genuine New England character is, what it has done, what it may do. Connecticut is, and has a right to be proud of its history, and of its long line of illustrious men. Not the least of these have been its Governors, of whom your county has furnished four during the century, whose names lend additional lustre to the already bright page of the history of the State.

This town was settled during the most eventful period of American history. One hundred years ago Connecticut was in a ferment of preparation for anticipated hostilities with the mother country. Jonathan Trumbull was Governor, one of the most wise and sagacious men America has ever produced, whose name and fame became so nationalized by the confidence reposed in him by Washington, that the country adopted for itself in honor of him, as one of its pet names, that of Brother Jonathan, by which endearing title he was called by the father of his country. The State was agitated by those apprehensions which reached their crisis in the spring of 1774. By this time the obnoxious tea had been thrown overboard in Boston harbor and British vengeance had concocted by way of retort the Boston port bll, and had struck by legislative act at the charter and government of Massachusetts. The first recorded evidence on the part of Connecticut, that indicated the general peril, was a proclamation issued by Governor Trumbull in May, 1774, which, after reciting the threatening aspect of Great Britain, enjoined a day of fasting and prayer. This proclamation was soon followed by an order to all the towns to double their quantity of powder, balls, and flints, and by resolutions passed in various town meetings, which declared the measures of the British parliament to be usurpations which placed life, liberty, and property at utter hazard, and unalterable determination of the people of Connecticut to maintain and transmit those rights to the latest generations. It is a matter of no surprise that the grand old Governor should have earned the title of rebel Governor, which was given him in London, in 1771, four years before the Declaration of Independence.

It was amidst such commotions as these stirring events would indicate, that this now thriving town was settled, twenty years after the organization of Litchfield county. How well it was located, how brave and hardy were its pioneers, through what dangers they passed, and what magnificent results crowned their efforts, struggles, and trials, has been ably and happily told you here to-day. It may not be amiss to briefly note how nobly the people made good the gallant Governor's prediction in the struggle for independence which ensued. During the revolution, Connecticut ranked fifth of the old thirteen States in population, Massachusetts, New York, Virginia, and South Carolina, being ahead of her.

In 1774 the population of the State was 198,010, and yet she furnished during the eight years of the war 39,831 continental troops and militia, which was the most furnished by any State except Massachusetts, which latter State furnished 83,092, New York furnishing 21,093, Virginia 30,835, and South Carolina but 5,508. Mr. Roger S. Baldwin said in the Senate, in reply to Mr. Mason of Virginia, "I can inform the senator that Connecticut, small as she was in territory and population compared with Virginia, had more troops in the war than the great State of Virginia. Virginia was obliged to offer tremendous bounties to induce her people to serve. The inhabitants of Connecticut rushed at once to the combat. They were at Ticonderoga, they were with Ethan Allen and his Green Mountain Boys, himself a native of Connecticut, on an expedition planned in Connecticut, and paid for by Connecticut, before the continental congress of 1776 had assembled—capturing that important fortress almost before the blood had grown cold that was shed at Concord and Lexington. They were at Bunker Hill with Putnam and Knowlton and Grosvenor, and their brave compatriots, who needed no bounties to induce them to engage in the service of their country."

The Hon. Henry C. Deming says in a letter to George M. Brown in 1857 :—"No State contributed more than Connecticut to our revolutionary literature, to those songs, and strains, and martial airs, more potent to move and change than even laws and arms. John Trumbull rushed into the war with a pen as sharp and effective as any sword. 'McFingal' was written at the urgent solicitation of John Adams and the members of the American Congress."

Connecticut furnished more salt beef and pork, and more live cattle, than any other State. So remarkable was she in this respect that she was known as the Provision State. In the winter of 1778, the darkest period of the revolution, while our discouraged and disheartened troops lay cold, naked, and hungry at Valley Forge, both officers and men nearly in despair, the commander-in-chief, as usual, turned his eyes longingly towards Connecticut, and made a strong appeal to Brother Jonathan for assistance. Nor was the call long unanswered, for, by order of the Governor, the chief commissary of the State, Colonel Champion, of Colchester, soon collected, and himself drove a large herd of cattle in mid winter, through almost impenetrable forests, over streams and mountains, more than three hundred miles, to the west bank of the Schuylkill, to the relief of more than ten thousand of our brave and starving men.

Such was Connecticut a hundred years ago—such in brief was the condition of affairs at the time of the first settlement of this town.

Our population small and scattered, our roads poor, and means of communication exceedingly difficult, steam and electricity still in the future, every man, woman, and child fully occupied in obtaining the means of subsistence, new towns to be laid out, built, and organized, everybody in a hand to hand struggle with nature, yet, no sooner were any of the rights of the colonists threatened or invaded, than there were found to be plenty of men, and time, and food, and clothing, and, best of all, pluck, with which to defend themselves against all invading forces. Is the present generation up to the standard of the one of which we have spoken ? Have we the elements of national growth and strength in as large a degree as had our forefathers ? Are we as honest, as frugal, as patriotic, as self-sacrificing, as those who have given us their high example ?

In following down the century which we are now contemplating, it would be proper, had we time, to dwell for a moment upon the distinguished services which your own Litchfield county Governors have rendered to the State, covering a period of seventeen years, the two Governors Wolcott, Smith, and Holley. It is perhaps sufficient for our purpose to know that they did not detract from, but added to the high estimation in which our governors had always been held. For (nearly) ninety years after Governor Trumbull's administration, no Governor had an opportunity equal to his, in which to show his ability, integrity, and patriotism. Such opportunities are granted to but few, however much they may be longed for. Nor had the people had any occasion to show their strength and loyalty. Nothing had called out the patriotism and devotion to country which lay dormant beneath the quiet exterior of peace and a stable government. But the storm finally came. After much murmuring, threatening, and commotion, there came another time in our history that our liberties were threatened, our rights invaded, that our constitution was sought to be overthrown by traitors in our midst, a time that demanded our entire strength if we would preserve intact that inheritance which we received from our fathers. The circumstances of this last great struggle in which Connecticut did her full share, are too fresh in your minds to need recapitulation. It was then found that we had a chief magistrate second only to Washington; that Connecticut had a Governor equal to any that had gone before; and that the people, as they sprang to arms to put down a gigantic rebellion, were worthy of both President and Governor.

If we may judge of the future by the past, it is safe to predict that the intelligence and patriotism of the people will be found equal to any demands which may be made upon them, and that in the future conflicts which are quite likely to come to the republic, the people of our grand old commonwealth will be found where they ever have been found, in the front rank, fighting for freedom, for liberty, and for law.

A handsome bouquet of flowers was presented to the Governor at the close.

The address of the Governor was heartily applauded.

THE PRESIDENT:—I am not instructed as to the manner in which the other exercises of the afternoon shall be conducted. There are many eminent gentlemen here who, if called upon, will, I presume, address you. It hardly belongs to me to suggest.

REV. JOSEPH ELDRIDGE, D. D., of Norfolk, being called for, said:

I need not say that this call upon me for a brief address is entirely unexpected. I am gratified, however, with these commemorative occasions, because I think they spring from sentiments, and are calculated to strengthen sentiments that are fitted to counteract a very strong social tendency of our times. The tendency to which I refer is that of excessive individualism, where each person shall set out, caring for himself and seeking his own advancement, irrespective of social or even domestic feelings.

There are circumstances in our country that favor this tendency. The members of families do not, as in the last century, remain long enough near the old home; nor do the children settle around in the vicinity of each other. They are early separated from their homes and scattered far and wide, becoming almost strangers to each other. And the consequences are a lack of local attachment and an almost dying out of family feeling. I therefore rejoice at every indication and every circumstance that operates to counteract this tendency to excessive individualism.

Among the circumstances that I think have this tendency to keep alive proper sentiments, one is the disposition on the part of families to trace out their genealogy. This is now becoming more and more common; and I think it is very desirable that as far as possible family pedigree should be traced out. Occasions of family gatherings of those of the same name and blood should be encouraged and become more frequent.

I know some men, especially in these days, who glory in being self-made men,—unfortunately, not very well made. I believe that most of those who have risen in the world and acquired distinction, if inquired of as to the principal cause to which they attribute their success, would ascribe it to what they had received of energy, intellect, and character from some devoted mother or some humble father. They do not feel themselves to be self made, although they may have made their fortunes.

Another circumstance that tends very much to counteract this tendency to excessive individualism is a commemorative occasion like this, when epochs in a town are marked and histories of its progress are written, such as we have listened to to-day with so much interest and so much profit. It is a low ambition to have a desire for the feeling of independence of the past, and of indifference to the future. These occasions awaken nobleness of thought and largeness of mind, leading us to feel that we are connected with the workers of the past and that we have responsibilities which reach on to the future; that we are but one link in the great chain of agencies, and responsible for our part in the progress of events as they transpire. Such occasions as this are calculated to awaken and cherish these appropriate sentiments in our hearts, and therefore I rejoice in their occurrence, and especially in the great interest that this occasion has brought forth. (Applause.)

The following telegram was here received and read by the President:

QUINCY, Ill., Aug. 16th, 1871.

To WINCHESTER CENTENNIAL:—In spirit I am with you. Business prevents personal attendance. I trust that our good works for the next one hundred years will surpass those of the last century.

Winsted's Son,
W. B. ANDREWS.

REV. HORACE WINSLOW, of Willimantic, followed, in a humorous speech, giving something of the experience he passed through in Winsted, and especially as connected with his being taken on one occasion for a horse-thief; the horse and the thief having been traced to Winsted from east of the Connecticut river, and Mr. Winslow being somewhat of a stranger here, and answering the description of the supposed thief.

REV. LEONARD BACON, D. D., of New Haven, was the next speaker. He said:

I have been enjoying the occasion to-day as I rarely enjoy an occasion of the kind; for it has been in my thoughts all the time that I had nothing to do but to enjoy it. And now, what shall I say? For I know not at what point to begin.

One thing has impressed my mind to-day as it has frequently of late. Looking at the changes which have been wrought within my own memory, in the character of the industry of Connecticut, in the employment of its people, in the distribution of its population, what is to be the destiny of Connecticut during the next hundred years? The changes from 1870 to 1970 we may venture to predict will be as great as the changes have been between 1771 and 1871. A hundred years ago, when Connecticut was ready to enter into the great conflict of the Revolution, it was the food-producing state for the armies of the revolution; while to-day Connecticut does not produce the food that supplies the wants of her own operative workmen. Within my memory Connecticut was a state exporting food to distant parts of the Union and to the West Indies. To-day the people of Connecticut would starve in less than two months, if it were not for food imported from abroad. The farms on these old hill sides and hill tops have been depreciating in value year by year, and the population which does not go away to California or the West or South, slides down from the hills into these valleys, where these mill sites are, where the rivers as they pass on their way lend their power to supplement the agencies and industry of man.

By and bye those who come after us will see a change. We begin to see indications of it now. The wealth produced and accumulated in the valleys will well up on the hill sides; and the destiny of Connecticut at some future day will be to become one great hive of manufacturing industry. From the water power working to produce, and from accumulating wealth, the farms on the hill-sides will become the garden spots, as it were, of these cities and towns filled with resounding machinery and alive with industry. I look forward to that coming time with confidence. When I see the forces that are at work to-day I am not disposed to be simply a praiser of the time that is past, but to be hopeful in regard to the future; and I believe that another generation after this, and another after that, will be more enlightened, more cultivated, more controlled by moral principles, more elevated by the principles of true and saving religion than any generation that has gone before; and so, as I look forward, I trust that this fair land of ours, this historic old state that has done so much heretofore for the good of humanity, shall continue to be a model state for the Union, a state from which all the influences going forth shall ever be what they have been in the past—influences that have made a "wilderness to rejoice and be glad, and the desert to blossom as the rose." (Applause.)

REV. F. A. SPENCER, of Vernon. N. Y., followed, saying

That though he was not born in Winsted, his father and mother were born in the town. He had found it a pleasant place to visit as he had often been here; but it was also a good place to go from. There are some noble men in central New York, who went from old Winchester. We have a county where old Winchester has planted its foot a great many times, and there is right behind me a blessed friend, Deacon Hills, who, nearly ninety years ago, opened his eyes upon Winchester hill, and went into the State of New York and succeeded his own father in the deaconship of the church. Forty years ago I used to look with reverence on his gray hairs, and he used to pat me on the head and tell me he hoped I would be a good boy. We have been friends always, and I persuaded him to come down here to see how Winchester looks.

About eighty years ago my grandfather, who lies buried on Winchester hill, said to my father, then twenty-one, "John, you have been a good boy, your time is now your own; you must now go out and take care of yourself. I can do no more than provide for your sisters"—there were seven or eight of them. John went out and worked by the month; and what did he do the first year? He came down here and bought the land on which Winsted now stands, the whole Higley farm, reaching from here away up to the old hemlock swamp. He worked every day as a farmer, and took it for his "stent" to make a pair of shoes every night, for he was a shoemaker as well as farmer. There was then no road and he finally persuaded the town authorities to make him a road. He bought the whole of Winsted for three dollars an acre.

I came down here just to look at my mother's and my grandfather's graves, one here, and one in the Old Society. I have enjoyed this occasion very much indeed.

Mr. Spencer closed by an allusion to some of the pleasing characteristics of his venerable uncle, Mr. Jonathan Coe, and made pleasant allusion to some other early residents.

REV. LEUMAS H. PEASE, of New Orleans, La., a native of Winsted, being on the platform, was called upon for some remarks, but declined on account of the already lengthy exercises of the occasion.

A brief address was made by MR. JOHN R. PITKIN, of Woodhaven, N. Y., who announced himself to have been a school teacher of the olden time who never used a whip, and who once worked on a farm in Winchester for $4.50 a month, and saved half of it. A. M. Perkins, of Winsted, volunteered a short poem.

Excellent music was furnished during the exercises by a volunteer chorus.

The exercises closed at 4 o'clock—all having passed off very pleasantly.

In the evening there was a social re-union at the residence of Normand Adams, Esq.

The returned children of Winchester were warm in praise of their cordial "welcome home."

COLLECTION OF ANTIQUITIES, &c.

A very interesting feature of the celebrations in both societies were the relics of old times, in the shape of portraits of citizens once resident here, old books, articles of furniture or of wearing apparel, ancient embroidery and needle-work, &c., &c. The collection at Winchester Center was at Bronson's Hall. Among these articles were a board from the front of the gallery of the first meeting house, embellished with sundry cuts and carvings, and several dates, among them 1773, 1775, deeply sunken by jack-knives, showing that in the good old times, in spite of tithing men and blue laws, boy nature was much the same as now; many of the joiner's tools used in framing the second church, erected in 1786–1788; also a piece of the carved ornaments about the pulpit of this church, and some of the trimmings from the top of the old square pews; several pitch pipes, including the one used for many years by Major Andrews, as chorister; several portraits, including those of Rev. Father Marsh and his lovely wife, Capt. Levi Munsill and wife, Esq. Beebe and his son Robert, Widow Mercy Bronson, Rev. Dr. Abel McEwen, for more than fifty years pastor of the church in New London, a number of the members of the Blake family formerly so numerous and prominent in the town; a printed sermon (probably the only copy in existence) preached by Rev. Ammi R. Robbins, of Norfolk, at the ordination of Rev. Joshua Knapp as first pastor of the church; an arm-chair, made by John McAlpine, Esq., from the timbers of the first meeting house, and occupied during the centennial exercises by Rev. Mr. Marsh.

There were many household articles in common use half a century ago and earlier, such as the spinning-wheel, rolls, little wheel, reel, hatchel, cards, the tall clock made by "Riley Whiting, Winchester," splint-bottomed kitchen chairs, durable Windsor chairs, andirons, long-handled spider, toasting iron, lanterns without a bit of glass giving their light through the holes arranged in curious figures punched in the tin, tall iron candlesticks, warming pans, and pewter tankards and platters, some of them polished to the last degree of brightness.

From the Starks family we had the old family cradle, and the bread tray of the first Deacon Wetmore, hollowed out of a log with a hatchet, "Granny Loveland's" family Bible, with other things.

The Loomis family exhibited a very ancient Bible, with a full family record; many curious pieces of antique earthen ware; a wonderful woolen blanket or rug made in 1775 by Hannah Dolbeare, given to the Foreign Mission School at Cornwall, and bought by Deacon Loomis when steward of the institution.

The Wetmores brought sundry cumbrous and rough tools, used by successive generations of workers in wood; a strange old decanter, or demi-john; Dr. Wetmore's spurs, used for years in his horseback rides over the hills, &c.

Col. Ozias Bronson's sword attracted much attention, as also his large dining table, where he lunched his company on training days.

The family Bible of the early McAlpines, with the covered blue wooden cradle, brought over the sea from the Scottish home, were worth much examination; while a covered pitcher, somewhat broken, presented to Mrs. Marsh many years ago, by Miss Sarah Benedict, and proved to have come over in the Mayflower, aimed at the preëminence.

We looked wonderingly at the queer old round table that Widow Hannah Everitt, the sturdy pioneer, spread before her guests when she kept tavern on the North road, where the latch string was always out, and we saw the veritable wooden latch, taken from her house, (torn down several years since,) lying upon the table. The funny old wrapper, with a square collar, said to have belonged to the landlady, was in keeping with the large glass tumblers, ornamented with wonderful figures, and in possession of the family more than a century.

Then we had Dr. Everitt's old square chair, his inkstand and account books, together with his spectacles with their huge round glasses and iron enough in the frames to make a small stove, while articles of crockery in common use by Mrs. Noble J. Everitt for more than fifty years, each with a different landscape painted upon it, and a quaint pepper-box with a cork in the bottom, completed the interesting collection from this family.

Mrs. Isaac Wade sent a large mug and bowl of strange pattern and great age, while the toddy tumbler of old Mr. Elijah Blake, always filled on Thanksgiving days and similar family occasions and passed around to the whole company, was exhibited by his granddaughter, and gave rise to endless jokes and mirth.

Some curious crockery from Henry Drake, a table-waiter used at the ordination of Rev. Mr. Marsh, a platter from Mrs. Harvey Andrews, tea cups from Mrs. Norris Coe, sundry tiles and some delicate old china from Mrs. Frank L. Whiting, with many old-fashioned household utensils from James L. Bragg, a linen table-cloth spun and woven by the wife of Dea. Eliphaz Alvord, with many towels and sheets of household manufacture in the early times, each received their share of examination.

The Munsill baby dress worn by six children of Capt. M., the youngest now about sixty years old, with a bedquilt pieced from the chintz wedding dress of the mother of Norris Coe, worn eighty years ago, and costing a dollar a yard, showed the durability of old-fashioned manufactures.

The collection at Winsted was arranged in the basement of the M. E. Church, from which the seats had been removed, two long tables receiving the various articles excepting such as were hung upon the walls or otherwise disposed of. A prominent feature of this collection was the large number of portraits of natives or former residents, among which were those of Gideon Hall, Sr., Dr. Luman Wakefield and wife, Rev. James Beach and wife, Capt. Wheelock Thayer and wife, Col. Hosea Hinsdale and wife, Dea. James H. Alvord and wife, Jonathan Coe and wife, Moses Camp, Sr., and wife, Rev. Daniel Coe and wife, Solomon Rockwell and wife, Alpha Rockwell and wife, Mrs. Hepzibah Rockwell, mother of the brothers Alpha and Solomon, Lorrin Whiting and wife, Riley Whiting and wife; and of later residents, Seth L. Wilder, William H. Phelps, S. Ward Coe, Lucius Clarke, Nelson D. Coe, Elliot Beardsley, Gideon Hall, Jr., and wife, Luman Hubbell.

There was a large variety of ancient relics, some of which were local in character and associations, while others illustrated old times without special reference to Winchester. The first tavern sign ever put up in Winsted, used at the "Hall place," on the hill beyond the East Village, attracted much attention. There were pewter platters, two silver teaspoons seventy-five years old, mugs, dishes, pans, spinning wheels, old chairs and tables, hatchels, cards, and all the paraphernalia of spinning and reeling, many small mantel ornaments, antique and unique; a piece of pottery from Mrs. R. L. Beecher that came over in the "Mayflower"; a child's shoe, handed down in the family of Mrs. Wm. C. Phelps, which was made for Mrs. Phelps's great-aunt, and known to be 140 years old; curious and beautiful articles of needle-work made by the girls of 70 to 100 years ago, among which was specially to be noted a silk-embroidered landscape sent by Mrs. Ezekiel Woodford; an old "Hussey"* or needle-case that belonged to the grand-mother of Mrs. Daniel Tuttle (herself 85 years old); a knitting sheath some six inches long, curiously carved in wood and made in 1732; some bed curtains with large, spreading figures, from 150 to 200 years old.

There was a bass-viol over 100 years old; a pitch-pipe, and a tuning-fork some six or eight inches long, the property of Jesse Williams, which were used to start the music in the first religious society in Winsted; a straw hat many years worn by "Uncle Jonny" Coe; a ponderous musket, used in the Revolutionary War, and a coat and vest, long and curious, 80 or 90 years of age, made here, and worn by a bridegroom exactly as it was shown.

Mrs. Caleb J. Camp furnished a capacious, old-time oaken chest, with carved front, a peculiar merit of which was, that it did *not* come over in the "Mayflower," although it was unquestionably aged when it came from England; a round dining table, old but elaborate; the first pulpit Bible of the first Congregational Church in Winsted; the private Bible of her father, the Rev. James Beach, having the texts he used marked, and bear-

---

* This word is supposed to be a corruption of "housewife."

ing evidence of faithful and long continued use; a newspaper published just after Washington's death, draped for him and containing his will; a pair of solid silver knee-buckles; a pair of linen stockings beautifully wrought by hand 60 to 75 years since, and two pairs of gloves whose gauntlets reached to the elbows.

J. J. Whiting brought a suit of child's clothes, made in the fashion of fifty years ago; a large pewter platter and dishes, in which were served baked beans and pork, which formed a part of the dinner of Gov. Jewell and others.

Benjamin Lawrence brought a large masonic pitcher, covered with emblems of all degrees of the order, and holding three or four quarts, for more than one hundred years in his family, and of foreign manufacture; and an old masonic suit was shown by Orrin White.

Various ancient books were displayed, especially one by Edward Clarke, a hymn book of great antiquity and interest; old papers by S. B. Forbes, Mrs. Plumb, and others. And finally, a quantity of arrow heads and other Indian relics dug up within our borders.

The room was beautifully decorated with evergreens, and presented an attractive appearance.

Nor should mention be forgotten of the ancient springless wagon in the procession, with small wheels having large spokes and long, tapering hubs, and with high-backed kitchen chairs for the occupants, whose feet rested on an abundant sprinkling of straw. The driver, arrayed in as old costume as could be found, plied his ox-whip faithfully, and was admirably supported by three ladies whose dress was equally representative in its character. And the riders on saddle and pillion gave an excellent exposition of that style of locomotion so universally in vogue when the town was settled.

POSTSCRIPT.

The death of Theron Bronson, Esq., late presiding officer of the Winchester church centennial exercises, occurring while these sheets are going through the press, we copy from the *Winsted Herald* the following obituary:

Died at Winchester Center, on the 20th of January, 1873, Theron Bronson, Esq., aged 63 years.

Mr. Bronson, by birth, ancestry, life-long residence, and active business, has been identified with all the interests of the town, and especially with those of the parish of his residence.

With activity, energy, and endurance, rarely equaled, he embarked in business at an early age, and prosecuted it in various forms, with increasing ardor, until the very close of his useful and exemplary life. As a farmer and stock dealer he became by far the largest land-owner in the town; while as a trader and produce dealer, he contributed largely to the prosperity of the community around him. His manly form and cheerful visage are indelibly impressed on the memory of a wide-spread circle of friends and acquaintances.

When to these characteristics are added a kind and generous heart and liberal hand, unquestioned integrity, large public spirit and private benevolence, and a pure Christian life, we have a man whose memory will be gratefully cherished, and whose loss will be deplored long after his mortal remains shall have mingled with kindred dust.

APPENDIX.

TOWN, COUNTY, AND LEGISLATIVE OFFICERS.

SENATORS.

Name	First	Last		Name	First	Last
Beardsley, Elliott	1853			Coe, Samuel W.	1850	
Beebe, James	1836	1837		Dudley, George	1863	
Boyd, John	1854			Hall, Gideon, Jr.	1847	
Clarke, Lucius	1846					

REPRESENTATIVES.

[NOTE.—Previous to the adoption of the Constitution of 1818, two sessions of the Legislature were held each year — in May and October.]

Name.	First.	Last.	No.	Name.	First.	Last.	No.
Adams, Matthew	1818	1831	5	Fanning, John J.	1863		1
" Normand	1851		1	Fyler, Florimond D.	1872		1
Alvord, Charles	1861		1	Gaylord, Nathaniel B.	1816	1818	2
" Eliphaz	1787	1811	11	Gilbert, Alvin	1850		1
Andrews, Daniel	1833		1	" William L.	1848	1868	2
" Harvey	1858		1	Gilman, Elias E.	1866		1
Beardsley, Elliot	1863		1	Hall, Gideon, Jr.	1838	1860	4
Beebe, James	1819	1826	3	Hatch, Washington	1844		1
Beecher, Rollin L.	1846	1864	2	Higley, Horace	1799	1806	7
Benedict, Benjamin	1787	1817	7	Hills, Huet	1792	1794	4
Bidwell, John W.	1855		1	" Seth	1781	1793	6
Bird, David	1852		1	Hinsdale, Bissell	1815	1815	2
Birdsall, James	1859		1	" Hosea	1821		1
Blake, Jonathan	1851		1	" Theodore	1837		1
Boyd, James	1804	1819	5	Hoadley, Samuel	1811		1
" John	1830	1835	2	Holmes, Joseph	1808	1814	6
Bronson, Isaac	1823	1832	3	Hubbard, Stephen A.	1855		1
" Isaac A.	1866		1	Hurlbut, Samuel	1791	1810	17
" Theron	1849		1	" "	1835		1
" William B.	1857		1	" Stephen	1856		1
Brownson, Ozias	1783	1784	3	Jenkins, Benjamin	1803	1804	2
Brown, Francis	1867		1	Loomis, Oliver	1834		1
Bull, Merrit	1817	1817	2	Marsh, Joseph M.	1871		1
Camp, John	1844		1	McCune, David	1791		1
" Moses	1865		1	" Robert	1781	1797	9
Case, Lyman	1839		1	Miller, Joseph	1829		1
Chase, Dudley	1854		1	Miner, Phineas	1809	1816	6
Clarke, Thomas M.	1857		1	Moore, Ralph H.	1870		1
Cleveland, George B.	1867		1	Munsill, Marcus	1847		1
" James C.	1834		1	Nash, Alva	1829	1830	2
Coe, Jonathan, Jr.	1822	1828	4	Pettibone, Ira W.	1868		1
" James R.	1845		1	Phelps, Daniel	1818	1828	2
" Norris	1838	1839	2	" Warren	1862		1
" Roger	1814	1815	3	Platt, Sylvester	1860		1
" William G.	1859	1865	2	Roberts, Harvey L.	1871		1
Cummings, J. T.	1809		1	Rockwell, Alpha	1807		1
Drake, Rufus	1836	1837	2	" John T.	1869		1
Dudley, George	1847		1	" Solomon	1820		1

618   ANNALS OF WINCHESTER,

Name.	First.	Last.	No.	Name.	First.	Last.	No.
Rowley, Artemas	1853		1	Wakefield, Luman	1826	1827	2
Russell, Giles	1810	1816	3	Watson, Thomas	1864		1
" Nathaniel	1801		1	Welch, James	1852		1
Sheldon, Philo G.	1850		1	Wetmore, Abel S.	1848		1
Smith, Asahel	1827	1831	2	" John G.	1862		1
" Elisha	1856		1	" Seth	1799	1802	4
" Heman	1795	1800	3	White, George	1861		1
" Zebina	1798	1802	2	Wheelock, Daniel B.	1849		1
Spencer, Grinnell	1824		1	Whiting, Riley	1818	1832	2
Strong, David	1872		1	Wilder, Seth L.	1858		1
Taylor, George	1853		1	Wilson, Abijah	1798	1802	2
Thayer, Wheelock	1833		1	Woodruff, Frederick	1870		1
Tolles, Amos	1812	1812	2	York, Charles J.	1869		1

JUSTICES OF THE PEACE.

Name.	First.	Last.	No.	Name.	First.	Last.	No.
Adams, Normand	1848	1850	2	Howe, John D.	1842		1
Alvord, Charles	1849		1	Holabird, William S.	1825	1855	28
" Eliphaz	1779	1817	18	Hubbard, Stephen A.	1860		1
Baldwin, Ezra	1848	1854	3	Hubbell, Luman	1833	1835	2
Beach, Albert N.	1870			" McPherson	1849	1851	2
Beebe, James	1817	1839	22	Humphrey, James	1852	1854	2
Beecher, Rollin L.	1854			Hurlbut, Samuel Jr.	1831	1849	9
Beers, Lewis F.	1866	1868	2	" Samuel	1798	1819	21
Blake, Jonathan	1839	1858	14	" William F.	1870		
Boyd, John	1828	1858	27	Kelsey, William	1848	1851	3
Bronson, Isaac	1822	1839	17	Loomis, Frederick L.	1864	1866	2
" Isaac A.	1868	1873	3	" Lewis E.	1843		1
" Theron	1842	1864	20	Marsh, William S.	1833	1838	5
Camp, Edward	1864	1866	2	McAlpine, John, Jr.	1846	1851	3
" Moses	1844	1860	8	" Silas H.	1835	1842	7
Carrington, Wm.	1844		1	Miller, Joseph	1817	1834	17
Case, Lyman	1838	1856	3	Munsell, Luman	1844	1850	6
" Lyman W.	1851		1	" Marcus	1860	1868	4
Clarke, Lucius	1844	1848	4	Nash, Alva	1832	1854	22
Coe, James R.	1848	1850	2	Norton, Charles S.	1862		
" Jonathan, Jr.	1824	1830	6	Oatman, Loyal	1870		1
" Norris,	1844	1850	5	Peck, William K.	1866	1869	3
" Samuel W.	1835	1868	33	Perkins, Augustus M.	1872		
" William G.	1858	1872	14	" Hiram	1850	1873	16
Crowell, Albert	1850		1	Pettibone, Ira W.	1866	1871	5
Dickerman, Wm. B.	1856	1858	2	Platt, Sylvester	1848	1860	11
Drake, Moses	1846	1851	2	Rockwell, Henry E.	1846		1
" Rufus	1844	1846	2	" Solomon	1803	1818	15
Dudley, George	1841	1846	3	Rood, William H.	1845	1871	4
Forbes, Samuel B.	1868	1872	4	Rowley, Stephen	1835	1838	3
Ford, Harvey	1842	1864	11	Senior, Thomas	1850		1
" Nelson D.	1864	1873	5	Weed, Charles B.	1858	1862	4
Foskett, Anson	1842	1850	8	Welch, James	1838	1841	3
Fyler, Florimond D.	1866			Wentworth, Chester	1850		1
Gaylord, Nathaniel B.	1841	1846	5	Wetmore, George W.	1850		1
Giddings, V. R. C.	1862	1864	2	" Truman S.	1819	1842	20
Gilbert, Alvin	1843		1	Wilder, Seth L.	1864	1866	2
" William L.	1854	1858	4	Woodford, Erastus S.	1845	1870	17
Hall, Gideon, Jr.	1832	1866	31	Woodruff, Frederick	1872		
Hallett, Charles B.	1862	1866	4	Soper, Chester	1831	1841	10
Hatch, William F.	1847	1849	2	Taylor, George	1851	1854	3
Hinsdale, Hosea	1831	1833	2	Thayer, Wheelock	1835	1847	5
" Theodore	1835	1842	7	Wakefield, John L.	1850	1852	
Hitchcock, Roland	1845			" Luman	1819	1848	29

APPENDIX. 619

JUDGES OF PROBATE.

Name.	First	Last	No.	Name.	First	Last	No.
Boyd, John	1838	1869	14	Hall, Gideon, Jr.	1839	1848	6
Camp, John	1861		1	Hitchcock, Roland	1846	1856	6
Coe, Daniel	1842		1	Perkins, Hiram	1869	1871	2
" Samuel W.	1843	1850	3	Rood, William H.	1847		1
Gilman, Elias E.	1871						

TOWN CLERKS.

Name	First	Last	No.	Name	First	Last	No.
Alvord, Charles	1851	1854	3	Goodwin, Theodore	1797		1
" Eliphaz	1771	1819	46	Hubbard, Stephen A.	1854		1
Boyd, John	1829	1873	26	North, Martin	1801		1
Camp, Moses, 2d	1846	1849	3	Platt, Levi	1819	1827	8
Coe, Samuel W.	1833	1841	11	Woodford, Erastus	1827	1829	2

SELECTMEN.

Name	First	Last	No.	Name	First	Last	No.
Adams, Matthew	1805	1825	5	Ford, Harvey	1855	1856	2
Alvord, Eliphaz	1773	1774	2	" Nelson D.	1869		1
" Jonathan	1771		1	Foskett, Anson	1843	1852	3
Andrews, Lloyd	1815	1817	3	Fyler, Hilamon	1857	1858	2
Andrus, Abraham	1773	1774	2	Gibbs, Warham	1772	1778	6
Austin, David	1772	1787	2	Goodwin, Theodore	1798		1
Beach, Adna	1799	1805	5	Hall, Gideon	1811	1846	9
Beardsley, Elliot	1858	1859	2	Hills, Beriah	1771		1
Beebe, James	1809	1822	5	" Huet	1796	1798	2
Beecher, Rollin L	1854		1	" Seth	1771	1788	12
Benedict, Benjamin	1780	1788	5	Hinsdale, Hosea	1808	1825	9
" Benjamin, Jr.	1804		1	" John	1861		1
Blake, Jonathan	1828	1845	3	Holmes, Joseph	1804		1
Boyd, James	1802	1803	2	Hoskins, Silas	1853		1
Bragg, James L.	1864		1	Hubbell, Luman	1835	1837	3
Branard, Othniel	1789	1794	2	Hurlbut, Lemuel	1831	1832	2
Bronson, Isaac A.	1862	1863	2	" Leonard	1823	1824	2
" Theron	1849		1	" Samuel	1781	1796	8
Brownson, Benoni	1792		1	Jopp, Orson W.	1853		1
" Isaac	1810	1820	4	Lee, John	1796		1
" Levi	1789	1812	2	Loomis, Abiel	1805		1
" Ozias	1780	1796	11	" Alanson	1841	1844	2
" Salmon	1802	1803	2	" Daniel	1789		1
Camp, Edward	1870		1	" Frederick L.	1872		1
" John	1847	1861	6	" Lorrain	1808		1
Case, Lyman	1836	1857	3	Malery, Elisha	1792		1
Chase, Dudley	1846	1848	3	Marshall, Reuben	1797	1801	3
Clarke, Lucius	1854		1	McAlpin, John	1808	1818	7
Coe, Eben	1814		1	McCune, Robert	1777	1788	6
" Jehial	1850		1	" Samuel	1787		1
" Jonathan	1778	1793	2	Miner, Phineas	1802	1803	2
" Jonathan, Jr.	1819	1825	7	Munsill, Marcus	1841	1843	3
" Nelson D.	1848		1	Murray, Ammi	1827		1
" Norris	1825	1826	2	" Daniel	1834	1835	2
" Roger	1806	1822	4	" Frederick	1857	1872	7
" Rozel	1786		1	Nash, Alva	1827	1833	5
Cook, Reuben	1831	1842	4	" John	1804	1814	3
" Urijah	1804		1	" Lorenzo S.	1861		1
Drake, Moses, Jr.	1829	1830	2	Newton, Samuel S.	1865		1
Doolittle, Jesse	1780	1788	5	Norton, Levi	1793	1801	4
Dunham, Jonathan	1792	1793	2	Perkins, Hiram	1855	1869	4
Everitt, Andrew	1796		1	Persons, Wing	1868		1
Frisbee, Joseph	1785	1789	2	Phelps, Daniel	1804	1826	2

ANNALS OF WINCHESTER.

SELECTMEN, continued.

Name.	First.	Last.	No.	Name.	First.	Last.	No.
Phelps, William C.	1860	1872	9	Thayer, Wheelock	1829	1833	3
Pine, Samuel W.	1870		1	Wetmore, John G.	1866	1867	2
Platt, Levi	1813	1814	2	" Samuel	1771	1775	4
" Sylvester	1836		1	" Samuel, 2d	1797	1798	2
Rice, Lorenzo	1860	1864	2	" Seth	1799	1801	3
Rockwell, Alpha	1802	1807	4	" Willard S.	1849	1856	3
Rood, Wm. H.	1865	1868	4	Whedon, Stephen	1817	1819	3
Rowley, Artemas	1836	1854	10	Wheeler, Nathan	1790	1793	3
Russell, Giles	1814	1818	5	Wilcoxson, Elisha	1779	1787	2
" Nathaniel	1789	1794	2	Wilder, Seth L.	1862	1863	2
Smith, Elisha	1817		1	Wilson, Abijah	1795	1801	7
" Heman	1790	1800	5	Wright, John	1774	1785	2
" Josiah	1776	1788	7	" Charles	1781		1
" Josiah, Jr.	1826	1827	2	Woodford, Erastus	1826	1830	4
" Zebina	1790	1813	8	Woodruff, Frederick	1869		1
Soper, Chester	1829		1	" Isaac B.	1862		1
Strong, David	1871		1				

COLLEGE GRADUATES.

Rev. Noble Everett, Yale,	1795	Rev. Orrin W. White, Oberlin,		
Abel McEwen, D. D., "	1804	Hiram Wilson, Wesleyan U.,		
George Baldwin, "	1811	John C. Holabird, "		
John Boyd, "	1821	Rev. Jonathan Coe, "		
Theodore Hinsdale, "	1821	Seth Church, "		
Edward Rockwell, "	1821	Charles F. Wetmore, Trinity,		
Rev. Samuel Rockwell, "	1825	James B. Wakefield, "		
Ira W. Pettibone, "	1854	Rev. Leumas H. Pease, Williams,	1835	
Edward R. Beardsley, "	1859	Rev. Henry B. Blake, "	1841	
Rev. John B. Doolittle, "	1863	George M. Carrington, "	1861	
Rev. John W. Alvord, Oberlin.		Benjamin W. Pettibone, Amherst,	1860	
Rev. Harmon E. Burr, "				

INDEX TO ANNALS OF WINCHESTER.

SUBJECTS.

Baldwin, Rev. John D., 356.
Bank, Hurlbut, 437.
"   Winsted, 436, 437.
"   Winsted Savings, 437.
Barkhamsted Light House, 25.
Bassett, Rev. Archibald, 213, 224, 233.
Beach, Rev. James, 356, 386–388.
Booge, Rev. Publius V., 182–184, 206, 212, 213.
Bride Stealing, 109.
Building Associations, 445–448.
Bulkley, Rev. C. H. A., 452.
Burying-grounds, 66, 72, 278.

Census, of 1756, 122; of 1771, 82; of 1774, 122; of 1782, 158.
Cheese-press, 337.
Clergymen, 56, 58, 63, 88, 89, 90, 95, 102–104, 107, 179, 183, 184, 206, 209, 212, 213, 224, 233, 234, 236, 237, 256, 356, 357, 396, 397, 453.
Clifton Borough, 431.
Cold Summer of 1816, 418.
Cooley, Rev. H. E., 357.
Cunningham, Rev. John, 256.

Dana, Rev. M. McG., 357.
Democratic Party, 206.
Dill, Rev. James H., 256.
Dwight, Rev. Timothy M., 356.

Eddy, Rev. Hiram, 452, 453, 466, 467.
Emigration from town, 44, 45, 223, 224.
Enoch Arden, 107, 108.

Fieldpiece (patriotic), 243, 244.
Fireplace, or " Smoke," 161.
Fish, 23, 26.
Freemen admitted, 143, 147, 148, 154, 171, 172, 175, 191, 192, 195, 198, 202, 207, 211, 213, 226, 228, 230, 231, 234, 236, 240, 241.
French War, 263, 291, 314.

Game, 23, 25, 26, 34.
Gay, Rev. Wm. M., 256.
Geese, 233.
General Training, 221, 222.
Goodenough, Rev. Arthur, 257.
"Great Exodus," 47, 224.
Green, Old Winchester, 221, 222.

Hard Winter of '83, 47, 48.
Harmer's Campaign, 53.
Hartford Jail-breaking of 1722, 11, 12.

Hartford Votes in town meeting, 10, 12.
Hawk Catching, 49.

Independence Day, Celebration of, 242, 243.
Indians, 25, 339.
Institute, Winchester, 257, 258.

Jefferson Flood, 224.

Knapp, Rev. Joshua, 89, 90, 179.
King, Rev. Salmon, 354.
Kinney, Rev. Aaron, 354–356.

Land Title, 9–14.
Land Grants to various towns, 9–14.
"   "   Votes in Hartford town meetings respecting, 10, 12.
Land, plan of division of, 17–19, 84.
"   reserved for highways, 19.
"   given to Hartford Ministers, 9, 32.
"   none reserved for Churches or Schools, 19, 32.
"   earliest deed of, recorded, 9.
Lawyers, 55, 342–344, 392, 393, 424.
Libraries, 500–504.

MANUFACTURES :—
    Axes, 511, 512.
    Augers, 521.
    Bolts and Nuts, 520.
    Cards, 516.
    Carriage springs, 522.
    Cheese Boxes, 506.
    Clocks, 515, 516.
    Coffin trimmings, 522.
    Condensed milk, 522.
    Cutlery, 520.
    Fire Irons, 521.
    Forges, 22, 95.
    Forks, 518.
    Foundries, 518.
    Grist Mills, 506, 507.
    Guns, 46.
    Iron and Steel, 363, 508–511.
    Joiners' tools, 522.
    Leather, 512–514.
    Linseed Oil, 518.
    Lumber, 522.
    Machinery, 518, 519.
    Nails, 511.
    Pins, 521.
    Plated ware, 522.
    Saw Mills, 62, 130–132.
    Scythes, 311, 507, 508.
    Tanneries, 371, 373.
    Tools, 519, 520.

INDEX TO SUBJECTS.

MANUFACTURES, *continued.*
   Wagons and Carriages, 516, 517.
   Whiskey. 517.
   Wire. 512
   Wooden Ware, 505, 506.
   Woolen Cloths, 514, 515.
Marsh, Rev. Frederick, 237, 238, 256.
Masonic Organizations, 499, 500.
Methodism, rise in town, 104, 402.
Methodist Church at Noppit, 256.
   "   " at Winsted, 402.
Miles, Rev. Thomas M., 357.
Minerals, 21.
New Town. petitioned for, 172.
Oath of Fidelity, 134.
Odd Fellows' Lodges, 500.
Parsons, Rev. Stephen, 349, 350.
Pearson, Rev. James B., 357.
Penitent Deacons, 130
Petitions for incorporation, 75, 76, 81-83.
Pettibone, Rev. Ira, 256. 257, 356.
Physicians, 50 68, 69, 396.
Pierson, Rev. Arthur T., 452.
Pioneer Settlers, 31-74.
Pomeroy, Rev. Augustus, 356.
Poor, care of by town, 255.
Post Offices, 362, 431-433.
Practical Jokes, 276, 277.
Protestant Episcopal Church, 439, 440.
Railroads.—Naugatuck, 437-439. Conn.
   Western, 491-493.
Revolutionary War. — Town Votes, 122,
   125-27, 128, 129, 134, 135, 137, 139.
   Declaration of Rights, 127, 129.—
   Soldiers of, 38, 44, 49, 50, 51, 53, 57,
   61, 65, 70, 71, 108, 109, 122, 129, 135,
   137, 139, 144, 146, 147, 149, 150, 151,
   161-166, 176, 191, 264, 265, 275, 291,
   298, 305, 314, 394.
Roads, 27-30, 102, 251-254, 358, 359, 376,
   404, 448, 449.
Russell, Rev. H. A., 357.
Sabba'day Houses, 79, 80.
St. Francis' R. C. Seminary, 445.
   "   " Parochial School, 445.
St. Joseph's R. C. Church, 444, 445.
St. Margaret's R. C. Fem. Seminary, 445.
Saracena, Fra. Leo da, 444.
Satan's Kingdom, 25.
School Costumes and Games, 380, 381.
School Houses, 33, 72, 218, 248, 358, 378,
   402, 403.
School Teachers, 381-383, 403, 428.
Schools, Common, 198, 217-221, 379-383.
Schools, Spelling in, 220, 221.
   " High and Seminaries, 257, 258,
   403, 404, 428.
Schools, Graded, 488.
Selectmen, 254.
Simons, Rev. Noah, 354.
Small-Pox, Inoculation for, 207, 208.
   "   " Pest-Houses, 208.
Smith, James C., Obituary of, 255.
Stocks, 242, 243.
Streams, 23, 24.

Sunday Traveling, 29, 148, 208.
Taverns, 29, 37, 97, 202, 210, 244, 358,
   378.
Temperance Reform & Societies, 493-499.
Trees, When Transplanted, 379.
Turnpikes, Green Woods, 211, 376.
   " Waterbury, 225.
Walker, Rev. J. B. R., 357.
War of 1812, 267, 274, 416-418.
War of 1861, 206, 460-487.
Wedding Customs, 109.
Wetherby, Rev. Charles, 453.
Whipping Post, 242, 243.
Will of First Settler, 33.
Winchester, First Ecclesiastical Society,
   Organization, 75-78.
Winchester Society, Petitioners for, 76.
   " First Meeting-House, 77, 80.
   " Second " 169, 202. 244.
Winchester, Third, " 244.
   " First Congregational Church,
   86, 88. .
Winchester Constituent Members, 87-
   " Early Admissions, 87, 88.
   " Creed and Covenant, 86, 87.
   " Ordination of 1st Pastor, 89.
   " Ordaining Covenant, 89.
   " Half-way Covenant, 102, 104,
   125, 140, 143.
Winchester, Township, Preliminary History, 9-14.
Winchester, Proprietors of, 15, 16.
   " Geological Formation, 21.
   " Physical " 20-24.
   " Proprietors' Meetings, 15, 16.
   " " Division of Lands,
   16-19, 31.
Winchester, Town, Incorporation, 81-83.
   " " Organization, 83-85.
   " " First Officers, 83.
   " " First Representation
   in General Assembly, 148.
Winchester, New Inhabitants, 93 to 383.
   " Meetings, 83 to 300.
Winsted Society, Petition for Incorporation, 281.
Winsted, Ancient, 346-355.
   " Modern, 355, 357.
   " Ecclesiastical History, 346-357.
   " First Cong. Church, 357, 453.
   " Second " " organized,
   357, 453.
Winsted, Buildings in 1803, 377-379.
   " Families " 380.
   " Villages, Early Aspect and
   Growth, 358-362, 430, 435, 436.
Winsted, Borough, 453-456.
   " Water Works, 455-457.
   " Roads, 358-62, 435, 440.
   " First Meeting-House, 346-54.
   " Second " 355, 360,
   361.
Winsted Parade Ground, 359, 362.
Woodworth, Rev. Ezra, 351-354.

SETTLERS AND INHABITANTS SPECIALLY NOTED WITH THEIR FAMILY RECORDS.

Ackley, Levi, 319.
Adams, Mathew, 226.
Adkins, James, 148.
Adkins, Isaac, 148.
Agard, Aaron. and Jos., 149.
Allen, John, 298.
Albro, Daniel, 407.
Alvord, Jonathan, 62.
Alvord, Eliphaz, 62-64.
Alvord, John, 64.
Alvord, David, 119.
Alvord, James H., 397.
Alvord, Ruel, 397.
Andrews, Abm. Sen., 105.
Andrews, Theophilus, 105.
Andrews, Abm. Jr., 106.
Andrews, Ens. Dan., 106.
Andrews, Eli, 106.
Andrews, Major Lloyd, 195.
Andrews, Dan'l Jr., 106.
Andrews, Elijah, 148.
Apley, Josiah, 344.
Arnold, Stephen, 268.
Avered, Capt. Josiah, 47.
Austin, David, 42.
Austin, David Jr., 43.
Austin, John, 267.

Bacon, Francis, John, 179.
Bailey, Theodore, 227.
Balcom, John Jr., 266.
Balcom, John Sr., 266.
Balcom, Jonathan, 266.
Balcom, Nathaniel, 266.
Balcom, Elias, 267.
Balcom, Elias Cabit, 267.
Baldwin, Samuel W., 236.
Baldwin, Norman, 236.
Baldwin, Reuben, 386.
Barbour, William, 136.
Barnstable, Wm , 146.
Bartlett, Samuel, 408.
Bassett, Lemuel, 123.
Beach, Caleb. 33.
Beach, Joel, 33-35.
Beach, Caleb (2), 35, 215.
Beach, John, 120.
Beach, Rev. James, 120, 386.
Beach, Adna, 186.
Beach, Horace V., 187.
Beach. Fisk, 187.
Beckley, Richard, 225.
Beckley, Daniel, Norris, 250.
Beebe, James. 231.
Beebe, David, 196.
Benedict, Capt. Benj., 71.
Benedict, Capt. Timothy. 72, 3.
Benedict, Timothy Jr., 72, 3.
Benedict, Timothy, (3) 72.
Benedict, Za'mon, 175.
Benedict, John, 175.
Benedict, Elijah, 344.
Bishop, Harry, Leverett, and Seth, 412.
Blackman, Peter, 131.
Blackman, Nathan, 131.
Blackman, Truman & J. P., 131
Blake, Elijah, 208
Blake, Jonathan, 209.

Blake, Harry, 209.
Blake, Ithuel, 210.
Blake, Allen, 210.
Boyd, James, 312-315.
Boyd, John, 316.
Boyd, James M , 316.
Boyd, Thomas, 321.
Boyd, Samuel, 316, 423.
Booge, Rev. P. V., 187.
Bragg, James, 245.
Bronson, Dea. Levi, 101.
Bronson, Col. Ozias, 109.
Bronson, Ozias Jr., 109.
Bronson, Levi (2), Salmon, and Asahel, 110.
Bronson, Abijah P. & Isaac, 111.
Bronson, Benoni, 154.
Bronson, Chauncey and Orentus, 15*.
Bronson, Parliament, 155.
Brooks, Asaph B., 239.
Brooks, Samuel and Chauncey, 239.
Broughton, Nathan, 175.
Bull, Merritt, 332.
Bull, Thomas R., 375.
Bunnell, Eliab, 386.
Bunnell, William, 210.
Burnham, Daniel, 392.
Burr, Allen, 228.
Burr, Jehiel, 325.
Burr, Salmon, 374.
Burr, Erastus, 385.
Burr, Roswell, 385.
Burr, Halsey, 385.
Burton, John, 307.
Butrick, Cyrus, 333.
Byington, Jesse, 398.

Camp, Samuel and Moses, 330 -332.
Cannon, Timothy, 322.
Cannon, Thomas, 145.
Carpenter, Bemsley, 391.
Case, Wm. R., 193.
Case, Asher, 239.
Castel, William, 119.
Castel, Elijah, 119.
Caul, William, 407.
Caul, Charles C., 406.
Chamberlin, Wm., Sr., & Jr., 155.
Champion. Nathan, 407.
Chase, Gedeliah, 345.
Chase. George, Dudley and Reuben, 248.
Chickley, William, 227.
Church, John, 144.
Church, Jonathan, Uri, 145.
Church, Hiram, 249.
Cleveland, James C., 409.
Cleveland. Orrin, 411.
Clark, Samuel. 131.
Clark, Daniel, 137.
Clark, Uzal, 288.
Clarke, Lemuel, 394.
Clarke, Lucius, 395, 410.
Clarke. Jesse, 373.
Clarke, Nathan W., 373.

Coe, Jonathan, 50.
Coe, Oliver, 51.
Coe, Robert, Jon., & Oliver, 52.
Coe, Jonathan, 53, 309.
Coe, David, 53.
Coe, Daniel, Eben, 54.
Coe, Roger, 198.
Coe, Jehial, Asahel, 55.
Coe, Nelson D., 55.
Coe, Jonathan, James R., 56.
Coit, Richard, 148.
Cone, Daniel H., 150.
Cone, Samuel, Warren, 239.
Cook, Aaron, 59.
Cook, Shubael, 303.
Cook, Urijah, 303.
Cook, Reuben. 303.
Cook, Anson, 304
Cook, Joseph, 333.
Corbin, Peter, 113.
Corbin, Peter Jr , Daniel, 114.
Crissey, David, 270.
Crissey, Preserved, Israel, 270.
Crocker, Wm., 199.
Crocker James,
Crowe, Henry B., 413.
Crum, William, 241.
Curtis, Jared, 232.

Davis, William, 314.
Dayton, Archibald, 250.
Deer, John, 150
Deer, Jonathan, 151.
Dodge, Joseph, 132.
Derby, John, 275.
DeWolf, Benjamin, 300.
DeWolf, Daniel, 301.
Doolittle, Jesse, 272.
Doolittle, Jesse Jr., Zera, 272.
Doolittle, Lyman, 272.
Douglass, Israel, 319.
Drake, Moses, 246.
Drake, Rufus. 249.
Dunham, Jonathan, 305.
Dudley, George. 333, 433.
Dutton, Nath., 73.

Eggleston, Daniel, 306.
Elmer, Hezekiah, 124.
Elmore, Joseph B., 176.
Elmore, Nathaniel, 196.
Everitt, Josiah, 47.
Everitt, Dr. Josiah. 49.
Everitt. Andrew, 50.
Everitt, Elihu, 230.
Everitt, Rev. Noble, 49.
Everitt, Noble J., 231.

Fay, Timothy and Wm., 132.
Fay, Gershom, 132.
Fay. Thaddeus, 308.
Filley, Wm., 40.
Filley, Abraham. 40.
Filley, Remembrance, 41
Forbes, Daniel, 126.
Ford. Harvey, 249.
Frisbie, Joseph. 112.
Frisbie, Elijah, 112.

INDEX OF SETTLERS.

Frisbie, Eli, 207.
Fyler, Silas, 188.
Fyler, Roman, 188.
Fyler, Stephen, Jr., 412.

Gaylord, Nathaniel B., (See Rockwell family.)
Gaylord, Henry L., 425.
Gaylord, Stephen, 207.
Gibbs, Warham, 65.
Gilbert, Samuel, 35.
Gilbert, Samuel D., 247.
Gleason, Noah, 60.
Gleason, Samuel D., 247.
Goff, David, 70.
Goodwin, Theodore, 189.
Goodwin, Russell, 190.
Goucher, William, 399.
Grant, Roswell, 176.
Grant, Miles, 428.
Grinnell, Michael, 305.
Grinnell, Rufus, 305.
Grinnell, Jasper, 395.
Griswold, Phineas, 112.
Griswold, Roswell, 136.
Griswold, Seth, 135.
Griswold, Phineas, Jr., 199.
Griswold, Matthew, 199.
Grover, Daniel, 60.
Grover, Timothy, 62.

Hale, James, 136.
Hall, John B., 192.
Hall, Sylvester, 203.
Hall, Gideon, 326.
Hall, Reuben, 411.
Handee, Barzillai, 282.
Handee, Clemons & Cyrenus, 282.
Hart, Lewis, 246.
Hart, Willard, 249.
Hart, Luke, Selah, 299.
Hart, Stephen, Samuel, 299.
Hatch, Zepheniah, 190.
Hatch, Moses, 164, 191.
Hawley, Samuel, 167.
Hawley, Salmon, 169.
Hawley, Eleazer, 406.
Hayden, Samuel, 273.
Hayden, Seth, 273
Hayden, Moses, 274.
Hewitt, Joshua, 399.
Higley, Horace, 322.
Hill, Wait, 192.
Hills, Benoni, 43.
Hills, Seth, 44.
Hills, John, Beria, 45.
Hills, Jesse, Chauncey, 46.
Hills, Benoni, Ira, 46.
Hills, Hewitt, 177.
Hinsdale, Bissell, 338, 341.
Hinsdale, Theodore, 341.
Hinsdale, Hosea, 371.
Hinsdale, Elizur, 391.
Hoadley, Samuel, 383, 384.
Hoadley, Luther, 384.
Holabird, Wm. S., 424.
Holcomb, Luther, 199.
Holmes, Ezra, Seth, 201.
Holmes, David, 298.
Holmes, Joseph, 334.
Holmes, Rufus, 335.
Holmes, Willard, 336, 412.
Holmes, Everett C , 336.
Horton, Jesse, 228.
Hoskin, Joseph, Sr., & Jr., 61.
Hoskin, Theodore, 61, 308.
Hoskin, Silas, 62, 415.
Hosmer, Thomas Jr., 41.
Hoyt, Nathaniel, 204.
Hoyt, Micajah, Zeri W., 204.
Hubbard, Elijah, 137.
Hubbell, Silliman, 214.
Hubbell, Luman, 214, 425.
Humphrey, Chauncey, 210.

Humphrey, Augustus, 215.
Hungerford, Reuben, 173.
Hurlbut, Capt. Samuel, 97.
Hurlbut, Leonard, 98.
Hurlbut, Samuel Jr., 98.
Hurlbut, Lemuel, 99.
Hurlbut, Stephen, Martin, 100.
Hurlbut, Joseph W., 100, 408.
Hurlbut, Erastus G., 239.
Hurlbut, Simeon, 144.

Jacklyn, Isaac, 230.
Jenkins, Benjamin, 311.
Johnson, Isaac, 399.
Johnson, Benjamin, 391.
Jopp, John, 295, 296.
Judd, Benjamin, 157.

Kellogg, Eleazer, 301.
Keyes, William, 172.
Kimberly, Jacob Sr., & Jr., 177.
Kingsbury, Geo., 204.
Kirkum, Philemon, 342.
Kinney, Rev. Aaron, 354.
Kinney, Sheldon, 411.
Kinney, Nisus, 415.
Knapp, Rev. Joshua, 107.
Knowlton, Stephen, 284.

Leach, Alex., 96.
Leach, William, 96.
Lemly, Solomon, 344.
Lemly, Jacob, 344.
Loomis, Simeon, 59.
Loomis, Ichabod, 117.
Loomis, Thaddeus, 117.
Loomis, Arphaxad, 118.
Loomis, Abiel, 118.
Loomis, Alanson, 425.
Loomis, Ichabod Jr., 119.
Loomis, Daniel, 123.
Loomis, Epaphras, 196.
Loomis, Dea. Lorrain, 196.
Loomis, Arah, 215.
Loomis, Wait, 234.
Loomis, Oliver, 250, 425.
Loomis, Asher, 323.
Loomis, Aaron, 371.
Lucas, John, 180.
Lyon, Christopher, 407.

McAlpine, John, 193.
McAlpine, Silas H., 194.
McEwen, Robert, 56.
McEwen, Gershom, 57.
McEwen, Robert, (2) 58.
McEwen. Samuel, 58.
McEwen, Rev. Abel, 58.
Maltbie, John, 406.
Mallory, Elisha, Sen., 286.
Mallory, Elisha Jr., Amasa, Asa, 287.
Marble, David, 408.
Mars, Jupiter, 229.
Marsh, Rev. Frederick, 238.
Marshall, John, 151.
Marshall, Reuben, 193.
Marshall, Daniel, 307.
Merriam, William, 320.
Merry, Cornelius, 41.
Miller, Lewis, 306.
Miller, Asahel, 329.
Miller, Joseph, 392.
Miller, Sheldon, 249, 307.
Mills, David, 271.
Mills, Chauncey, 271.
Miner, Reuben, 107.
Miner, John, 124.
Miner, Phineas, 124.
Miner, William, 125.
Mitchell, Joseph, 320.
Mitchell, Selden, 400.
Moore, Simeon, Jr., 170.
Moore, Dr. Aaron, 325.

Mott, Adam, 36.
Mott, Jonathan, 37.
Mott, Adam Jr., Lent., 38.
Mott, Lent Jr., 213.
Mott, Loammi, 39, 200.
Munsill, Zacheus, 321.
Munson, Caleb, 301.
Munson, Hermon, 396.
Murray, David, 178.
Murray, Daniel, 234.
Murray, Ammi, 240.
Murray, William, 400.

Nash, John, 170.
Nash, Alva, 171.
North, Martin, 126, 127.
North, Martin Jr., 127.
North, Rufus, 127.
Norton, Levi, 151.
Norton, Levi (2), 333.

Oakley, Hawley, 385.
Oakley, Alvah, 385.

Palmer, Enoch, 59.
Palmer, Ambrose, 113
Palmer, Solomon, 308.
Parks, Nathaniel, 336.
Parks, Jonathan, 337.
Pease, Asaph, 423.
Persons, Alpheus, 376.
Persons, Timothy, 376.
Phelps, Daniel, Sr., & Jr., 200.
Phelps, Lancelot, 237.
Phelps, Benj., Frederick. 247.
Phillips, John, 375.
Pinney, Elijah, 232.
Platt, Daniel, 73.
Platt, Joseph, 157.
Platt, Levi, 180.
Platt, Sylvester, Levi Jr., 181.
Porter, Eleazer, 285.
Potter, Daniel, 269.
Potter, Phineas, 269.
Potter, Sheldon, 269.
Pratt, Andrew, 320.
Preston, Ebenezer, 35.
Preston, Joseph, 36.
Preston, Samuel, 36.
Preston, Benjamin, 113.
Priest, Philip, 126.

Reynolds, Horace, 408.
Rice, Daniel, 230.
Richards, Eli, 241.
Riley, John C , 200.
Roberts, Joel, 113.
Roberts, George, 408.
Roberts, Samuel, 152.
Rockwell, Elihu, 334.
Rockwell, Solomon, 363.
Rockwell, Alpha, 364.
Rockwell, Edward, Samuel, 370.
Rockwell, John T., 370.
Rockwell, B. B., 365.
Rockwell, Henry E., 428.
Rogers, Simeon, 284.
Rogers, Jonathan, 309.
Rohrabacker, John, 400.
Root, Roger, 235.
Root, Gurdon, 235.
Rowley, Ebenezer, 276.
Rowley, Alpha, 410.
Rowley, Asher, 278.
Rowley, Elias, 279.
Rowley, Reuben, 334.
Rowley, Samuel, 391.
Rowley, Stephen, 422.
Russell, Nathaniel, 291.
Russell, Giles, 293.

Sanford, Henry, 337.
Sanford, William, 337.

INDEX OF SETTLERS. 625

Schovil, Stephen, 146.
Scovill, Reuben, 317.
Seymour, Truman, 324.
Seymour, Jacob, John, 374.
Shattuck, Randall, 328.
Shaw, John, 297.
Shepard, Ebenezer, 265.
Shepard, Didymus, 168.
Shepard, James, 373.
Skinner, Isaac, 185.
Skinner, Benjamin, 393.
Smith, Eleazer, 60.
Smith, Elisha, Esq., 101.
Smith, Chauncey, 153.
Smith, Heman, 178.
Smith, Oliver, 229.
Smith, Asahel, 235.
Smith, Josiah, 267.
Smith, Zebina, 296.
Smith, Elisha, 297.
Smith, Riley, 423.
Smith, Theodore, 337.
Soper, Chester, 413.
Spencer, Thomas, 93.
Spencer, John, 94.
Spencer, Thomas (2), 95.
Spencer, Grinnell, 95.
Spencer, Stephen, 144.
Spencer, Elisha, 284.
Spencer, Ozias, 285.
Spencer, Norman (1), 416.
Stanclift, Comfort, 287.
Stanclift, Samuel, 288.
Stannard, Abel, 73.
Stannard, Lemuel, 73.
Stannard, William, 74.
Stannard, Seth, Ezra, 74.
Starkweather, Elijah, 205.
Starkweather, Roger, 237.
Storer, John, 240, 400.
Strong, David, Edwin M., 205.
Strong, Lyman, 396.
Sweet, Jonathan, 108, 123.
Sweet, James, Reuben, 123
Sweet, Peleg, 168.

Sweet, John, 288.
Swift, Zephaniah, 246.

Talcott, Wm. O., 424.
Tallmadge, David, 395.
Taylor, Eliud, 192.
Taylor, Silas, 201.
Thayer, Wheelock, 413.
Thompson, Elijah, 153.
Thompson, Dan., Samuel, 153.
Thrall, Reuben, 101.
Thrall, Erastus, 197.
Tibballs, Abel, 225
Tibballs, Nathan, 225.
Tolles, Amos, 324.
Treat, Salmon, 306.
Tucker, Reuben, 62.
Tucker, Isaac, 232.
Turrell, Darius, 406.
Tuttle, Geo., 240.
Tuttle, Daniel G., 414.

Videto, John Sr.,& Jr., 114.

Wade, Amasa, Stephen, 115.
Wade, Isaac, Stephen, 116.
Wade, Amasa Jr., 116.
Wakefield, Luman, 409.
Walter, John, 275.
Walter, Andrew, Lemuel, 275.
Walter, Daniel, 276.
Ward, David, 153.
Ward, Daniel, 157.
Waterman, Wm. Jr , 306.
Wells, Asahel, 211.
West, David Jr., 289.
West, Judah, 289.
Westlake, Samuel, 327.
Westlake, William, John, 327.
Westlake, Thomas, 328.
Wetmore, Samuel, 66.
Wetmore, John, Abel. 67.
Wetmore, Seth, Samuel Jr., 67.
Wetmore, Samuel (2), 68.
Wetmore, Truman S., 68.

Wetmore, John (4), 69.
Wetmore, John 2d (4), 69.
Wetmore, Sam'l H., Abel S., 70.
Wheadon, Solomon, 194.
Wheadon, Stephen, 194.
Wheeler, Benjamin, 295.
Wheeler, Nathan, 296.
Wheeler, Isaac, 298.
White, Oliver, Sen. & Jr., 328.
White, Daniel, 332.
Whiting, Christopher, 137.
Whiting, Lorrin, 138.
Whiting, Riley, 138.
Whiting, Benjamin, 319.
Wilcox, Daniel, 329.
Wilcoxson, Gideon, 108.
Wilcoxson, Elisha, 125.
Wilkinson, Lewis, 65.
Wilkinson, Jesse, 65.
Wilkinson, Levi, 66.
Wilkinson, Miles, 201.
Williams, Jesse, 414.
Wilson, Abijah, 317.
Wilson, Zenas, 318.
Wilson, Reynold, 318.
Wilson, Abijah Jr., 318.
Wilson, Nelson, 415.
Wilson, Daniel B., 319.
Woodford, Ezekiel, 388.
Woodford, Erastus, 388.
Woodford, Ezekiel Jr., 389.
Woodford, Lester, 389.
Woodford, Benjamin B., 390.
Woodford, E. Sterling, 390.
Woodford, Lucius J., 390.
Woodruff, Hawkins, 107.
Woodruff, Jonah, 133.
Wright, Justus, 171.
Wright, Lieut. John, 262.
Wright, Samuel, 263.
Wright, John Jr., 264 .
Wright, Charles, 264.
Wright, Freedom, 265.
Wright, Norton, 302.
Wright, Joel, 334.

INDEX

ABBOTT, 248
ABBY, 16
ABERNETHY, 101
ABREW, Or Abro 149
ACKLEY, 62 64 74 228 319 Levi 319
ADAMS, 139 149 189 226 374 378 410 422 425-426 431 434 461 Mathew 226
ADKINS, 43 148 158 162 468 476 Isaac 148 James 148
AGARD, 46 51 87 126 147-149 Aaron And Jos 149
ALBERT, 464 468
ALBRO, 300 327 407 Daniel 407
ALDEN, 162
ALDRIDGE, 292
ALEXANDER, 314
ALLEN, 29 46 67 174 226 298-299 334 474 John 298
ALVORD, 26 62-64 67 83-85 88 107 119 129 134 140 143 146-148 150-152 157-158 164-165 168 172 180-181 184 203-204 206 211-212 217-218 225 244 289 297 299 319 321 365 372 395 397 404 451 458 478 489 494 520 David 119 Eliphaz 62-64 James H 397 John 64 Jonathan 62 Ruel 397
AMES, 274
ANDERSON, 116
ANDREWS, 33 52 55 57-58 65 71-72 105-106 134 147-148 160 165 173 179-180 185 188 193 195-196 198 204 207 213 217 226 243 249 273 299-300 399 427 464 468 470 478 494 Abm Jr 106 Abm Sen 105 Dan'l Jr 106 Eli 106 Elijah 148 Ens Dan 106 Major Lloyd 195 Theophilus 105
ANDROS, 9-10 33 92
ANDRUS, 15 64 158 165 373
APLEY, 228 271 338 344 380 Josiah 344

ARCULARIUS, 371
ARMSTRONG, 521
ARNOLD, 15 144 161-163 165 268 274 281 283 469 479 Stephen 268
ASHLEY, 16 394
ATKINS, 45 340 385 463
ATWATER, 396
ATWOOD, 227
AUSBON, 346
AUSTIN, 22 42-43 57 70-71 76-77 83 85 87 94 105 107 129 134 143 148 150 153-154 160 163-166 192 219 258 267 280 288 293 345-346 351 355 358 363 377 506-507 David 42 David Jr 43 John 267
AVERED, Averet Averit And Averet (see Everitt) 41 47 76 83 85 87 164 Capt Josiah 47
AYRAULT, 426 513
BACHELDER, 478
BACON, 179-180 188 195-196 317 328 334 506 Francis John 179
BAIL, 248
BAILEY, 52 61-62 187 226-227 230 278 411 415 464 Theodore 227
BAIRD, 343 378 391 401 479 517
BAKER, 11 115 365 368
BALCOM, 29 135 160-163 165 228 266-267 272 275 281 283 288 305 346 506 Elias 267 Elias Cabit 267 John Jr 266 John Sr 266 Jonathan 266 Nathaniel 266
BALDWIN, 120 175 191 236 240 248 296-297 317 324 334 356 386-388 391 401 451 476-479 Norman 236 Reuben 386 Rev John D 356 Samuel W 236
BALL, 516
BANCROFT, 196 464
BANDLE, 249 300 516
BANK, Hurlbut 437 Winsted 436-437 Winsted Savings 437
BANKS, 478

BANNING, 302
BARBER, 115 195 199 203 207 210
  226 230 233 237 270 296 388 478-
  479
BARBOUR, 102 135-136 150 William
  136
BARKER, 327
BARKHAMSTED, Light House 25
BARNES, 110 298 321 324 384
BARNSTABLE, 144 146 Wm 146
BARNUM, 465
BARRETT, 16
BARTLETT, 116 408-409 419-420
  Samuel 408
BARTON, 144 189 227 230 363 369
  457 489 520
BASNEY, 476-477
BASS, 335 367
BASSETT, 109 120 123 132 134 158
  173 213 224 231 233-234 236 300
  Lemuel 123 Rev Archibald 213 224
  233
BATCHELLER, 413-414 430 434 464
  468 478
BATTELL, 58
BEACH, 5 17 32-35 40 44 70 75-76 83-
  84 87 97 108 120 134 148 158 165
  177 186-187 199 208-210 215 234
  241 311-312 317 323 331 349 356
  375 377-378 386-387 427 440 453
  464 469 476-477 494 Adna 186
  Caleb 33 Caleb (2) 35 215 Fisk 187
  Horace V 187 Joel 33-35 John 120
  Rev James 120 356 386 386-388
BEARDSLEY, 211 265 301 306-307
  309 312 321-322 328-329 333-334
  336 341 344 364 368-369 373 378
  385 401 403 413 427 434 436 451
  458 485 489 501 508 510 519-520
BECK, 314
BECKLEY, 73 108 176 199 225 228
  250 Daniel Norris 250 Richard 225
BECKWITH, 330
BEEBE, 38 58 111 162-163 196 213
  231 257 259 367 369 David 196
  James 231
BEECHER, 70 138 156 211 272 335
  383 404 419 454
BEEMAN, 509
BEERS, 249 316
BELDEN, 348
BELKNAP, 314

BELL, 424
BELLAMY, 88-89 185
BELLOWS, 336 463 468 470-471 479
BEMIS, 203
BENEDICT, 62 71-73 85 89 105 110
  114 117 124 129 134 146-148 158
  163-165 167-168 170 175 185 192
  198-199 203 208 210-211 213 217
  226 232 236 249 300 338 344 Capt
  Benj 71 Capt Timothy 3 72 Elijah
  344 John 175 Timothy (3) 72
  Timothy Jr 3 72 Za'mon 175
BENHAM, 296 341 427
BENJAMIN, 16
BENTLEY, 110
BENTON, 16 340
BERNHARDT, 465
BERRY, 440
BEVINS, 398 404
BIDWELL, 16 187 227-228 340 451
BIEDERMAN, 470 472 479
BILLS, 420
BIRD, 50 259 316 515
BIRDSALL, 434 451
BIRMINGHAM, 476
BISHOP, 296 328 388 399 412 437-438
  Harry 412 Leverett 412 Seth 412
BISSELL, 64 208 271 340
BLACKMAN, 57 130-131 148 158 162
  171 175 192 196 J P 131 Nathan
  131 Peter 131 Truman 131
BLAKE, 41 46 100 154 187 200 205
  208-210 228 232 240 258-259 408-
  409 513 Allen 210 Elijah 208
  Harry 209 Ithuel 210 Jonathan
  209
BLAKESLEE, 35 327 384
BLAKESLEY, 215
BLIGH, 319
BLISS, 476
BLUIT, 464
BOICE, 193
BOOGE, (Bogue) 119 124 182-184 187
  192 197 206 212-213 Rev P V 187
  Rev Publius V 182-184 206 212-
  213
BOOTH, 520
BORDEN, 249 486 522
BOSWELL, 5 502
BOSWORTH, 318
BOUTON, 71
BOWDISH, 239

INDEX.   629

BOWERS, 203
BOWN, 158 283
BOYD, 4 53 95 100 144 207-208 213-
    214 271 298 311-316 321 324 327
    342 363 367 375 378 385 395 401-
    402 404 410 413 419-420 423 426-
    428 430 433 440 451 457 466 499
    507-512 518-520 James 312-315
    James M 316 John 316 Samuel
    316 423 Thomas 321
BRADFORD, 426
BRADLEY, 73 85 89 125 163 165 463
BRADNER, 314
BRADSHAW, 520
BRAGG, 155-156 179 245 James 245
BRAINARD, 62 270 295 347 351 358
BREEN, 199
BREW, 476-477
BREWER, 322
BRIDE, Stealing 109
BRINSMAID, 89 185
BRINTNELL, Or Brindle 214
BRONSON, (see Brownson) 40 45 50
    52 59 65 67-68 71 74 78 80 93 97
    101 110-112 116-117 123 135 169
    171 186 188-189 193-194 202 207
    209-210 218 221-222 226 232-233
    241-242 244 250 274 396 423 428
    434 522 Abijah P 111 Asahel 110
    Benoni 154 Chauncey 155 Col
    Ozias 109 Dea Levi 101 Isaac 111
    Levi (2) 110 Orentus 155 Ozias Jr
    109 Parliament 155 Salmon 110
BROOKS, 62 89 113-114 127 152 168
    181 192 200 204 227 239 247 258-
    259 337 396-397 Asaph B 239
    Chauncey 239 Samuel 239
BROUGHTON, 175 Nathan 175
BROWN, 46 96 188 235 296 309 320
    334 350 353 393 399 412 461 463-
    464 468 473-475 479 491-492 518
BROWNSON, (see Bronson) 109-112
    129 134 139 143 147 154-155 157-
    158 162-164 173 177-180 184 191
    207 217-218 231
BRUSIE, 400 406
BUCHANAN, 244
BUCHLER, 292
BUCKINGHAM, 15 452 462-463 467
BUCKLAND, 64 312
BUCKMAN, 279
BUEL, 233

BUILDING ASSOCIATIONS, 445-448
BULCROFT, 476 478
BULKLEY, 452 Rev C H A 452
BULL, 16 59 213 230 278 298 332 339
    375 377 385 401 408 507 Merritt
    332 Thomas R 375
BUNCE, 16 403 509
BUNNELL, 46 203 210 243 328 386
    412 464 476 Eliab 386 William 210
BURDICK, 470 472 479
BURGOYNE, 28 44 163
BURNHAM, 15-16 241 271 330 391-
    392 394 Daniel 392
BURNSIDE, 474
BURR, 15-16 29 54 115 228 269-270
    286 289 306 319 323 325 328 333
    371 374 385-386 419 457 494 508-
    509 Allen 228 Erastus 385 Halsey
    385 Jehiel 325 Roswell 385
    Salmon 374
BURRALL, 275 366 424
BURRITT, 340
BURROUGHS, 501
BURT, 287 370-371 426 511
BURTON, 307 329 380 411 465-466
    479 John 307
BURYING-GROUNDS, 66 72 278
BUSHNELL, 50 279 317 500
BUTLER, 16 125 162 314 332 491 501
    518
BUTRICK, 226 288 301 333 380 Cyrus
    333
BYINGTON, 398 404 408 418 511
    Jesse 398
BYRON, 337
CABLE, 293
CADWELL, 374 423
CADY, 114 320
CALAHAN, 469
CALLER, 346
CALLOWAY, 139 384
CALVERT, 245
CAMP, 16 19 52 94 119 121 138 187
    228 249 269 284 287 299 305 309
    317 319-322 324 326 330-332 337
    358 371 378-379 388 391 400 410
    425 433-434 444 451-452 454 465
    489 500 512 Samuel And Moses
    330 332
CAMSELL, 478
CANFIELD, 89 175 185 348 367

CANNON, 144-145 322 Thomas 145
   Timothy 322
CAPRON, 55
CARHART, 370
CARMAN, 476
CARPENTER, 391 Bemsley 391
CARRIER, 62
CARRINGTON, 239 476
CARROL, 476-477
CARTER, 95 152 211 301
CASE, 46 55 95 98 131 139-140 155
   193 195-196 210 226 228 235 239
   241 264 295 312 367 389 415 494
   507 Asher 239 Wm R 193
CASTEL, (Castle) 109 119 134 158-
   159 165 171 306 Elijah 119
   William 119
CATLIN, 11 45 69 424
CATLING, 36 281
CAUL, 210 234 406-407 Charles C 406
   William 407
CENSUS, Of 1756 122 Of 1771 82 Of
   1774 122 Of 1782 158
CHAMBERLIN, 154-155 159 173 187
   214 236 241 245 371 500 Wm Sr &
   Jr 155
CHAMBERS, 294
CHAMPION, 269 296 337 394 407 518
   Nathan 407
CHAPIN, 285 365
CHAPMAN, 100
CHARLES II, 128
CHASE, 58 74 109 136 150-151 248
   253 338 345 380 Gedeliah 345
   George Dudley And Reuben 248
CHATTERTON, 286
CHAUGUM, 25 230-231
CHAUNCEY, 291
CHEESE-PRESS, 337
CHICKLEY, 226-227 William 227
CHRISTY, 293
CHUBB, 267 272 284
CHURCH, 15 98 134 144-145 154 159
   163 165 177 190 192 229 236 240
   248-249 299 336 400 Hiram 249
   John 144 Jonathan Uri 145
CLANCEY, 469
CLAPP, 376
CLARK, 38-39 100 107 125 130-131
   134 136-137 159-160 177 192 200
   210 218 228 234 240 247 258-259
   271 283 286 324 327 373-374 394

CLARK (cont.)
   475-476 500 521 Daniel 137
   Samuel 131 Uzal 283
CLARKE, 287 312 315 335 392 394-
   395 402 410 423 435-436 476 489
   500 502 507 509-510 516 520 Jesse
   373 Lemuel 394 Lucius 395 410
   Nathan W 373
CLARY, 457 520
CLAUDET, 465
CLAYBORN, 278
CLEMENT, 301
CLEMMONS, 207 301 322
CLERGYMEN, 56 58 63 88-90 95 102-
   104 107 179 183-184 206 209 212-
   213 224 233-234 236-237 256 356-
   357 396-397 453
CLEVELAND, 56 209 234 297 307 332
   392 409 411 420 465 476 James C
   409 Orrin 411
CLIFTON, Borough 431
COCKEY, 99
COE, 37 46 50-56 61 65 69 76 82-83 85
   89 93-94 101-102 108 113 116 118
   124-126 129 134-135 142-143 148
   154 156-157 159 161-165 172 175
   180 186 192 195 198-199 202 206-
   207 214 217-218 228 230 235 240
   246 248 257 270 286 288-289 300
   302 306 309 316 318 321-322 329
   332 335 343-344 358 372 379-380
   390 395 399 412 414 416 419-420
   423 425 439-440 464-465 468 470
   478-479 516 Daniel Eben 54 David
   53 Jehial Asahel 55 Jonathan 50
   52-53 309 Jonathan James R 56
   Nelson D 55 Oliver 51-52 Robert
   52 Roger 198
COGSWELL, 474-475 480
COIT, 134 148 157-158 163 165 172
   184 197 205 221 240 244 250
   Richard 148
COLD, Summer Of 1816 418
COLE, 15 340 397
COLEMAN, 226
COLLIER, 188
COLLINS, 322 335 509 512
COLT, 465-466
COLTON, 16
COMINS, 476-477 479
COMMERFORD, 248

CONE, 98 134 148 150 159 162 239 245 384 451 489 Daniel H 150 Samuel Warren 239
CONKLIN, 465 467
CONVERSE, 162
COOK, 15-16 50-52 59 76 83 85 132 148 154 156 158-159 162 165 171 225-226 241 248 284 286 293 302-304 306 323 327 333 341 375 380 393 397 402-403 407 416 419 451 454 457 464 466 476-479 494 506 509-510 512-513 519-521 Aaron 59 Anson 304 Joseph 333 Reuben 303 Shubael 303 Urijah 303
COOLEY, 357 453 472 Rev H E 357
COOPER, 132 291 465 467-468 476-477
CORBIN, 49 71 109 113-114 134 147 154 159 162-163 165 192 207 Peter 113 Peter Jr Daniel 114
COREY, 93 96
CORLEY, 370
COTHREN, 282
COUCH, 465 478
COVEY, 248 516
COVILL, 104
COWDRY, 110
COWLES, 114 148 174 215 247 282 301 306 317 336 371 422
COY, 174 176 188 226
CRAMER, 124
CRANE, 195 317 407 494
CRAVATH, 64
CRESSWELL, 433
CRISSE, 160 165
CRISSEY, 143 152 235 265 268-270 283 309 322 371 David 270 Preserved Israel 270
CRITTENDEN, 465
CROCKER, 72 148 170 191 199 209 211 225 236 Wm 199
CROMWELL, 484 499
CROSBY, 521
CROSS, 304 499
CROWE, 281 287 352 401 411 413 420 516 Henry B 413
CRUM, 171 241 William 241
CULVER, 71 107 298 408 415
CUMMING, 391 473
CUMMINGS, 236 401
CUMMINS, 322
CUNNINGHAM, 256 Rev John 256

CURRIE, 54
CURRY, 278
CURTICE, 204
CURTIS, 40 70 113 137 156 232 234-235 248 279 317 322 331 335 340 Jared 232
CUTLER, 476
DALEY, 469
DANA, 357 395 453 Rev M Mcg 357
DANIELS, 463 468 470 475-477 480-481
DARBE, 268 275 281 300
DAVIS, 272 290 312 326 333 338 344 376 380 404 William 314
DAW, 72 203 226
DAY, 16 47 89 185
DAYTON, 110 186 247 250 463 474 476 478 480 Archibald 250
DEAN, 245 270
DEAR, (Deer) 150-151 159 180 192 228
DEARTHICK, 320-321
DECKER, 465 478
DEER, John 150 Jonathan 151
DELAND, 285
DEMING, 16 263 291 335 384 472
DEMOCRATIC, Party 206
DEMPSEY, 463 468 470-471 480
DENNAN, 465
DENNEN, 463
DENNIS, 373
DENNY, 162
DENSLOW, 427
DERBY, 161 165 275 John 275
DETERT, 478
DEWEY, 461 478
DEWOLF, 292 300-301 309 336 380 Benjamin 300 Daniel 301
DEXTER, 214 287 384 427
DIBBLE, 339
DICKINSON, 16 100 267 304 373
DIDSBURY, 464
DILL, 256 Rev James H 256
DILLEY, 476
DIMICK, 152
DIMOCK, 516
DIOMEDES, 445
DIXON, 432
DODD, 16 366
DODGE, 130 132 134 159 164 Joseph 132
DOLPHIN, 147 159 163 480

DOOLITTLE, 40 57-58 147 160 202 213 226 271-272 275 283 285 296 299 318-319 337 347 349 355 358-359 367 378 383 423 506 Jesse 272 Jesse Jr Zera 272 Lyman 272
DORMAN, 453
DOUGHTY, 465 489
DOUGLASS, 207 226 319 333 380 480 Israel 319
DOWD, 266 272 318
DOWNS, 302 476-477 480 482
DOYLE, 476
DRAKE, 6 32 40-41 52 60 170 174 177 188 195 232 246 249 256 365 371 Moses 246 Rufus 249
DUBOIS, 384
DUCHER, 162
DUDLEY, 118 150 182 250 289 312 329-331 343 373 378 404 425-426 433-434 436 451 454 474 488-489 513-514 George 333 433
DUGAN, 478
DUNHAM, 160 278 286 301 305 Jonathan 305
DUNN, 469
DUNNING, 178 204
DURAND, 476
DURGIN, 439
DUTTON, 73 85 202 331 Nath 73
DWIGHT, 356 Rev Timothy M 356
EARNE, 462
EASTON, 15-16
EATON, 370
EDDY, 452-453 462-463 466-467 Rev Hiram 452-453 466-467
EDGECOMB, 271
EDWARDS, 313 411 501
EELLS, 191
EGGLESTON, 53 93 100 119 190 201 207 228 239 245 301 306 322 330 473-474 478 480 482 Daniel 306
ELDRIDGE, 387
ELLSWORTH, 11 226
ELMER, 51 72 123-124 134 159 165 180 184 218 Hezekiah 124
ELMORE, 100 116 154 156 192 196 202 207 218 287 299 478 Joseph B 156 Nathaniel 196
ELWELL, 227 231 380
EMERSON, 369
EMIGRATION, From Town 44-45 223-224

EMMONS, 326 340
ENO, 126 249 335 368
ENOCH, Arden 107-108
ENSIGN, 12 15-16 42 136 347 367-368 374
EVANS, 465
EVARTS, 476-477 480
EVERETT, 47 127 392
EVERITT, 38 45 47-50 59 73 78 101 105 113-114 117 123 126-127 134 137 139 143 149 151 153-154 157 159 169-170 182 184 188-189 200 202 204 207 218 220-221 230-231 241 246-247 Andrew 50 Dr Josiah 49 Elihu 230 Josiah 47 Noble J 241 Rev Noble 49
EVITTS, 465
F, Miss Roxy 382
FAIRCHILD, 270
FAIRWEATHER, 13
FANNING, 113 192 199 204
FARNSWORTH, 16
FARRAGUT, 472
FARRAND, 89 102-103 185
FAY, 126-127 129-130 132 134 154 159 162-163 165 180 308 Gershom 132 Thaddeus 308 Timothy And Wm 132
FELIX, 292
FERRIS, 249 469 476-477 480
FIELD, 100 408
FIELDPIECE, (Patriotic) 243-244
FILER, 165
FILLEY, 34 38 40-41 76-77 83 85 87 134 148 150 154 156-157 159 162-163 165 186 226 298 395 Abraham 40 Remembrance 41 Wm 40
FINN, 469 478
FIREPLACE, Or "smoke" 161
FISH, 23 26
FISK, 465
FITCH, 11-12 388
FITZ, Gerald 476 478 480
FITZPATRICK, 465
FLEMING, 474-475 480
FLOWERS, 374
FLYNN, 469
FOOT, (Foote) 176 179 191
FORBES, 16 126 369 403 419-420 499 Daniel 126
FORCIER, 478

INDEX. 633

FORD, 110 187 194 249 506 Harvey 249
FORESBY, 151
FOSKET, 267 323-324 326 329 337 434
FOSTER, 328 426 478 513
FOWLER, 278 349
FOX, 226 325
FRASIER, 333
FREEMAN, 152 391 395
FREEMEN, Admitted 143 147-148 154 171-172 175 191-192 195 198 202 207 211 213 226 228 230-231 234 236 240-241
FREMONT, 244
FRENCH, 478 War 263 291 314
FRISBEE, 109 134 164 191
FRISBEY, 151
FRISBIE, 112 159 207 233 321 324 336 439 Eli 207 Elijah 112 Joseph 112
FRISSELL, 239
FULLER, 160 190 284 414
FYLER, 45 155 165 187-189 191 193 200 207-208 256 297 317 322 325 337 374 390 410 412 415 Roman 188 Silas 188 Stephen Jr 412
GAGE, 118
GALE, 463
GALLAGHER, 250 259 515
GALPIN, 190
GAME, 23 25-26 34
GANNON, 469
GARDINER, 470
GARRETT, 58 478
GARRISON, 461
GARSON, 469
GASCOIGNE, 458 520
GASKILL, 294
GASTON, 374 516
GATES, 266
GAY, 256 Rev Wm M 256
GAYLORD, 64 167 173 207 209 230 335 365 367 403 410 422 425 440 512 518 522 Henry L 425 Stephen 207
GEESE, 233
GENERAL, Training 221-222
GIBBS, 65-66 77 83 85 88 126-127 134 161-162 217 336 374 476-477 480 Warham 65
GIDDINGS, 461

GILBERT, 16 18 35 54 106 112 153 174-175 226 246-247 300 325 391 406 434 470-471 480 488 507 516 Samuel 35 Samuel D 247
GILLECK, 444
GILLES, 501
GILLETT, 212 286 290 303 323 337 346 389
GILMAN, 16 296 376 488-489 522
GLEASON, 36 41 60 83 85 126 161 178 180 275-276 Noah 60 Samuel D 247
GLOSTER, 469
GLYNN, 463
GODDARD, 56
GOFF, (Goffe) 70 76 82-83 85 87-88 160-161 163 286 320 David 70
GOLD, 29
GOODENOUGH, 257 Rev Arthur 257
GOODMAN, 16
GOODRICH, 96 266
GOODWIN, 16 94 100 131 189-190 239 328 330 366 Russell 190 Theodore 189
GOUCHER, 399 William 399
GOULD, 245 424
GRANGER, 431 465 468 476-477
GRANT, 46 106 116 136 176 197 205 211 225 228 247 279 289 315 324 330 365 428 478 Miles 428 Roswell 176
GRAVES, 304
GRAY, 203 245 469
GREAT, Exodus 47 224
GREELEY, 312
GREEN, 95 187 225 407 476-477 480 517 Old Winchester 221-222
GREENE, 329
GREGORY, 489
GREINER, 274
GRENELL, 94
GRIFFIN, 308 322 478 501
GRINNELL, 96 228 305 395 Jasper 395 Michael 305 Rufus 305
GRISOLD, Roswell 136
GRISWOLD, 54 59 68 71 107 109 112-113 117 127 134 136 143 148 159 165 188 194 199 205 209 217-218 221 235 240 245-246 375 394 422 451 Matthew 199 Phineas 112 Phineas Jr 199 Seth 135

GROVER, 60 62 114 156 159 165
   Daniel 60 Timothy 62
HAGGARTY, 478-480
HAGUE, 478
HALE, 55 88 115 135-136 156 159 411
   516 James 136
HALL, 21 50 54 59 98 105-106 119 192
   203 207 228 273 295 326 332 339
   347 379 392 397 411 420 431 440
   476 Gideon 326 John B 192
   Reuben 411 Sylvester 203
HALLETT, 409 419 488 513
HAMILTON, 228 375 412 436
HAMLIN, 208 290
HANCOCK, 344
HANDEE, 282 Barzillai 282 Clemons
   282 Cyrenus 282
HARD, Winter Of '83 47-48
HARDEN, 53
HARMER, 53 163
HARMER'S, Campaign 53
HARRIS, 313 463 465 469 486 507
HARRISON, 369 432
HART, 62 72 89 107 175 185 213-214
   226 237 246-249 275 299 301 332
   340 380 385-386 476-477 480 482
   Lewis 246 Luke Selah 299
   Stephen Samuel 299 Willard 249
HARTFORD, Jail-breaking Of 1722
   11-12 Votes In Town Meeting 10
   12
HATCH, 69 96 144 155 157 164 188
   190-191 200-201 226 237 253 275
   386 451 465 Moses 164 191
   Zepheniah 190
HAWK, Catching 49
HAWKINS, 287
HAWKS, 339
HAWLEY, 167 169 175 296 323 367
   371 406 470-471 513 Eleazer 406
   Salmon 169 Samuel 167
HAYDEN, 29 138 160 226 246 273-274
   276 283 326 349-350 365 375 382
   386 Moses 274 Samuel 273 Seth
   273
HAYES, 294
HAYNES, 16 278
HAZLETINE, 16
HAZZARD, 480
HEALY, 293
HENDERSON, 516
HENDRICKEN, 444

HENSHAW, 18 228 295
HERMANCE, 516
HERMANDY, 469
HERRICK, 307
HEWITT, 178 289 399-400 470 479
   507 Joshua 399
HICKOX, 384
HICKS, 401 488
HIGLEY, 199-200 211 237 299 322-
   323 358 378 402 423 427 500
   Horace 322
HILL, 97 192 249 285 Wait 192
HILLS, 5 9 41 43-47 50 66-67 69-70
   76-78 81 83 85 87 89-90 95 107
   111 116 123 129-130 134 139 143-
   144 146-148 150-151 153 159 163-
   165 171 175 177 179 184 186 188
   192-193 196-197 203 207 210-211
   217 221 341 377 389 Benoni 43
   Benoni Ira 46 Hewitt 177 Jesse
   Chauncey 46 John Beria 45 Seth
   44
HINKLEY, 196
HINMAN, 47 49 51 161
HINSDALE, 32 53 90 153 234 276
   298-299 304 316 334 338-342 367-
   368 371-373 378 391-392 398 400-
   401 404 410 415-416 419 426-428
   440 451 454 473 479 499 501 508
   511 513-514 516 518 Bissell 338
   341 Elizur 391 Hosea 371
   Theodore 341
HISCOCK, 95
HITCHCOCK, 272 318-319 330 349
HOADLEY, 23 115 138-139 230-231
   383-384 392 401-402 417 419 506-
   507 512 515-516 518 Luther 384
   Samuel 383-384
HODGE, 399
HODGES, 371 465
HOLABIRD, 269 296 334 362 408 420
   424 439 465 494 517 Wm S 424
HOLCOMB, 35 192 199 226 230
   Luther 199
HOLLISTER, 478
HOLMES, 56 200-201 207 226 228 298
   321-322 334-336 344 380 395 412-
   413 424 435 494 David 298
   Everett C 336 Ezra Seth 201
   Joseph 334 Rufus 335 Willard 336
   412
HOMAN, 314

INDEX. 635

HOOKER, 120 162 233 238 366 387 396
HOPKINS, 15 355
HORNE, 463 468 474-475 482 486
HORTON, 228 265 318 424 Jesse 228
HOSFORD, 162 464-465 468 474-477 480 482
HOSKIN, 61-62 82-83 85 102 112 119 134-135 137 142 159-160 163 192 267 295 308 320 380 385 407 415 465 468 478 Joseph Jr 61 Joseph Sr 61 Silas 62 415 Theodore 61 308
HOSMER, 16 31 41 49 76-77 85 Thomas Jr 41
HOTCHKISS, 239 424
HOUSE, 422 426
HOWARD, 64 397 465 468
HOWE, 424 445 521
HOYT, 27 114 192 204-205 226 232 423 Micajah Zeri W 204 Nathaniel 204
HUBBARD, 16 41 66 100 137 159 232 287 315 394 398 433 476-477 480 Elijah 137
HUBBELL, 53-54 108 132 156 200 214 228 258 312 315 390 399 420 425 440 Luman 214 425 Silliman 214
HUDSON, 147 162-163 190 266 314 317 374 414
HULBERT, 312 327 363 377 403 407 451 509-510
HULL, 106 191 206 469 474 476-477 480
HUMISTON, 476 480
HUMPHREY, 28 46 49 74 98 110 114 125 194-195 210 215 230 330 434 451 509 Augustus 215 Chauncey 210
HUNGERFORD, 173 230 246 256 271 Reuben 173
HUNTINGTON, 348 365-366
HUNTTING, 116
HURD, 271
HURFORD, 315
HURLBUT, 25 46 69 93 96-101 112 119 125-126 134-135 144-148 150 154 157 159 162 164-165 169 173 179-180 182 185 187 190-192 194 200 202-203 207-208 210-211 221-223 226 233-234 239-240 243-244 246-247 249 252 259 293 298 302

HURLBUT (cont.)
305 320 328 341 344 367 408 414 437 474 476-477 480 482 Capt Samuel 97 Erastus G 239 Joseph W 100 408 Lemuel 99 Leonard 98 Samuel Jr 98 Simeon 144 Stephen Martin 100
HYDE, 121 201 388
INDEPENDENCE DAY, Celebration Of 242-243
INDIANS, 25 339
INSTITUTE, Winchester 257-258
IRVING, 502
ISAACS, 370
ISAIAH, Da Scanno 445
IVES, 38 195 201 213
JACKLYN, 136 196 204 230-231 Isaac 230
JACKSON, 342 424
JAMES, Ii 10
JAQUA, (Jaques) 107 304 394
JARVIS, 68
JEFFERSON, 224 431 Flood 224
JENCKS, 511
JENKINS, 95 144 207 213-214 271 273-274 311-312 315 327 363 375 378 385 391 401 408-409 419 433 507-509 511-512 Benjamin 311
JENNINGS, 114
JOHNSON, 34 118 125 138 215 218 231 301 339 368 391 399 407 502 Benjamin 391 Isaac 399
JONES, 15 190 321 499
JONSON, 88
JOPP, 272 276 295-296 John 295-296
JOSLIN, 414
JUDD, 16 72 154 157 159 408 Benjamin 157
JUDSON, 88
KEEGAN, 476
KEELER, 521
KEEN, 316
KEENEY, 15-16
KELLOGG, 16 159 165 170 219 241 270 281 301 305 331-332 346 348-349 384 451 463 467 477-478 Eleazer 301
KELSEY, 16 112-113 202 265 329
KENT, 173 312 370 476-477 480
KERMANN, 465
KEYES, 54 90 134 172 288 (Kies) 165 William 172

KEYS, 468
KILBORN, 16 434
KILBOURN, 9 96 118 373
KILBURN, 69
KIMBERLY, 177-178 230 Jacob Jr 177
  Jacob Sr 177
KING, 274 354 Rev Salmon 354
KINGSBURY, 204-205 Geo 204
KINNEY, 264 298-299 319-320 325
  333-334 354-356 389 400 404 411-
  412 415 420 474 478 483 501 516
  Nisus 415 Rev Aaron 354 354-356
  Sheldon 411
KIRBY, 186 417
KIRKHAM, 54 338
KIRKUM, 342-344 378 395 401-402
  Philemon 342
KNAPP, 62 89-90 102-105 107 126
  134-135 139-143 147-148 160 167
  173 178-179 182 185 189 217 244
  331 412 Rev Joshua 89-90 107 179
KNOWLTON, 160 162 226 269 276
  283-284 330-331 358 Stephen 284
LAIRD, 293
LAKE, 108
LAMB, 427
LAMBERT, 210 337
LAND, Earliest Deed Of Recorded 9
  Given To Hartford Ministers 9 32
  Grants To Various Towns 9-14
  Grants Votes In Hartford Town
  Meetings Respecting 10 12 None
  Reserved For Churches Or Schools
  19 32 Plan Of Division Of 17-19 84
  Reserved For Highways 19 Title 9-
  14
LANDON, 372 398
LARNED, 58
LATHAM, 279 465
LATHROP, 144 339 363 365 457 520
LATIMER, 58 97
LATOURETTE, 110 174
LAWRENCE, 27 176 368 378
LAWTON, 203
LAWYERS, 55 342-344 392-393 424
LEACH, 93 96 159 162-163 165 192
  329 Alex 96 William 96
LEAMING, 67
LEAVITT, 101
LEE, 55 70 89 104 185 233 243 317
  368
LEMLEY, 338 344 380

LEMLY, Jacob 344 Solomon 344
LEO, Da Saracena 444-445 472
LEONARD, 131 170 178 195 234 463
  468-469
LEROY, 285 399 476-477
LEWIS, 64 108 117 123 187 304-305
  324 378 388 426 440 473 513
LIBRARIES, 500-504
LINA, 478
LINCOLN, 461 463 475 516-517
LITCHFIELD, 139
LOCKWOOD, 187 275 286 297 303
LONDON, 172
LONG, 369
LOOMIS, 44 52 54 59-61 71 73 76 85
  87-88 101 109 111 117-119 123
  134-135 139 148 151 154 159 163
  165 186 188 193 196-198 203 207-
  208 211 215-216 227-228 234 243
  250 270 301-303 309 319 323 329
  332 358 365 371 380-381 419 423
  425 427 433 466 513-514 521
  Aaron 371 Abiel 118 Alanson 425
  Arah 215 Arphaxad 118 Asher 323
  Daniel 123 Dea Lorrain 196
  Epaphras 196 Ichabod 117
  Ichabod Jr 119 Oliver 250 425
  Simeon 59 Thaddeus 117 Wait 234
LORD, 15 461
LOSAW, 475
LOTHERINGTON, 474
LOVEJOY, 461
LOVELAND, 67 191
LUCAS, 101 111 162 180 207 308 321
  323 John 180
LYMAN, 66 189 324 378 389
LYNCH, 444
LYON, 61 315 407 Christopher 407
MADDRA, 478-479
MALLORY, 138 240 268 286-287 295
  306 318 324 330 334 349 373 413
  Amasa 287 Asa 287 Elisha Jr 287
  Elisha Sen 286
MALTBIE, 317 406 John 406
MANCHESTER, 54 64 107 284 288
  322 478
MANGAN, 444
MANUFACTURES, Augers 521 Axes
  511-512 Bolts And Nuts 520 Cards
  516 Carriage Springs 522 Cheese
  Boxes 506 Clocks 515-516 Coffin
  Trimmings 522

INDEX.

MANUFACTURES (cont.)
  Condensed Milk 522 Cutlery 520
  Fire Irons 521 Forges 22 95 Forks
  518 Foundries 518 Grist Mills 506-
  507 Guns 46 Iron And Steel 363
  508-511 Joiners' Tools 522 Leather
  512-514 Linseed Oil 518 Lumber
  522 Machinery 518-519 Nails 511
  Pins 521 Plated Ware 522 Saw
  Mills 62 130-132 Scythes 311 507-
  508 Tanneries 371 373 Tools 519-
  520 Wagons And Carriages 516-
  517 Whiskey 517 Wire 512
  Wooden Ware 505-506 Woolen
  Cloths 514-515
MARBLE, 296 408-409 419-420 424
  David 408
MARCUM, 137
MARS, 229 Jupiter 229
MARSH, 6 63 90 97 102-103 109 114
  159 170 180 212 234 237-239 250
  256 317 465 468 478 Rev
  Frederick 237-238 238 256
MARSHALL, 45 50 53 94-95 150-151
  159 173 188 192-193 195 199-200
  207-209 213 221 228 230 288 307
  321 323 327 332-333 336 369 416
  501 514 Daniel 307 John 151
  Reuben 193
MARTIN, 327 465 476-477 481
MARVIN, 270 411
MASON, 264
MASONIC, Organizations 499-500
MATHER, 296 386
MATHEWS, 341
MATSON, 396
MAYBEE, 273
MCALPINE, 70 98 111-112 130 154-
  155 193-194 207 228 257-259 478-
  479 506 John 193 Silas H 194
MCBETH, 258
MCCAULEY, 463
MCCRARY, 384
MCCULLOCK, 307
MCDERMOT, 478
MCDOEL, 315
MCDONALD, 278 409
MCENTIRE, 266
MCEWEN, (Mccune Mackune And
  Macune) 6 33 41 45 56-59 68 76 83
  85 87 89 108 129 131 134 137 139
  143-144 146-148 159 165 184 203

MCEWEN (cont.)
  207 217-218 221 226 231 367
  Gershom 57 Rev Abel 58 Robert 56
  Robert (2) 58 Samuel 58
MCFARLAND, 444
MCGUIRE, 465
MCNEIL, 190
MEACHAM, 170 243
MEAD, 266 305 334
MEEKER, 100
MEEKIN, 16
MEIGS, 162
MERRIAM, 320 William 320
MERRILL, 15 39 100 238 268 408
MERRIMAN, 194
MERRY, 41 Cornelius 41
METHODISM, Rise In Town 104 402
METHODIST, Church At Noppit 256
  Church At Winsted 402
MILES, 187 319 357 416 453 Rev
  Thomas M 357
MILLARD, 317
MILLER, 39 52-53 205 241 249 274
  288 304 306-309 320 329 373 380
  382 391-392 403-404 409 411 483-
  484 501 513 516 Asahel 329
  Joseph 392 Lewis 306 Sheldon 249
  307
MILLIMAN, 470
MILLS, 77 140 150 160 165 167 182-
  184 192 207 212 226 230 271-272
  281 283 297 321 344 349 393-394
  465 Chauncey 271 David 271
MINER, (Minor) 80 105 107-108 123-
  125 131-132 134 139 143 150 159
  165 171 179 187 202 205 211-212
  219 234-235 240 249 325 John 124
  Phineas 124 Reuben 107 William
  125
MINERALS, 21
MITCHELL, 209 226 258 320 400-401
  404 413 516 Joseph 320 Selden
  400
MONEL, 314
MONROE, 431
MONSON, 171
MOONEY, 469
MOORE, 11 68 156 170 209 227 236
  286 307 325 344 352 395 409 465
  468 476 478 488 520 522 Dr Aaron
  325 Simeon Jr 170
MOORIS, 478

MORE, 302
MORGAN, 110 422 500 512
MORLEY, 428
MORRIS, 163
MORSE, 226 396 403 463
MOTT, 5 17 29 36-41 59 76 82-83 85 87 108 112 132-134 143 159 161-162 165 197 200 213 Adam 36 Adam Jr Lent 38 Jonathan 37 Lent Jr 213 Loammi 39 200
MUDGE, 270
MULLEN, 444 466 472
MUNGER, 181 248
MUNRO, 315
MUNSILL, 41 57 59 78 93 111 127 144 149 192 195 201-202 231 241 321 Zacheus 321
MUNSON, 94 154-155 198 235 245 299 301 318 376 380-381 396 411-412 436 494 507 Caleb 301 Hermon 396
MURDOCK, 318
MURRAY, 51 107 125 131 137 178 193 195 206 218 228 234 239-240 400 408 469 Ammi 240 Daniel 234 David 178 William 400
NASH, 69 112 119 156 170-173 184 218 241 259 515 Alva 171 John 170
NEAL, 37 237
NEARING, 114
NETH, 36
NEVINS, 465
NEW, Town Petitioned For 172
NEWELL, 89 102-103 185 268
NEWMAN, 454 463 468 478 486
NEWTON, 246 396
NOBLE, 47 312 372 408
NORCROSS, 293
NORTH, 50 101 114 126-127 129 134 137 140 143 152 159 172 174 188 234 240 256 Martin 126-127 Martin Jr 127 Rufus 127
NORTHRUP, 393 409
NORTHWAY, 136
NORTON, 6 26 74 96 120 150-152 154 159 179-180 201 219 228 233-234 257 263-264 272 279 287 298 305 320 329 331 333-334 365 386 401 406 413 428 489 Levi 151 Levi (2) 333
O'GORMAN, 444

OAKLEY, 61 228 299 308 385 Alvah 385 Hawley 385
OATH, Of Fidelity 134
ODD, Fellows' Lodges 500
OGDEN, 509
OLCOTT, 16
OLMSTED, 16
ORR, 311 507
ORTON, 293
ORVIS, 131
OSBORN, 336 380 384 414
OVERTON, 476 479
OVIATT, 289
OWEN, 404
PACKARD, 465 468 474
PAGE, 153 406 453 474
PALMER, 59 61 76 83 85 89 101 109 113 135 139 159-160 162 165 188 281 283 305 308 328 334 349 351 464 468-471 481 494 517 Ambrose 113 Enoch 59 Solomon 308
PANTRY, 16 41 43
PARCELS, 241
PARKANT, 469
PARKE, 392 403 427 434
PARKER, 293
PARKS, 336 Jonathan 337 Nathaniel 336
PARMELE, 180
PARSONS, 125 147 163 320 330 349-350 362 414 451 489 Rev Stephen 349-350
PARTRIDGE, 305 478
PATTERSON, 5 368
PATTON, 214
PAYNE, 227
PEAKE, 393
PEARSON, 357 453 466 Rev James B 357
PEASE, 49-50 202 272 336 378 423 470 474 478 483 494 Asaph 423
PECK, 315 397 428 466 468
PEET, 327
PELLETT, 15-16
PENDLETON, 174 465
PENITENT, Deacons 130
PERCIVAL, 21 154
PERKINS, 308 386
PERRET, 65
PERRY, 175 332 399 427
PERSONS, 344 376 507 Alpheus 376 Timothy 376

INDEX.

PETITIONS, For Incorporation 75-76 81-83
PETTIBONE, 193 256-257 342 347 356 453 472 Rev Ira 256-257 356
PETTIT, 476
PHELPS, 15 29 61 99-100 123 181 200 216 231-232 234 237 247 304 322 340 349 352 355 376 391 410 436-437 454 488-489 515 521 Benj Frederick 247 Daniel Sr & Jr 200 Lancelot 237
PHILLIPS, 136 174 230 274 375-376 380 449 451 John 375
PHIPPENNY, 237
PHYSICIANS, 50 68-69 396
PICKETT, 57
PIERCE, 95-96 299 319 333 335 369 389 415 478
PIERPONT, 291
PIERSON, 452 Rev Arthur T 452
PINE, 476
PINNEY, 176 232 329 409 Elijah 232
PIONEER, Settlers 31-74
PITKIN, 15 17 28 32 77 341
PLATT, 57 60 64 73 85 106 126 135 142 154 157 159 165 180-181 195 203 217-218 220 226 259 514 Daniel 73 Joseph 157 Levi 180 Sylvester Levi Jr 181
PLUMB, 340
PLUMMER, 370
POISSON, 16
POLK, 432
POMEROY, 356 Rev Augustus 356
POND, 177 194 325 337 407 465 489
POOL, 473
POOR, Care Of By Town 255
PORSON, 162
PORTER, 15-16 54 117 160 180 226 231 269 285 346 358 Eleazer 285
POST, Offices 362 431-433
POTTER, 73 88 111 143 157 160 165 229-230 269-270 281 283-284 290 296 358 369 378 384 463 Daniel 269 Phineas 269 Sheldon 269
PRACTICAL, Jokes 276-277
PRATT, 15-16 74 100 175 226 244 288 320 366 381-382 Andrew 320
PRESBER, 463 465
PRESCOTT, 274 292 294
PRESTON, 17 33 35-36 40 42 59 74 76 85 87-89 108-109 113 126 135-136

PRESTON (cont.)
143 147 159 162-163 165 186 211 217 226 241 331 476-477 481 Benjamin 113 Ebenezer 35 Joseph 36 Samuel 36
PRICE, 167 175 196 465
PRIEST, 59 73 126 135 165 217 Philip 126
PRINCE, 367 (Negro) 144 146 162
PROPER, 469
PROTESTANT, Episcopal Church 439-440
PRYOR, 187 189
PUTNAM, 151 164 329 499
QUIGLEY, 470
QUINN, 444
RACE, 374
RAILROADS, -- Conn Western 491-493 -- Naugatuck 437-439
RAINSFORD, 197
RANKIN, 478
RANNEY, 416 420 426 513
RANSOM, 374
RAYMOND, 177 271
REED, 151 230 367
REEVE, 63 124
REIDY, 489
REVOLUTIONARY, War -- Declaration Of Rights 127 129 War -- Soldiers Of 38 44 49-51 53 57 61 65 70-71 108-109 122 129 135 137 139 144 146-147 149-151 161-166 176 191 264-265 275 291 298 305 314 394 War -- Town Votes 122 125-129 134-135 137 139
REYNOLDS, 111 329 408 476-477 Horace 408
RHODES, 207
RICE, 230 235 398 457 520 Daniel 230
RICHARDS, 119 241 393 513 Eli 241
RICHARDSON, 111 407 471 478
RILEY, 191 200-201 207 226 John C 200
RISING, 331 339
ROADS, 27-30 102 251-254 358-359 376 404 448-449
ROBBINS, 86 88-90 109 167 182-185 212 233 236 238 243 291-292 476
ROBERTS, 15 29 65 67 86 88-89 102-103 109 113 127 150 152 159 162 165 174-175 185 240 285 333-334

ROBERTS (cont.)
369 408 463 465 468 474 478 481
George 408 Joel 113 Samuel 152
ROBINS, 17 369
ROBINSON, 187-188 212
ROCKWELL, 58 105-106 108 113 123
131-132 150 228 265 288 298 303
312 316 319 321 329-330 334-335
341-342 358-359 363-372 375 377-
379 389 392-393 396 401 403 406
409 411 413 415 418-420 425-426
428 451 454 457 494 500 507-510
513-514 516 Alpha 364 B B 365
Edward Samuel 370 Elihu 334
Henry E 428 John T 370 Solomon
363
RODMAN, 470
ROGERS, 160 195 214 279 283-284
309 358 476 478 481 Jonathan 309
Simeon 284
ROHRABACKER, John 400
ROOD, 98 196 375
ROOT, 16 19 119 124 234-235 331
Gurdon 235 Roger 235
RORABACK, (Roherbacher
Rohrabacher) 272 374 400 406
ROSE, 326 469
ROSSITER, 70
ROWE, 476 478 481 483
ROWLEY, 97 101 120 160 162 188 200
219 226 228 240-241 263 266-267
276-279 281 283-284 305 318 320
322 328 330 334 358 375 385 391
397 406 409-411 415 422 425-426
470 479 483 Alpha 410 Asher 278
Ebenezer 276 Elias 279 Reuben
334 Samuel 391 Stephen 422
ROYCE, 181
RUGG, 94 96 119-120 157 176 187-188
232 332 469 476
RUSSELL, 16 192 211 235 286 290-
294 297 303 347 357 380 382 389
453 466 501 Giles 293 Nathaniel
291 Rev H A 357
RUTHERFORD, 99
SABBA'DAY, Houses 79-80
SACKET, 297 399
SAGE, 55 138 171 195 246 324 394
407 465 476
SAINT CLAIR, 469
SAINT FRANCIS, 444 488 Parochial
School 445 Seminary 445

SAINT JOSEPH'S, Church 444-445
SAINT MARGARET, Of Cortona 444
488 R C Fem Seminary 445
SALTER, 370
SANDERFORTH, 107-108 125 171
SANFORD, 54 62 116 292 337 378 412
440 Henry 337 William 337
SARACENA, Fra Leo Da 444
SATAN'S, Kingdom 25
SAXTON, 185 247
SCHERMERHORN, 406
SCHMIDT, 469
SCHOFIELD, 146
SCHOOL, Costumes And Games 380-
381 Houses 33 72 218 248 358 378
402-403 Teachers 381-383 403 428
SCHOOLS, Common 198 217-221 379-
383 Graded 488 High And
Seminaries 257-258 403-404 428
Spelling In 220-221
SCHOVIL, 144 146 162 190 Stephen
146
SCOTT, 117 478
SCOVILL, Rueben 317
SCOVILLE, 226 317 395 399 406
SCRIMGEOUR, 313
SEAMAN, 464
SEDGWICK, 16 38 51 71 161 190 264-
266
SELDEN, 72 414
SELECTMEN, 254
SENIOR, 328
SEXTON, 287
SEYMOUR, 11-12 15-17 55 150 214
228 230 324 374 403 476-477 509
Jacob John 374 Truman 324
SHATTUCK, 145 278 285 308 328 374
411 Randall 328
SHAW, 297-298 John 297
SHEFFIELD, 307
SHELDON, 145 240 297 327-328 330
346-347 386 392 400 404
SHELLEY, 476
SHELTON, 373
SHEPARD, 16 161 168 265-266 268
270 304 329 370-373 388 401 513
516 Didymus 168 Ebenezer 265
James 373
SHERIDAN, 473
SHERIDEN, 444
SHERMAN, 57-58 131 162 167 382
393

INDEX.

SHORT, 439
SHORTMAN, 271
SHOWERS, 187
SILLIMAN, 501
SIMONS, 175 354 Rev Noah 354
SIMONSON, 279 434
SKINNER, 16 68 155 185 340 365 393-394 407 427 464 468 475-477 483 Benjamin 393 Isaac 185
SLACK, 474 481
SLOCUM, 216
SMALL-POX, Inoculation For 207-208 Pest-houses 208
SMALLEY, 348
SMITH, 15 22 41 53 60 67 76 93 101 109 126 135 141 147-150 153-155 157 159 161-162 164-165 172 176 178 182 192 217 226-231 234-235 240 246 255 264 266-268 271 273-274 281 283 286-287 292-293 296-298 301 305-306 313 318 323-324 329 337-339 344 346-349 351 355 365 374 386 391 393 395-396 423 427 440 451 465 468 476-477 494 499 509 Asahel 235 Chauncey 153 Eleazer 60 Elisha 297 Elisha Esq 101 Heman 178 James C Obituary Of 255 Josiah 267 Oliver 229 Riley 423 Theodore 337 Zebina 296
SMOLLET, 501
SNEDIKER, 465
SOPER, 44-45 59 273 302 314 329 386 413 425 515 517 522 Chester 413
SPAULDING, 176 246
SPENCER, 16 53 60 65 68-70 74 93-96 135 143-145 152 154 159-160 164-165 177 179 190-192 226 239 284-285 288 299 305 311 322 341 377 380 394 397 415-416 439-440 451 509 513 Elisha 284 Grinnell 95 John 94 Norman (1) 416 Ozias 285 Stephen 144 Thos 93 Thos (2) 95
SPERRY, 433
SPICER, 225
SPRING, 304
SQUIRE, 374 509
STABELL, 144 252 270 301 321 391 476
STACK, 175
STANCLIFF, 154 160
STANCLIFT, 61 159-160 287-288 Comfort 287 Samuel 288

STANDLEY, 9
STANLEY, 50 187 221 370
STANNARD, 60 73-74 82 85 125 135 159 161-163 165 192 228 329 Abel 73 Lemuel 73 Seth Ezra 74 William 74
STANTON, 236 278 328
STAPLES, 341
STARKS, 54 67 205-206 216 228 234 476 478 481
STARKWEATHER, 67 204-206 237 241 249 307 Elijah 205 Roger 237
STARR, 88-89 185
STEARNS, 290
STEELE, 282
STEESE, 391
STETSON, 393
STEUBEN, 176
STEVENS, 73 110
STEVENSON, 130 133 165
STEWART, 465
STICKNEY, 517
STILLMAN, 291
STOCKS, 242-243
STONE, 171 234 322
STONEMAN, 104
STORER, 145 240 400 John 240 400
STOW, 150
STOWE, 291
STREAMS, 23-24
STRICKLAND, 375
STRONG, 108 124 176 205 214 241 283 298 396 403 463 489 515 522 David Edwin M 205 Lyman 396
STUART, 374
SUMNER, 396 461
SUNDAY, Traveling 29 148 208
SWAIN, 234
SWEET, 54 59 72 74 94 108 123 130 133 135 160-162 165 168 172 207 226 231 234 239 274 281 288-289 329 333 347 380 388 401 417 465 James Reuben 123 John 288 Jonathan 108 123 Peleg 168
SWIFT, 5 47 50 162 220 246 259 303 320 Zephaniah 246
TALCOTT, 9 12 17 56 424-425 Wm O 424
TALLMADGE, 317 395 David 395
TAVERNS, 29 37 97 202 210 244 358 378
TAYLER, 16

TAYLOR, 105 136 167 192 201 214
    259 339 348 409 427-429 434 469
    518-519 Eliud 192 Silas 201
TEETER, 476-477 481
TEMPERANCE, Reform & Societies
    493-499
TENCELLENT, 470
TERRILL, 478
TERRY, 470-471 521
TEW, 215
THAYER, 62 413 426 430 499 508
    Wheelock 413
THOMPSON, 33 69 96 150 153 159-
    160 181-182 229 289 314 318 416
    458 511 520 Dan Samuel 153
    Elijah 153
THORBURN, 411
THORNE, 469 481
THORNTON, 515
THORP, 35 215 463
THRALL, 52 93 101-102 136 155 197-
    198 217 Erastus 197 Reuben 101
TIBBALLS, 64-65 105 203 225 Abel
    225 Nathan 225
TILER, 173
TIMPSON, 327
TODD, 118 289 445
TOLLES, 207 324 Amos 324
TOWNE, 246
TRACY, 152
TRAFFORD, 187
TREAT, 228 268 287 305-306 369 428
    Salmon 306
TREES, When Transplanted 379
TRENCK, 501
TROWBRIDGE, 204
TRULL, 203
TRUMBULL, 11 13 143 501
TUCKER, 16 62 66 82 85 135 143 159
    165 201 232 240 Isaac 232 Reuben
    62
TULLER, 150-151 156 171 253
TURNER, 144 180 265 293 478
TURNPIKES, Green Woods 211 376
    Waterbury 225
TURRELL, 406 426 Darius 406
TUTTLE, 55 72 240 275 277 300-301
    303 332 389-390 414 474 477 481
    Daniel G 414 Geo 240
TWISS, 474-475 481
TYLER, 33 164 432 467-468 522
UTLEY, 211

VAILL, 331
VAN, Buren 461-462 Deusen 476
    Kleek 313 Oustrom 465
VAUGHN, 474
VEBER, 465
VIDETO, 109 113-114 135 139 159
    175 231 John Jr 114 John Sr 114
VOGEL, 463
VOORHIES, 54
VORE, 302
VROOMAN, 65
WADE, 59 73 102 109 115-116 126 135
    154 157 159 165 171 177 180 207
    218 226 228 230 245 259 337 513
    Amasa Jr 116 Amasa Stephen 115
    Isaac Stephen 116
WADSWORTH, 15-16 107 125 299 309
    388 465 478
WAKEFIELD, 227 325 367 409-410
    415 419 439-440 445 469 512
    Luman 409
WALKER, 357 453 465 Rev J B R 357
WALTER, 107 136 148 159-162 165
    275-276 281 283 285 300 327 346
    380 386 517 Andrew Lemuel 275
    Daniel 276 John 275
WAR, Of 1812 267 274 416-418 Of
    1861 206 460-487
WARD, 53 100 150 153-154 157 159
    204-205 320-321 411 Daniel 157
    David 153
WARNER, 228 403 463 476
WARREN, 228 463
WASHINGTON, 143 428 431 501
WATERMAN, 306 Wm Jr 306
WATSON, 16 275 368 390 397-398 465
    478-479 481
WATTLES, 329
WAUGH, 313
WEAVER, 272 328 518
WEBB, 64
WEBSTER, 16 139 467
WEDDING, Customs 109
WEDGE, 187
WEED, 281 338 342 351 378 435 454
    500
WEIRS, 420
WEISS, 469
WELCH, 231 321 338 342 402 419 434
    451 465 473 481 489
WELD, 162
WELLES, 413

WELLS, 15-16 28 117 194 197 207 211
  365 Asahel 211
WENTWORTH, 338 412 434
WENZELL, 476-477
WESLEY, 502
WEST, 154 157 159-160 162 289 297
  318 325 330 378 385 David Jr 289
  Judah 289
WESTCOTT, 289
WESTLAKE, 99 138 226 240 275 278
  319 327-328 380 386 401 407
  Samuel 327 Thomas 328 William
  John 327
WETHERBY, 453 Rev Charles 453
WETMORE, 6 28 41 45 47 53 57 66-70
  76 83 85 88-89 94 98 111-112 119
  124 126-127 129-130 135 139 141
  143 147 154 159 164 171 186-187
  194 201 203-205 210 212 224 226
  228 236 258 272 325-326 378 389
  434 445 454 479 489 500 521 John
  (4) 69 John 2d (4) 69 John Abel 67
  Sam'l H Abel S 70 Samuel 66
  Samuel (2) 68 Seth Samuel Jr 67
  Truman S 68
WHAPLES, 16
WHEADON, 110 136 194-195 211 213
  236 Solomon 194 Stephen 194
WHEELER, 45 100 152 192 207 269
  272 287 294-296 298-299 304 319
  322 326 351 358 373 378-379 386
  399 408 412 465 469 478-479 481
  Benjamin 295 Isaac 298 Nathan
  296
WHEELOCK, 138 464 468 478 519
WHIFFLER, 472
WHIPPING, Post 242-243
WHITE, 105 116 154 157 159 175 232
  236 241 326 328 331-332 339-340
  385 394 476 478 518 Daniel 332
  Oliver Sen & Jr 328
WHITEHEAD, 465 469 476-477
WHITFORD, 281 306 347
WHITING, 15 69 71 112 114 131 137-
  138 159 171 175 211 241 246 255
  258 268 273 284 286-287 309 319
  327 331 380 383-384 400 404 409-
  410 415 429 434 451 507 515-516
  518-519 Benj 319 Christopher 137
  Lorrin 138 Riley 138
WHITMAN, 56
WHITMORE, 190

WHITNEY, 28
WHITTLESEY, 341
WICKER, 424
WILBRAHAM, 399
WILBUR, 465
WILCOX, 72 137 184 216 226 236 329
  377 451 514 Daniel 329
WILCOXSON, 57 105 108 123 125 135
  141 143-144 159 162 164 215 218
  Elisha 125 Gideon 108
WILDER, 139 410 414 427 434
WILKES, 234
WILKINSON, 65-66 77 83 85 87 123
  135 159 161-162 165 168 175 201
  211 Jesse 65 Levi 66 Lewis 65
  Miles 201
WILL, Of First Settler 33
WILLARD, 291 340
WILLIAM, And Mary 10
WILLIAMS, 15-16 55 115-116 118 289
  295-296 299 331 395 399 407 414
  419 440 463 Jesse 414
WILMOT, 270
WILSON, 29 44 53 226 228 231 265-
  266 272 287 302 317-319 323 337
  412-413 415-416 422 449 515
  Abijah 317 Abijah Jr 318 Daniel B
  319 Nelson 415 Reynold 318 Zenas
  318
WINCHESTER, Constituent Members
  87 Creed And Covenant 86-87
  Early Admissions 87-88 First
  Congregational Church 86 88 First
  Ecclesiastical Society
  Organization 75-78 First Meeting-
  house 77 80 Geological Formation
  21 Half-way Covenant 102 104 125
  140 143 Meetings 83-300 New
  Inhabitants 93-383 Ordaining
  Covenant 89 Ordination Of 1st
  Pastor 89 Physical Formation 20-
  24 Proprietors Of 15-16
  Proprietors' Division Of Lands 16-
  19 31 Proprietors' Meetings 15-16
  Second Meeting-house 169 202 244
  Society Petitioners For 76 Third
  Meeting-house 244 First Officers
  83 Town First Representation In
  General Assembly 148 Town
  Incorporation 81-83 Town
  Organization 83-85 Township
  Preliminary History 9-14

WINSTED, Ancient 346-355 Borough 453-456 Buildings In 1803 377-379 Ecclesiastical History 346-357 Families In 1803 380 First Cong Church 357 453 First Meeting-house 346-354 Modern 355 357 Parade Ground 359 362 Roads 358-362 435 440 Second Cong Church Organized 357 453 Second Meeting-house 355 360-361 Society Petition For Incorporation 281 Villages Early Aspect And Growth 358-362 430 435-436 Water Works 455-457
WITHERSPOON, 501
WOLCOTT, 153 209 327 332
WOOD, 155 314 328 384 411 426 476
WOODALL, 385 457 521
WOODFORD, 23 53-55 70 174 286 288 379 388-391 401 410 414 419 423 425-426 476-478 481 488 494 500 521 Benjamin B 389 E Sterling 390 Erastus 388 Ezekiel 388 Ezekiel Jr 389 Lester 389 Lucius J 390

WOODRUFF, 52 105 107 130 133 135 144 146 150 159 161 202 270 272 295 299 319 360 376 378 385 406 419 423 426 465 476 489 507-508 513-514 521 Hawkins 107 Jonah 133
WOODS, 111 293
WOODWARD, 68 327
WOODWORTH, 215 268 274 350-354 476 Rev Ezra 351-354
WOOSTER, 162 307 315
WORTHINGTON, 332
WRIGHT, 29 53 85 97 110 135 139 147 160-164 171-173 175 202 207 226 263-265 281 283 292 302 318 320 330 334 346-347 355 366 380 386 414 478-479 481 Charles 264 Freedom 265 Joel 334 John Jr 264 Justus 171 Lieut John 263 Norton 302 Samuel 263
WYLLYS, 25 230 283
YALE, 29 410
YORK, 489
YOUNG, 105-106

ERRORS AND CORRECTIONS.

The Compiler, being disqualified by inexperience and defective eyesight for proof-reading, assigned that special duty to other hands, and only read over the proof-sheets, without comparing them with the copy. A subsequent revision has revealed a list of errors which is here given with their corrections.

Page 12, Line 3, for 1773 read 1723.
" 21, " 15, " quantity " quality.
" 34, " 3, " long " large.
" " " 39, " Concator " Concolor.
" 37, " 33, " 1653 " 1753.
" 41, " 21, " Coventry " Country.
" 41, " 38, " 1754 " 1764.
" 45, " 16, " 1788 " 1782.
" 46, " 5, " Chamery, " Chauncey.
" 46, " 22, " Jan. " June.
" 50, " 17, " Henry " Harvey.
" 51, " 39, after 1784, insert Mary Ledyard.
" 54, " 16, for 1838 read 1832.
" 56, " 11, " Ason, " A son.
" 57, " 30, " terms, read tours.
" 75, " 15, " 1757 " 1767.
" 86, " 19, " and " out.
" 86, " 22, strike out wh.
" 89, " 37, for, these read their.
" 91, " 2, " so " to.
" 97, " 8, insert comma after Sarah.
" 100, " 43, for VI read IV.
" 102, " 2, " May 20 read May 23.
" 111, " 37, " 1851 " 1852.
" 114, " 15, " N. J. " Conn.
" 116, " 24, " Booth, " Booge.
" 116, " 29, strike out July 15, 1811.
" 119, " 4, add Coe (7) after Alanson.
" 125, " 3, strike out W. after Zerviah.
" 125, " 14, for Sept. 22 read Sept. 13.
" 130, " 28, " abjurgations read objurgations.
" 138, " 4, for 1785 read 1786.
" 138, " 7, " 1796 " 1794.
" 138, " 16, " Loritta, read Lorilla.
" 141, " 38, " by " to.
" 142, " 4, before forbearance insert proper.
" 173, " 23, insert after and, " Reuben, who."
" 195, " 9, for John Joes read John Ives.
" 195, " 10, " Laurence " Luman.
" 196, " 29, " June " January.
" 200, " 2, " 1797 " 1799.
" 205, " 16–17, for New Pultz, read New Paltz.
" 209, " 39, for Newbern read Wilmington.
" 224, " 25, insert 1801 between paragraphs.
" 226, " 10, for Levi read Zeri.
" 226, " 33, " Coe " Case.
" 229, " 22, " pounds read dollars.
" 231, " 19, " 1805 " 1806.
" 236, " 2, " March 16, read March 10.
" 248, " 19, " 1858 " 1854.
" 253, " 13, " Pineknot " Pine knoll.
" 256, " 28, " Alexander " John.
" 267, " 23, " grantor " grantee.
" 268, " 35, " 1784 " 1774.
" 271, " 31, " Seloen " Selven.
" 271, " 33, " Fyler " Fyla.
" 285, " 2, " April " March.
" 286, " 1, " lot " plot.
" 287, " 6, " June 13, 1838, read January 13, 1838.
" 287, " 7, " aged 36, read aged 66.
Page 288, line 35, for Bertrick read Butrick.
" 290, between lines 3, 4, insert title, 1784.

Page 290, line 22, for Nov. 12, read Nov. 22.
" 291, " 6, for (daughter of?) read He was.
" 292, " 33, " Sept. 11, read Sept 18.
" 294, " 17, " 1827 " 1847.
" 298, " 5, " Nishus " Nisus.
" 302, " 7, " 1781 " 1791.
" 302, " 24, " Sarah Vare read Sarah Vore.
" 303, " 21, " 73 " 78.
" 303, " 33, 34, for January " June.
" 305, " 5, for Treal " Treat.
" 305, " 23, " statute " statue.
" 313, " 23, " Wargh " Waugh.
" 313, " 37, " Schrimgeozir read Scrimgeour.
" 314, " 11, " Monsell read Monell.
" 314, " 27, after ROBERT, insert " AND."
" 322, " 11, for Brown read Brewer.
" 323, " 20, for Higby read Higley.
" 324, " 31, insert b. May 16, 1830, and for m. Dec. 16, 1830, read Dec. 13, 1846.
" 325, " 10, for Hulsey read Halsey.
" 329, " 12, " 1796 " 1797.
" 332, " 33, " hop " shop.
" 333, " 1, " 1827, " 1817.
" 335, " 29, " May 4, 1857 read May 4, 1837.
" 336, " 13, " April read August.
" 343, " 14, " Bird " Baird.
" 345, " 1, " Lyman " Luman.
" 351, " 1, " Anstus " Austin's.
" 363, " 8, " a nuisance read miasma.
" 367, " 37, " Jan. 8, " Jan. 18.
" 368, " 28, " entirely " intently.
" 368, " 42, " 1856 " 1836.
" 368, " 43, strike out by second wife.
" 383, " 19, for saturnian read saturnine.
" 397, " 10, " Sept. 11, " Sept. 1.
" 398, " 33, " b. Aug. 2, 1859, read b. Aug. 2, 1858.
" 403, " 17, " Bunn read Bunce.
" 414, " 12, " Sept. 10, 1840, read June 23, 1857.
" 419, " 35, " Hulsey read Halsey.
" 422, " 1, " XVIII " XXVIII.
" 423, " 8, " Dec. 25, 1865 read April 2, 1856.
" 423, " 9, " Erase "He died June 16, 1865, aged 68."
" 424, " 6, " 1849 read 1847.
" 428, " 18, " 1830 " 1838.
" 434, " 29, " Stoves " Stores.
" 437, " 28, " 1854 " 1864.
" 444, " 11, " Henricken, read Hendricken.
" 453, " 26, " Cooky " Cooley.
" 462, " 8, " April 4, " April 13.
" 462, " 17, " 5th " 14th.
" 463, " 27, " Day " Dayton.
" 471, " 23, " Feb. 24, 1864, read Feb. 20, 1864.
" 471, " 38, " Dec. 22, 1864, " Dec. 22, 1863.
" 489, " 34, " 1872 " 1871.
" 500, " 27, 32, for Orion " Union.
" 500, " 29, 33, " Union " Orion.
" 515, " 12, for Isaac " David.
" 516, " 4, " 1870 " 1871.
" 520, " 1, " 1868 " 1858.

www.ingramcontent.com/pod-product-compliance
Lightning Source LLC
Chambersburg PA
CBHW071230300426
44116CB00008B/974